THE FORMS OF THE OLD TESTAMENT LITERATURE

Editors

ROLF P. KNIERIM • GENE M. TUCKER • MARVIN A. SWEENEY

*Published

ISAIAH 40–66

MARVIN A. SWEENEY

The Forms of the Old Testament Literature

WILLIAM B. EERDMANS PUBLISHING COMPANY
GRAND RAPIDS, MICHIGAN

Wm. B. Eerdmans Publishing Co.
2140 Oak Industrial Drive N.E., Grand Rapids, Michigan 49505

© 2016 Marvin A. Sweeney
Published 2016
Printed in the United States of America

22 21 20 19 18 17 16   1 2 3 4 5 6 7

Library of Congress Cataloging-in-Publication Data

Names: Sweeney, Marvin A. (Marvin Alan), 1953–   author.
Title: Isaiah 40–66 / Marvin A. Sweeney.
Description: Grand Rapids: Eerdmans Publishing Company, 2016. |
Series: The forms of the Old Testament literature; [19] |
Includes bibliographical references.
Identifiers: LCCN 2016013062 | ISBN 9780802866073 (pbk.: alk. paper)
Subjects: LCSH: Bible. Isaiah, XL–LXVI—Commentaries.
Classification: LCC BS1520 .S94 2016 | DDC 224/.1066—dc23
LC record available at http://lccn.loc.gov/2016013062

www.eerdmans.com

Dedicated
to the Memory of
Roy F. Melugin
In Friendship and Gratitude

Contents

Abbreviations and Symbols

I. MISCELLANEOUS ABBREVIATIONS AND SYMBOLS

ca.	about, approximately
cf.	compare
col(s).	column(s)
Diss.	Dissertation
DtrH	Deuteronomistic History
ed.	editor(s), edited by; edition
e.g.	for example
esp.	especially
ET	English translation
et al.	et alii (and others)
f(f).	following verse(s), page(s), line(s)
Fest.	Festschrift
HB	Hebrew Bible
idem	the same
i.e.	id est (that is)
l(l).	line(s)
LXX	Septuagint
MT	Masoretic Text
n(n).	note(s)
NT	New Testament
OT	Old Testament
p(p).	page(s)
pl(s).	plate(s)
PN	personal name
repr.	reprint
rev.	revised
sic	so, thus (indicating an error transcribed from the original)
s.v.	*sub voce* (under the word)
TJ	Targum Jonathan
tr.	translator(s), translated by
v(v).	verse(s)

viz.	*videlicet* (that is to say; namely)
vol(s).	volume(s)
*	When placed after a text citation, the asterisk indicates a hypothetical form presumed to underlie the present form of the text
→	The arrow indicates a cross reference to another section of the glossary
=	Equals, is equivalent to

II. PUBLICATIONS

AASOR	Annual of the American Schools of Oriental Research
ÄAT	Ägypten und Altes Testament
AB	Anchor Bible
ABD	*Anchor Bible Dictionary*
ACEBT	*Amsterdamse Cahiers voor Exegese en Bijbelse Theologie*
AcOr	*Acta Orientalia*
AGSU	Arbeiten zur Geschichte des Spätjudentums und Urchristentums
AIL	Ancient Israel and Its Literature
AION	*Annali dell'istituto universitario orientale di Napoli, Pubblicazioni*
AJSL	*American Journal of Semitic Languages and Literatures*
AJT	*American Journal of Theology*
ALUOS	*Annual of the Leeds University Oriental Society*
AnBib	*Analecta Biblica*
ANET	J. B. Pritchard, ed., *Ancient Near Eastern Texts Relating to the Old Testament* (3rd ed.; Princeton: Princeton University, 1969)
AnOr	Analecta Orientalia
AOAT	Alter Orient und Altes Testament
ArOr	*Archiv orientální*
ARW	*Archiv für Religionswissenschaft*
ASTI	*Annual of the Swedish Theological Institute in Jerusalem*
ATANT	Abhandlungen zur Theologie des Alten und Neuen Testaments
ATD	Das Alte Testament Deutsch
ATR	*Anglican Theological Review*
ATSAT	Arbeiten zu Text und Sprache im Alten Testament
AUM	Andrews University Monographs
AusBR	*Australian Biblical Review*
AUSS	*Andrews University Seminary Studies*
AzT	Arbeiten zur Theologie
BA	*Biblical Archaeologist*
BASOR	*Bulletin of the American Schools of Oriental Research*
BAT	Botschaft des Alten Testaments
BBB	Bonner biblische Beiträge
BBET	Beiträge zur biblischen Exegese und Theologie

BDB	F. Brown, S. R. Driver, and C. A. Briggs, *Hebrew and English Lexicon of the Old Testament* (rev. ed.; Oxford: Oxford University Press, 1957)
BEATAJ	Beiträge zur Erforschung des Alten Testaments und Antike Judentums
BETL	Bibliotheca Ephemeridum Theologicarum Lovaniensium
BEvT	Beiträge zur evangelischen Theologie
BHS	K. Elliger and K. Rudolph, eds., *Biblia hebraica Stuttgartensia* (Stuttgart: Deutsche Bibelstiftung, 1977)
Bib	*Biblica*
BibB	Biblische Beiträge
BibIll	*Bible Illustrator*
BibInt	*Biblical Interpretation*
BibInt	Biblical Interpretaton Series
BibLeb	*Bibel und Leben*
BibOr	Biblica et orientalia
BibS(N)	Biblische Studien (Neukirchen, 1951-)
Bijdr	*Bijdragen*
BIOSCS	*Bulletin of the International Organization of Septuagint and Cognate Studies*
BJRL	*Bulletin of the John Rylands University Library of Manchester*
BJS	Brown Judaic Studies
BKAT	Biblischer Kommentar: Altes Testament
BMS	BIBAL Monograph Series
BN	*Biblische Notizen*
BO	*Bibliotheca orientalis*
BOuT	De Boeken van het Oude Testament
BR	*Biblical Research*
BSac	*Bibliotheca Sacra*
BT	*The Bible Translator*
BTB	*Biblical Theology Bulletin*
BTFT	*Bijdragen: Tijdschrift voor Filosofie en Theologie*
BTS	Biblisch-Theologische Studien
BVC	*Bible et Vie Chrétienne*
BWANT	Beiträge zur Wissenschaft vom Alten und Neuen Testament
BZ	*Biblische Zeitschrift*
BZAW	Beihefte zur Zeitschrift für die alttestamentliche Wissenschaft
CAT	Commentaire de l'Ancien Testament
CBC	Cambridge Bible Commentary
CBQ	*Catholic Biblical Quarterly*
CBQMS	Catholic Biblical Quarterly Monograph Series
CBSC	Cambridge Bible for Schools and Colleges
CentB	Century Bible
CHANE	Culture and History of the Ancient Near East
ConBOT	Coniectanea biblica, Old Testament
ConJud	*Conservative Judaism*
CRBS	*Currents in Research: Biblical Studies*

CTM	Calwer theologische Monographien
DBAT	*Dielheimer Blätter zum Alten Testament*
DBSup	*Dictionnaire de la Bible, Supplément*
DD	*Dor le-Dor*
DJD	Discoveries in the Judaean Desert
EB	Echter Bibel
EBib	Études bibliques
EBR	*The Encyclopedia of the Bible and Its Reception* (ed. H.-J. Klauck et al.; Berlin: de Gruyter, 2009–)
ECC	Eerdmans Critical Commentary
EF	Erträge der Forschung
EHAT	Exegetisches Handbuch zum Alten Testament
EJL	Early Judaism and Its Literature
EncBib	*Encyclopaedia Biblica*
EncJud	*Encyclopedia Judaica (1971)*
ErF	Erträge der Forschung
ErIs	*Eretz Israel*
EstBib	*Estudios biblicos*
ETL	*Ephemerides theologicae lovanienses*
ETR	*Études Théologiques et Religieuses*
EvT	*Evangelische Theologie*
ExAud	*Ex Auditu*
Exp	*The Expositor*
ExpB	Expositor's Bible
ExpTim	*Expository Times*
FAT	Forschungen zum Alten Testament
FB	Forschung zur Bibel
FOTL	Forms of the Old Testament Literature
FRLANT	Forschungen zur Religion und Literatur des Alten und Neuen Testaments
GBS	Guides to Biblical Scholarship
HAR	*Hebrew Annual Review*
HAT	Handbuch zum Alten Testament
HBS	Herders Biblische Studien
HBT	*Horizons in Biblical Theology*
HCOT	Historical Commentary of the Old Testament
HDR	Harvard Dissertations in Religion
Hen	*Henoch*
HKAT	Handkommentar zum Alten Testament
HSAT	*Die heilige Schrift des Alten Testaments* (Kautzsch) (4th ed.; Tübingen: Mohr Siebeck, 1922-23), ed. Bertholet
HSM	Harvard Semitic Monographs
HSS	Harvard Semitic Series
HTR	*Harvard Theological Review*
HTS	Harvard Theological Studies
HUCA	*Hebrew Union College Annual*
HUCM	Hebrew Union College Monographs

IB	*Interpreter's Bible*
IBT	Interpreting Biblical Texts
ICC	International Critical Commentary
IDB	*Interpreter's Dictionary of the Bible*
IDBSup	Supplementary volume to *IDB*
IEJ	*Israel Exploration Journal*
Int	*Interpretation*
IOS	*Israel Oriental Studies*
IRT	Issues in Religion and Theology
JANES	*Journal of the Ancient Near Eastern Society*
JAOS	*Journal of the American Oriental Society*
JARCE	*Journal of the American Research Center in Egypt*
JBL	*Journal of Biblical Literature*
JBQ	*Jewish Bible Quarterly*
JBR	*Journal of Bible and Religion*
JCS	*Journal of Cuneiform Studies*
JEA	*Journal of Egyptian Archaeology*
JETS	*Journal of the Evangelical Theological Society*
JNES	*Journal of Near Eastern Studies*
JNSL	*Journal of Northwest Semitic Languages*
JQR	*Jewish Quarterly Review*
JR	*Journal of Religion*
JSJSup	Journal for the Study of Judaism Supplement
JSOT	*Journal for the Study of the Old Testament*
JSOTSup	Journal for the Study of the Old Testament Supplement Series
JSS	*Journal of Semitic Studies*
JSSM	Journal of Semitic Studies Monograph
JTS	*Journal of Theological Studies*
KAT	Kommentar zum Alten Testament
KEH	Kurzgefasstes exegetisches Handbuch zum Alten Testament
KHC	Kurzer Hand-Commentar zum Alten Testament
LBC	Layman's Bible Commentary
LD	Lectio divina
LHBOTS	Library of Hebrew Bible/Old Testament Studies
LQ	*Lutheran Quarterly*
LUA	Lunds universitets årsskrift
MC	Mesopotamian Civilizations
MGWJ	*Monatsschrift für Geschichte und Wissenschaft des Judentums*
MIOF	*Mitteilungen des Instituts für Orientforschung*
NCB	New Century Bible
NewCathEnc	*New Catholic Encyclopedia*
NGTT	*Nederduitse Gereformeerde Teologiese Tydskrif*
NIB	*New Interpreter's Bible*
NIBC	New International Biblical Commentary
NICOT	New International Commentary on the Old Testament
NRSV	New Revised Standard Version
NRTh	*Nouvelle revue théologique*

NTT	*Nederlands Theologisch Tijdschrift*
OBO	Orbis biblicus et orientalis
ÖBS	Österreichische biblische Studien
OBT	Overtures to Biblical Theology
OLZ	*Orientalistische Literaturzeitung*
OrAnt	*Oriens antiquus*
OTE	*Old Testament Essays*
OTG	Old Testament Guides
OTL	Old Testament Library
OtSt	*Oudtestamentische Studiën*
OTWSA	Ou-Testamentiese Werkgemeenskap in Suid-Afrika
PEFQS	*Palestine Exploration Fund Quarterly Statement*
PEGLMBS	*Proceedings, Eastern Great Lakes and Midwest Biblical Societies*
PEQ	*Palestine Exploration Quarterly*
PIBA	*Proceedings of the Irish Biblical Association*
PJ	*Palästinajahrbuch*
POS	Pretoria Oriental Series
Proof	*Prooftexts*
PTMS	Pittsburgh Theological Monograph Series
RB	*Revue biblique*
REJ	*Revue des Études Juives*
RevQ	*Revue de Qumran*
RevScRel	*Revue des sciences religieuses*
RGG	Die Religion in Geschichte und Gegenwart
RHPR	*Revue d'histoire et de philosophie religieuses*
RHR	*Revue de l'histoire des religions*
RivB	*Rivista biblica*
ROT	Reading the Old Testament
RSPT	*Revue des Sciences Philosophiques et Théologiques*
RSR	*Recherches de science religieuse*
RSV	Revised Standard Version
SacPag	*Sacra Pagina*
SANT	Studien zum Alten und Neuen Testaments
SAT	Die Schriften des Alten Testaments
SB	Sources bibliques
SBB	Stuttgarter biblische Beiträge
SBL	Society of Biblical Literature
SBLDS	Society of Biblical Literature Dissertation Series
SBLMS	Society of Biblical Literature Monograph Series
SBLSCS	Society of Biblical Literature Septuagint and Cognate Studies
SBLSP	Society of Biblical Literature Seminar Papers
SBLSym	Society of Biblical Literature Symposium Series
SBM	Stuttgarter biblische Monographien
SBS	Stuttgarter Bibelstudien
SBT	Studies in Biblical Theology
SEA	*Svensk exegetisk årsbok*

Sem	*Semitica*
SJLA	Studies in Judaism in Late Antiquity
SJOT	*Scandinavian Journal of the Old Testament*
SJT	*Scottish Journal of Theology*
SOTSMS	Society for Old Testament Studies Monograph Series
SSN	Studia Semitica Neerlandica
ST	*Studia Theologica*
StBibLit	Studies in Biblical Literature
StPB	Studia Post-biblica
TB	Theologische Bücherei
TBC	Torch Bible Commentary
TBT	*The Bible Today*
TDOT	G. J. Botterweck, H. Ringgren, and H.-J. Fabry, eds., *Theological Dictionary of the Old Testament* (ET; 17 vols.; Grand Rapids: Eerdmans, 1974–)
THAT	*Theologisches Handwörterbuch zum Alten Testament*
ThStK	*Theologische Studien und Kritiken*
TLZ	*Theologische Literaturzeitung*
TRu	*Theologische Rundschau*
TS	*Theologische Studien*
TThSt	*Trierer Theologische Studien*
TTZ	*Trierer theologische Zeitschrift*
TynB	*Tyndale Bulletin*
TZ	*Theologische Zeitschrift*
UF	*Ugarit-Forschungen*
USQR	*Union Seminary Quarterly Review*
UUÅ	Uppsala universitets Årsskrift
VF	*Verkündigung und Forschung*
VT	*Vetus Testamentum*
VTSup	Vetus Testamentum, Supplements
WAW	Writings from the Ancient World
WBC	Word Biblical Commentary
WMANT	Wissenschaftliche Monographien zum Alten und Neuen Testament
WO	*Die Welt des Orients*
WuD	*Wort und Dienst*
WZHalle	*Wissenschaftliche Zeitschrift der Martin-Luther-Universität*
ZAH	*Zeitschrift für Althebräistik*
ZAR	*Zeitschrift für Altorientalische und Biblische Rechtsgeschichte*
ZAW	*Zeitschrift für die alttestamentliche Wissenschaft*
ZBK	*Zürcher Bibelkommentare*
ZDMG	*Zeitschrift der deutschen morgenländischen Gesellschaft*
ZDPV	*Zeitschrift des deutschen Palästina-Vereins*
ZKTh	*Zeitschrift für Katholische Theologie*
ZRGG	*Zeitschrift für Religions- und Geistesgeschichte*
ZTK	*Zeitschrift für Theologie und Kirche*

Editors' Foreword

This volume is the nineteenth published in the commentary of *The Forms of the Old Testament Literature (FOTL)*. This foreword complements the forewords to volumes published thus far.

The reader will realize the difference between the chronological sequence in which the individual volumes appear and their positions in the order of the commentary. The dates of the published volumes depend on the working schedules of the individual contributors, which are also influenced by their participation in the ever-widening range of research. The order of the volumes in the commentary follows the sequential order of the books in the Protestant Churches, even where on occasion more than one biblical book is treated in the same volume or where two volumes are used for one biblical book. Excepted from this order are the books of Job, Proverbs, Ruth, Song of Songs, Ecclesiastes/Qoheleth, and Esther, whose combined treatment is published in the volume on *Wisdom Literature*. The commentary on Lamentations likewise appears in the volume *Psalms, Part 2*.

An international, interconfessional, and eventually interreligious team of scholars contributes to the project, originally launched by Rolf Knierim and Gene M. Tucker over five decades ago. Its membership has changed and expanded over the years. After many years as coeditor together with Knierim, Tucker relinquished his position after retiring from the Candler School of Theology. Sweeney, since 1994 Professor at the Claremont School of Theology and since 2000 Professor at the Academy for Jewish Religion California as well, has succeeded Tucker as coeditor of the series.

During the early stages of deliberations, it had become clear that the project should not be a handbook about the results of the work of form criticism, including method and exemplification. Nor should it be an encyclopedia of the identified genres and their settings in their typical societal traditions. These aspects are already on record through the results of the history of the discipline originally — and appropriately — called form *history* (Form *Geschichte*) rather than form *criticism*. The expression "form criticism" is only retained in this commentary with the conscious implication that form criticism involves the study of the genres and settings of the societal traditions of the texts. Instead of the two above-mentioned options for conceiving, organizing, and publishing the project, the coeditors determined that it should be a commentary, in which all texts throughout all books of the Hebrew Bible are form-critically interpreted. This goal is the result of both programmatic and didactic considerations.

The coeditors recognized programmatically that form-critical work must include all of what had been done only in part in the past, and what originally had been considered to be outside the task of biblical form criticism in its search for the oral traditions behind the written texts: the form-critical interpretation of all literary texts of the Bible, including the extant texts of the biblical books. The reality of the Bible as not oral but written literature exists in its own right, with its own societal genres and settings and traditions. This fact also applies to the specific texts of our extant Bibles.

The coeditors also recognized that the original form-critical method was inadequately conceived, since the search for societal traditions or conditions behind the texts was conducted without form-critical study of the social and literary conditions in which these texts were produced and in which they function. As long as the societal identity of our texts themselves was not first established independently, the inherited method could not demonstrate how the societal conditions behind the text, which were claimed to be discovered by investigators, would indeed be the matrices of the texts' own societal identity. More than once could it be said or thought that the structure of a genre claimed to be found in a text indeed fails to explain that text.

The inclusion in form-critical study of the written, and especially the texts which are before us as readers, has meant that this study begins with the form-critical interpretation of the unique expression of the texts, because it encounters them in their individuality in the first place. In whatever way they reflect or represent typical traditions, they exist in their individuality. The unique character of texts consists of diverse elements and aspects; but these elements are subservient to the texts conceived in their entireties. These texts are formed in conceptually-structured units, which represent the order of the texts. The study of this sort of structure reveals the aspects by which the text is governed or controlled as an entirety. And its results lead to the investigation of whether or not such structure reflects the tradition of a particular genre and its setting(s), or forms of expression outside the traditional societal conventions.

Because the commentary is based on the fundamental aspects of the contribution of form criticism's legacy to biblical interpretation, preeminently of genre and setting, it is the presentation and interpretation of the structure of each identified text before everything else, from the large to the small units, that represents the essential addition to the form-critical method in this commentary. For a discussion of this current state in the form-critical study of the Hebrew Bible, see *The Changing Face of Form Criticism for the Twenty-First Century,* ed. Marvin A. Sweeney and Ehud Ben Zvi (Grand Rapids: Eerdmans, 2003).

Didactically speaking, by beginning the interpretation of a text with the presentation and discussion of its own structure, the method established in this commentary should offer all readers the opportunity to be guided into the study of a biblical text as such to begin with, into their involvement in understanding its presented structure, from which they may then be led to the subsequent discussion of the traditions of genre, setting, and intention/function/meaning.

Indeed, the study of the texts' structures can be carried out independently, and by all. It is also important for any kind of biblical exegesis, and for the study of any text as well, not only as the first step of form-critical work.

The use of the present commentary is by and large self-explanatory and in line with the policy of this series. It is to be used alongside the Hebrew text and/or a translation of the text. Major literary corpora are introduced by general bibliographies covering wider information, while form-critical bibliographies relevant for the discussion of the individual units are placed at the end of such units. The system of the sigla used for the presentation of the texts' structure indicates the relationship of the parts, including the super- and/or subordination of the parts within the unity of a text. The traditional chapter and verse divisions of the Hebrew/Aramaic text are supplied in the right-hand margin of the structure diagrams.

The present volume includes a glossary of the genres and formulas discussed in the commentary. The definitions of the genres and formulas were provided by Professor Sweeney, based on earlier work from the FOTL project.

The coeditors acknowledge with profound appreciation the contribution of numerous persons and institutions to the work of the project. All of the individual contributors and editors have received significant financial, administrative, and student assistance from their respective institutions.

ROLF P. KNIERIM
MARVIN A. SWEENEY

Preface

This volume is dedicated to the memory of my late friend and colleague, Roy F. Melugin. Roy was originally contracted to write this volume, but his passing on April 9, 2008, prevented him from doing so. I learned about his illness only a few weeks before he died. One Sunday evening during the winter trimester at the Academy for Jewish Religion California, my cell phone rang about 6:25 p.m. as I was just sitting down to begin my 6:30 p.m. course on Isaiah. I started by telling Roy that I was about to begin class and would have to call him back, but as the words left my mouth I realized that something must be wrong. And so I asked him what was happening, and he told me about his recent diagnosis. We talked at length the next day. Roy asked me to write the FOTL Isaiah 40-66 volume, which I readily agreed to do. We made plans to meet at the upcoming Society of Biblical Literature Annual Meeting in Boston, but unfortunately, Roy passed just a few weeks after we talked.

I first met Roy while I was in graduate school, when he spent a semester at Claremont to do research for his FOTL Isaiah 40–66 volume. He had written a brilliant dissertation on Isaiah 40–55, published as *The Formation of Isaiah 40–55* (BZAW 141; Berlin: de Gruyter, 1976), which examined the literary relationships between the various generic units of Deutero-Isaiah with a view toward defining the literary coherence and characteristics of Isaiah 40–55. I used his work extensively in my own dissertation, published as *Isaiah 1–4 and the Post-Exilic Understanding of the Isaianic Tradition* (BZAW 171; Berlin: de Gruyter, 1988), which sought to establish the final form of the book of Isaiah as a basis for redaction-critical work in Isaiah 1–39. I got to know Roy better as co-chair of the early "Israelite Prophetic Literature" Section at SBL, and after I was invited to write the FOTL Isaiah 1–39 volume, we found that we had much in common in our work on Isaiah. We eventually founded the SBL Seminar on "The Formation of the Book of Isaiah," which proved to be a very important and stimulating seminar that heavily influenced contemporary research on Isaiah and the other prophetic books. We coedited the first volume of essays published by the SBL Isaiah Seminar, *New Visions of Isaiah* (JSOTSup 214; Sheffield: Sheffield Academic, 1996).

My own engagement with Isaiah is practically life-long. When I became a Bar Mitzvah in 1966, my Torah portion was Ekev, Deuteronomy 7:12–11:25, and the Haftarah reading was Isaiah 49:14–51:3. I read portions of the passage and wrote a D'var Torah on the passage. Later as an undergraduate at the University of Illinois, I discovered Isaiah again while studying with Neil Irons and David L. Petersen and wrote my first exegetical paper on the narratives concerning Sennacherib's siege of Jerusalem in Isaiah 36–39/2 Kings 18–20. Later at Claremont, I studied Isaiah from various angles, among other topics, with my doctoral advisor, Rolf Knierim, as well as my committee members, James A. Sanders and William H. Brownlee. When Rolf had to be away for a class session in a course that I was taking, he asked me to teach it. The class session was on genres in Isaiah 1–5, and on teaching the class, I found a basis for my dissertation work on Isaiah.

After publishing my FOTL volume on Isaiah 1–39 in 1996 (*Isaiah 1–39, with an Introduction to Prophetic Literature* [Grand Rapids: Eerdmans, 1996]), I went on to other topics in prophetic literature and other concerns in the Hebrew Bible and Jewish studies, e.g., King Josiah of Judah, the Twelve Prophets, 1-2 Kings, Jewish biblical theology, Ezekiel, and Jewish mystical literature, and ultimately, Jeremiah. But Isaiah has always been the foundation of my work and view of the field. Unfortunately, Roy left little useable material, and so this volume is entirely the product of my own work, even as I've read Roy's publications and reflected on our long collaboration. My volume is both different from the volume he would have produced — mine is very much concerned with formal issues and redaction-criticism — and yet is very much influenced by Roy's concern with literary features and perspectives.

I am indebted to many Isaiah scholars in addition to Roy over the course of my career who have been influential in my developing views on Isaiah; unfortunately, they are too many to mention by name here. I would like to mention my research assistants at Claremont for the role they played in the research and writing of this work. Ms. Soo Jung Kim, Ph.D. candidate in Hebrew Bible at the Claremont School of Theology, did extensive bibliographical research. Dr. Pamela J. W. Nourse, Ph.D. student in Hebrew Bible at the Claremont School of Theology, expertly proofread the entire volume. I am grateful to both of these students for their work. Any lapses and errors are my own.

I am also grateful to my students at Claremont School of Theology, the Academy for Jewish Religion California, Claremont Graduate University, and Yonsei University for their enthusiasm, wisdom, and diligence in the study of the Hebrew Bible and the history of Judaism and Jewish thought.

Finally, I would to like to thank my family, my wife Muna, our daughter Leah, and our son-in-law Brian, for their love and support throughout the duration of this project and beyond. Nothing would be possible without them.

MARVIN A. SWEENEY
San Dimas, California
January, 2015/Tevet, 5775

Chapter 1

Introduction to the Book of Isaiah

Bibliography

R. Abma, *Bonds of Love: Methodic Studies of Prophetic Texts with Marriage Imagery (Isaiah 50:1-3 and 54:1-10, Hosea 1–3, Jeremiah 2–3)* (SSN 40; Assen: Van Gorcum, 1999); P. R. Ackroyd, "Isaiah," in *The Interpreter's One-Volume Commentary on the Bible* (ed. C. M. Layman; Nashville: Abingdon, 1971) 329-71; idem, *Studies in the Religious Tradition of the Old Testament* (London: SCM, 1987); J. W. Adams, *The Performative Nature and Function of Isaiah 40–55* (LHBOTS 448; London: T. & T. Clark, 2006); R. Albertz, "Darius in Place of Cyrus: The First Edition of Deutero-Isaiah (Isaiah 40.1–52.12) in 521 BCE," *JSOT* 27 (2003) 371-83; idem, "On the Structure and Formation of the Book of Deutero-Isaiah," in Bautch and Hibbard, eds., *The Book of Isaiah*, 21-40; J. M. Allegro, *Qumran Cave 4: I (4Q158-4Q186)* (DJD 5; Oxford: Clarendon, 1968); O. T. Allis, *The Unity of Isaiah: A Study in Prophecy* (Philadelphia: Presbyterian and Reformed, 1950); B. W. Anderson, "Exodus and Covenant in Second Isaiah," in *Magnalia Dei/The Mighty Acts of G-d* (Fest. G. E. Wright; ed. F. M. Cross et al.; Garden City: Doubleday, 1976) 339-60; idem, "Exodus Typology in Second Isaiah," in Anderson and Harrelson, eds., *Israel's Prophetic Heritage,* 177-95; B. W. Anderson and W. Harrelson, eds., *Israel's Prophetic Heritage* (Fest. J. Muilenburg; ed. B. W. Anderson and W. Harrelson; New York: Harper, 1962); M. Baillet et al., *Les 'Petites Grottes' de Qumcian* (DJD 3; Oxford: Clarendon, 1962); K. Baltzer, *Deutero-Isaiah* (Hermeneia; Minneapolis: Fortress, 2001); H. M. Barstad, *The Babylonian Captivity of the Book of Isaiah: "Exilic" Judah and the Provenance of Isaiah 40–55* (Oslo: Instituttet for Sammenlignende Kulturforskning, 1997); idem, *The Myth of the Empty Land: A Study in the History and Archaeology of Judah During the "Exilic" Period* (Oslo: Instituttet for Sammenlignende Kulturforskning, 1996); idem, *A Way in the Wilderness: The "Second Exodus" in the Message of Second Isaiah* (JSSM 12; Manchester: University of Manchester Press, 1989); H. Barth, *Die Jesaja-Worte in der Josiazeit: Israel und Assur als Thema einer produktiven Neuinterpretation der Jesajaüberlieferung* (WMANT 48; Neukirchen-Vluyn: Neukirchener, 1977); G. Baumann, *Love and Violence: Marriage as Metaphor for the Relationship between YHWH and Israel in the Prophetic Books* (Collegeville: Liturgical, 2003); R. J. Bautch, "Lament Regained in Trito-Isaiah's Penitential Prayer," in *Seeking the Favor of G-d: The Origins of Penitential Prayer in Second Temple Judaism* (EJL 21; ed. M. J. Boda et al.; Atlanta: SBL, 2006) 83-99; R. J. Bautch and J. T. Hibbard, eds., *The Book of Isaiah: Enduring Questions Answered Anew* (*Fest.* J. Blenkinsopp; Grand Rapids: Eerdmans, 2014); E. Beaucamp, "D'Isaïe à son livre: A propos d'un ouvrage récent," *Liber Annuus* 33 (1983) 75-98; J. Becker, *Isaias — Der Prophet und sein Buch* (SBS 30; Stuttgart: Katholisches Bibelwerk, 1968); J. Begrich, *Studien zum Alten Testament* (TBü 21; Munich: Kaiser, 1964); idem, *Studien zu Deuterojesaja* (TBü 20; Munich: Kaiser, 1969); P. Benoit et al., *Les Grottes de Murabba'ât* (DJD 2; Oxford: Clarendon, 1961); U. Berges, *Das Buch Jesaja: Komposition und Endgestalt* (HBS 16; Freiburg: Herder, 1998); idem, "Farewell to Deutero-Isaiah or Prophecy without a Prophet," in *Congress Volume: Ljubljana 2007* (VTSup 133; ed. A. Lemaire; Leiden: Brill, 2010) 575-95; idem, *Isaiah: The Book of Isaiah: Its Composition and Final Form* (Sheffield: Sheffield Phoenix, 2012); idem, *Isaiah: The Prophet and His Book* (Sheffield: Sheffield Phoenix, 2012); idem, *Jesaja 40–48* (HThKAT; Freiburg: Herder, 2008); idem, "Kingship and Servanthood in the Book of Isaiah," in Bautch and Hibbard, eds., *The Book of Isaiah,* 159-78; W. A. M. Beuken, "The Main Theme of Trito-Isaiah: The Servants of Yhwh," *JSOT* 47 (1990) 67-87; idem, "Major Interchanges in the Book of Isaiah Subservient to Its Umbrella Theme: The Establishment of Yhwh's Sovereign Rule at Mt. Zion (Chs. 12–13; 27–28; 39–40; 55–56)," in Bautch and Hibbard, eds., *The Book of Isaiah,* 113-32; J. A. Bewer, *The Book of Isaiah* (2 vols.; New York: Harper, 1950); H. Birkeland, *Zum hebräischen Traditionswesen: Die Komposition der prophetischen Bücher des Alten Testaments* (Oslo: Dybwad, 1938); S. H. Blank, *Prophetic Faith in Isaiah* (New York: Harper, 1958); idem, "Traces of Prophetic Agony in Isaiah," *HUCA* 27 (1956) 81-92; J. Blenkinsopp, "The Cosmological and Protological Language of Deutero-Isaiah," *CBQ* 73 (2011) 493-510; idem, *Isaiah 1–39* (AB 19; New York: Doubleday, 2000); idem, *Isaiah 40–55* (AB 19A; New York: Doubleday, 2002); idem, *Isaiah 56–66* (AB 19B; New York: Doubleday, 2003); idem, "The Servant and the Servants in Isaiah and the Formation of the Book," in Broyles and Evans, eds., *Writing and Reading the Scroll of Isaiah,* 155-75; idem, "The Servants of the L-rd in Third Isaiah," *PIBA* 7 (1983) 1-23; P.-E. Bonnard, *Le Second Isaïe, Son Disciple et leurs Éditeurs: Isaïe 40–66* (EBib; Paris: Gabalda, 1972); D. Bourguet, "Pourquoi à-t-on rassemblé des oracles si divers sous le titre d'Esaïe?" *ETR* 58 (1983) 171-79; G. H. Box, *The Book of Isaiah* (London: Pitman, 1908); C. J. Bredenkamp, *Der Prophet Jesaia* (Erlangen: Deichert, 1887); W. H. Brownlee, *The Meaning of the Qumran Scrolls for the Bible, with Special Attention to the Book of Isaiah* (Oxford: Oxford University Press, 1964); C. C. Broyles and C. A. Evans, eds., *Writing and Reading the Scroll of Isaiah: Studies of an Interpretive Tradition* (VTSup 70/1-2; 2 vols.; Leiden: Brill, 1997); W. Brueggemann, *Isaiah 1–39; Isaiah 40–66* (2 vols.; Louisville: Westminster John Knox, 1998); idem, "Unity and Dynamic in the Isaiah Tradition," *JSOT* 29 (1984) 89-107; D. M. Carr, "Reaching for Unity in Isaiah," *JSOT* 57 (1993) 61-80; idem, "What Can We Say about the Tradition History of Isaiah?" in *SBL 1992 Seminar Papers* (ed. E. H. Lovering, Jr.; Atlanta: Scholars, 1992) 583-97; R. P. Carroll, *When Prophecy Failed: Cognitive Dissonance in the Prophetic Traditions of the Old Testament* (New York: Seabury, 1979); T. K. Cheyne, *Introduction to the Book of Isaiah* (London: Black, 1895); idem, *The Prophecies of Isaiah* (2 vols.; London: Paul, Trench, Trübner, 1889); B. S. Childs, *Introduction to the Old Testament as Scripture* (Philadelphia: Fortress, 1979) 311-38; idem, *Isaiah* (OTL; Louisville: Westminster John Knox, 2001); R. E. Clements, "Beyond Tradition-History: Deutero-Isaianic Development of First Isaiah's Themes," *JSOT* 31 (1985) 95-113; idem, "Isaiah," in *The Books of the Bible,* vol. 1: *The Old Testament/The Hebrew Bible* (ed.

B. W. Anderson; New York: Scribners, 1989) 247-79; idem, *Isaiah 1–39* (NCB; London: Marshall, Morgan, and Scott; Grand Rapids: Eerdmans, 1980); idem, "Isaiah: A Book without Ending?" *JSOT* 97 (2002) 109-26; idem, *Old Testament Prophecy: From Oracles to Canon* (Louisville: Westminster John Knox, 1996); idem, "The Unity of the Book of Isaiah," *Int* 36 (1982) 117-29; R. J. Clifford, *Fair Spoken and Persuading: An Interpretation of Second Isaiah* (New York: Paulist, 1984); A. Condamin, *Le Livre d'Isaïe: Introduction* (EBib; Paris: Gabalda, 1940); idem, *Le Livre d'Isaïe: Traduction critique avec notes et commentaires* (EBib; Paris: Lecoffre, 1905); E. W. Conrad, "The Fear Not Oracles in Second Isaiah," *VT* 34 (1984) 129-52; idem, "Isaiah and the Abraham Connection," *AJT* 2 (1988) 382-93; idem, E. W. Conrad, *Fear Not Warrior: A Study of 'al tîrā' Pericopes in the Hebrew Scriptures* (BJS 75; Chico: Scholars, 1985); idem, *Reading Isaiah* (OBT 27; Minneapolis: Fortress, 1991); idem, "The Royal Narratives and the Structure of the Book of Isaiah," *JSOT* 41 (1988) 67-81; S. L. Cook, *Conversations with Scripture: 2 Isaiah* (Harrisburg: Morehouse, 2008); C. H. Cornill, "Die Composition des Buches Jesajas," *ZAW* 4 (1884) 83-105; G. I. Davies, "The Destiny of the Nations in the Book of Isaiah," in Vermeylen, ed., *The Book of Isaiah,* 93-120; F. Delitzsch, *The Prophecies of Isaiah* (trans. J. Martin; 2 vols.; Grand Rapids: Eerdmans, 1954); S. J. Dille, *Mixing Metaphors: G-d as Mother and Father in Deutero-Isaiah* (JSOTSup 398; London: T. & T. Clark, 2004); A. Dillmann, *Der Prophet Jesaia* (Leipzig: Hirzel, 1890); B. R. Doak, "Legalists, Visionaries, and New Names: Sectarianism and the Search for Apocalyptic Origins in Isaiah 56–66," *BTB* 40 (2010) 9-26; S. R. Driver and A. Neubauer, *The "Suffering Servant" of Isaiah According to Jewish Interpreters* (Eugene: Wipf and Stock, 1877/1999); B. Duhm, *Das Buch Jesaia* (5th ed.; HKAT; Göttingen: Vandenhoeck & Ruprecht, 1968; 1st ed., 1892); W. J. Dumbrell, "The Purpose of the Book of Isaiah," *TynB* 36 (1985) 111-28; J. H. Eaton, *Festal Drama in Deutero-Isaiah* (London: SPCK, 1979); idem, "The Isaiah Tradition," in *Israel's Prophetic Tradition* (*Fest.* P. R. Ackroyd; ed. R. Coggins et al.; Cambridge: University Press, 1982) 58-76; idem, "The Origin of the Book of Isaiah," *VT* 9 (1959) 138-57; A. B. Ehrlich, *Randglossen zur hebräischen Bibel, textkritisches, sprachliches und sachliches,* vol. 4: *Jesaia, Jeremia* (Leipzig: Hinrichs, 1912); K. Elliger, *Deuterojesaja in seinem Verhältnis zu Tritojesaja* (BWANT 63; Stuttgart: Kohlhammer, 1933); idem, *Deuterojesaja: Jesaja 40,1–45,7* (BKAT XI/1; Neukirchen-Vluyn: Neukirchener, 1978); idem, *Die Einheit des Tritojesaia (Jesaia 56–66)* (BWANT 45; Stuttgart: Kohlhammer, 1928); G. I. Emmerson, *Isaiah 56–66* (OTG; Sheffield: Sheffield Academic, 1996); C. A. Evans, "On Isaiah's Use of Israel's Sacred Tradition," *BZ* 30 (1986) 92-99; idem, "On the Unity and Parallel Structure of Isaiah," *VT* 38 (1988) 129-47; A. J. Everson and H. C. P. Kim, eds., *The Desert Will Bloom: Poetic Visions in Isaiah* (AIL 4; Atlanta: SBL, 2009); H. Ewald, *Die Propheten des Alten Bundes* (3 vols.; 2nd ed.; Göttingen: Vandenhoeck & Ruprecht, 1867); F. Feldman, *Das Buch Isaias* (EHAT 14/1; Münster: Aschendorff, 1925); A. Feuillet, "Bibliographie choisie sur le livre d'Isaïe," in *Études d'exégèse et de la théologie biblique A. T.* (Paris: Gabalda, 1975) 501-8; idem, "La communauté messianique dans la predication d'Isaïe," *BVC* 20 (1957-58) 38-52; idem, "Introduction au livre d'Isaïe," in *Études d'exégèse et de la théologie biblique A. T.* (Paris: Gabalda, 1975) 19-201; idem, "Isaïe (Le livre d')," *DBSup,* 647-729; idem, "Le messianisme du livre d'Isaïe: Ses rapports avec l'histoire et les traditions d'Israël," in *Études d'exégèse et de la théologie biblique A. T.* (Paris: Gabalda, 1975) 223-59 (repr. from *RSR* 36 [1949] 182-228); I. Fischer, *Tora für Israel, Tora für die Völker: Das Konzept des Jesajabuches* (SBS 164; Stuttgart:

Katholisches Bibelwerk, 1995); G. Fohrer, *Das Buch Jesaja* (ZBK; 3 vols.; 2nd ed.; Zürich: Zwingli, 1964-67); idem, "Wandlungen Jesajas," in *Studien alttestamentlichen Texten und Themen (1966-1972)* (BZAW 155; Berlin: de Gruyter, 1981) 11-23 (repr. from *Fest.* Wilhelm Eilers [ed. G. Wiessner; Wiesbaden: Harrassowitz, 1967] 58-71); C. Franke, *Isaiah 46, 47, and 48: A New Literary-Critical Reading* (Biblical and Judaic Studies 3; Winona Lake: Eisenbrauns, 1994); K. Fullerton, "The Book of Isaiah: Critical Problems and a New Commentary," *HTR* 6 (1913) 478-520; W. Gesenius, *Philologisch-kritischer und historiker Commentar über den Jesaia* (3 vols.; Leipzig: Vogel, 1821); H. Gevaryahu, "Isaiah: How the Book Entered Holy Writ," *JBQ* 18 (1989-90) 206-12; idem, "The School of Isaiah: Biography and Transmission of the Book of Isaiah," *DD* 18 (1989-90) 62-68; H. L. Ginsberg, "Isaiah, First Isaiah," *EncJud* 9; idem, *The Supernatural in the Prophets, with Special Reference to Isaiah* (Cincinnati: Hebrew Union College Press, 1979); Y. Gitay, "The Effectiveness of Isaiah's Speech," *JQR* 75 (1984) 162-72; idem, "Isaiah and His Audience," *Proof* 3 (1983) 223-30; idem, *Prophecy and Persuasion: A Study of Isaiah 40–48* (Bonn: Linguistica Biblica, 1981); J. Goldingay, *Isaiah* (NIBC 13; Peabody: Hendrickson, 2001); idem, *Isaiah 56–66* (ICC; London: Bloomsbury, 2014); idem, *The Message of Isaiah 40–55: A Literary-Theological Commentary* (London: T. & T. Clark, 2005); J. Goldingay and D. Payne, *Isaiah 40–55* (ICC; 2 vols.; London: T. & T. Clark, 2006); M. J. Goulder, "Deutero-Isaiah of Jerusalem," *JSOT* 28 (2004) 351-62; A. Graffy, *A Prophet Confronts His People* (*AnBib* 104; Rome: Biblical Institute, 1984); H. Gressmann, "Die literarische Analyse Deuterojesajas," *ZAW* 34 (1914) 254-97; H. Gross, *Die Idee des ewigen und allgemeinen Weltfriedens im Alten Orient und im Alten Testament* (TThSt 7; Trier: Paulinus, 1956); H. Haag, *Der G-ttesknecht bei Deuterojesaja* (Erträge der Forschung 223; Darmstadt: Wissenschaftliche Buchgesellschaft, 1985); R. Halas, "The Universalism of Isaias," *CBQ* 12 (1950) 162-70; P. D. Hanson, *The Dawn of Apocalyptic* (Philadelphia: Fortress, 1975); idem, *Isaiah 40–66* (Interpretation; Louisville: Westminster John Knox, 1995); M. Haran, "The Literary Structure and Chronological Framework of the Prophecies in Isa XL–XLVIII," in *Congress Volume: Bonn 1962* (VTSup 9; Leiden: Brill, 1963) 127-55; A. J. Hauser, ed., *Recent Research on the Major Prophets* (Sheffield: Sheffield Phoenix, 2008); R. Hendel, "Isaiah and the Transition to Apocalyptic," in *Birkat Shalom* (*Fest.* S. M. Paul; ed. C. Cohen et al.; Winona Lake: Eisenbrauns, 2008) 261-79; H.-J. Hermisson, *Deuterojesaja: Jesaja 45,8–49,13* (BKAT 11/2; Neukirchen-Vluyn: Neukirchener, 2003); idem, *Deuterojesaja: Jesaja 49,14–53,12* (BKAT XI/12-16; Neukirchen-Vluyn: Neukirchener, 2007-12); idem, "Einheit und Komplexität Deuterojesajas: Probleme der Redaktionsgeschichte von Jes 40–55," in Vermeylen, ed., *The Book of Isaiah,* 287-312; W. Hill, "Book of Isaiah," *NewCathEnc* 7, 666-71; F. Hitzig, *Der Prophet Jesaja* (Heidelberg: Winter, 1833); W. L. Holladay, *Isaiah: Scroll of a Prophetic Heritage* (Grand Rapids: Eerdmans, 1978); G. Hölscher, "Jesaja," *TLZ* 77 (1952) 683-94; B. Hrobon, *Ethical Dimension of Cult in the Book of Isaiah* (BZAW 418; Berlin: de Gruyter, 2010); I. J. de Hulster, *Iconographic Exegesis and Third Isaiah* (FAT 36; Tübingen: Mohr Siebeck, 2009); B. Janowski and P. Stuhlmacher, *The Suffering Servant: Isaiah 53 in Jewish and Christian Sources* (Grand Rapids: Eerdmans, 2004); Joseph Jensen, "Weal and Woe in Isaiah: Consistency and Continuity," *CBQ* 43 (1981) 167-87; idem, "YHWH's Plan in Isaiah and in the Rest of the Old Testament," *CBQ* 48 (1986) 443-55; K. Joachimsen, *Identities in Transition: The Pursuit of Isa. 52:13–53:12* (VTSup 142; Leiden: Brill, 2011); D. Jones, "Traditio of the Oracles of Isaiah of Jerusalem," *ZAW* 67 (1955) 226-46; O. Kaiser, "Geschichtliche Erfahrung und eschatologische

Erwartung: Ein Beitrag zur Geschichte der alttestamentlichen Eschatologie im Jesaja-buch," in *Von der Gegenwartsbedeutung des Alten Testaments* (Göttingen: Vandenhoeck & Ruprecht, 1984) 167-80; idem, "Literaturkritik und Tendenzkritik. Überlegungen zur Methode des Jesajaexegese," in Vermeylen, ed., *The Book of Isaiah*, 55-71; J. S. Kaminsky, "The Concept of Election and Second Isaiah," *BTB* 31 (2001) 135-44; J. S. Kaminsky and A. Stewart, "G-d of All the World: Universalism and Developing Monotheism in Isaiah 40–66," *HTR* 99 (2006) 139-63; Y. Kaufmann, *The Babylonian Captivity and Deutero-Isaiah* (New York: Union of American Hebrew Congregations, 1970); R. H. Kenneth, *The Composition of the Book of Isaiah in the Light of History and Archaeology* (London: British Academy, 1910); K. Kiesow, *Exodustexte im Jesajabuch: Liter-arkritische und motivgeschichtliche Analysen* (OBO 24; Göttingen: Vandenhoeck & Ruprecht; Fribourg: Éditions Universitaires, 1979); H. C. P. Kim, *Ambiguity, Tension, and Multiplicity in Deutero-Isaiah* (StBibLit 52; New York: Lang, 2003); idem, "Little Highs, Little Lows: Tracing Key Themes in Isaiah," in Bautch and Hibbard, eds., *The Book of Isaiah*, 133-58; idem, "The Song of Moses (Deuteronomy 32.1-43) in Isaiah 40–55," in *G-d's Word for Our World* (Fest. S. J. DeVries; ed. J. H. Ellens et al.; JSOTSup 388; London: T. & T. Clark, 2004) 1:147-71; E. J. Kissane, *The Book of Isaiah* (vol. 1; Dublin: Browne and Nolan, 1941; 2nd ed. 1960); J. Klausner, *The Messianic Idea in Israel* (trans. W. F. Stinespring; New York: Macmillan, 1955); A. W. Knobel, *Der Prophet Je-saia* (KEH; Leipzig: Weidmann, 1843); K. Koch, "Damnation and Salvation — Prophetic Metahistory and the Rise of Eschatology in the Book of Isaiah," *ExAud* 6 (1990) 5-13; idem, *The Growth of the Biblical Tradition* (trans. S. M. Cupitt; New York: Scribner's, 1969); idem, "Ugaritic Polytheism and Hebrew Monotheism in Isaiah 40–55," in *The G-d of Israel* (ed. R. P. Gordon; Cambridge: Cambridge University Press, 2007) 205-28; idem, "Zur Geschichte der Erwählungsvorstellung in Israel," *ZAW* 67 (1955) 205-26; K. Koenen, *Ethik und Eschatologie im Tritojesajabuch* (WMANT 62; Neukirchen-Vluyn; Neukirchener 1990); L. Köhler, *Deuterojesaja (Jesaja 40–55) Stilkritsch Unter-sucht* (BZAW 37; Giessen: Töpelmann, 1923); E. König, *Das Buch Jesaja* (Gütersloh: Bertelsmann, 1926); J. L. Koole, *Isaiah III*. Vol. 1: *Isaiah 40–48* (HCOT; Leuven: Peeters, 1997); idem, *Isaiah III*. Vol. 2: *Isaiah 49–55* (HCOT; Leuven: Peeters, 1998); idem, *Isaiah III*. Vol. 3: *Isaiah 56–66* (HCOT; Leuven: Peeters, 2001); R. G. Kratz, *Kyros im Deuterojesaja-Buch* (FAT 1; Tübingen: Mohr Siebeck, 1991); A. Laato, "The Composi-tion of Isaiah 40–55," *JBL* 109 (1990) 207-28; R. Lack, *La symbolique du livre d'Isaïe* (AnBib 59; Rome: Biblical Institute, 1973); F. Landy, "Exile in the Book of Isaiah," in *The Concept of Exile in Ancient Israel and Its Historical Contexts* (ed. E. Ben Zvi and Ch. Levin; BZAW 404; Berlin: de Gruyter, 2010) 241-56; idem, "The Ghostly Prelude to Deutero-Isaiah," *BibInt* 14 (2006) 332-63; idem, "I and Eye in Isaiah, or Gazing at the Invisible," *JBL* 131 (2012) 85-97; idem, "Spectrality in the Prologue to Deutero-Isaiah," in Everson and Kim, eds., *The Desert Will Bloom*, 131-58; B. Langer, *G-tt als "Licht" in Israel und Mesopotamien* (ÖBS 7; Klosterneuburg: Österreichisches Katholisches Bi-belwerk, 1989); W. Lau, *Schriftgelehrte Prophetie in Jes 56–66* (BZAW 225; Berlin: de Gruyter, 1994); T. L. Leclerc, *YHWH Is Exalted in Justice: Solidarity and Conflict in Isaiah* (Minneapolis: Fortress, 2001); E. A. Leslie, *Isaiah, Chronologically Arranged, Translated, and Interpreted* (New York: Abingdon, 1963); L. J. Liebreich, "The Compi-lation of the Book of Isaiah," *JQR* 46 (1955-56) 259-77; *JQR* 47 (1956-57) 114-38; O. Lip-schits et al., eds., *Judah and the Judeans in the Achaemenid Period: Negotiating Identity in an International Context* (Winona Lake: Eisenbrauns, 2011); H. Løland, *Silent or*

Salient Gender? The Interpretation of Gendered G-d Language in the Hebrew Bible, Exemplified in Isaiah 42, 46 and 49 (FAT 32; Tübingen: Mohr Siebeck, 2007); R. Lowth, *Isaiah: A New Translation, with a Preliminary Dissertation* (5th ed.; 2 vols.; Edinburgh: Caws, 1807); Ø. Lund, *Way Metaphors and Way Topics in Isaiah 40–55* (FAT 2/28; Tübingen: Mohr Siebeck, 2007); P. Machinist, "Mesopotamian Imperialism and Israelite Religion: A Case Study from the Second Isaiah," in *Symbiosis, Symbolism, and the Power of the Past* (ed. W. G. Dever and S. Gitin; Winona Lake: Eisenbrauns, 2003) 237-64; R. Margalioth, *The Indivisible Isaiah: Evidence for the Single Authorship of the Prophetic Book* (New York: Yeshiva University, 1964); K. Marti, *Das Buch Jesaja* (KHC 10; Tübingen: Mohr Siebeck, 1900); F. Matheus, *Singt dem H-rrn ein neues Lied: Die Hymnen Deuterojesajas* (SBS 141; Stuttgart: Katholisches Bibelwerk, 1990); C. Matthews McGinnis and P. K. Tull, eds., *"As Those Who Are Taught": The Interpretation of Isaiah from the LXX to the SBL* (SBLSym 27; Atlanta: SBL, 2006); J. McInnes, "A Methodological Reflection on Unified Readings of Isaiah," in *Colloquium: The Australian and New Zealand Theological Review* 42 (2010) 67-87; J. L. McKenzie, *Second Isaiah* (AB 20; Garden City: Doubleday, 1968); S. A. Meier, *Speaking of Speaking: Marking Direct Discourse in the Hebrew Bible* (VTSup 46; Leiden: Brill, 1992); R. F. Melugin, "The Conventional and the Creative in Isaiah's Judgment Oracles," *CBQ* 36 (1974) 301-11; idem, "Form Criticism, Rhetorical Criticism, and Beyond in Isaiah," in Mathews McGinnis and Tull, eds., *"As Those Who Are Taught,"* 263-78; idem, *The Formation of Isaiah 40–55* (BZAW 141; Berlin: de Gruyter, 1976); idem, "Isaiah 40–66 in Recent Research: The 'Unity' Movement," in Hauser, ed., *Recent Research on the Major Prophets,* 142-94; idem, "Israel and the Nations in Isaiah 40–55," in *Problems in Biblical Theology* (*Fest.* R. Knierim; ed. H. T. C. Sun and K. L. Eades; Grand Rapids: Eerdmans, 1997) 249-64; idem, "Poetic Imagination, Intertextuality, and Life in a Symbolic World," in Everson and Kim, eds., *The Desert Will Bloom,* 7-15; R. F. Melugin and M. A. Sweeney, eds., *New Visions of Isaiah* (JSOTSup 214; Sheffield: Sheffield Academic, 1996); R. P. Merendino, *Der Erste und der Letzte: Eine Untersuchung von Jes 40–48* (VTSup 31; Leiden: Brill, 1981); T. N. D. Mettinger, *A Farewell to the Servant Songs: A Critical Examination of an Exegetical Axiom* (Lund: Gleerup, 1983); J. Middlemas, "Divine Reversal and the Role of the Temple in Trito-Isaiah," in *Temple and Worship in Biblical Israel* (ed. J. Day; London: T. & T. Clark, 2005) 164-87; idem, "Trito-Isaiah's Intra- and Internationalism," in Lipschits et al., eds., *Judah and the Judeans in the Achaemenid Period,* 105-25; P. D. Miscall, *Isaiah* (Sheffield: JSOT, 1993); idem, "Isaiah: The Labyrinth of Images," *Semeia* 54 (1991) 103-21; J. Morgenstern, "Further Light from the Book of Isaiah upon the Catastrophe of 485 B.C.," *HUCA* 37 (1966) 1-28; W. S. Morrow, "Comfort for Jerusalem: The Second Isaiah as Counselor to Refugees," *BTB* 34 (2004) 80-86; S. Mowinckel, *He That Cometh* (Nashville: Abingdon, 1954); idem, *Jesaja-disiplene: Profetien fra Jesaja til Jeremia* (Oslo: Dybwad, 1926); idem, "Die Komposition des Deuterojesajanischen Buches," *ZAW* 49 (1931) 87-112, 242-60; idem, *Prophecy and Tradition* (Oslo: Dybwad, 1946); J. Muilenburg, "The Book of Isaiah: Chapters 40–66," in *IB,* 5:381-773; D. F. Murray, "The Rhetoric of Disputation: Reexamination of a Prophetic Genre," *JSOT* 38 (1987) 95-121; C. Nihan, "Ethnicity and Identity in Isaiah 56–66," in Lipschits et al., eds., *Judah and the Judeans in the Achaemenid Period,* 67-104; C. R. North, "Isaiah," *IDB,* 7:131-44; idem, *The Second Isaiah: Introduction, Translation and Commentary to Chapters XL–LV* (Oxford: Clarendon, 1964); R. Nurmela, *The Mouth of the L-rd Has Spoken: Inner Biblical Allusions in Sec-*

ond and *Third Isaiah* (Lanham: University Press of America, 2006); H. Odeberg, *Trito-Isaiah (Isaiah 56–66): A Literary and Linguistic Analysis* (UUÅ; Uppsala; Lundquist, 1931); J. van Oorschot, *Von Babel zum Zion: Eine literarkritische und redaktions-geschichtliche Untersuchung* (BZAW 206; Berlin: de Gruyter, 1993); R. Oosting, "The Counsellors of the L-rd in Isaiah 40–55," *JSOT* 32 (2008) 353-82; idem, *The Role of Zion/Jerusalem in Isaiah 40–55: A Corpus-Linguistic Approach* (SSN 59; Leiden: Brill, 2013); H. M. Orlinsky and N. Snaith, *Studies on the Second Part of the Book of Isaiah* (VTSup 14; Leiden: Brill, 1967); J. N. Oswalt, *The Book of Isaiah, Chapters 1–39* (NICOT; Grand Rapids: Eerdmans, 1986); idem, *The Book of Isaiah, Chapters 40–66* (NICOT; Grand Rapids: Eerdmans, 1998); S. M. Paul, "Deutero-Isaiah and Cuneiform Royal Inscriptions," in *Divrei Shalom,* 11-22; idem, "Deuteronom(ist)ic Influences on Deutero-Isaiah," in *Mishneh Todah (Fest.* J. Tigay; ed. N. Sacher Fox et al.; Winona Lake: Eisenbrauns, 2009) 219-27; idem, *Divrei Shalom: Collected Studies of Shalom M. Paul on the Bible and the Ancient Near East, 1967-2005* (CHANE 33; Leiden: Brill, 2005); idem, *Isaiah 40–66* (ECC; Grand Rapids: Eerdmans, 2012); idem, "Literary and Ideological Echoes of Jeremiah in Deutero-Isaiah," in *Divrei Shalom,* 399-416; K. Pauritsch, *Die neue Gemeinde: G-tt sammelt Ausgestossene und Arme (Jesaia 56–66)* (AnBib 47; Rome: Biblical Institute 1971); A.-M. Pelletier, "Le livre d'Isaïe et le temps de l'histoire," *NRTh* 112 (1990) 30-43; A. Penna, "Isaias," *EncBib;* A. Petitjean, "Représentations littéraires de Dieu chez Isaïe: Introduction à la theologie isaïenne," *Revue Diocésaine de Namur* 21 (1967) 143-62; K. Pfisterer Darr, *Isaiah's Vision and the Family of G-d* (Louisville: Westminster John Knox, 1994); G. J. Polan, *In the Ways of Justice Toward Salvation: A Rhetorical Analysis of Isaiah 56–66* (New York: Lang, 1986); M. Polliack, "Deutero-Isaiah's Typological Use of Jacob in the Portrayal of Israel's National Renewal," in *Creation in Jewish and Christian Tradition* (ed. H. Graf Reventlow and Y. Hoffman; JSOTSup 319; Sheffield: Sheffield Academic 2002) 72-110; Y. T. Radday, "Two Computerized Statistical-linguistic Tests Concerning the Unity of Isaiah," *JBL* 89 (1970) 319-24; idem, *The Unity of Isaiah in the Light of Statistical Linguistics* (Hildesheim: Gerstenberg, 1973); idem, "Vocabulary Eccentricity and the Unity of Isaiah," *Tarbiz* 39 (1969-70) 323-41 (Hebrew); R. Rendtorff, "The Book of Isaiah: A Complex Unity; Synchronic and Diachronic Reading," in *SBL 1991 Seminar Papers* (ed. E. H. Lovering, Jr.; Atlanta: Scholars 1991) 8-20 (repr. in Melugin and Sweeney, eds., *New Visions of Isaiah,* 32-49); idem, *Canon and Theology: Overtures to an Old Testament Theology* (OBT; trans. M. Kohl; Minneapolis: Fortress, 1993); idem, "Isaiah 56:1 as a Key to the Formation of the Book of Isaiah," in *Canon and Theology,* 181-89; idem, "Jesaja 6 im Rahmen der Komposition des Jesajabuches," in Vermeylen, ed., *The Book of Isaiah,* 73-82; idem, "Zur Komposition des Buches Jesajas," *VT* 34 (1984) 295-320; L. G. Rignell, *A Study of Isaiah Ch. 40–55* (Lund: Gleerup, 1956); A. Rofé, "The Extent of Trito-Isaiah According to Kuenen and Elliger: Chaps. 54–66," *Hen* 26 (2004) 128-35; idem, "How Is the Word Fulfilled? Isaiah 55:6-11 within the Theological Debate of Its Time," in *Canon, Theology, and Old Testament Interpretation (Fest.* B. S. Childs; ed. G. M. Tucker et al.; Philadelphia: Fortress, 1988) 246-61; M. Rosenbaum, "You are my Servant: Ambiguity and Deutero-Isaiah," in *Bringing the Hidden to Light (Fest.* S. A. Geller; ed. K. F. Kravitz and D. M. Sharon; Winona Lake: Eisenbrauns, 2007) 187-216; A. R. Rosenberg, *The Book of Isaiah* (Judaica Books of the Bible; 2 vols.; New York: Judaica, 1982, 1983); H. H. Rowley, *The Servant of the L-rd* (Oxford: Blackwell, 1965); J. Ruck, "Isaiah and the Prophetic Disciple," *TBT* 21 (1983) 399-405; J. van Ruiten and M. Vervenne, eds.,

Studies in the Book of Isaiah (Fest. W. A. M. Beuken; BETL 132; Leuven: Peeters, 1997); J. F. A. Sawyer, "Daughter of Zion and Servant of the L-rd in Isaiah: A Comparison," *JSOT* 44 (1989) 89-107; idem, *Isaiah* (Daily Study Bible; 2 vols.; Philadelphia: Westminster, 1984-86); B. Scheur, *The Return of YHWH: The Tension between Deliverance and Repentance in Isaiah 40–55* (BZAW 377; Berlin: de Gruyter, 2008); H. Schmidt, *Die Grossen Propheten* (SAT 2/2; Göttingen: Vandenhoeck & Ruprecht, 1915); W. H. Schmidt, "Die Einheit der Verkündigung Jesajas: Versuch einer Zusammenschau," *EvT* 37 (1977) 260-72; idem, "Jerusalemer El-Traditionen bei Jesaja: Ein religionsgeschichtlicher Vergleich zum Vorstellungskreis des göttlichen Königtums," *ZRGG* 16 (1964) 302-13; J. J. Schmitt, *Isaiah and His Interpreters* (New York: Paulist, 1986); A. Schoors, *I Am G-d Your Saviour: A Form-Critical Study of the Main Genres in Is. XL–LV* (VTSup 24; Leiden: Brill, 1973); B. Schramm, *The Opponents of Third Isaiah: Reconstructing the Cultic History of the Restoration* (JSOTSup 193; Sheffield: Sheffield Academic, 1995); J. Schreiner, "Das Buch jesajanischer Schule," in *Wort und Botschaft: Eine theologische und kritische Einführung in die Probleme des Alten Testaments* (Würzburg: Echter, 1967) 143-62; idem, *Sion-Jerusalem, JHWHs Königssitz* (SANT 7; Munich: Kumosel, 1963); E. Sehmsdorf, "Studien zur Redaktionsgeschichte von Jesaja 56–66: Jes 65:16b-25; 66:1-4; 56:1-8," *ZAW* 84 (1972) 517-76; C. R. Seitz, "The Book of Isaiah 40–66," in *NIB,* 6:309-552; idem, "The Divine Council: Temporal Transition and New Prophecy in the Book of Isaiah," *JBL* 109 (1990) 229-47; idem, "How Is the Prophet Isaiah Present in the Latter Half of the Book? The Logic of Chapters 40–66 within the Book of Isaiah," *JBL* 115 (1996) 219-40; idem, "Isaiah 1–66: Making Sense of the Whole," in *Reading and Preaching the Book of Isaiah* (Philadelphia: Fortress, 1988) 105-26; idem, *Zion's Final Destiny: The Development of the Book of Isaiah* (Minneapolis: Fortress, 1991); S. Sekine, *Die tritojesajanische Sammlung (Jes 56–66) redaktionsgeschichtliche Untersucht* (BZAW 175; Berlin: de Gruyter, 1989); G. T. Sheppard, "The Book of Isaiah: Competing Structures According to a Late Modern Description of Its Shape and Scope," in *SBL 1992 Seminar Papers* (ed. E. H. Lovering, Jr.; Atlanta: Scholars 1992) 549-82; J. Skinner, *The Book of the Prophet Isaiah, Chapters 40–66* (CBC; Cambridge: University Press, 1929); I. W. Slotki, *Isaiah* (London: Soncino, 1949); J. D. Smart, *History and Theology in Second Isaiah: A Commentary on Isaiah 35, 40–66* (Philadelphia: Westminster, 1965); G. A. Smith, *The Book of Isaiah* (ExpB; 2 vols.; New York: Armstrong, 1905); P. A. Smith, *Rhetoric and Redaction in Trito-Isaiah: The Structure, Growth, and Authorship of Isaiah 56–66* (VTSup 62; Leiden: Brill, 1995); B. D. Sommer, *A Prophet Reads Scripture: Allusion in Isaiah 40–66* (Stanford: Stanford University Press, 1998); H. C. Spykerboer, *The Structure and Composition of Deutero-Isaiah, with Special Reference to the Polemics against Idolatry* (Meppel: Krips, 1976); T. Staubli, "Maat-Imagery in Trito-Isaiah," in *Images and Prophecy in the Ancient Eastern Mediterranean* (ed. M. Nissinen and C. E. Carter; Göttingen: Vandenhoeck & Ruprecht, 2009) 41-50; O. H. Steck, *Bereitete Heimkehr: Jesaja 35 als redaktionelle Brücke zwischen dem Ersten und dem Zweiten Jesaja* (SBS 121; Stuttgart: Katholisches Bibelwerk, 1985); idem, *Friedensvorstellungen im alten Jerusalem: Psalmen, Jesaja, Deuterojesaja* (TS 111; Zürich: Theologischer, 1972); idem, *G-ttesknecht und Zion* (FAT 4; Tübingen: Mohr Siebeck, 1992); idem, *Studien zu Tritojesaja* (BZAW 203; Berlin: de Gruyter, 1991); idem, "Tritojesaja im Jesajabuch," in *Studien zu Tritojesaja,* 3-45; J. Stromberg, *An Introduction to the Study of Isaiah* (London: T. & T. Clark, 2011); idem, *Isaiah after Exile: The Author of Third Isaiah as Reader and Redactor of the Book* (Oxford Theological Monographs;

Oxford: Oxford University Press, 2011); J. Strugnell, "Notes en Marge du volume V des 'Discoveries in the Judean Desert of Jordan,'" *RevQ* 7 (1970) 163-276; C. Stuhlmueller, *Creative Redemption in Deutero-Isaiah* (AnBib 43; Rome: Biblical Institute Press, 1970); M. A. Sweeney, "The Book of Isaiah as Prophetic Torah," in Melugin and Sweeney, eds., *New Visions of Isaiah,* 50-67; idem, "The Book of Isaiah in Recent Research," *CRBS* 1 (1993) 141-62 (repr. in Hauser, ed., *Recent Research on the Major Prophets,* 78-92); idem, "Eschatology in the Book of Isaiah," in Bautch and Hibbard, eds., *The Book of Isaiah,* 179-95; idem, *Form and Intertextuality in Prophetic and Apocalyptic Literature* (FAT 45; Tübingen: Mohr Siebeck, 2005); idem, "Isaiah," in *Oxford Bibliographies in Biblical Studies* (ed. C. Matthews; New York: Oxford University Press, http://www.oxford bibliographies.com/view/document/obo-9780195393361/obo-9780195393361-0058.xml); idem, *Isaiah 1–4 and the Post-exilic Understanding of the Isaianic Tradition* (BZAW 171; Berlin: de Gruyter, 1988); idem, *Isaiah 1–39, with an Introduction to Prophetic Literature* (FOTL; Grand Rapids: Eerdmans, 1996); idem, "Isaiah and Theodicy after the Shoah," in *Strange Fire: Reading the Bible after the Holocaust* (ed. T. Linafelt; Sheffield: Sheffield Academic 2000) 208-19; idem, "Isaiah, Prophet and Book," *EBR;* idem, *King Josiah of Judah: The Lost Messiah of Israel* (Oxford: Oxford University Press, 2001); idem, "The Legacy of Josiah in Isaiah 40–55," in Everson and Kim, eds., *The Desert Will Bloom,* 109-29 (repr. in *Reading Prophetic Books,* 114-32); idem, "On Multiple Settings in the Book of Isaiah," in *SBL 1993 Seminar Papers* (ed. E. H. Lovering, Jr.; Atlanta: Scholars, 1993) 267-73 (repr. in *Form and Intertextuality in Prophetic and Apocalyptic Literature* [FAT 45; Tübingen: Mohr Siebeck, 2005] 28-35); idem, "On the Road to Duhm: Isaiah in Nineteenth Century Critical Scholarship," in Mathews McGinnis, and Tull, eds., *"As Those Who Are Taught,"* 243-62; idem, "Prophetic Exegesis in Isaiah 65-66," in Broyles and Evans, eds., *Writing and Reading the Scroll of Isaiah,* 455-74; idem, *The Prophetic Literature* (IBT; Nashville: Abingdon, 2005); idem, *Reading Prophetic Books: Form, Intertextuality, and Reception in Prophetic and Post-biblical Literature* (FAT 89; Tübingen: Mohr Siebeck, 2014); idem, "The Reconceptualization of the Davidic Covenant in Isaiah," in van Ruiten and Vervenne, eds., *Studies in the Book of Isaiah,* 41-61 (repr. in *Reading Prophetic Books,* 94-113); L.-S. Tiemeyer, *For the Comfort of Zion: The Geographical and Theological Location of Isaiah 40–55* (VTSup 139; Leiden: Brill, 2011); idem, "Isaiah 40–55: A Judahite Reading Drama," in *Daughter Zion: Her Portrait, Her Response* (AIL 13; ed. M. J. Boda et al.; Atlanta: SBL, 2012) 55-75; idem, "The Watchman Metaphor in Isaiah LVI–LXVI," *VT* 55 (2005) 378-400; L.-S. Tiemeyer and H. M. Barstad, eds., *Continuity and Discontinuity: Chronological and Thematic Development in Isaiah 40–66* (FRLANT 255; Göttingen: Vandenhoeck & Ruprecht, 2014); C. C. Torrey, *The Second Isaiah: A New Interpretation* (New York: Scribner's, 1928); P. K. Tull, "One Book, Many Voices: Conceiving of Isaiah's Polyphonic Message," in Mathews McGinnis and Tull, eds., *As Those Who Are Taught,* 279-314; idem, "Rhetorical Criticism and Beyond in Second Isaiah," in *The Changing Face of Form Criticism for the Twenty-First Century* (ed. M. A. Sweeney and E. Ben Zvi; Grand Rapids: Eerdmans, 2003) 326-34; P. K. Tull Willey, *Remember the Former Things: The Recollection of Previous Texts in Second Isaiah* (SBLDS 161; Atlanta: Scholars 1997); D. W. Van Winkle, "The Relationship of the Nations to YHWH and to Israel in Isaiah XL–LV," *VT* 35 (1985) 446-58; J. Vermeylen, ed., *The Book of Isaiah/Le livre d'Isaïe* (BETL 81; Leuven: University Press and Peeters, 1989); idem, *Du prophète Isaïe à l'apocalyptique* (EBib; 2 vols.; Paris: Gabalda, 1977-78); idem, "L'unité du livre d'Isaïe," in *The Book of Isaiah,* 11-53; J. M. Vincent, *Studien zur literarischen Eigenart und zur geistigen Heimat von Jesaja, Kap. 40–55* (BBET 5; Frankfurt a.M.: Lang, 1977); P. Volz, *Jesaia II* (KAT 9/2; Hildesheim: Olms, 1974); T. C. Vriezen, "Essentials of the Theology of Isaiah," in Anderson and Harrelson, eds., *Israel's Prophetic Heritage,* 128-46; G. W. Wade, *The Book of the Prophet Isaiah* (Westminster Commentary; London: Methuen, 1911); J. M. Ward, "Isaiah," *IDBSup,* 456-61; J. D. W. Watts, *Isaiah 1–33* (WBC 24; Waco: Word, 1985); idem, *Isaiah 34–66* (WBC 25; Waco: Word, 1987); B. G. Webb, "Zion in Transformation: A Literary Approach to Isaiah," in *The Bible in Three Dimensions* (ed. D. J. A. Clines et al.; JSOTSup 87; Sheffield: Sheffield Academic, 1990) 65-84; R. D. Wells, "'They All Gather, They Come to You': History, Utopia, and the Reading of Isaiah 49:18-26 and 60:4 -16," in Everson and Kim, eds., *The Desert Will Bloom,* 197-216; W. Werner, *Studien zur alttestamentlichen Vorstellung vom Plan JHWS* (BZAW 173; Berlin: de Gruyter, 1988); C. Westermann, *Basic Forms of Prophetic Speech* (trans. H. C. White; Philadelphia: Westminster, 1967; repr. Cambridge: Lutterworth, 1991); idem, *Isaiah 40–66* (OTL; Philadelphia: Westminster, 1969); idem, *Sprache und Struktur der Prophetie Deuterojesajas* (CTM 11; Stuttgart: Calwer, 1981); R. N. Whybray, *Isaiah 40–66* (NCB; Grand Rapids: Eerdmans; London: Marshall, Morgan, and Scott, 1975); idem, *The Second Isaiah* (OTG 1; Sheffield: Sheffield Academic, 1983); H. G. M. Williamson, *The Book Called Isaiah: Deutero-Isaiah's Role in Composition and Redaction* (Oxford: Clarendon 1994); H. W. Wolff, "Die Begründungen der prophetischen Heils- und Unheilssprüche," in *Gesammelte Studien zum Alten Testament* (TB 22; Munich: Kaiser, 1964) 9-35 (repr. from *ZAW* 52 [1934] 1-22); E. J. Young, *The Book of Isaiah* (3 vols.; NICOT; Grand Rapids: Eerdmans, 1965-72); J. Ziegler, *Das Buch Isaias* (EB; Würzburg: Echter, 1958); W. Zimmerli, "Zur Sprache Tritojesajas," in *G-ttes Offenbarung: Gesammelte Aufsätze zum Alten Testament* (Munich: Kaiser, 1969), 217-33.

INTRODUCTION TO THE BOOK OF ISAIAH: THE VISION OF ISAIAH BEN AMOZ: PROPHETIC EXHORTATION TO JERUSALEM/ JUDAH TO ADHERE TO YHWH, ISAIAH 1:1–66:24

Structure

I. Concerning YHWH's plans for worldwide sovereignty at Zion — 1:1–33:24
A. Prologue to the book of Isaiah: introductory parenesis concerning YHWH's intention to purify Jerusalem — 1:1-31
B. Prophetic instruction concerning YHWH's projected plans to establish worldwide sovereignty at Zion: announcement of the Day of YHWH — 2:1–33:24
  1. Prophetic announcement concerning the preparation of Zion for its role as the center for YHWH's world rule — 2:1–4:6
  2. Prophetic instruction concerning the significance of Assyrian judgment against Jacob/Israel: restoration of Davidic rule — 5:1–12:6
  3. Prophetic announcement concerning the preparation of the nations for YHWH's world rule — 13:1–27:13

Although the superscription for the book of Isaiah in 1:1 identifies the entire book as "The Vision of Isaiah ben Amoz which he saw concerning Judah and Jerusalem in the days of Uzziah, Jotham, Ahaz, and Hezekiah, kings of Judah," interpreters have long recognized Isaiah to be a composite book. Thus, the Babylonian Talmud in *b. Baba Batra* 14b-15a states that the book of Isaiah was written by "Hezekiah and his colleagues." The Talmud's statement does not anticipate an author from the Babylonian period, but it does recognize that someone other than Isaiah ben Amoz had a hand in the composition of the book. The medieval Jewish exegete R. Abraham ibn Ezra (d. 1167) recognized later composition beginning in ch. 40, where he states,

This chapter has been placed here for the following reason: in the preceding chapter it is predicted that all the treasures of the king, and even his sons, will be carried away to Babylon; this sad prediction is properly followed by the words of comfort. These first comforting promises, with which the second part of the book of Isaiah begins, refer, as R. Moses Hakkohen believes, to the restoration of the temple by Zerubbabel; according to my opinion to the coming redemption from our present exile; prophecies concerning the Babylonian exile are introduced only as an illustration, showing how Cyrus, who allowed the captive Jews to return to Jerusalem. . . (read, "showing that Cyrus allowed the captive Jews to return to Jerusalem," MAS). About the last section of the book there is no doubt, that it refers to a period yet to come, as I shall explain. — It is to be borne in mind, that the opinion of the orthodox, that the book of Samuel was written by Samuel, is correct as regards the first part, till the words, 'And Samuel died' (1 Sam xxv.1); this remark is confirmed by the fact that the book of Chronicles contains the names (of the descendants of David) in genealogical order down to Zerubbabel. — The words 'Kings shall see and arise, princes and (they, MAS) shall worship' (xlix.7) support this view, though they might also be explained as follows: "Kings and princes will arise, etc., when they hear the name of the prophet, even after his death." The reader will adopt the opinion which recommends itself most to his judgment. (M. Frieländer, Ph.D., *The Commentary of Ibn Ezra on Isaiah* [New York: Philipp Feldheim, n.d.; 1st ed., London: N. Trübner, 1873] 1:169-71; my corrections are noted)

Just as Ibn Ezra had earlier followed the Talmud in recognizing that not all of the Torah was written by Moses, so he concluded that ch. 40 began a section of the book of Isaiah that was written when Cyrus decreed that Jews could return to Jerusalem.

With the coming of the age of Enlightenment, modern critical scholars began to recognize that ch. 40 marked the beginning of a segment of Isaiah composed by an author from the period of the Babylonian exile. Interpreters identify J. C. Doederlein's 1775 Latin translation of Isaiah and notes as well as J. B. Koppe's notes to the 1780 translation of Robert Lowth's commentary as the beginning of critical research on Isaiah (Doederlein, *Esaias ex recensione textus hebraei ad fidem codd. Manuscriptorum et versionum antiquarum latine vertit notasque varii argumenti subiecit Jo. Christoph. Doederlein D.* [Altdorf, 1775, cited from Gesenius, *Jesaia,* 1/1:140, n. 21]; Friedman, "Isaiah," *EncJud* 9:45; Seitz, "Isaiah, Book of," *ABD* 3:473; Sweeney, "On the Road"). The first full discussions of the hypothesis appeared in E. F. C. Rosenmüller's 1791-93/1811-20 notes on Isaiah and especially J. G. Eichhorn's widely influential 1780-83 introduction to the Old Testament (Rosenmüller, *Scholia in Vetus Testamentum. T. III. Jesaiae vaticinia complectens* [Leipzig: Barth, 1791-93, cited from Gesenius, *Jesaia,* 1/1:137, n. 6]; Eichhorn, *Einleitung in das Alte Testament* [4th ed.; Göttingen: Rosenbusch, 1820-24, 1st ed., 1780-83] 76-146; Friedman, "Isaiah," *EncJud* 9:46). Indeed, Eichhorn did not limit himself to chs. 40-66, but identified chs. 15–16; 21:1-10; and 24–27 as compositions that must also come from later prophets. Wilhelm Gesenius identified chs. 13; 14; 21; 24–27; 34; 35; and

40–66 as the work of an exilic-period prophet whom he called "Pseudo-Jesaia" (Gesenius, *Jesaia,* ad loc; Sweeney, "On the Road," 248-51). The views of Eichhorn and Gesenius were generally followed by their students, Ferdinand Hitzig *(Der Prophet Jesaia),* Heinrich Georg August Ewald (*Die Propheten des Alten Bundes,* 3:7-140, 159-76), and August Dillmann (*Der Prophet Jesaia;* Sweeney, "On the Road to Duhm," 251-60). G. A. Smith's expositional commentary on Isaiah and S. R. Driver's critical introduction to the Old Testament cleared the way for the hypothesis in the English-speaking world (Smith, *The Book of Isaiah,* 2:3-25; Driver, *An Introduction to the Literature of the Old Testament* [Cleveland: World, 1965, 1st ed., 1891] 236-46).

Most interpreters recognize that Bernhard Duhm's 1892 commentary marks the beginning of modern critical research on Isaiah. Nevertheless, Duhm was highly dependent on the work of the scholars mentioned here who had identified an exilic-period prophet as the author of chs. 40–55 and of much material in chs. 1–39. Duhm followed his predecessors in identifying chs. 40–55 as the work of an anonymous prophet from the period of the Babylonian exile, although he placed Deutero-Isaiah in Phoenicia rather than in Babylon. Over the course of the 20th century, most interpreters have come to accept Deutero-Isaiah as the product of an anonymous 6th-century prophet of the Babylonian exile. Early-20th-century research tended to follow Duhm in positing that chs. 40–55 comprise numerous short oracular texts that were assembled into a sequence of collections, and early form-critics, such as J. Begrich *(Gesammelte Studien)* and L. Köhler *(Deuterojesaja),* tended to define those short, self-contained units on generic grounds. But in the aftermath of World War II, the rise of redaction criticism (see esp. Westermann, *Isaiah 40–66;* Elliger, *Deuterojesaja*) and rhetorical criticism (see esp. Muilenburg, "Isaiah 40–66") prompted scholars to abandon their prior focus on the short self-contained unit in an effort to understand the larger structural and rhetorical patterns that might inform the reading of biblical texts. Thus scholars combined synthetic forms of literary criticism with diachronic concerns in attempts to define the overall structure of chs. 40–55 (e.g., Melugin, *Formation;* Spykerboer, *Structure and Composition*) or chs. 40–48 (e.g., Merendino, *Der Erste*), whereas others focused on rhetorical criticism as a means to define coherence in chs. 40–48 (e.g., Gitay, *Prophecy and Persuasion*) or 40–55 (e.g., Clifford, *Fair Spoken*). German scholarship, while largely accepting the redactional coherence of chs. 40–55, has attempted to trace the compositional processes by which these chapters arrived at their present form (Steck, *G-ttesknecht;* Kratz, *Kyros;* Kiesow, *Exodustexte;* van Oorschott, *Von Babel;* Berges, *Das Buch Jesaja*). Although some have attempted to challenge the Babylonian setting of chs. 40–55 in favor of a Judean setting (e.g., Tiemeyer, *For the Comfort*), the argument is not entirely persuasive. It is clear that a Judean population continued to reside in Judah during the Babylonian exile, but chs. 40–55 indicate an author or authors who well understood Babylonian culture, particularly the Akitu or New Year's festival, and called upon exiled Jews to return to Jerusalem to rebuild the temple following Cyrus's decree. Such understanding does not preclude the possibility that the author of chs. 40–55 returned to Jerusalem in the late 6th century to complete the work and to see it performed liturgically in the context of the restored temple.

Duhm's truly original contribution to modern research on Isaiah was the identification of Trito-Isaiah as another anonymous prophet who wrote in Judah during the mid-5th century B.C.E., immediately prior to the time of Nehemiah and Ezra, in an effort to build support for the newly-reconstructed Jerusalem temple. Some interpreters, particularly Elliger (*Die Einheit; Deuterojesaja*), have attempted to defend the contention first made by Duhm that Trito-Isaiah is the product of a single author, but most scholars hold that the various views of the temple, as either completed or still in ruins, and the lack of linguistic consistency point to multiple hands in the composition of chs. 56–66 (see Hanson, *Dawn;* Stromberg, *Isaiah after Exile,* 1-40; Goldingay, *Isaiah 56–66,* 1-9). Although many view Trito-Isaiah as a Persian-period redactional and rhetorical unity (e.g., Hanson, *Dawn;* P. A. Smith, *Rhetoric and Redaction*), others maintain that Trito-Isaiah shows evidence of redactional expansion and growth well into the later-Persian or Hellenistic periods (e.g., Steck, *Studien;* Sekine, *Die tritojesajanische Sammlung;* Koenen, *Ethik;* Blenkinsopp, *Isaiah 56–66*). Still others hold that there is no Trito-Isaiah at all, insofar as linguistic affinities with chs. 40–55 indicate that chs. 56–66 are simply a continuation of Deutero-Isaiah (e.g., Haran, "Literary Structure"; Sommer, *A Prophet Reads Scripture;* Paul, *Isaiah 40–66*), although such a view fails to account for the marked interest in the differentiation between the righteous and the wicked in chs. 56–66 versus the view of Israel as a single nation in chs. 40–55.

Twentieth-century scholarship generally followed Duhm in asserting a Proto- or First Isaiah, i.e., the late-8th-century prophet Isaiah ben Amoz, in chs. 1–39; an anonymous 6th-century prophet dubbed Deutero- or Second Isaiah in chs. 40–55; and a 6th- /4th-century section of oracles in chs. 56–66 identified as Trito- or Third Isaiah, but the three-part structure of chs. 1–39; 40–55; and 56–66 defines neither the synchronic nor the diachronic forms of the book. Ackroyd, "An Interpretation of the Babylonian Exile: A Study of 2 Kings 20, Isaiah 38–39," *Studies,* 152-71; Clements, "The Unity"; idem, "Beyond Tradition-History"; Seitz, "Divine Council": idem, "How Is the Prophet Isaiah Present"; and Kiesow, *Exodustexte,* pointed to a variety of links between First and Second Isaiah, such as the anticipation of the Babylonian exile in chs. 1–12 and 36–39 (Ackroyd, "Isaiah 1–12: Presentation of a Prophet," *Studies,* 79-104; cf. B. Gosse, *Isaumie 13,1–14,23 dans la tradition littéraire du livre d'Isaïe et dans la tradition des oracles contre les nations* [OBO 78; Göttingen: Vandenhoeck & Ruprecht; Freiburg: Universitätsverlag, 1988]); the interrelationships between Second Isaiah's statements concerning the former and the new things, the concern to open the eyes, ears, and minds, and the new exodus from Babylonia with their counterparts in chs. 1–39 (Clements, "The Unity"; idem, "Beyond Tradition-History"; Kiesow, *Exodustexte*); and the interrelationships between the call narratives in ch. 6 and 40:1-11 (Seitz, "The Divine Council"; idem, "How Is the Prophet Isaiah Present"). Rendtorff noted links between Trito-Isaiah and First Isaiah, such as the interest in justice (*mišpāṭ*) and righteousness (*ṣĕdāqâ*), that pointed to Trito-Isaiah and First Isaiah as a redactional envelope around Second Isaiah (Rendtorff, "Isaiah 56:1"; cf. Jones, "The Traditio"; see now Stromberg, *Isaiah after Exile*). Scholars began to experiment with attempts to build upon these interrelationships to define a basis either for reading First and Second Isaiah together (e.g., Williamson, *The Book Called Isaiah*) or for reading the final form of the book of Isaiah as a whole (e.g., Becker, *Isaias;* Lack, *La symbolique;* Childs, *Introduction;* idem, *Isaiah;* Sweeney, *Isaiah 1–4;* idem, *Isaiah 1–39;* Leclerc, *YHWH Is Exalted*). Many have also focused on redaction-critical attempts to explain the formation of the book of Isaiah as a whole (Berges, *Das Buch Jesaja;* Blenkinsopp, *Isaiah 1–39;* idem, *Isaiah 40–55;* idem, *Isaiah 56–66;* Steck, *Bereitete Heimkehr;* idem, *G-ttesknecht;* Sweeney, *Isaiah 1–39;* Vermeylen, "L'unité").

Several key factors must be considered in any attempt to define the formal structure of the book of Isaiah. The first is the degree to which chs. 1–39 anticipate the Babylonian exile and the downfall of the Babylonian Empire. Isaiah 13–14 explicitly calls for the downfall of the Babylonian Empire on the Day of YHWH, and ch. 21 does so surreptitiously, identifying Elam and Media, two countries involved in the downfall of Babylon, as Babylon's attackers. Likewise, ch. 39 presents Isaiah's condemnation of King Hezekiah for receiving a Babylonian delegation in Jerusalem and announces that someday his sons will be carried off to Babylon.

Second is the degree to which chs. 1–39; 40–55; and 56–66 all focus on the theme of a second exodus in which exiled Judeans and Israelites will return to Jerusalem and the land of Israel from foreign captivity. Examples of the return from foreign exile appear in 11:10-16; 27:2-13; 35:1-10; 40:1-11; 43:1-21; 48:20-21; 49:7-26; 51:9-11; 54:1-17; 60:1–62:12; 63:11-14; and 66:18-21, indicating that the motif permeates the entire book. Other exodus-related motifs include the portrayal of Israel rendered blind, deaf, and dumb so that it cannot repent and be saved in ch. 6, much like Pharaoh's heart is hardened in the exodus narratives; the portrayal of Assyrian oppression of Israel like that of Egypt in 10:24-26; and the slaying of 185 thousand Assyrian soldiers by the angel of YHWH in chs. 36–39, much like the angel of death slew the firstborn of Egypt in the exodus narratives.

Third is the degree to which chs. 40–55 and 56–66 take up language and motifs from Isaiah's commissioning narrative in ch. 6, particularly the problematic commands to the prophet to render the people blind, deaf, and dumb so that the people will not repent and be saved from the impending judgment. Second Isaiah repeatedly calls upon the people of Israel to open their eyes and ears so that they might see, hear, and understand the new things that YHWH is doing now that the Babylonian exile is coming to an end. Such calls appear in 42:7; 42:13-25; 43:8; 48:3-8; 44:18-22; and 56:10. The concern with the holy seed in 6:13 also comes to expression in 65:9, which describes the seed from Jacob that will possess YHWH's holy mountain, and in 66:22, which speaks about the continuity of Israel's seed and name. Indeed, chs. 65–66 also develop the tree imagery of chs. 6 and 11 to portray the return of the exiles to YHWH's holy mountain (Sweeney, "Prophetic Exegesis in Isaiah 65–66," in *Form and Intertextuality,* 46-62). Other intertextual motifs include the light experienced by the people who walk in darkness (9:1; 42:16; 50:10-11; 60–62); the revelation of YHWH's Torah to all the nations as well as to Israel (2:2-4; 42:4; 51:4); the development of the motif of rejoicing from 8:6 in 66:10-14 (Sweeney, "On *ûměśôś* in Isaiah 8:6" in *Form and Intertextuality,* 36-45); the hidden face of G-d

(8:16-17; 54:8; 64:6); the interrelationship between ensign in 11:10-16 and the references to the ensign in 49:22; 62:10; the multitude of intertextual relationships between ch. 1 and chs. 65–66 (Sweeney, *Isaiah 1–39;* idem, "Prophetic Exegesis in Isaiah 65–66"); and the many other intertextual relationships between chs. 1–39 and 40–66.

Fourth is the deliberate contrast between the portrayal of Ahaz in 7:1–9:6 and the portrayal of Hezekiah in chs. 36–39. Ackroyd ("Isaiah 36–39: Structure and Function," in *Studies,* 105-20) points out the parallels: both kings are portrayed in a time of crisis; both narratives focus on the upper pool by the Fullers' Field as the location for the primary encounters on which the plot turns; both narratives emphasize divine zeal. He also points out the contrast, namely, Ahaz fails to show faithfulness in YHWH and the nation thereby suffers for his faithlessness, whereas Hezekiah turns to YHWH in faithfulness and thereby saves Jerusalem. The contrast between the two highlights the portrayal of the causes for punishment in the first half of the book versus the sought-for reaction of the people in the second half of the book.

Finally, the parallels between chs. 1 and 34–35 must be considered. This issue begins with the observation of the gap in the Great Isaiah Scroll from Qumran (1QIsaᵃ) between chs. 33 and 34. Although clearly the product of the Qumran scribe, the gap represents his apparent understanding of the structure of the book. Indeed, Brownlee *(Meaning)* and Evans ("On the Unity") laid out the case for the apparent parallels, and Sweeney developed it as the key feature of the structure of the book of Isaiah *(Isaiah 1–39)*. Ch. 1 points to coming judgment and restoration for the people of Israel, whereas chs. 34–35 point to coming judgment against the nations, beginning with Edom, and restoration for Israel. The two texts have parallel calls to attention in 1:2 and 34:1; the focus on YHWH's vengeance in 1:24 and 34:8; unquenchable burning of YHWH's enemies in 1:31 and Edom in 34:10; the "mouth of YHWH that speaks" in 1:20 and 34:16; YHWH's sword of punishment in 1:20 and 34:5, 6; the sacrificial blood and fat of cattle in 1:11-15 and 34:6-7; the references to Sodom and Gomorrah in 1:7-9, 10 and 34:9-11; and the references to wilting leaves in 1:30 and 34:4. As the parallel concerns with judgment of first Israel and then the nations followed by restoration indicates, each of these chapters functions as an introduction to each half of the book. Indeed, ch. 1, with its interest in announcing to Israel the judgment of Jerusalem and its subsequent restoration, and chs. 34–35, with their interest in announcing to the nations that their judgment has been realized and that Jerusalem's restoration is at hand, function as introductions to their respective segments of Isaiah.

These considerations indicate that chs. 1–33 and 34–66 function as the two major components of the formal synchronic structure of the book of Isaiah. Whereas chs. 1–33 focus on Jerusalem's impending judgment and restoration in anticipation of YHWH's worldwide sovereignty over all creation and humanity at Zion, chs. 34–66 focus on the nations' punishment, beginning with Edom, and restoration of Jerusalem as the realization of YHWH's worldwide sovereignty over all creation and humanity at Zion. A number of further considerations support this contention. Isaiah 1–33 point to impending judgment against Jerusalem, Judah, and Israel as well as Assyria (10:5-34; 14:24-27), Babylon (13:1–14:23), and the other nations mentioned in chs. 13–27 as a prelude to the restoration of righteous Davidic kingship and recognition of YHWH in Jerusalem (2:2-4; 9:1-6; 11:1-16; 32–33). Isaiah 34–66 point to the realization of judgment against Edom (Isaiah 34; 63:1-6) as well as the other nations, most notably Babylon (Isaiah 46–47), as the basis for the impending restoration of Jerusalem (Isaiah 35; 49–54; 60–62) and the recognition of YHWH's role as the true sovereign of all creation and humanity (Isa 40:12–48:22; 65–66). But whereas chs. 1–33 point to the restoration of righteous Davidic kingship (9:1-6; 11:1-16; 32–33), chs. 34–66 point to Cyrus as YHWH's messiah and temple-builder (44:28; 45:1) and to YHWH as the true sovereign (65:1). Instead of an eternal covenant between YHWH and the house of David, chs. 34–66 anticipate an eternal covenant between YHWH and the people of Israel based on the model of David (ch. 55). Instead of oppression of Jerusalem, Judah, and Israel by the nations as portrayed in chs. 1–33, chs. 34–66 anticipate that the nations will play a key role in enabling the restoration of the Israelite and Judean exiles to Jerusalem (chs. 34–35; 60–62; 65–66).

The formal synchronic literary structure, discussed in detail in Sweeney, *Isaiah 1–39,* then enables the presentation of this aforementioned scenario. The book of Isaiah as a whole constitutes the Vision of Isaiah ben Amoz as a prophetic EXHORTATION to Jerusalem and Judah to adhere to YHWH. It presents its argument in two basic segments, each of which points to YHWH as the sovereign of the universe at large and Jerusalem, Judah, and Israel in particular. The first segment in chs. 1–33 constitutes a PROPHETIC ANNOUNCEMENT concerning YHWH's plans for worldwide sovereignty in Zion. The second segment in chs. 34–66 constitutes a PROPHETIC ANNOUNCEMENT concerning the realization of YHWH's plans for worldwide sovereignty in Jerusalem. Both sections understand the events of Jerusalem's history from the late-8th-century invasions of Israel and Judah by the Assyrian Empire, through the Babylonian exile and the Persian-period restoration of Jerusalem, as deliberate acts of YHWH who planned the entire process as a means to demonstrate divine sovereignty to Jerusalem, Judah, and Israel as well as to all the nations of the world.

Chs. 1–33 include a sequence of textual blocks in chs. 1; 2–4; 5–12; 13–23; 24–27; and 28–33 that are discussed in detail in Sweeney, *Isaiah 1–39.* Chs. 1–33 begin with a prologue in ch. 1, which constitutes an introductory PARENESIS concerning YHWH's intention to purify Zion for its role as the site for YHWH's rule of all creation. By pointing to both the judgment and the restoration of Jerusalem, it calls upon the people to abandon allegedly evil conduct and to adhere to YHWH so that they might be included among those who will be included in YHWH's world rule.

Chs. 2–33, introduced by a superscription in 2:1, then follow with an announcement of the Day of YHWH, which presents detailed prophetic instruction concerning YHWH's projected plans to establish worldwide sovereignty at Zion. Chs. 2–33 comprise four basic subunits, each of which is demarcated formally and focuses on a specific concern that anticipates YHWH's plans. Chs. 2–4 constitute a prophetic announcement concerning the Day of YHWH which focuses on the preparation of Zion for its role as the center for YHWH's world rule. Isaiah 5–12 shifts its focus to prophetic instruction concerning the significance of Assyrian judgment against Jacob/Israel and the anticipated restoration of righteous Davidic rule. Isaiah 13–27, introduced once again by its own superscription in 13:1, constitutes a prophetic announcement concerning the preparation of the nations for YHWH's world rule. Chs. 13–27 comprise two subunits which focus on the two key elements of the announcement, namely, the pronouncements concerning the nations in chs. 13–23 and the prophetic announcement of YHWH's new world order based upon the restoration of Zion and Israel in chs. 24–27. Finally, chs. 28–33 constitute prophetic instruction concerning YHWH's plans for Jerusalem, particularly the announcement of a royal deliverer who will oversee the people on YHWH's behalf.

Chs. 34–66 include textual blocks in chs. 34–35 and 36–39 that are discussed in detail in Sweeney, *Isaiah 1–39*, as well as chs. 40–54 and 55–66 with all of their subunits that are discussed in detail in the present volume. Chs. 34–66 constitute the PROPHETIC ANNOUNCEMENT concerning YHWH's plans for worldwide sovereignty in Zion. It includes two basic subunits, each of which is defined by its distinctive formal and thematic features, in chs. 34–54 and chs. 55–66.

Isaiah 34–54 constitute prophetic INSTRUCTION concerning the realization of YHWH's worldwide sovereignty in Zion. It begins in chs. 34–35 with prophetic instruction concerning YHWH's power to return the redeemed exiles to Zion, including announcements concerning YHWH's punishment of the nations that oppressed Israel in ch. 34 and the portrayal of return of the exiles to Zion in ch. 35. The second major subunit appears in chs. 36–39, which constitute royal narratives concerning YHWH's deliverance of Jerusalem and Hezekiah during Sennacherib's siege. These narratives provide a contrast between the allegedly faithless Ahaz in chs. 5–12, esp. 7:1–9:6, who brings judgment against Jerusalem and the people for his failure to trust in YHWH, and Hezekiah in chs. 36–39, who turns to YHWH in faith during a time of crisis and thereby delivers the city and its people. Such a model provides an example for the readers of the book who are asked to adhere to YHWH as the true sovereign of the universe. Chs. 40–54 then present prophetic INSTRUCTION that YHWH is indeed maintaining the covenant and restoring Zion as promised in chs. 1–33.

The formal synchronic structure of the prophetic instruction that YHWH is maintaining covenant and restoring Zion in chs. 40–54 is discussed in detail in the present volume. Many interpreters note that chs. 40–48 focus broadly on the return of Jacob, i.e., personified Israel, to Jerusalem and the land of Israel whereas Isaiah 49–55 focuses broadly on the figure of Bat Zion/Daughter Zion as a personification of Jerusalem who waits for the return of her husband, YHWH, and her children, the exiled people of Jerusalem, Judah, and Israel (Tull Willey, *Remember the Former Things,* who identifies Jacob/Israel and Bat Zion as the male and female servant figures of Second Isaiah). Although some hold that these blocks of material must be treated as separate blocks of text, closer attention to the rhetorical and persuasive features of these chapters calls for a different reading that highlights their argumentative character and the interplay of the two metaphorical figures, Jacob and Bat Zion (cf. P. K. Tull, "Rhetorical Criticism and Intertextuality," in *To Each Its Own Meaning: An Introduction to Biblical Criticisms and Their Application* [ed. S. L. McKenzie and S. R. Haynes; Louisville: Westminster John Knox, 1999] 156–80; P. Trible, *Rhetor-*

ical Criticism: Context, Method, and the Book of Jonah [GBS; Minneapolis: Fortress, 1994], for methodological perspective).

Isaiah 40:1-11 constitutes a brief prologue for chs. 40–54, insofar as it introduces the overarching themes of comfort for the people and the end of Jerusalem's punishment, the return of YHWH and the exiles to Zion through the wilderness in a new exodus, the response of creation to YHWH's return, the proclamation of a new prophetic commission to speak, the constancy of YHWH's word, and the announcement to Zion that YHWH is returning. Interpreters have focused especially on the so-called call or commissioning elements of this text and its interrelationship with Isaiah 6, which constitutes the original commissioning narrative of Isaiah ben Amoz (e.g., Seitz, "The Divine Council"; "How Is the Prophet Isaiah Present"). Isaiah 40:1-11 thereby functions as a new commissioning narrative for the diachronically-defined exilic prophet, Second Isaiah, and his/her book in chs. 40–55. But when this text is read in the synchronic framework of the book of Isaiah as a whole, it cannot function as the commissioning narrative of a new prophet; it can only function as a recollection of the earlier commissioning narrative in ch. 6, perhaps from a different perspective of the Seraph who touched Isaiah's lips with the burning coal and the prophet himself. When read in this fashion, 40:1-11 probes more deeply into the interaction between the Seraph and the prophet at the time of the latter's commissioning in an effort to lay out the agenda for the following chapters. Interpreters have noted that 40:1-8, with its interests in the comfort of the people, the second exodus, and the role of creation, anticipates the concerns of chs. 40–48 (40:12–48:22), whereas 40:9-11, with its concern with announcing the return of YHWH and the people to Zion, anticipates the concerns of chs. 49–55 (49–54). Ch. 55, with its focus on a renewed Davidic covenant with the people of Israel, has a very different set of concerns to be discussed below, but 40:1-11 appears to function as a prologue for both 40:12–48:22 and chs. 49–54. Consequently, 40:1-11; 40:12–48:22; and 49–54 must be read together as a coherent block that proclaims the renewed prophetic commission to announce YHWH's restoration of Zion.

Turning to 40:12–54:17, two distinctive elements emerge. One is the argumentative or persuasive character of the text (cf. Gitay, *Prophecy and Persuasion*), and the other is the appearance of liturgical or hymnic elements that demarcate the various subunits of the text (Matheus, *Singt dem H-rrn*). Close examination of the text indicates that 40:12–54:17 puts forward a series of arguments in a sequence of five formally defined subunits that culminate in the contention that YHWH is restoring Zion.

The first is 40:12-31, which is formally defined by its disputational character, including its introductory rhetorical questions, "Who measured with the hollow of his hand the waters and measured with his finger the heavens?" in v. 12 and its closing assertion, "those who hope in YHWH shall renew strength," in v. 31. Altogether, 40:12-31 argues that YHWH is the master of all creation who may therefore act in the world as the following texts contend.

The second is 41:1–42:13, which is formally defined by its introductory forensic summons to the coastlands and the nations to contend with YHWH in court in 41:1, "Be silent before me, O coastlands, and let the nations renew their strength," and by its closing hymn in 42:13, "YHWH like a warrior goes out; like a man of war, he awakens zeal; he shouts, indeed, he roars!" The passage contends throughout that YHWH is the master of human events, beginning with the assertion expressed by the rhetorical question, "Who has aroused from the east, one who is righteous? Called him to his feet (i.e., his service)?" in reference to King Cyrus of Persia, who will later emerge in the text as YHWH's anointed king and temple-builder who will see to the return of the exiles and the restoration of Jerusalem.

The third is 42:14–44:23, which is formally defined by YHWH's introductory exclamation, "I was silent from the past, I was quiet and restrained. Like a woman giving birth, I will scream, I will pant and gasp together," in 42:14 and closes in 44:23 with the hymn, "Sing out, O Heavens, because YHWH has acted; shout aloud, O Depths of the Earth! Break out, O Mountains in song; O Forest and every Tree in it! For YHWH has redeemed Jacob, and magnified himself in Israel!" Clearly, there is a lot of drama in this text, which draws upon past acts by YHWH and assertions of YHWH's continued action to contend that YHWH is the redeemer of Israel.

The fourth is 44:24–48:22, which begins in 44:24 with a PROPHETIC MESSENGER SPEECH ascribed to "YHWH, your redeemer," and reiterates YHWH's role as creator and redeemer of Israel to assert that YHWH can employ Cyrus, the foreign king of Persia, as messiah and temple-builder as part of the larger effort to restore Jerusalem. One would have expected a Davidic figure for this role, but lacking a viable Davidic monarch at the end of the Babylonian exile, our text turns to the only viable royal figure at the time, Cyrus of Persia. In this respect, the text recognizes the political realities of the time, and it prepares for the passing of the eternal Davidic covenant to the people of Israel as a whole in ch. 55. Isaiah 44:24–48:22 concludes with the hymnic call to "go forth from Babylon" in 48:20-21 and the statement in 48:22, reiterated in 57:21, "There is no peace, says YHWH, for the wicked."

The fifth and final subunit of the sequence appears in 49:1–54:14, which is demarcated formally by its introductory summons to attention concerning YHWH's intentions to restore the servant, Jacob/Israel; its overall focus on Bat Zion or Jerusalem as the metaphorical portrayal of the bride to whom YHWH returns and the mother to whom Jacob/Israel returns; and its closing liturgical summons to the barren mother, Bat Zion, to widen her tent because her children, Jacob/Israel, and her husband, YHWH, are returning to her. Overall, Isaiah 49–54 contends that YHWH is restoring Jerusalem.

The second and concluding unit of the prophetic announcement concerning the realization of YHWH's plans for worldwide sovereignty at Zion in chs. 34–66 appears in chs. 55–66, which constitute the rhetorical goal of the book as a prophetic exhortation to adhere to YHWH's covenant. The introductory passage to this unit is ch. 55, which is formally defined by its introductory metaphorical summons to listen to YHWH, its overall concern to grant the eternal Davidic covenant to the people of Israel, and its concluding sign in vv. 11-13 that YHWH's word is reliable and will stand forever. Although scholars have correctly argued that ch. 55 was composed as the concluding element for Second Isaiah, its concern with the reliability of YHWH's word and the eternal nature of

YHWH's covenant with Israel prompt it to function synchronically within the final form of the text as an introduction to chs. 56–66, diachronically defined as Trito-Isaiah, which function synchronically as prophetic instruction concerning the reconstituted covenant. Specifically, ch. 55 functions as an exhortation to adhere to YHWH's covenant, and chs. 56–66 function as prophetic instruction as to how one might observe that covenant.

Fundamentally, the instruction in chs. 56–66 distinguishes between the righteous who adhere to YHWH's covenant and the wicked who do not. The contrasting fates of the righteous and wicked reiterate concerns from ch. 1 and serve as motivation in the exhortation to adhere to YHWH's covenant: those who adhere to YHWH's covenant will be part of the restored Zion to which the nations will convey the exiles and the wicked will perish. Isaiah Chs. 56–66 comprise three subunits, each of which contributes to the instruction concerning the reconstituted nation of Israel in Zion.

The first subunit is chs. 56–59, which provides prophetic instruction concerning the proper observance of YHWH's covenant. The passage is demarcated by its initial subunit concerned with the inclusion of foreigners among the restored people, which holds that foreigners who observe YHWH's covenant, beginning with Shabbat observance, will be included in what can only be considered as a form of conversion to Judaism. It continues with 56:9–57:21, which focuses on YHWH's willingness to forgive those who repent; 58:1-14, which admonishes the people to repent, including specific instructions for covenant observance; and it concludes with 59:1-21, which presents a lament concerning YHWH's willingness and ability to deliver those who repent.

The second subunit is chs. 60–62, which constitutes a proclamation of salvation or restoration for Jerusalem. Although some consider the servant figure in ch. 61 to be a royal, close study of the portrayal of the figure indicates that he is a priest, which points to the restoration of the temple as the foundation for the restoration of Jerusalem.

Finally, the third subunit is chs. 63–66, which focuses on the process by which the restoration is to be achieved. It begins in 63:1-6 with the portrayal of YHWH's return after slaying the wicked in Edom, which recalls the initial concern with Edom and the nations in ch. 34. It continues in 63:7–64:11 with the prophet's LAMENT and APPEAL for mercy on behalf of the righteous among people, and it concludes in chs. 65–66 with YHWH's response to the prophet's appeal with an announcement of salvation for the righteous, who will be returned to Jerusalem by the nations at large, and the wicked, who will perish at YHWH's hand. Such a differentiation between the fates of the righteous and the wicked serves as motivation for the people to choose to adhere to YHWH's covenant and therefore to be a part of the restored Jerusalem, rather than to be considered among the wicked so that they perish.

Genre

The book of Isaiah is an example of a PROPHETIC BOOK. Although interpreters have attempted to identify sets of characteristics for the genre, e.g., a three-part pattern of judgment against Israel, judgment against the nations, and restoration for both Israel and the nations, close attention to each of the prophetic books indicates that there are no typical patterns characteristic of a prophetic book other than a SUPERSCRIPTION or narrative introduction that identifies the material of the book in question as the "words," "pronouncement," "vision," etc. of the prophet named in the superscription.

Prophetic books appear in a variety of forms. The book of Jeremiah may be identified as an ACCOUNT of the prophecies of Jeremiah, insofar as its superscription in MTJer 1:1 appears as "the words of (*dibrê*) Jeremiah ben Hilkiah from the priests who were in Anathoth in the Land of Benjamin, when the word of YHWH came to him in the days of Josiah ben Amon, king of Judah, in the thirteenth year of his reign, and it came in the days of Jehoiakim ben Josiah, king of Judah, until the completion of the eleventh year of Zedekiah ben Josiah, king of Judah, until the exile of Jerusalem in the fifth month." Following the initial identification of the work as "the words of Jeremiah. . . . when the word of YHWH came to him, etc.," the book is organized according to a sequence of syntactically-independent PROPHETIC WORD FORMULAS, e.g., "The word (*haddābār*) which came to Jeremiah from YHWH, saying . . ." as found in MTJer 7:1 or 11:1 (cf. Jer 1:2). Subunits within each segment defined by the syntactically-independent instance of the prophetic word formulas are identified by a syntactically-dependent example of the formula introduced by a *wāw*-consecutive form, "and the word of YHWH came (*wayĕhî dĕbar yhwh*) to him/me, saying . . ." as found in MTJer 1:4, 11, 13; 2:1 and elsewhere. LXXJeremiah is organized along similar lines (M. A. Sweeney, "The Masoretic and Septuagint Versions of the Book of Jeremiah in Synchronic and Diachronic Perspective," in *Form and Intertextuality,* 65-77; idem, "Differing Perspectives in the LXX and MT Versions of Jeremiah 1–10," in *Reading Prophetic Books,* 135-53).

Although the book of Ezekiel employs the same types of PROPHETIC WORD FORMULAS as Jeremiah, it must be considered generically different. Ezekiel appears in the form of an AUTOBIOGRAPHICAL CHRONICLE of the prophecies of Ezekiel, insofar as its narrative introduction appears in a first person narrative form that supplies chronological references for the events that it narrates. Although Ezek 1:2-3 appears in third person narrative form, these verses function only to explain the first person statement in Ezek 1:1. Otherwise, the book appears in first person narrative form throughout, and it is organized according to a sequence of first person chronological formulas in Ezek 1:1-3; 8:1; 20:1; etc. that define the formal structure of the book so that it spans the length of Ezekiel's twenty-year career from the age of thirty, when he would have been ordained for active service as a Zadokite priest, until his fiftieth year, the year in which he would have completed active priestly service, when he presents his final vision of the restored temple in Ezekiel 40–48. Within the major blocks of the book, subunits are defined by instances of the PROPHETIC WORD FORMULAS as in Jeremiah (M. A. Sweeney, *Reading Ezekiel: A Literary and Theological Commentary* [ROT; Macon: Smyth and Helwys, 2013]; idem, "Ezekiel: Zadokite Priest and Visionary Prophet of the Exile," in *Form and Intertextuality,* 125-43).

The Book of the Twelve Prophets presents a very distinctive problem insofar as it is read as one book comprising twelve prophets in Judaism and as twelve distinct Minor Prophets in Christianity. There is no formal superscription that identifies the work as the Book of the Twelve, but each of the individual twelve prophets has its own superscription or narrative introduction, which provides the name of the prophet and some generic and sometimes historical indications. Thus, Hosea is "the word of YHWH which came to Hosea ben Beeri in the days of Uzziah, Jotham, Ahaz, Hezekiah, kings of Judah, and in the days of Jeroboam ben Joash, king of Israel" (Hos 1:1). Joel is "the word of YHWH which came to Joel ben Pethuel" (Joel 1:1). Amos is "the words of Amos, who was among the sheepbrokers from Tekoa, who envisioned concerning Israel in the days of Uzziah, king of Judah, and in the days of Jeroboam ben Joash, king of Israel, two years before the earthquake" (Amos 1:1). Obadiah is "the vision of Obadiah" (Obad 1). Jonah begins in narrative form, "and the word of YHWH came to Jonah ben Amittai, saying . . ." (Jonah 1:1). Micah is "the word of YHWH which came to Micah the Morashtite in the days of Jotham, Ahaz, Hezekiah, kings of Judah, which he envisioned concerning Samaria and Jerusalem" (Mic 1:1). Nahum is identified as "the Pronouncement of Nineveh; the Book of the Vision of Nahum the Elqoshite" (Nah 1:1). Habakkuk is "the Pronouncement which Habakkuk the Prophet saw" in Hab 1:1 and "A Prayer of Habakkuk the Prophet concerning Laments" in Hab 3:1. Zephaniah is "the Word of YHWH which came to Zephaniah ben Cushi ben Gedaliah ben Amariah ben Hezekiah in the days of Josiah ben Amon, king of Judah" (Zeph 1:1). Haggai begins in narrative form, "In the second year of King Darius, in the sixth month, on the first of the month, the word of YHWH came to Haggai the Prophet, to Zerubbabel ben Shealtiel, Governor of Judah, and to Joshua ben Jehozadak, the High Priest, saying . . ." (Hag 1:1). Zechariah likewise begins in narrative form, "In the eighth month, in the second year of Darius, the word of YHWH came to Zechariah ben Berechiah ben Iddo the Prophet, saying . . ." (Zech 1:1). And Malachi begins, "A Pronouncement: The Word of YHWH to Israel by the Hand of Malachi" (Mal 1:1). When read as a whole, the Book of the Twelve Prophets could be read as a COMPENDIUM of the Twelve Prophets. When read individually, each of the Twelve has its own distinctive generic identity. Some resemble Jeremiah insofar as they are identified as "the words of Amos" (Amos) or as "the word of YHWH which came to PN" (Hosea; Joel; Micah; Zephaniah). Some resemble Ezekiel insofar as they appear in chronological narrative form (Haggai; Zechariah). None, however, is formally identical to Jeremiah or Ezekiel.

The book of Isaiah is identified by its SUPERSCRIPTION as "The Vision (ḥāzôn) of Isaiah ben Amoz which he envisioned (ḥāzâ) concerning Judah and Jerusalem in the days of Uzziah, Jotham, Ahaz, Hezekiah, kings of Judah" (Isa 1:1). Only Obadiah employs the Hebrew term ḥāzôn, "vision, perception," to describe the book, and Amos, Micah, and Habakkuk employ the verb ḥāzâ, "he envisioned, perceived," to describe the action of the prophet in terms like Isaiah. But again, no other prophet is portrayed in identical terms. Isaiah can be understood generically as a VISION ACCOUNT, insofar as the book presents Isaiah's vision. Readers of English may object to such a term because the book employs visionary events on only a limited basis, e.g., Isaiah 6, but the Hebrew and Aramaic verb *ḥāzâ/ḥāzā'* does not mean, "to see," as it is so frequently translated. Rather, it means "to perceive," insofar as *ḥāzâ* includes both visual and audial perception in its full meaning. Hence, the book of Isaiah presents truly visionary accounts like Isaiah 6, but it also includes a large amount of oracular material that is perceived audially. The translation "to envision" attempts to encapsulate the meaning of the verb, and "vision" attempts to encapsulate the noun.

But the rhetorical dimensions of the book of Isaiah must also be considered in relation to its generic character. As discussed in *Isaiah 1–39, 50-52,* EXHORTATION must be considered as an important element in the generic character of the book insofar as it is designed to persuade its audience to adhere to YHWH as true G-d of creation and human events. Chs. 40–55 and 56–66 are formulated with this concern in mind. Chs. 1 and 55 are especially identified as EXHORTATIONS that are explicitly designed to call upon the audience of the text to adhere to YHWH. As the present commentary indicates, ch. 55, although written as part of Deutero-Isaiah, functions synchronically to introduce the Trito-Isaian material in chs. 56–66 and thereby make the rhetorical goals of the book clear, namely that the audience is exhorted to identify with YHWH and adhere to YHWH's will in order that they will be included in YHWH's covenant for a restored Jerusalem at the center of creation. To fail to adhere to YHWH in the portrayal of the book of Isaiah means to die as an enemy of YHWH. Such a fate functions as a powerful incentive to the audience to adhere to YHWH and abide by YHWH's covenant. Indeed, chs. 34–35 and 36–39 make this purpose clear as well. Chs. 34–35 portray judgment against the wicked nations of the world as the prelude to the return of exiled Jews to Jerusalem. Chs. 36–39 portray Hezekiah's deliverance from the Assyrian siege when he turns to YHWH in faith, unlike his father, Ahaz, who reputedly refused to show faith in YHWH and thereby saw his nation overrun as a result (7:1–9:6). Likewise, chs. 1–33 point to the judgment suffered by Jerusalem, Judah, and Israel, all of which is portrayed as in accordance with YHWH's will as a necessary means to lead to YHWH's worldwide recognition as the true creator of the universe and redeemer of Israel and the nations when YHWH acts to restore Zion following the (Babylonian) exile as conceived in ch. 6. Other generic elements, such as the prophetic INSTRUCTION, in which the prophet offers guidance to the audience of the book concerning YHWH's identity, role in history, and expectations, play an especially important role in both chs. 40–54 and 56–66 as well as throughout the book of Isaiah as whole. The DISPUTATION SPEECH and RHETORICAL QUESTIONS play key roles in facilitating the arguments of the texts, especially contentions that YHWH is the true creator of the universe, redeemer of Israel, and sovereign of Israel and all creation. The PROPHETIC JUDGMENT SPEECH, which announces judgment against Israel and other parties who have failed to observe YHWH's will, and the PROPHETIC ANNOUNCEMENT OF SALVATION or RESTORATION, which announce restoration for those who adhere to YHWH, also play key roles throughout the book, and especially in chs. 40–55, in giving expression to the interplay between judgment and restoration that functions as the means to identify the realization of YHWH's will throughout the book. Such announcements of judgment and restoration play constituent roles in explaining Jerusalem's and Judah's history from the Assyrian invasions of the late 8th century through the 6th-century Babylonian exile and the Persian-period restoration of the late 6th, 5th, and early 4th centuries b.c.e.

Finally, the liturgical dimensions of the book must also be considered in relation to its generic identity. Interpreters have long noted the liturgical character of the language of chs. 40–55, not to mention texts such as 2:2-4; 12; 24–27; and 35, which suggests that the book may have been composed for performance in a liturgical context, perhaps at the restored Jerusalem temple. Such a public venue would be an ideal means to convey the book of Isaiah to its audience, much like Psalms. Indeed, D. L. Petersen's study, *Late Israelite Prophecy: Studies in Deutero-Prophetic Literature and Chronicles* (SBLMS 23; Missoula: Scholars 1977), demonstrates that prophets, who so frequently sang the liturgy of the Jerusalem temple, were changed into Levites in the presentation of the book of Chronicles. Such a phenomenon would support the view that the book of Isaiah was composed as a type of Liturgy for performance at the Jerusalem temple.

Setting

Although the present volume focuses specifically on Isaiah 40–66, consideration of the setting of these chapters requires consideration of the setting for the book of Isaiah as a whole. Isaiah 40–55 and Isaiah 56–66 each appear to have distinctive compositional histories, but there is currently no firm empirical evidence that either set of texts ever constituted a discrete or self-standing body of literature. They appear only within the present form of the book of Isaiah as a whole, and any arguments concerning the setting of these texts and the possibility that they may once have formed independent discrete textual forms must begin with analysis of the final form of the book. Biblical books come to the reader by the hands of their final composers, and the final form of the text must be the indisputable basis for any arguments concerning the compositional history of the book (R. P. Knierim, "Criticism of Literary Features, Form, Tradition, and Redaction," in *The Hebrew Bible and Its Modern Interpreters* [ed. D. A. Knight and G. M. Tucker; Chico: Scholars 1985] 123-65). Only when critical examination of the final form of the text shows evidence of earlier composition may such claims be made. The interpreter cannot impose a preconceived model concerning the compositional history of the text.

The earliest known forms of the book of Isaiah appear among the Judean Wilderness scrolls from Qumran. The oldest manuscript is 1QIsaᵃ, a proto-Masoretic Hebrew scroll from the latter quarter of the 2nd century b.c.e. which displays considerable evidence of interpretative readings in the text (P. F. Flint and E. Ulrich, *Qumran Cave 1. II. The Isaiah Scrolls* [DJD 32; Oxford: Clarendon, 2010] 2:61). The second major Isaiah manuscript from Qumran, 1QIsaᵇ, is another proto-Masoretic Hebrew scroll that dates to the second third of the 1st century b.c.e. Eighteen additional fragmentary Isaiah manuscripts were found in Qumran Cave 4 (4QIsaᵃ⁻ʳ, including pap4QIsaᵖ; E. Ulrich et al., *Qumran Cave 4. X. The Prophets* [DJD 15; Oxford: Clarendon, 1997] 7-143), one in Cave 5 (5QIsa; M. Baillet et al., *Les 'Petites Grottes'*), and one at Wadi Murabbʿaat

(Mur 3; Benoit et al., *Les Grottes*). Five fragmentary pesher manuscripts for Isaiah were found in Cave 4 (4QpIsa[a-e]; Allegro, *Qumran Cave 4. I*; J. Strugnell, "Notes en Marge du volume V des 'Discoveries in the Judean Desert of Jordan'," *RevQ* 7 [1970] 163-273). Although there are variations, these manuscripts present a largely proto-Masoretic text. The Septuagint Greek form of Isaiah appears in two 4th-century C.E. manuscripts, Codex Vaticanus and Codex Sinaiticus. Although both codices present variant readings in Greek, interpreters generally agree that they presuppose a largely proto-Masoretic Hebrew text. The earliest Masoretic Hebrew text of Isaiah appears in Codex Cairo of the Prophets dated to 896 C.E. Other key manuscripts include the St. Petersburg Codex of the Bible dated to 1008 C.E. and the Aleppo Codex dated to ca. 920 C.E. and considered by Maimonides to be the most authoritative text of the Bible.

The Masoretic Text of Isaiah may have undergone minor textual modification during the course of its transmission, but it must remain the basis for any analysis of the book of Isaiah. Some scholars have attempted to argue that the formation of the book extends into the Hellenistic period, but apart from minor glossing or interpretative modifications, none of which can be demonstrated empirically, there is no overt evidence of Hellenistic-period composition in the book of Isaiah. Considering the formal structure, generic character, and concerns of the book, its final compositional form appears to date to the Persian period, specifically to the period of Nehemiah and Ezra, during the late 5th and early 4th centuries B.C.E. Ezra-Nehemiah presents many historical difficulties, but one of its major historical claims is to present the return to Jerusalem by Nehemiah and Ezra, both of whom undertook efforts to restore the centrality of Jerusalem in Judean/Jewish life and to ensure that the Jerusalem temple would function as the holy center of Judaism and indeed all creation as understood in ancient (and modern) Jewish thought.

To this end, Nehemiah, who returned to Jerusalem as the Persian-appointed governor in 445 B.C.E., rebuilt the city walls of Jerusalem, moved ca. one-tenth of the local Judean population into the city, and undertook various religious reforms, such as the observance of Shabbat, tithing to support the temple, a prohibition of intermarriage, and other measures. Ezra, a priest trained in Torah and appointed by the Persians to oversee religious affairs in Jerusalem, arrived in the city during the 7th year of King Artaxerxes of Persia. If the text refers to Artaxerxes I (465-424), there are historical problems, as the date for Ezra's arrival would be 458, some thirteen years prior to Nehemiah, who pursued a less comprehensive reform program than Ezra. Others maintain that Ezra arrived during the 7th year of Artaxerxes II (404-359), i.e., 397, which would fit better with the portrayal of Nehemiah insofar as Ezra's reforms, based on the copy of the Torah which he brought to Jerusalem, were far more comprehensive and complete.

In either case, both figures were concerned with establishing the role of the temple as the central institution of Persian-period Jerusalem and Judaism at large and with calling upon the Jewish population of the time to observe YHWH's covenant as articulated in the Torah. The book of Isaiah has similar aspirations, e.g., it calls for the recognition of YHWH's Torah (2:2-4); it calls for the return to Jerusalem and the temple (chs. 40–66); and it maintains that observance of YHWH's covenant, beginning with the Shabbat, is expected for the righteous who would reside in the restored Jerusalem (56:1-8; 65–66). Indeed, Ezra-Nehemiah portrays Ezra's return to Jerusalem as fulfillment of Isaiah's prophecies, particularly the restoration of the "holy seed" of Israel (Ezra 9:2; Isa 6:13) and the new exodus from Babylonia (Ezra 9; see Klaus Koch, "Ezra and the Origins of Judaism," *JSS* 19 [1974] 173-97).

The final form of Isaiah supports such a contention insofar as it is formulated in two major parts to achieve its purposes. Chs. 1–33 present YHWH's judgment of Jerusalem and the expected restoration in an effort to demonstrate YHWH's sovereignty over creation and humanity. Chs. 34–66 maintain that the restoration is at hand, again to demonstrate YHWH's sovereignty from Zion and to confirm YHWH's credibility as the true G-d over all creation and humanity whose word both stands forever (40:8) and does what YHWH intends it to do (55:11). The purpose of the final form of the book is to exhort or persuade its audience that YHWH is the true G-d of creation and humanity, that YHWH brought about the punishment and restoration of Jerusalem in part to demonstrate divine sovereignty over all creation and humanity from Zion, that YHWH calls for the return of exiled Jews to return to Jerusalem from exile in Babylonia and elsewhere in the world, particularly Assyria and Egypt, and that YHWH will deliver the righteous who tremble at YHWH's presence and observe YHWH's expectations. The wicked who reject such observance will perish. Such an agenda fully supports the efforts of Nehemiah and Ezra.

Additional reasons for dating the final form of the book of Isaiah to the period of Nehemiah and Ezra begin with the book's worldwide perspective which identifies YHWH's worldwide sovereignty with the rise of the Persian Empire. The pronouncements concerning the nations in chs. 1–39 are especially important insofar as they are nations that comprise the Persian Empire, including Babylon (13:1–14:23; cf. chs. 46–47), Assyria (14:24-27; cf. 10:5-34), Philistia (14:28-32), Moab (chs. 15–16), Aram and Israel (ch. 17; cf. ch. 5; 9:7–10:4), Ethiopia and Egypt (chs. 18–20), Midbar-Yam (i.e., the Tigris-Euphrates Delta region; 21:1-10), Dumah (21:11-12), Arabia (the north Arabia desert region; 21:13-17), Jerusalem (ch. 22; cf. chs. 1–4; 28–31), and Tyre (ch. 23). The former territory of Edom (ch. 34; 63:1-6) was also included in the Persian Empire. Greece is absent, which eliminates a date in the Hellenistic period. Persia is not listed as one of the nations subjected to YHWH's judgment, but 21:1-10 identifies Elam and Media as the powers responsible for the fall of Babylon (identified with Midbar-Yam). Isaiah 44:24-28 and 45:1-7 identify the Persian monarch Cyrus as YHWH's anointed king and temple-builder.

Babylon (13:1–14:23; 46–47) appears as the head of the nations and as the major enemy of YHWH in the book of Isaiah. In 539 B.C.E., Babylon submitted to the Achaemenid Persian king Cyrus. In the context of the 5th- /4th-century edition of Isaiah, Cyrus and the later Persian monarchs serve as the agents for YHWH's rule over the nations from Zion. Although chs. 1–33 look forward to the rule of an ideal Davidic monarch (9:1-6; 11; 32), chs. 34–66 presuppose the rule of Cyrus (45:1-7) and YHWH (chs. 65–66), but not that of a Davidic monarch. Rather, the Davidic promise is applied to the people of Israel at large (55:3). The lack of a Davidic monarch fits the pattern for Persian rule of Judah.

Both Nehemiah and Ezra were appointed by the Persians to govern and administer Judah on behalf of the Persian Empire.

The clear distinction between the righteous and the wicked in the present form of the book of Isaiah likewise points to a setting in the period of Nehemiah and Ezra. The book of Isaiah calls upon its audience to identify with the righteous by observing YHWH's will. Many scholars follow Hanson *(The Dawn of Apocalyptic),* who argues that such a distinction in Trito-Isaiah indicates a conflict between a prophetic-visionary party and a priestly group within the postexilic Jewish community. In relation to the book of Isaiah, such a conflict would pit the authors of Trito-Isaiah, who advocate a covenant that will include eunuchs, foreigners, and the nations at large (cf. 56:1-8; 66:18-24), against the supporters of Ezra and Nehemiah, who advocate a covenant based on Mosaic Torah that excludes foreign participation. This position presupposes that the inclusion of eunuchs and gentiles in Trito-Isaiah stands in conflict with the prohibition against intermarriage enacted under Ezra and Nehemiah (Ezra 9–10; Neh 13:23-31).

But closer analysis of this material indicates that Hanson overlooks several important considerations. First, the Trito-Isaiah texts do not address the issue of intermarriage; they address the issue of proper observance of the covenant. They argue that a eunuch or a foreigner who keeps the covenant by observing the Shabbat and refraining from evil shall be accepted in YHWH's temple. Ezra-Nehemiah does not exclude the eunuch or the foreigner who adopts the covenant of Judaism. It only excludes foreign women who do not adopt Judaism and thereby become part of the Jewish people (Neh 13:23-28). Ezra-Nehemiah prohibits intermarriage as a means to avoid the idolatry of the gentiles and thereby to protect the covenant (Ezra 9). This prohibition is based upon Exod 34:11-16 and Deut 7:1-5, which prohibit intermarriage with various nations as a means to avoid apostasy, and upon Deut 23:3-8, which excludes Ammonites and Moabites from the community, as well as Edomites and Egyptians to the third generation.

The Ezra-Nehemiah narrative indicates that foreign wives and children are banished, but it says nothing about foreign husbands. The reason for this is clear; foreign men would have continued their foreign worship, and would not have taken part in worship at the Jerusalem temple. But interpreters do not consider the possibility that foreign husbands might have adopted Judaism and thereby become part of the Jewish people. In the case of such a conversion, there would have been no need to banish a foreign husband since he would have become a part of the community by observing the covenant. The foreigners mentioned in Trito-Isaiah are not those banished by Ezra; they are foreign men — and possibly men who were born to mixed marriages between Jews and Gentiles — who observe the covenant and therefore convert to Judaism.

The use of the term *ḥārēd,* "he who trembles," to refer to those who observe the covenant as "those who tremble" *(ḥărēdîm)* at the word of YHWH also points to the interrelationship between Isaiah and Ezra-Nehemiah. J. Blenkinsopp *(Ezra-Nehemiah* [OTL; Philadelphia: Westminster, 1988] 178) notes that both Trito-Isaiah (66:2, 5) and Ezra (Ezra 9:4; 10:3) employ the noun forms *ḥārēd,* and *ḥărēdîm,* to refer to those who observe YHWH's covenant. Apart from 1 Sam 4:13, these are the only occurrences of this term in the Hebrew Bible. Both Isaiah and Ezra-Nehemiah employ the same terminology to describe those who observe the covenant in the early Persian period; both polemicize against those who fail to observe the covenant; both emphasize observance of the Shabbat as the cornerstone of the covenant (56:1-8; 58:13-14; Neh 9:14; 10:31; 13:15-22); both emphasize YHWH's Torah; both support the centrality of the temple; and neither precludes the participation of eunuchs or those foreigners who convert to Judaism. Both Ezra-Nehemiah and the final form of Isaiah are in fundamental agreement on the nature of covenant observance in Persian-period Judaism.

As noted throughout the commentary to chs. 40–66, these texts indicate that the book of Isaiah may well have been employed liturgically in the Jerusalem temple. Baltzer *(Deutero-Isaiah)* points to the performance-oriented aspects of chs. 40–55 throughout his commentary, although he errs by locating the setting for such performance in Hellenistic-period theatrical performance. Other scholars have pointed to a Levitical context for the preservation and reinterpretation of the Isaiah tradition which in turn raises the question of liturgical function (Eaton, *Festal Drama;* idem, "Isaiah Tradition"; idem, "Origin"). Such a Levitical context might be identified with the so-called Isaianic school posited by Mowinckel *(Jesaja-disiplene; Prophecy and Tradition)* and Schreiner ("Das Buch jesajanischer Schule"). The Levites are identified as the interpreters of Torah in Neh 8:7-8, and Levitical singers are identified as prophets in the Second Temple period (1 Chronicles 15; 25; 2 Chronicles 20; 29; for a full discussion, see R. J. Tournay, *Seeing and Hearing G-d with the Psalms: The Prophetic Liturgy of the Second Temple in Jerusalem* [JSOTSup 118; tr. J. E. Crowley; Sheffield: JSOT 1991]; Petersen, *Late Israelite Prophecy*).

Such a liturgical context might include the reading of Isaiah in the context of the temple, much as Ezra read the Torah to the people in Nehemiah 8–10. Ezra's reading took place during the festival of Sukkot, or Booths, which stresses the themes of both the ingathering of the fruit and olive harvest, the beginning of the rainy season, and the ingathering of the people of Israel from the exodus at the end of the forty years of wandering in the wilderness. Such themes would correspond well to those of the book of Isaiah, which stresses the ingathering of the harvest and renewed creation together with the ingathering of the exiles (e.g., 11:11-16; 12:6; 27:12-13; 35:8-10; 40:1-11; 49:8-12; 62:10-12; and 65–66). This would facilitate the community's understanding of the Torah by pointing out that the experiences of disaster at the hands of Assyria and Babylonia, as well as restoration under Persian rule, were designed to lead to the purification of Jerusalem and renewal of the covenant that was currently underway in the time of Ezra. A reading of the book of Isaiah, with its EXHORTATION to adhere to YHWH's covenant and its emphasis on YHWH's Torah, would then provide an ideal means to garner support for Ezra's program of reform and restoration (cf. J. L. Wright, *Rebuilding Identity: The Nehemiah-Memoir and Its Earliest Readers* [BZAW 348; Berlin: de Gruyter, 2004]); Dalit Rom-Shiloni, *Exclusive Inclusivity: Identity Conflicts between the Exiles and the People Who Remained (6th-5th Centuries BCE)* [LHBOTS 543; London: Bloomsbury, 2013]).

The final form of the book of Isaiah is best understood as the product of a mid-5th- to early-4th-century redaction that was designed to support Nehemiah's and Ezra's efforts to restore Jerusalem and the temple as the holy center of Judaism and creation at large. Although the final redaction of Isaiah comprises all sixty-six chapters of the book, it appears to be an expansion of the 6th-century edition of the book to be discussed below. This redaction produced the present form of several major textual blocks in Isaiah, including chs. 1; 2–4; 28–33; 34–35; and 55–66. In each case, it employed earlier textual material but added its own material and organized earlier material to produce the present form of the text. Thus, the 5th-/4th-century redaction of the final form of Isaiah is responsible for the composition of 1:1, 19-20, 27-28; 2:1; 4:3-6; 33; 34; 56–59; 63:1-6; and 65–66 (see esp. Sweeney, *Isaiah 1–39,* passim, for discussion of Isaiah 1–39; and Stromberg, *Introduction;* idem, *Isaiah after Exile,* for discussion of the history of Trito-Isaiah research).

Although Duhm argued that Isaiah 56–66 was the work of a single anonymous prophet whom he labeled Trito-Isaiah (see also Elliger, *Die Einheit*), subsequent scholarship recognizes that chs. 56–66 are actually the work of multiple hands. Such a conclusion entails a redaction-critical explanation for the present form of chs.56–66 as a block of material within the final form of the book of Isaiah. As noted above, the differentiation between the righteous and the wicked plays a key role in distinguishing this material from other elements of Isaiah; chs. 40–55 do not differentiate between the righteous and the wicked among either Israel/Jacob or Jerusalem/Bat Zion, but simply assume that these terms refer to a single nation or city that must learn to recognize YHWH. Although much of the First Isaiah materials condemn Judah and Jerusalem for wrongdoing against YHWH, one sees little differentiation of the righteous and the wicked apart from those texts identified above as part of the 5th-/4th-century edition of the book, i.e., 1:1, 19-20, 27-28; 2:1; 4:3-6; 33; 34; 56–59; 63:1-6; and 65–66.

Within chs. 56–66, several texts stand outside the Trito-Isaian paradigm of distinguishing between the righteous and the wicked in Judah and Jerusalem. Chs. 60–62 have long been recognized as a potentially Deutero-Isaian text because of their affinities with chs. 40–55. Although they call for a return of the exiles to Jerusalem along lines similar to those of Deutero-Isaiah, their portrayal of the servant figure in Isaiah 61 points to a priestly figure rather than to a royal or prophetic figure as many interpreters suppose. As the analysis below indicates, such a portrayal fits best with the late-6th-century rebuilding of the temple led by Zerubbabel ben Shealtiel and Joshua ben Jehozadak. Indeed, the priestly portrayal of the servant in ch. 61 suggests that Joshua ben Jehozadak, who was ordained for service as the high priest in the restored temple (see Zechariah 3), may well be the servant figure portrayed in the text. Such a conclusion points to the role played by chs. 60–62 in the late-6th-century edition of the book of Isaiah.

The portrayal of YHWH's approach as Divine Warrior in 63:1-6 does not indicate a differentiation between the righteous and the wicked among the people of Jerusalem or Judah. Instead, it presumes the wickedness of Edom, which then serves as the basis for YHWH's attack against the nation. Indeed, 63:1-6 has affinities with ch. 34, which employs Edom as the exemplar of wickedness among the nations as the justification for YHWH's punishment against them. Isaiah 63:1-6 is best set against the background of the demise of Edom in the 6th/5th centuries B.C.E. as Edom was supplanted by or assimilated into the Nabateans. It therefore appears to be a text that was taken up and incorporated within chs. 56–66 as part of the final formation of Trito-Isaiah and the book of Isaiah as a whole.

The prophet's lament in 63:7–64:11 indicates no differentiation between the righteous and the wicked, but instead understands the people as a whole. It also indicates that the temple lies in ruins (63:18; 64:9-10), and it raises questions about YHWH's righteousness by pointing to the hiding of YHWH's face (64:6) and YHWH's hostile actions against Jerusalem and Judah as cause for viewing YHWH as the one who caused the people to sin (63:17). Such a portrayal precludes identification with the Trito-Isaian texts, although it is a subunit within this block. Isaiah 63:7–64:11 also indicates little relation with chs. 40–55, which are overwhelmingly designed to demonstrate YHWH's righteousness and fidelity to the people of Israel. Instead, 63:7–64:11 appears to be lamentation text, akin to the book of Lamentations, which may well have posed the questions that chs. 40–55 and 56–66 are designed to answer.

The remaining texts that form chs. 56–66 as Trito-Isaiah (56:1-8; 56:9–57:21; 58:1-14; 59:1-21; and 65:1–66:24) all presuppose the differentiation between the righteous and the wicked among Israel as the overarching perspective of this block within Isaiah and indeed of the final edited form of the book as a whole. Isaiah 56:1-8 sets the agenda for the block by calling upon its audience to do justice and righteousness by observing YHWH's covenant; 56:9–57:21 focuses on YHWH's willingness to forgive the repentant; 58:1-14 admonishes the people to repent and return to YHWH; 59:1-21 focuses on YHWH's intent and ability to deliver those who repent; and 65:1–66:24 exhorts the audience to include themselves among the righteous and thereby avoid the death that awaits the wicked. As noted above, such an agenda well serves the agendas of Nehemiah and Ezra, who exhorted the people of Jerusalem and Judah to observe YHWH's covenant and to make the Jerusalem temple the holy center of Judaism and creation at large. The incorporation of chs. 60–62; 63:1-6; and 63:7–64:11 into the Trito-Isaian framework facilitates its agenda by pointing to the coming return to Jerusalem by the righteous in chs. 60–62, the judgment of the wicked Edom in 63:1-6, and appeal to YHWH's capacity to deliver the people in 63:7–64:11.

Duhm understands Trito-Isaiah to be the concluding collection of prophetic oracles for the book of Isaiah. More recently, interpreters point to the role played by chs. 56–66 in the final redaction of the book. Rendtorff argues that the emphasis on *mišpāṭ*, "justice," and *ṣĕdāqâ*, "righteousness," in 56:1-8 points to a motif that extends throughout the entire book and thereby points to the references to these terms as the "key" to understanding the redaction of Isaiah ("Isaiah 56:1"). Steck points especially to the exodus motif in chs. 60–62 and 66:18-24 as a redactional link with other exodus texts in 49:14-26; 35:1-10; 27:12-13; 11:10-16; and others to explain the redactional formation of the book (*Bereitete Heimkehr; Studien*). The present commentary points to the intertextual relationships between the texts in chs. 56–66 and others throughout the rest of the book to point to an ongoing purpose in the interpretation and reinterpretation of Isaiah. Examples include the extensive interest throughout chs. 56–66 in ch. 6, which raises questions about the righteousness of G-d who renders the people blind, deaf, and dumb; the use of 8:6 to portray the rejoicing of the restored Jerusalem in 66:10-14; the portrayal of YHWH as the righteous monarch in 65:1 in place of Cyrus in 44:28; 45:1 and the righteous house of David in 9:1-6; 11:1-16; and 32; the exodus motif as indicated in Steck's work; the revelation of YHWH's great life from 9:1 in ch. 61; and many others as well. Essentially, chs. 56–66 are designed to reflect on adherence to YHWH's eternal Davidic covenant to Israel as articulated in ch. 55; the status of those who act upon YHWH's calls to repent and return to Jerusalem as articulated throughout the book, including the status of those who were the products of intermarriage, assimilation, and conversion during the Babylonian exile; the role of Shabbat as the signature observance of YHWH's covenant; and YHWH's identification with the Persian Empire.

Underlying the final form of the book of Isaiah is a late-6th-century edition of Isaiah that comprises chs. 2–62*, including chs. 2–32*; 35–55; and 60–62. The late-6th-century edition of Isaiah was composed in relation to the rebuilding of the Jerusalem temple in 520-515 B.C.E., and it may well have served as a liturgical text for the dedication of the new temple. The 6th-century edition appears to illustrate Rendtorff's principle that the book of Isaiah is built around the core of chs. 40–55 ("Zur Komposition"). The late-6th-century edition of Isaiah composed redactional blocks, in some cases based on earlier Isaian materials, in 2:2–4:2; 24–27; 35; and 60–62; edited the earlier 7th-century edition of the book in chs. 5–37*; and employed these materials to provide a framework for the work of the late-6th-century prophet, Second Isaiah, in chs. 40–55. Redactional work within chs. 5–37* included the reworking of an earlier oracle concerning the death of the Assyrian monarch, Sargon II, and its reformulation into an oracle condemning Babylon and the Babylonian king in 13:1–14:27 and the reformulation of 2 Kings 18–20 in Isaiah 36–39 to point beyond the Assyrian period to the Babylonian exile. Altogether, the late-6th-century redaction places Deutero-Isaiah's prophetic instruction concerning YHWH's restoration of the covenant and call for the exiles to return to Jerusalem in chs. 40–55.

Chs. 2–4; 13–14; 24–27; 35; 36–39 are discussed in Sweeney, *Isaiah 1–39*. Isaiah 60–62 is discussed in detail in the commentary below. It is a late-6th-century composition with affinities to Deutero-Isaiah that envisions the restoration of Jerusalem and the establishment of a servant figure portrayed in ch. 61 who has been appointed to serve as YHWH's agent to proclaim the restoration and see to the welfare of the people of Israel at large. Although many presume this figure is a prophetic or royal figure, close examination of his dress and his task indicates that he is a priestly figure, very likely a portrayal of Joshua ben Jehozadak, the priest who returned to Jerusalem from Babylonian exile with Zerubbabel ben Jehozadak to be ordained to serve as high priest in the newly-rebuilt Jerusalem temple. Chs. 60–62 make intertextual references to earlier texts, particularly the portrayals of the great light to be seen by the people in 9:1-6 and the various references to the return of the exiled people to Jerusalem as a second exodus in 11:10-16; 27:12-13; 35; and throughout chs. 40–55 to make the case that the restoration is at hand with the return of the people to Zion and the building of the Second Temple. Chs. 60–62 therefore form the culmination of the late-6th-century edition of the book of Isaiah (cf. Sekine, *Das tritojesajanische Sammlung;* Steck, *Studien*). The focus on the restoration in relation to the rebuilding of the temple and Joshua ben Jehozadak suggests that chs. 60–62 and the whole of the late-6th-century redaction were composed in Jerusalem, perhaps to function as part of the liturgy that celebrated the dedication of the new temple.

Isaiah 40–55 constitutes the work of the anonymous prophet of the Babylonian exile known only as Deutero- or Second Isaiah. Unlike Trito-Isaiah, chs. 40–55 show enough consistency of style to posit that one hand was responsible for the entire composition, even when the focus shifts from Jacob/Israel in chs. 40–48 to Bat Zion/Jerusalem in chs. 49–55 and back again to Israel in ch. 55. Although some have tried to claim that this prophet wrote from Jerusalem (Tiemeyer, *For the Comfort of Zion*), there is little evidence to support such a claim, although it is not impossible that the prophet returned from Babylonia to Jerusalem, either with those who returned with Sheshbazzar in 539 B.C.E. or with those who returned with Zerubbabel ben Shealtiel and Joshua ben Jehozadak in 522. The institutional setting for the composition of the text in Babylon remains murky, but the hymnic language of the work indicates that the prophet appears to function as a liturgical singer along the lines of those who were recognized as Levites in the book of Chronicles (cf. Petersen, *Late Israelite Prophecy*). Insofar as Ezekiel had his own house in Babylonia where the elders of Israel gathered, presumably for consultation and instruction by the Zadokite priest and prophet Ezekiel, it is possible that Second Isaiah lived under similar circumstances that would have prompted the composition of chs. 40–55.

Second Isaiah displays a number of concerns that point to a context in late-6th-century Babylonia at the time of the submission of the city to King Cyrus of Persia. Of course, the first indication of this concern is the identification of Cyrus as YHWH's messiah and temple-builder in 44:28 and 45:1. Such notices indicate Second Isaiah's presence in Babylon at the time of Cyrus's entry into the city in 539 B.C.E. and his recognition by the priests of Marduk as Babylon's next king. As the famed Cyrus Cylinder indicates, the outset of Cyrus's reign as Babylon's new monarch saw his decree that the various nations that had been exiled by the Babylonians could return to their homelands with their gods and reestablish their temples while maintaining loyalty to Cyrus and the Persian Empire (*ANET,* 315-16). Although Judah is not mentioned in the Cyrus Cylinder, Cyrus's decree to allow Jews to return to Jerusalem to rebuild the temple is in keeping with the announcement recorded in the Cyrus Cylinder (Ezra; 2 Chr 36:22-23). Indeed, the portrayal in Isaiah 46 of the burdens imposed by the images of Bel and Nebo on their animals suggests the imagery of the Akitu or New Year festival in Babylon, when the images of the gods of Babylonian and foreign subject nations are paraded through the city at the time when the king is authorized by Marduk to rule for another year. Cyrus was proclaimed king of Babylon at the Akitu festival of 539, and it is likely that Deutero-Isaiah's images from Isaiah 46 represent an eyewitness account of that event.

The imagery of the Akitu festival with the nations bearing their gods before Marduk may well influence Deutero-Isaiah's views of the second exodus, in which the nations will play a role in bearing and returning the exiles to Jerusalem in 49:14-26 (cf. chs. 60–62). The proclamation of Cyrus as king of Babylon appears to inform Deutero-Isaiah's arguments that YHWH is the true sovereign of creation and redeemer of Israel. At the time of the Akitu festival, the Babylonian king is authorized to rule on Marduk's behalf, and Cyrus's decrees as the new Babylonian monarch would have been based in the power granted him by Marduk's recognition at the Akitu festival. Deutero-Isaiah's claims that YHWH's Torah and *mišpāṭ* ("justice") will be sent out to the nations appears to be based on such a model and helps to explain how YHWH is identified as the true power behind Cyrus: Cyrus acts as YHWH's regent in Deutero-Isaiah, much as the Davidic monarch served as YHWH's regent throughout the monarchic period. When YHWH restores the exiled Judeans to Jerusalem, all the nations are to witness YHWH's act of sovereignty and fidelity and thereby recognize YHWH as the true monarch of the world who authorizes Cyrus to rule on YHWH's behalf. Within the broader context of the 6th-century edition of Isaiah, YHWH's teaching of Torah to Jacob and to the nations is already signaled in 2:2-4, and it extends throughout Deutero-Isaiah (Sweeney, "Prophetic Torah").

The portrayal in Deutero-Isaiah (and in the broader 6th-century edition of Isaiah) of a second exodus in which the Judean exiles return to Jerusalem (40:1-11; 43:16-21) indicates that Deutero-Isaiah is rooted among the intelligentsia who were exiled by the Babylonians in 597, 587, and 582 B.C.E. It was normal practice for conquering Mesopotamian empires to take the educated and skilled survivors of a conquered nation and put them to work for their own purposes throughout the empire. Deutero-Isaiah would hardly have been alive in 587, but the prophet would likely have been descended from educated exiled parents who provided their offspring an education. Although modern interpreters will never know, the book of Isaiah's interest in Isaiah's children indicates that Deutero-Isaiah was possibly a descendant of Isaiah ben Amoz who preserved, reflected upon, and expanded the great ancestor's tradition. Indeed, the prophet knows some version of the pentateuchal traditions, including creation, Noah's flood and covenant, the ancestors Abraham, Sarah, and Jacob, Moses and the exodus from Egypt, and the wilderness narratives. But the prophet also appears to know the earlier Isaian traditions as indicated by the repeated emphasis on opening the eyes of the blind, the ears of the deaf, and the hearts or minds of the dumb from ch. 6. Such knowledge has prompted scholars to recognize that the prophet's references to the former and new things indicate references to the earlier Isaian tradition (Clements, "Unity"; "Beyond Tradition History").

The prophet's political shift from David to Cyrus likewise points to a Babylonian setting for chs. 40–55. Babylon became the seat of Persian Achaemenid power in 539 B.C.E., and Deutero-Isaiah recognized the significance of such a shift by identifying YHWH with the Persians and by granting YHWH's eternal covenant with David to the people of Israel at large (Isa 55:11). It would have been unthinkable for Second Isaiah to announce the restoration of the house of David in Babylon. Such a move would have brought a quick end to any possibilities of a return of Jewish exiles to Jerusalem to restore the temple. But interpreters must keep in mind that sentiment in favor of the restoration of the house of David would have remained strong among any Judean population left in Judah. It was, after all, the people of the land who placed King Josiah of Judah on the throne when an internal palace coup led to the assassination of his father, Amon. It was also the people of the land who placed Josiah's second son, Jehoahaz, on the throne in place of his older brother Jehoiakim in 609, only to see Jehoahaz deposed by Necho six months later. Sentiment for the house of David was apparently quite strong among the people of the land of Judah prior to the revolts. Even when the exiles returned in 522, the prophet Haggai, whom some identify as an indigenous Judean, called for the overthrow of the Persian Empire and the recognition of Zerubbabel ben Shealtiel, King Jehoiachin's grandson, as YHWH's new Davidic monarch. Of course, the Persian monarch would have none of that, and Zerubbabel disappeared from history by the time the Second Temple was dedicated. Deutero-Isaiah's — and the book of Isaiah's — political stance affirms the Persian monarchy in the end — and not the house of David.

Finally, the liturgical character of chs. 40–55 must be considered. Scholars have recognized both Deutero-Isaiah's performative (Baltzer, *Deutero-Isaiah*) and its liturgical characteristics (Eaton, *Festal Drama*). Although the 6th-century edition of Isaiah may well have been performed liturgically at the dedication of the newly-restored temple in 515 B.C.E., it is not so clear that chs. 40–55 were initially composed for performance at the temple. The emphasis on return from Babylon to Jerusalem points to a Babylonian setting for the book. Such a message is best understood as directed to a population of exiles in Babylonia rather than to a population of Judeans, even returned Judeans, in Jerusalem. Deutero-Isaiah is designed to convince its audience to return to Jerusalem from Babylon. The setting for the performance of such a work in Babylonia is elusive, however, unless we consider the roles of priests in Babylonia. Ezekiel had a house in Babylonia to which the elders would come to consult the prophet and priest (Ezek 1:1). Ezekiel 11 speaks of a little sanctuary that would help to ensure the survival of Jewish identity in exile; some identify it with an early form of synagogue. Ezra 8:17 makes reference to "the place Casiphia," from which Levites under the direction of Iddo would return to Jerusalem. Insofar as the Hebrew term *māqôm* often designates a site for worship, some have proposed that Casiphia must have been a priestly community in exile and a center for Jewish worship in the exile. A place like Casiphia would have been the location for the composition and performance of a work like that of Deutero-Isaiah.

As for the earlier editions of the book of Isaiah prior to the composition of Second Isaiah — the late-7th-century Josianic edition of Isaiah that pointed to Josiah as the righteous monarch who would restore Israel on YHWH's behalf and the late-8th-century oracles of Isaiah ben Amoz — they are discussed in Sweeney, *Isaiah 1–39,* ad loc.

Interpretation

The interpretation of chs. 40–66 must be considered in relation to their context within the full form of the book of Isaiah. As noted in the discussion of the formal structure of Isaiah above, the book constitutes the vision of Isaiah ben Amoz, which is formulated as an exhortation to Judah and Jerusalem to adhere to YHWH. The book is therefore inherently persuasive in orientation insofar as it attempts to persuade its audience to recognize YHWH as the true sovereign G-d of creation and human events, based in Zion, whose will and word have remained constant throughout history from the time of the prophet, Isaiah ben Amoz, who lived during the period of the Assyrian subjugation of Judah and Jerusalem through the time of the audience of the book. As indicated in the present commentary, the setting of the final edition of Isaiah is the time of Nehemiah and Ezra in the latter 5th through the early 4th century B.C.E. The book is designed to support the efforts of Nehemiah and Ezra to restore the Jerusalem temple as the holy center of creation, humanity, and Judaism at large and to encourage its audience to observe YHWH's covenant with them as part of those efforts.

The final form of the book of Isaiah comprises two major components. The first portion of the book in chs. 1–33 focuses on YHWH's plans to reveal worldwide sovereignty from Zion. Detailed discussion concerning this portion of the book appears in Sweeney, *Isaiah 1–39,* ad loc. This portion of the book charges that the people of Israel do not know YHWH nor do they adhere to YHWH's expectations properly; hence there is a need to purge Jerusalem and Judah in order to rectify this problem and to demonstrate YHWH's sovereignty to Jerusalem and Judah and to the world at large. This portion of the book presents its understanding of the experience of Israel, Judah, and Jerusalem during the lifetime of the prophet in the latter half of the 8th century B.C.E., when the Assyrian Empire destroyed the northern kingdom of Israel and subjugated Jerusalem and Judah. It maintains that the Assyrian invasions were brought about by YHWH as punitive actions taken because of the people's alleged ignorance of YHWH and failure to observe YHWH's expectations, but it also anticipates that YHWH will punish Assyria as well and restore Jerusalem and Judah once the process is completed. Isaiah therefore represents a form of theodicy insofar as it attempts to defend the power, presence, and righteousness of YHWH over against charges that YHWH had failed to protect Jerusalem and Judah from Assyrian and later Babylonian invasion, exile, and destruction. Such an understanding is crucial in relation to the Davidic/Zion covenant tradition in which YHWH is sworn to protect the house of David and the city of Jerusalem forever (2 Samuel 7). The fact of the matter is that YHWH did not protect the house of David and Jerusalem, but the book of Isaiah is designed to demonstrate that YHWH kept fidelity to the covenant by restoring Jerusalem and Judah under Persian rule by asserting that the covenant of David is actually with the people of Israel.

The first portion of the book begins with the prologue of the book in ch. 1 which presents an introductory parenesis concerning YHWH's intentions to purify Jerusalem. The chapter includes the superscription of the book, which identifies the prophet, his concerns, and the time in which he lived and points to YHWH's plans to bring punishment upon Jerusalem and Judah as well as restoration for those who adhere to YHWH (see esp. 1:27-28). The second portion of the first half of the book in chs. 2–33 then presents the agenda of ch. 1

in detail with a prophetic instruction concerning YHWH's projected plans to establish worldwide sovereignty at Zion with an announcement of the Day of YHWH. This segment of the book comprises four elements which articulate its agenda. The first in chs. 2–4, introduced by its own superscription in 2:1, presents a prophetic announcement concerning the preparation of Zion for its role as the holy center of creation and YHWH's world rule. The second element in chs. 5–12 shifts its focus to Israel as well as to Jerusalem and Judah to present prophetic instruction concerning the significance of Assyrian judgment against Jacob/Israel and points to the establishment of righteous Davidic rule. The third element in chs. 13–27, again introduced by a superscription in 13:1, presents a prophetic announcement concerning the preparation of the nations, beginning with Babylon, for YHWH's world rule, including the prophet's pronouncements against the nations in chs. 13–23 and the prophecy of salvation in chs. 24–27, which announces YHWH's new world order. The fourth and final element in chs. 28–33 presents prophetic instruction concerning YHWH's plans for Jerusalem by announcing a royal savior or deliverer for the city.

The second half of the book appears in chs. 34–66, which focus on the realization of YHWH's plans for worldwide sovereignty at Zion. Again, detailed discussion of chs. 34–39 appears in Sweeney, *Isaiah 1–39*, ad loc., and detailed discussion of chs. 40–66 appears in the present volume. Chs. 40–66 comprise two major subunits. The first presents prophetic instruction concerning the realization of YHWH's worldwide sovereignty at Zion in chs. 34–54. The second presents prophetic exhortation to adhere to YHWH's covenant in chs. 55–66, which constitutes the rhetorical or argumentative goal of the book.

The prophetic instruction concerning the realization of YHWH's worldwide sovereignty at Zion in chs. 34–54 comprises three major elements. The first in chs. 34–35 introduces the second half of the book with a presentation of prophetic instruction concerning YHWH's power to punish the nations and to return the redeemed exiles to Zion. This section sets the agenda for the second half of the book by portraying the downfall of Edom as an example of YHWH's judgment against the nations — and later against the alleged wicked in Israel — as well as the redemption and return of the (righteous) exiles.

The second element in chs. 36–39 presents royal narratives concerning YHWH's deliverance of Jerusalem and Hezekiah. This block presents a deliberate contrast between the portrayal of King Ahaz in 7:1–9:6, whose alleged lack of faith in YHWH's fidelity during a time of invasion led to the Assyrian subjugation of Jerusalem and Judah, whereas Hezekiah's turn to YHWH led to the deliverance of Jerusalem and Hezekiah from Sennacherib's invasion. Nevertheless, the narrative anticipates the Babylonian Exile when Isaiah declares that Hezekiah's sons will be exiled to Babylon due to his initial alliance with the Babylonian prince, Merodach Baladan, rather than relying upon YHWH as expected.

The third element in chs. 40–54 presents prophetic instruction that YHWH is maintaining the covenant and restoring Zion. This segment is especially concerned with establishing YHWH's credibility and reliability at the close of the Babylonian exile by arguing that YHWH is the creator and redeemer who planned the whole process from the beginning. The segment begins with a brief prologue in 40:1-11 that constitutes a renewed prophetic commission, although it never names the prophet, in order to announce YHWH's restoration of Zion. A key element here is the assertion in v. 8, that the word of our G-d stands forever, which aids in defending YHWH's fidelity to Israel. The instruction proper appears in Isa 40:12–54:17, which presents a series of formally defined sub-units, each of which presents an argument that progressively demonstrates that YHWH is the true G-d of creation and human events who brought about both exile and restoration according to a preconceived and preannounced plan. The first argument appears in 40:12-31, which draws upon Israel's creation traditions to contend that YHWH is the true G-d of creation, thereby countering any argument that Marduk, the city god of Babylon, or any other god should be recognized as such. The second argument appears in 41:1–42:13, which identifies Jacob/Israel as YHWH's servant and asks its audience to consider the former things, understood in context as a reference to Isaiah's vision in the first half of the book, to argue that YHWH is the master of human events. The third argument in 42:14–44:23 draws upon Israel's ancestral and exodus traditions to argue that YHWH is the redeemer of Israel. This section attempts to demonstrate YHWH's fidelity to the covenant promises made to the founding generations and to demonstrate that YHWH is once again carrying out an exodus that will redeem the servant Israel from Babylonian Exile and return Israel to Jerusalem and the land of Israel. Many interpreters have attempted to read the servant songs as references to a coming messiah, but the context of chs. 40–55 and 49:1-6 in particular make it clear that Jacob/Israel is indeed the servant, despite the problems that the passage presents. The fourth argument in 44:24–48:22 contends that YHWH will use Cyrus, the foreign King of Persia, for the restoration of Zion. This argument is key because it becomes clear in the early Persian period that the Davidic monarchy will not be restored under Persian rule. By arguing that YHWH will use Cyrus as messiah and temple-builder (44:28; 45:1), the subunit builds upon the earlier arguments that YHWH is creator, master of human events, and redeemer of Israel while indicating the identification of YHWH with Persian rule. Such a contention demonstrates that the book of Isaiah favors submission to Persian rule rather than revolt to reestablish Judean independence under a Davidic monarch as advocated by the Book of the Twelve Prophets, the LXX form of the book of Jeremiah, and to a lesser degree, the book of Ezekiel, who envisions a Davidic monarch, but merely presents him as a figure who will lead Israel in worship to the temple. The fifth and final element in the sequence is 49:1–54:17, which contends that YHWH is restoring Zion, here personified as a second female servant figure, Bat Zion or Bat Jerusalem, a metaphorical portrayal of Jerusalem as YHWH's restored bride and Israel's mother to whom her exiled children return. The teleological theological view of the book is evident in viewing the restoration of Jerusalem — and not the intervening abandonment of the city — as the key element in YHWH's relationship with Jerusalem and Israel.

The prophetic exhortation to adhere to YHWH's covenant in chs. 55–66 constitutes the rhetorical goal of the book, insofar as it attempts to persuade the audience to abide by YHWH's covenant, beginning with observance of the Shabbat, as the means to be a part of the restoration of Jerusalem. To fail to do so means death, which entails that the audience has a very powerful motivation to be included among the righteous! This unit is based upon ch. 55, which constitutes the exhortation proper insofar as it assigns the Davidic covenant to Israel at large as a sign of YHWH's fidelity and that YHWH's word accomplishes what YHWH intends it to do. By opening with a metaphorical invitation to eat and drink, the passage exhorts the people to take part in the covenant. Chs. 56–66 then follow with prophetic instruction concerning the means to adhere to the covenant and thereby be part of the restoration in Zion which serves as a detailed substantiation of the exhortation in ch. 55. Chs. 56–66 comprise three major subunits. The first in chs. 56–59 presents prophetic instruction concerning proper observance of the covenant, which calls for Shabbat observance as exemplification of the covenant, even by foreigners and eunuchs. For foreigners, such observance entails a form of conversion to Judaism. For eunuchs, inclusion recognizes the injustices inflicted upon Jews during the Babylonian exile. The second in chs. 60–62 constitutes a prophetic announcement of salvation or restoration for the entire nation with a special emphasis on the role of the Jerusalem temple as the holy center of creation, Jerusalem, and Judaism at large. The third in chs. 63–66 presents prophetic instruction concerning the process of restoration, that the wicked among the nations will be punished and the righteous among the nations will return exiled Jews, some of whom will be selected to serve as priests and Levites for service in the temple, to Jerusalem.

The 6th-century edition of the book of Isaiah in chs. 2–55* runs along similar lines to the final 5th- /4th-century edition of the book, except that it does not distinguish between the righteous and the wicked. Instead, it treats Israel as a whole and the nations receive similar treatment. It further differs by beginning with an emphasis on the ascent of the nations and Jacob to Zion to learn YHWH's Torah and thereby to bring peace to the world at large instead of war. Both the nations and Israel will suffer YHWH's punishment on the Day of YHWH as part of the process leading to restoration in chs. 2–4*. Chs. 5–12 portray Israel's punishment and restoration under the rule of a righteous Davidic monarch; chs. 13–27 portray the punishment of the nations and their restoration; and chs. 28–33 portray the punishment of Jerusalem and its restoration. Ch. 35 introduces the new exodus by the exiles to Jerusalem, and chs. 36–39 again highlight Hezekiah's faithfulness to YHWH as the basis for YHWH's deliverance of Jerusalem and Hezekiah in a time of crisis, but the final reference to Babylonian exile continues to introduce chs. 40–55. Chs. 40–55 once again begin with a prologue in 40:1-11, which portrays YHWH's restoration of Jerusalem, and follow by presenting the arguments that YHWH is the creator in 40:12-31, the master of human events in 41:1–42:13, the redeemer of Israel in 42:14–44:23, the true G-d who uses Cyrus as messiah and temple-builder in 44:24–48:22, and the redeemer of Bat Zion/Jerusalem in chs. 49–54. Ch. 55 constitutes the culmination of the arguments by asserting that the Davidic covenant is still in force, although it is now applied to all Israel rather than specifically to the Davidic King. Chs. 60–62, which celebrate the return of exiled Jews to the restored temple in Jerusalem, then serve as the culmination of the 6th-century edition of the book. It is possible that chs. 40–55 were composed for liturgical performance in the exilic community in Babylonia, in which case they were likely read with earlier Isaian texts in chs. 2–39*.

Discussion of the interpretation of the 7th-century Josianic edition of Isaiah and the 8th-century oracles of Isaiah ben Amoz appears in Sweeney, *Isaiah 1–39,* ad loc, and in idem, *King Josiah of Judah,* ad loc.

Chapter 2

The Individual Units of Isaiah 40–66

THE ACCOUNT OF ISAIAH'S RENEWED PROPHETIC COMMISSION 40:1-11

Structure

I. The announcement of YHWH's instructions to comfort the people and Jerusalem	40:1-2
A. Instruction to comfort My people	40:1
1. Instruction proper	40:1a
2. Divine speech formula	40:1b
B. Instruction to comfort Jerusalem	40:2
1. Twofold instruction to comfort Jerusalem	40:2aα
a. Speak intimately to Jerusalem	40:2aα$^{1-4}$
b. Proclaim to her	40:2aα$^{5-6}$
2. Threefold statement of reasons for comfort	40:2aβ-b
a. Because she has fulfilled her service	40:2aβ
b. Because her guilt is pardoned	40:2aγ
c. Because she has received double punishment for sins	40:2b
II. The proclamation of instructions to the people to prepare a highway in the wilderness for the revelation of YHWH's return	40:3-5
A. Proclamation/speech formula: anonymous angelic voice	40:3aα
B. Proclamation proper	40:3aβ-5
1. Twofold announcement to prepare the way for YHWH's return	40:3aβ-b
a. Face/turn to the way of YHWH in the wilderness	40:3aβ
b. Make straight in the desert the highway for our G-d	40:3b
2. Threefold statement of paired results/consequences	40:4-5
a. First pair: raised valley and downcast mountains/hills	40:4a
1) Raised valley	40:4aα
2) Downcast mountains and hills	40:4aβ
b. Second pair: rough ground to plain and ridges to valleys	40:4b
1) Rough ground transformed to plain	40:4bα
2) Ridges transformed to valleys	40:4bβ

c. Third pair: revelation of YHWH's glory and all flesh
see   40:5
    1) Revelation of YHWH's glory   40:5a
    2) All flesh see   40:5b
       a) Basic statement   40:5bα
       b) Reason: YHWH has spoken   40:5bβ
III. The announcement of instructions to the Herald of Zion/Jerusalem to proclaim YHWH's return   40:6-11
   A. Instruction speech by anonymous voice to proclaim   40:6aα
     1. Speech formula   40:6aα$^{1-2}$
     2. Instruction speech proper: proclaim   40:6aα^3
   B. Responses by prophet and voice of G-d/angel   40:6aβ-11
     1. Response by prophet   40:6aβ-8
      a. Speech formula   40:6aβ^1
      b. Speech proper: what shall I proclaim?   40:6aβ^2-8
       1) Question: what shall I proclaim?   40:6aβ$^{2-3}$
       2) Contrast of transitory creation/humans with eternal word of G-d   40:6b-8
         a) Metaphor: flesh as grass and endurance like flower   40:6b
           (1) Flesh as grass   40:6bα
           (2) Endurance like flower   40:6bβ
         b) YHWH withers both grass and flower   40:7a
           (1) Withers grass   40:7aα
           (2) Fades flower   40:7aβ
         c) Word of YHWH stands forever   40:7b-8
           (1) Interjection: people are grass   40:7b
           (2) YHWH's word stands forever   40:8
     2. Response by voice of G-d/angel: instruction to proclaim YHWH's return to Zion   40:9-11
      a. Go up to a high mountain   40:9aα
      b. Raise your voice   40:9aβ
      c. Announce reassurance   40:9bα
       1) Announcement formula   40:9bα^1
       2) Announcement proper: reassurance formula   40:9bα$^{2-3}$
      d. Announce YHWH's return to Zion   40:9bβ-11
       1) Instruction to announce formula   40:9bβ
       2) Instruction proper   40:9bγ-11
         a) Behold: your G-d   40:9bγ
         b) Behold: YHWH's approach with strength   40:10a
         c) Behold: YHWH's approach with compensation and action   40:10b-11
           (1) Basically stated   40:10b
           (2) Metaphorical depiction of YHWH as shepherd   40:11
             (a) YHWH shepherds flock   40:11aα
             (b) YHWH gathers sheep in arm   40:11aβ
             (c) YHWH carries lambs in bosom   40:11bα
             (d) YHWH leads mother sheep   40:11bβ

Isaiah 40:1-11 constitutes a discrete unit within the larger literary framework of the book of Isaiah. The unit follows the narrative material in chs. 36–39, which present an account of Sennacherib's siege of Jerusalem in 701 B.C.E. and other related material. Isaiah 40:1-2 begins with a syntactically-independent statement that recounts YHWH's words of comfort to the people and instructions to speak intimately to the city of Jerusalem that her term of punishment is coming to an end. Whereas chs. 36–39 present the account of the anonymous narrator of the book, 40:1-2 appears to be the words of the prophet. Although critical scholarship has correctly identified the prophet in chs. 40–55 as an anonymous prophet of the Babylonian exile known simply as Deutero- or Second Isaiah, within the synchronic literary context of the book, the prophet must be identified as Isaiah ben Amoz. Other anonymous voices speak in syntactically-discrete subunits in vv. 3-5 and 6-8, respectively, concerning the people's task to prepare in the wilderness the highway for the revelation of YHWH's return to Zion and the prophet's task to announce YHWH's return. A fourth syntactically-discrete subunit in vv. 9-11 presents the announcement that the prophet, here identified as *měbaśśeret șîyôn*, "the Herald of Zion," and *měbaśśeret yěrûšālāim*, "the Herald of Jerusalem," is to proclaim to Jerusalem/Zion, namely, that YHWH is returning to Jerusalem/Zion. Isaiah 40:12 marks the beginning of a new unit concerned with establishing YHWH's role as the unchallengeable creator of the universe.

Interpreters commonly argue that the internal structure of 40:1-11 includes subunits in vv. 1-8, which recount the call of the prophet or the like, and vv. 9-11, which recount the prophet's instructions to speak to Jerusalem. Reasons for such a division generally include reference to the masculine plural imperatives of vv. 1-2 and 3-5 directed to the people and the view that the voices of vv. 3-5 and 6-8 are the voices of angels or YHWH's attendants in the divine council, whereas vv. 9-11 employ feminine singular imperatives directed to Jerusalem/Zion. An additional reason is the view that the concerns with the people of Israel in vv. 1-8 and Jerusalem in vv. 9-11 anticipate the concerns with Israel/Jacob in chs. 40–48 and Jerusalem/Zion in chs. 49–54 (Melugin, *Formation*). But such a view misses an important aspect of this text, that the instructions to proclaim to Jerusalem in vv. 9-11 are the response to the question uttered by an anonymous voice in v. 6aβ, "what shall I proclaim?" Although the comments concerning the transitory nature of the natural and human world and the permanence of YHWH's word in vv. 6b-8 are often viewed as the answer to the question, they do not express the proclamation per se. Rather, they present the presumptions that lie behind the proclamation, that although generations have suffered and perished during the period of Jerusalem's punishment, YHWH's promise to defend Jerusalem is eternal, and it is about to be realized in the following proclamation of vv. 9-11.

Such a view calls for a different understanding of the internal structure of 40:1-11. Interpreters are correct to identify YHWH's heavenly council as the setting for this text (e.g., Cross, "The Council of YHWH in Second Isaiah"), and they are also correct in identifying this text as a reprise of Isaiah ben Amoz's original commissioning narrative or vocational account in ch. 6 (Seitz, "The Divine Council"; "How Is the Prophet?"). And finally, they are correct to differentiate between addresses to Israel that anticipate chs. 40–48 and to Jerusalem that anticipate chs. 49–54. But the dynamics of the address appear in a three-part structure in vv. 1-2, 3-5, and 6-11, in which the initial account of YHWH's instructions to comfort the people in vv. 1-2 is followed by two other voices in vv. 3-5 and 6-11 that respectively convey instructions to prepare a way in the wilderness for the revelation of YHWH's presence and instructions to announce YHWH's return to Jerusalem.

Isaiah 40:1-2 constitutes the prophet's announcement of YHWH's instructions to comfort the people and Jerusalem. The divine speech formula in v. 1b makes it clear that another party conveys YHWH's speech in these verses. The basic structure of this passage falls into two major portions, defined by the masculine plural imperatives, *naḥămû*, "comfort," in v. 1a and *dabběrû*, "speak," in v. 2, that demarcate vv. 1 and 2-3 as the two basic components of this subunit. Verse 1 includes YHWH's instruction to "comfort my people" in v. 1a followed by the above-noted speech formula in v. 1b. Here, the masculine plural imperative form is directed to the angelic members of the heavenly court who will convey YHWH's instructions to the prophet. Verse 2 includes the twofold instruction to speak *(dabběrû)* intimately to (lit. "upon the heart of") Jerusalem in v. 2aα$^{1-4}$ and to proclaim *(wěqirû)* to her in v. 2aα$^{5-6}$. The reason for the use of the idiom, "speak upon the heart of Jerusalem," is that Jerusalem is portrayed metaphorically throughout Second Isaiah, esp. chs. 49–54, as the bride of YHWH to whom YHWH now returns. Such language conveys the manner in which a man might speak to his wife. Three *kî*, "for, because," clauses then follow in vv. 2aβ-b to provide the reasons for YHWH's instructions to comfort Zion: because her term of service is over (v. 2aβ), because her guilt is pardoned (v. 2aγ), and because she has received a double punishment from YHWH for all of her sins (v. 2b). The 3rd-person reference to YHWH is no cause for concluding that YHWH is not the speaker, as this speech is to be conveyed by the angelic attendants at YHWH's court to the prophet and ultimately to the people.

Isaiah 40:3-5 presents the announcement of instructions to the people to prepare the way for the revelation of YHWH's return to Zion. This subunit is demarcated by an initial reference to an anonymous proclaiming voice in v. 3aα, which may be identified with the voice of one of the angelic attendants at YHWH's heavenly court who conveys YHWH's message to the prophet. A second reference to an anonymous speaking voice at the outset of v. 6 marks the beginning of the next subunit.

Following the initial reference to the proclaiming voice in v. 3aα, vv. 3aβ-5 present the speech to be conveyed by the angel to the prophet. A twofold instruction appears in 3aβ-b, defined by masculine plural imperatives directed to the people. The first in v. 3aβ instructs the people in the wilderness to "face *(pannû)* the way of YHWH," and the second in v. 3b instructs the people to "make straight *(yaššěrû)* in the desert the highway for our G-d." A statement of the results of such action then appears in v. 4 in the form of three paired outcomes, all of which are joined by conjunctive *wāw*'s. The first pair in v. 4a includes the uplifting of every valley in v. 4aα and the downfall of every mountain and hill in v. 4aβ. The second in v. 4b includes the transformation of rough ground to a plain in v. 4bα and ridges into a valley in v. 4bβ. The third in v. 5 includes the revelation of the glory or presence of YHWH in v. 5a and viewing of such revelation by all flesh in v. 5b. Indeed, the latter includes the rationale for the whole, "because the mouth of YHWH has spoken," in v. 5bβ, i.e., because YHWH has decreed that this will happen.

Isaiah 40:6-11 presents the announcement of instructions to the Herald of Zion/Jerusalem to proclaim YHWH's return to Jerusalem. The subunit is demarcated initially by the syntactically-independent reference to a voice in v. 6aα instructing another party to proclaim. Verses 6aβ-8 then follow with a syntactically-joined account of the response asking, "what shall I proclaim?" together with statements indicating the transitory nature of creation and human experience contrasted with the permanence of the word of G-d. Verses 9-11 then present the answer to the question with instructions to the Herald of Jerusalem/Zion to announce YHWH's return to the city. The initial rhetorical question in 40:12 marks the beginning of a new unit.

Discussion of the internal structure of 40:6-11 has been complicated by the text-critical problem of the reading of wĕ'āmar, "and he said," in v. 6aβ[1]. LXX, Vulgate, and 1QIsa[a] read this term as a 1st-person verb, i.e., respectively, *kai eipa*, "and I said," in the LXX, *et dixi*, "and I said," in Latin, and *w'wmrh*, "and I said," in the unpointed Qumran Hebrew text. Such a reading presumes the prophet's response to the question posed by the anonymous voice. But both Targum Jonathan and the Syriac Peshitta support the Masoretic Text. Insofar as the MT text is the more difficult reading, it would seem to represent the more authentic text that indeed portrays the prophet's response, but does so from the perspective of the heavenly council itself. In such a case, the MT reading presupposes that our text describes the statements made by YHWH or an angel of YHWH to the prophet while standing in the presence of the divine council. Such a reading makes for an interesting counterpoint to ch. 6, which is narrated from the standpoint of the prophet.

Isaiah 40:6-11 therefore falls into two major subunits. The first appears in v. 6aα, in which the anonymous voice of YHWH or one of YHWH's angels instructs the prophet to proclaim. This text includes the speech formula in v. 6aα[1-2] followed by the instruction per se in v. 6aα[3]. The second subunit appears in vv. 6aβ-11 which relates the prophet's response to the question in v. 6aβ-8 followed by the voice's response to the prophet's question, "what shall I proclaim?" in vv. 9-11.

The inner structure of vv. 6aβ-8 includes the speech formula in v. 6aβ[1] followed by an account of the prophet's speech in vv. 6aβ[2]-8. The prophet's speech expresses concern with what should be proclaimed. It begins with the question in v. 6aβ[2-3], followed by the prophet's statements indicating the transitory nature of creation and human life in contrast to the eternal character of the word of G-d in vv. 6b-8. Verses 6b-8 employ three sets of syntactically-independent paired statements to make this point. The first in v. 6b employs the metaphorical portrayal of flesh as grass and its endurance (ḥesed, "fidelity") as a flower of the field that lives for only a very short period of time. The second in v. 7a continues the metaphor by attributing the transitory nature of grass and flowers to the breath of YHWH that withers them both. The culminating statement in v. 7b-8 begins with an interjection, "indeed, the people are grass," in v. 7b, which many interpreters view as a gloss. Nevertheless, the statement appears in all major textual witnesses, and it appears to function as an introduction that applies the metaphor to the people, thereby asserting that people may wither or fade like grass and flowers, but the word of G-d stands forever. In this respect, the text in v. 8 asserts that generations of human beings may pass but YHWH remains true to the divine word. Within the present context, such statements reinforce the prophet's question, "what shall I proclaim?" i.e., given that YHWH's word remains constant, what should the prophet say?

The answer comes in vv. 9-11. No speech formula identifies the anonymous voice as the speaker. That is done simply by the syntactical break at v. 9 and the characterization of the subunit as an instruction speech directed to the Herald of Zion/Jerusalem, i.e., the prophet. The structure of the instruction speech is defined by the sequence of four feminine singular imperative verbal statements directed to the Herald of Zion/Jerusalem in vv. 9aα, 9aβ, 9bα, and 9bβ. The four-part sequence includes instructions to go up to a high mountain (v. 9aα), raise your voice (v. 9aβ), announce the reassurance formula, "do not fear" (v. 9bα, including both the announcement formula in v. 9bα[1] and the announcement of the reassurance formula in v. 9bα[2-3]), and speak the message of YHWH's return to Zion (v. 9bβ). The message of YHWH's return to Jerusalem per se appears in vv. 9bγ-11 in three basic segments, each of which is introduced by the particle *hinnēh*, "behold!" The first in v. 9bγ introduces the sequence with the simple exclamation, "behold, your G-d!" The second in v. 10a portrays YHWH's approach with strength and a powerful arm that will presumably defeat the nation's oppressors. The third in vv. 10b-11 begins in v. 10b with the twofold statement that YHWH approaches with compensation (*śĕkārô*, "his wage") and action (*ûpĕ'ullātô*, "and his deed"). Verse 11 then employs four verbal statements to portray YHWH metaphorically as a shepherd who shepherds his flock (v. 11aα), who gathers sheep with his arm (v. 11aβ), who carries lambs in his bosom (v. 11bα), and who leads the mother sheep (v. 11bβ). The use of the shepherding metaphor introduces an element of divine compassion to reinforce the initial premise of the passage that the people's and Jerusalem's time of suffering is over.

Genre

Interpreters generally recognize 40:1-11 as an example of a prophetic Vocation Account. The basis for such identification lies in the normative diachronic reading of this passage as the introduction to the prophecies attributed to the Babylonian-period prophet, Second Isaiah, as well as the clear instruction to an individual figure in v. 6 to "proclaim!" followed by the response, "what shall I proclaim?" Habel's analysis of the genre ("The Form") indicates six standard elements, including 1) a divine confrontation, 2) an introductory word, 3) a commission, 4) an objection by the prophet, 5) a reassurance, and 6) a sign. The divine confrontation may be identified with YHWH's instruction to comfort "My people" and "Jerusalem" in vv. 1-2. The introductory word might include both the instructions to comfort in vv. 1-2 and to prepare a way in the wilderness in vv. 3-5. The commission followed by the prophet's response appears in vv. 6-8. Readers must note that no clear objection by the prophet appears here, although the statements concerning the transitory nature of grass, flowers, and the people might suggest some doubt. Nevertheless, the prophet appears to answer any potential doubts by stating that YHWH's word will stand forever. Finally, the divine response in vv. 9-11 concerning YHWH's return to Jerusalem appears to function as a sign of YHWH's fidelity. Although there is some variation from the form in this text, the basic elements all appear in one form or another.

In addition to the prophetic vocation account, the genre of INSTRUCTION also permeates this text to indicate YHWH's instructions to people, prophet, and heavenly court that the time for restoration has come. Furthermore, the PROPHETIC ANNOUNCEMENT OF SALVATION appears in 40:9-11 to convey the basic content of YHWH's message concerning Israel and Jerusalem.

Nevertheless, a problem emerges in that the prophet is never clearly identified. Of course, this is the problem of the entirety of chs. 40–66 insofar as the synchronic presentation of these chapters presumes the identity of the 8th-century prophet, Isaiah ben Amoz, as the primary prophetic figure of the entire book. Indeed, if Isaiah was commissioned in ch. 6, the need for a second commission in 40:1-11 is not entirely obvious. But the diachronic character of chs. 40–66 demands a vocation account for the anonymous prophet of the exile at or near the outset of the prophet's oracles, and 40:1-11 ably fills that need. Furthermore, Seitz ("The Divine Council"; "How Is the Prophet?") correctly argues that 40:1-11 relates intertextually with ch. 6, so that the present text emerges as a renewed prophetic commission within the synchronic literary form of the book. The anonymity of the prophet facilitates such an intertextual reading insofar as Deutero-Isaiah is implicitly identified with Isaiah ben Amoz in the larger literary context of the book.

But readers must note that this passage does not present the same kind of autobiographical account of the prophet's encounter with YHWH as one finds in ch. 6. Although most interpreters read the Hebrew phrase in v. 6aβ[1], wĕ'āmar, "and he said," as wa'ōmar, "and I said," in keeping with 1QIsaiah[a], w'wmrh, and LXX, kai eipa, the MT deliberately reads the verb as a 3rd-person descriptive statement. Insofar as this is the only potential indication of a 1st-person narrative perspective, 40:1-11 must be read as a 3rd-person account of the prophet's encounter with YHWH. The narrative is not recounted from the prophet's perspective, whoever the prophet might be, but from the perspective of the anonymous narrator of the text. Such a perspective suggests that the MT presents an account of YHWH's commission of the prophet in the heavenly council analogous to the account of Micaiah ben Imlah's commission in 1 Kgs 22:19-23. In the present context, such an account takes Isaiah's commission further than that of ch. 6. Isaiah ben Amoz asked YHWH in ch. 6 how long he was to ensure judgment against the people by keeping them blind, deaf, and dumb, and YHWH responded by stating the prophet must continue until the entire land and people were laid waste with only about one-tenth left to survive. But 40:1-11 takes up the last elements of hope that appear in the earlier commission account in ch. 6, i.e., the portrayal of the "holy seed" from the ravaged stump that was left to strike roots to renew itself in 6:13. Presupposing the broader synchronic literary context of the book, 40:1-11 announces that the time of restoration has come.

Setting

Isaiah 40:1-11 follows the account of YHWH's deliverance of Jerusalem and Hezekiah in chs. 36–39, and it stands at the head of the oracles that presuppose the Babylonian exile and beyond in chs. 40–66. Ch. 39 closes with Isaiah's condemnation of Hezekiah for his alliance with Prince Merodach Baladan of Babylonia, and it notes that Hezekiah will suffer the exile of his own sons to Babylon, where they will serve as eunuchs in the palace of the king of Babylon. Following immediately upon such a statement, 40:1-11 presupposes the impending end of the Babylonian exile and announces the anticipated return of the exiles to Jerusalem. No account of Jerusalem's destruction appears in Second Isaiah — or indeed anywhere in Isaiah at all — but the material beginning in ch. 40 presupposes the disaster that overtook Jerusalem and Judah a century and a half after the reign of King Hezekiah. Insofar as 40:1-11 introduces the oracles of Second Isaiah in chs. 40–55 — and indeed the oracles of Trito-Isaiah in chs. 56–66 as well — it functions as a means to signal to the readers the worldwide recognition of YHWH's role as sovereign over creation and redeemer of Israel and Jerusalem that will dominate the rest of the book.

The historical setting of 40:1-11 is the impending end of the Babylonian exile and the rise of the Persian Empire under King Cyrus the Great. Such a setting is evident throughout the oracles of Second Isaiah in chs. 40–55, particularly indicated by the explicit references to Cyrus as YHWH's messiah and temple-builder in 44:28 and 45:1, as well as the general scenario of Babylon's downfall and Israel's impending return to Jerusalem that permeates these chapters. Isaiah 40:1-11 is therefore part of the 6th-century edition of the book of Isaiah that anticipates the end of the Babylonian exile and the impending restoration of Jerusalem.

But 40:1-11 must also be recognized as part of the final 5th-century edition of the book of Isaiah as a whole. Although the conclusion of the Babylonian exile is long past by this time, the full realization of the restoration of Jerusalem and the recognition of YHWH throughout the world is yet to be achieved. Isaiah 40:1-11 introduces the oracles of Trito-Isaiah in chs. 56–66 as well which continue to look forward to the restoration but explain its delay by contending that the wicked who do not fully adhere to YHWH remain to be purged from the nation before the restoration of Jerusalem and recognition of YHWH can be fully achieved.

Finally, the social setting or *Sitz im Leben* of 40:1-11 must be considered. Cross ("The Council of YHWH") long ago recognized that this text is set in the heavenly divine court of YHWH. Based upon the analogy with the portrayal of YHWH's court in 1 Kgs 22:19-23, he correctly maintains that the divine council of YHWH is the setting in which YHWH commissions prophets to speak the divine message to the people of Israel, Jerusalem, and indeed the entire world. Just as Micaiah ben Imlah stood in YHWH's court in 1 Kgs 22:19-23, so our anonymous prophet stands in the divine court of YHWH in Isa 40:1-11. Although the court is not explicitly described, the interaction between YHWH's voice calling for the comfort of Jerusalem in vv. 1-2 and other voices in vv. 3-5, presumably those of the angelic attendants of the divine court calling for the clearing of a way in the desert to enable YHWH's return to Jerusalem, combine to point to the setting of the divine court. The indication of the prophet's responses to the command to proclaim in vv. 6-8 builds the case for the divine court insofar as the prophet will serve as the human agent to convey the divine message to Israel and Jerusalem. YHWH's own response to the prophet in vv. 9-11 seals the instruction to the prophet to announce the divine return.

Interpretation

The interpretation of 40:1-11 is determined by a combination of its formal structure, its generic characteristics, and its various settings.

Isaiah 40:1-11 depicts a scene in the heavenly court of YHWH in which YHWH gives instruction to those gathered about, presumably angelic attendants and the prophet, to announce the comfort and restoration of Israel and Jerusalem. The account of YHWH's initial instructions includes the basic instruction in v. 1 to comfort YHWH's people, i.e., the people of Israel, and in v. 2 to comfort Jerusalem. Jerusalem is here portrayed in feminine terms, in keeping with the traditional portrayal of Jerusalem as the bride of YHWH (cf. Zeph 3:14-20; Ezekiel 16; Isaiah 54). The language employed therefore presumes an intimate conversation between husband and wife in which the husband will tell his wife that a period of difficulty has now come to an end. In the present instance, the difficulty includes a term of punishment for wrongdoing that is now coming to an end. Indeed, the reference to Jerusalem's receiving double for her sins presupposes the punishment for theft in Exod 22:7; although the crime is not the same — indeed, the crime is never named — the imposition of double restoration emerges as the basis on which the punishment of Jerusalem is calculated.

A second set of announcements appears in vv. 3-5, this time directed to the people of Israel who are about to return home to Jerusalem from Babylonian exile. The command to clear a way in the desert for YHWH's return pointedly draws upon the wilderness tradition of the Pentateuch, which portrays Israel's exodus from Egypt and its journey to the promised land of Israel under the leadership of YHWH and Moses. History will repeat itself here, although this time the journey to the land of Israel will originate in Babylonia, where the people of Israel were subjected to the rule of the Babylonian Empire. In making the case that YHWH is the redeemer of Israel once again, the present text points to the cooperation of the elements of creation: valleys and hills cooperate to provide a smooth roadway home from Babylon, just as nature cooperated in the wilderness journey from Egypt to Israel by providing food in the form of manna and quails and water from previously unknown sources. As a result of creation's cooperation with YHWH in bringing the people home, all the nations will recognize YHWH's glory and the truth of YHWH's word.

The third set of announcements in 40:6-11 includes the initial instruction to the prophet to proclaim in v. 6aα, followed by the responses of the prophet and G-d or G-d's angel in vv. 6aβ-11. The instruction to proclaim, spoken by an anonymous heavenly attendant at the royal court, provides no details of what the prophet should proclaim, although the prior segments will have made the basic content of the message clear. The prophet's response in vv. 6aβ-8, beginning with the question, "what shall I proclaim?" may indicate resistance or hesitation, although it best seems to function as a means to highlight some fundamental perspectives of the text. The prophet is able to consider the permanence of YHWH's word over against the transitory character of the natural and human worlds. The contention that YHWH's word will stand forever makes an important point within the full context of the book of Isaiah, namely, the prophecies of restoration spoken by Isaiah ben Amoz in the late 8th century B.C.E. may not have been realized immediately — indeed, Jerusalem and Judah were devastated by Sennacherib's invasion in 701 — but YHWH's word will nevertheless be realized with the end of the Babylonian exile and the impending restoration of Jerusalem. Even if Jerusalem is not yet fully restored and YHWH not fully recognized by the late 6th century, such restoration and recognition are yet to come once the wicked have been purged from the world.

YHWH's response to the prophet in vv. 9-11 then answers the prophet's question: announce the return of YHWH to Jerusalem. The prophet is addressed as the Herald of Good Tidings to Zion/Jerusalem. The feminine form of the title, *měbaśśeret ṣîyôn/yěrûśālāim*, "Herald of Good Tidings to Zion/Jerusalem," and the feminine address forms have prompted many to speculate that Deutero-Isaiah might be a woman, but the forms indicate that it is Jerusalem herself who is addressed and who in turn will announce to the cities of Judah that YHWH is returning home with the exiles, who will now restore the land and the city. The imagery of YHWH's return continues to draw on the imagery of the exodus and wilderness traditions, especially by emphasizing YHWH's powerful arm employed in the exodus and again in Isaiah to punish Israel's enemies and to redeem the people (5:25-29; 9:7–11:16). The pastoral imagery of YHWH leading the people as a shepherd would lead a flock of sheep draws on common Israelite and ancient Near Eastern depictions of kings as shepherds who lead their people and protect them from harm. In the present instance, the metaphor functions as a means to argue that YHWH intended the restoration of the people from the outset of the period of punishment in the time of Isaiah ben Amoz.

Bibliography

H. M. Barstad, "Isaiah 40,1-11: Another Reading," in *Congress Volume Basel 2001* (VTSup 92; Leiden: Brill, 2002) 225-40; D. M. Carr, "Isaiah 40:1-11 in the Context of the Macrostructure of Second Isaiah," in *Discourse Analysis of Biblical Literature* (ed. W. R. Bodine (SemeiaSt; Atlanta: Society of Biblical Literature, 1995) 117-32; F. M. Cross, "The Council of YHWH in Second Isaiah," *JNES* 12 (1953) 274-77; R. Davidson, "The Imagery of Isaiah 40:6-8 in Tradition and Interpretation," in *The Quest for Context and Meaning (Fest.* J. A. Sanders; ed. C. A. Evans and S. Talmon; BibInt 28; Leiden: Brill, 1997) 37-55; G. Fischer, "Die Redewendung *daber 'al lev* im AT: Ein Beitrag zum Verständnis von Jes 40,2," *Bib* 65 (1984) 244-50; J. P. Fokkelmann, "Stylistic Analysis of Isaiah 40:1-11," *OtSt* 21 (1981) 68-90; D. N. Freedman, "The Structure of Isaiah 40:1-11," in *Perspectives on Language and Text (Fest.* F. I. Andersen; ed. E. W. Conrad and E. G. Newing; Winona Lake: Eisenbrauns, 1987) 167-93; S. A. Geller, "A Poetic Analysis of Isaiah 40:1-2," *HTR* 77 (1984) 413-20; N. Habel, "The Form and Significance of the Call Narratives," *ZAW* 77 (1965) 297-323; F. Hartenstein, "'. . . dass erfüllt ist ihr Frondienst' (Jesaja 40,2): die Geschichtshermeneutik Deuterojesajas im Licht der Rezeption von Jesaja 6 in Jesaja 40,1-11," in *'Sieben Augen auf einem Stein' (Sach 3,9): Studien zur Literatur des Zweiten Tempels (Fest.* I. Wili-Plein; ed. Hartenstein und M. Pietsch; Neukirchen-Vluyn: Neukirchener, 2007) 101-19; K. Holter, "Zur Funktion der *Städte* Judas in Jesaja xl 9," *VT* 46 (1996) 119-21; R. Kilian, "Baut eine Strasse für unseren G-tt!," in *Künder des Wortes (Fest.* J. Schreiner; ed. L. Ruppert et al.; Würzburg: Echter, 1982) 53-60; M. C. A. Korpel, "Second Isaiah's Coping with the Religious Crisis: Reading Isaiah 40 and 55," in *The Crisis of Israelite Religion* (ed. B. Becking and Korpel; OtSt 42; Leiden: Brill, 1999) 90-113; R. G. Kratz, "Der Anfang des Zweiten Jesaja in Jes 40,1f. und das Jeremiabuch," *ZAW* 106 (1994) 243-61; idem, "Der Anfang des Zweiten Jesaja in Jes 40,1f. und seine literarischen Horizonte," *ZAW* 105 (1993) 400-419; L. Krinetzki, "Zur Stilistik von Jes 40,1-8," *BZ* 16 (1972) 54-69; L. J. Kuyper, "The Meaning of *ḥasdo* Isa xl 6," *VT* 13 (1963) 489-92; O. Loretz, "Die Gattung des Prologs zum Buche Deuterojesaja," *ZAW* 96 (1984) 210-20; idem, "Der Sprecher der Götterversammlung in Is 40,1-8," *UF* 6 (1974) 489-91; R. Mosis, "Der verlässliche Grund der Verkündigung. Zu Jes 40,6-8" in *Der Dienst für den Menschen in Theologie und Verkündigung (Fest.* A. Brems; ed. R. M. Hübner et al.; Regensburg: Pustet, 1981) 113-25; A. Phillips, "Double for All Her Sins," *ZAW* 94 (1982) 130-32; K. K. Sacon, "Isaiah 40:1-11: A Rhetorical-Critical Study," in *Rhetorical Criticism (Fest.* J. Muilenburg; ed. J. J. Jackson and M. Kessler; Pittsburg, 1974) 99-116; A. Scheiber, "Der Zeitpunkt des Auftretens von Deuterojesaja," *ZAW* 84 (1972) 242-43; A. Scherer, "Hyperbolisch oder juridisch? Zu einigen Deutungen von כפלים in Jes 40,2 und zur Semantik der übrigen Belege der Wurzel כפל im Alten Testament," *ZAW* 115 (2003) 231-40; T. Seidl, "Offene Stellen in Jesaja 40,1-8," in *Goldene Apfel in silbernen Schalen* (ed. K. D. Schunck and M. Augustin; Frankfurt: Lang, 1992) 49-56; C. R. Seitz, "The Divine Council"; idem, "How Is the Prophet Isaiah Present?"; H.-J. Stoebe, "Überlegungen zu Jesaja 40,1-11, zugleich der Versuch eines Beitrages zur G-ttesknechtfrage," *TZ* 40 (1984) 104-13; S. Wagner, "Ruf G-ttes und Aufbruch (Jes 40,1-11)," in *Meilenstein (Fest.* H. Donner; ed. M. Weippert and S. Timm; ÄAT 30; Wiesbaden: Harrassowitz, 1995) 308-15; A. L. H. M. van Wieringen, "Jesaja 40,1-11: eine drama-linguistische Lesung von Jesaja 6 her," *BN* 49 (1989) 82-93; B. M. Zapff, "Jes 40 und die Frage nach dem Beginn des deuterojesajanischen Corpus," in *G-ttes Wege Suchend: Beiträge zum Verständnis der Bibel und ihrer Botschaft (Fest.* R. Mosis; ed. F. Sedlmeier; Würzburg: Echter, 2003) 355-73.

DISPUTATION: YHWH IS THE MASTER
OF CREATION 40:12-31

Structure

I. Threefold rhetorical assertion: YHWH is the creator who will redeem Jacob	40:12-20
A. First rhetorical assertion: YHWH measured out the waters, heavens, and earth	40:12
1. Initial paired rhetorical questions	40:12aα
a. First rhetorical question of pair: who measured water with the palm of the hand?	40:12aα$^{1-4}$
b. Second rhetorical question of pair: who gauged the heavens with the span of the hand?	40:12aα$^{5-7}$
2. Elaboration with three continuing rhetorical questions	40:12aβ-b
a. First rhetorical question of the three: who completed with a measure the dust of the earth?	40:12aβ
b. Second and third paired rhetorical questions of the three	40:12b
1) First rhetorical question of the pair: who weighed with a scale the mountains?	40:12bα
2) Second rhetorical question of the pair: who weighed with a scale the hills?	40:12bβ
B. Second paired rhetorical assertion: no one can measure the mind of YHWH	40:13
1. First rhetorical assertion of pair: no one can measure the mind of YHWH	40:13a
2. Second rhetorical assertion of pair: no one can make known YHWH's counsel	40:13b
C. Third set of paired rhetorical assertions: no one is like YHWH	40:14-20
1. First set of two paired rhetorical assertions: no one can impart understanding to or teach YHWH	40:14
a. First pair of rhetorical assertions	40:14a
1) Who will counsel or impart understanding to YHWH?	40:14aα
2) Who will teach the path of justice to YHWH?	40:14aβ
b. Second pair of rhetorical assertions	40:14b
1) Who will teach knowledge to YHWH?	40:14bα
2) Who will make known the path of understanding to YHWH?	40:14bβ
2. Second set of two paired rhetorical assertions: no one can compare to YHWH	40:15-20
a. Declarative assertions that the nations of the world cannot challenge YHWH	40:15-17
1) First set of two declarations	40:15a
a) The nations are like a drop in a bucket	40:15aα
b) The nations are considered like dust on scales	40:15aβ
2) Second set of three declarations	40:15b-16
a) The coastlands are like dust balls	40:15b

52

a) The one who views princes as nothing   40:23a
b) The one who makes judges of the earth as void   40:23b

  2) Elaboration: human rulers are like chaff before YHWH   40:24
    a) Threefold metaphorical portrayal of rulers' lack of
      staying power   40:24a
      (1) They are not planted   40:24aα$^{1-3}$
      (2) They are not sown   40:24aα$^{4-6}$
      (3) They are not rooted in the earth   40:24aβ
    b) Twofold portrayal of YHWH's ability to blow
      them away   40:24b
      (1) They wither when YHWH blows on them   40:24bα
      (2) They blow away like chaff before a storm   40:24bβ
  2. Presentation of culminating rhetorical question: to whom
    can YHWH be compared?   40:25-26
    a. Presentation of rhetorical question proper: to whom can
      I be compared?   40:25
      1) Question proper   40:25a
      2) Speech formula identifying YHWH as the Holy One   40:25b
    b. Instructions to view YHWH's power   40:26
      1) Twofold instruction   40:26aα
      a) Raise your eyes on high   40:26aα$^{1-3}$
      b) See who created these things   40:26aα$^{4-7}$
      2) Depiction of YHWH's power   40:26aβ-b
      a) YHWH's actions   40:26aβ
      (1) Brings out by number their host   40:26aβ$^{1-3}$
      (2) Calls them by name   40:26aβ$^{4-6}$
      b) Response by YHWH's hosts: not one is missing
      due to YHWH's power   40:26b
III. Assertion: YHWH can deliver Jacob   40:27-31
  A. First set of rhetorical questions: challenge to Israel's belief
    that they are hidden from YHWH   40:27
    1. Twofold question: why do you say/speak?   40:27a
      a. Why do you say, O Jacob?   40:27aα
      b. Why do you speak, O Israel?   40:27aβ
    2. Twofold premise that they are hidden from YHWH   40:27b
      a. My way is hidden from YHWH   40:27bα
      b. My case passes away from my G-d   40:27bβ
  B. Second set of rhetorical questions with answers: YHWH is
    all-powerful creator and master of the earth   40:28-31
    1. Twofold initial questions   40:28aα$^{1-5}$
      a. Do you not know?   40:28aα$^{1-2}$
      b. Have you not heard?   40:28aα$^{3-5}$
    2. Answer: YHWH is master of creation   40:28aα^{6}-31
      a. Basically stated   40:28aα$^{6-11}$
      1) YHWH is G-d of the world   40:28aα$^{6-8}$
      2) YHWH is creator of the ends of the earth   40:28aα$^{9-11}$
      b. Elaboration on YHWH's attributes   40:28aβ-31

1) First set: endurance and wisdom 40:28aβ-b
   a) Paired statements on YHWH's endurance 40:28aβ
     (1) YHWH does not tire .... 40:28aβ$^{1-2}$
     (2) YHWH does not grow weary .... 40:28aβ$^{3-4}$
   b) There is no examining YHWH's understanding 40:28b
2) Second set: twofold statement on YHWH's support
   of the weak 40:29
   a) Gives strength to the tired 40:29a
   b) Increases power to those who lack vigor 40:29b
3) Third set: summation of YHWH's power to sustain 40:30-31
   a) Paired premise that the young may grow weak 40:30
     (1) Youths may grow tired and weary 40:30a
     (2) Young men may stumble 40:30b
   b) Paired declarations that those who trust in YHWH
   grow strong 40:31
     (1) First set 40:31a
       (a) Those who trust in YHWH renew strength ... 40:31aα
       (b) Those who trust in YHWH renew what is
       lost like eagles 40:31aβ
     (2) Second set 40:31b
       (a) They run and do not grow weary 40:31bα
       (b) They walk and do not grow tired 40:31bβ

Isaiah 40:12-31 is demarcated initially by the syntactically-independent rhetorical question in v. 12, "who measured waters with the hollow of his hand?" This initial question signals the disputational character of the unit, which focuses on demonstrating that YHWH is the master of creation who is able to redeem Jacob. This disputational focus of the text, supported by the repeated use of rhetorical questions to aid in convincing the reader of the truth of its claims, continues through v. 31, which portrays the support enjoyed by those who trust in YHWH. The command in 41:1, "remain silent before Me, O coastlands," marks the beginning of a new disputational unit that employs an initial summons to trial as part of a larger interest in demonstrating YHWH's role as master of human events.

Isaiah 40:12-31 comprises three major subunits in vv. 12-20, 21-26, and 27-31, each of which addresses Israel or Jacob with rhetorical questions that assert YHWH's role as master of creation and ability to redeem Jacob.

Isaiah 40:12-20 employs a threefold rhetorical assertion that YHWH is the creator who will redeem Jacob. The first rhetorical assertion of YHWH's role as creator appears in 40:12. This verse employs a series of paired rhetorical questions that assert YHWH's role as creator. The initial set of syntactically-independent paired rhetorical questions appears in v. 12aα. The first question of the pair, "who measured waters with the hollow of his hand?" in v. 12aα$^{1-4}$, is answered obviously with "YHWH" and points to YHWH's role as the creator who set the waters of the world into place. The second question of the pair in 12aα$^{5-7}$, "who gauged the heavens with the span of a hand?" is likewise answered with YHWH who set the heavens into place. Verse 12aβ-b, joined to the preceding material by a conjunctive *wāw*, then employs a set of three continuing rhetorical questions, each of which is linked together by a conjunctive *wāw*, to elaborate upon the first pair. The first question of the three appears in v. 12aβ, "and (who) completed with a measure the dust of the earth?" Again, the answer is obviously YHWH acting in the role of creator. The second and third questions then appear as a paralleled pair in v. 12b. The second, "and (who) weighed with a scale the mountains" in v. 12bα, and the third, "and (who weighed) with a scale the hills?" in v. 12bβ, likewise both point to YHWH's role as creator as the only possible answer to the questions.

The second set of paired rhetorical assertions, which focus on convincing the audience that no one can measure the mind of YHWH, appears in 40:13. The pair is syntactically independent from the preceding subunit, but the two questions are joined by a conjunctive *wāw*. The first question in v. 13a, "who can measure the mind of YHWH?" asserts that no one has such ability. The second in v. 13b, "and (which) man makes his (YHWH's) counsel known?" again asserts that no man is able to do so.

The third set of paired rhetorical assertions, which drive home the point that no one is like YHWH, appears in 40:14-20. This subunit begins in v. 14 with a syntactically-independent set of two paired rhetorical questions, joined together by a conjunctive *wāw*, that assert that no one can teach YHWH anything. The first pair in v. 14a, joined together by a conjunctive *wāw*, asks "who will take counsel and impart understanding to him (YHWH)?" in v. 14aα, and the second in v. 14aβ asks, "and (who) will teach him (YHWH) the path of justice?" The obvious answers are once again, "no one." The second pair of rhetorical assertions, joined to the preceding subunit by a conjunctive *wāw*, appears in v. 14b, where they, too, are joined together by a conjunctive *wāw*. The first question in v. 14bα asks, "and (who) will teach him (YHWH) knowledge?" and the second question in v. 14bβ asks, "and (who) will teach him (YHWH) the path of understanding?" As always in this text, the answer is "no one."

The second subunit of vv. 14-20 appears in 40:15-20 as a second set of two paired rhetorical assertions that no one can compare to YHWH. The rhetorical questions are embedded in vv. 18-20 as part of a much larger unit. That unit begins with a set of syntactically-independent declarative assertions in vv. 15-17 that introduce the questions by asserting that the nations of the world — implicitly indicating their gods — cannot challenge YHWH. The first set of two declarations, joined together by a conjunctive *wāw*, appears in v. 15a. The first in v. 15aα asserts that the nations are like a drop in a bucket (before YHWH), and the second in v. 15aβ asserts that the nations are considered (by YHWH) to be like dust on scales. The second set of three declarations, joined together by conjunctive *wāw*'s, appears in vv. 15b-16. The first in v. 15b asserts that the coastlands are like dust balls (to YHWH). The second and third form a parallel in v. 16 based on their metaphorical uses of Lebanon as a source for whole burnt offerings to YHWH. The first declaration of the pair in v. 16a asserts that not even Lebanon, which was known in antiquity for its abundant forests, could provide sufficient wood for a suitable burnt offering to YHWH. The second declaration of this pair in v. 16b likewise asserts that Lebanon's forests could not provide sufficient animals to make up a suitable burnt offering for YHWH.

The third set of paired declarations concerning the nations appears in v. 17 to constitute the culmination of the declarative sequence. They are syntactically independent, and no *wāw* joins the elements of the pair. The first declaration of the pair in v. 17a asserts that the nations are nothing before YHWH, and the second declaration in v. 17b asserts that the nations are considered void before YHWH. The second set of rhetorical questions (the first was in v. 14) then appears in vv. 18-20 and asserts YHWH's incomparability. This subunit is joined to vv. 15-17 by a conjunctive *wāw*, which indicates its dependent character within the larger structure of the unit. The paired rhetorical questions proper appear in v. 18, where they are joined together by a conjunctive *wāw*. The first in v. 18a asks, "and to whom will you compare G-d?" and the second in v. 18b asks, "and how will you portray (arrange) him (G-d)?" As always, the obvious answer is that such comparisons or portrayals cannot be made. The syntactically-independent subunit in vv. 19-20 then elaborates on the preceding portrayal of YHWH by depicting the useless character of idols manufactured by a craftsman. The first element in the portrayal in v. 19 depicts a metalworker casting idols, including the pouring of metal in v. 19aα, the hammering of gold in v. 19aβ, and the hammering of chains of silver in v. 19b. The second element of the elaboration in v. 20 depicts the actions of a woodworker in manufacturing an idol, including the choice of mulberry wood in v. 20aα, the choice of quality wood that will not rot in v. 20aβ, and the choice of a craftsman who will build an idol that will not fall apart in v. 20b. Of course, this last statement is a jab at the idols of the nations which fall apart when made of defective materials, whereas YHWH is incomparable.

The second major unit of 40:12-31 appears in 40:21-26, which asserts that YHWH is the master of creation. It begins in v. 21 with syntactically-independent rhetorical questions that challenge the audience's knowledge of the foundations of the world and then present the rhetorical answer in vv. 22-26 that YHWH is the master. The rhetorical questions in v. 21 appear as a fourfold sequence, each of which is introduced by a rhetorical *hê*, that shames the audience into admitting that they know of YHWH's power. The first in v. 21aα[1-2] asks, "Do you not know?" The second in v. 21aα[3-4] asks, "Have you not heard?" The third in v. 21aβ asks, "Has it not been told to you from the beginning?" And the fourth and culminating question in v. 21b asks, "Do you not know the foundations of the earth?" The effect is like asking a school child if she or he knows the most basic lessons from first grade.

The rhetorical answer to the questions posed in v. 21 then appears in vv. 22-26, that YHWH is the master of creation. Although the name YHWH does not appear in the present verses, the attributes are all those of YHWH, and the larger context supplies the name. The syntactically-independent vv. 22-24 presents three paired rhetorical answers, in which each pair is joined together by a conjunctive *wāw*. The first paired answer in v. 22a presents YHWH as the one who sits above the earth in v. 22aα and as the one who views the earth's inhabitants like grasshoppers in v. 22aβ. The second paired answer in v. 22b presents YHWH as the one who stretches out the heavens like gauze in v. 22bα and as the one who spread out the heavens like a tent in v. 22bβ. The third paired answer in vv. 23-24 includes both the paired answers proper in v. 23 and an elaboration on the answers in v. 24 that compares human powers to chaff before YHWH. The first answer in v. 23a portrays YHWH as the one who views human princes as nothing, and the second in v. 23b portrays YHWH as the one who makes void the judges of the earth. The elaboration in v. 24 first employs a threefold metaphorical portrayal of the limited staying power of human rulers in v. 24a who are not planted in v. $24a\alpha^{1-3}$, are not sown in v. $24a\alpha^{4-6}$, and are not rooted in the earth in v. $24a\beta$. A twofold portrayal of YHWH's ability to blow them away follows in v. 24b, including the fact that they wither when YHWH blows on them in v. $24b\alpha$ and that they will blow away like chaff before a storm in v. $24b\beta$. The culminating rhetorical questions then appear in vv. 25-26 where they are joined to vv. 22-24 by a conjunctive *wāw*. The presentation of the rhetorical question proper appears in v. 25 in the form of a quotation of the Holy One, YHWH. The question proper, "and to whom will you compare Me that I would resemble?" appears in v. 25a followed by the speech formula, "says the Holy One" in v. 25b. Again, the question is obviously answered by "no one," thereby asserting YHWH's incomparability. Verse 26 then follows this rhetorical assertion with instructions to view YHWH's power. It begins with a twofold instruction in v. $26a\alpha$ to raise your eyes on high in v. $26a\alpha^{1-3}$ and to see who created these things in v. $26a\alpha^{4-7}$. The depiction of YHWH's power then follows in v. $26a\beta$-b. The portrayal of YHWH's actions in v. $26a\beta$ includes bringing out by number the heavenly host in v. $26a\beta^{1-3}$ and calling them by name in v. $26a\beta^{4-6}$. Verse 26b accentuates YHWH's power by noting the response of the heavenly host, i.e., YHWH's overwhelming power ensures that not one of them will fail to appear.

The third and culminating unit of 40:12-31 appears in 40:27-31, which asserts that YHWH can deliver Jacob. Again, the unit begins with syntactically-independent rhetorical questions that provide the basis for argumentation: if YHWH is the creator (vv. 12-20), if YHWH is the master of creation (vv. 21-26), then YHWH is able to redeem Jacob (vv. 27-31). The unit comprises two sets of rhetorical questions in v. 27 and vv. 28-31. The first set in v. 27 challenges the premise that Israel's way is hidden from YHWH. It begins with a twofold question in v. 27a that asks, "why do you say, O Jacob?" in v. $27a\alpha$ and "why do you speak, O Israel?" in v. $27a\beta$. The twofold premise for the question then follows in v. 27b, including the premise that "my way is hidden from YHWH" in v. $27b\alpha$ and "my case passes away from my G-d" in v. $27b\beta$. Both questions and premises state the belief among Israelites that YHWH is somehow unaware and unconcerned with Israel's current troubles, i.e., they are exiled in Babylon away from their homeland in the land of Israel and the city of Jerusalem. The passage seeks to assert that YHWH is aware and concerned and that YHWH is about to act to remedy their situation.

The second set of rhetorical questions and their rhetorical answers appears in vv. 28-31, which asserts that YHWH is the all-powerful master of heaven and earth who is able to address the needs of the people. The twofold questions appear in v. $28a\alpha^{1-5}$, including the question, "do you not know?" in v. $28a\alpha^{1-2}$ and "have you not heard?" in v. $28a\alpha^{3-5}$. The answer, that YHWH is the master of creation, then follows in vv. $28a\alpha^{6}$-31, including a basic statement of the answer in v. $28a\alpha^{6-11}$ and an elaboration on YHWH's attributes that demonstrate YHWH's power to act in vv. 28aβ-31. The basic statement of the answer in 28aα$^{6-11}$ includes two elements: the assertion that YHWH is G-d of the world in v. 28aα$^{6-8}$ and that YHWH is the creator of the ends of the earth in v. 28aα$^{9-11}$. The elaboration on YHWH's attributes in 28aβ-31 then follows with three syntactically-independent sets in vv. 28aβ-b, 29, and 30-31. The first set of attributes in v. 28aβ-b takes up YHWH's endurance and wisdom. It begins with a paired statement on YHWH's endurance in v. 28aβ, including the statement that YHWH does not tire in v. 28aβ$^{1-2}$ and the statement that YHWH does not grow weary in v. 28aβ$^{3-4}$. Verse 28b concludes with a statement that there is no examining YHWH's wisdom. The second set in v. 29 presents a twofold statement of YHWH's support for the weak, including the statement that YHWH gives strength to the tired in v. 29a and that YHWH increases power to those who lack vigor in v. 29b. The third set in vv. 30-31 sums up YHWH's power to sustain. The first element in v. 30 presents a paired premise that the young may grow weak, including the statement that the young may grow faint and weary in v. 30a and that young men may stumble in v. 30b. The unit concludes in v. 31 with paired declarations that those who trust in YHWH grow strong. The first set in v. 31a includes declarations that those who trust in YHWH renew strength in v. 31aα and renew plumage like eagles in v. 31aβ. The second set in v. 31b includes declarations that those who trust in YHWH run and do not grow weary in v. 31bα and they walk and do not grow tired in v. 31bβ, thereby demonstrating YHWH's capacity to support and redeem Jacob.

Genre

Interpreters have generally recognized the overarching role of the DISPUTATION speech in the construction of 40:12-31, although they differ considerably in assessing the formal structure of the passage and the extent to which the genre appears in its constitutive elements (see Graffy, *A Prophet Confronts*, 6-15). A DISPUTATION designates a dispute between two or more parties in which one party challenges the viewpoint of another. Common settings for the genre include wisdom literature, which examines contrasting points of view (e.g., Job); legal settings which judge competing legal claims (e.g., Gen 31:36-43); and prophetic literature in which the prophet attempts to persuade an audience to abandon an opponent's viewpoint and accept the prophet's view in its place (e.g., Mic 2:6-11; Hag 1:2-11; Mal 1:6-2:9). The genre frequently employs two basic elements, a statement of the opponent's viewpoint followed by argumentation in which the speaker attempts to refute the opponent's viewpoint and argue for a different view (Graffy, *A Prophet Confronts*). Prophetic examples of the genre frequently employ three elements within the deep structure of the text; the thesis to be disputed, the counterthesis for which the prophet argues, and the argumentation proper (Murray, "Rhetoric of Disputation").

The argumentation frequently employs examples of the RHETORICAL QUESTION, i.e., a question that has an obvious answer and therefore requires no response. RHETORICAL QUESTIONS frequently serve an argumentative agenda insofar as they enable the speaker to assert an obvious point and thereby win the audience over to his or her position because the audience agrees with the assertion made by the question.

Setting

As a work of Second Isaiah, the historical setting of 40:12-31 is the late 6th century B.C.E., when the Babylonian Empire fell to the Achaemenid Persian monarch Cyrus the Great. Although many interpreters maintain that Second Isaiah's work may have been written in anticipation of Cyrus's conquest of the city, the depiction of the Babylonian Akitu or New Year's festival in Isaiah 46 suggests that the city had already fallen and that Cyrus had been named the new king of Babylon. Isaiah 40:12-31 would have been incorporated into the late-6th-century edition of the book of Isaiah, which included much of chs. 2–55 and 60–62, which viewed the fall of Babylon to Cyrus and Cyrus's decree that Jews could return to Jerusalem to rebuild the Jerusalem temple and the Jewish homeland as an act of YHWH.

The social setting of 40:12-31 would be the city of Babylon itself and the celebration of the Akitu or New Year's festival in Babylonia. The Akitu festival honored Marduk, the city god of Babylon, who in Babylonian mythology had set the world of creation into order and established the city of Babylon as his capital for ruling the nations of the world. The Akitu festival included a ritual procession in which the king of Babylon and the gods of all the cities and nations that Babylon ruled would be paraded through the streets of the city in a procession that would lead to the Entemenanki, the ziggurat or stepped pyramid that had been built for the worship of Marduk. According to the Babylonian creation epic, *Enuma Elish,* Marduk was the hero deity who set creation into order after defeating Tiamat, the goddess of the oceans and of chaos, who had threatened to kill all the gods and goddesses of the Babylonian pantheon. After killing Tiamat in battle, Marduk cut her body in half, setting up one half as the heavens and the other as the earth to begin the process of creation. As a result of Marduk's victory over Tiamat and his ordering the world of creation, the gods build the Entemenanki in Babylon to honor Marduk as creator, thereby authorizing Babylon to serve as Marduk's capital for ruling all of the nations of the world. During the annual Akitu festival, the Babylonian king was brought before Marduk at the Entemenanki, where he was designated by Marduk to serve as his regent for ruling the empire.

Isaiah 40:12-31 also serves as an element within the larger structure of the final 5th-century edition of the book of Isaiah, where it continues to assert YHWH's role as creator of the universe and redeemer of Israel during the course of the early Second Temple period when Persia ruled Judea. It would therefore anticipate the time when Judah and the rest of the world would be purged of evil so that YHWH's worldwide sovereignty over creation and human affairs would be universally recognized. The temple reforms enacted by Nehemiah and Ezra would be part of the process of purging the temple, the nation, and the world of impurity, thereby preparing the temple to serve once again as the holy center of creation and the locus for YHWH's worldwide sovereignty.

Interpretation

The interpretation of 40:12-31 presupposes its formal structure, its generic characteristics, and its settings.

Isaiah 40:12-31 employs the DISPUTATION genre to challenge the prevailing attitude among exiled Jews that YHWH was impotent before Marduk, the city god of Babylon. The Babylonian destruction of Jerusalem and the temple and the exile of large numbers of the Judean population to Babylonian would have convinced many that YHWH was unable or unwilling to defend the nation and that the disaster was the result of Marduk's victory over YHWH. The audience's view might well presume the claims of Babylonian mythology. According to the *Enuma Elish,* the Babylonian creation epic, the world was put into order when Marduk defeated Tiamat, the Babylonian goddess of the seas and chaos, who threatened to destroy all of the gods and goddesses of the Babylonian pantheon. The *Enuma Elish* was presented each year during the Babylonian Akitu or New Year festival, which celebrated Marduk's victory over chaos, his creation of the world, and his designation of the Babylonian king to rule as his regent for the coming year. The *Enuma Elish* asserts that the gods built the Entemenanki, the ziggurat or stepped pyramid temple that stood in Babylon, to commemorate Marduk's victory, to acknowledge Marduk as chief of the Babylonian pantheon, and to identify Babylon as Marduk's capital for ruling the world. To Judean exiles, the Akitu festival and the *Enuma Elish* would have been very powerful statements of Marduk's role as creator and victor over any who challenged the Babylonian power structure that Marduk had put into place. To Judeans exiled in Babylonia, YHWH would have been identified with Tiamat's forces of chaos. Babylonia's defeat of Judah would have been understood mythologically as Marduk's defeat of YHWH.

No such statement of Marduk's power is made; it is presumed throughout the text as the prophet focuses instead on convincing the audience that YHWH is the true creator of the universe. Second Isaiah employs a threefold rhetorical argument in the first major subunit of this text in 40:12-20 to assert the counterthesis that YHWH is the creator of the universe and that therefore YHWH has the capacity to redeem Israel from Babylonian exile. The prophet employs paired rhetorical questions to make the case. Such a device is especially useful in the context of argumentation insofar as it employs multiple questions to pile on assertions that the audience cannot refute.

In the first instance, 40:12 employs two sets of rhetorical questions to make the prophet's essential points. The first set in v. 12aα asserts that YHWH employed YHWH's own hands to measure the waters of creation and to set the heavens into place. The second set in v. 12aβ-b elaborates with three further questions that assert that YHWH measured the dust of the earth, that YHWH weighed the mountains with a scale, and that YHWH weighed the hills with a scale. The import of these questions is to convince the audience that YHWH is the creator of the universe. Curiously, v. 12 offers no evidence to support its claims. The audience would presumably be familiar with creation texts such as Genesis 1–2; Psalm 74; Job 38–42 or others, but such a perspective indicates that the prophet addresses a Judean audience that already knows its own sources and narratives.

In the second instance, 40:13 employs a paired set of rhetorical questions to assert that no one, presumably human or divine, can measure or fathom the mind of YHWH. The first question of the pair asserts that no one can measure the mind of YHWH, and the second asserts that no one can make known YHWH's counsel or decisions. Again, v. 13 presents no evidence to support its claims, which suggests that the prophet speaks largely to an audience that is already familiar with the sources that assert YHWH's omniscience and power.

In the third and final instance, 40:14-20 employs two further sets of paired rhetorical questions together with declarative statements to assert that no one, again either human or divine, is like YHWH. The first set of two paired rhetorical questions in v. 14 asserts in 14a that no one can counsel YHWH or teach YHWH the path of justice and in v. 14b that no one will teach knowledge to YHWH or make known to YHWH the path of understanding. Both sets of questions presume that YHWH already possesses such knowledge. The second set of paired rhetorical questions appears in the context of a much larger subunit in vv. 15-20. The subunit begins with three sets of paired declarative statements in vv. 15-17 that argue that the nations of the world cannot challenge YHWH. The first set in v. 15a denigrates the nations by claiming that they are like a drop in the bucket or dust on the scales before YHWH. The second set of three declarations in vv. 15b-16 asserts that the coastlands are like dust balls and that even heavily forested Lebanon lacks sufficient wood and animals to make a whole burnt offering suitable for YHWH's greatness. The third set of two declarations in v. 17 then concludes with assertions that the nations are nothing and void before YHWH. These declarations prepare the way for the concluding set of paired rhetorical questions in vv. 18-20. The paired rhetorical questions in v. 18 assert that YHWH can be compared to no one and that YHWH cannot be portrayed or described at all. The concluding elaboration then employs the imagery of idols manufactured by a craftsman from metal and wood to demonstrate their useless character.

The second major subunit of this text in 40:21-26 again employs the rhetorical question as an argumentative device to assert that YHWH is the master of creation. Four rhetorical questions appear in v. 21 to begin the process of making such an assertion. The four questions focus on the audience's knowledge, asserting that they already know that YHWH is the master of creation because they were taught as much already. Again, the questions presume an educated Judean audience that already knows its sources concerning YHWH and creation. Verses 22-26 then present the rhetorical answers to the questions. Verses 22-24 employ three sets of paired rhetorical answers to assert in v. 22a that YHWH sits enthroned above the earth and views its inhabitants as grasshoppers, in 22b that YHWH spreads out the heavens like gauze and like a tent, and in 23-24 that YHWH views human rulers as powerless. The culminating vv. 25-26 return to the device of rhetorical questions to assert that YHWH, the Holy One, can be compared to no one. YHWH's ability to call out the entire host of heaven by name provides the evidence for this assertion.

Presupposing the earlier arguments that YHWH is the creator and the master of creation, the third major section in 40:27-31 turns to the argument that YHWH can deliver Jacob. Two sets of rhetorical questions make this point. The first in v. 27 employs two sets of paired questions to counter the beliefs of the people of Israel that their way is hidden from YHWH and that YHWH does not consider their case — in short, that YHWH does not exercise power over them. The second set of questions in vv. 28-31 begins in v. 28aα$^{1-5}$ by asserting that the audience already knows the answer to the question. The remainder of the passage then provides the answer: YHWH is the G-d of the world and creator of the ends of the earth, who does not tire or grow weary, whose understanding is not to be examined, and who gives strength to the tired and the weak. In the end, the passage asserts that YHWH's roles as creator and master of creation fully qualify YHWH to give strength to those who trust in YHWH, i.e., YHWH is fully qualified and able to redeem Israel.

Bibliography

S. Anthonioz, "À qui me comparerez-vous?" (Is 40,25): La Polémique contre l'idolâtrie dans le Deutéro-Isaïe (LD 241; Paris: Cerf, 2011); D. Arenhoevel, "Die Kraft des Glaubens (Jes 40,27-31)," in Propheten in Israel: Bibeltheologische Betrachtungen zu Jesaja, Deuterojesaja, Jeremia, Hosea und Micha (Fribourg: Paulus, 1994); K. Baltzer, "Jes 40, 13-14 — ein Schlüssel zur Einheit Deutero-Jesajas?" BN 37 (1987) 7-10; A. Fitzgerald, "The Technology of Isaiah 40:19-20 + 41:6-7," CBQ 51 (1989) 426-46; A. Graffy, A Prophet Confronts His People (AnBib 104; Rome: Biblical Institute, 1984); N. C. Habel, "He Who Stretches Out the Heavens," CBQ 34 (1972) 417-30; R. de Hoop, "Isaiah 40.13, the Masoretes, Syntax and Literary Structure: A Rejoinder to Reinoud Oosting," JSOT 33 (2009) 453-63; R. F. Melugin, "Deutero-Isaiah and Form Criticism," VT 21 (1971) 326-37; T. N. D. Mettinger, "The Elimination of a Crux? A Syntactic and Semantic Study of Isaiah xl 18-20," in Studies on Prophecy: A Collection of Twelve Papers (VTSup 26; Leiden: Brill, 1974) 77-83; J. C. de Moor, "The Integrity of Isaiah 40," in Mesopotamica, Ugaritica, Biblica (Fest. K. Bergerhof; ed. M. Dietrich and O. Loretz; Neukirchen-Vluyn: Neukirchener, 1993) 181-216; D. F. Murray, "The Rhetoric of Disputation: Re-Examination of a Prophetic Genre," JSOT 38 (1987) 95-121; B. D. Naidoff, "The Rhetoric of Encouragement in Isaiah 40:12-31," ZAW 93 (1981) 62-76; P. Trudinger, "To Whom Then Will You Liken G-d?" VT 17 (1967) 220-25; R. N. Whybray, The Heavenly Counsellor in Isaiah xl 13-14 (SOTSMS 1; Cambridge: Cambridge University Press, 1971); H. G. M. Williamson, "Isaiah 40:20: A Case of Not Seeing the Wood for the Trees," Bib 67 (1986) 1-20; B. M. Zapff, "Jes 40 und die Frage nach dem Beginn des deuterojesajanischen Corpus," in G-ttes Wege Suchend: Beiträge zum Verständnis der Bibel und ihrer Botschaft (Fest. R. Mosis; ed. F. Sedlmeier; Würzburg: Echter, 2003) 355-76.

DISPUTATION: YHWH IS MASTER OF HUMAN EVENTS 41:1–42:13

Structure

I. YHWH's address to court (trial speech): contention that
YHWH is master of human events   41:1-4

a) Each helps the other   41:6a

b) Each tells the other to be strong   41:6b

  2) Elaboration on their encouragement: building of idols   41:7

    a) Craftsman encourages the smith   41:7a

     (1) Basic statement   41:7aα

     (2) Elaboration on the smith   41:7aβ

      (a) The one who hammers metal flat   41:7aβ$^{1-2}$

      (b) The one who strikes the anvil   41:7aβ$^{3-5}$

    b) Craftsman finishes the idol by nailing it securely   41:7b

     (1) Says the smith's riveting work is good   41:7bα

     (2) Fastens it securely with nails   41:7bβ

B. YHWH's address to Israel: reassurance/salvation speech   41:8-20

  1. Introductory address to YHWH's servant Israel, with appellations   41:8-9

    a. Initial invocation to Israel, my servant   41:8aα

    b. Jacob, whom I have chosen   41:8aβ

    c. Seed of Abraham, my beloved   41:8b

    d. Whom I grasped from the ends of the earth   41:9aα

    e. Whom I called from the earth's farthest edges   41:9aβ

    f. To whom I said, "you are my servant, I have chosen you, I did not reject you"   41:9b

  2. First reassurance speech to Israel: I am with you   41:10-13

    a. Twofold reassurance statement   41:10a

     1) Fear not for I am with you   41:10aα

     2) Do not be afraid for I am your G-d   41:10aβ

    b. Elaboration   41:10b-13

     1) YHWH's statements of support   41:10b

      a) I strengthen you   41:10bα^{1}

      b) I help you   41:10bα$^{2-3}$

      c) I support you with my righteous right hand   41:10bβ

     2) YHWH's defeat of Israel's enemies   41:11-13

      a) Defeat of enemies   41:11-12

       (1) All who oppose you will be ashamed and embarrassed   41:11a

       (2) All who contend with you shall be nothing and perish   41:11b

       (3) Disappearance of men who struggle with you   41:12a

       (4) Men who battle you will be nothing and nonexistent   41:12b

      b) Reason for defeat: YHWH helps you   41:13

       (1) I am YHWH, your G-d who grasps your right hand   41:13a

       (2) Who says to you, "Do not fear; I will help you"   41:13b

  3. Second reassurance speech to worm Jacob: I will help you   41:14-20

    a. Twofold reassurance statement   41:14

     1) First reassurance statement: do not fear, worm Jacob, men of Israel   41:14a

2) I will help you   41:14b
    a) Basically stated   41:14bα
    b) Expanded oracular formula   41:14bβ
   b. Elaboration   41:15-20
    1) I will defeat your enemies   41:15-16
     a) I will make you into a sharp threshing sledge   41:15a
     b) You will thresh mountains to dust and hills to chaff   41:15b
     c) You will winnow them so the wind carries and
      scatters them   41:16a
     d) You will rejoice in YHWH and praise the Holy
      One of Israel   41:16b
    2) I will provide water to your poor and needy   41:17-20
     a) Poor and needy unsuccessfully seek water   41:17a
     b) YHWH will respond   41:17b-20
      (1) Basically stated   41:17b
       (a) I YHWH will answer them   41:17bα
       (b) G-d of Israel will not abandon them   41:17bβ
      (2) Elaboration   41:18-20
       (a) I will open streams in hills and springs in
        the valleys   41:18a
       (b) I will turn the desert to ponds and parched
        land to water sources   41:18b
       (c) I will plant cedars, acacia, myrtle, oleaster,
        box tree, elm in the wilderness   41:19
       (d) Purpose: so that they will see, know, con-
        sider, and understand that YHWH the Holy
        One of Israel did this   41:20
III. YHWH's address to court   41:21–42:4
  A. Trial speech: YHWH's contention, viz., YHWH alone is G-d   41:21-29
   1. YHWH's dismissal of opponents: disputation   41:21-24
    a. YHWH's challenge to opponents   41:21-23
     1) Initial twofold challenge to bring arguments to court   41:21
     a) Bring near your case   41:21a
     b) Bring forward your contentions   41:21b
     2) Elaboration   41:22-23
     a) Come forward and declare what will happen   41:22
      (1) Challenge statements proper   41:22a-bα$^{1-4}$
       (a) First statement: come and tell us what will
        happen   41:22a
       (b) Second statement: declare to us the first
        things   41:22bα$^{1-4}$
      (2) Purpose: threefold statement that we will know
       the future   41:22bα$^{5-8}$-β
       (a) First statement: that we may consider   41:22bα$^{5-6}$
       (b) Second statement: that we will know their
        outcome   41:22bα$^{7-8}$
       (c) Third statement: inform us of what is coming   41:22bβ

b) Declare the signs of the future/demonstrate that
   you are gods   41:23a
   (1) Challenge statement proper   41:23aα
   (2) Purpose: so we will know that you are gods   41:23aβ
c) Do good or evil that we may stand in awe   41:23b
   (1) Challenge statement proper   41:23bα
   (2) Purpose: that we may be awed when we see   41:23bβ
b. Result: opponents are worthless   41:24
  1) Twofold statement that opponents are nothing   41:24a
   a) You are nothing   41:24aα
   b) Your actions are null   41:24aβ
  2) Whoever chooses you commits abomination   41:24b
2. YHWH's declaration of actions proving that YHWH is G-d   41:25-29
  a. YHWH's declaration that servant comes from north and
    east   41:25
   1) YHWH's actions   41:25a
   a) I arouse him from the north and he comes   41:25aα
   b) I arouse him from the rising sun and he calls my
     name   41:25aβ
   2) Results   41:25b
   a) He comes upon officers like mud   41:25bα
   b) He tramples them as a potter would clay   41:25bβ
  b. Elaboration: demonstration of YHWH's claims   41:26-29
   1) YHWH's opponents could not do these things   41:26
   a) Twofold rhetorical questions   41:26a
   (1) First: no else declares these things so that we
     know   41:26aα
   (2) Second: no one else declares these things so
     that we say he is right   41:26aβ
   b) Rhetorical answers: no one did this other than
     YHWH   41:26b
   (1) No one declares these things   41:26bα[1-3]
   (2) No one announces these things   41:26bα[4-6]
   (3) No one listens to you   41:26bβ
  2) Counter argument: YHWH did these things   41:27-29
   a) Former predictions concerning Zion have come true   41:27
   (1) Former things concerning Zion have come to pass 41:27a
   (2) I now send a herald to Jerusalem   41:27b
   b) No one else can do this   41:28-29
   (1) I find no one capable   41:28
   (a) I look and there is no one capable nor a
      counselor   41:28a
   (b) I question them and no one can answer   41:28b
   (2) They are all nothing   41:29
   (a) All of them are nothing   41:29aα
   (b) Their deeds are nothing   41:29aβ
   (c) Their metal images are wind and void   41:29b

B. Presentation of servant Israel to court	42:1-4
1. Presentation of servant Israel proper with YHWH's qualifications	42:1a-bα
a. Behold my servant whom I uphold	42:1aα
b. My chosen one whom I approve	42:1aβ
c. I have placed my spirit upon him	42:1bα
2. Qualities of the servant	42:1bβ-4
a. Brings out law to the nations	42:1bβ
b. Does not raise voice	42:2
1) Does not cry out or shout	42:2a
2) Does not make voice heard in the street	42:2b
c. Does not disturb	42:3a
1) Does not break a weak reed	42:3aα
2) Does not put out a dim wick	42:3aβ
d. Brings out law for truth	42:3b
e. Does not desist until accomplishes goal	42:4
1) Does not grow dim or run	42:4aα
2) Until establishes law and Torah in the world	42:4aβ-b
a) Establishes law on earth	42:4aβ
b) Coastlands await his Torah/teaching	42:4b
IV. YHWH's address to servant: commission	42:5-9
A. Expanded prophetic messenger formula	42:5
1. Messenger formula proper	42:5aα$^{1-4}$
2. YHWH's attributes	42:5aα$^{5-7}$-b
a. Created/stretched out the heavens	42:5aα$^{5-7}$
b. Founded the earth and its contents	42:5aβ
c. Gave soul and breath to people	42:5b
1) Soul to people on it	42:5bα
2) Breath to those who walk on it	42:5bβ
B. YHWH's commissioning speech	42:6-9
1. YHWH's commission to servant	42:6-7
a. Commission	42:6a-bα
1) I YHWH have called you in righteousness	42:6aα
2) I have grasped you by the hand	42:6aβ
3) I created you	42:6bα^1
4) I appointed you	42:6bα^2
b. Purpose of commission	42:6bβ-7
1) For a covenant of the people	42:6bβ$^{1-2}$
2) For a light of the nations	42:6bβ$^{3-4}$
3) To open the eyes of the blind	42:7a
4) To rescue prisoners from dark dungeons	42:7b
2. YHWH's self-identification and announcement of action	42:8-9
a. YHWH's self-identification	42:8
1) Announcement of divine name	42:8a
2) Does not concede identity to others	42:8b
a) Does not give glory to others	42:8bα
b) Nor praise to idols	42:8bβ

Isaiah 41:1–42:13 is demarcated initially by the syntactically-independent address form in 41:1, which introduces the TRIAL SPEECH in vv. 1-4. Indeed, the trial speech in 41:1-4 introduces a series of subunits in 41:1-4; 41:5-20; 41:21–42:4; and 42:5-9 which constitutes elements of a disputational trial scene that is designed to demonstrate that YHWH is the master of human events. Each subunit presumes a different addressee. Isaiah 41:1-4 presents to the court YHWH's contention that YHWH controls human events. Isaiah 41:5-20 constitutes YHWH's address to Israel that contrasts the coastlands' and Israel's response to YHWH, emphasizing the coastlands' fear of YHWH due to their reliance on idolatry and Israel's reassurance due to their reliance on YHWH. Isaiah 41:21–42:4 once again presents YHWH's contention to the court that YHWH alone is G-d and that YHWH therefore presents the servant, Israel, to the court. Isaiah 42:5-9 then presents YHWH's address to the servant in which YHWH commissions the servant to serve as a covenanted people to bring YHWH's light to the nations. The unit concludes in 42:10-13 with a hymn that calls upon the coastlands, sailors, and the inhabitants of the wilderness to give glory and praise to YHWH as the master of human events. Isaiah 42:14 begins a new unit in which YHWH claims the role of redeemer of Israel.

The first subunit of the passage is 41:1-4, which constitutes YHWH's address to the court contending that YHWH is the master of human events. YHWH's role as speaker is evident by the use of 1st-person address language throughout the subunit, culminating in YHWH's self-identification in v. 4. The initial summons to trial in v. 1 is formulated as a syntactically-independent imperative address to the coastlands that commands them to remain silent as the courtroom proceedings begin. The command proper appears in v. 1aα, and the motivations for the command then follow in v. 1aβ-b. The motivation includes three subunits that portray the reasons for the command for silence as the courtroom scene begins: the nations must prepare themselves for the trial in v. 1aβ, they must draw near and present their case in v. 1bα, and finally YHWH's summation that YHWH and the nations must approach the court for a legal proceeding then concludes the subunit.

Having introduced the proceeding in v. 1, YHWH then proceeds to make the first contentions before the court in vv. 2-4, specifically claiming to control human events. This segment comprises two subunits, each of which begins with a rhetorical question that is designed to build the case for YHWH's claim to serve as master of human events. The first rhetorical question and its associated material appear in vv. 2-3. Rhetorical questions employ the form of a question which has an obvious answer, but they function rhetorically as a means to assert the substance of the answer. The present question begins in v. 2aα by asking who has awakened a righteous figure from the east who will serve YHWH in defeating hostile nations. The question thereby answers itself by asserting that YHWH is the one who has carried out such an action. Verses 2aβ-3 then elaborate upon the role of the righteous one awakened by YHWH with four assertions. Verse 2aβ identifies the figure as righteous and asserts that YHWH has summoned him to serve at YHWH's feet, i.e., to serve YHWH. Verse 2bα states that YHWH places nations before this righteous one in v. 2bα$^{1-3}$, and v. 2bα$^{4-5}$ follows by asserting that the purpose of this placement is so that the righteous figure will dominate kings. Verse 2bβ-γ asserts that YHWH renders the weapons of the nations useless, including the statement in v. 2bβ that their swords will be like dust and the statement in v. 2bγ that their bows will be like chaff. Finally, v. 3 portrays the righteous one's pursuit of the nations, including the statement in v. 3a that he will pursue them at will without any opposition and the statement in v. 3b that the road does not come upon, i.e., hinder, his feet. Isaiah 41:4 then presents the second and culminating rhetorical question that contends that YHWH is the one who has done this. The rhetorical question appears in v. 4a, including the question proper in v. 4aα and an elaboration upon the question in v. 4aβ that contends that YHWH is the one who announced such an action to the generations from the beginning. The unambiguous rhetorical answer then appears in v. 4b, that YHWH is the one who has done this, including 1st-person statements in 4bα in which YHWH claims to be the first and in v. 4bβ in which YHWH claims to be the last.

Isaiah 41:5-20 then constitutes YHWH's address to Israel as part of the court proceeding initiated in vv. 1-4. Although vv. 5-7 appear in 3rd-person descriptive form, the 1st-person formulation of vv. 8-20, which is tied syntactically to vv. 5-7 with a conjunctive *wāw*, demonstrates that YHWH remains the speaker in this subunit. Overall, 41:5-20 is formulated to portray in vv. 5-7 the coastlands as fearful of YHWH as they rely on idols whereas vv. 8-20 portray Israel as reassured insofar as Israel relies on YHWH.

Isaiah 41:5-7 portrays the coastlands' fear as they approach the court.

Verse 5a portrays their fear with three successive verbal statements. Verse 5aα¹⁻²
states that the coastlands see; v. 5aα³ states that they fear; and v. 5aβ states that
the ends of the earth tremble. Verses 5b-7 then follow this initial portrayal by
identifying the cause for the nations' fear, i.e., their own idolatry. Verse 5b
begins the sequence with a syntactically-independent paired verbal statement
indicating that the nations draw near in v. 5bα and that they come in v. 5bβ.
Verses 6-7 then turn to the issue of their idolatry. Verse 6 employs a paired
verbal statement to portray their encouragement to each other as each helps his
neighbor in v. 6a and tells his brother to "be strong" (ḥăzāq) in v. 6b. Verse 7
then employs wordplay involving the verb root ḥzq to elaborate upon this scene
of encouragement with a portrayal of the building of idols. Verse 7a portrays
the craftsman or woodworker encouraging (wayĕḥazzēq, "and he strengthens")
the metalsmith. The encouragement begins with a basic statement in v. 7aα
followed by an elaboration on the smith in v. 7aβ as the one who hammers the
metal flat in v. 7aβ¹⁻² and as the one who strikes the anvil in v. 7aβ³⁻⁵. After the
smith has completed his work, v. 7b portrays the craftsman or woodworker
finishing the idol by declaring the smith's riveting to be good in v. 7bα and by
nailing it securely so that it doesn't wobble in v. 7bβ.

Isaiah 41:8-20 then presents YHWH's address to Israel in the form of a
REASSURANCE or SALVATION SPEECH based on the PROPHETIC ANNOUNCE-
MENT OF SALVATION. YHWH's speech appears throughout in 1st-person address
form directed to a 2nd-person masculine addressee identified explicitly at the
outset as "Israel, my servant," in v. 8. The unit comprises three subunits, each
of which is identified by its initial 2nd-masculine singular address form in vv.
8-9, which constitutes the introduction to YHWH's address; vv. 10-13, identified at the outset by the introductory 2nd-masculine singular REASSURANCE
FORMULA, 'al tîrā', "do not fear!"; and vv. 14-20, again identified at the outset
by the introductory REASSURANCE FORMULA in 2nd-person feminine singular
form, 'al tîrĕ'î, "do not fear!"

Isaiah 41:8-9 constitutes YHWH's introductory address to the servant
Israel. The subunit is formulated with a 2nd-masculine singular address form
in v. 8aα, "and you (wĕ'attâ), O Israel, My servant," that functions as an invocation. The rest of the subunit then constitutes a series of appellations for the
servant that then follow from the invocation, including "Jacob, whom I have
chosen," in v. 8aβ; "seed of Abraham, my beloved" in v. 8b; "whom I grasped
from the ends of the earth" in v. 9aα; "whom I called from the earth's farthest
edges" in v. 9aβ; and "to whom I said, 'you are my servant, I have chosen you,
I did not reject you'" in v. 9b.

Isaiah 41:10-13 constitutes YHWH's first REASSURANCE SPEECH to Israel
within the larger framework of 41:8-20. The speech is demarcated at the outset
by the REASSURANCE FORMULA, 'al tîrā', "do not fear!" The subunit is formulated through v. 13 as YHWH's 1st-person address to Israel. The appearance of
the feminine REASSURANCE FORMULA, 'al tîrĕ'î, "do not fear!" in v. 14 marks
the beginning of YHWH's second REASSURANCE SPEECH. The phrase "for I
am with you" immediately following the reassurance formula in v. 10 defines
the primary theme of the speech. The subunit begins with a twofold reassurance statement in v. 10a, including the statement "fear not for I am with you,"

in v. 10aα and the statement "do not be afraid for I am your G-d," in v. 10aβ. Verses 10b-13 then elaborate on these statements. Verse 10b presents YHWH's three statements of support for Israel, including "I strengthen you" in v. 10bα¹, "indeed, I help you" in v. 10bα²⁻³, and "indeed, I support you with my righteous right hand" in v. 10bβ. YHWH then announces the defeat of Israel's enemies in vv. 11-13. This subunit includes the fourfold announcement of the defeat of enemies in vv. 11-12, including the statement that "all who oppose you will be ashamed and embarrassed" in v. 11a, "all who contend with you shall be nothing and perish" in v. 11b, the announcement of the disappearance of all who struggle with Israel in v. 12a, and the announcement that those who battle with Israel will become nothing and nonexistent in v. 12b. YHWH announces the reason for the defeat of Israel's enemies in v. 13. This statement begins with YHWH's self-identification, "I am YHWH, your G-d, who grasps your right hand" in v. 13a, followed by the qualifying statement in v. 13b, "who says to you, 'Do not fear, I will help you.'"

YHWH's second REASSURANCE SPEECH to Israel then follows in 41:14-20. As noted above, it begins with the 2nd-feminine singular REASSURANCE FORMULA, 'al tîrě'î, "do not fear!" The oracle employs the feminine form to account for the address to Israel as "worm, Jacob." The feminine singular Hebrew term tôla'at, "worm," indicates Israel's vulnerability compared to its enemies (cf. Koole, Isaiah III: Isaiah 40–48, 167). The speech focuses on YHWH's efforts on behalf of Israel through v. 20. YHWH's speech shifts the address to the court once again in v. 21. The subunit begins with a twofold reassurance statement in v. 14, including the first reassurance statement, "do not fear, worm Jacob, men of Israel," in v. 14a followed by the statement, "I will help you" in v. 14b. This second statement includes two components: the basic statement "I will help you" in v. 14bα and an expanded ORACULAR FORMULA, "oracle (ně'um) YHWH, and your redeemer, 'the Holy One of Israel,'" in v. 14bβ. Verses 15-20 then elaborate on these statements. Verses 15-16 focus on YHWH's promises to defeat Israel's enemies with four statements: "I will make you into a sharp threshing sledge" in v. 15a, "you will thresh mountains to dust and hills to chaff" in v. 15b, "you will winnow them so the wind carries and scatters them" in v. 16a, and "you will rejoice in YHWH and praise the Holy One of Israel" in v. 16b. Verses 17-20 then shift to YHWH's promises to sustain Israel with water for the poor and needy. The subunit begins in v. 17a with a portrayal of the poor and needy attempting unsuccessfully to find water. Verses 17b-20 then present YHWH's response. The response is basically stated in v. 17b with two statements: that "I YHWH will answer them" in v. 17bα and that "the G-d of Israel will not abandon them" in v. 17bβ. Verses 18-20 then elaborate on this premise with a fourfold portrayal of YHWH's actions to help the thirsting poor and needy. YHWH states in v. 18a that "I will open the streams in the hills and springs in the valley" and in v. 18b that "I will turn the desert to ponds and parched land to water sources"; states in v. 19 that YHWH will plant seven types of trees in the wilderness; and concludes in v. 20 by stating that the purpose of these actions is so that the poor and needy will know, consider, and understand that YHWH, the Holy One of Israel, did this.

Isaiah 41:21–42:4 constitutes YHWH's second address to the court. It is formulated entirely as YHWH's speech, but it falls into two subunits as indicated by the change in topic. YHWH claims that YHWH alone is G-d in the first subunit in 41:21-29, and then YHWH presents the servant, Israel, to the court in the second subunit in 42:1-4. Isaiah 42:5 marks YHWH's address to the servant as the beginning of a new subunit.

Isaiah 41:21-29 is formulated as a TRIAL SPEECH in which YHWH attempts to demonstrate to the court that YHWH alone is G-d. The passage is heavily dependent upon the DISPUTATION form, in which a party challenges the viewpoint of the audience and argues instead for an alternative viewpoint. The first segment of this text appears in 41:21-24, in which YHWH refutes the claims of the opponents that they must be recognized as gods. The second segment of the text in 41:25-29 then argues that YHWH alone must be recognized as G-d.

Isaiah 41:21-24 begins with YHWH's challenge to the opponents in vv. 21-23. This subunit begins in v. 21 with YHWH's twofold challenge formulated with imperative verbs that demand of the opponents that they bring their arguments for their divine status before the court. The first appears in v. 21a, which calls upon the opponents to "bring near your case," and the second appears in v. 21b, which calls upon them to "bring forward your contentions." Verses 22-23 then elaborate upon this challenge by demanding that the opponents prove their case by declaring what will happen in the future. The first instance of this challenge appears in v. 22, in which YHWH employs 3rd-person descriptive language to demand that they come forward and declare what will happen. This segment begins in v. 22a-bα^{1-4} with a twofold challenge statement in which YHWH first demands in v. 22a that they come and tell us what will happen and then demands in v. 22bα^{1-4} that they declare to the court the first things, i.e., those statements and events of the past that led to the present situation. Verse 22bα^5-β then follows with a threefold statement of the purposes of such declarations by the opponents, i.e., so that the court may know the future. The three statements include v. 22bα^{5-6}, which states that the court may consider the claim; v. 22bα^{7-8}, which states that the court may know the outcome; and v. 22bβ, which states that the opponents may inform the court of what is coming. Verse 23a returns to 2nd-person plural address language to demand that the opponents declare the signs of the future so that they might demonstrate that they are gods. YHWH's challenge statement proper appears in v. 23aα and the purpose follows in v. 23aβ. Finally, YHWH demands in v. 23b that the opponents do good or evil so that the court might stand in awe. Again, the challenge statement proper appears in v. 23bα and the purpose follows in v. 23bβ. The subunit concludes in v. 24 with YHWH's 2nd-person plural declaration to the opponents that they are worthless. Verse 24a comprises a twofold statement that the opponents are worthless, including v. 24aα, in which YHWH declares that they are nothing, and v. 24aβ, in which YHWH declares that their actions are null. Verse 24b then declares that whoever chooses them commits abomination *(tôʿēbâ)*, which denotes a religiously objectionable act (Lev. 18:22; Deut 13:15; Ezek 16:50).

Isaiah 41:25-29 then presents YHWH's arguments that prove that YHWH is G-d. They are formulated in 1st-person form and addressed to the court. The subunit begins in v. 25 with YHWH's declaration that YHWH is bringing the servant from the north and from the east (sunrise). YHWH's declaration begins in v. 25a with a twofold declaration of YHWH's actions: "I arouse him from the north and he comes" in v. 25aα and "I arouse him from the rising sun and he calls my name" in v. 25aβ. The results of YHWH's declaration then follow in v. 25b: "he comes upon officers like mud" in v. 25bα and "he tramples them as a potter would clay" in v. 25bβ. Verses 26-29 then present an elaboration on these initial declarations that are designed to demonstrate YHWH's claims. Verse 26 employs rhetorical questions coupled with rhetorical answers to assert that YHWH's opponents cannot do these things. The twofold rhetorical questions in v. 26a assert in v. 26aα that no one else can declare these things so that the court will know and in v. 26aβ that no one else declares these things so that the court can say that he is right. The rhetorical answers in v. 26b employ three statements to assert that no one other than YHWH does these things: no one declares these things in v. 26bα$^{1-3}$, no one announces these things in v. 26bα$^{4-6}$, and no one listens to the opponents in v. 26bβ. Verses 27-29 then present YHWH's counterargument, that YHWH did these things. This segment begins with YHWH's assertion in v. 27 that YHWH's former predictions concerning Zion have now come true. Verse 27a asserts that the former things concerning Zion have come to pass, and v. 27b asserts that YHWH is now sending a herald to Jerusalem to announce the restoration. Verses 28-29 then follow with YHWH's refutation that no one else can do this. Verse 28 presents YHWH's two statements that no one else can do this: "I look and there is no one capable nor is there a counselor" in v. 28a and "I question them and no one can answer" in v. 28b. Verse 29 then concludes the segment with a threefold statement that YHWH's opponents are nothing: all of them are nothing in v. 29aα, their deeds are nothing in v. 29aβ, and their metal images are wind and void in v. 29b.

Isaiah 42:1-4 then turns to YHWH's presentation of the servant, Israel, to the court. The unit continues YHWH's 1st-person address language as in 41:21-29. It includes the initial presentation of the servant proper with YHWH's threefold qualifications in v. 1a-bα. YHWH begins with the statement "behold my servant whom I uphold" in v. 1aα, followed by "my chosen one whom I approve" in v. 1aβ, and "I have placed my spirit upon him" in v. 1bα. Verses 1bβ-4 then follow with a fivefold statement of the qualities of the servant. Verse 1bβ presents him as one who brings out law to the nations. Verse 2 describes him as one who does not raise his voice, including the statement that he does not cry out or shout in v. 2a and does not make his voice heard in the street in v. 2b. Verse 3a describes him as one who does not disturb, including the statement that he does not break a weak reed in v. 3aα and the statement that he does not put out a dim wick in v. 3aβ. Verse 3b describes him as one who brings out law for truth. Finally, v. 4 presents him as one who does not desist until he accomplishes his goal. Verse 4aα states that he does not grow dim or run, and v. 4aβ-b states that he will continue until he establishes law and Torah in the world, including the statement that he will establish law on earth in v. 4aβ and that the coastlands await his Torah or teaching in v. 4b.

Isaiah 42:5-9 continues with YHWH's address to the servant. Again, the passage employs 1st-person address language, but in this case YHWH's statements are addressed to the servant, Israel. The address appears in the form of a commissioning speech in which YHWH commissions the servant to serve as YHWH's covenant of the people and as a light to the nations. The unit begins with an expanded Prophetic MESSENGER FORMULA in v. 5 which includes the messenger formula proper in v. 5aα$^{1-4}$ and an expansion in v. 5aα$^{5-7}$-b which includes YHWH's attributes. Three attributes appear, including YHWH's role as the one who created and stretched out the heavens in v. 5aα$^{5-7}$, the one who founded the earth and its contents in v. 5aβ, and the one who gave soul and breath to people in v. 5b. Verse 5bα refers to the granting of soul to people on earth, and v. 5bβ refers to breath given to those who walk on it. In keeping with the messenger speech form, YHWH's commissioning speech follows in vv. 6-9. The commission to the servant appears in vv. 6-7. It begins the fourfold commission in v. 6aα-bα, including YHWH's statements that "I YHWH have called you in righteousness" in v. 6aα, "I have grasped you by the hand" in v. 6aβ, "I created you" in v. 6bα^1, and "I appointed you" in v. 6bα^2. The four-fold statement of the purpose of the commission appears in v. 6bβ-7, including statements that the servant is commissioned as a covenant of the people in v. 6bβ$^{1-2}$, for a light to the nations in v. 6bβ$^{3-4}$, to open the eyes of the blind in v. 7a, and to rescue prisoners from dark dungeons in v. 7b. YHWH's self-identification and announcement of action then concludes the unit in vv. 8-9. YHWH's self-identification in v. 8 includes two elements: the 1st-person announcement of the divine name in v. 8a and the statement in v. 8b that YHWH does not concede the divine identity to others. This later statement includes the provision that YHWH does not give glory to others in v. 8bα and that YHWH does not give praise to idols in v. 8bβ. Verse 9 then follows with YHWH's twofold announcement of coming action. YHWH announces in v. 9a the new things, including former things that came to pass in v. 9aα and the declaration of new things in v. 9aβ. Verse 9b follows with YHWH's announcement that "I inform you before they come to pass."

Isaiah 41:1–42:13 closes with a concluding hymn in 42:10-13. The song is formulated as a HYMN OF PRAISE, and it includes three basic elements. The first is the initial call to sing YHWH's praise in v. 10. The call is formulated with the masculine plural imperative verb *šîrû*, "sing!" The call proper appears in v. 10a, and it is followed by the addressees in v. 10b, including sailors on the sea in v. 10bα and the coastlands and their inhabitants in v. 10bβ. A second or renewed call to sing YHWH's praise appears in vv. 11-12, formulated in 3rd-person jussive language. The renewed call includes three elements: a call to let the desert and the towns of Kedar cry out in v. 11a, a call to let the inhabitants of Sela sing out from the mountaintops in v. 11b, and a call to let them praise YHWH in v. 12, including a call to let them give glory to YHWH in v. 12a and a call to let them declare YHWH's praise to the coastlands in v. 12b. The hymn concludes with the basis for praise, that YHWH defeats enemies in v. 13. Verse 13a presents a twofold declaration that YHWH goes forth against enemies, including statements that YHWH goes forth like a warrior in v. 13aα and that YHWH awakens rage like a man of war in v. 13aβ. Verse 13b then follows with a twofold declaration of YHWH's actions against enemies, including a portrayal of YHWH's yelling and roaring in v. 13bα and a portrayal of YHWH acting like a warrior against enemies in v. 13bβ.

Genre

Interpreters generally recognize the influence of the Trial Genres in 41:1–42:13. The Trial Genres refer to elements related to a trial setting or legal procedure in the courts. In the present instance, YHWH begins in 41:1-4 with an address to the court, here portrayed as the coastlands of the earth who will stand as witnesses or judges to the legal proceeding between YHWH, the G-d of Israel, and the gods of the other nations of the earth. These verses portray the beginning of such a proceeding in which YHWH calls for silence in the courtroom as both YHWH and the nations prepare to begin the proceeding.

The passage also makes heavy use of the Disputation genre, insofar as YHWH argues before the court that YHWH alone must be recognized as the true G-d of all the nations. YHWH states the contention in 41:2-4 and buttresses the argument by claiming to be the first and the last, who brings the servant figure from the east and renders nations and their weapons useless when they attempt to oppose YHWH's actions. In 41:5-20, YHWH argues first in vv. 5-7 that the nations fear to approach because their gods are nothing more than wooden and molten constructions, whereas YHWH counterargues in vv. 8-20 that YHWH has chosen the servant, Israel, that YHWH supports the servant, that YHWH will defeat the servant's enemies, and that YHWH will open streams in the wilderness as the servant returns to the land of Israel in a journey patterned as a second exodus, this time from Babylonia rather than from Egypt.

In making these contentions, YHWH's speech makes use of other genres as well. The Rhetorical Question, i.e., a question with a self-evident answer, appears throughout the passage in 41:2, 4 as a means to assert that YHWH and no one else has guided human events by rousing a righteous one from the east who will ultimately return to the land of Israel. Although Rhetorical Questions appear in the form of questions, their self-evident answers enable them to function instead as assertions by appealing to the audience's sense of reason that no other answers could be given to the questions. Rhetorical Questions appear again in 41:26 as a means to assert that no one but YHWH foretold the events that are now taking place and that no one but YHWH could ever be recognized as the true G-d of creation.

YHWH's speech also makes use of the Reassurance Formula, *'al tîrā'*, "do not fear!" in 41:10, 14 in both 2nd-masculine singular and 2nd-feminine singular address forms depending upon the formulation of the addressee (Conrad, *Fear Not Warrior,* 80-90). The Reassurance Formula functions as a means to reassure the addressee, in this case Israel or Jacob, of YHWH's support in 41:10-13 and 41:14-20. In 41:10, an example of the Assistance Formula ("for I am with you!") follows to reinforce the message of reassurance to Israel. Both the Reassurance Formula and the Assistance Formula are common elements of the Prophetic Announcement of Salvation, which appears to have influenced the present passage as well insofar as YHWH's reassurances to Israel in YHWH's Announcement of Salvation in 41:8-20 are intended to convince them that YHWH will stand by them and restore them to the land of Israel in the aftermath of the Babylonian exile.

The Trial Genre and the Disputation are evident once again in 41:21-29 as YHWH demands that the nations bring their arguments before the court and then proceeds to demolish them by demonstrating that they are incapable of foretelling the events that are now unfolding in the world of ancient Israel. In the end, YHWH contends that YHWH alone is capable of such action and that no one listens to the gods of the nations because they are nothing.

Following YHWH's presentation of the servant Israel to the court in 42:1-4, YHWH addresses the servant in 42:5-9 with a COMMISSION SPEECH that commissions the servant as YHWH's covenant of the people and light to the nations to open the eyes of the blind and to release those imprisoned so that all might recognize YHWH as the true G-d of creation. The passage begins with an expanded example of the Prophetic MESSENGER FORMULA, *kōh 'āmar hā'ēl yhwh,* "thus says the G-d, YHWH," followed by a string of YHWH's attributes that identifies YHWH as the source of the Servant's commission.

Finally, the passage concludes with an example of the HYMN OF PRAISE in 42:10-13. The HYMN OF PRAISE has a simple two-part structure, including a CALL TO PRAISE, which appears in twofold form in vv. 10-12, and the BASIS FOR PRAISE, which appears in v. 13. In the present case, the hymn in vv. 10-13 demarcates the conclusion of 41:1–42:13 with its focus on YHWH's role as master of human events and signals that the next unit will begin with the next stage of argumentation, that YHWH is the redeemer of Israel (Mattheus, *Singt dem H-rrn ein neues Lied,* 63-67).

Setting

Isaiah 41:1–42:13 stands in the sequence of argumentation in the work of Second Isaiah. It argues that YHWH is the master of human events, and it attempts to demonstrate this role by demonstrating that YHWH has defeated the nations to bring the servant, Israel, back from exile in the east to the land of Israel. The passage follows 40:12-31, which argues that YHWH is the master of creation, and it precedes 42:14–44:23, which argues that YHWH is the redeemer of Israel. Isaiah 41:1–42:13 therefore stands as one element in a larger sequence of oracles in chs. 40–54 that argues that YHWH is returning to Zion and restoring Bat Zion, i.e., Jerusalem personified as YHWH's bride. The references to YHWH's having foretold the events that have now come to pass as well as those yet to come in 42:9, together with the inability of the gods of the nations to do so, presuppose the earlier prophecies of Isaiah ben Amoz in the first portion of the book of Isaiah. Isaiah ben Amoz announced judgment against Israel and Judah throughout chs. 1–33, but also pointed to restoration once the punishment was over in texts such as 2:2-4; 8:23–9:6; 11:1–12:6; 13:1–14:23; 24–27; 32; and 33. The present passage looks back to those earlier prophecies and proclaims that the time of restoration previously announced in the book of Isaiah has now come to pass. Furthermore, the passage is fully aware of the pentateuchal Wilderness narratives as well in Exodus 16–18 and Numbers 11–36. The passage argues that, just as YHWH led Israel from Egyptian bondage to the promised land of Israel in antiquity, the time for a journey through the wilderness has come once again, but this time the Wilderness journey will take Israel from Babylonia back to the land of Israel. The references to YHWH's providing water in the wilderness during this journey in 41:18-20 presuppose YHWH's provision of water for Israel in Exod 17:1-7 and Numbers 20. YHWH's commission to the servant that he will open the eyes of the blind and rescue prisoners confined to prisons of darkness demands that the readers of this text will recall Isaiah's commission in Isaiah 6 to render the people blind so that YHWH might bring about the great works now coming to fruition and the announcement in 9:1 that the people walking in darkness would see a great light. From the perspective of 41:1–42:13, these events are now coming to pass with the restoration of the servant, Israel.

The historical setting for this oracle is the late 6th century B.C.E., when King Cyrus of Persia defeated Babylonia and became the king of Babylonia. The passage appears to presuppose Cyrus's decree of 539 B.C.E. that Jews could return to the land of Israel and rebuild the temple in Jerusalem with the support of the Persian monarchy (2 Chr 36:22-23; Ezra 1:1-4). Interpreters have tended to assume that Second Isaiah's oracles may have anticipated Cyrus's rise to power and thereby date as early as 545 B.C.E., but the presumption of the servant, Israel's, return to the land of Israel throughout the passage appears to presuppose that Cyrus's decree has already been issued. The place references to the servant as one whom YHWH has aroused from the east in 41:2, from the ends of the earth and its distant edges in 41:9, and from the north and sunrise in 41:25 suggest that the location for the prophet's discourse could be Jerusalem rather than Babylonia as most interpreters presume (Tiemeyer, *For the Comfort,* 130-35). Indeed, the concluding hymn in 42:10-13 suggests a temple or at least a temple-site setting. Insofar as scholars know of no liturgical setting used by Jews in Babylonia, the site of the temple, whether rebuilt or not, would provide an appropriate setting for the liturgical performance of the book of Isaiah.

As part of the 6th-century edition of the book of Isaiah, 41:1–42:13 celebrates Cyrus's decree that Jews could return to Jerusalem to rebuild the temple. As part of the 5th-century edition of Isaiah, 41:1–42:13 celebrates the return of Jews to Jerusalem. It looks forward to the time when Jerusalem will be fully restored and YHWH recognized both in Judah and throughout the world as the master of human events.

Interpretation

From the early work of B. Duhm, 41:1–42:13 has been read as a collection of independent oracles loosely grouped together. But with the advances in exegetical theory and the reading of Isaiah over the past century, particularly the recognition that the so-called Servant Songs of Second Isaiah must be read in context, a new, fully-integrated reading is now possible. Mettinger's insight that the servant of 42:1-4 must be recognized as Israel in keeping with the other elements of Second Isaiah that identify the servant as Israel/Jacob (e.g., 41:8) makes such a reading mandatory *(Farewell to the Servant Songs).*

Isaiah 41:1–42:13 is both a formal and rhetorical unit that argues that YHWH is the master of human events. It presupposes the rise of Cyrus the

Great, king of Persia, to the throne of Babylon in 539 B.C.E. and Cyrus's decree that subject nations, including Judah, might return to their homelands and rebuild the sanctuaries for their gods (see the Cyrus Cylinder in *ANET,* 315-16; 2 Chr 36:22-23; Ezra 1:1-4). From the standpoint of Second Isaiah, the anonymous prophet of the exile, and both the 6th- and 5th-century editions of the book of Isaiah, Israel is the servant that YHWH reveals in this passage. YHWH's ability to defeat the nations to bring the servant forward as a covenant to the people (Israel) and a light to the (foreign) nations becomes the key argument that YHWH must be recognized as the true G-d of all the nations of the world. The argument is buttressed by the references to YHWH's announcements in chs. 1–33 that Israel's restoration would take place once its punishment was over. The gods of the nations were unable to anticipate or bring about such an event.

The passage begins with a courtroom scene in 41:1-4, in which YHWH summons the nations and their gods to court before the coastlands to contend that YHWH alone — and not the foreign gods — controls human events. The references to the righteous figure summoned by YHWH from the east to defeat the nations to make such restoration possible presupposes Cyrus as YHWH's agent and points to YHWH — and not Marduk or Zoroaster or any other — as the G-d who brought Cyrus to power. The references to YHWH's having proclaimed such an action from the beginning likewise point to YHWH's role as G-d of the nations as well as the first and the last.

YHWH's address to Israel in 41:5-20 contrasts the gods of the nations with YHWH. Israel is after all the true addressee of Second Isaiah and the book of Isaiah as a whole, insofar as Isaiah is intended to rouse Israel to action, to accept the contention that YHWH is the true G-d, and to return to Jerusalem to restore YHWH's temple. The nations are portrayed in vv. 5-7 as fearful because they rely on idols and the idols on which they rely are nothing more than artful creations made of wood and hammered or molten metal. YHWH's reassurance or salvation speech in vv. 8-20 reinforces the claim that YHWH has chosen Israel from the very beginning, i.e., the time of Abraham and Jacob, and that YHWH has not rejected Israel. Such an argument is intended to defend YHWH against charges of divine absence, impotence, indifference, and even evil, insofar as it attempts to argue that both the exile and the restoration were part of YHWH's plans for Israel from the beginning (see, e.g., ch. 6) for recognition by all the nations of the world. The speech also contends that YHWH will remain faithful to Israel for the future as well, so that the effort to return to the land of Israel and rebuild the temple will proceed with divine support. YHWH will defeat any enemies that stand in Israel's way, much as YHWH defeated Egypt and Amalek in the exodus and wilderness narratives, and YHWH will stand with Israel on the journey home just as YHWH did in the wilderness (Exodus 14–15; 17; Numbers 20).

YHWH's address to the court in 41:21–42:4 argues that YHWH alone must be recognized as the true G-d of the nations. YHWH demands in 41:21-24 that the foreign gods show evidence that they are capable of foretelling and carrying out such actions and dismisses them as unable to do so. Now YHWH turns to the arousal of the servant Israel to demonstrate YHWH's claim to be the true G-d. YHWH's description in 41:25-29 of efforts to raise the servant from the north and east who calls upon YHWH's name demonstrates that YHWH is G-d and that the gods of the nations are not. Finally, YHWH presents the servant in 42:1-4 as YHWH's servant and chosen one whom YHWH supports and whose task it is to bring YHWH's rule and justice to the nations. The servant is portrayed as a gentle figure, not as a violent figure, who will bring YHWH's rule and teaching to the world as an act of peace.

YHWH commissions the servant in 42:5-9 to serve as YHWH's covenant to the people Israel and as YHWH's light to the nations. With YHWH's commission of the servant to serve as the central sign of YHWH's role as master of human events, both Israel and the nations of the world will recognize YHWH as the true G-d of all the world, Israel and the nations.

The concluding hymn in 42:10-13 celebrates YHWH's newly-recognized status. Any enemies that rise against YHWH will suffer defeat.

Bibliography

E. Beaucamp, "Chant nouveau de retour (Is 42:10-17)," *RevScRel* 56 (1982) 145-58; U. Berges, "'Ich gebe Jerusalem einen Freudenboten': Synchrone und diachrone Beobachtungen zu Jes 41,27," *Bib* 87 (2006) 319-37; C. Bergmann, "'Like a Warrior' and 'Like a Woman Giving Birth': Expressing Divine Immanence and Transcendence in Isaiah 42:10-17," in *Bodies, Embodiment, and Theology in the Hebrew Bible* (LHBOTS 465; ed. S. T. Kamionkowski and W. Kim; London: T. & T. Clark, 2010) 38-56; W. A. M. Beuken, "*Mišpāṭ:* The First Servant Song and Its Context," *VT* 22 (1972) 1-30; L. Boadt, "Isaiah 41:8-13: Notes on Poetic Structure and Style," *CBQ* 35 (1973) 20-34; R. E. Clements, "A Light to the Nations," in *Forming Prophetic Literature* (*Fest.* J. D. W. Watts; ed. J. W. Watts and P. R. House; JSOTSup 236; Sheffield: Sheffield Academic 1996) 57-69; E. W. Conrad, *Fear Not Warrior: A Study of* 'al tîrā' *Pericopes in the Hebrew Scriptures* (BJS 75; Chico: Scholars, 1985); M. Dijkstra, "He Who Calls the Eras from the Beginning (Isa 41:4): From History to Eschatology in Second Isaiah," in *The New Things: Eschatology in Old Testament Prophecy* (*Fest.* H. Leene; ed. F. Postma, K. Spronk, and E. Talstra; ACEBTSup 3; Maastricht: Shaker, 2002) 61-76; H. M. Dion, "The Patriarchal Traditions and the Literary Form of the 'Oracle of Salvation,'" *CBQ* 29 (1967) 198-206; P. E. Dion, "Institutional Model and Poetic Creation," in *Ascribe to the L-rd* (*Fest.* P. C. Craigie; ed. L. Eslinger and G. Taylor; JSOTSup 67; Sheffield: Sheffield Academic 1988) 319-39; A. Fitzgerald, "The Technology of Isaiah 40:19-20 + 41:6-7," *CBQ* 51 (1989) 426-46; G. Fohrer, "Zum Text von Jes. XLI 8-13," *VT* 5 (1955) 239-49; J. Goldingay, "The Arrangement of Isaiah XLI-XLV," *VT* 29 (1979) 289-99; E. Hessler, "Die Struktur der Bilder bei Deuterojesaja," *EvT* 25 (1965) 349-69; D. R. Hillers, "*Běrît 'ām:* Emancipation of the People," *JBL* 97 (1978) 175-82; J. Jeremias, "מִשְׁפָּט im ersten G-ttesknechtlied (Jes xlii, 1-4)," *VT* 22 (1972) 31-42; G. H. Jones, "Abraham and Cyrus," *VT* 22 (1972) 304-19; R. Kilian, "Anmerkungen zur Beudeutung von *mišpāṭ* im erste G-ttesknechtlied," in *Die Freude an G-tt, unsere Kraft* (*Fest.* O. B. Knoch; ed. J. J. Degenhardt; Stuttgart: Katholisches Bibelwerk, 1991) 81-88; H. C. P. Kim, "An Intertextual Reading of 'A Crushed Reed' and 'A Dim Wick' in Isaiah 42.3," *JSOT* 83 (1999) 113-24; K. Koch, "Zur Geschichte der Erwählungsvorstellung in Israel," *ZAW* 67 (1955) 205-26; A. Lauha, "'Der Bund des Volkes': ein Aspekt der deuterojesajanischen Missionstheologie," in *Beiträge zur alttestamentlichen Theologie* (*Fest.* W. Zimmerli; ed. H. Donner, R. Hanhart, and R. Smend; Göttingen: Vandenhoeck & Ruprecht, 1977) 257-61; F. Mattheus, *Singt dem H-rrn ein neues Lied: die Hymnen Deuterojesajas* (Stuttgart: Katholisches Bibelwerk, 1990; R. P. Merendino, "Literarkritisches, Gattungskritisches und Exegetisches zu Jes 41,8-16," *Bib* 53 (1972) 1-42; T. Milinovich, "Form Criticism and the *rîb* in Isaiah 41,21–42,4," *BN* 136 (2008) 44-57; C. R. North, "The 'Former Things' and the 'New Things' in Deutero-Isaiah," in *Studies in Old Testament Prophecy* (*Fest.* T. H. Robinson; ed. H. H. Rowley; Edinburgh: T. & T. Clark, 1950) 111-26; D. Odendaal, "The 'Former' and the 'New Things' in Isaiah 40–48," in *Old Testament Studies: Papers Read at the Tenth Meeting of the Ou-testamentiese Werkgemeenskap in Suid-Afrika* (ed. A. H. van Zyl; Leiden: Brill, 1967) 64-75; H. M. Orlinsky, "A Covenant (of) People, A Light of Nations," in *Essays in Biblical Culture and Bible Translation* (New York: Ktav, 1974) 166-86; K. Pfisterer Darr, "Like Warrior, Like Woman: Destruction and Deliverance in Isaiah 42:10-17," *CBQ* 49 (1987) 560-71; W. S. Prinsloo, "Isaiah 42:10-12: 'Sing to the L-rd a New Song,'" in *Studies in the Book of Isaiah* (*Fest.* W. A. M. Beuken; ed. J. van Ruiten and M. Vervenne; BETL 132; Leuven: Peeters, 1997) 289-301; B. Renaud, "La mission du Serviteur en Is. 42,1-4," *RevScRel* 64 (1990) 101-13; A. Schoors, "Les choses antérieures et les choses nouvelles dans les oracles deutéro-Isaïens," *ETL* 40 (1964) 19-47; H. Schweizer, "Prädikationen und Leerstellen im I. G-ttesknechtslied," *BZ* 26 (1982) 251-58; B. J. Spencer, "The 'New Deal' for Post-Exilic Judah in Isaiah 41,17-20," *ZAW* 112 (2000) 583-97; J. J. Stamm, "*Berît 'am* bei Deuterojesaja," in *Probleme biblischer Theologie* (*Fest.* G. von Rad; ed. H. W. Wolff; Munich: Kaiser, 1971) 510-24; W. B. Stevenson, "The Interpretation of Isaiah xli 8-20 and li 1-8," *Exp* 8 (1913) 209-21; C. C. Torrey, "Isaiah 41," *HTR* 44 (1951) 121-36; J. T. Walsh, "The Case for the Prosecution," in *Directions in Biblical Hebrew Poetry* (ed. E. R. Follis; JSOTSup 40; Sheffield: Sheffield Academic, 1987) 101-18; idem, "Summons to Judgment: A Close Reading of Isaiah xli 1-20," *VT* 43 (1993) 351-71; H. G. M. Williamson, "First and Last in Isaiah," in *Of Prophets' Visions and the Wisdom of Sages* (*Fest.* R. N. Whybray; ed. H. A. McKay and D. J. A. Clines; JSOTSup 162; Sheffield: JSOT, 1993) 95-108; A. van der Woude, "What Is New in Isaiah 41:14-20? On the Drama Theories of Klaus Baltzer and Henk Leene," in Postma, Spronk, and Talstra, *The New Things,* 261-67.

THE ACCOUNT OF YHWH'S ANNOUNCEMENT THAT YHWH IS THE REDEEMER OF ISRAEL 42:14–44:23

Structure

I. Announcement of YHWH's plan for the redemption of Israel	42:14–43:8
A. Announcement proper	42:14-17
1. YHWH's announcement that YHWH will speak	42:14
a. Twofold statement of YHWH's prior silence	42:14a
1) I have kept silent for a long time	42:14aα
2) I have constrained myself to remain quiet	42:14aβ
b. Metaphorical announcement that YHWH will scream like a woman in labor	42:14b
1) I will scream like a woman in labor	42:14bα

β. Hidden in prisons	42:22aβ
(b) People are without deliverance	42:22b
α. Plundered without a deliverer	42:22bα
β. Despoiled without an advocate	42:22bβ
c. Rhetorical questions asserting YHWH's role as cause of punishment	42:23-25
1) Rhetorical questions proper	42:23-24aα
a) First set of questions: Israel needs to listen	42:23
(1) Who among you listens?	42:23a
(2) Who will pay attention for the future?	42:23b
b) Second set of questions: YHWH brought the punishment	42:24aα
(1) Who gave Jacob to despoilment?	42:24aα¹⁻⁴
(2) Who gave Israel to plunderers?	42:24aα⁵⁻⁶
2) Rhetorical answer: YHWH brought the punishment	42:24aβ-25
a) Rhetorical question as answer: was it not YHWH?	42:24aβ
b) Qualification	42:24b-25
(1) Against whom they sinned	42:24bα
(2) They were not willing to walk in YHWH's path	42:24bβ
(3) They did not listen to YHWH's Torah	42:24bγ
(4) YHWH poured out wrath upon them	42:25aα
(5) YHWH poured out the fury of war	42:25aβ
(6) It burned all about them, but they didn't know	42:25bα
(7) It burned among them, but they didn't pay attention	42:25bβ
2. Twofold oracle of salvation for Jacob: punishment is now over	43:1-8
a. Conjunctive expanded messenger formula	43:1a
1) Conjunctive messenger formula proper	43:1aα¹⁻⁴
2) Qualifications of YHWH	43:1aα⁵-β
a) YHWH created Jacob	43:1aα⁵⁻⁶
b) YHWH formed Israel	43:1aβ
b. Twofold oracle proper	43:1b-8
1) First reassurance oracle: I/YHWH am with you	43:1b-4
a) Reassurance statement	43:1bα
(1) Reassurance formula	43:1bα¹⁻²
(2) Reason: for I will redeem you	43:1bα³⁻⁴
b) Elaboration	43:1bβ-4
(1) You are mine	43:1bβ
(a) I have called you by name	43:1bβ¹⁻²
(b) You are mine	43:1bβ³⁻⁴
(2) Qualification	43:2-4
(a) I am with you (assistance formula)	43:2
α. When you pass through water, I am with you	43:2aα
β. When you pass through streams, they will not submerge you	43:2aβ

      2) Peoples have assembled — 43:9aα$^{5-6}$
   b. Rhetorical questions: denial of nations' claims — 43:9aβ
      1) Who among them has declared this? — 43:9aβ$^{1-4}$
      2) Who makes known the former things? — 43:9aβ$^{5-6}$
   c. Challenge to nations: let them produce witnesses to
     substantiate their claim — 43:9b
  2. YHWH's counterclaim: I am G-d — 43:10-13
   a. You are my witnesses — 43:10
      1) Twofold declaration of witnesses — 43:10a
        a) First declaration with oracular formula: you are
          my witnesses — 43:10aα
        b) Second declaration: my chosen servant — 43:10aβ
      2) Purpose of the declaration: you will know, believe,
        and understand — 43:10b
        a) You will know — 43:10bα$^{1-4}$
        b) You will believe in me — 43:10bα$^{5-6}$
        c) You will understand I am the one — 43:10bα^{7}-γ
          (1) Basically stated — 43:10bα$^{7-10}$
          (2) Qualification: there is no other G-d before or
             after me — 43:10bβ-γ
   b. YHWH's counterclaims — 43:11-13
      1) Self-identification: I am YHWH — 43:11
        a) Basically stated — 43:11a
        b) Qualification: none beside me — 43:11b
      2) Self-identification: I am G-d — 43:12-13
        a) I declared it and delivered — 43:12aα
          (1) I declared — 43:12aα$^{1-2}$
          (2) I delivered — 43:12aα^{3}
        b) I announced it and there is no foreign god among you — 43:12aβ
          (1) I announced — 43:12aβ^{1}
          (2) There is no foreign god among you — 43:12aβ$^{2-4}$
        c) You are my witnesses that I am G-d — 43:12b
          (1) You are my witnesses with oracular formula — 43:12bα
          (2) I am G-d — 43:12bβ
         d) Substantiation — 43:13
          (1) I am the one from the beginning — 43:13a
             (a) From the first day I am the one — 43:13aα
             (b) No one delivers from my hand — 43:13aβ
          (2) No one reverses my actions — 43:13b
             (a) I act — 43:13bα
             (b) No one reverses it — 43:13bβ
B. Substantiation of YHWH's claim: overthrow of Babylon — 43:14-15
  1. Expanded messenger formula — 43:14a
  2. Announcement of YHWH's role as holy creator and king — 43:14b-15
   a. YHWH will bring down Babylon for your sake — 43:14b
      1) For your sake I send to Babylon — 43:14bα$^{1-3}$
      2) I will bring down her bars — 43:14bα$^{4-6}$

3) Babylonians will lament 43:14bβ
b. Self-identification: I am YHWH, your holy creator and
king 43:15
C. Presentation of YHWH's contention: YHWH is the redeemer
of Israel 43:16–44:5
1. Proclamation of salvation to Israel 43:16-21
a. Expanded messenger formula 43:16-17
1) Messenger formula proper 43:16aα
2) Qualifications of YHWH 43:16aβ-17
a) Who made road in the sea and path in mighty waters 43:16aβ-b
(1) Road in the sea 43:16aβ
(2) Path in mighty waters 43:16b
b) Who defeated chariots and horses 43:17
(1) YHWH's actions: defeat of chariots and horses 43:17a
(2) Results: they went down and were extinguished 43:17b
(a) Went down and did not rise 43:17bα
(b) Extinguished and quenched like a wick 43:17bβ
b. Oracle proper: proclamation of salvation/YHWH's new
action for Israel 43:18-21
1) Do not recall the past 43:18
a) Do not remember former things 43:18a
b) Do not ponder earlier things 43:18b
2) I am doing something new 43:19a
a) Doing something new 43:19aα$^{1-3}$
b) Now it will blossom 43:19aα$^{4-5}$
c) Rhetorical question: do you not know? 43:19aβ
3) I make a road through the wilderness/rivers in desert 43:19b
a) Road through the wilderness 43:19bα
b) Rivers in the desert 43:19bβ
4) Response by desert wildlife 43:20-21
a) Wild animals will honor me 43:20a
b) Reason: I make water in the wilderness for my
chosen people to praise me 43:20b-21
(1) I make water in the wilderness/rivers in desert 43:20bα
(a) Water in the wilderness 43:20bα$^{1-4}$
(b) Rivers in the desert 43:20bα$^{5-6}$
(2) Purpose: to give water to my chosen people 43:20bβ-21
(a) To give water to my chosen people 43:20bβ
(b) Qualification: people that I formed to
praise me 43:21
2. Israel's response to YHWH 43:22–44:5
a. Basis for punishment: Israel's past rejection of YHWH 43:22-28
1) Israel's past rejection of YHWH 43:22-24
a) You have not called me 43:22
(1) Basically stated 43:22a
(2) You wearied me instead 43:22b
b) You have not brought me offerings 43:23

(1) Twofold accusation — 43:23a
  (a) You did not bring me whole burnt offerings — 43:23aα
  (b) You did not honor me with peace offerings — 43:23aβ
(2) Twofold response by YHWH — 43:23b
  (a) I did not cause you to serve with grain
    offerings — 43:23bα
  (b) I did not trouble you about incense — 43:23bβ
c) You have not bought reed for me — 43:24
  (1) Twofold accusation — 43:24a
    (a) You did not offer cash — 43:24aα
    (b) You did not offer fat — 43:24aβ
  (2) Twofold response by YHWH — 43:24b
    (a) You burdened me with sin — 43:24bα
    (b) You troubled me with iniquity — 43:24bβ
2) YHWH's justification for past punishment — 43:25-28
  a) YHWH's role: I forgive your sins — 43:25
    (1) I erase transgressions for my own sake — 43:25a
    (2) I forget sins — 43:25b
  b) Appeal for Israel's testimony — 43:26
    (1) Remind me — 43:26aα
    (2) Let us arbitrate — 43:26aβ
    (3) Tell your story to justify yourselves — 43:26b
  c) YHWH's testimony and action — 43:27-28
    (1) Israel's past sins — 43:27
      (a) Your first ancestor sinned — 43:27a
      (b) Your representative transgressed — 43:27b
    (2) YHWH's reaction: punishment — 43:28
      (a) I profaned the holy princes — 43:28a
      (b) I gave Jacob/Israel to destruction and mockery — 43:28b
        α. Jacob to the ban — 43:28bα
        β. Israel to mockery — 43:28bβ
b. Oracle of reassurance for Jacob — 44:1-5
  1) Summons to hear — 44:1
    a) Hear, O Jacob, my servant — 44:1a
    b) Israel whom I have chosen — 44:1b
  2) Oracle of reassurance — 44:2-5
    a) Expanded messenger formula — 44:2a
      (1) Messenger formula — 44:2aα
      (2) Qualification of YHWH: creator who helps you — 44:2aβ
    b) Oracle proper — 44:2b-5
      (1) Reassurance formula — 44:2b
        (a) Directed to my servant Jacob — 44:2bα
        (b) Directed to my chosen Jeshurun — 44:2bβ
      (2) Metaphorical announcement of blessing — 44:3-5
        (a) YHWH's action: pour out spirit and blessing — 44:3
          α. Metaphor of pouring water and rain — 44:3a
            aa. Water — 44:3aα

β. He kindles and bakes bread 44:15aγ

γ. He makes a god/idol 44:15b

    aa. Makes a god and bows down to it 44:15bα

    bb. Makes an idol and worships it 44:15bβ

  (b) Elaboration 44:16-17

    α. Mundane uses for wood 44:16

      aa. He burns half with fire 44:16aα

      bb. He eats meat with that half 44:16aβ

      cc. He roasts and is full 44:16aγ

      dd. He warms himself .... $44:16b\alpha^{1-2}$

      ee. And says Ah! I am warm! I see coals ... $44:16b\alpha^{3}$-β

    β. Sacred use of wood 44:17

      aa. He makes an idol for a god with the
         rest 44:17a

      bb. He worships it, bows down, and prays
         to it 44:17bα

      cc. He says 'Save me for you are my G-d' ... 44:17bβ

  2) Derision of craftsmen who make idols 44:18-20

    a) They don't know what they are doing 44:18-19

      (1) They don't know and don't understand ... 44:18

        (a) Basically stated 44:18a

        (b) Reason: their eyes and minds are prevented
           from seeing and thinking 44:18b

      (2) They lack knowledge to say 44:19

        (a) Basically stated .... $44:19a\alpha^{1-9}$

        (b) Statement: rhetorical question .... $44:19a\alpha^{10}$-b

          α. Circumstances: I burned, baked, roasted,
            ate .... $44:19a\alpha^{10-18}$β

          β. Twofold rhetorical question 44:19b

            aa. Do I make the rest into an abomination? 44:19bα

            bb. Do I worship wood? 44:19bβ

    b) Final evaluation 44:20

      (1) He pursues ashes 44:20aα

      (2) A deluded heart leads him astray 44:20aβ

      (3) He doesn't say 'Isn't this a lie in my right hand?' 44:20b

E. Final exhortation to Israel to return to YHWH 44:21-22

  1. Remember these things Jacob/Israel 44:21a

    a. Remember Jacob/Israel .... $44:21a\alpha^{1}$

    b. Reason: you are my servant .... $44:21a\alpha^{2-4}$-β

      1) You are my servant .... $44:21a\alpha^{2-4}$

      2) I formed you as my servant 44:21aβ

  2. Israel, do not forget me 44:21b-22a

    a. Basically stated 44:21b

    b. Reason: I wipe away sins and transgressions ... 44:22a

      1) I wipe away your sins like a cloud 44:22aα

      2) Your transgressions are like mist 44:22aβ

  3. Return to me 44:22b

Isaiah 42:14–44:23 constitutes the account of YHWH's announcement that YHWH is the redeemer of Israel. The unit begins in 42:14-17 with YHWH's 1st-person announcement that YHWH will speak, whereas 42:10-13 concluded the previous unit with a 3rd-person hymn of praise in which the prophet called upon an unidentified audience to sing praise for YHWH. Isaiah 42:14–44:23 is concerned throughout with demonstrating that YHWH is the true redeemer of Israel. It comprises three basic subunits. The first is the announcement of YHWH's plan for the redemption of Israel in 42:14–43:8. The second is a disputational trial sequence in 43:9–44:22, in which YHWH attempts to substantiate in court the claim to be the true redeemer of Israel. The third is a concluding hymn of praise in 44:23. Isaiah 44:24 introduces a new subunit that is concerned with demonstrating that YHWH can use a foreign monarch, King Cyrus of Persia, as the agent for redeeming Israel and rebuilding the temple in Jerusalem.

Isaiah 42:14–43:8 presents YHWH's announcement of YHWH's plan for the redemption of Israel as the first major subunit of this passage. It is demarcated at the outset by YHWH's 1st-person speech in 42:14-17, which presents the announcement proper. The elaboration on this announcement which spells out the details and implications of YHWH's announcement appears in 42:18–43:8.

The announcement proper of YHWH's plans in 42:14-17 begins with a syntactically-independent 1st-person statement by YHWH concerning YHWH's prior silence. Indeed, 42:14 constitutes a two-part announcement of YHWH's intention to speak that begins in v. 14a with a twofold statement of YHWH's prior silence in v. 14aα and YHWH's self-restraint in v. 14aβ, followed by the announcement in v. 14b that YHWH will now scream like a woman in labor. The use of this metaphorical simile accentuates YHWH's intention to speak in contrast to the prior silence. The metaphor likewise accentuates the birth of something new that is about to happen. Again, the announcement appears in twofold form, including YHWH's announcement that "I will scream like a woman in labor" in v. 14bα and "I will pant and gasp together" in v. 14bβ. Isaiah 42:14 thereby introduces the announcement of YHWH's actions on Israel's behalf in 42:15-16.

Isaiah 42:15-16 presents YHWH's announcement concerning YHWH's ac-

tions on Israel's behalf. It begins with a presentation of YHWH's actions on Israel's behalf in vv. 15-16bα, specifically YHWH's guiding Israel, here identified
also as the blind, through the wilderness. This presentation comprises three aspects of YHWH's guidance. First is the focus on the mountains and hills in v. 15a
with a twofold statement concerning YHWH's intention to parch mountains
and hills in v. 15aα and YHWH's intention to dry up all of their grass in v. 15aβ.
Second is YHWH's statement concerning the rivers and ponds or marshes in
v. 15b, which again presents a twofold statement concerning YHWH's intention
to turn rivers into islands in v. 15bα, i.e., dry them up so that islands appear in the
riverbeds, and to dry up the ponds or marshes in v. 15bβ. The third is YHWH's
statement concerning the blind or Israel in v. 16a-bα. This subunit comprises
two elements. It begins with YHWH's twofold statement in v. 16a concerning
YHWH's guidance of the blind Israel, including YHWH's intention to lead the
blind on a path that they do not know in v. 16aα and YHWH's intention to lead
them on routes that they do not know in v. 16aβ. YHWH's twofold statement
concerning the intention to turn darkness into light then follows in v. 16bα,
including the change of darkness into light in v. 16bα$^{1-4}$ and the transformation
of valleys into plains in v. 16bα$^{5-6}$. The summary appraisal statement in v. 16bβ
then closes out the subunit with YHWH's statement that these are the things
that I have done and I have not abandoned them.

Isaiah 42:18–43:8 elaborates upon YHWH's announcement concerning the
plan for the redemption of Israel in vv. 14-17. The elaboration includes two basic
subunits. The first is a disputation speech in 42:18-25 that argues that Israel's
past suffering during the Babylonian exile was due to YHWH's punishment of
Jacob/Israel for sin. Such an argument is intended to demonstrate that YHWH
is the true deity in the world who controls Israel's fate. The second is a twofold
oracle of salvation for Jacob in 43:1-8 that maintains that Israel's punishment
is now over.

The disputation speech concerning YHWH's role in Israel's punishment
in 42:18-25 comprises three basic subunits. The first is a twofold call to attention
in 42:18 that calls upon the blind and the deaf, here used in reference to Israel
(cf. ch. 6), to give their attention to YHWH's discourse. The call breaks down
into two basic components, including the call to the deaf to listen in v. 18a and
the call to the blind to see in v. 18b.

The second major subunit is the presentation of a set of rhetorical questions in vv. 19-22 that are intended to demonstrate Israel's sin as the basis
for YHWH's decision to punish Israel with Babylonian exile. The rhetorical
questions appear in v. 19 in two sets. The first set in v. 19a includes a twofold
rhetorical question, including "who is blind like my servant (i.e., Israel?)" in
v. 19aα and "who is deaf like my messenger (Israel)?" in v. 19aβ. Of course,
the answer is no one, as Israel is the blind and deaf party addressed here. The
second set of rhetorical questions appears in v. 19b. Again, the questions are
twofold, including "who is blind like Meshullam?" (apparently a name applied
to Israel in v. 19bα) and "who is blind like the servant of YHWH?" (again apparently a reference to Israel in v. 19bβ). The rhetorical answers to these questions
then follow in vv. 20-22, which contrast YHWH's purpose with the people's
response. Isaiah 42:20 introduces this subunit with a depiction of the servant's

or Israel's inability to understand, including Israel's inability to see despite seeing in v. 20a and its inability to hear despite open ears in v. 20b. Verses 21-22 then focus on YHWH's purpose in contrast to the people's situation. Verse 21 presents YHWH's purpose as an interest in promoting righteousness among the people, including a statement that YHWH desires righteousness in v. 21a and a statement that YHWH's Torah (instruction) is intended to bring about the people's righteousness in v. 21b. Verse 22 then presents the desperate situation of the people in two parts. Verse 22a portrays the people as plundered and despoiled, including a statement to this effect in v. 22aα and a statement indicating that they are imprisoned in v. 22aβ. Verse 22b then portrays the people without deliverance with statements that the people are plundered without a deliverer in v. 22bα and that they are despoiled without an advocate in v. 22bβ.

The third major subunit of 42:18-25 is a second set of rhetorical questions in 42:23-25 that focuses on asserting YHWH's role as the cause of Israel's punishment. The questions proper appear in vv. 23-24aα in two sets. The first set in v. 23 focuses on Israel's need to listen, including the question "who among you listens?" in v. 23a and "who will pay attention for the future?" in v. 23b. Of course, the answer in both cases is no one. The second set of questions follows in v. 24aα, including "who gave Jacob to despoilment?" in v. 24aα¹⁻⁴ and "who gave Israel to plunderers?" in v. 24aα⁵⁻⁶. Of course, the answer in both cases is YHWH. The rhetorical answer then follows in vv. 24aβ-25 with a detailed presentation of YHWH as the responsible party. This segment begins in v. 24aβ with another rhetorical question, "was it not YHWH?" which presents the basic answer. Verses 24b-25 then qualify this answer with a sequence of seven circumstances and actions that specify the process by which YHWH brought punishment upon Israel. The first in v. 24bα identifies YHWH as the one against whom they sinned. The second in v. 24bβ states that they were not willing to walk in YHWH's path. The third in v. 24bγ states that they did not listen to YHWH's Torah. The fourth in v. 25aα states that YHWH poured out wrath upon them. The fifth in v. 25aβ states that YHWH poured out the fury of war. The sixth in v. 25bα states that it burned all about them, but they didn't know what it was about. And the seventh in v. 25bβ states that it burned among them, but they didn't pay attention to its significance.

The second major subunit of 42:18–43:8, joined to 42:18-25 by the conjunction wĕ'attâ, "and now," is 43:1-8. Isaiah 43:1-8 presents a twofold oracle of salvation for Jacob (Israel) that announces that the punishment is now over. It begins in v. 1a with a conjunctive expanded messenger formula that identifies YHWH as Jacob's creator and the one who formed Israel. The basic messenger formula appears in v. 1aα¹⁻⁴, and the qualifications on YHWH's identity appear in v. 1aα⁵-β, including the qualification that YHWH is the creator of Jacob in v. 1aα⁵⁻⁶ and that YHWH is the one who formed Israel in v. 1aβ.

The twofold oracle of salvation for Israel then follows in 43:1b-8. The first element of this oracle appears in 43:1b-4 in the form of a reassurance oracle in which YHWH states to Israel "I am with you." It begins with the reassurance statement in v. 1bα, which includes the reassurance formula in v. 1bα¹⁻² followed by the reason for YHWH's reassurance, i.e., "for I will redeem you" in v. 1bα³⁻⁴. Isaiah 43:1bβ-4 then follows with an elaboration on this point. The elaboration begins in v. 1bβ with YHWH's twofold statement that "Israel is mine," including the statements "I have called you by name" in v. 1bβ¹⁻² and "You are mine" in v. 1bβ³⁻⁴. Verses 2-4 then qualify YHWH's statements. Verse 2 presents four qualifications for YHWH's assertion that "You are mine." The first in v. 2aα states that "when you pass through water, I am with you." The second in v. 2aβ asserts that "when you pass through streams, they will not submerge you." The third in v. 2bα states that "when you walk through fire, you will not be burned." The fourth in v. 2bβ states that "when you walk through flame, it will not scorch you." Isaiah 43:3-4, which is introduced by causative *kî*, "because," then follows with the reasons for YHWH's assertion that "Israel in mine," i.e., "I am YHWH, your G-d and deliverer." This subunit begins in v. 3a with YHWH's self-identification as "YHWH, your G-d and deliverer," including the statement in v. 3aα that "I am YHWH your G-d" and the statement in v. 3aβ that "I am the Holy One of Israel, your deliverer." Verses 3b-4 then follow with YHWH's deeds on behalf of Israel in two sections. The first in v. 3b specifies that YHWH appoints North African nations for Israel, i.e., that these nations will recognize and honor Israel, including Egypt in v. 3bα and Ethiopia and Saba in v. 3bβ. The second in v. 4 is a more generalized statement that YHWH gives peoples and nations for Israel, including the condition or protasis "because you are precious in my eyes" in v. 4a and the apodosis in v. 4b that "I give people [in v. 4bα] and nations [in v. 4bβ] for you."

The second element in the oracle is a second reassurance oracle in 43:5-8, in which YHWH once again asserts, "I am with you." The subunit begins in v. 5a with YHWH's reassurance, including the reassurance formula, "do not fear," in v. 5aα and the assistance formula, "I am with you," in v. 5aβ. Verses 5b-8 then follow with an enumeration of YHWH's deeds on behalf of Israel. The first element in v. 5b focuses on what YHWH does for Israel, including the statement in v. 5bα that "I bring your seed from the east" and the statement in v. 5bβ that "I gather you from the west." Verses 6-8 then focus on what YHWH says. The portion in v. 6a focuses on what YHWH says to the north and the south, including the command to "give," i.e., return Israel, to the north in v. 6aα and the command to the south, "do not hide (Israel)," in v. 6aβ. Verses 6b-8 then follow with YHWH's statements to all to "bring my people home." Verse 6b takes up the sons and the daughters, including the command to "bring sons from afar" in v. 6bα and the command to "bring daughters from the ends of the earth" in v. 6bβ. Verse 7 specifies that these commands refer to all that are YHWH's, including "all that are called by my name and my glory that I created" in v. 7a and "all that I formed and made" in v. 7b. Verse 8 concludes the oracle with a command to "set my people free," including the command to "set free my blind people who have eyes" in v. 8a and the command to "set free my deaf people who have ears" in v. 8b.

Isaiah 43:9–44:22 constitutes the second major subunit of 42:14–44:23 as the trial scene in which YHWH substantiates in court YHWH's claims to be the redeemer of Israel. This segment includes five major subunits, including the challenge to the opponents in 43:9-13; the substantiation of YHWH's claims with the overthrow of Babylon in 43:14-15; the presentation of YHWH's contention that YHWH is the redeemer of Israel in 43:16–44:5; YHWH's summary statements in 44:6-20; and the final exhortation to Israel to return to YHWH in 44:21-22.

Isaiah 43:9-13 constitutes the initial call for the nations to make their claim in court. The segment is formulated as the prophet's presentation of YHWH's speech as indicated by the oracular formula, *nĕ'um yhwh,* "oracle of YHWH," in v. 10 and the 1st-person formulation of the speech. The subunit includes three basic elements. The first is the call for the nations to make their claim in 43:9. This segment includes three elements. The first element is the portrayal of the gathering of the nations in v. 9aα, including the portrayal of the nations gathered together in v. 9aα$^{1-4}$ and the people assembled in v. 9aα$^{5-6}$. The second element is the presentation of the rhetorical questions in v. 9aβ that are designed to deny the nations' claims, including the questions "who among them has declared this?" in v. 9aβ$^{1-4}$ and "who makes known the former things?" in v. 9aβ$^{5-6}$. The unspoken answer in both cases is clearly no one. The third element in v. 9b then closes the subunit in v. 9 with a challenge to the nations to let them produce witnesses to substantiate their claims. The expectation is that they will not be able to do so.

The second basic element of 43:9-13 is the presentation of YHWH's contention in vv. 10-13 that I am G-d. This segment begins with in v. 10 with YHWH's declaration that you, i.e., the people of Israel who constitute the audience of this text, are YHWH's witnesses to the claim that YHWH is the redeemer of Israel. Verse 10 begins with a twofold declaration that "you are my witnesses" in v. 10a, including the first declaration with the oracular formula in v. 10aα that "you are my witnesses" and the second declaration in v. 10aβ that "you are my chosen servant." Verse 10b then follows with a statement of the purpose of the declaration, that you will know, believe, and understand that YHWH is the true G-d. Verse 10b includes three components based on these verbs: that "you will know" in v. 10bα$^{1-4}$, that "you will believe in me" in v. 10bα$^{5-6}$, and that "you will understand that I am the one" in v. 10bα^{7}-γ. Indeed, this last segment is further divided into the basic statement in v. 10bα$^{7-10}$ and the qualification that before YHWH no G-d was created and there will be no other after YHWH in v. 10bβ-γ.

Isaiah 43:11-13 then follows with YHWH's counterclaims. This segment begins in v. 11 with YHWH's self-identification as YHWH, including the basic statement in v. 11a and the qualification that there is none beside YHWH in v. 11b. A second and more detailed self-identification follows in vv. 12-13, in which YHWH self-identifies as G-d. This segment includes four basic elements that together make the argument that YHWH is G-d. The first appears in v. 12aα, in which YHWH declares that "I declared" in v. 12aα$^{1-2}$ and "I delivered" in v. 12aα^{3}. The second element appears in v. 12aβ, in which YHWH declares that "I announced it," including the basic declaration in v. 12aβ^{1} and the announcement that "there is no foreign god among you" in v. 12aβ$^{2-4}$. The third element appears in v. 12b in which YHWH declares that "you are my witnesses that I am G-d," including the declaration that "you are my witnesses" with the oracular formula in v. 12bα and the declaration that "I am G-d" in v. 12bβ. The fourth element is the substantiation for the claim in v. 13. This element begins with YHWH's declaration that "I am the one from the beginning" in v. 13a, including the statement that "from the first day I am the one" in v. 13aα and that "no one delivers from my hand" in v. 13aβ. The declaration that "no one reverses my actions" follows in v. 13b and includes the statements that "I act" in v. 13bα and "no one reverses it (my action)" in v. 13bβ.

Isaiah 43:14-15 substantiates YHWH's claims to be G-d by pointing to the overthrow of Babylon as the second major subunit of 43:9–44:22. This subunit begins with an expanded messenger formula in v. 14a, which identifies YHWH as Israel's redeemer and the Holy One of Israel, and it follows in vv. 14b-15 with YHWH's announcement of YHWH's role as the holy creator and king. The announcement begins in v. 14b with YHWH's claims to bring down the Babylonian Empire for the sake of Israel, here identified by the 2nd-person plural pronouns as the addressee of the announcement. The announcement includes three elements, including the statement that "for your sake I send to Babylon" in v. 14bα$^{1-3}$, "I will bring down her bars" in v. 14bα$^{4-6}$, and the statement that "the Babylonians will lament" in v. 14bβ. YHWH's self-identification as Israel's creator and king in v. 15 then constitutes the second major element of the announcement.

Isaiah 43:16–44:5 then constitutes the third major subunit of 43:9–44:22, with a presentation of YHWH's contention that YHWH is the redeemer of Israel. This subunit begins with the proclamation of salvation to Israel in 43:16-21. The proclamation begins with a heavily expanded messenger formula in vv. 16-17, which includes the messenger formula proper in v. 16aα and the qualifications of YHWH in vv. 16aβ-17. The first qualification appears in v. 16aβ-b by describing YHWH as the one who brought Israel through the sea and mighty waters, including statements that YHWH made a road in the sea in v. 16aβ and a path in mighty waters in v. 16b. The second qualification in v. 17 claims that YHWH is the one who defeated chariots and horses, including the statement of YHWH's actions in defeating chariots and horses in v. 17a and the twofold statement of results, i.e., that they went down and were extinguished in v. 17b, including statements that "they went down and did not rise" n v. 17bα and that "they were extinguished and quenched like a wick" in v. 17bβ.

The presentation of the oracle then continues in 43:18-21. The presentation of YHWH's new action for Israel in 43:18-21 includes four basic elements. The first is YHWH's instruction not to recall the past in v. 18, which includes statements not to remember the former things in v. 18a and not to ponder earlier things in v. 18b. The second is YHWH's announcement that "I am doing something new" in v. 19a, including statements that YHWH is doing something new in v. 19aα$^{1-3}$, that now it will blossom in v. 19aα$^{4-5}$, and finally, a rhetorical question "do you not know?" in v. 19aβ which asserts to the audience that indeed they do or must know. The third is YHWH's announcement in v. 19b about making roads through the wilderness to lead Israel home, including the statement in v. 19bα concerning the road through the wilderness and the statement in v. 19bβ concerning rivers in the desert. The fourth presents the response to YHWH's actions in vv. 20-21 by creation in the form of the desert wildlife. This segment begins with YHWH's claim that "the wild animals will honor me" in v. 20a, followed by a statement concerning the reason for the animals' action, that YHWH makes water in the wilderness "for my chosen people to praise me" in vv. 20b-21. This segment begins with YHWH's statement concerning the making of water in the wilderness in v. 20bα, including statements that YHWH makes water in the wilderness in v. 20bα$^{1-4}$ and rivers in the desert in v. 20bα$^{5-6}$. Verses 20bβ-21 follow with YHWH's statement that the purpose is "to give water to my chosen people," including the basic statement in v. 20bβ and the qualification that the chosen people are "the people that I formed to praise me" in v. 21.

Isaiah 43:22–44:5 constitutes the announcement of Israel's response to YHWH. It includes two basic elements: the basis for punishment in Israel's past rejection of YHWH in 43:22-28 and the oracle of reassurance for Jacob in 44:1-5.

The presentation of the basis for punishment in 43:22-28 focuses on Israel's past rejection of YHWH. It begins in 43:22-24 with an account of Israel's rejection of YHWH in three basic components. The first is the charge that "you have not called me" in v. 22, which is basically stated in v. 22a and expanded with the charge that "you have wearied me instead" in v. 22b. The second is the charge that "you have not brought me offerings" in v. 23. This charge begins with the twofold accusation in v. 23a that "you did not bring me whole burnt offerings" in v. 23aα and that "you did not honor me with peace offerings" in v. 23aβ. The twofold response by YHWH follows in v. 23b, including statements that "I did not cause you to serve with grain offerings," i.e., I did not ask for them, in v. 23bα and that "I did not trouble you about incense," i.e., I did not ask for it, in v. 23bβ. The third charge, that "you have not bought reed [something purchased with a receipt] for me" appears in v. 24. This segment begins with the twofold accusation that "you did not offer reed," i.e., cash, in v. 24aα and that "you did not offer fat" in v. 24aβ. YHWH's twofold response follows in v. 24b with accusations that "you burdened me with sin" in v. 24bα and that "you troubled me with iniquity" in v. 24bβ.

Isaiah 43:25-28 follows as the second element of 43:22-28 with YHWH's justification for past punishment. The segment includes three subunits. The first in v. 25 announces YHWH's role in forgiving Israel's sins, including statements that "I erase transgressions for my own sake" in v. 25a and that "I forget sins" in v. 25b. The second appears as an appeal for Israel's testimony in v. 26, including statements that Israel must remind YHWH in v. 26aα, an appeal to arbitrate in v. 26aβ, and an appeal to tell your story to justify yourselves in v. 26b. The third appears in vv. 27-28 with a presentation of YHWH's testimony and action. The first portion in v. 27 concentrates on Israel's past sins with statements that "your first ancestor sinned" in v. 27a and that "your representative [presumably the same as the ancestor just mentioned] transgressed" in v. 27b. The second portion in v. 28 presents YHWH's reaction to these misdeeds: punishment. This segment begins with YHWH's claim that "I profaned the holy princes" in v. 28a and the claim that "I gave Jacob/Israel to destruction and mockery" in v. 28b, including statements that "I gave Jacob to the ban" in v. 28bα and that "I gave Israel to mockery" in v. 28bβ.

Isaiah 44:1-5 constitutes the second major subunit of 43:22–44:5 with an oracle of reassurance for Jacob. Following the account of Israel's sins in 43:22-28, YHWH now proposes that as the G-d and redeemer of Israel, YHWH will now respond to Israel if Israel will call upon YHWH. The oracle begins in v. 1 with a summons to hear directed to Israel. It includes commands "hear O Jacob, my servant" in v. 1a and "(hear), O Israel, whom I have chosen" in v. 1b. YHWH's oracle of reassurance then follows in vv. 2-5. It begins with an expanded messenger formula in v. 2a that includes the messenger formula proper in v. 2aα and the qualification of YHWH as the creator who helps you in v. 2aβ. The oracle proper then follows in vv. 2b-5. It begins with the reassurance formula, 'al tîrā', "do not fear!" in v. 2b directed to two recipients, each of which is a name for Israel: "my servant Jacob" in v. 2bα and "my chosen Jeshurun" in v. 2bβ. Verses 3-5 then constitute a metaphorical announcement of YHWH's blessing for Israel. It begins in v. 3 with a metaphorical announcement of YHWH's action of pouring out spirit and blessing for Israel. The metaphor of pouring water and rain appears in v. 3a, including statements concerning the pouring of water in v. 3aα and rain in v. 3aβ. Verse 3b follows with a depiction of YHWH's pouring spirit or blessing on Israel's offspring, including spirit on Israel's descendants in v. 3bα and blessing on Israel's offspring in v. 3bβ. Verses 4-5 then portray the results of YHWH's actions. Verse 4 portrays the results in metaphorical terms: Israel's descendants will sprout like grass in v. 4a and they will grow like willows in v. 4b. Isaiah 44:5 then describes Israel's projected response to this blessing in four parts: "they will say that I am YHWH's" in v. 5aα, "they will call on the name Jacob" in v. 5aβ, "they will write hand of YHWH" in v. 5bα, and "they will use the name of Israel" in v. 5bβ.

Isaiah 44:6-20 constitutes the fourth major subunit of the trial scene in 43:9–44:22 as YHWH's summary statement. The summary statement in 44:6-8 asserts YHWH's claim to be the true G-d and redeemer of Israel. It is followed by a satire against idolatry in 44:9-20 which attempts to demonstrate the futility of reliance on foreign gods.

The summary statement in 44:6-8 begins with an expanded messenger formula in v. 6a, which includes the messenger formula proper in v. 6aα and a qualification of YHWH Seba'ot as redeemer of Israel in v. 6aβ. The oracular summary statement then appears in vv. 6b-8. It begins with YHWH's self-assertion that YHWH is the true G-d. The first segment of this self-assertion appears in the twofold statement in v. 6b, which includes 1st-person statements that YHWH is the first and the last in v. 6bα and that there is no other G-d beside YHWH in v. 6bβ. Verse 7 then follows with the presentation of rhetorical questions that are intended to support YHWH's assertions. The twofold rhetorical questions appear in v. 7aα, including the question "who can announce (the future) like me?" in v. 7aα$^{1-3}$ and "who can declare and arrange (events) for me?" in v. 7aα$^{4-6}$. Verse 7aβ-b then follows with statements of the objects or goals inherent in the previous question. The first states the interest in establishing an eternal people, i.e., Israel, in v. 7aβ. The second in v. 7b states the interest in establishing the future signs and what will come, including statements concerning the establishment of signs and what will come in v. 7bα and the challenge to let any contender for the role of G-d declare it in v. 7bβ. Verse 8 concludes the present subunit with YHWH's reassurance to Israel in v. 8, including the reassurance statement in v. 8aα and a following set of supporting rhetorical questions in 8aβ-b. The rhetorical questions are organized into two paired groups. The first in v. 8aβ focuses on YHWH's claims to have foretold and declared, including the questions "have I not foretold?" in v. 8aβ$^{1-3}$ and "have I not declared and you are witnesses?" in v. 8aβ$^{4-6}$. The second segment in v. 8b presents a rhetorical question and answer that there is no other G-d beside

YHWH, including the question "is there a G-d beside me?" in v. 8bα and the rhetorical answer in v. 8bβ that "there is no other rock (apparently a metaphor for G-d); I don't know one."

The satire against idol worship in 44:9-20 is frequently viewed as an independent unit by many scholars, but it appears here as a means to demonstrate the futility of worshipping foreign gods. The text is organized into three major subunits, each of which focuses on a different description of the craftsmen who make the idols that represent the foreign gods. The first in vv. 9-11 focuses on the makers of idols in general. The second in v. 12 focuses on the metalsmith who makes cast idols. The third in vv. 13-20 focuses on the woodworker who makes idols of wood.

The satirical portrayal of the makers of idols in vv. 9-11 begins with the portrayal per se in v. 9. The initial element in v. 9a focuses on the purposelessness of their work and includes statements that their work is worthless in v. 9aα and that it constitutes useless treasures in v. 9aβ. The second element in v. 9b asserts that incapable idols lead the idol-maker to shame, insofar as they give witness to idols that neither see nor know in v. 9bα, with the consequence that idol-makers are shamed in v. 9bβ. Verses 10-11 then follow as the second element of this subunit with the rhetorical assertion that the idol-makers shall be ashamed. This segment begins in v. 10 with the presentation of a rhetorical question that asks "who would do such a thing?" The question appears in twofold form in v. 10a, including the question "who would fashion G-d?" in v. 10aα and "who would cast an image?" in v. 10aβ. Verse 10b then closes this segment with the rhetorical qualification that such would be to no purpose. The rhetorical answer to the questions then appears in v. 11, which asserts that the idol-makers should be ashamed. This segment begins in v. 11a with the assertion that all idol-makers should be ashamed, including the assertion proper in v. 11aα and the reason for the assertion, i.e., that they are human, in v. 11aβ. Verse 11b then closes the segment with the declaration that they should all stand together fearful and ashamed.

The second subunit of the satire against idols appears in 44:12 as a satire against craftsmen in metal who make idols. This brief subunit begins in v. 12a-bα with a four-part portrayal of the ironworker and his work: the initial portrayal of the ironworker and his tools in v. 12aα, a description of how he works with charcoal in v. 12aβ, a description of how he forms his work by hammering in v. 12aγ, and a description of how he makes his work with a strong arm in v. 12bα. Verse 12bβ-γ then follows with the assertion that the metalworker is susceptible to weakness, including statements that he loses his strength when he is hungry in v. 12bβ and that he grows faint when he lacks water in v. 12bγ.

The third and final subunit of the satire against idols appears in 44:13-20 as a satire against craftsmen who work in wood. This subunit includes two major elements. The first is the portrayal of the craftsman's work in 44:13-17, and the second is the derision of the craftsmen who make idols in 44:18-20.

The description of the craftsman's work in 44:13-17 includes four basic elements. The first appears in v. 13aα$^{1-4}$ as a description of the craftsman measuring with a line. The second appears in v. 13aα$^{5-6}$ as a description of the craftsman forming his work with a stylus. The third appears in v. 13aβ-b with a description of the building process with three basic segments. The first segment in v. 13aβ describes how he makes the idol with tools. The second segment in v. 13aγ describes how he marks it with a compass. The third segment in v. 13b describes how he makes the idol into the pattern of a man, including a basic statement that it is the pattern of a man in v. 13bα and the qualification that it appears like the beauty of a man to dwell in a temple in v. 13bβ. Finally, the fourth basic element of 44:13-17 appears in vv. 14-17 with a lengthy discourse concerning the craftsman's use of wood. It begins in v. 14 with a description in three subunits of his cutting the wood. The first in v. 14aα states that he cuts cedars. The second in v. 14aβ states that he takes plane trees and oak. And the third in v. 14b states that he prepares trees of the forest for himself to use in the construction of idols. The satire concerning the fact that wood is used for burning then follows in vv. 15-17. Verse 15 begins with the assertion in three elements that fuel wood is used to make an idol. The first in v. 15aαβ asserts the wood is used for fuel and includes statements that wood is for burning in v. 15aα and that wood is for keeping warm in v. 15aβ. The second is the assertion that he kindles wood to bake bread in v. 15aγ. The third in v. 15b is that he uses this same wood to make a god or an idol, including statements that he makes a god and bows down to it in v. 15bα and that he makes an idol and worships it in v. 15bβ. Verses 16-17 then follow with an elaboration on this point by delineating the mundane uses for wood in v. 16 and the sacred uses for wood in v. 17. There are five mundane uses, including burning half the wood with fire in v. 16aα, eating meat with that half in v. 16aβ, roasting and becoming sated in v. 16aγ, warming himself with the fire in v. 16bα[1-2], and saying "Ah! I am warm! I see coals!" in v. 16bα[3]-β. The sacred use of the wood in v. 17 includes three elements: making an idol for a god with the rest of the wood in v. 17a, worshipping it, bowing down, and praying to it in v. 17bα, and saying to the wood, "Save me, for you are my G-d!" in v. 17bβ.

The derision of the craftsman who makes idols in 44:18-20 then follows. The first major subunit appears in vv. 18-19, which focus on an attempt to claim that such woodworkers do not know what they are doing. It begins with the assertion in v. 18 that they don't know or understand, which is basically stated in v. 18a and follows with the explanation that their eyes and minds are prevented from seeing and thinking in v. 18b. Verse 19 then follows with the assertion that they lack the knowledge to say anything worthwhile on the matter. This is basically stated in v. 19aα[1-9] and follows with a presentation of rhetorical questions that are designed to reinforce the point in v. 19aα[10]-b. This segment begins with a statement of the circumstances by the craftsman: "I burned, baked, roasted, and ate," in v. 19aα[10-18]-β. The circumstances are followed by a twofold rhetorical question in v. 19b, including the rhetorical questions "do I make the rest into an abomination [i.e., an idol]?" in v. 19bα and "do I worship wood?" in v. 19bβ. Verse 20 then concludes the subunit with a final evaluation in three parts: a statement that the craftsman pursues ashes in v. 20aα, that a deluded heart or mind leads him astray in v. 20aβ, and that he doesn't say, "Isn't this a lie in my right hand?" in v. 20b.

The final exhortation to Israel to return to YHWH in 44:21-22 then closes the trial scene in 43:9–44:22. This subunit begins in v. 21a with an exhortation to Israel/Jacob to remember these things, including the statement in v. 21aα[1] to Jacob/Israel to remember and the statement of the reason, that "you are my servant," in v. 21aα[2]-β. The latter element includes YHWH's statements that "you are my servant" in v. 21aα[2-4] and that "I formed you as my servant" in v. 21aβ. The second element of the final exhortation is YHWH's appeal to Israel, "do not forget me!" in v. 21b-22a. This is basically stated in v. 21b and the reason is given: "I wipe away sins and transgressions" in v. 22a. The latter statement includes two elements: "I wipe away your sins like a cloud" in v. 22aα and "your transgressions are like mist" in v. 22aβ. The final element is YHWH's final exhortation, "return to me!" in v. 22b. This is basically stated in v. 22bα and the reason given in v. 22bβ, "I deliver you."

The concluding hymn of praise in 44:23 then closes the entire unit in 42:14–44:23. It includes two basic subunits. The first appears in v. 23aα[1-5] as a call to the heavens to praise YHWH. It includes two elements: the call to the heavens proper in v. 23aα[1-2] and the reason for the call, that YHWH has acted, in v. 23aα[3-5]. The second basic subunit appears in v. 23aα[6]-b as a call to the depths, mountains, and forests to praise YHWH. It begins in v. 23aα[6]-γ with the call proper, including the call to the depths in v. 23aα[6-8], the call to the mountains in v. 23aβ, and the call to the forests in v. 23aγ. The reason for the call, that YHWH has redeemed Jacob/Israel, appears in v. 23b in two parts: that YHWH redeemed Jacob in v. 23bα and that YHWH magnified the divine self through Israel in v. 23bβ.

Genre

Isaiah 42:14–44:23 employs a variety of genres in its presentation of YHWH's announcement that YHWH is the redeemer of Israel. At the most fundamental level, the unit is an ACCOUNT of YHWH's announcement, which means that the prophet plays the fundamental role in conveying or reporting YHWH's ANNOUNCEMENT to the reading audience of the book of Isaiah. The unit is not a prose account; rather, it is an oracular account of YHWH's words to be conveyed to Israel.

Isaiah 42:14–44:23 includes three major subunits, each of which is defined by its overarching generic character.

The first is the announcement of YHWH's plan for the redemption of Israel in 42:14–43:8. The subunit constitutes an ANNOUNCEMENT, which is a very basic generic category in which one party announces a set of content to another party. In this case, YHWH is the subject of the announcement and Israel or the reading audience of the book of Isaiah is the object of the announcement. Announcements have no defined form and simply convey a set of contents that may have its own distinctive generic character. In the case of 42:14–43:8, an important dimension of this subunit is its argumentative character, insofar as it is designed to convince its reading or hearing audience that YHWH is indeed the redeemer of Israel. Such a contention would have been questionable during the course of the Babylonian exile in that YHWH had proved unable or unwilling to defend Judah from the Babylonians during the course of three invasions in

598-597, 588-586, and 582 B.C.E. that saw the exile of King Jehoiachin ben Jehoiakim of Judah and major elements of the Judean population, the destruction of the city of Jerusalem and the Jerusalem temple, and the virtual destruction of much of the nation of Judah. For those Jews exiled to Babylonia, the contention that YHWH continues to be the redeemer of Israel would have been a difficult contention to accept. Consequently, the DISPUTATION genre plays an important role in this text. Although past scholarship has identified 42:18-25 as an example of the DISPUTATION genre, in fact the entire unit is permeated by the concerns and features of a disputation. A disputation is designed to challenge the beliefs of an audience on a specific point of contention and convince the audience to adopt a different set of beliefs. The genre frequently displays three elements, including the thesis to be disputed, the counterthesis for which the speaker argues, and the dispute or argumentation proper (Begrich, *Gesammelte Studien* 48-53; Graffy, *A Prophet Confronts;* Murray, "The Rhetoric of Disputation"). YHWH's assertion that YHWH is the redeemer of Israel appears at several points in this text, including 43:1bα; 43:3a; 43:10-13; and 44:6-8. The thesis against which YHWH argues, the notion that foreign gods are powerful or even active in the world, is never directly stated, but the satirical dismissal of the roles and claims of other gods appears throughout the passage, particularly in 43:9 and 44:9-20.

The argumentation appears throughout 42:14–43:8. YHWH emphasizes YHWH's actions on Israel's behalf with appeals to contemporary events and past Israel/Judean traditions. The contemporary event presumed throughout Second Isaiah is the rise of King Cyrus the Great of Persia, who would be named King of Babylon in 539 B.C.E. and who would issue a decree allowing exiled Jews to return to Jerusalem to rebuild the city, the temple, and Jewish life in the land (2 Chr 36:22-23; Ezra 1:1-4). Cyrus is not mentioned in the present text, but appears in the next major unit of the book in 44:28 and 45:1. The appeal to past tradition focuses on several important texts and traditions. One is the reference to Israel as the blind and the deaf that draws especially on the vocation account of Isaiah ben Amoz in ch. 6, in which YHWH instructs the prophet that his role is to render the people blind, deaf, and senseless so that YHWH can work out the divine plan for the recognition of YHWH's role as G-d throughout the entire world. In the present case, YHWH refers to Israel as blind and deaf in 42:15-16 and 42:18-25 as part of an effort to contend that the time for Israel's blindness and deafness is at an end and that it is now time to recognize that YHWH brought about Israel's exile and restoration as part of the larger plan to gain recognition as G-d throughout all creation. In addition to the Isaian motif of Israel's blindness and deafness, YHWH's argument asserts YHWH's role as creator and sustainer of creation insofar as YHWH both establishes creation (Gen 1:1–2:3) and ensures that the rains come in their season to provide food and substance for the earth's inhabitants (e.g., Deuteronomy 28–33). Again in Isa 42:15-16, YHWH announces to the blind and deaf Israel that YHWH is capable of drying up all creation and turning light into darkness to redeem Israel. Indeed, this latter point is a concern in 8:23–9:6, in which YHWH claims to lead Israel in darkness until they see a great light. The third set of traditions employed is the exodus and wilderness traditions of Exodus-Numbers, which present YHWH's efforts to free Israel from Egyptian bondage and sustain and guide them in the wilderness in their journey to the promised land of Israel. Isaiah 42:15-16 again makes reference to YHWH's guiding the blind and the deaf through the wilderness in an effort to demonstrate that YHWH is now replicating the ancient guidance from Egypt to the promised land, except that now YHWH will guide Israel from Babylonian exile back to the promised land once again.

Other generic elements also play important roles in 42:14–43:8. The CALL TO ATTENTION in 42:18 is directed to Israel in an effort to focus Israel's attention on YHWH's argumentation that YHWH is the redeemer of Israel. RHETORICAL QUESTIONS also play a key role in this text, insofar as they are a common rhetorical device that engages the audience to accept an assertion that is patently obvious from the standpoint of the speaker. They appear in 42:19-22 as part of YHWH's argument that Israel's suffering is due to its sins against YHWH, i.e., YHWH is still the powerful master of creation and redeemer of Israel, so Israel's suffering is due to Israel's own wrongdoing. The ORACLE OF SALVATION in 43:1-8 is designed to announce YHWH's intentions to bring restoration or deliverance to Israel in the aftermath of its exile. It again functions as a means to express YHWH's power. It employs the PROPHETIC MESSENGER FORMULA, "Thus says YHWH," at the outset of the oracle to indicate that YHWH is the source of the following oracle. Included in the oracle of salvation is the REASSURANCE FORMULA, "Do not fear!" and the ASSISTANCE FORMULA, "I am with you!" both of which are designed to assure Israel of YHWH's power and fidelity to the covenant with Israel.

The second major subunit of 42:14–44:23 is the trial scene of 43:9–44:22. This is an example of the broader category of TRIAL GENRES that employs forensic language, organization, and argumentation to make a point or collection of points to the audience at hand. The presumption of a legal setting adds to the persuasive purpose of the genre, which is closely related to the above-noted DISPUTATION genre. In the present instance, the text is organized in four subunits to convey the points made before a court of law. Of course in this case, the audience is the final judge of the argumentation of the text. Thus, the first subunit is an initial TRIAL SPEECH in 43:9-13 that challenges YHWH's opponents to make their claims to be G-d versus YHWH's claim to be G-d. Again, RHETORICAL QUESTIONS in 43:9 play a role here in denying any legitimacy to the claims of the foreign gods. The second subunit is the substantiation of YHWH's claim to be G-d, namely that YHWH is responsible for the overthrow of Babylon, in 43:14-15. The third subunit is the presentation of YHWH's contention that YHWH is the redeemer of Israel in 43:16–44:5. This text includes a PROPHETIC ANNOUNCEMENT OF SALVATION to Israel in 43:16-21, which begins with an expanded Prophetic MESSENGER FORMULA in 43:16-17 to identify YHWH as the source of the proclamation. The oracle itself in 43:18–44:5 once again relies on past traditions, such as the exodus/wilderness tradition to make the case that YHWH is doing something new, redeeming Israel from Babylonian bondage as opposed to the past experience of Egyptian bondage. The wilderness motif enters when YHWH claims to make a road through the wilderness for Israel in 43:19b, 20-21. The oracle again reiterates YHWH's power in 43:22–44:5 by explaining Israel's suffering as a result of its rejection of YHWH. An ORACLE OF SALVATION, again with its own REASSURANCE FORMULA in 44:2b, appears in 44:1-5. The oracle is introduced by a SUMMONS TO HEAR to attract the audience's attention to the claims made in the oracle. The oracle once again relies on YHWH's role as creator and sustainer of creation to portray YHWH's blessing of Israel metaphorically as YHWH's pouring rain on Israel in 44:3-5. The fourth major subunit is the summary statement in 44:6-20 that reiterates YHWH arguments to be the true G-d and redeemer of Israel. Again, the Prophetic MESSENGER FORMULA appears in 44:6a to identify YHWH as the source of the following oracle, and RHETORICAL QUESTIONS appear in 44:7 to reinforce the point that no one but YHWH can announce coming events and therefore be recognized as G-d. The REASSURANCE FORMULA and further RHETORICAL QUESTIONS in 44:8 likewise reinforce the point. The SATIRE against idol worship undermines the contentions of foreign gods that they are indeed G-d. RHETORICAL QUESTIONS in 44:10 and 19 likewise aid in convincing the audience of these points. The final EXHORTATION in 44:21-22 reiterates YHWH's main concern in the TRIAL SPEECH to ensure that Israel recognizes YHWH as G-d and thereby returns to YHWH.

The third major generic element in this unit is the concluding HYMN OF PRAISE in 44:23. The hymn employs the standard elements, i.e., call to praise YHWH and a statement of the reasons to praise YHWH, in both of its two basic subunits, 44:23aα$^{1-5}$ and 44:23aα^{6}-b. The hymn of course reinforces the message of the whole.

Setting

The historical setting of this text is the late period of the Babylonian exile or its immediate aftermath in the early Persian period in the late 6th century B.C.E. The text presupposes the end of the Babylonian exile and the rise of King Cyrus of Persia as the new king of Babylonia. The expectation that Jews are about to return to the land of Israel to rebuild Jerusalem and the temple is the key criterion in coming to such a conclusion. Although the text presumes a coming return home, it seems to presuppose that Cyrus is already on the throne and that return to the land of Israel is an imminent possibility. Such a setting would then be placed in ca. 539 B.C.E., when Cyrus made his famous decree.

The social setting or *Sitz im Leben* of the text appears to be the courtroom, as indicated by the extensive use of the disputation and trial genres discussed above. Of course the courtroom must be recognized as a fictive setting for the text. The true social setting appears to be liturgical insofar as the unit concludes with the HYMN OF PRAISE in 44:23. We do not know of liturgical settings in Babylonia that would have been employed for Jewish worship, although such settings might have been found in locations such as the homes of temple priests, as presupposed by the gathering of the elders of Israel at the Babylonian home of the prophet and priest Ezekiel in Ezek 8:1. Alternatively, the present text may presuppose the setting of the ruined Jerusalem temple at the time of Sheshbazzar's return to Jerusalem (Ezra 1).

The literary setting is the book of Isaiah. At the synchronic level, 42:14–44:23 plays a role in the final 5th-century edition of the text, where it functions as part of the argument that is designed to persuade returned exiles to return to YHWH and to support the rebuilt Jerusalem temple. Its earlier form would have been as part of the 6th-century edition of the book of Isaiah, where it would have functioned in a similar manner, although return to YHWH would have meant actually returning to Jerusalem and taking part in the reestablishment of the city and the Jerusalem temple.

Interpretation

Isaiah 42:14–44:23 is the prophet's account of YHWH's announcement that YHWH is the redeemer of Israel. This text is designed to convince its audience that YHWH is indeed the redeemer of Israel even in the aftermath of the Babylonian exile. The text essentially argues that YHWH had planned for Israel's redemption long ago, but that Israel first had to go through a process of punishment for its alleged abandonment of YHWH. Now that the punishment is completed, 42:14–44:23 argues that the time for Israel's redemption, i.e., return to the land of Israel to rebuild Jerusalem and the temple, has come. The impetus for such an announcement is the rise of King Cyrus of Persia to the position of King of Babylon in 539 B.C.E. and his announcement that Jews could return to the land of Israel to rebuild Jerusalem, the Temple, and their national life albeit under Persian rule. Throughout the unit, YHWH claims to have announced this outcome long ago. In other words, YHWH claims to have brought Cyrus to the throne of Babylon for just such a purpose.

Isaiah 42:14–44:23 falls into three major subunits, each of which contributes to the argumentative strategy of this text.

The first is the announcement of YHWH's plan for the redemption of Israel in 42:14–43:8. The announcement proper in 42:14-17 acknowledges YHWH's past silence concerning Israel during its period of suffering as a means to acknowledge the realities of Israel's exile from its homeland. Such a claim is designed to overcome doubts about YHWH's power and efficacy in the face of the Babylonian Empire, by claiming instead that YHWH has been the powerful and righteous G-d of Israel all along and that YHWH had planned for Israel's redemption from the beginning. Such an argument is teleological insofar as it points to the goal of YHWH's actions with regard to Israel. An ontological perspective would question whether YHWH's punishment of Israel is indeed justified, particularly since the book of Isaiah contends that YHWH commissioned Isaiah in ch. 6 to render the people blind, deaf, and dumb so that YHWH could carry out this divine purpose. The portrayal of YHWH's actions on behalf of Israel, i.e., guiding the blind and deaf people through the dried wilderness, draws on several textual bases to make its point. One, of course, is ch. 6, which portrays the people as blind and deaf. Another is YHWH's role as creator and bringer of rain in Gen 1:1–2:3 and Deuteronomy 28–30, and a third is the exodus and wilderness tradition in Exodus-Numbers, which presents YHWH's guidance of Israel from Egyptian bondage through the wilderness to the promised land of Israel. Altogether, the use of these traditions builds the case that YHWH is doing something new for Israel: now that the exile is over, YHWH will lead

Israel in a new exodus from Babylonia through the wilderness to return to the land of Israel. Those who doubted YHWH and relied on idols instead will now be ashamed in the face of YHWH's redemptive actions.

The elaboration on the basic announcement in 42:18–43:8 provides background and an enhanced perspective on YHWH's announcement. The disputation speech in 42:18-25 argues that Israel's suffering during the course of the Babylonian exile was due to its own sins against YHWH. The text never becomes specific concerning the nature of Israel's sin other than intimations that Israel did not observe YHWH's Torah or follow the divine will. Again, the motif of Israel's blindness and deafness enters the discussion, but this time the motif functions as a means to explain Israel's sin: Israel did not recognize YHWH's purposes for Israel nor did it listen to YHWH's instruction. YHWH therefore brought punishment on Israel as a result. Such a contention is designed to explain evil in the world, but it does so by holding the victim to be responsible for its own suffering. Such an argument might be considered as morally questionable today, particularly in the aftermath of the Shoah, in which some six million Jews were murdered simply because they were Jewish, but contemporary readers must understand that the prophet was attempting to make sense of the suffering of the people of Israel and could best do so in anticipation of the prospect of Israel's restoration. The twofold oracle of salvation for Israel in 43:1-8 announces YHWH's restoration of Israel by drawing especially on the role of YHWH as the creator of Jacob/Israel. The REASSURANCE FORMULA "do not fear," coupled with the assistance formula "I am with you," in 43:1b-4 provides the basis for Israel's restoration. Again, exodus and wilderness tradition make their appearance when YHWH asserts that the people will walk through water and streams, but they are enhanced by the addition of the reference to walking through fire and flame to accentuate the novel character of YHWH's new redemption of Israel. The portrayal of North African nations given to Israel as ransom draws on earlier oracles in chs. 18–19 (see esp. 19:16-23) and 30–31 that depict the recognition of YHWH by Egypt and its neighbors, who will play a role in gathering Israel from exile to bring the people home (e.g., 11:15-16; 19:23; 27:12-13; 35:1-10). The unit concludes in 43:8 with YHWH's demand that Israel be set free.

The second major subunit of 42:14–44:23 is the trial scene in 43:9–44:22, in which YHWH substantiates the claim to be redeemer of Israel in a courtroom setting. The setting is fictive of course, but it adds to the persuasive character of the speech. It begins in 43:9-13 with the courtroom preliminaries in which YHWH calls upon the nations to make their claim that their gods are the true deities of the world versus YHWH's counterclaim that YHWH is indeed the true G-d of Israel and creation at large. The bases for YHWH's claims are that YHWH declared what would happen, that YHWH had indeed delivered Israel, and that the people of Israel, identified as YHWH's servant, are witness to the whole event. The substantiation for YHWH's claims in 43:14-15 draws upon the rise of Cyrus to become king of Babylon. YHWH claims credit for sending Cyrus to break down the bars of Babylon, which would presume Cyrus's defeat of Babylon's army and his approach to the city in 539 B.C.E. The presentation of YHWH's chief contention, that YHWH is the redeemer of Israel, appears in

43:16–44:5, beginning with a proclamation of salvation for Israel in 43:16-21, in which YHWH once again refers to the guidance of Israel through the Red Sea at the time of the exodus as the basis for YHWH's claims to lead a similar exodus from Babylonia. YHWH's challenge to not remember the past or former things, but to think instead on YHWH's new action, is designed to convince the people that the new exodus from Babylon is about to take place as YHWH will once again guide the people through the desert to the promised land of Israel. YHWH reiterates the claim in 43:22–44:5 that Israel's suffering in the Babylonian exile was the result of its past rejection of YHWH. YHWH's claims not to have burdened the people with requirements for offerings draws upon 1:10-17, and the claims that "your first ancestor sinned" presuppose the Jacob narratives in Genesis 25–35. But YHWH's oracle of reassurance in 44:1-5 announces that the time of punishment is over and the time for restoration has come. The summary statement in 44:6-20 reiterates YHWH's arguments that YHWH is the redeemer of Israel in 44:6-8 and presents a polemical satire against idolatry in 44:9-20 that is designed to undermine anyone who might still be inclined to trust in foreign gods. These things are wood! How could anyone worship them?

The final exhortation to Israel to return to YHWH in 44:21-22 identifies the primary purpose of YHWH's discourse: to convince Israel that YHWH is indeed the true G-d and redeemer of Israel.

The third subunit of 42:14–44:23, the concluding HYMN OF PRAISE for YHWH in 44:23, likewise reinforces the message of the whole. YHWH must be praised because YHWH has redeemed Israel.

Bibliography

R. Baldlauf, "Jes 42,18-25," in *Ein G-tt — Eine Offenbarung* (*Fest.* N. Füglister; ed. F. V. Reiterer; Würzburg: Echter, 1991) 13-36; K. Baltzer, "Liberation from Debt Slavery after the Exile in Second Isaiah and Nehemiah," in *Ancient Israelite Religion* (*Fest.* F. M. Cross, Jr.; ed. P. D. Miller; Philadelphia: Fortress, 1987) 477-84; idem, "Schriftauslegung bei Deuterojesaja? Jes 43,22-28 als Beispiel," in *Die Väter Israels* (*Fest.* J. Scharbert; ed. A. Görg and A. R. Müller; Stuttgart: Katholisches Bibelwerk, 1989) 11-16; T. Booij, "Negation in Isaiah 43$_{22-24}$," *ZAW* 94 (1982) 390-400; C. C. Broyles, "The Citations of YHWH in Isaiah 44:26-28," in Broyles and Evans, eds., *Writing and Reading the Scroll of Isaiah,* 399-421; R. E. Clements, "Who Is Blind But My Servant? (Isaiah 42:19): How Then Shall We Read Isaiah?" in *G-d in the Fray* (*Fest.* W. Brueggemann; ed. T. Linafelt and T. Beal; Minneapolis: Fortress, 1998) 143-56; D. Dempsey, "The Verb Syntax of the Idol Passage of Isaiah 44:9-20," in *Imagery and Imagination in Biblical Literature* (CBQMS 32; *Fest.* A. Fitzgerald; ed. L. Boadt and M. S. Smith; Washington: Catholic University of America, 2001) 145-56; M. D. Dick, "Prophetic *poeïsis* and Verbal Icon," *CBQ* 46 (1984) 226-46; P. E. Dion, "The Structure of Isaiah 42:10-17 as Approached Through Versification and Distribution of Poetic Devices," *JSOT* 49 (1991) 113-24; J. Goldingay, "The Arrangement of Isaiah xli–xlv," *VT* 29 (1979) 289-99; idem, "Isaiah 42.18-25," *JSOT* 67 (1995) 43-65; A. Graffy, *A Prophet Confronts His People* (*AnBib* 104; Rome: Biblical Institute, 1984); W. Grimm, *Die Heimkehr der Jakobskinder (Jes 43,1-7): Bedeutungen eines Prophetenwortes für die Biblische Theologie* (Frankfurt:

Lang, 1985); C. Hardmeier, "'Geschwiegen habe ich seit langem . . . wie die Gebärende schreie ich jetzt': Zur Komposition und Geschichtstheologie von Jes 42,14–44,23," *WuD* 20 (1989) 155-79; E. Kutsch, "Ich will meinen Geist ausgiessen auf deine Kinder," in *Das Wort, das weiterwirkt (Fest.* K. Frör; ed. R. Riess and D. Stolberg; Munich: Kaiser, 1981) 157-68; F. Matheus, "Jesaja xliv. 9-20," *VT* 37 (1987) 312-26; idem, *Singt dem H-rrn ein neues Lied,* 67-73; D. F. Murray, "The Rhetoric of Disputation: Re-examination of a Prophetic Genre," *JSOT* 38 (1987) 95-121; K. Pfisterer Darr, "Like Warrior, Like Woman: Destruction and Deliverance in Isaiah 42:10-17," *CBQ* 49 (1987) 560-61; H. C. Schmitt, "Erlösung und Gericht: Jes 43,1-7 und sein literarischer und theologischer Kontext," in *Alttestamentlicher Glaube und Biblische Theologie (Fest.* H. D. Preuss; ed. J. Hausmann and H.-J. Zobel; Stuttgart: Kohlhammer, 1992) 120-31; G. M. Soares-Prabhu, "Laughing at Idols," in *Reading from This Place* (ed. F. F. Segovia and M. A. Tolbert; Minneapolis: Fortress, 1995) 109-31; P. Stern, "The 'Blind Servant' Imagery of Deutero-Isaiah and Its Implications," *Bib* 75 (1994) 224-32; D. W. Thomas, "Isaiah xliv. 9-20," in *Hommages à André Dupont-Sommer* (Paris: Adrien-Masonneuve, 1971) 319-30; D. Vieweger and A. Böckler, "Ich gebe Ägypten als Lösegeld für dich," *ZAW* 108 (1996) 594-607; D. W. van Winkle, "Proselytes in Isaiah xl–lv?" *VT* 47 (1997) 341-59; L. Wächsler, "Israel und Jeschurun," in *Schalom: Studien zu Glaube und Geschichte Israels (Fest.* A. Jepsen; ed. K.-H. Bernhardt; Stuttgart: Calwer, 1971) 58-64; H. E. von Waldow, *". . . denn ich erlöse di" Eine Auslegung von Jeseja 43* (BibS[N] 29; Neukirchen: Neukirchener, 1960); B. Willmes, "G-tt erlöst sein Volk: Gedanken zum G-ttesbild Deuterojesajas nach Jes 43,1-7," *BN* 51 (1990) 61-93.

THE ACCOUNT OF YHWH'S ANNOUNCEMENT THAT YHWH WILL USE CYRUS FOR THE RESTORATION OF ISRAEL 44:24–48:22

Structure

I. Announcement of plan to use Cyrus	44:24–45:8
A. To Israel: disputation; YHWH's self-predication	44:24-28
1. Expanded messenger speech formula	44:24a
2. YHWH's speech proper; disputation; self-predication	44:24b-28
a. Initial self-identification: I am YHWH	44:24bα$^{1-2}$
b. Self-predication	44:24bα$^{3-4}$-28
1) Creator	44:24bα^{3}-γ
a) Does all	44:24bα$^{3-4}$
b) Stretches out heavens alone	44:24bβ
c) Spreads out earth oneself	44:24bγ
2) Overturns diviners and sorcerers	44:25a
a) Annuls signs of diviners	44:25aα
b) Confounds sorcerers	44:25aβ
3) Turns back sages and their knowledge	44:25b
a) Turns back sages	44:25bα
b) Overturns their knowledge	44:25bβ
4) Supports servant and messengers	44:26a

a) Establishes word of YHWH's servant — 44:26aα

b) Confirms counsel of YHWH's messengers — 44:26aβ

5) Restores Jerusalem and Judah — 44:26b

  a) Says to Jerusalem "you will be restored" — 44:26bα¹⁻³

  b) (Says) to cities of Judah "you will be rebuilt" — 44:26bα⁴⁻⁶

  c) (Says) to its ruins "I will restore them" — 44:26bβ

6) Controls waters of chaos — 44:27

  a) Says to deep "be dry" — 44:27a

  b) (Says) to your rivers "I will dry them up" — 44:27b

7) Uses Cyrus to restore Jerusalem and the temple — 44:28

  a) Cyrus — 44:28a

    (1) Says to Cyrus "my shepherd" — 44:28aα

    (2) He will fulfill my will — 44:28aβ

  b) Jerusalem and temple — 44:28b

    (1) Says to Jerusalem she will be rebuilt — 44:28bα

    (2) (Says) to temple she will be reestablished — 44:28bβ

B. To Cyrus: royal commission; self-predication by YHWH — 45:1-7

  1. Expanded messenger formula directed to Cyrus — 45:1

    a. Messenger formula proper directed to Cyrus, YHWH's anointed — 45:1aα¹⁻⁵

    b. Predication of Cyrus — 45:1aα⁶⁻b

      1) I grasp his hand to subdue nations — 45:1aα⁶⁻¹¹

        a) Action: grasp right hand — 45:1aα⁶⁻⁸

        b) Purpose: to subdue nations — 45:1aα⁹⁻¹¹

      2) I ungird kings to open gates — 45:1aβ-b

        a) Action: I open the loins of kings — 45:1aβ

        b) Purpose: to open doors and ensure that gates are not closed — 45:1b

          (1) To open doors before him — 45:1bα

          (2) To ensure that gates do not remain closed — 45:1bβ

  2. YHWH's royal commissioning speech to Cyrus — 45:2-7

    a. YHWH's actions for recognition by Cyrus — 45:2-3

      1) YHWH's actions for Cyrus — 45:2-3a

        a) I walk before you — 45:2aα

        b) I level hills — 45:2aβ

        c) I break down doors of bronze — 45:2bα

        d) I cut down bars of iron — 45:2bβ

        e) I give you treasures of darkness and secret stores — 45:3a

      2) Purpose of YHWH's actions: so you will know that I YHWH G-d of Israel call you by name — 45:3b

    b. YHWH calls Cyrus by name for the sake of YHWH's servant Jacob/Israel — 45:4

      1) Purpose of YHWH's action: for the sake of Jacob my servant and Israel my chosen one — 45:4a

      2) YHWH's action: I give you title — 45:4b

        a) Basically stated: I give you title — 45:4bα

        b) Qualification: you did not know me — 45:4bβ

c. Summation: so that all may know that I am YHWH   45:5-7
  1) Premise: I am YHWH and there is no other G-d   45:5a
    a) Basic premise: I am YHWH and there is no other   45:5aα
    b) Elaboration: beside me there is no G-d   45:5aβ
  2) YHWH's action and purpose   45:5b-7
    a) YHWH's action: I gird you   45:5b
      (1) Basically stated   45:5bα
      (2) Qualification: but you don't know me   45:5bβ
    b) Purpose of action: world will know that I am YHWH   45:6-7
      (1) Basically stated: so all the world will know
        that there is none but me   45:6a
      (2) Elaboration: YHWH's self-predication   45:6b-7
        (a) Basic premise: I am YHWH   45:6b
        (b) Role as creator   45:7a
          α. Creating light and darkness   45:7aα
          β. Making peace and disaster   45:7aβ
        (c) Summation: I YHWH do all these things   45:7b
C. Hymn of Praise   45:8
  1. Attributes of creation   45:8a-bα
    a. Let heavens pour rain and righteousness   45:8a
      1) Let the heavens pour rain from above   45:8aα
      2) Let the skies rain righteousness   45:8aβ
    b. Let the earth produce victory and righteousness   45:8bα
      1) Let earth open and produce victory   45:8bα$^{1-4}$
      2) Let righteousness sprout   45:8bα$^{5-7}$
  2. YHWH's claim of responsibility: I YHWH created it   45:8bβ
II. Trial scene concerning YHWH's use of Cyrus   45:9–48:19
  A. Preliminary arguments   45:9-25
    1. Disputation: Israel has no right to challenge YHWH   45:9-13
      a. Woe speeches that deny the right to question YHWH's
        actions   45:9-10
        1) First woe speech against those who contend with
          maker   45:9
          a) Woe statement against one who challenges his
            maker   45:9a
          b) Rhetorical challenges that reinforce point: does
            clay rebuke potter?   45:9b
            (1) Rhetorical question: what are you doing?   45:9bα
            (2) Challenge: your work has no handles   45:9bβ
        2) Second woe speech against those who challenge
          parents   45:10
          a) Woe statement against one who would challenge
            father   45:10a
          b) Against one who would challenge mother   45:10b
      b. YHWH's messenger speech denying right to challenge
        YHWH   45:11-13
        1) Expanded messenger formula   45:11a

bb. All who fashion Images should walk
    in disgrace together   45:16b
    δ. Address to Israel: you are delivered by
        YHWH   45:17
        aa. Israel is delivered by YHWH forever   45:17a
        bb. You shall not be ashamed/disgraced
           forever   45:17b
b. Trial speech: YHWH's position is unchallengeable 45:18-25
  1) Expanded YHWH messenger formula   45:18a
    a) Basic YHWH messenger formula $45{:}18a\alpha^{1\text{-}4}$
    b) YHWH's attributes as creator $45{:}18a\alpha^{5}\text{-}\beta$
      (1) Creator of heaven is G-d $45{:}18a\alpha^{5\text{-}8}$
      (2) Creator of the earth and its maker $45{:}18a\alpha^{9}\text{-}\beta$
        (a) Basically stated $45{:}18a\alpha^{9\text{-}11}$
        (b) Elaboration $45{:}18a\alpha^{12}\text{-}\beta$
        α. YHWH established it $45{:}18a\alpha^{12\text{-}13}$
        β. Not for chaos YHWH created it $45{:}18a\beta^{1\text{-}3}$
        γ. For dwelling YHWH formed it $45{:}18a\beta^{4\text{-}5}$
  2) YHWH's speech: disputational trial speech:
    I YHWH am G-d   45:18b-25
    a) YHWH's assertion: I am G-d   45:18b-19
      (1) Basic premises   45:18b
        (a) I am YHWH   45:18bα
        (b) There is no other   45:18bβ
      (2) Elaboration   45:19
        (a) I did not speak while hiding in a place of
           darkness   45:19aα
        (b) I did not say to the seed of Jacob "seek me
           in chaos"   45:19aβ
        (c) I YHWH speak rightly and truly   45:19b
        α. I YHWH speak what is right   45:19bα
        β. I declare what is straight   45:19bβ
    b) Summons to opponents   45:20
      (1) Summons proper   45:20a
        (a) Gather and come   45:20aα
        (b) Draw near fugitives of the nations   45:20aβ
      (2) Dismissal of opponents: those who carry
        wooden idols and pray to a god who gives no
        success do not know   45:20b
    c) YHWH's assertion of proof of G-d: foretold
      current events   45:21
      (1) Rhetorical challenge to opponents to prove
        their case   45:21a
        (a) Let them declare and draw near   45:21aα
        (b) Let them take counsel together   45:21aβ
      (2) Rhetorical questions: assertions that YHWH
        is G-d   45:21b

(a) Threefold rhetorical questions	45:21bα$^{1\text{-}9}$
α. Who foretold this from before?	45:21bα$^{1\text{-}4}$
β. Who declared it from the past?	45:21bα$^{5\text{-}6}$
γ. Was it not I, YHWH?	45:21bα$^{7\text{-}9}$
(b) Twofold assertion that YHWH is G-d	45:21bα^{10}-β
α. There is no G-d besides me	45:21bα$^{10\text{-}13}$
β. There is no G-d righteous and delivering but me	45:21bβ
d) Appeal for ends of the earth to turn to YHWH	45:22
(1) Appeal proper	45:22a
(2) Basis for appeal: for I am G-d and there is no other	45:22b
e) YHWH's concluding oath: all the world will recognize YHWH	45:23-25
(1) YHWH's statement of oath	45:23
(a) Elaborated oath formula	45:23a
α. I have sworn by myself	45:23aα
β. Righteousness comes forth from my mouth, a word that remains true	45:23aβ
(b) Substance of oath: all world will recognize YHWH	45:23b
α. Every knee shall bend	45:23bα
β. Every tongue shall swear	45:23bβ
(2) Elaboration of oath	45:24-25
(a) By YHWH come righteousness and strength	45:24
α. Righteousness and strength come from YHWH	45:24a
β. Enemies are put to shame	45:24b
(b) By YHWH all the seed of Israel is vindicated and praised	45:25
B. Presentation of evidence: YHWH's power	46:1–47:15
1. Disputation: demonstration of the weakness of Babylon's gods in relation to YHWH	46:1-13
a. Premise to be disputed: people carry idols of gods that cannot act	46:1-2
1) Portrayal of Bel and Nebo bowing	46:1aα
a) Bel bows	46:1aα$^{1\text{-}2}$
b) Nebo bends down	46:1aα$^{3\text{-}4}$
2) Elaboration: gods are burdens	46:1aβ-2
a) Their idols are burdens for animals and beasts	46:1aβ-γ
b) What you carry is a tiresome load	46:1b
c) Summation: gods unable to act	46:2
(1) They bow and bend together	46:2aα
(2) They cannot deliver a burden	46:2aβ
(3) They walk in captivity	46:2b
b. YHWH's counterargument: I am the true G-d who delivers	46:3-13

1) First address: I bear and deliver — 46:3-4
  a) Address form — 46:3
    (1) Basic address: listen to me — 46:3a
      (a) Directed to house of Jacob — 46:3aα
      (b) Directed to all the remnant of the house of Israel — 46:3aβ
    (2) Elaboration on addressees — 46:3b
      (a) Those carried from the belly — 46:3bα
      (b) Those born from the womb — 46:3bβ
  b) Substance of address: I am the one who acts — 46:4
    (1) I am the one — 46:4a
      (a) I am the one until old age — 46:4aα
      (b) I am the one who bears you until you turn gray — 46:4aβ
    (2) Summation — 46:4b
      (a) I act — 46:4bα
      (b) I carry — 46:4bβ
      (c) I bear — 46:4bγ
      (d) I deliver — 46:4bδ
2) Second address: I am incomparable — 46:5-7
  a) Rhetorical questions — 46:5
    (1) First set of rhetorical questions: to whom will you compare me as equivalent? — 46:5a
    (2) Second set of rhetorical questions: to whom will you liken me as the same? — 46:5b
  b) Rhetorical answer: the gods are not equivalent because they cannot act — 46:6-7
    (1) They spend money on gods — 46:6a
      (a) Lavish gold from the purse — 46:6aα
      (b) Weigh out silver with a measuring scale — 46:6aβ
    (2) Craftsman builds gods for worship — 46:6b
      (a) They hire a craftsman who builds it — 46:6bα
      (b) They worship it and bow down — 46:6bβ
    (3) Gods cannot move — 46:7a
      (a) They carry it on the shoulder — 46:7aα[1-3]
      (b) They bear it — 46:7aα[4]
      (c) They set it in place — 46:7aα[5-6]
      (d) It stands — 46:7aα[7]
      (e) It does not move from its place — 46:7aβ
    (4) Gods cannot answer or deliver — 46:7b
      (a) He cries out to it but it does not answer — 46:7bα
      (b) It does not deliver him from his threat — 46:7bβ
3) Third address: exhortation: remember and stand firm from sins — 46:8
  a) Exhortation: remember and stand firm — 46:8a
  b) Consider that which is sinful — 46:8b
4) Fourth address: remember that I am G-d — 46:9-11

a) Initial pair of commands: get down in the dust and
sit on the ground, addressed to the virgin daughter
of Babylon 47:1aα
b) Summative command with explanation: sit without
throne, addressed to the daughter of the Chaldeans 47:1aβ-b
   (1) Command proper addressed to the daughter of
   the Babylonians: sit on the ground without
   a throne 47:1aβ
   (2) For you shall no longer be soft and spoiled 47:1b
2) Second set of commands with elaboration: become a
slave woman 47:2-4
a) Initial set pair of commands: take a hand mill and
grind meal 47:2a
   (1) Take a hand mill 47:2aα
   (2) Grind meal 47:2aβ
b) Subsequent quartet of commands with elaboration: remove clothing to ford river 47:2b
   (1) Remove your veil 47:2bα$^{1-2}$
   (2) Strip your train 47:2bα$^{3-4}$
   (3) Bare your thigh 47:2bβ$^{1-2}$
   (4) Ford rivers 47:2bβ$^{3-4}$
c) Results: Babylon exposed and YHWH avenged 47:3
   (1) Babylon exposed 47:3a
      (a) Your nakedness is revealed 47:3aα
      (b) Your shame is seen 47:3aβ
   (2) YHWH avenged 47:3b
      (a) I will take vengeance 47:3bα
      (b) No one will stop me 47:3bβ
d) Hymn of praise for YHWH Seba'ot, redeemer and
holy one of Israel 47:4
3) Third set of commands with elaboration: sit silent in
darkness 47:5
a) Initial paired commands addressed to the daughter
of the Chaldeans: sit silently in darkness 47:5a
   (1) Sit silently 47:5aα
   (2) Enter into darkness 47:5aβ
b) Explanation: for you will not be called the mistress of kingdoms 47:5b
b. Second address to the daughter of Babylon: prophetic
judgment speech 47:6-11
1) Basis for judgment: Babylon's failure to show mercy
to Israel 47:6-7
a) YHWH's actions against Israel 47:6a
   (1) I was angry against my people 47:6aα$^{1-2}$
   (2) I profaned my inheritance by placing them in
   your power 47:6aα^{3}-β
      (a) I profaned my inheritance 47:6aα$^{3-4}$

(b) I placed them in your power	47:6aβ
b) Babylon's failure to show mercy to Israel	47:6b-7
(1) First charge: you did not show mercy to Israel	47:6bα
(2) Second charge with elaboration: you made your yoke heavy upon the old	47:6bβ-7
(a) Basically stated	47:6bβ
(b) Elaboration: you didn't think	47:7
α. Charge: you thought you would be mistress forever	47:7a
β. Twofold further charges: you didn't think about the aftermath	47:7b
aa. You didn't take these matters to heart	47:7bα
bb. You didn't think about the aftermath	47:7bβ
2) Announcement of judgment: evil and disaster will render you a childless widow	47:8-11
a) Call to attention directed to Babylon metaphorically described	47:8
(1) Call to attention proper	47:8aα$^{1-4}$
(2) Metaphorical elaboration on Babylon	47:8aα^5-b
(a) First instance: who lives securely	47:8aα$^{5-6}$
(b) Second instance: who believes herself safe from harm	47:8aβ-b
α. Who says to herself/narrative tag	47:8aβ$^{1-2}$
β. Content of what she says	47:8aβ^3-b
aa. There is no one but me	47:8aβ$^{3-5}$
bb. I will not become a widow	47:8bα
cc. I will not be left childless	47:8bβ
b) Announcement of judgment	47:9-11
(1) Basically stated	47:9
(a) Childlessness and widowhood will come upon you suddenly on one day	47:9a
(b) Elaboration: they come in full measure despite your enchantments and spells	47:9b
(2) Elaboration on Babylon's presuppositions	47:10-11
(a) You thought you were secure in your evil	47:10aα
α. You were secure in your evil	47:10aα$^{1-2}$
β. You said there is no one who sees me	47:10aα$^{3-5}$
(b) Your wisdom and knowledge led you astray	47:10aβ-b
α. Basically stated	47:10aβ
β. You said there is no one but me	47:10b
(c) Announcement of judgment reprised: evil, disaster, and destruction are coming upon you	47:11
α. Evil is coming upon you	47:11aα
aa. Basically stated	47:11aα$^{1-3}$
bb. Elaboration: you don't know its power	47:11aα$^{4-6}$
β. Disaster is falling upon you	47:11aβ-γ
aa. Basically stated	47:11aβ

  (a) They are called into exile from the holy city 48:2aα
  (b) They are dependent on G-d of Israel/YHWH 48:2aβ-b
   α. Dependent on G-d of Israel 48:2aβ
   β. Specification: YHWH is the name 48:2b
 b. Disputation speech proper concerning YHWH's control
 of events 48:3-11
  1) YHWH's past announcements of what will come 48:3-5
   a) I announced what would happen and it did 48:3
    (1) Paired statement 48:3a
     (a) I declared what would happen from the
      beginning 48:3aα
     (b) From my mouth it came out and I made it
      known 48:3aβ
    (2) Summary: I acted immediately and it happened 48:3b
   b) Reason for YHWH's announcement: so you would
   not attribute to idols 48:4-5
    (1) YHWH's qualifications for declaration 48:4
     (a) I knew you were stubborn 48:4a
     (b) And the sinews of your neck are like iron 48:4bα
     (c) And your forehead is bronze 48:4bβ
    (2) Declaration with reason 48:5
     (a) Twofold declaration statement 48:5a
      α. I declared it then 48:5aα
      β. I made it known before it happened 48:5aβ
     (b) Reasons for declaration: attribute to idols 48:5b
      α. Lest you say my idol did these things 48:5bα
      β. My carved and molten images com-
       manded them 48:5bβ
  2) Obligation to acknowledge YHWH with qualifications 48:6-8
   a) Israel's obligation to acknowledge YHWH 48:6
    (1) You have heard and you must declare 48:6a
     (a) You have heard 48:6aα
     (b) Rhetorical question: you must declare 48:6aβ
    (2) What to acknowledge 48:6b
     (a) YHWH made new things known in the past 48:6bα
     (b) Hidden things that you did not know 48:6bβ
   b) Reason for obligation: now they come to pass 48:7
    (1) Now YHWH's past predictions come to pass 48:7a
     (a) Now they come to pass 48:7aα
     (b) You did not hear of them before today 48:7aβ
    (2) You cannot claim that you knew about them 48:7b
   c) Qualification: I know that you are treacherous and
   rebellious 48:8
    (1) Threefold statement that you did not know 48:8a
     (a) You did not hear 48:8aα[1-3]
     (b) You did not know 48:8aα[4-6]
     (c) Your ears were not opened before today 48:8aβ

(1) I spoke to him	48:15aα
(2) I called him	48:15aβ
(3) I brought him and he will succeed in his path	48:15b
(a) I brought him	48:15bα
(b) He will succeed	48:15bβ
c) Presentation of Cyrus	48:16
(1) Call to attention	48:16aα
(a) Draw near	48:16aα$^{1-2}$
(b) Hear this	48:16aα$^{3-4}$
(2) I announced this before	48:16aβ-γ
(a) I did not speak in secret	48:16aβ
(b) I was there	48:16aγ
(3) Cyrus's statement: YHWH sent me and YHWH's spirit	48:16b
d) Concluding oracle: exhortation to heed YHWH	48:17-19
(1) Prophetic messenger formula	48:17a
(2) Oracle of salvation: exhortation to heed YHWH	48:17b-19
(a) YHWH's self-identification	48:17b
α. Self-identification proper	48:17bα$^{1-3}$
β. First qualification: teaching you to profit	48:17bα$^{4-5}$
γ. Second qualification: guiding your path	48:17bβ
(b) Exhortation: heed YHWH's commands	48:18-19
α. Condition to be fulfilled: heed YHWH's commands	48:18a
β. Results: peace, righteousness, offspring	48:18b-19
aa. Peace and righteousness	48:18b
α) Peace like river	48:18bα
β) Righteousness like waves of sea	48:18bβ
bb. Numerous offspring	48:19
α) Like sand and grains	48:19a
aa) Sand	48:19aα
bb) Grains	48:19aβ
β) Name not cut off or destroyed before YHWH	48:19b
aa) Name not cut off	48:19bα
bb) Name not destroyed	48:19bβ
III. Concluding hymnic command with warning	48:20-22
A. Presentation of hymn: call to leave Babylon	48:20-21
1. Depart from Babylon	48:20aα$^{1-2}$
2. Flee from the Chaldeans	48:20aα$^{3-4}$
3. Declare with a joyous voice	48:20aα$^{5-7}$
4. Announce this	48:20aα$^{8-9}$
5. Bring it out to the ends of the earth	48:20aβ
6. Say that YHWH has redeemed servant Jacob	48:20b-21
a. Command: say	48:20bα
b. Content of announcement: hymn of praise for YHWH's deliverance of Israel	48:20bβ-21

1) Announcement that YHWH redeemed servant Jacob	48:20bβ
2) Means of deliverance: water in the wilderness	48:21
a) They did not thirst	48:21aα
b) YHWH provided water	48:21aβ-b
(1) Water flowed for them	48:21aβ
(2) The rock split	48:21bα
(3) Water gushed out	48:21bβ
B. Warning: there is no peace for the wicked	48:22

Isaiah 44:24–48:22 constitutes the account of YHWH's announcement that YHWH will use Cyrus, the king of Persia, for the restoration of Israel (cf. Westermann, *Sprache*, 81; Merendino, *Der Erste*, 403, Melugin, *Formation*, 126). The unit follows immediately upon the hymn in 44:23 that closed the previous unit. The prophet presents YHWH's speeches throughout that focus on the question of YHWH's use of Cyrus, a foreign monarch, to return Israel from Babylonian exile to the land of Israel and to rebuild Jerusalem and the temple. YHWH's speeches in this unit appear in the form of an announcement and argument that YHWH as G-d of creation and Israel is fully capable of employing Cyrus to fulfill the divine will. Although a hymnic element appears at the conclusion of the initial announcement of YHWH's plans to use Cyrus in 44:24–45:8, the hymn in 45:8 both summarizes YHWH's role as the creator who controls the waters of creation and anticipates YHWH's plans to bring righteousness and deliverance to the world. Isaiah 45:9–48:19 then presents a disputational trial scene in which YHWH offers arguments in court to support the claims made in 44:24–45:8. Although Cyrus is not explicitly named as he was in 44:28 and 45:1, 45:9–48:19 makes repeated reference to him in 45:13; 46:10-11; and 48:14-16. Preliminary arguments that reject Israel's right to challenge YHWH and that assert YHWH's right to act appear in 45:9-25. The presentation of the evidence of YHWH's power that focuses on the weakness of Babylonia's gods in relation to YHWH appears in 46:1–47:15. The summary speeches appear in 48:1-19. The unit concludes with a command in hymnic form in 48:20-21(22) to depart from Babylon as YHWH has now freed Israel from Babylonian control. The presentation in 48:22 of YHWH's statement that there is no peace for the wicked may well be a gloss from 57:21 (e.g., Westermann, *Isaiah 40–66*, 205), but in the present form of the text it functions as a qualification of the preceding command by specifying that YHWH's restoration of Israel will not include the wicked, i.e., those who do not adhere to YHWH. Such a gloss reflects the editing of the final 5th-century form of the book. Isaiah 49:1 opens with a statement by YHWH's servant and therefore constitutes the opening of the next unit of the book.

    Isaiah 44:24–45:8 constitutes the announcement of YHWH's plan to use Cyrus as YHWH's agent for the restoration of Israel. It includes three basic subunits. The first is the announcement addressed to Israel in 44:24-28 of YHWH's plans to use Cyrus in this fashion. The second is the announcement addressed to Cyrus in 45:1-7 of YHWH's plans. The third is the concluding hymn in 45:8, which lacks any particular addressee and reiterates YHWH's roles as creator and the one who brings righteousness and victory.

Isaiah 44:24-28 constitutes the prophet's presentation of YHWH's address to Israel concerning YHWH's self-identification as creator and G-d of Israel. The address is disputational in form because it is designed to overcome doubts concerning YHWH's ability to function as G-d of creation and Israel given the realities of the Babylonian exile. It begins with an expanded messenger formula in 44:24a which identifies as YHWH as the speaker of the following material in vv. 24b-28. The expansion of the messenger formula identifies YHWH as the redeemer of Israel and its creator from the womb. YHWH's speech focuses on YHWH's self-identification and self-predication. Although its use of participial forms to describe YHWH's actions might suggest a hymnic composition, each statement ends with a finite verbal form that asserts YHWH's actions as a means to convince the audience of this text of YHWH's ability to function as Israel's creator and redeemer. The speech begins with YHWH's self-identification in 44:24bα$^{1-2}$, "I am YHWH."

The balance of the speech in 44:24bα^3–45:7 is a series of seven self-predications in which YHWH announces YHWH's roles, beginning with roles that are known to Israel, such as creator, opponent to diviners and sorcerers, etc., and culminating with the announcement of YHWH's plan to use Cyrus to restore Jerusalem and the temple. The argument proceeds by establishing that YHWH makes all, creates the heavens, confounds diviners and the wise, etc., and thereby establishes that YHWH is fully capable of using Cyrus to restore Jerusalem and the temple. The first predication in 44:24bα^3-b focuses on YHWH's role as creator in three statements, each of which is based on a participle. YHWH claims to be the one who makes everything in v. 24bα$^{3-4}$; who stretches out the heavens alone in v. 24bβ; and who spreads out the earth oneself in v. 24bγ. The second predication in 44:25a employs two verbal statements linked by a conjunctive *wāw* which focus on YHWH's ability to overturn diviners and sorcerers, including YHWH's annulment of the signs of diviners in v. 25aα and the confounding of sorcerers in v. 25aβ. The third predication in 44:25b again employs two verbal statements joined by a conjunctive *wāw* to identify YHWH's role as the one who confounds sages, including statements in v. 25bα that YHWH turns back sages and in v. 25bβ that YHWH overturns their knowledge. The fourth predication in 44:26a employs two verbal statements joined by a conjunctive *wāw* to assert that YHWH supports servants and messengers, including statements in v. 26aα that YHWH supports YHWH's servant and in v. 26aβ that YHWH confirms the counsel of YHWH's messengers. The fifth predication in 44:26b employs one participial statement that refers to YHWH's three addressees: YHWH is the one who says to Jerusalem that "you will be restored" in v. 26bα$^{1-3}$, to the cities of Judah that "you will be rebuilt" in v. 26bα$^{4-6}$, and to its ruins that "I will restore them" in v. 26bβ. The sixth predication in 44:27 employs another participle to present YHWH's two statements to the waters of creation: to the deep YHWH says "be dry" in v. 27a and to your (i.e., the deep's) streams YHWH says "I will dry them up" in v. 27b. The seventh and final predication in 44:28 employs a more complicated structure to address both Cyrus in v. 28a and Jerusalem and the temple in v. 28b. Verse 28a employs the participle, *hā'ōmēr,* "the one who says," to address Cyrus with two statements joined with a conjunctive *wāw:* "you are my shepherd" addressed directly to Cyrus in v. 28aα and "all my will he will fulfill" which speaks about Cyrus in v. 28aβ. Verse 28b employs the infinitive *lē'mōr,* "saying," to follow up with an address to Jerusalem and the temple stating that Jerusalem will be rebuilt in v. 28bα and that the temple will be reestablished in v. 28bβ.

The address to Israel in 44:24-28 prepares the way for YHWH's address to Cyrus in 45:1-7. Having demonstrated that YHWH is able to employ Cyrus to restore Jerusalem and the temple in 44:24-28, then YHWH in 45:1-7 commissions Cyrus to do so. The subunit begins in 45:1 with an expanded messenger formula directed to Cyrus in which YHWH directs the following message to the Persian king. The basic messenger formula appears in v. 1aα$^{1-5}$ directed to Cyrus, identified here as YHWH's anointed. Verse 1aα^{6}-b then lays out the predication of Cyrus as YHWH's anointed in two parts. Verse 1aα$^{6-11}$ identifies YHWH's support for Cyrus with a 1st-person statement that YHWH will grasp the right hand of Cyrus in v. 1aα$^{6-8}$ and follows with a statement that YHWH's purpose in supporting Cyrus is to subdue nations before him in v. 1aα$^{9-11}$. The second predication of Cyrus in v. 1aβ-b focuses on YHWH's actions against the kings of the nations in support of Cyrus. YHWH states in v. 1aβ that "I open the loins of kings," i.e., that YHWH will disarm kings by removing the belts that hold their weapons and prepare them for war. YHWH then states the purpose of this act in v. 1b in two parts: to open doors before Cyrus in v. 1bα and to ensure that gates do not remain closed in v. 1bβ. Such statements recall the opening of the gates of Babylon to welcome Cyrus as its next king.

YHWH's royal commissioning speech to Cyrus then follows in 45:2-7. The first portion of the speech appears in 45:2-3, which defines YHWH's actions on behalf of Cyrus in vv. 2-3a and the purpose of YHWH's action, i.e., so that Cyrus will recognize YHWH, in v. 3b. YHWH's actions on behalf of Cyrus include five elements, each of which is defined by 1st-person verbs. YHWH states that 1) "I walk before you" in v. 2aα; 2) "I level hills" in v. 2aβ; 3) "I break down doors of bronze" in v. 2bα; 4) "I cut down bars of iron" in v. 2bβ; and 5) a dual statement in v. 3a in which YHWH states "I give you treasures of darkness and secret stores." Verse 3b employs a purpose clause to state YHWH's objective: "so that you will know that I YHWH G-d of Israel call you by name." Such a statement makes YHWH's identity clear and highlights the fact that YHWH employs a foreign king to accomplish YHWH's purposes.

The second element of YHWH's commissioning speech to Cyrus immediately follows in 45:4 with a much fuller statement of YHWH's purpose. It begins with a purpose clause in v. 4a which states that YHWH acts on behalf of "my servant Jacob and "Israel my chosen one." Verse 4b then follows with a statement of YHWH's actions, "I call you by name" in v. 4bα followed by the qualification, "I give you title, but you did not know me," in v. 4bβ. Such a statement constitutes the main act of designating Cyrus as YHWH's king.

The third element of YHWH's commissioning speech in 45:5-7 constitutes a summation of the whole: it maintains that YHWH has commissioned Cyrus so that all the world may know YHWH. The basic premise of this segment appears in v. 5a with the statement "I am YHWH and there is no other" in v. 5aα followed by the elaboration in v. 5aβ, "beside me there is no G-d." Verses 5b-7 then follow with a reiteration of YHWH's actions and the purposes for which

YHWH acts. Verse 5b states YHWH's action on behalf of Cyrus: YHWH girds Cyrus in v. 5bα and then qualifies the action in v. 5bβ by stating that Cyrus does not know YHWH. Verses 6-7 then define the purpose of YHWH's action: "so that all the world will know that I am YHWH." This premise is basically stated in v. 6a. Verses 6b-7 then elaborate on this basic premise. Verse 6b states the premise in simplified form, "I am YHWH"; v. 7a elaborates by laying out YHWH's role as creator of light and darkness in v. 7aα and maker of peace and disaster in v. 7aβ; and v. 7b sums up with a statement, "I YHWH do all these things."

The concluding hymn of praise in 45:8 then closes 44:24–45:8 by reiterating the themes of the whole. Verse 8a-bα employs a combination of imperative and jussive verbs to proclaim the attributes of creation in two parts. Verse 8a calls upon the heavens to pour rain in v. 8aα and the heavens to rain righteousness in v. 8aβ. Verse 8bα then follows with a twofold call for the earth to produce victory in v. 8bα$^{1-4}$ so that righteousness will sprout in v. 8bα$^{5-7}$. Verse 8bβ then closes the hymn with YHWH's claim of responsibility, "I YHWH created it."

Isaiah 45:9–48:19 constitutes a trial scene concerning YHWH's use of Cyrus to redeem Israel and to restore Jerusalem and the temple. The prophet presents YHWH's speeches throughout, which focus on an attempt to demonstrate YHWH's right and ability to use the Persian king Cyrus as YHWH's agent for action in the world. The passage includes three major subunits based on a combination of formal and thematic factors. Isaiah 45:9-25 presents the preliminary arguments in the courtroom scene in which YHWH attempts to deflect challengers and to assert the divine right to act. Isaiah 46:1–47:15 presents the evidence of YHWH's right to act by focusing on the weakness of Babylon's gods in 46:1-13 and YHWH's control of Babylon in 47:1-15. Isaiah 48:1-19 then presents a summation of YHWH's arguments reiterating YHWH's identity as the G-d of Israel and all creation together with YHWH's commitment to the restoration of Israel.

The presentation of the preliminary arguments in 45:9-25 includes two basic components. The first is a disputation speech that denies Israel's right to challenge YHWH in 45:9-13, and the second is a twofold messenger speech that asserts YHWH's right to act on Israel's behalf. Together, these subunits prepare the reader for the presentation of evidence in 46:1–47:15.

Isaiah 45:9-13 begins with a presentation of two woe speeches in 45:9-10 that deny the right to challenge YHWH's action, followed by a messenger speech in 45:11-13 that focuses on the same theme. The woe speeches appear respectively in 45:9 and 45:10. The first woe speech begins with the stereotypical woe statement in v. 9a which warns anyone who would argue with his or her own creator, metaphorically portraying such a person as a potsherd that would challenge other earthenware potsherds. A set of paired rhetorical questions then follows in v. 9b to reinforce the point. The first in v. 9bα questions whether clay can say to the potter, "what are you doing?" which of course it can not, and the second in v. 9bβ reiterates the point by questioning whether the same clay can challenge its maker by pointing out that the potter's work has no handles. Again, such a scenario is patently absurd. The second woe speech in 5:10 shifts metaphors to make the same point. This speech appears simply as a twofold woe statement without reinforcing rhetorical questions. The first portion of the woe statement which appears in v. 10a presents the absurd situation of one who says to his or her father, "what did you sire?" and the second in v. 10b presents the parallel situation of one who says to his or her mother, "what did you bear?, i.e., for what did you go into labor?" Both cases presume that a child has no right to question the parents' actions of giving birth.

The following prophetic messenger speech in 45:11-13 then focuses on the same point as the woe speeches. The oracle begins with an expanded messenger formula in v. 11a which pointedly identifies YHWH as both the Holy One of Israel and as Israel's maker (*yōṣrô*, lit., "his creator"), which reiterates the language employed for the potter in v. 9bα. The oracle proper follows in vv. 11b-13bβ in the form of a disputation speech that presents a twofold rhetorical question in v. 11b, followed by three counterassertions in vv. 12a, 12b, and 13a-bβ. The twofold rhetorical question in v. 11b employs a 3rd-person plural rhetorical question in v. 11bα to deny the right of Israel to question YHWH's signs concerning YHWH's children, i.e., the sons (Israel) have no right to challenge the parent's (YHWH's) future plans for them. The second in v. 11bβ employs a 2nd-person plural to state to Israel that "you do not have the right to command the work of my hands." The three counterassertions then follow. The first in v. 12a presents YHWH's 1st-person statement asserting that YHWH is the creator, i.e., "I made the earth" in v. 12aα and "I created humans upon it (the earth)" in v. 12aβ. The second in v. 12b employs similar 1st-person statements to assert that YHWH is creator of the heavens and their hosts, i.e., "I, my hand, stretched out the heavens," in v. 12bα, and "I commanded all their hosts (the stars)" in v. 12bβ. The third in v. 13a-bβ employs a combination of 1st- and 3rd-person statements to assert YHWH's role in bringing Cyrus. Verse 13a employs two 1st-person statements to assert that YHWH roused him (Cyrus) in righteousness in v. 13aα and that YHWH cleared his (Cyrus's) path in v. 13aβ. Third-person statements concerning the results of YHWH's actions then follow in v. 13bα-β. Verse 13bα$^{1-3}$ asserts that "he (Cyrus) will build my city (Jerusalem)," and v. 13bα$^{4-5}$ states that "he (Cyrus) will release my exiles (Israel)." The conditions for Cyrus's actions then follow in v. 13bβ: these actions will be performed without cost in v. 13bβ$^{1-2}$ and without the need for a bribe in v. 13bβ$^{3-4}$. The concluding YHWH speech formula in v. 13bγ then closes the entire subunit.

Isaiah 45:14-25 then follows with the disputational assertion of YHWH's right to act, which comprises two messenger speeches in vv. 14-17 and 18-25 linked by a conjunctive *kî*, "for." The first messenger speech in vv. 14-17 focuses on Egypt's recognition of YHWH's role as deliverer of Israel, which of course plays intertextually on the narratives of YHWH's redemption of Israel from Egyptian bondage in Exodus 1–15, albeit on different grounds than the plagues. The subunit begins with the messenger formula in v. 14aα$^{1-3}$, followed by YHWH's speech per se in vv. 14aα^4-17. YHWH's speech constitutes an announcement in four parts of Egypt's recognition of YHWH's role as deliverer of Israel. The first part in v. 14aα$^{4-14}$ constitutes an announcement that "the produce of Egypt and the commerce of Ethiopia and the tall Sabeans will pass over to you (i.e., to Israel)." The second announcement in v. 14aβ states that "they (the Egyptians, Ethiopians, and Sabeans) will follow you (Israel) and be yours." The third announcement in v. 14aγ states that "they (the Egyptians, Ethiopians, and Sabeans) will walk after you in fetters and pass by." The fourth announcement in vv. 14b-17 presents an elaborate portrayal of the Egyptians, Ethiopians, and Sabeans bowing down and praying to Israel. The announcement of the bowing appears in v. 14bα$^{1-2}$, and the announcement of the prayer appears in vv. 14bα^3-17 in an elaborate form. The basic prayer/speech formula appears in v. 14bα$^{3-4}$, followed by an elaboration on the motif that YHWH is G-d in vv. 14bβ-17 in four parts. The first appears in v. 14bβ, introduced by the particle *'ak*, "indeed!" Verse 14bβ asserts that "YHWH is indeed G-d among you (Israel)," including the basic statement in v. 14bβ$^{1-3}$ and the following assertion, joined by a conjunctive *wāw*, that "there is no other G-d." The second appears in v. 15, introduced by *'ākēn*, "indeed," which functions with both asseverative and conjunctive force (cf. 49:4; 53:4; Zeph 3:7). Verse 15 constitutes a twofold statement of YHWH's identity as a concealed G-d who delivers, including the statement that "you are a hidden G-d" in v. 15a and qualified by the statement that "(YHWH is) G-d of Israel who delivers" in v. 15b. The third appears in v. 16, which constitutes a twofold statement that idolaters, i.e., those who worship gods other than YHWH, should be ashamed. The first statement in v. 16a asserts that "all idolaters should be ashamed and disgraced," and the second in v. 16b asserts that "all who fashion images should walk in disgrace together." The fourth appears in v. 17 and asserts in two parts that Israel is delivered by YHWH. The first part in v. 17a employs a *niphal* or passive verb to assert that "Israel is delivered by YHWH with eternal deliverance." The second part in v. 17b employs a negative verbal address form to assert that "you (Israel) shall neither be ashamed nor disgraced forever."

The second messenger speech in 45:18-25 then follows with an introductory *kî*, "for," which links this subunit to the preceding messenger speech in 45:14-17. Having asserted the recognition of YHWH as deliverer in 45:14-17, 45:18-25 then follows with a disputational trial speech that argues that YHWH's position is unchallengeable. The subunit begins with an expanded YHWH messenger formula in v. 18a that focuses on YHWH's role as creator. Following the basic YHWH messenger formula in v. 18aα$^{1-4}$, v. 18aα^5-β presents YHWH's attributes as creator. Verse 45:18aα$^{5-8}$ asserts that as creator of heaven, YHWH is G-d, and v. 45:18aα^9-β identifies YHWH as creator of the earth and its maker. Following the basic statement of this premise in v. 45:18aα$^{9-11}$, v. 18aα^{12}-β elaborates with threefold statements that 1) "YHWH established it" in v. 18aα$^{12-13}$, 2) "YHWH did not create it for chaos" in v. 18aβ$^{1-3}$, and 3) "YHWH formed it for dwelling" in v. 18aβ$^{4-5}$.

YHWH's speech then follows in 45:18b-25 in the form of a disputational trial speech that argues that YHWH is G-d. The speech includes five major syntactically-independent elements in vv. 18b-19, 20, 21, 22, and 23-25.

The first in 45:18b-19 is YHWH's 1st-person assertion that YHWH is G-d. The basic premises for this assertion appear in v. 18b in two parts: the 1st-person statement, "I am YHWH," in v. 18bα and "there is no other" in v. 18bβ. Verse 19 presents YHWH's 1st-person elaboration on these premises in three parts: 1) "I did not speak while hiding in a place of darkness" in v. 19aα; 2) "I did not say to the seed of Jacob 'seek me in chaos'" in v. 19aβ; and 3) "I YHWH speak rightly and truly" in v. 19b. The last elaboration in v. 19b includes statements by YHWH that "I YHWH speak what is right" in v. 19bα and "I declare what is straight" in v. 19bβ.

The second in 45:20 constitutes YHWH's summons to opponents. The basic summons appears in v. 20a in two parts: a summons to gather and come in v. 20aα and a summons to the fugitives of the nations to draw near together in v. 20aβ. The following qualification in v. 20b dismisses YHWH's opponents, as those who carry a god of wood cannot possibly know anything as they pray to a god that does not deliver.

The third element in 45:21 presents YHWH's ability to foretell current events as proof that YHWH is the true G-d. Verse 21a constitutes a rhetorical challenge in two parts to YHWH's opponents to prove their case: "let them declare and draw near" in v. 21aα and "let them take counsel together" in v. 21aβ. Verse 21b then follows with rhetorical questions and assertions that YHWH is G-d. The three rhetorical questions appear in v. 21bα$^{1-9}$, including 1) "Who foretold this from before?" in v. 21bα$^{1-4}$; 2) "(Who) declared it from the past?" in v. 21bα$^{5-6}$; and 3) "Was it not I, YHWH?" in v. 21bα$^{7-9}$. The rhetorical assertions in v. 21bα^{10}-β, linked to the questions by a conjunctive *wāw*, then lay out the rather obvious conclusions to draw in two parts: "there is no G-d besides me" in v. 21bα$^{10-13}$ and "there is no G-d righteous and delivering but me" in v. 21bβ.

The fourth element in 45:22 presents YHWH's appeal for the ends of the earth to turn to YHWH. The appeal proper appears in v. 22a, and the basis for the appeal, "for I am G-d and there is no other," appears in v. 22b.

The fifth element in 45:23-25 presents YHWH's concluding oath that all the world will recognize YHWH. The statement of the oath appears in v. 23. The elaborated oath formula in v. 23a includes two statements by YHWH: "I have sworn by myself" in v. 23aα and "righteousness comes forth from my mouth, a word that remains true (lit., and it does not return)" in v. 23aβ. The substance of the oath appears in v. 23b, including the assertion that "every knee shall bend to me" in v. 23bα and "every tongue shall swear (to me)" in v. 23bβ. The elaboration of the oath then appears in vv. 24-25. Verse 24 asserts that righteousness and strength come by or through YHWH, including the basic statement of this premise in v. 24a and the corresponding statement that YHWH's enemies will be put to shame in v. 24b. Verse 25 concludes with the statement that "by YHWH all the seed of Israel is vindicated and praised."

The presentation of the evidence concerning the weakness of Babylonia's gods and the power of YHWH appears in 46:1–47:15. Isaiah 46:1-13 presents a disputation speech, addressed to Israel, in which YHWH argues that the Babylonian gods are powerless in comparison to YHWH. Isaiah 47:1-15 employs YHWH's direct address to Babylon, portrayed metaphorically as a destitute woman, to demonstrate YHWH's power over Babylonia.

Isaiah 46:1-13 appears as a disputation speech, addressed by YHWH to Israel, that attempts to demonstrate the powerless nature of the Babylonian gods when compared to YHWH. The premise to be disputed appears in 46:1-2 with a portrayal of the Babylonian gods as they are carried through the streets of Babylon during the Akitu or New Year festival that celebrated the role of Marduk, the city god of Babylon, as the creator of the universe and Marduk's authorization of the King of Babylon to rule on Marduk's behalf. Isaiah 46:3-13 then presents YHWH's counterarguments that are intended to demonstrate that YHWH is the true G-d by comparing the weakness of the Babylonian gods to the power of YHWH.

The premise in 46:1-2 portrays the Babylonian gods as they are carried through the streets. The Akitu festival called for a parade through the streets of Babylon in which images of the Babylonian gods and the gods of all the nations that were subservient to Babylon were carried through the streets of the city to the Etemenanki, the ziggurat or stepped pyramid structure that served as the temple of Marduk, the city god of Babylon and the chief of the Babylonian pantheon. The purpose of the holiday was to celebrate Marduk's victory over Tiamat, the dragon goddess of the sea, who threatened to turn the universe into chaos following the murder of her husband, Apsu, the god of fresh water, who had planned to kill all of the gods for interrupting his sleep with their noise. The Babylonian creation epic, the *Enuma Elish*, "When on High," recounts the events of creation. The gods gather to discuss how they will defend themselves against Tiamat and select Marduk as their champion. The two armies meet in battle, and Marduk advances to challenge Tiamat to one-on-one combat. Using his weapons, the wind, the bow, and the net, he is able to kill Tiamat, divide her body to create heaven and earth, and by use of the blood of her commander, Kingu, create human beings to do the work of the gods. Marduk sets up the various gods and goddesses as stars, planets, etc., and the gods respond by building him the Etemenanki to serve as his temple in recognition of Marduk's role as creator of the universe and chief of the gods. When the parade reaches the Etemenanki, the king of Babylon ascends to the top, where he is slapped in the face by a woman priest to remind him of his subservience to Marduk and presented with the tablets of destiny which authorize him to rule on Marduk's behalf for another year.

Although 46:1-2 presents the Babylonian gods in procession during the Akitu festival, it portrays them in disparaging terms as burdens to those who carry them to emphasize their lack of power in relation to YHWH. The two divine names mentioned here include Bel, "Lord," a title for Marduk, the city god of Babylon and chief of the Babylonian pantheon, and Nebo, the son of Marduk and lord of writing and wisdom who recorded the destinies of all gods and humans. Indeed, Nebo is the author of the tablets of destiny that authorize the Babylonian king to rule on Marduk's behalf. But in 46:1-2, the reader does not see the powerful chief gods of the Babylonian pantheon. Instead, the reader sees Bel and Nebo bowing and bending down as their images are carried through the streets. They thereby appear as burdens to their bearers.

Indeed, the structure of this subunit makes their burdensome characters clear. Verse 1aα introduces the subunit with a portrayal of Bel and Nebo bowing and bending as their bearers are not able to carry the weight of the heavy images. It employs a combination of the perfect verb *kāraʿ*, "he bowed," and the participle *qōrēs*, "(he is) bending," to indicate that the bowing and bending of these gods is both accomplished and ongoing. Verses 1aβ-2 then elaborate on the initial portrayal with three syntactically-independent statements that emphasize the burdensome character of these gods. Verse 1aβ-γ states that their images are burdens for animals and beasts. Verse 1b indicates that those things that you carry, i.e., the idols of the gods, are a wearisome burden. Verse 2 presents a summation in a sequence of three syntactically-independent verbal statements that collectively demonstrate that these gods are incapable of acting. Verse 2aα states that the two bow and bend together, v. 2aβ states that they cannot deliver a burden, and v. 2b states that they walk into captivity.

Isaiah 46:3-13 then presents YHWH's counterargument in 1st-person declarative language, stating in v. 4, "I am he," i.e., "I am the true G-d," and in v. 9b, "I am G-d and there is no other; I am G-d and there is none like me." The structure of this subunit is based on five 2nd-masculine plural address forms in vv. 3, 5, 8, 9, and 12, each of which addresses the people of Israel as a whole. Each address form introduces a statement by YHWH which progressively asserts YHWH's role as the true G-d and creator who acts to deliver Zion and Israel from Babylon.

The first address appears in 46:3-4, which presents YHWH's assertions that YHWH bears (the people) and delivers them. The subunit begins with an address form in v. 3 that is constituted by a masculine plural imperative, "listen (šim'û) to me, O house of Jacob," a variation of the standard call to attention, in v. 3aα. The verb does double duty to govern the second clause in v. 3aβ as well, "listen to me, O remnant of the house of Israel." Verse 3b then elaborates on the initial address forms by defining the addressees as "those who were carried from the belly" in v. 3bα and as "those born from the womb" in v. 3bβ. The purpose of these statements is to highlight the contention that true gods, such as YHWH, are not themselves borne or carried by their adherents; rather, YHWH carries the people of Israel from birth. The substance of the address appears in v. 4 with YHWH's assertions to be the true G-d. Verse 4a is joined to v. 3 by a conjunctive wāw to emphasize the relationship between these elements of the text and the two parallel portions of v. 4a, in which YHWH claims that "I am he," the one true G-d. Verse 4aα claims that "YHWH is the one from old age," and v. 4aβ follows with a parallel statement that "YHWH is the one who bears you until you turn gray." Both of these statements highlight YHWH's role as sustainer of life as well as creator. Verse 4b then closes the subunit with a summation constituted by four finite verbal formations that state that YHWH is the one who acts (v. 4bα), carries (v. 4bβ), bears (v. 4bγ), and delivers (v. 4bδ), i.e., all of the things that the Babylonian gods are incapable of doing.

The second address form appears in 46:5-7, which focuses on YHWH's incomparability. The subunit begins with two sets of rhetorical questions in v. 5 which set the theme by focusing on the audience's inability to compare YHWH to any other deity. The first set appears in v. 5a with two verbal statements governed by the initial particle lĕmî, "To whom will you compare me? And (to whom) will you consider me equivalent?" The initial particle, "to whom?" likewise governs the second set of rhetorical questions in v. 5b, "and (to whom) will you liken me and we will be the same?" Verses 6-7 then follow with the rhetorical answer to these questions that focuses on the foreign gods who can never be equivalent to YHWH because they cannot act. This subunit comprises four paired statements in vv. 6a, 6b, 7a, and 7b, each of which is syntactically self-contained. They present a succession of images intended to demonstrate that the foreign gods are completely incapable of action in the world. Verse 6a focuses on the money spent to build the images of the foreign gods, including a statement that those who would have such images spend gold from the purse lavishly in v. 6aα, followed by a statement that those who would build such images weigh silver by measure in v. 6aβ. The second appears in v. 6b, which focuses on the worship of gods built by a craftsman. The first element in v. 6bα states that these people hire a craftsman to build a god, and the second statement in v. 6bβ then portrays them worshipping and bowing down to the newly-built idol. Verse 7a emphasizes that these gods are simply idols that cannot move and must be carried where they would go. Five elements appear within v. 7a, each of which is based on a verbal statement. The first element in v. 7aα$^{1-3}$ states that it is carried on the shoulder. The second in v. 7aα^4 states that it is borne. The third in v. 7aα$^{5-6}$ states that the idol is set in place. The fourth in v. 7aα^7 states that the idol stands. Finally, v. 7aβ states that it does not move from its place. The final segment of the rhetorical answer appears in v. 7b, which emphasizes that the gods cannot deliver or answer. It includes two elements. The first in v. 7bα indicates that one may cry out to the idol, but it will not answer. The second in v. 7bβ indicates that the idol is unable to deliver him from his threat.

The third address in 46:8 is an exhortation that reminds the audience to remember what it learns here and to stand firm in its adherence to YHWH. It includes two basic elements. The first in v. 8a employs two masculine plural imperative verbs to call on the audience to remember *(zikrû)* this and to stand firm *(wĕhiṯ'ōšāšû*, reading with Kimḥi, who derives the term from *'îš* and understands it to mean something on the order of "to be a man"; cf. H. Leene, "Isaiah 46.8 — Summons to Be Human? *JSOT* 30 [1984] 111-21). The second in v. 8b then follows with an admonition to consider sins *(hāšîmû pôšĕ'îm 'al-lēb)*, lit., "place sins on the heart."

The fourth address in 46:9-11 calls upon the audience to remember that YHWH is G-d. It begins with the masculine imperative verb *zikrû*, "remember" (the former things from the past). It comprises two basic elements, including the exhortation to remember (that YHWH is G-d) in vv. 9-11a and a concluding summation in v. 11b. The exhortation includes the basic exhortation based on the imperative verb in v. 9a and a specification in vv. 9b-11a, linked by the particle *kî*, "for," that specifies the former things from the past that the audience is asked to remember. The specification comprises four paired statements by YHWH that describe YHWH's attributes in an effort to demonstrate that YHWH is the G-d who acts and is therefore the true G-d. The first appears in v. 9b with YHWH's statements that "I am G-d and there is no other" in v. 9bα, followed by "(I am) G-d, and there is none like me." The second appears in v. 10a with YHWH's statements that "(I am) the one who declares the future *('aḥărît)* from former times" in v. 10aα followed by "(I am the one who declares) from the past that which is not yet done" in v. 10aβ. The third appears in v. 10b with YHWH's statements that "(I am) the one who says my counsel shall stand" in v. 10bα, followed by "and all my will I will do" in v. 10bβ. The fourth appears in v. 11a, which focuses on YHWH's summons of a champion, here designated as *'ayiṭ*, "bird of prey." Ancient Mesopotamian literature frequently employed the metaphor of a bird of prey to designate monarchs. The first element appears in

v. 11aα with YHWH's statement "(I) summon from the east a bird of prey," and
v. 11aβ follows with "(I summon) from a far land a man of my counsel," i.e., a
man who will carry out my will. The second major element of the address then
appears in v. 11b with two sets of paired statements in which YHWH declares
the ability to carry out what YHWH claims. The initial particle, 'ap, "indeed,"
sets this half verse off from the exhortation in vv. 9-11a and thereby emphasizes
the main point of the address. The first paired statement in v. 11bα presents
YHWH's statement, "Indeed I spoke; indeed I brought it about," and the second
in v. 11bβ follows with "I created; indeed, I act." Both sets of paired statements
are designed to support YHWH's claim to be the true G-d of creation.

The fifth and final address in 46:12-13 focuses on YHWH's capacity to
bring righteousness and deliverance, i.e., to carry out true action in the world
in contrast to the foreign idols referenced above. It begins with the masculine
plural imperative šim'û 'ēlay, "listen to me," a variation of the standard call to
attention. It includes two basic components. The first is the address form in
v. 12 which calls on the audience to listen to what YHWH has to say. The first
element of the address form appears in v. 12a based on the imperative "listen
to me" and addressed to those who are stubborn of heart, i.e., those inclined
to reject YHWH's disputation. The second presupposes the imperative and
addresses those who are far from righteousness. Such a statement is persuasive in character because it suggests to the audience that if they do not follow
YHWH's instructions they will commit a transgression. The substance of the
address, an announcement of salvation, then follows in v. 13. It comprises two
sets of paired statements by YHWH. The first appears in v. 13a, which focuses
on YHWH's capacity to bring deliverance of salvation. The first element of
the pair is YHWH's statement "I bring near my righteousness and it is not far"
in v. 13aα, and the second follows in v. 13aβ with YHWH's statement "(I bring
near) my deliverance/salvation and it does not tarry." The second set of paired
statements in v. 13b focuses on YHWH's capacity to bring deliverance/salvation
and glory to Zion and Israel. The first element in the pair in v. 13bα presents
YHWH's statement "And I will bring deliverance/salvation to Zion," and the
second in v. 13bβ follows with "(and I will bring) my glory to Israel." Again,
the passage underscores the point that YHWH acts whereas the foreign gods do
not. The conclusion to draw is that YHWH alone is the true G-d.

Isaiah 47:1-15 presents YHWH's address to Babylon, metaphorically
portrayed as a defeated and humiliated lady who now finds herself as a slave
and a refugee. The unit is configured largely as a prophetic judgment speech,
although it also employs elements of the taunt to demonstrate Babylon's lack
of power before YHWH. The unit is demarcated by its formulation as YHWH's
2nd-person feminine singular address to Babylon throughout in contrast to the
2nd-person masculine plural addresses to Israel/Jacob in chs. 46 and 48.

Isaiah 47:1-15 comprises three subunits, each of which is based on a combination of 1st-person singular address language, which indicates YHWH's
speech, and feminine singular imperative forms directed to Babylon. The first
subunit in 47:1-5 presents YHWH's initial address to Babylon, which employs
feminine singular address forms to command her to sit in the dust, grind grain
like a slave woman, strip herself of her fine garments, and otherwise assume her

new role as a slave woman. The second subunit in 47:6-11 begins with YHWH's 1st-person address in which YHWH explains how, in anger, YHWH had turned Israel over to Babylon, but Babylon's failure to show mercy to Israel resulted in Babylon's judgment. The feminine singular address forms do not appear until v. 8, where they appear as part of an announcement of judgment that is joined syntactically to the basis for judgment in vv. 6-7. The third and final subunit appears in 47:12-15 in the form of a taunt which once again employs feminine singular imperative forms to address Babylon with a declaration that none of her former powers and supporters can save her from YHWH.

The first subunit in 47:1-15 employs three sets of feminine singular imperatives in vv. 1, 2-4, and 5 to command Babylon to take up her new status as a defeated and humiliated slave woman. Each of these subunits includes additional material that explains the background, circumstances, and meanings of the commands. The metaphorical portrayal of Babylon as a woman enables the address to contrast Babylon's past status as the pampered and powerful mistress and ruler of the world with her new status as a slave girl who sits stripped in the dirt, grinding grain and exposing herself as she lifts her skirts to ford rivers when she goes into exile.

The first set of imperatives in v. 1 includes an initial pair of feminine singular imperatives in v. 1aα that commands "the virgin daughter of Babylon" to get down and sit *(rĕdî ûšĕbî)* in the dirt. Verse 1aβ-b then follows with a summative command that "the daughter of the Chaldeans (i.e., Neo-Babylonians)" is to sit *(šĕbî)* on the ground without a throne because she will no longer be considered soft and spoiled. The command proper appears in v. 1aβ, and the explanation of her new status appears in v. 1b. This subunit focuses on the change in status that the personified city is about to experience as the soft and spoiled lady is commanded to get down from her throne and sit in the dirt. What will follow cannot be good for her.

The second set of imperatives together with their elaborating material appears in vv. 2-4. The subunit begins with an initial pair of feminine singular imperatives in v. 2a that command the deposed lady to take *(qĕḥî)* a hand mill in v. 2aα and to grind *(ṭaḥănî)* meal in v. 2aβ. Such a menial and tedious task was generally relegated to the slave girls of the household, which of course signifies Babylon's new status. A subsequent quartet of imperatives in v. 2b then elaborates on Babylon's newly-lowered status by depicting her stripping her clothing to ford rivers. The commands demand that she remove *(gallî)* her veil in v. 2bα$^{1-2}$, strip *(ḥeśpî)* her train in v. 2bα$^{3-4}$, bare *(gallî)* her thigh in v. 2bβ$^{1-2}$, and ford *(ʿibrî)* rivers in v. 2bβ$^{3-4}$. The last verb, *ʿibrî*, "cross, ford," calls to mind the similar sounding Hebrew term *ʿibrî*, "Hebrew," that was employed to portray Israel's homeless status before settling into the land of Israel. The results of Babylon's new status are stated in v. 3: Babylon is exposed and YHWH is avenged. Babylon's exposure in v. 3a is deliberately pornographic to portray the once pampered and powerful lady exposed on the street like a woman who is about to be sold or raped, as the case may be, insofar as her nakedness is revealed in v. 3aα and her shame, apparently a metaphor for her vagina, is seen by all in v. 3aβ. Such exposure of women might be expected in a slave market or in the aftermath of the conquest of a city in which surviving women are stripped and sold to the highest bidder to do with what he pleases. Verse 3b then follows with a twofold statement of YHWH's vengeance against Babylon, including 1st-person statements that YHWH will take vengeance in v. 3bα and that no one can stop YHWH in v. 3bβ. A hymn of praise in v. 4 that celebrates YHWH's role as Israel's redeemer and the Holy One of Israel then closes the subunit with an affirmation of YHWH's name and power.

The third set of imperatives with explanation appears in 47:5. The paired imperatives in v. 5a first reprise the commands to sit *(šĕbî)* from v. 1, but this time, Babylon is commanded to sit silently in v. 5aα and to enter *(ûbō'î)* into darkness in v. 5aβ, apparently a play on the notion that YHWH dwells in the Holy of Holies of the Jerusalem temple in abject darkness (see, e.g., 1 Kgs 8:12): Babylon will sit in darkness before her master, YHWH. The explanatory material in v. 5b likewise reprises the initial premise of the subunit by explaining that Babylon will no longer be called the mistress or lady of the kingdoms *(geberet mamlākôt):* Babylon has lost her status as the ruling city of the world.

The second address to Babylon in 47:6-11 once again includes an imperative feminine singular verb, *wĕ'attâ šim'î zō't,* "and now hear this!" but the imperative does not appear until v. 8, and it is linked to the preceding material by the introductory conjunctive particle *wĕ'attâ,* "and now." The unit begins in v. 6 with a 1st-person speech by YHWH addressed to Babylon in 2nd-person feminine singular form. The 1st-person speech by YHWH continues only through v. 7. Following the above-mentioned conjunctive particle in v. 8, the speech shifts to a neutral 3rd-person announcement form in vv. 8-11, but YHWH continues to serve as speaker throughout. The next unit begins in v. 12 with the syntactically-independent feminine singular imperative, *'imdî-nā',* "stand now!" again addressed to Babylon personified as a woman. Overall, 47:6-11 is formulated as a prophetic judgment speech in which YHWH serves as the speaker. Isaiah 47:6-7 presents the grounds for judgment, and 47:8-11 presents the announcement of judgment proper.

The announcement concerning the grounds for Babylon's judgment in 47:6-7 begins with YHWH's statement of actions taken against Israel in v. 6a, including two basic elements. YHWH states in the first element in v. 6aα$^{1-2}$, in 1st-person form, that YHWH was angry against YHWH's own people. In the second element in v. 6aα^{3}-β, YHWH continues with a 1st-person statement that YHWH had placed the people in Babylon's power as a means to punish them. This statement comprises two basic elements. The first in v. 6aα$^{3-4}$ indicates that YHWH had profaned YHWH's own inheritance (i.e., Israel), and the second in v. 6aβ indicates that YHWH had placed the people in Babylon's power. Isaiah 47:6b-7 then shifts to YHWH's accusation that Babylon had failed to show mercy to Israel, which stands as the basic ground for punishment against Babylon. The first element of this charge appears in v. 6bα, which stands as a basic statement of the charge of Babylon's failure to show mercy. The second element which appears in vv. 6bβ-7 adds a second charge that Babylon made her yoke heavy upon the old. This charge is basically stated in v. 6bβ, and v. 7 then follows with an elaboration. The elaboration charges that Babylon did not think about what she was doing in abusing Israel. The elaboration employs two elements. The first in v. 7a charges Babylon with thinking that she would be mistress forever, and the second element in v. 7b presents a twofold charge that she did not think about the aftermath or consequences of her actions. Verse 7bα states that she did not take these matters to heart, and v. 7bβ charges that she did not think about the aftermath.

The announcement of judgment appears in 47:8-11. The announcement of judgment is joined to the statement of the grounds for judgment in 47:6-7 by the conjunctive particle *wĕ'attâ*, "and now," as stated above. The announcement of judgment comprises two basic elements: the call to attention in v. 8 and the announcement of judgment proper in vv. 9-11.

The call to attention in 47:8 functions as a means to direct Babylon's and the reader's attention to the following announcement of judgment in vv. 9-11. Following the introductory conjunctive particle *wĕ'attâ*, "and now," it employs the feminine imperative verb *šim'û zō't*, "hear this!" to signal what is to follow. The call to attention proper appears in v. 8aα$^{1-4}$ directed to *'ădînâ*, "pampered one," a metaphorical portrayal of Babylon as a spoiled or pampered lady. Verse 8aα^5-b then follows with a metaphorical elaboration on Babylon to extend her initial portrayal as *'ădînâ*, "pampered one." The first instance in v. 8aα$^{5-6}$ portrays her as a woman who dwells securely, as royal women in ancient Mesopotamia would have lived in a protected environment. The second instance in v. 8aβ-b shifts to Babylon's understanding of her own status: she believes herself to be safe from harm. Her self-conceptualization is conveyed initially by a narrative tag in v. 8aβ$^{1-2}$, "who says in her heart (i.e., who thinks to herself)," and the content of her thoughts follows in v. 8aβ^3-b in three discrete statements. These statements include "there is no one but me" in v. 8aβ$^{3-5}$, "I will not sit as a widow (i.e., become a widow)" in v. 8bα, and "I will not know childlessness" in v. 8bβ.

An introductory *wāw*-conjunctive form joins the announcement of judgment in 47:9-11 to the call to attention in 47:8. The announcement of judgment comprises two basic elements: a basic statement of the judgment in v. 9 followed by an elaboration on Babylon's presuppositions, which further explores metaphorically the great lady's mindset, in vv. 10-11. The purpose of the elaboration is to highlight Babylon's arrogance in thinking that no one could overpower her, but of course the text asserts that YHWH is precisely the One to do so.

The basic statement of the announcement of judgment includes two elements. The first is the statement in v. 9a that childlessness and widowhood will come upon Babylon in one instance. The second elaborates on the first by stating that these misfortunes will come upon her in full measure despite her enchantments and spells, apparently a reference to Babylonian magic and astrology that was designed to anticipate the actions of the gods by tracking the heavenly bodies, thereby enabling humans to avoid divine misfortune by planning their activities in full knowledge of divine plans.

The elaboration on Babylon's presuppositions in 47:10-11 is joined to the basic statement of the announcement of judgment in 47:9 by an introductory *wāw*-consecutive to show that it flows naturally from the announcement. The elaboration comprises three basic elements, including a reprise of Babylon's thoughts in v. 10aα, a charge that Babylon's wisdom and knowledge led her astray in v. 10aβ-b, and a reprise of the announcement of judgment in v. 11. The first element in v. 10aα focuses on Babylon's presuppositions of security. It includes two elements: a 2nd-person feminine singular statement in v. 10aα$^{1-2}$ that charges Babylon with feeling secure in her own evil and another 2nd-feminine singular statement in v. 10aα$^{3-5}$ that charges Babylon with thinking that no one sees her. The second element in 10aβ-b again employs 2nd-person feminine address forms to charge that Babylon's own wisdom and knowledge led her astray. The subunit comprises two elements, including the basic statement of the charge in v. 10aβ and her statement that "there is no one but me" in v. 10b. Finally, the third element in the sequence focuses on reprising the announcement of judgment against Babylon in v. 11. It is joined to the preceding by a $w\bar{a}w$-consecutive that shows that judgment is a natural consequence of Babylon's previously stated presuppositions. The subunit comprises three basic elements, each of which is joined by a $w\bar{a}w$. The first element in v. 11aα employs 2nd-feminine address language to announce that evil is coming upon Babylon, including a basic statement in v. 11aα$^{1-3}$ and an elaboration in v. 11aα$^{4-6}$ that states that Babylon does not know its power, i.e., the source of the power that is bringing judgment upon her. The second element in v. 11aβ-γ again employs 2nd-feminine singular address forms to announce that disaster ($h\bar{o}w\hat{a}$) is falling upon Babylon, including a basic statement in v. 11aβ and a statement that she will not be able to atone for it — and thereby avoid the disaster — in v. 11aγ. The third element in v. 11b again employs 2nd-feminine address forms to announce that destruction ($\check{s}\hat{o}'\hat{a}$, i.e., Shoah, the Hebrew term now employed for the Holocaust) is coming upon Babylon, including a basic statement in v. 11bα and an elaboration in v. 11bβ that states that Babylon will not know, i.e., a destruction that she has never experienced before.

The third and final address to the daughter of Babylon appears in 47:12-15 in the form of a taunt that calls attention to her lack of power before YHWH. The subunit employs imperative and 2nd-feminine singular address language throughout, beginning with the syntactically-independent feminine singular imperative '$imd\hat{i}$-$n\bar{a}$', "stand, please," and continuing until 48:1, which employs a masculine plural imperative to address Israel as the house of Jacob.

Isaiah 47:12-15 includes two basic subunits. The first is the command to Babylon to stand by her enchantments and spells in v. 12, and the second is the taunt proper in vv. 13-15, which points out that her powers are useless. There is no syntactical join between the two subunits, but the continued focus on Babylon's powers ties the two elements together.

The command to stand in 47:12 includes two basic elements. The first is the basic statement of the command to Babylon to stand by her enchantments and spells in v. 12a. The second is a speculative statement, marked by two occurrences of the Hebrew term '$\hat{u}lay$, "perhaps," that mockingly raises the possibilities that she might profit from her powers in v. 12bα or that she might intimidate someone, e.g., YHWH, in v. 12bβ. From the standpoint of the unit in ch. 47, such possibilities are patently absurd, which contributes to the taunting nature of this subunit.

The taunt proper appears in 47:13-15, which maintains that Babylon's powers are useless before YHWH. The basic statement of the taunt appears in v. 13a, which states that Babylon is helpless even with all of her counsels or advice from her supporters. Verses 13b-15 then elaborate upon the uselessness of Babylon's astrologers and visionaries. The subunit begins with a call to let the "joiners of the heavens" and "those who envision the stars" stand and deliver Babylon. The "joiners of the heavens" refers to those who track the movements of the stars and other heavenly bodies as a means to determine the wills of the gods with which each astral body is associated, and "those who gaze on or envision the stars" refers to those who track the stars for the same purpose. In both cases, these figures attempt to inform Babylon what will happen next in the world. The satirical character of these proposals is evident from the larger context of ch. 47 and ch. 46 before — it is obvious that these figures are completely incapable of carrying out any such action. Such an outcome is evident from the final subunit in vv. 14-15, which strings together a sequence of four factors that demonstrate the inefficacy of Babylon's astrologers and stargazers: they are like straw that fire consumes in v. 14aα; they cannot save even themselves from the flame in v. 14aβ; v. 14b intimates that this flame is no fire for mere cooking or sitting before, as it is presumably a fire of judgment from YHWH; and v. 15 concludes with a summary-appraisal form that states that no one will be able to save Babylon. The summary-appraisal breaks down into two basic components. The first is a taunting judgment in v. 15a that claims that this is what Babylon gets for trafficking with such traders from her youth. The second in v. 15b mocks Babylon and her associates by claiming that each has wandered off on his own way in v. 15bα so that there is no one to save Babylon in v. 15bβ.

Isaiah 48:1-19 concludes the trial scene in 45:9–48:19 with a presentation of YHWH's summary speeches that reiterate the arguments made throughout the unit and exhort the audience to accept YHWH as the true G-d of creation and human events who will use the Persian monarch Cyrus to achieve Israel's return from Babylonian exile to the land of Israel. The passage employs 2nd-person masculine address language throughout to address Israel, characterized collectively as Israel and the house of Jacob and metaphorically as Jacob. This contrasts with the feminine forms of address employed for Babylon in ch. 47 and the masculine plural address to the coastlands in ch. 49.

The formal structure of 48:1-19 includes two major addresses in 48:1-11 and 48:12-19, each of which begins with a call to attention formulated with masculine imperative verbs. Isaiah 48:1-11 begins with the masculine plural imperative šim'û-zō't, "hear this," directed collectively to "the house of Jacob which is called by the name Israel and has come forth from the waters (seed) of Judah," in vv. 1-2. The house of Jacob is further qualified in vv. 1-2, but it is clear that imperative plural is employed here because the house of Jacob is a corporate or collective designation for the people of Israel. Isaiah 48:12-19 by contrast employs a masculine singular imperative verb, šĕma' 'ēlay, "listen to me," directed individually to "Jacob" and "Israel my called one" in v. 12a. The metaphorical portrayal of Israel as the patriarchal ancestor Jacob justifies the use of the imperative singular verb in this instance. Isaiah 48:1-11 presents a disputation speech that contends that YHWH is the true G-d who both predicts and controls the events that are unfolding with the rise of Cyrus of Persia as the new king of Babylon and the potential for the return of the Babylonian exiles to the land of Israel. Isaiah 48:12-19 presents YHWH's summary speech in which YHWH asks the audience to accept YHWH's claims and thereby realize YHWH's promises to make Israel a great nation. Together, they prepare the audience for the following exhortation in 48:20-22 to leave Babylon.

The disputation speech in 48:1-11 argues that YHWH is the true G-d because YHWH planned and foretold the events that were currently taking place in Babylonia, namely, the fall of Babylon, the rise of Cyrus of Persia as the new king of Babylon, and the potential for Jewish exiles to return to rebuild the land of Israel. It initially employs masculine plural imperative language to address the people as the house of Jacob in vv. 1-2, although it shifts to masculine singular forms in vv. 3-11. The unit falls into two basic components, the call to attention in vv. 1-2 and the disputation speech proper concerning YHWH's control of events in vv. 3-11.

The call to attention in 48:1-2 introduces the following disputation speech by alerting the audience to "listen to this," i.e., what is to follow. The basic call to attention appears in v. 1aα$^{1-4}$, where it employs the masculine plural verb *šim'û-zō't*, "hear this," to address the audience defined collectively as "the house of Jacob," an appellation employed in 2:5 at the outset of the book to characterize Israel as a whole. Three qualifications for the house of Jacob then follow in vv. 1aα^5-2. The first in v. 1aα^5-β specifies that the house of Jacob is called by the name Israel and descended from the waters (seed or semen) of Judah. The reference to the name Israel appears in v. 1aα$^{5-7}$, and the reference to descent from Judah appears in v. 1aβ. The second qualification appears in v. 1bα, with the twofold statement that the house of Jacob is sworn by the name of YHWH in v. 1bα$^{1-3}$ and that it invokes the G-d of Israel in v. 1bα$^{4-6}$. The third qualification in vv. 1bβ-2 is more complex than its two predecessors in that it challenges or negates the first two qualifications, apparently to lay the foundation for YHWH's acts of punishment against Israel by bringing about the exile in the first place. The subunit begins in v. 1bβ with the basic statement "not in truth and not in righteousness (is Jacob called Israel and sworn by YHWH)." The reason for such a negation follows in v. 2, which begins with a causative *kî*, "for, because," and contends that they are exiled by YHWH and therefore dependent upon YHWH. The statement that they are called from the holy city in v. 2aα signals their exile from Jerusalem. The following twofold statement in v. 2aβ-b points to YHWH as the cause of Jacob's current state of exile by establishing that they are dependent upon YHWH in v. 2aβ and specifying that YHWH is the name in v. 2b.

The disputation speech proper, which argues that YHWH is the true G-d who controls events, then follows in 48:3-11. It is formulated with a combination of 1st-person subject references to YHWH as the speaker and 2nd-masculine singular address forms to refer to Israel or Jacob as the addressee. The unit comprises three syntactically-independent subunits in vv. 3-5, 6-8, and 9-11 that present the constituent arguments for YHWH's case.

The first subunit in 48:3-5 presents YHWH's arguments that YHWH announced in the past what would come to pass, and it contends that these events are happening now. This contention appears in basic form in v. 3. Verse 3a presents paired assertions that "I declared what would happen from the beginning" in v. 3aα and "from my mouth it came out and I made it known" in v. 3aβ. The summary follows immediately in v. 3b with YHWH's statement that "I acted immediately and it happened." Such a statement functions as a means to confirm YHWH's prior assertions. The reason for YHWH's announcement, so that the people would not attribute current events to idols, then follows in vv. 4-5. Verse 4 states three qualifications for YHWH's declaration: YHWH knows that the people are stubborn in v. 4a, that the sinews of their necks are like iron in v. 4bα, and that their foreheads are bronze in v. 4bβ. YHWH's declaration together with the reasons for the declaration then appears in v. 5. The declaration itself appears in v. 5a in two parts; first is the statement that "I declared it then" in v. 5aα and then the statement, "I made it known before it happened" in v. 5aβ. The reasons in v. 5b also include two parts: "lest you say my idol did these things" in v. 5bα and "my carved and molten images commanded them" in v. 5bβ.

The second subunit in 48:6-8 presents Israel's obligations to acknowledge YHWH, with qualifications. This subunit includes three components in vv. 6, 7, and 8. The first component in v. 6 states Israel's obligation to acknowledge YHWH. It begins with a statement of Israel's obligation in v. 6a that contains the statement "you have heard" in v. 6aα, followed by the rhetorical question "will you not declare it?" in v. 6aβ, which functions as an assertion that you must declare it. Verse 6b then follows with statements of what Israel must declare, including that "YHWH made new things known in the past" in v. 6bα and that "(YHWH made known) the hidden things that you did not know" in v. 6bβ. The second component in v. 7 then states reasons for the obligation, i.e., now YHWH's past declarations are coming to pass. This assertion is basically stated in v. 7a as a twofold statement, including assertions that "now they come to pass" in v. 7aα and that "you did not hear of them before today" in v. 7aβ. Verse 7b then follows with the assertion that "you cannot claim that you knew about them," to underscore the point that YHWH had declared them long ago. YHWH's qualification that the people are treacherous and rebellious then follows as the third component in v. 8. It begins with a threefold statement in v. 8a that the people did not know, including the assertions that "you did not hear" in v. 8aα$^{1-3}$, that "you did not know" in v. 8aα$^{4-6}$, and that "your ears were not opened before today" in v. 8aβ. Of course, each of these statements presupposes the commission of Isaiah ben Amoz as a prophet in 6:9-10. The twofold statement of YHWH's qualification follows in v. 8b, including assertions that YHWH knows that the people are treacherous in v. 8bα and that they are rebellious in v. 8bβ. Such a statement subtly addresses the questions of theodicy posed to Isaiah's commission by positing that YHWH knew that the people were culpable from the beginning.

The third subunit in 48:9-11 defines the purpose for Israel's exile as an opportunity for YHWH to test and refine the people for the sake of YHWH's name (cf. 1:20-26). Again, the subunit comprises three basic parts in vv. 9, 10, and 11. The first component in v. 9 defends YHWH's reputation by claiming that YHWH shows restraint in punishing Israel for the sake of the divine name (i.e., reputation). The statement is twofold in that YHWH states that YHWH is patient for the sake of the divine name in v. 9a and that YHWH holds back on punishing Israel for the sake of YHWH's reputation in v. 9b. The second component in v. 10 presents YHWH's twofold contention that YHWH was refining the people in v. 10a and testing them in v. 10b. Finally, the third component in v. 11 presents YHWH's defense that YHWH was acting to safeguard the divine reputation. The basic statement of this assertion, i.e., that "I act for my own sake," appears in v. 11aα. The qualification for this assertion then follows in v. 11aβ-b in two parts, including the claim that there will be no profanation of the divine name in v. 11aβ and that YHWH's glory will not go to another in v. 11b. Altogether, this subunit justifies the Babylonian exile as a case of self-defense.

Isaiah 48:12-19 presents YHWH's summation speech, in which YHWH asks the audience to accept the claims that YHWH has been making throughout this unit, as the second major element of 48:1-19. Like its counterpart in 48:1-11, 48:12-19 begins with a call to attention in v. 12a, although the present instance is a much shorter form. It begins with the masculine singular imperative verb, *šĕmaʿ ʾēlay,* "listen to me," addressed to Jacob in v. 12aα. The use of the singular form of the verb is justified by the personification of Israel as Jacob. The verb likewise governs the second element in the call to attention in v. 12aβ, in which "Israel my called one," serves as the addressee. Here again, the use of Israel would refer to Jacob personified with his alternative name.

The summation of YHWH's claims then follows in 48:12b-19. The unit falls into two components, YHWH's claims to be the founder of creation in vv. 12b-14a and YHWH's claim to employ Cyrus, the king of Persia, to act on YHWH's behalf in vv. 14b-19.

The presentation of YHWH's claims to be the founder of creation in 48:12b-14a comprises three 1st-person assertions spoken by YHWH. The first in v. 12b presents YHWH's claim to be the first and the last. It includes three elements: the claim that "I am the one" in v. 12bα$^{1-2}$, "I am the first" in v. 12bα$^{3-6}$, and "I am the last" in v. 12bβ. The second in v. 13a presents YHWH's claims to be the founder of earth and the heavens, including the earth in v. 13aα and the heavens in v. 13aβ. The third in vv. 13b-14a is more complex. It presents YHWH's call to heaven and earth to confirm YHWH's role as creator. It begins in v. 13b with YHWH's introduction to the address, in which YHWH states "I call to them" in v. 13bα and commands that they stand together to testify in v. 13bβ. YHWH then addresses heaven and earth directly in v. 14a. In the first instance, YHWH presents a call to attention that employs masculine plural imperative verbs in v. 14aα calling upon all of them (heaven and earth) to gather (*hiqqābĕṣû*) in v. 14aα$^{1-2}$ and to listen (*šămāʿû*) in v. 14aα^3. The address to heaven and earth then follows in v. 14aβ with the rhetorical question "who among you has foretold these things?" — i.e., heaven and earth were incapable of doing so, and so YHWH their creator must be the only possible source for such foreknowledge.

Isaiah 48:14b-19 presents YHWH's announcement that Cyrus will act on YHWH's behalf. This is a radical claim, as it entails that a foreign monarch will act to carry out the divine will. It includes four major components in vv. 14b, 15, 16, and 17-19 which lay out the various elements of this assertion. The first in v. 14b presents YHWH's announcement that Cyrus will act on YHWH's behalf. This segment includes the statement "YHWH loves him, he will do (YHWH's) will in Babylon" in v. 14bα and the assertion that he will act with YHWH's strength, literally, "his arm," against the Chaldeans in v. 14bβ. The second component in v. 15 presents YHWH's assertions that YHWH brought him and that he will succeed. It includes three elements, YHWH's assertions that "I spoke to him" in v. 15aα, that "I called him" in v. 15aβ, and the twofold assertion in v. 15b that "I brought him" in v. 15bα and that "he will succeed in his path" in v. 15bβ. The third component in v. 16 constitutes YHWH's presentation of Cyrus. It begins with a call to attention in v. 16aα$^{1-4}$, which includes the masculine plural imperatives *qirbû 'ēlay*, "draw near to me," in v. 16aα$^{1-2}$ and *šim'û-zō't*, "hear this," in v. 16aα$^{3-4}$. Verse 16aβ-γ then follows with YHWH's two-part announcement reminding the audience that YHWH had announced this before, including the statements that "I did not speak in secret" in v. 16aβ and that "I was there (at the beginning)" in v. 16aγ. Verse 16b then concludes this component with Cyrus's statement that YHWH sent him with YHWH's spirit.

The fourth component in 48:17-19 is much more complex. It presents the concluding oracle of the subunit, which functions as an exhortation to heed YHWH. It begins with the prophetic messenger formula in v. 17a, which certifies that the following oracle comes from YHWH. The oracle itself appears in vv. 17b-19 as an oracle of salvation which functions as an exhortation to heed YHWH. The oracle begins with YHWH's self-identification in v. 17b, including three parts. The first is YHWH's self-identification proper in v. 17bα$^{1-3}$, the second is the first qualification which maintains that YHWH will guide you (the audience) to profit in v. 17bα$^{4-5}$, and the third is the second qualification which maintains that YHWH's purpose is to guide you (the audience) on your path in v. 17bβ. The self-identification then functions as an introduction to the following exhortation to heed YHWH's commands in vv. 18-19. Verse 18a employs the conditional particle *lû'*, "if," to state the condition to be fulfilled, that the people heed YHWH's commands. Verses 18b-19 then state the results of doing so. Verse 18b asserts that peace and righteousness will result from following YHWH's commands, including peace like a river in v. 18bα and righteousness like the waves of the sea in v. 18bβ. Both serve as natural metaphors for order, serenity, and beauty in the world. Verse 19 then asserts that the people will enjoy numerous offspring as a result of heeding YHWH's commands. Verse 19a maintains that their offspring will be like sand in v. 19aα and grain in v. 19aβ. Verse 19b then concludes the sequence with the claim that the people's name will not be cut off in v. 19bα and that their name will not be destroyed in v. 19bβ.

Finally, 48:20-22 closes the entirety of 44:24–48:22 with a concluding hymnic command to flee Babylon, coupled with a warning. The hymnic command, identified by its imperative forms, appears in vv. 20-21. The warning then follows in v. 22.

The hymnic command in 48:20-21 comprises a series of six commands, each formulated with a masculine plural imperative, that orders Israel to depart from Babylon as YHWH has now redeemed Jacob from Babylonian exile. The first calls on the people to depart from Babylon in v. 20aα$^{1-2}$; the second calls on the people to flee from the Chaldeans in v. 20aα$^{3-4}$; the third commands the people to declare with a joyous voice in v. 20aα$^{5-7}$; the fourth commands the people to announce this in v. 20aα$^{8-9}$; the fifth commands the people to bring it out to the ends of the earth in v. 20aβ; and the sixth and final imperative then tells them to say that YHWH has redeemed Jacob in vv. 20b-21. This segment begins with the command to "say" in v. 20bα, followed by the content of the announcement that the people are to make, a hymn of praise for YHWH's deliverance of Israel, in vv. 20bβ-21. The hymn begins with the announcement that YHWH has redeemed the servant Jacob in v. 20bβ. The means of deliverance, YHWH's provision of water in the wilderness, then follows in v. 21. This portion of the hymn begins with the announcement that the people did not thirst in v. 21aα. Verse 21aβ-b then follows with a threefold specification of YHWH's provision of water, including the statement that the water flowed for them in v. 21aβ, that the rock split in v. 21bα, and that the water gushed out in v. 21bβ.

The concluding warning that there is no peace for the wicked in 48:22 qualifies the preceding hymn by asserting that those who are wicked will indeed suffer. It thereby supports the exhortation to heed YHWH's commands by promising suffering for those who do not.

Genre

The overarching genre of 44:24–48:22 is a combination of the DISPUTATION and the TRIAL GENRES. The disputation is well represented in Deutero-Isaiah as the basic argumentative genre that presents the succession of arguments throughout chs. 40–55. Following upon earlier arguments to contend that YHWH is the master of creation in 40:12-31, that YHWH is the master of human events in 41:1–42:13, and that YHWH is the redeemer of Israel in 42:14–44:23, 44:24–48:22 employs the DISPUTATION as a means to argue that YHWH will use Cyrus, a foreign monarch, to redeem Israel, restore Jerusalem, and rebuild the temple.

The DISPUTATION presumes an opponent who holds an opposing viewpoint, and in this case the opponents are those nations that put their trust in idols and foreign gods. Specific elements identified as disputations include 44:24-28; 45:9-13, 18-25; 46:5-11; 48:1-11, 12-15 (e.g., Köhler), but the interrelationships of these elements within the larger text indicate that they characterize 44:24–48:22 as a whole. The present text is designed to argue that YHWH, and not the idols of the nations, is the true G-d. A major element in this argumentative strategy is to demonstrate that YHWH exercises power in the world as master of creation, master of human events, and redeemer of Israel and that the foreign gods or idols that the nations worship are incapable of such action. A complementary element in the strategy is the argument that YHWH foretold all of the events that are currently unfolding, e.g., Israel's punishment and exile to a foreign land, the collapse of Israel's enemies, the emergence of a righteous monarch, and the return of Israel to a restored Jerusalem as the holy center of YHWH's creation. A third element is the claim that YHWH has brought Cyrus, the king of Persia, to accomplish YHWH's purposes. Within the full form of the book of Isaiah and even within the 6th-century edition of the book, such an argument presumes the announcements of these events in the first portion of the book in chs. 1–39. Altogether, such arguments presume the statements in 40:8 that YHWH's word will stand forever and in 55:11 that YHWH's word performs YHWH's purpose. Consequently, the intertextual elements of the book, both within chs. 40–55 and in relation to the book as a whole, function within the framework of the

DISPUTATION to argue that YHWH is the true G-d of creation and the human world. In the end, 44:24–48:22 employs this point as part of a larger argument to convince the exiled people to leave Babylon, to return to Jerusalem, and to reestablish the temple for the worship of YHWH.

Isaiah 46:1-13 is an example of the DISPUTATION genre that makes such claims. Past scholars viewed the passage as a combination of elements, one of which is a disputation (cf. Melugin, *Formation,* 131-35). But indeed, the entire unit is a disputation, which includes the premise to be disputed in 46:1-2, that the foreign gods are true gods who should be honored by carrying them in the streets, whereas YHWH's counterargumentation in 46:3-13 contends that YHWH is the true G-d who is able to act to bring deliverance to the people of Zion and Israel. In order to make such a claim, 46:1-13 employs variations of the CALL TO ATTENTION in vv. 3 and 12 to catch the audience's attention and it concludes with an ANNOUNCEMENT OF SALVATION in vv. 12-13, viz., that YHWH brings righteousness, deliverance, and glory to Zion and Israel.

The TRIAL GENRES also play a key role in 44:24–48:22 insofar as the DISPUTATION appears within the context of a forensic or trial framework. The text is formulated as though it were a legal proceeding in which YHWH must summon the opponents before the court and present arguments to demonstrate the truth of YHWH's claims. The organization of the unit points to the influence of the TRIAL GENRES insofar as 44:24–45:8 presents YHWH's announcement of the plan to use Cyrus for the restoration of Israel, and 45:9–48:19 presents the trial scene in which YHWH presents preliminary arguments in 45:9-25 that YHWH is indeed G-d; evidence that YHWH indeed exercises the power of a G-d in relation to the weak Babylonian gods in 46:1-13 and YHWH's power to bring down Babylon in 47:1-15; and finally a summation of YHWH's arguments in 48:1-19 that YHWH's ability to control events cannot be refuted. The use of the TRIAL GENRES does not demonstrate a legal setting for the text; indeed, the TRIAL GENRE functions as a rhetorical device in biblical literature to aid in convincing an audience of the truth of the claims argued within the text. Job, an example of wisdom literature, makes extensive use of the TRIAL GENRES as part of its attempt to examine YHWH's true character.

The concluding HYMNS OF PRAISE in 45:8 and 48:20-22 also play a key role in this text insofar as they point to its liturgical character. Isaiah 44:24–48:22 is fundamentally a liturgical text that was meant to be performed in public before an audience of Israelites or Judeans who are well aware of the Babylonian exile. Indeed, the text is designed to convince them that YHWH is the true G-d and that YHWH employs Cyrus as YHWH's anointed redeemer to accomplish the return of Jews to Jerusalem and the land of Israel.

Other generic elements also figure prominently in 44:24–48:22. The Prophetic MESSENGER SPEECH with its characteristic MESSENGER FORMULA, *kōh 'āmar yhwh,* "thus says YHWH," and its variations appears in 45:1-7, 14-17, and 18-25 as a means to identify YHWH as the speaker in the text and to validate YHWH's claims to be the true G-d who employs a foreign king to redeem Israel and to restore Jerusalem and the temple. The ROYAL COMMISSION in 45:2-7 provides the means by which YHWH identifies Cyrus as YHWH's agent for the redemption of Israel, the restoration of Jerusalem, and the recognition of YHWH as the true G-d. The WOE SPEECHES in 45:9-10 provide a means to delegitimize those who would challenge YHWH's claims to divine status so that they could continue to adhere to idols.

The RHETORICAL QUESTION plays an important role in 45:9, 11b, 21b, and 46:5 to appeal to the audience so that they might better accept YHWH's claims. The RHETORICAL QUESTION appears throughout the unit as well. A rhetorical question is one with an obvious answer. The purpose of such a question is not to find the answer to a question whose answer is not known. Rather, it is a rhetorical device that employs the form of a question to draw in the interest and attention of the audience which is expected to recognize the answer to the question immediately. By employing the obvious answer, the rhetorical question then functions as an assertion, with which the audience will agree because it knows the answer. In this manner, the rhetorical question functions as means to win the audience over to the position of the speaker.

The ANNOUNCEMENT OF SALVATION in 46:12-13 functions as a means to support YHWH's claims to be the true G-d in 46:1-13, that YHWH — and not the idols — is the only one who is able to act to bring deliverance and glory to Zion and to Israel.

Finally, the OATH in 45:23 employs a modified form of the OATH FORMULA to present YHWH's oath to vindicate, praise, and ultimately to restore Israel from Babylonian exile.

Isaiah 47:1-15 functions within the larger context of the disputation in 45:9-48:19 concerning YHWH's use of Cyrus as messiah and temple-builder. Like 46:1-13, it presents evidence concerning YHWH's claims to power. But whereas 46:1-13 is an announcement concerning YHWH's power directed to Israel/Jacob, 47:1-15 is directed to Babylon, metaphorically portrayed as a royal lady who has fallen upon hard times and must now serve as a slave girl.

Isaiah 47:1-15 represents a mixed genre of TAUNT and PROPHETIC ANNOUNCEMENT OF JUDGMENT. The TAUNT is a statement or composition that is designed to denigrate its subject. It appears at the beginning and end of the passage in 47:1-5 and 47:12-15, where it mocks Babylon for her humiliation and reduced circumstances. Isaiah 47:1-5 proceeds by issuing commands to the once great lady Babylon that she should now get down and sit in the dirt where she will take up a hand mill and grind meal, a task whose tedious nature normally ensured that it is assigned to the lowest slave girls of the palace. In addition to her new work assignment — particularly remarkable for a lady who likely had never done any menial work before in her life — she is commanded to strip off her fine garments, bare her thighs, and ford rivers rather than be carried across as a lady would have expected. The metaphor reaches a crescendo by stating that her nakedness or shame will be revealed, which in turn suggests not simply a pornographic exposure of the once secure woman, but the possibility that she would suffer rape as part of her overall experience of humiliation and deposition. Isaiah 47:1-5 makes sure to remind her that she was once a soft and pampered woman who would never have experienced such degradation. And so the TAUNT makes sure to hold her up as a mocking example of denigration of a once great lady who served as mistress of the nations, but is now reduced to slave status.

The PROPHETIC ANNOUNCEMENT OF JUDGMENT appears in 47:6-11, in which YHWH both announces judgment against Lady Babylon and explains the reasons for her downfall. The passage begins with YHWH's announcement of the BASIS FOR JUDGMENT in 47:6-7, in which YHWH explains that YHWH had judged Israel/Judah and placed them under the authority of Babylon, but that Babylon had abused her role as YHWH's agent of punishment, refusing to show any mercy to YHWH's people. The passage makes sure to present Babylon's own thoughts, i.e., that she would always enjoy her position of authority as mistress of the nations and that no one would ever call her to account. The PROPHETIC ANNOUNCEMENT OF JUDGMENT then appears in 47:8-11. It begins with an example of the CALL TO ATTENTION FORMULA in 47:8, which typically opens a public address and attempts to call attention to the following statements. Normally, the CALL TO ATTENTION includes 1) an invitation to listen, here expressed by the phrase "and now hear this," 2) mention of the addressees, here metaphorically expressed as "the pampered one," together with the following portrayal of Babylon as a spoiled lady who thinks that no one could possibly challenge or afflict her, and 3) an indication of what is to be heard, here expressed through the metaphorical portrayal of the woman as one who never thought she would know widowhood or childlessness, and yet that is precisely what she will now experience. The ANNOUNCEMENT OF JUDGMENT per se appears in 47:9-11, which announces that "these two things will come upon you," the aforementioned widowhood and childlessness that would leave her without family or support in the world as she grows older, assuming of course that she will survive. The announcement pauses to portray the uselessness of Babylon's previous sources for security, her reliance on spells and enchantments associated with the Babylonian gods, priests, diviners, etc., that actually have no power before YHWH. The announcement ends by reiterating that "evil," "disaster," and "destruction" are coming upon her and she has no power to thwart them.

The passage then returns to the TAUNT in 47:12-15; having announced judgment against Babylon and portrayed the powerlessness of her spells, these verses then taunt her by calling upon her to stand by spells and enchantments, suggesting that maybe she can profit from their use as she has throughout her lifetime. But the passage makes it clear that her sorcerers and soothsayers are nothing more than straw before a fire. They will be consumed and there will be no one to save Babylon when her need is the greatest.

The summation speeches in 48:1-19, including both 48:1-11 and 48:12-19, continue the use of the DISPUTATION genre within the context of the TRIAL SPEECHES. Once again, the issue of the dispute is YHWH's claim to be recognized as the true G-d of all creation instead of the foreign gods that the people of Israel would encounter in Babylonian exile. The twist here is that the passage attempts to explain Israel's suffering by conquest and exile as a righteous act of YHWH brought on by allegations that Israel had abandoned YHWH and refused to observe YHWH's expectations. Such an argumentative strategy seeks to overcome the underlying charge that YHWH was somehow negligent or powerless in refusing or failing to defend Israel against a foreign enemy. The allegation essentially blames the victim for its own suffering rather than assigning responsibility to the deity, who was charged with securing Israel from harm. Like earlier examples of the DISPUTATION in 44:24–48:12, the present text argues that YHWH must be recognized as the true G-d because YHWH is the creator of heaven and earth and because YHWH foretold the events that were transpiring in the late 6th century B.C.E., namely the rise of Cyrus to power, the downfall of the Babylonian Empire, and the opportunity for exiled Israelites to return to their homeland. YHWH's predictions will be found in the first part of the book of Isaiah in chs. 1–33, which speaks about impending invasion by a foreign power, the rise of a righteous monarch, and the return of the scattered people to Jerusalem.

Both of the DISPUTATION SPEECHES in vv. 1-11 and 12-19 begin with the CALL TO ATTENTION FORMULA, respectively in vv. 1-2 and v. 12a, to direct the audience's attention to the following argumentation in the DISPUTATION SPEECHES. Isaiah 48:1-2 presents a modified example of the CALL TO ATTENTION formula which qualifies the address to the house of Jacob by defining Jacob in relation to both Israel and Judah, by pointing to its relationship with YHWH, and by asserting that the people had somehow violated this relationship. Isaiah 48:12a hints at such a relationship by identifying Israel as called by YHWH. Additional examples of the CALL TO ATTENTION appear in 48:14aα and 48:16aα$^{1-4}$, which function as part of YHWH's disputation speech in vv. 12b-19 concerning the selection of Cyrus as YHWH's agent. In the first instance, the CALL TO ATTENTION in 48:14aα invokes heaven and earth to recognize YHWH as the one who predicted the events that they are now witnessing. The CALL TO ATTENTION in 48:16aα$^{1-4}$ introduces YHWH's claims in v. 16 to have predicted the rise of Cyrus.

YHWH's disputation speeches in 48:12-19 also make use of other devices. The RHETORICAL QUESTION in 48:14aβ both denies that anyone in the audience has foretold these events and asserts that YHWH is the only one who did so. The concluding oracle in 48:17-19 employs a number of generic elements. First is the Prophetic MESSENGER FORMULA in v. 17a, which certifies the following oracle as an oracle by YHWH. Second is the overall character of the oracle as an EXHORTATION which is designed to call upon YHWH's audience to accept YHWH's claims and to observe YHWH's commands. Within the oracle, YHWH employs an example of the SELF-IDENTIFICATION formula in v. 17b to assert YHWH's role as the G-d of Israel.

The concluding hymn in 48:20-22 makes use of an example of a HYMN OF PRAISE in 48:20bβ-21. The HYMN announces that YHWH has redeemed YHWH's servant Jacob, and it identifies the means of deliverance as the provision of water in the wilderness. Such an announcement draws upon the wilderness traditions concerning YHWH's provision of water in the wilderness (Exodus 17; Numbers 20) to point to the journey that Israel will undertake to return to the land of Israel from Babylonian captivity as an analogy to the ancient tradition of returning to the land of Israel from Egyptian captivity.

The WARNING in 48:22 functions as a means to reinforce the argumentative agenda of 44:24–48:22, that those who do not accept and act on the claims which YHWH puts forward in this text will never know the peace that is promised to those who do so.

Setting

Isaiah 44:24–48:22 functions as a component of the final form of the book of Isaiah, which dates to the times of Nehemiah and Ezra in the mid- to late 5th century B.C.E. As noted above, 44:24–48:22 functions as one element among a larger chain of arguments that maintains that YHWH is the master of creation (40:12-31), master of human events (41:1–42:13), and redeemer of Israel (42:14–44:23), and it anticipates the next argument in the chain in chs. 49–54, that YHWH is restoring Jerusalem. As a component of Deutero-Isaiah, however, the compositional setting of this text must date to the time of the rise of King Cyrus of Persia, in the latter portion of the 6th century, i.e., ca. 545-538, when Cyrus became king of Babylon and decreed that exiled Jews could return to Jerusalem to rebuild the Jerusalem temple. The explicit mentions of Cyrus by name in 44:28 and 45:1 make it clear that this text cannot predate Cyrus, although the effort to convince Jews to leave Babylon in order to return to Jerusalem could continue to function for years afterward. Nevertheless, the reference to Cyrus alone — and not to Cambyses, Darius, or other Persian monarchs — suggests that the text presumes that Cyrus is still alive. Some have noted the metaphorical reference to Cyrus in 46:11 as *'ayiṭ,* "a bird of prey," particularly since Cyrus employed the image of the eagle to represent himself. But the use of *'ayiṭ* is appropriate, particularly since Cyrus was able to defeat Babylonian armies in the field before negotiating his peaceful entrance into the city of Babylon. Given his military strength and his ability to use it, the imagery of a bird of prey that swoops down and captures its enemies is entirely fitting and helps to build the case that YHWH's use of Cyrus is a demonstration of YHWH's power. So the historical setting for the composition of this text may be placed in the years 545-530 B.C.E.

Although 44:24–48:22 employs the DISPUTATION and TRIAL GENRES, the social setting of the text appears to be neither wisdom nor the Israelite court system. DISPUTATIONS are widely employed in wisdom literature (e.g., Job), but they make frequent appearances in prophetic literature as well, where they function as a means to convince an audience of a point in question. It is also unlikely that this text ever functioned within a courtroom setting, as the TRIAL GENRES are frequently employed as rhetorical devices within the prophetic literature as a means to impress upon the audience the importance of the issue at hand as well as to aid in convincing the audience of the truth of the claims made therein. The social setting therefore presumes a context in which Israelites must be convinced that YHWH is the true G-d. Such a context can presume exiled Judeans who witness Cyrus's rise to power as the new king of Babylon in 539 B.C.E. or Judeans who have returned to the land of Israel to rebuild the temple as a result of Cyrus's rise.

Indeed, the HYMNS OF PRAISE in 45:8 and 48:20-21 point to a liturgical setting as the social setting of this text. The exact location, either in Babylonian exile or at the site of the Jerusalem temple, must remain in doubt. Clearly, ch. 46 demonstrates that the text presupposes knowledge of the Babylonian Akitu or New Year festival in which Cyrus was named as king of Babylon, but it is not certain whether this is presented as a current or as a retrospective event.

Interpreters have little evidence for liturgical settings in Babylonia in which Jews would have been able to present a liturgy that made such claims for either YHWH or Cyrus. It is possible, however, that such a liturgy could have been presented at the site of the ruined Jerusalem temple when the first Jews returned to the city under the leadership of Sheshbazzar in 538 (Ezra 1, esp. vv. 8, 11). In such an instance, the presentation of 44:24–48:21 would have served as a means to legitimize those Jews who returned to Jerusalem from Babylonian exile and their efforts to reestablish the temple.

The portrayal of the downfall and humiliation of Lady Babylon in 47:1-15 offers an especially interesting example for reflection upon setting. Overall, it portrays her as a powerful, spoiled, and pampered lady who suffers the humiliation of reduction to slave status and the realization that the spells, enchantments, astrologers, and soothsayers who had once served as the bases for her standing in the world had proved to be entirely useless to her now that she is debased. This imagery is all the more remarkable when we recognize that Babylon was not sacked or humiliated by Cyrus and his army when they took control of the city in 539. Indeed, Cyrus had defeated the Babylonian army in the field, in part by virtue of the defection of the Babylonian general Gobryas, and his relationship with Gobryas then played an important role in Cyrus's negotiations with the priests of Marduk to accept Cyrus as the next Babylonian king. The priests' dissatisfaction with the previous Babylonian monarch, Nabonidus, enabled Cyrus to negotiate with them a peaceful submission of the city. Consequently, Babylon opened its gates to Cyrus, paraded him through the city as part of the Akitu festival, and named him as Marduk's chosen monarch. Babylon therefore did not suffer the humiliations described in this text; rather, Babylon continued to serve as the administrative capital for Persia's western empire until the early 5th century B.C.E. The humiliations portrayed here appear to represent the experiences of Israelite or Judean exiles, who were forcibly removed from their homeland by the Babylonians following their initial invasion of Judah in 598-597, the second invasion which resulted in the destruction of Jerusalem and the temple in 588-586, and perhaps a third invasion following the assassination of their Judean governor, Gedaliah ben Ahikam ben Shaphan, in 582. Therefore, the humiliation of Babylon as portrayed in this chapter appears to be anticipatory of what might happen when Cyrus would seize the city. Judean women would have experienced the humiliation of becoming slave girls, exposing themselves to cross rivers on the journey to Babylon, as well as exposure and rape, and so the portrayal of Lady Babylon's humiliation would most likely reflect memories of such experiences by Judean women in exile. As it happens, Babylon would not actually experience hardship under Cyrus; the city was only sacked much later in 486.

The summary speeches in 48:1-19 resume the disputational trial language of 45:9–48:19. Such language is characteristic of a courtroom setting in which the parties to a dispute are attempting to convince the judge and surrounding audience that their respective positions are correct. But insofar as YHWH is a party — indeed, the principal party in this dispute — it would appear that the audience is the judge. In the end, the speech is designed to convince the audience to accept YHWH as the true G-d based upon YHWH's roles as creator of heaven and earth, redeemer of Israel, and the one who foretold these events from the beginning. It therefore crosses a line from courtroom to ritual gathering. We know little of the worship practices of exiled Israelites during the Babylonian exile. Some speculate with some basis that the institution of the synagogue finds its roots in the Babylonian exile. Just as the temple would have served as the final appeal court in an Israelite or Judean judicial setting, so it would have served as the setting for religious instruction. Although we know little of nascent synagogues or worship centers in Babylonian exile, it would seem that such centers would serve as the initial settings for the performance of this text. Once the exiles had returned to Jerusalem and rebuilt the temple, the temple would then join any nascent synagogues as the setting for 45:9–48:19 and indeed Second Isaiah and the book of Isaiah as a whole.

Isaiah 48:1-19 functions as a component of a much larger literary work, and so the literary setting of 48:1-19 is clearly 45:9–48:19 and beyond that 44:24–48:22 and the book of Isaiah as a whole. But interpreters must recognize the intertextual nature of YHWH's claims to have predicted present events long in the past. Such claims point to the larger context of the book of Isaiah as a whole for claims that YHWH had predicted the judgment and exile of Israel, the downfall of Babylon, the emergence of a righteous king, and the return to Jerusalem and the land of Israel of the exiled Judean and Israelite population. Scenarios of judgment against Israel and Judah together with scenarios of restoration appear throughout the first part of Isaiah in ch. 1; 2–4; 5–12; and 28–32. Judgment against Babylon appears in chs. 13–14; 21 and perhaps 24–27. The oracles concerning a future monarch are problematic, however, insofar as 9:1-6 and 11:1-16 appear to presuppose a righteous Davidic monarch, whereas 44:24–48:22 presupposes Cyrus, the king of Persia, as YHWH's choice. Interpreters must note, however, that 9:6 presupposes a righteous monarch who will sit upon David's throne, but it does not specifically state that he must be a descendant of David. The references to a monarch who will arise from the stump or root of Jesse in 11:1, 10, nevertheless anticipate a Davidic figure. Isaiah 32 envisions a monarch, but does not identify him specifically as a Davidic figure. It would seem that Second Isaiah read the monarchic oracles in such a way that Cyrus could be seen as YHWH's agent, even if ultimately a Davidic monarch might emerge when all Israel returned to Jerusalem and the land of Israel from foreign exile.

Finally, the appearance of a HYMN OF PRAISE in 48:20-21 marks this subunit as the closing element of 44:24–48:22. Such an appearance presupposes the setting of the Jerusalem temple as well as any nascent synagogues or worship centers that may have been created during the Babylonian exile.

Interpretation

Isaiah 44:24–48:22 presents the account of YHWH's announcement that YHWH will use Cyrus for the restoration of Israel. This is a disputational text that is designed to persuade its audience of Judean exiles and returnees that YHWH is G-d of all creation and nations and that YHWH is therefore able to use a foreign monarch such as Cyrus to bring about the redemption of Israel/Judah from Babylonian exile so that they might return to Jerusalem to rebuild the Jerusalem temple.

The text begins in 44:24–45:8 with YHWH's announcement of plans to use Cyrus for the redemption of Israel and the restoration of Jerusalem and the temple. This text is initially addressed to Israel in 44:24-28 to convince the Israelite/Judean audience that YHWH is capable of such an act. It employs a prophetic messenger speech in which YHWH self-predicates or self-identifies as the creator of heaven and earth, who overturns both diviners and sages, supports servants and messengers, restores Jerusalem and Judah, controls chaos, and finally uses Cyrus to restore Jerusalem and the temple. Essentially, the text presupposes Cyrus's remarkable rise to power and ascension to the Babylonian throne, and argues that Cyrus's rise is an act of YHWH. Isaiah 45:1-7 presents YHWH's announcement of these claims to Cyrus, although it is unlikely that this text was ever presented to Cyrus; it is more likely that it continues to address its Israelite/Judean audience. Here, YHWH commissions Cyrus by claiming that Cyrus's victories are the result of YHWH's efforts to defeat his enemies. YHWH names Cyrus as YHWH's servant as a means to demonstrate that YHWH is indeed G-d of all the earth and there is no other G-d than YHWH. The purpose of YHWH's actions is so that all the world will recognize YHWH as G-d, particularly those among Israel/Judah whom the text is designed to convince that they should return to Jerusalem to rebuild the temple. The concluding hymn in 45:8 reinforces YHWH's claims to be the creator and therefore reinforces YHWH's claims to have brought Cyrus to bring about Israel's redemption and Jerusalem's restoration.

The trial scene that attempts to demonstrate the veracity of YHWH's use of Cyrus follows in 45:9–48:22. The first segment of this text appears in 45:9-25, which presents the preliminary arguments for YHWH's claims. The subunit begins with an attempt to fend off any challenges to YHWH by pointing to YHWH's role as creator, master of human events, and redeemer of Israel as argued respectively in 40:12-31; 41:1–42:13; and 42:14–44:23. The two woe speeches in 45:9-10 effectively argue that nothing or no one created has the capacity or right to challenge its creator: as the products of YHWH's creation, the text's Israelite/Judean audience has no right to deny YHWH's claims. The argument continues in a somewhat different form in 45:11-13, which employs a messenger speech to maintain that the audience has no right to challenge YHWH's signs concerning the future of the people, here identified as the work of YHWH's hands. By signs, the text appears to refer to earlier prophecies concerning the future of Israel that appear in the first portion of the book of Isaiah in chs. 1–33. It appears to presuppose texts that identify YHWH as the creator of the world and of Israel in Genesis, the Psalms, and perhaps elsewhere. Insofar as the text identifies Cyrus as YHWH's agent for restoration, it appears to presuppose Cyrus's decree that exiled Israelites/Judeans might return to Jerusalem to rebuild the temple (2 Chr 36:22-23; Ezra 1; cf. the Cyrus Cylinder, *ANET*, 315-16).

The argument continues with the assertion of YHWH's right to act in 45:14-25. This segment presents two messenger speeches, each of which contributes a new element to the argument. The first in 45:14-17 claims that the wealth of Egypt, Ethiopia, and the Sabeans will be presented to Israel. Such an argument presupposes Cyrus's perceived plans to invade Egypt following the conquest of Babylonia. Indeed, Cyrus's largess to Jerusalem and Judah appears to be designed to secure Judean support for an Egyptian invasion, insofar as Judah and surrounding territories would be the starting point and base of support and communications for any such invasion. Cyrus never succeeded even in launching such an invasion. That would ultimately be left to his son and successor Cambyses (530-525 B.C.E.) and his son-in-law, Darius (525-486). Nevertheless, expectations would have been high for a Persian invasion of Egypt in 539 when Cyrus ascended the Babylonian throne, and those expectations appear to inform the present text. Such an appeal would be particularly effective to a Judean audience, who would read such an action in relation to the exodus narratives. Once again, YHWH would bring down an Egyptian pharaoh as part of the larger scenario of Israel's redemption from bondage and exile.

Isaiah 45:18-25 then follows with repeated arguments concerning YHWH's power and efficacy. As creator, YHWH does not bring chaos, but order in the world. YHWH acts to bring order and security to Israel, and that is what is happening now. Whereas the nations pray to idols made of wood, stone, and metal that remain silent and have no power, YHWH had already announced what is about to happen in prior times, specifically, in the earlier portions of the book of Isaiah now found in chs. 1–33; 36–39. Consequently, all the world — and especially all Israel and Judah — must recognize YHWH as G-d of all creation and humankind who is about to redeem Israel from Babylonian exile, return them to the city of Jerusalem, and reestablish the Jerusalem temple as the holy center of creation. At that point, all the world will bow down to YHWH and swear to YHWH as G-d, and all Israel will be vindicated and praised.

Isaiah 46–47 then presents evidence of YHWH's power. Isaiah 46:1-13 presents YHWH's arguments to the Israelite audience that YHWH should be recognized as the true G-d. Isaiah 47:1-15 presents YHWH's address to Babylon, metaphorically portrayed as a defeated and abandoned woman sitting in the dust, explaining to her that YHWH has brought punishment upon her for oppressing YHWH's people when they were placed under her charge.

The disputation speech in 46:1-13 presents arguments that YHWH must be recognized as the true G-d because YHWH is able to act in the world of creation and human events whereas the Babylonian gods, being mere idols built by craftsmen from gold and silver, have no capacity to act. Indeed, the initial portrayal of Bel, a title for Marduk, the city god of Babylon, and Nebo, Marduk's son who was in charge of wisdom, writing, and the tablets of destiny that determined rule in the Babylonian world, presents them as mere idols who must be carried through the streets. The scene presupposes the Babylonian Akitu or New Year festival celebrated in the spring, when images of all the Babylonian gods and the gods of nations subservient to Babylon were carried in procession to the Etemenanki, the central ziggurat or stepped pyramid temple of Marduk, so that Marduk could authorize the Babylonian king to rule for another year. Following Cyrus's peaceful conquest of the city in 539 B.C.E., following his defeat of the Babylonian army in the field and the dissatisfaction of the priests of Marduk with Nabonidus, the prior Babylonian king, Cyrus was named as the new king of Babylon at the Babylonian Akitu festival. He was paraded through the city, brought to the top of the Etemenanki, slapped in the face by a female priest to remind him that he served Marduk, and then given the tablets of destiny to rule Babylon on Marduk's behalf for the coming year.

But 46:1-2 is not intended simply as a portrayal of the Akitu procession. As part of the larger disputation pattern in 46:1-13, it articulates the premise to be challenged in the disputation, that Bel/Marduk and Nebo are the true gods of Babylon and indeed of creation as a whole. The portrayal of the gods bowing and bending as they are carried through the streets of the city is intended as a caricature to show that they are nothing more than heavy burdens, built from wood, gold, and silver, that can do nothing in the world other than wear out the animals and men who were carrying them through the city's streets. Isaiah 46:1-2 makes points of saying that these images are burdensome to the beasts and animals that carry them; that they bend and bow together with the animals on whose backs they are placed; that they are unable to deliver anyone, particularly the animals and the people who must carry them; and finally, they are portrayed as walking into captivity. Bel and Nebo were the chief gods of Babylon, but now they are subservient to Cyrus, the king of Persia, who is now to be named king of Babylon as well.

YHWH's counterargument appears in 46:3-13 in five parts, each of which begins with a masculine plural address form that directs YHWH's words to the Israelite/Judean audience that must be convinced that YHWH — and not Bel and Nebo — is the true G-d of creation and Israel/Judah.

The first segment of YHWH's argument in 46:3-4 begins with a call to attention formula addressed to the house of Jacob and the remnant of the house of Israel, which suggests that the Judeans, whether in Babylonia or in the land of Israel, would constitute the primary audience of this text. YHWH stresses that they were carried or borne from the belly and the womb in a deliberate contrast with Bel and Nebo in vv. 1-2. But YHWH's address stresses that YHWH is the one (lit., "I am he" in v. 4) who has carried or sustained them from birth and who will carry, sustain, and deliver them through old age.

The second segment of YHWH's speech in 46:5-7 poses rhetorical questions to the audience: "to whom will you compare me and we will be alike?" and "to whom will you liken me that we will be the same?" The obvious answer to the questions is no one: there is no G-d like YHWH. The balance of this segment then focuses on the inability of the Babylonian gods to act. They are made with gold and silver. A craftsman must be paid to build their images to which the people then bow down. They have to be carried about on the shoulder, much as they were in vv. 1-2, and when they are set down, they remain stationary and do not move. When someone cries out to them for help, there is no answer because, indeed, these gods are incapable of delivering anyone.

The third segment of YHWH's speech in 46:8 calls for the audience to remember these arguments and to be strong. When it calls upon the audience to consider sins, it calls upon them to remember past sins for which they were punished and present sins, such as believing in the Babylonian gods, that must be avoided.

The fourth segment of YHWH's speech in 46:9-11 calls upon the audience to remember the former things from the past. In the context of the book of Isaiah, this would refer to YHWH's actions with regard to Jerusalem, Judah, Israel, Assyria, and the other nations as articulated in the first portion of the book of Isaiah. The argument proceeds with an initial statement by YHWH: "I am G-d and there is no other. I am G-d and there is none like me." YHWH's attributes then follow, emphasizing especially YHWH's ability to foretell what will happen, YHWH's ability to see to it that YHWH's will is done, YHWH's ability to call a bird of prey (i.e., Cyrus) from the east to carry out YHWH's will. In each case, the argument focuses on an attribute that demonstrates that YHWH is G-d. The first part of Isaiah spoke about YHWH's punishment of Israel and Judah (chs. 1; 2–4; 5–9), but it also spoke about YHWH's punishment of Assyria and Babylonia (chs. 10; 13–14), and it spoke about YHWH's intentions to raise up a righteous monarch who would deliver the people (chs. 9; 11; 32). All of this is coming true now. In all cases, YHWH is doing what YHWH said YHWH would do. The Babylonian gods were unable to do this. Consequently, YHWH is the true G-d.

Finally, the fifth segment of YHWH's speech in 46:12-13 is YHWH's culminating appeal to those who might doubt YHWH's power. It is addressed to those strong or stubborn of heart and those who are far from righteousness, i.e., those who might not trust in YHWH's power. YHWH's final statements are that YHWH is bringing righteousness and deliverance — they are not far off — and that YHWH is bringing deliverance to Zion and glory to Israel. Again, these acts become the decisive criteria that demonstrate that YHWH is truly G-d.

Isaiah 47:1-15 then shifts the argument to a direct address to Babylon, here personified as a spoiled and pampered great lady who now finds herself in the position of a slave girl who will do menial work, be stripped of her fine clothing, and be exposed before all. The rhetorical purpose of the text is to demonstrate that Babylon has no power before YHWH, and the text accomplishes this goal by announcing judgment against Babylon in vv. 6-11 in the midst of a taunt in vv. 1-5 and 12-15. Metaphor plays an important role as Babylon is portrayed as a great lady who once ruled the world and now finds herself a humiliated slave.

The passage begins with a taunt against Lady Babylon in 47:1-5 that commands her to get down off of her throne and sit in the dust so that she might take up a hand mill and grind meal as any slave girl in the palace would be expected to do. The metaphorical portrayal of Babylon as a great lady piles on the adjectives to heighten the contrast between her past greatness and her present lowly status. She is described in v. 1 as "the virgin daughter of Babylon" and as "the daughter of the Chaldeans" to highlight her lofty and protected status. The speaker taunts her by claiming that never again will she be called "the soft and dainty one." In contrast to her past high station, she must now take up a hand mill and grind meal, a tedious task that is assigned to the lowest of the slave girls, requiring them to sit on their knees and grind raw grain with stones into meal or flour that can be baked or cooked into cakes, bread, and other grain-based goods. The portrayal of Lady Babylon commanded to strip off her veil is pornographic to a degree and designed to highlight her humiliation and the danger in which she finds herself. These commands emphasize the abrupt loss of her status, stripping off her veil and train as she must bare herself to cross rivers, emulating the movements of exiles traveling across the Euphrates River to find a new home of servitude in Babylonia. The fact that the text mentions that her nakedness and shame are exposed emphasizes her vulnerability. Not only are her most intimate body parts exposed for public view, such exposure suggests the threat of rape that women — and men — so frequently experience in wartime and captivity. All of this forms YHWH's vengeance against Babylon, who will no longer be viewed as the Mistress of the Kingdoms, an allusion to Babylon's role as capital city of an empire that once ruled western Asia.

Isaiah 47:6-11 then turns to the judgment to be leveled against Babylon. The first portion of this passage in vv. 6-7 provides the reasons for Babylon's judgment, employing imagery that also raises some questions about YHWH. YHWH claims to have delivered the people of Israel/Judah up for judgment. The reason for this judgment is not stated; presumably the rest of the book, particularly chs. 1–33, provides this information. Nevertheless, YHWH's claim to pass judgment on Judah suggests an attempt to conceal the fact that YHWH was not able to defend the people against the Babylonians and chose to blame the victims instead for their own suffering. In any case, YHWH turns the people over to Babylon, and YHWH charges that Babylon refused to show them mercy. Whatever the grounds for the punishment of Judah might have been, now Babylon becomes culpable as well for failing to treat YHWH's people properly. The text explores Babylon's attitude by positing her inner thoughts, that she will always be the great lady or mistress of the nations, and that no one will call her to account.

The announcement of judgment in 47:8-11 again highlights Babylon's spoiled and pampered character and her thoughts that there is no one but her in the world, that there is no power that can oversee her actions. Her inner thoughts are revealed once again: she thinks that she will never know widowhood or childlessness, but this is precisely what the announcement of judgment prescribes for her. She will know both, and the taunt continues to a degree by highlighting the fact that none of her usual spells and enchantments will save her. The Babylonians were known for the use of such devices as well as soothsayers, astrologers, etc., who would track the astral bodies and thereby predict the attitudes and actions of the gods in order to plan the actions of human beings and protect them from divine capriciousness. Despite her past reliance on such means, however, evil, disaster, and destruction will nevertheless fall upon the once powerful Lady Babylon.

Isaiah 47:12-15 then returns to the taunt by baiting Babylon, calling upon her to stand by her spells and enchantments so that they can be proven to be useless. The text highlights her reliance on these devices from her youth, but now is the time to redouble her humiliation by demonstrating publically that everything she has thought, believed, and relied upon since her childhood is a lie. The text mocks her by suggesting that perhaps she will profit from the aid of her astrologers and stargazers who predict the future, but it also makes it clear that such figures are as useless and powerless as straw before fire. This flame is not benign — there will be no cooking or warming oneself before this flame. Instead, it consumes everything, driving away Babylon's astrologers and stargazers, and leaving her alone with no one rescue her.

Isaiah 48:1-19 provides the summary or closing arguments for the trial scene presented in 45:9–48:19. Isaiah 48:1-19 therefore sums up and reiterates the arguments that YHWH has put forward earlier in the passage. These arguments include the demand to be recognized as the true G-d of heaven and earth, the true G-d of Israel, the one who brings Cyrus as the new king to carry out YHWH's will, the one who will restore the people of Israel and Judah to Jerusalem and the land of Israel, and the one who foretold all of this long ago.

The summary arguments begin in 48:1-11 with a disputation speech addressed to the house of Jacob that asserts YHWH's control of events. It begins with a call to attention in vv. 1-2 that defines the house of Jacob as a combination of Israel and Judah and thereby envisions the return of all the exiles, those exiled by Assyria as well as by Babylonia. But in defining its audience, the call to attention includes statements concerning the people's sworn relationship to YHWH and indications that they have not been completely loyal to that commitment. The passage thereby lays the groundwork for the assertion that the Babylonian exile was not due to YHWH's lack of presence, power, fidelity, or righteousness. Rather, it was due to Israel's and Judah's failure to live up to their obligations to YHWH. Such an agenda serves the larger purpose to identify YHWH as the true G-d of creation and of Israel.

The disputation speech proper in 48:3-11 then focuses on YHWH's control of events. YHWH's assertion that YHWH foretold these events becomes a key element in the argument. Such claims can only be supported by reference to the first portion of the book of Isaiah in chs. 1–33, where the scenario of YHWH's judgment against Israel and Judah, the exile of the people, the downfall of Babylon, the rise of a future king, and the return of the exiled people to Jerusalem and the land of Israel constitutes the major concerns of the first part of the book. From the perspective of the second part of the book, now is the time that these events are to be realized. YHWH claims to know that the people would be stubborn, and therefore the people must know that YHWH — and not foreign gods — was responsible for the exile and the impending restoration. Now that the restoration is about to take place, YHWH claims that Israel is obligated to recognize YHWH's true role in these events. Any claims that the people did not hear, know, or have their ears opened cannot be sustained because these events were foretold in chs. 1–33; indeed, YHWH commanded Isaiah to make sure that the people could not see, hear, or know what was to happen to them in ch. 6, but ch. 32 announces that in the end, they will be able to see, hear, and know, and that time has now come. YHWH concludes the disputation by claiming that the purpose of the exile was to refine and test the people and thereby to preserve the divine reputation in keeping with 1:20-26, which uses similar imagery to state YHWH's purpose in bringing judgment.

The summation speech in 48:12-19 focuses on convincing the people to accept YHWH's claims and to act upon them. It begins with a brief call to attention in v. 12a addressed to Jacob, whom YHWH calls Israel. The body of the speech in vv. 12b-19 focuses on two major claims: YHWH's claim to be the founder of creation in vv. 12b-14a and YHWH's claim to the right to choose Cyrus, king of Persia, as YHWH's designated monarch to carry out Israel's return from exile. Indeed, the first claim serves as a basis for the second. Isaiah 48:12b-14a focuses on the major elements of YHWH's claim to be the founder of creation: YHWH is the first and the last, the founder of earth and heaven, and the one who calls upon heaven and earth to assemble before YHWH. None in heaven and earth can foretell these things. The claim to choose Cyrus is more controversial because Cyrus is neither Israelite nor a member of the house of David. Nevertheless, YHWH claims to love him, which employs classic language used for the Davidic monarch (cf. Psalm 2), to call him and make him succeed, and to have announced this before. As noted above, this claim is somewhat difficult in that earlier prophecies concerning a righteous monarch appear to anticipate a Davidic monarch, but none mentions Cyrus per se or even a foreign king. The concluding oracle then exhorts Israel to recognize and heed YHWH. Should they do so, they will enjoy peace, righteousness, and offspring in keeping with YHWH's initial promises in the book of Isaiah (e.g., 9:1-6) and the ancestral tradition at large.

The concluding hymn in 48:20-22 then closes 44:24–48:22 by calling upon Israel to depart from Babylonian exile and by citing a hymn of praise that celebrates YHWH's provision of water in the wilderness. Such a citation indicates that YHWH is acting once again to redeem Israel from foreign exile. This time, the oppressor is not Egypt — it is Babylon — but YHWH will lead Israel through the wilderness once again to return to the promised land. The concluding warning in v. 22 makes sure that these promises do not extend to the wicked, which of course provides further incentive to accept YHWH and to act upon YHWH's instructions.

Bibliography

R. Achenbach, "Das Kyros-Orakel in Jesaja 44,24–45,7 im Lichte altorientalischer Parallelen," *ZAR* 11 (2005) 155-94; S. E. Balentine, "Isaiah 45: God's 'I Am,' Israel's 'You Are,'" *HBT* 16 (1994) 103-20; N. C. Baumgart, "JHWH . . . erschafft Unheil: Jes 45,7 in seinem unmittelbaren Kontext," *BZ* 49 (2005) 202-36; J. Becker, "Zur Beurteilung von Jes 48,22 und 57,21," *BN* 119/120 (2003) 5-7; W. A. M. Beuken, "The Confession of G-d's Exclusivity by All Mankind," *Bijdr* 35 (1974) 335-56; C. C. Broyles, "The Citations of YHWH in Isaiah 44:26-28," in Broyles and Evans, eds., *Writing and Reading*, 399-421; C. Cohen, "The 'Widowed' City," *JANES* 5 (1973) 75-81; A. Condamin, "Les prédictions nouvelles du chapitre xlviii d'Isaïe," *RB* 7 (1910): 200-216; J. L. Crenshaw, "YHWH ṣᵉbā'ôt šᵉmô," *ZAW* 81 (1969) 156-75; M. Deroche, "Isaiah LXV 7 and the Creation of Chaos?" *VT* 42 (1992) 11-21; M. Dijkstra, "Zur Deutung von Jesaja 45 15ff," *ZAW* 89 (1977) 215-22; H. M. Dion, "Le genre littéraire sumérien de l' 'Hymne à soi-même' et quelques passages du Deutéro-Isaïe," *RB* 74 (1967) 215-34; M. Eng, "What's in a Name? Cyrus and the Dating of Deutero-Isaiah," in *Inspired Speech: Prophecy in the Ancient Near East* (*Fest.* H. B. Huffman; ed. J. Kaltner and L. Stulman; JSOTSup 378; Sheffield: Sheffield Academic, 2004) 216-24; J. P. Fokkelmann, "The Cyrus Oracle (Isaiah 44,24–45,7)," in van Ruiten and Vervenne, eds., *Studies,* 303-23; C. Franke, "The Function of the Satiric Lament over Babylon in Second Isaiah," *VT* 41 (1991) 408-18; idem, *Isaiah 46, 47, and 48;* idem, "Reversals of Fortune in the Ancient Near East: A Study of the Babylon Oracles in the Book of Isaiah," in Melugin and Sweeney, eds., *New Visions of Isaiah,* 104-23; M. Franzmann, "The City as Woman: The Case of Babylon in

Isaiah 47," *AusBR* 43 (1995) 1-19; L. Fried, "Cyrus the Messiah? The Historical Background to Isaiah 45:1," *HTR* 95 (2002) 373-93; W. Gross, "Das Negative in Schöpfung und Geschichte: YHWH hat auch Finsternis und Unheil Erschaffen (Jes 45,7)," in *"Ich Schaffe Finsternis und Unheil!" Ist G-tt Verantwortlich für das Übel?* (ed. W. Gross and K.-J. Kuschel; Mainz: Grünwald, 1992) 34-46; H. Haag, "Ich BEWIRKE Heil und erschaffe Unheil (Jes 45,7)," in *Wort, Lied und G-ttesspruch.* vol. 2: *Beiträge zu Psalmen und Propheten (Fest.* J. Ziegler; FB 2; ed. J. Schreiner; Würzburg: Echter, 1972) 179-85; K. Holter, "The Wordplay on El ("G-d") in Isaiah 45,20-21," *SJOT* 7 (1993) 88-98; R. Kittel, "Cyrus und Deuterojesaja," *ZAW* 18 (1898) 149-62; J. L. Koole, "Zu Jesaja 45,9ff," in *Travels in the World of the Old Testament (Fest.,* M. A. Beek; SSN 16; ed. M. S. H. G. Heerma van Voss, P. H. J. Houwinck ten Cate, and N. A. Uchelen; Assen: Van Gorcum, 1974) 170-75; H. Leene, "Isaiah 46.8 — Summons to Be Human?" *JSOT* 30 (1984) 111-21; idem, "Universalism and Nationalism? Isaiah XLV 9-13 and Its Context," *Bijdr* 35 (1974) 309-34; F. Lindeström, *G-d and the Origins of Evil* (CBOTS 21; Lund: Gleerup, 1983) 179-99; R. Martin-Achard, "Esaïe 47 et la tradition prophétique sur Babylone," in *Prophecy: Essays Presented to Georg Fohrer* (BZAW 150; ed. J. A. Emerton; Berlin: de Gruyter, 1980) 83-105; B. D. Naidoff, "The Two-Fold Structure of Isaiah XLV 9-13," *VT* 31 (1981) 180-85; T. D. Nilsen, "The Creation of Darkness and Evil (Isaiah 45:6C-7)," *RB* 115 (2008) 5-25; G. S. Ogden, "Moses and Cyrus," *VT* 28 (1978) 195-203; C. M. Pilkington, "The Hidden G-d in Isaiah 45:15," *SJT* 48 (1995) 285-300; H. Rechenmacher, *Jungfrau, Tochter Babel: Eine Studie zur sprachwissenschaftlichen Beschreibung althebräischer Texte am Beispiel von Jes 47* (ATSAT 44; St. Ottilien: EOS, 1994); H. Schaudig, "Bēl Bows, Nabû Stoops! The Prophecy of Isaiah XLVI 1-2 as a Reflection of the Babylonian Processional Omens," *VT* 58 (2008) 557-52; H.-C. Schmitt, "Prophetie und Schuldtheologie im Deuterojesajabuch," in *Studia biblica et semitica (Fest.* T. C. Vriezen; Wageningen: Veenman, 1966) 356-66; M. A. Sweeney, "On Multiple Settings in the Book of Isaiah," in *Form and Intertextuality,* 28-35; M. Weippert, "Erwägungen zu Jesaja 44,24-28," *DBAT* 21 (1985) 121-32.

THE ANNOUNCEMENT OF THE RESTORATION OF YHWH'S RELATIONSHIP WITH ZION 49:1–54:17

Structure

Isaiah 49:1–54:17 constitutes the next major subunit of the book of Isaiah. Following the concluding hymn of the previous subunit, 49:1–54:17 is demarcated at the outset by a summons to hear directed to the coastlands and the people. Although a concluding hymn also appears in 49:13, the introductory *wāw*-consecutive formation, *wattō'mer ṣîyôn,* "and Zion said," in 49:14 indicates a connection with the following material concerning Zion in 49:14–54:17. Indeed, the conjunction in 49:14 establishes a relationship not only between subunits within the text, but between the concern with the servant, Israel, addressed in 49:1-13, and Zion, the subject of concern in 49:14–54:17 throughout. As Tull Willey's study, *Remember the Former Things,* demonstrates, the interplay between the (male) servant, Israel, and the female (servant) Zion permeates Second Isaiah, insofar as the two figures provide an adaptation of the marriage motif in which the servant/sons, Israel, returns to the bride, Bat Zion, whom YHWH had abandoned, leaving her alone and bereft of children.

With the return of Israel and the restoration of the "marriage" between YHWH and Bat Zion, 49:1–54:17 presents the restoration of YHWH's relationship with Zion. To that end, 49:1-13 announces the restoration of YHWH's servant, Israel. It includes three major subunits, each demarcated by its distinctive speaker and generic character: the servant's announcement of his commission in 49:1-6, YHWH's proclamation of salvation to the servant, Israel, in 49:7-12, and the concluding hymn of praise in 49:13. Isaiah 49:14–52:12 constitutes YHWH's announcement of restoration for Zion. This subunit speaks of salvation for Zion throughout, and it concludes with hymnic material in 52:7-10 followed by a command to depart Babylon to join YHWH in 52:11-12. It includes three subunits, each of which is defined by its distinctive speaker and generic character. Isaiah 49:14-26 is a disputation in which YHWH assures Zion of salvation; 50:1-11 presents a trial scene in which YHWH states conditions for salvation; and 51:1–52:12 constitutes the prophet's proclamation of salvation for Zion. Isaiah 52:13–53:12, generally recognized as the culminating Servant Song, returns the focus to YHWH's servant, Israel, with YHWH's announcement of the exaltation of the servant. Finally, 54:1-17 employs the metaphorical portrayal of Bat Zion as YHWH's previously abandoned bride to proclaim the restoration of the covenant between YHWH and Zion. Isaiah 55:1, with its introductory exclamation, *hôy,* introduces an entirely new subunit in chs. 55–66 concerned with exhorting the people to return to Jerusalem to join in YHWH's restored covenant with the city.

Genre

Isaiah 49–54 constitutes an ANNOUNCEMENT of the restoration of YHWH's relationship with Zion. It employs a number of generic elements, such as the ANNOUNCEMENT OF SALVATION, the DISPUTATION, the TRIAL SPEECH, the HYMN OF PRAISE, and others that are identified in the detailed discussion of its constituent subunits.

Setting

Isaiah 49–54 focuses especially on the return of the exiled Israelites to the city of Jerusalem and thus on the restoration of YHWH's relationship with the city. Such a concern would be paramount in the late 6th century B.C.E. when King Cyrus of Persia and Babylonia decreed in 539 that exiled Jews could return to their homeland to rebuild the temple and when the rebuilding of the temple was actually accomplished in 520-515 during the reign of Darius the Great. Together with the presence of the hymnic material throughout chs. 40–55 and indeed the rest of the book, such a concern indicates that the 6th-century edition of the book of Isaiah was formulated to function as a liturgical work that would have been performed to celebrate the dedication of the Second Temple in 515. Once the book of Isaiah was completed during the late 5th- through early-4th-century administrations of Nehemiah and Ezra, chs. 49–54 would have been read as anticipating the time when the full restoration of Israel to Jerusalem would ultimately be realized.

Interpretation

Overall, chs. 49–54 envision the return of the servant, Israel, to the city of Je-rusalem. The unit employs motifs from the marriage metaphor to portray Israel as YHWH's long-suffering servant who will return to Jerusalem as the children of Mother Zion, who had been lost to her throughout the Babylonian exile. Not only do the children return, but YHWH, Bat Zion's long estranged husband, finally returns to her to restore the marriage/covenant that had been moribund throughout the ca. seventy years of Babylonian captivity, 587-585 through 515.

Bibliography

M. A. Sweeney, *Isaiah 1–4*, 81-87.

THE ANNOUNCEMENT CONCERNING YHWH'S COMMISSION OF THE SERVANT 49:1-13

Structure

I. Servant's announcement of his commission	49:1-6
A. Call to attention	49:1a
1. Listen, O coastlands, to me	49:1aα
2. Give ear, O nations from afar	49:1aβ
B. Announcement of commission proper	49:1b-6
1. Statement of call	49:1b
a. YHWH called me from the womb	49:1bα
b. YHWH named me from the belly of my mother	49:1bβ

The announcement concerning the role of YHWH's servant, Israel, in the restoration of YHWH's relationship with Zion in 49:1-13 is demarcated at the outset by the syntactically-independent call to attention in 49:1a. Although this call to attention introduces the servant's announcement of his commission in 49:1-6, the following oracles in 49:7-12 present YHWH's proclamation of salvation to the servant, which functions as means to elaborate on YHWH's deliverance of the servant. The concluding hymn in 49:13 closes the subunit with a hymn of praise that celebrates YHWH's deliverance of the people from their exile throughout the world. Isaiah 49:1-13 serves as an introduction to the following material in 49:14–54:17, which is joined to 49:1-13 by the introductory *wāw*-consecutive formation.

The first component of the passage is the servant's announcement of his commission in 49:1-6. As noted above, it begins with a call to attention in v. 1a, which is directed to the coastlands and the nations from far away. Such an audience indicates the worldwide perspective for the fictive audience of the passage and indeed of Second Isaiah at large. In the present instance, such an audience reinforces the book's claims that YHWH is the G-d of all creation.

The announcement of the servant's commission proper then follows in vv. 1b-6 with a sequence of six 1st-person subunits in vv. 1b, 2a, 2b, 3, 4, and 5-6, each of which is defined thematically and introduced by a *wāw*, that lays out the basic elements of the servant's commission. The 1st-person formulation indicates that the servant is the speaker throughout. The first appears in v. 1b, which presents a twofold statement concerning the servant's call. Verse 1bα states that "YHWH called me from the womb," and v. 1bβ states that "YHWH named me from the belly of my mother." The second in v. 2a presents a metaphorical portrayal of the servant's mouth as a sharpened blade that is hidden in YHWH's hand. Verse 2aα presents the metaphor of the sharpened blade, and v. 2aβ presents the metaphor of the blade hidden in YHWH's hand. The third statement in v. 2b presents a metaphorical portrayal of the servant as a polished arrow in YHWH's quiver. Verse 2bα presents the metaphor of the polished arrow, and v. 2bβ presents the metaphor of the quiver. The fourth statement in v. 3 presents the servant's statement that "YHWH has named me as the servant," including the basic statement in v. 3a and the elaborated statement in v. 3b that names the servant as "Israel in whom I (YHWH) am glorified." The fifth statement in v. 4 presents the servant's reflection on his role as YHWH's servant in two components. The first in v. 4a presents the servant's thoughts about the futility of his labor, including the statement that "I labored for nothing" in v. 4aα and the statement that "I spent my strength uselessly" in v. 4aβ. The second in v. 4b presents the servant's thoughts concerning his trust in YHWH, including the statement that "my case is with YHWH" in v. 4bα and the statement that "my deed is with my G-d" in v. 4bβ. The sixth and final element in vv. 5-6 concludes the unit with the servant's presentation of YHWH's twofold statement about the servant. The first statement in v. 5 focuses on YHWH's statements concerning the restoration of the servant. This statement comprises two basic elements. The first in v. 5a presents YHWH's statement concerning the servant's restoration, including YHWH's expanded speech formula in v. 5aα and the subject of YHWH's speech, that YHWH's purpose is to restore Jacob/Israel in v. 5aβ. The second element in v. 5b presents the servant's response, including statements that "I am honored in the sight of YHWH" in v. 5bα and that "my G-d was my strength in v. 5bβ.

The statement concerning the restoration of Israel in v. 6 then announces the servant's role as a light to the nations, including the statement in v. 6a that it is too little for YHWH to restore the tribes of Jacob and the survivors of Israel and the statement in v. 6b concerning YHWH's intent to make the servant into a light to the nations in order to deliver the earth.

The second major component of the passage is the presentation of YHWH's proclamation to the servant in 49:7-12. This subunit comprises two oracular proclamations of salvation by YHWH in vv. 7 and 8-12, each of which is introduced by an expanded MESSENGER FORMULA to identify YHWH as the source of the oracle. The first in v. 7 presents the basic proclamation, and the second in vv. 8-12 elaborates upon the first.

The first oracular proclamation of salvation for the servant in v. 7 begins with an expanded MESSENGER FORMULA in v. 7aα. The messenger formula identifies YHWH as the source of the oracle. It qualifies YHWH as the holy redeemer of Israel, and it states that YHWH's oracle is directed to the servant, who in turn is qualified as one despised of soul, abhorred by the nations, and who is a slave to (foreign) kings. Such qualification of the servant facilitates the contrast between the servant's present state and his future state as defined in YHWH's oracle in v. 7aβ-b, that kings shall rise and princes shall bow in the servant's presence in v. 7aβ and that the object of such rising and bowing is to honor YHWH, the Holy One of Israel, in v. 7b.

The second oracular proclamation of salvation for the servant in vv. 8-12 elaborates upon the first with an oracle of salvation. The subunit begins with a basic messenger formula in v. 8aα$^{1-3}$ that simply identifies YHWH as the source of the oracle. The oracle of salvation then follows in vv. 8aα^4-12. The oracle begins with a brief twofold reference to the time and day of YHWH's deliverance in v. 8aα^4-β, including the statement that YHWH will answer in a time of favor in v. 8aα$^{4-6}$ and the statement that YHWH helps in the day of salvation in v. 8aβ.

The announcement of salvation proper, that the servant Israel is to be a people in covenant with YHWH, then follows in vv. 8b-12. It begins with a basic statement of the premise of the oracle, that "I created you and appointed you as a covenant people," in v. 8bα. The following statements in vv. 8bβ-9a then specify the four purposes of the covenant people: to restore the land in v. 8bβ, to restore desolate inheritances in v. 8bγ, to say to the captives that they can go free in v. 9aα, and to say to those who are in darkness that they can now show themselves in v. 9aβ. Verses 9b-12 then lay out the results of the servant's appointment as YHWH's covenant people in five statements. The first in v. 9bα metaphorically states that the people will graze by the roads much like sheep. The second in v. 9bβ continues the grazing sheep metaphor with a statement that their pasture will be on every height. The third in v. 10aα states that they will neither hunger nor thirst. The fourth in v. 10aβ states that the *sharav,* the dry desert wind, and the sun will not strike them. Finally, the fifth in vv. 10b-12 provides the reasons for projected tranquility of the people: that YHWH will lead them. Verse 10b states this reason in two parts: v. 10bα specifies that the one who shows mercy will lead them, and v. 10bβ states that YHWH will guide them to water. Verses 11-12 then present YHWH's statements that illustrate YHWH's capacity and intent to carry out the deliverance announced in v. 10b. YHWH announces in two parts in v. 11 the intention to build a road for the return of the exiled people, including the announcement that "I will make my mountains into a road" in v. 11a and the announcement that "my highways will rise" in v. 11b. YHWH then announces in v. 12 the results of these actions: that the people will return to the land of Israel on these roads, in three parts, including the announcement that "behold, they come" in v. 12a, the announcement that "behold, they come from north and west" in v. 12bα, and finally, the announcement that "they come from Syene" (i.e., from the south) in v. 12bβ.

The third major component of the passage is the hymn of praise in v. 13 that concludes the subunit. The hymn of praise celebrates YHWH's announcement of salvation for the servant so that all the world will know YHWH's role as creator and redeemer of Israel. The hymn includes the two basic elements of the genre. The call to praise in v. 13a calls upon heaven and earth to shout aloud and celebrate in v. 13aα and the hills to break forth in song in v. 13aβ. Verse 13b then follows with the basis for such praise in two parts: YHWH has comforted the people in v. 13bα and YHWH has shown mercy to the afflicted ones in v. 13bβ.

Genre

Isaiah 49:1-13 presents an announcement of YHWH's commission of the servant, Israel. It includes three basic subunits, each of which comprises a distinct generic character, including the servant's announcement of his commission in 49:1-6, YHWH's proclamation of salvation to the servant in 49:7-12, and the concluding hymn of praise in 49:13.

The servant's announcement of his commission in 49:1-6 is based on the ANNOUNCEMENT of a COMMISSION. A commission is an authoritative charge given by a superior, in this case YHWH, to a subordinate, in this case Israel. In the present text, the servant, Israel, announces his own commission by YHWH. Prior scholarship has focused either on attempts to dismiss Israel from the text or to define the type of commission at hand. Attempts to dismiss Israel from the text have been based largely on the tension created within the text by the individual portrayal of the servant and the collective portrayal of Israel as well as by the servant's task to raise up the tribes of Jacob and to restore the survivors of Israel (v. 6). But Mettinger's study has demonstrated that there are no grounds for the dismissal of Israel. There is no text-critical warrant for such a move, and scholars proposing the excision of Israel from the text have failed to appreciate the metaphorical character of the portrayal of Israel in this text simultaneously as an individual as well as a national or collective group. Whereas past discussion has attempted to define the servant's role as monarch or prophet, the task of the servant is decisive in the present context. The servant's task is to restore Jacob/Israel. Interpreters must recognize that a major role of any nation or group is to assert its own identity and interests — in this case, to carry out the return of the people of Israel to their homeland and thereby to serve as a light to the nations concerning YHWH's role as creator of the universe and redeemer of Israel, in keeping with the overall concerns of chs. 40–55 within the book of Isaiah as a whole.

The announcement of the servant's commission in 49:1-6 makes use of other generic elements as well. The CALL TO ATTENTION formula appears in v. 1a. A call to attention opens a public presentation or address and attempts to attract the attention of an audience to the speech that follows. The present example in 49:1a includes the three basic elements: an invitation to listen indicated by the verbs *šim'û,* "listen (to me)" and *haqšîbû,* "give ear"; the mention of the addressees, "coastlands" and "nations from afar"; and an indication of what is to come. This last element is only implicit in the present text, i.e., the imperative signal that something to be heard is to follow. The SPEECH FORMULA for YHWH in v. 5, *'āmar yhwh,* "said YHWH," introduces the following statement by YHWH in v. 5a that is quoted by the servant to support his claims that his commission includes his appointment as a light of the nations. Some interpreters note the influence of the COMMUNAL THANKSGIVING PSALM, such as the indications of past troubles and YHWH's deliverance in vv. 4-5, but other characteristic elements of the Thanksgiving Psalm are missing. In the present instance, the references to past troubles and YHWH's deliverance in vv. 4-5 support the commission of Israel to play the key role in overcoming past reverses.

YHWH's proclamation of salvation to the servant in 49:7-12 comprises two basic subunits, the oracular proclamation of salvation in v. 7 and the elaboration in vv. 8-12. Both are based in the PROPHETIC ANNOUNCEMENT OF SALVATION. Westermann, in *Prophetic Oracles of Salvation,* argues that the genre is best labeled as proclamation of salvation. The genre typically includes three basic elements: the reassurance formula, "fear not!"; the basis for reassurance; and the future orientation of the proclamation. The present examples lack the reassurance formula, but they include the other two elements. The oracular proclamation of salvation in 49:7 begins with an expanded PROPHETIC MESSENGER FORMULA in v. 7aα to identify YHWH as the source of the following oracle. The oracle itself presents the basis for reassurance and the future orientation with its statements that "kings shall see and rise" and that "princes shall (see and) bow down" before the formerly despised and abhorred servant who served as a slave. In this case, the brief proclamation of salvation announces that the servant Israel will no longer serve in its role as a defeated nation, exiled to a foreign land. Instead, kings and princes will recognize the servant Israel's restoration as a signal for YHWH's sovereignty over the entire world as author of creation and redeemer of Israel.

The elaboration in 49:8-12 is likewise based on the PROPHETIC ANNOUNCEMENT OF SALVATION insofar as it elaborates with a far more detailed statement YHWH's deliverance of Israel to its new role as YHWH's servant. The passage once again begins with a Prophetic MESSENGER FORMULA in v. 8aα$^{1-3}$ to identify YHWH as the source for the following oracle. The oracle again lacks the reassurance formula, "fear not," but it presents a detailed announcement of YHWH's deliverance of Israel so that they might become once again YHWH's covenant people. Isaiah 49:8aα^4-β refers to the time of YHWH's deliverance, and vv. 8b-12 present the announcement of salvation proper, both in terms of the basis for Israel's deliverance and the future orientation of that deliverance. The basic statement in v. 8bα, "and I created you and appointed you as a covenant people," presents the gist of the matter. The following material in vv. 8bβ-9a and vv. 9b-12, respectively, present the purpose of the servant as the covenant people and the results of the servant's role. The purposes of the covenant people include restoration of the land, restoration of Israel's inheritance in the land, the release of captives, and the appearance of those hidden away. The results include a metaphorical portrayal of the returning exiles as sheep grazing by the roads and on top of every height, the lack of hunger and thirst, and protection from the *sharav,* the hot desert sirocco, and the sun. The results conclude with statements of the reasons for deliverance in vv. 10b-12, that YHWH will lead them home, and makes a statement certifying that the return will take place.

The final subunit of the passage is the HYMN OF PRAISE in 49:13. Some identify it as an eschatological hymn of praise to express a sense of the end time, but the hymn refers simply to YHWH's comforting and restoration of the servant Israel. The typical hymn of praise includes two basic elements: the call to praise and the basis for praise. Both elements appear in the present instance. The call to praise appears in v. 13a with the dual commands, "Shout aloud, O Heavens, and celebrate, O Earth" and "Break out in song, O Mountains!" The basis for praise then follows with the twofold statement in v. 13b that YHWH has comforted the people and that YHWH has shown mercy to the afflicted ones.

Setting

The historical setting for 49:1-13 is the end of the Babylonian exile and the return of Jews to Jerusalem and the land of Israel at the outset of the Persian period. The text anticipates the restoration of Israel, which has prompted many interpreters to argue that it must have been written sometime between 545 B.C.E., when Cyrus began his advance against Babylonia, and 539, when Cyrus entered the city of Babylon and was named King of Babylonia. Interpreters cannot be certain that this text actually anticipates the end of the exile; such a composition may have been penned retrospectively to celebrate the end of the exile and the return of Jews to the land of Israel as part of a liturgical celebration of the event at the site of the Jerusalem temple or even at the dedication of the Second Temple in 515.

The literary setting of 49:1-13 must be considered as well. It follows immediately upon 44:24–48:22, which focuses on the contention that YHWH will use Cyrus to carry out the restoration of Zion. Isaiah 49:1-13 appears at the outset of chs. 49–54, which contend that YHWH is actually carrying out the restoration of Zion. By featuring the announcement of the commissioning of the servant Israel at the outset of this section, 49:1-13 signals the interest in chs. 49–54 in the restoration of YHWH's relationship with Zion. The commission of the servant in 49:1-6 presupposes that Israel has now been called to undertake a new task, demonstrating YHWH's role as the sovereign of all creation as well as of Israel, and the pronouncement of salvation in 49:7-12 reinforces the commission by elaborating upon the task that the servant Israel is to undertake. The concluding hymn in 49:13 points to the liturgical dimension of this text, which appears to have been composed for performance in a ritual setting. Insofar as the dedication of the Second Temple in 515 would have celebrated the return of Jews to Jerusalem and YHWH's roles as Creator of the Universe and the Redeemer of Israel, 49:1-13 appears to presuppose the social setting of the rededication of the Jerusalem temple.

Interpretation

The announcement concerning the commission of the servant Israel in 49:1-13 introduces the larger unit in chs. 49–54, which announces the restoration of YHWH's relationship with Zion. The commission of Israel as YHWH's servant entails the restoration of Israel from Babylonian captivity to the land of Israel and the recognition of YHWH by the nations as the Creator of the Universe and the Redeemer of Israel. The passage presupposes Cyrus's 539 B.C.E. decree that Jews may return to Jerusalem to rebuild the temple (2 Chr 36:22-23; Ezra 1:1-4). It appears to be set in relation to the temple dedication ceremony related in Ezra 6.

The passage begins in 49:1-6 with Israel's announcement of his commission as YHWH's servant. The call to attention in 49:1a places the announcement in the context of all creation by calling upon coastlands at ends of the earth and the nations from afar to listen and give heed to what the servant is about to announce. Although such a worldwide perspective is typical in Judean prophetic literature, it is especially poignant in the present context because of the claim it makes concerning YHWH's worldwide sovereignty in the aftermath of the Babylonian exile. Essentially, the servant's announcement portrays YHWH in the place of Cyrus as the true sovereign of the world.

The servant's announcement of the commission proper follows in 49:1b-6. It begins with the servant's recollection of YHWH's call from the womb in v. 1b, which evokes memories of the prophet Jeremiah's call from the womb as well (Jer 1:4-10). Such a portrayal indicates that Israel was always destined for its role, much as Jacob was destined for his role from the very beginning when he struggled with his brother Esau while still in the womb of their mother Rebekah (Gen 25:19-26). The following metaphorical portrayals of the servant's mouth as a hidden sharp blade in v. 2a and as a concealed polished arrow in v. 2b recall portrayals of Mesopotamian kings with their weapons and their bows drawn, but the motif of hiddenness and concealment emphasizes that Israel's role as the figure who will facilitate the worldwide recognition of YHWH's true power has been concealed only to be revealed in the present. The servant's announcement in v. 3 that YHWH names him, Israel, as servant ensures that readers or hearers of the text will have no doubt that the restoration of Israel points to YHWH's greatest act of redemption for the people of Israel since the time of exodus from Egypt. The servant's retrospective view in v. 4a of the futility of his labor and the spending of his strength accounts for the period of Babylonian subjugation, and the expression of trust in YHWH in v. 4b accounts for Israel's trust in YHWH throughout the ordeal. The concluding reference to YHWH's twofold statement about the servant in vv. 5-6 both reinforces the servant's claims and takes them a step further. The first statement in v. 5 reiterates the servant's task to restore Jacob/Israel as well as the servant's confidence in YHWH. The second statement in v. 6 then emphasizes that there is a task beyond that of restoration: the servant will serve as a light to the nations to proclaim YHWH's worldwide sovereignty to them as well.

The presentation of YHWH's proclamation of salvation to the servant Israel in 49:7-12 then reinforces the servant's own proclamation and elaborates upon it. The passage begins with YHWH's first oracular proclamation in 49:7, which announces that kings shall rise and princes shall bow before the servant in order to recognize and honor YHWH as the Holy One of Israel. Isaiah 49:8-12 then follows with an elaboration on this theme. Following the prophetic messenger formula, the subunit begins with an announcement concerning the time and day of YHWH's deliverance in v. 8aα⁴-β, that the time and day have come. The announcement of salvation then follows in vv. 8b-12. It begins with YHWH's basic statement of the servant's commission in v. 8bα, "and I created you and appointed you as a covenant people," followed by the purposes of the commission in vv. 8bβ-9a and the results of the commission in vv. 9b-12. The purposes of YHWH's commission of the servant are to restore the land, restore Israel's desolate inheritances, to release the captives, and to bring forth those who were hidden to light. The result is a metaphorical portrayal of a people freed from captivity as sheep who peacefully graze by the road under the watchful eye of their master: they graze by the road, they pasture on the hilltops, they do not hunger or thirst, and the *sharav,* the dry desert sirocco, and the sun do not harm them. Finally, the reasons for such tranquility appear at the end of the passage with statements that it is YHWH who leads them to water as in the Wilderness wanderings following the exodus. YHWH's statements in vv. 11-12 that YHWH will create a road on which the people will return home from all around the world, i.e., from north and west and from Syene (the ancient Egyptian town located by modern Aswan; n.b., the text reads "from the land of *sînîm* (China)," but most scholars emend *sînîm* to *sēwēnēh,* "Syene"), then point to YHWH's restoration of Jacob/Israel to the land of Israel.

The unit then concludes with a hymn of praise in 49:13 which calls upon the heavens and earth and the hills to rejoice because YHWH has comforted the people and shown mercy to them. The hymn once again points to YHWH's role as the Creator of the Universe and Redeemer of Israel.

Bibliography

T. N. D. Mettinger, *A Farewell to the Servant Songs;* C. Westermann, *Prophetic Oracles of Salvation in the Old Testament* (trans. Keith Crim; Louisville: Westminster John Knox, 1991).

YHWH'S ANNOUNCEMENT OF SALVATION FOR ZION 49:14–52:12

Structure

I. Disputation: YHWH assures Zion of salvation	49:14-26
A. Prophet's presentation of Zion's dilemma: YHWH has forsaken me (premise to be disputed)	49:14
1. Speech formula	49:14aα
2. Zion's speech	49:14aβ-b
a. YHWH has abandoned me	49:14aβ
b. My L-rd has forgotten me	49:14b
B. Prophet's presentation of YHWH's response to Zion: assurance of salvation (refutation)	49:15-26
1. First oracular response: I have not forgotten you	49:15-21
a. Rhetorical questions	49:15a
1) Can a woman forget her baby?	49:15aα
2) Can a woman forget the child of her womb?	49:15aβ
b. YHWH's response: assurance of salvation	49:15b-21
1) Initial response: I don't forget you	49:15b
a) She might forget	49:15bα
b) I will not forget you	49:15bβ
2) Extended response: I will deliver you	49:16-21
a) I remember you	49:16
(1) Upon the palms of my hands I engraved you	49:16a

(2) Your walls are before me always   49:16b

b) Concerning the return of your children   49:17-21

  (1) Your children hurry   49:17a

  (2) Those who ruined you depart   49:17b

  (3) Raise your eyes and see: they are assembled and come   49:18a

  (4) YHWH's oath concerning return   49:18b-21

    (a) Oath formula with oracle formula $49{:}18b\alpha^{1\text{-}4}$

      α. Oath formula $49{:}18b\alpha^{1\text{-}2}$

      β. Oracle formula $49{:}18b\alpha^{3\text{-}4}$

    (b) You shall wear your children like jewels of bride $49{:}18b\alpha^{5}\text{-}\beta$

      α. You shall wear them like jewelry $49{:}18b\alpha^{5\text{-}8}$

      β. You shall bind them on like a bride $49{:}18b\beta$

    (c) Your ruined land and places will be crowded with inhabitants while your enemies stay far away   49:19

    (d) Your lost children will say the place is too crowded, make room for me to live   49:20

    (e) You will say to yourself: where did they come from?   49:21

      α. Speech formula $49{:}21a\alpha^{1\text{-}2}$

      β. Speech proper $49{:}21a\alpha^{3}\text{-}b$

        aa. Who bore them? $49{:}21a\beta^{3}\text{-}b\alpha^{2}$

        bb. Who raised them? $49{:}21b\alpha^{3}\text{-}\gamma^{4}$

        cc. Where have they been? $49{:}21b\gamma^{5\text{-}6}$

2. Second oracular response: I will signal the nations to bring your children home   49:22-23

  a. Messenger formula $49{:}22a\alpha^{1\text{-}4}$

  b. Oracle proper: oracle of deliverance $49{:}22a\alpha^{5}\text{-}23$

    1) I will raise my hand/ensign $49{:}22a\alpha^{5}\text{-}\beta$

      a) Raise my hand to nations $49{:}22a\alpha^{5\text{-}9}$

      b) Lift my ensign to peoples $49{:}22a\beta$

    2) They will bring your children home   49:22b

      a) Bring your sons in bosoms $49{:}22b\alpha$

      b) Carry your daughters on shoulders $49{:}22b\beta$

    3) Kings and queens shall care for your children $49{:}23a\alpha$

      a) Kings will be your caretakers $49{:}23a\alpha^{1\text{-}3}$

      b) Queens will be your wet nurses $49{:}23a\alpha^{4\text{-}5}$

    4) They bow to you/lick dust of your feet $49{:}23a\beta\text{-}\gamma$

      a) Bow to you $49{:}23a\beta$

      b) Lick dust of your feet $49{:}23a\gamma$

    5) Qualified recognition formula: you will know that I am YHWH   49:23b

      a) Recognition formula $49{:}23b\alpha$

      b) Those who wait for me will not be shamed $49{:}23b\beta$

3. Third oracular response: I will ensure your salvation   49:24-26

a. Rhetorical questions   49:24
  1) Can spoil be taken from a warrior?   49:24a
  2) Can captives be released from one who is righteous?   49:24b
b. Presentation of YHWH's oracular answer   49:25-26
  1) Messenger formula   49:25aα^{1-4}
  2) Oracle proper   49:25aα^{5}-26
    a) Captives and spoil will be taken   49:25aα^{5}-β
      (1) Captives will be taken from a warrior   49:25aα^{5-8}
      (2) Spoil will be retrieved from a tyrant   49:25aβ
    b) I will contend with adversaries and deliver children   49:25b
      (1) I will contend with your adversaries   49:25bα
      (2) I will deliver your children   49:25bβ
    c) I will make your oppressors eat their flesh and drink their blood   49:26a
      (1) Eat their own flesh   49:26aα
      (2) Drink their own blood   49:26aβ
    d) Elaborated recognition formula   49:26b
      (1) Recognition formula: all will know that I am YHWH your deliverer   49:26bα
      (2) Elaboration: your redeemer, the Mighty One of Jacob   49:26bβ
II. Trial scene: YHWH's conditions for salvation   50:1-11
  A. Trial speech: people are responsible for breaking covenant   50:1-3
    1. Messenger formula   50:1aα^{1-3}
    2. Trial speech proper   50:1aα^{4}-3
      a. First set of rhetorical questions: I brought the punishment on account of your sins   50:1aα^{4}-b
      1) Rhetorical questions proper   50:1aα^{4}-β
        a) Where is the divorce document of your mother whom I divorced?   50:1aα^{4-10}
        b) Who are my creditors to whom I sold you?   50:1aβ
      2) Rhetorical answers   50:1b
        a) For your sins you were sold   50:1bα
        b) For your sins your mother was divorced   50:1bβ
      b. Second set of rhetorical questions: I am the power in the universe   50:2-3
      1) Rhetorical questions proper   50:2a
        a) First subset: you didn't appear or answer   50:2aα
          (1) Why was no one there when I came?   50:2aα^{1-4}
          (2) Why did no one answer when I called?   50:2aα^{5-7}
        b) Second subset: I have strength to redeem and deliver   50:2aβ-γ
          (1) Is my hand too short to redeem?   50:2aβ
          (2) Do I lack the strength to deliver?   50:2aγ
      2) Rhetorical answers   50:2b-3
        a) I dried up the sea and rivers   50:2bα
          (1) I dried the sea   50:2bα^{1-4}
          (2) I made the rivers a desert   50:2bα^{5-7}

C. Prophet's concluding parenesis: presentation of YHWH's
   declaration of conditions — 50:10-11
   1. Prophet's exhortation to trust in YHWH — 50:10
      a. Rhetorical questions: trust YHWH and listen to servant — 50:10a-bα
         1) Who among you trusts in YHWH? — 50:10a
         2) Who among you listens to the servant who walks in
            darkness without light? — 50:10bα
      b. Exhortation: trust in YHWH and rely on G-d — 50:10bβ-γ
         1) Trust in YHWH — 50:10bβ
         2) Rely on G-d — 50:10bγ
   2. YHWH's admonition: abandon your resistance to YHWH — 50:11
      a. YHWH's observation: you are immersed in fire — 50:11a
         1) You kindle fire — 50:11aα
         2) You gird on sparks — 50:11aβ
      b. YHWH's challenge: walk in your fire — 50:11bα
         1) Walk in the light of your fire — 50:11bα$^{1-3}$
         2) Walk in the sparks which you have kindled — 50:11bα$^{4-5}$
      c. You will suffer because this comes from me — 50:11bβ-γ
         1) This comes to you from my hand — 50:11bβ
         2) You will lie in pain — 50:11bγ
III. Proclamation of salvation for Zion — 51:1–52:12
   A. Threefold exhortation to listen and see — 51:1-8
      1. First exhortation to those who seek YHWH — 51:1-3
         a. Call to attention — 51:1a
            1) Basically stated — 51:1aα
            2) Addressees — 51:1aβ
               a) You who pursue justice — 51:1aβ$^{1-2}$
               b) You who seek YHWH — 51:1aβ$^{3-4}$
         b. Twofold call to see — 51:1b-2
            1) First call to see: rock and quarry — 51:1b
               a) Look to the rock from which you were cut — 51:1bα
               b) Look to the quarry from which you were carved — 51:1bβ
            2) Second call to see: Abraham and Sarah — 51:2
               a) Call proper — 51:2a
                  (1) Look to Abraham your father — 51:2aα
                  (2) Look to Sarah who bore you — 51:2aβ
               b) Basis for second call — 51:2b
                  (1) For he was one when I called him — 51:2bα
                  (2) I blessed and multiplied him — 51:2bβ
         c. Basis for exhortation: announcement of YHWH's com-
            fort for Zion — 51:3
            1) Comfort for Zion and ruins — 51:3aα
               a) Comfort for Zion — 51:3aα$^{1-4}$
               b) Comfort for Zion's ruins — 51:3aα$^{5-7}$
            2) Transformed wilderness and desert — 51:3aβ-γ
               a) Transformed wilderness like Eden — 51:3aβ
               b) Transformed desert like garden of YHWH — 51:3aγ

3) Gladness and thanksgiving will be found in her	51:3b
a) Gladness and joy	51:3bα
b) Thanksgiving and the sound of music	51:3bβ
2. Second exhortation for my nation	51:4-6
a. Call to attention with basis	51:4-5
1) Twofold call to attention proper	51:4a
a) First call to my people	51:4aα
b) Second call to my nation	51:4aβ
2) Basis for call: YHWH's Torah as light for nations	51:4b-5
a) Basis proper	51:4b
(1) My Torah goes out	51:4bα
(2) My law I establish as light for nations	51:4bβ
b) Elaboration: nations wait for my arm/rule	51:5
(1) My arm will rule nations	51:5a
(a) My righteousness and victory go forth	51:5aα
α. My righteousness is near	$51:5a\alpha^{1\text{-}2}$
β. My victory goes forth	$51:5a\alpha^{3\text{-}4}$
(b) My arm will rule nations	51:5aβ
(2) Coastlands hope/wait for me	51:5b
(a) Coastlands hope for me	51:5bα
(b) Coastlands wait for my arm	51:5bβ
b. Exhortation to see YHWH's victory	51:6
1) Twofold exhortation proper	51:6a
a) Lift your eyes to the heavens	51:6aα
b) Look to the earth below	51:6aβ
2) Bases for exhortation	51:6b
a) Heavens will dissipate like a cloud	$51:6b\alpha^{1\text{-}4}$
b) Earth will wear out like a garment	$51:6b\alpha^{5\text{-}7}$
c) Its inhabitants will die like gnats	$51:6b\beta^{1\text{-}4}$
d) My victory shall be forever	$51:6b\beta^{5\text{-}7}$
e) My righteousness shall not be dismayed	51:6bγ
3. Third exhortation with basis for nation with my Torah in their heart	51:7-8
a. Exhortation	51:7
1) Twofold call to attention	51:7a
a) Listen to me you who know righteousness	51:7aα
b) Listen to me nation with my Torah in their heart	51:7aβ
2) Twofold reassurance speech	51:7b
a) Reassurance speech: do not fear the shame of humans	51:7bα
b) Do not be dismayed by their jeers	51:7bβ
b. Basis for exhortation	51:8
1) Shaming/jeering humans will pass away	51:8a
a) Moths will eat them like garment	51:8aα
b) Moths will eat them like wool	51:8aβ
2) My righteousness/victory are forever	51:8b
a) My righteousness is forever	51:8bα

b) My victory is for all generations   51:8bβ
B. Announcement of the restoration of Zion   51:9–52:12
  1. Answered lament: YHWH will act   51:9-16
    a. Quotation of lament: appeal for YHWH to act   51:9-11
      1) Metaphorical appeal for YHWH's arm to awaken   51:9a
        a) Awake and clothe yourself with strength   51:9aα
        b) Awake as in days of old and past generations   51:9aβ-γ
      2) Rhetorical questions   51:9b-11
        a) Did you not defeat sea monsters?   51:9b
          (1) Did you not cleave Rahab?   51:9bα
          (2) Did you not pierce the Dragon?   51:9bβ
        b) Did you not dry the sea so the exiles could return?   51:10-11
          (1) Did you not dry the sea?   51:10aα
          (2) Did you not dry the great deep?   51:10aβ
          (3) Did you not make a road for the redeemed to pass?   51:10b-11
            (a) Question proper   51:10b
            (b) Elaboration   51:11
              α. Twofold statement concerning return   51:11aα-β
              aa. Ransomed of YHWH will return   51:11aα
              bb. They come to Zion with shouting   51:11aβ
              β. Threefold statement concerning rejoicing   51:11aγ-b
              aa. Eternal joy on their head   51:11aγ
              bb. Joy and gladness they attain   51:11bα
              cc. Worry and groaning flee   51:11bβ
    b. YHWH's answer: I will deliver you as my people   51:12-16
      1) Initial response: I YHWH comfort you   51:12a
      2) Elaboration concerning YHWH's resolve: rhetorical questions and answers   51:12b-14
        a) First question with answer   51:12b-13a
          (1) Question: why do you fear mortals?   51:12b
            (a) Men who will die?   51:12bα
            (b) Humans who are like grass?   51:12bβ
          (2) Response: you have forgotten YHWH and you fear the oppressor   51:13a
            (a) You have forgotten YHWH your maker who spread out the heavens and founded the earth   51:13aα$^{1-7}$
            (b) You fear all the time the wrath of the oppressor who prepares to destroy (you)   51:13aα^{8}-β
        b) Second question with answer   51:13b-14
          (1) Question: where is the anger of the oppressor?   51:13b
          (2) Response: the oppressed is freed   51:14
            (a) Quickly the oppressed is freed   51:14a
            (b) He does not die   51:14bα
            (c) He does not lack bread   51:14bβ
      3) Hymnic response: I am YHWH and you are my people   51:15-16

a) I am YHWH your G-d 51:15
 (1) Basically stated 51:15aα
 (2) Who stirs up the sea so its waves roar 51:15aβ
 (3) Declaration: YHWH Seba'ot is the Name 51:15b
b) Actions: what I will do 51:16
 (1) I place my words in your mouth 51:16aα
 (2) In the shadow of my hand I conceal you 51:16aβ
 (3) To spread out the heavens and to found the earth 51:16bα
 (4) To say to Zion: you are my people 51:16bβ
2. Salvation speech: suffering of Zion is over 51:17-23
 a. Call to Jerusalem to awaken and rise 51:17
  1) Commands to Jerusalem to awaken and rise 51:17aα
   a) Awaken 51:17aα^1
   b) Awaken 51:17aα^2
   c) Arise, O Jerusalem 51:17aα$^{3-4}$
  2) Qualification of Jerusalem: drunk cup of YHWH's wrath 51:17aβ-b
   a) First qualification: drunk cup of YHWH's wrath 51:17aβ
   b) Second qualification: drain goblet of reeling 51:17b
 b. Salvation speech proper: suffering of Zion is over 51:18-23
  1) Basis for salvation: Zion's current state of ruin 51:18-20
   a) Lack of guidance due to lack of sons 51:18
    (1) No one to guide her from all the sons she bore 51:18a
    (2) No one to hold her hand from all the sons she
     raised 51:18b
   b) Two things have befallen you: destruction and
    hunger 51:19
    (1) Basic statement: two things have befallen you 51:19aα
    (2) Specification through rhetorical questions 51:19aβ-b
     (a) Destruction and ruin: who will console you? 51:19aβ
     (b) Hunger and the sword: who will comfort you? 51:19b
   c) Your sons lie punished by YHWH 51:20
    (1) Portrayal of Zion's sons lying faint like a
     trapped antelope 51:20a
    (2) They are filled with the wrath of YHWH/
     rebuke of Zion's G-d 51:20b
  2) Announcement of salvation 51:21-23
   a) Therefore plus call to attention 51:21
    (1) Addressed to humbled one 51:21a
    (2) Addressed to one drunk but not with wine 51:21b
   b) Oracle of salvation for Zion 51:22-23
    (1) Prophetic messenger formula 51:22aα
     (a) From your L-rd, YHWH 51:22aα$^{1-4}$
     (b) From your G-d who contends for the people 51:22aα$^{5-7}$
    (2) Salvation oracle proper 51:22aβ-23
     (a) I have taken the cup of reeling from you 51:22aβ-b
      α. Twofold basic statement 51:22aβ-bα
      aa. Cup of reeling 51:22aβ

γ. Second elaboration: my name is reviled 52:5bβ
(2) Twofold announcement of YHWH's intent to
    act on behalf of Israel/Bat Zion 52:6
    (a) First announcement: my people shall know
        my name 52:6a
    (b) Second announcement: I am the one who
        speaks 52:6b
4. Vision of herald: YHWH's return to Zion 52:7-10
  a. Vision of the herald proper 52:7
    1) Vision statement 52:7aα
    2) First qualification: announcing peace 52:7aβ$^{1-2}$
    3) Second qualification: proclaiming goodness 52:7aβ$^{3-4}$
    4) Third qualification: announcing deliverance 52:7aβ$^{5-6}$
    5) Saying to Zion: your G-d rules 52:7b
      a) Speech formula 52:7bα
      b) Announcement proper: your G-d rules 52:7bβ
  b. Shout of the watchmen 52:8
    1) Announcement of the watchmen's shout 52:8a
      a) The voice of the watchmen 52:8aα
      b) They have raised their voices 52:8aβ
      c) Together they sing out 52:8aγ
    2) Reason for announcement: they see YHWH's return
       to Zion 52:8b
  c. Call for Jerusalem/Israel to shout for YHWH 52:9-10
    1) Call proper to ruins of Jerusalem 52:9a
    2) Bases for call 52:9b-10
      a) YHWH has comforted the people 52:9bα
      b) YHWH has redeemed Jerusalem 52:9bβ
      c) YHWH bares arm so all the nations see 52:10
        (1) YHWH has bared the holy arm in the sight of
            all the nations 52:10a
        (2) All the ends of the earth see the deliverance of
            our G-d 52:10b
5. Command to depart and join YHWH 52:11-12
  a. Commands proper addressed to bearers of the vessels
     of YHWH 52:11
    1) First command sequence: turn, go out, and touch
       nothing impure 52:11a
    2) Second command sequence: go out, be pure 52:11b
  b. Bases for commands 52:12
    1) First basis: you will not depart in haste/flee 52:12a
      a) You will not depart in haste 52:12aα
      b) You will not flee 52:12aβ
    2) Second basis: YHWH goes with you 52:12b
      a) YHWH goes before you 52:12bα
      b) G-d of Israel guards your rear 52:12bβ

ISAIAH 40–66

Isaiah 49:14–52:12 begins with a *wāw*-consecutive construction, *wattō'mer ṣîyôn,* "and Zion said," that serves several functions. First, it connects 49:14–52:12 to the preceding unit in 49:1-13, which announces YHWH's commissioning of the servant Israel. Second, it opens the new subunit Isa 49:14–52:12 with the prophet's presentation of Zion's speech that shifts concern from the servant, Israel, in 49:1-13 to YHWH's announcement of salvation of Zion or the city of Jerusalem, to which Israel will return. Third, it serves as the basis for the presentation of YHWH's disputation in 49:14-26, in which YHWH assures Zion of salvation. Two other subunits then follow, each of which is syntactically-independent but builds upon the concerns of the preceding subunit. Isaiah 50:1-11 constitutes a trial scene which presents YHWH's conditions for the salvation of Zion, and 51:1–52:12 then actually proclaims salvation for Zion. Thus, 49:14–52:12 as a whole focuses on YHWH's announcement of salvation for Zion. Isaiah 52:13 then shifts the focus back to the servant, Israel, to introduce a new subunit in 52:13–53:12, which stands as the next major subunit of 49:1–54:17.

Isaiah 49:14-26 constitutes a disputation speech in which YHWH assures Zion of salvation. It begins with the aforementioned Zion speech formula, *wattō'mer ṣîyôn,* "and Zion said," which introduces the prophet's presentation of Zion's statement of her dilemma in v. 14: YHWH has forsaken me. Verse 14 begins with a speech formula in v. 14aα which identifies Zion as the speaker. Her speech then follows in v. 14aβ-b in two parallel statements that express her dilemma: "YHWH has abandoned me" in v. 14aβ and "My L-rd has forgotten me" in v. 14b. Zion's statements then constitute the premise that is to be disputed throughout the rest of the subunit.

Isaiah 49:15-26 then constitutes the balance of the unit as the prophet's presentation of YHWH's response to Zion, in which YHWH assures Zion of salvation. Within the context of the disputation genre, such a response constitutes YHWH's refutation of Zion's premise, i.e., YHWH has not abandoned her; indeed, YHWH is acting to deliver her. YHWH's response includes three oracular units that develop YHWH's three major points: "I have not forgotten you" in the first oracular response of vv. 15-21; "I will signal the nations to bring your children home" in the second oracular response of vv. 22-23; and "I will ensure your salvation" in the third oracular response of vv. 24-26.

The first oracular response in 49:15-21 lacks the prophetic messenger formula that is characteristic of the other two. Its oracular character is evident in v. 18bα[1-4], which includes an example of YHWH's oath formula, *ḥay-'ānî,* "by my life," followed by the oracle formula, *nĕ'um yhwh,* "utterance of YHWH." YHWH's response begins in v. 15a with a pair of rhetorical questions: "can a woman forget her baby?" in v. 15aα and "can a woman forget the child of her womb?" in v. 15aβ. The answer to both questions is obviously "no!" indicating that they function as a means to assert that YHWH will not forget or abandon Zion. Consequently, YHWH's response in vv. 15b-21 assures Zion of salvation and begins with a two-part initial statement of YHWH's basic premise in v. 15b: even if these women could forget their babies in v. 15bα, I (YHWH) will not forget you (Zion) in v. 15bβ. Such a statement places YHWH's commitment to Zion even above that of the two women cited in the rhetorical questions of v. 15a. YHWH's extended response, which develops the theme that YHWH will

178

deliver Zion, then follows in vv. 16-21. It begins with YHWH's pledge to remember Zion in v. 16 expressed metaphorically by YHWH's twofold statement that "upon the palms of my hands I have engraved you" in v. 16a and "your walls are before me always" in v. 16b. Verses 17-21 then shift to YHWH's pledge to return Zion's children, with a four-part portrayal of the process of return. The first in v. 17a asserts that "your children hurry to you." The second in v. 17b asserts that "those who have ruined you will now depart." The third in v. 18a asserts that "you will raise your eyes to see that the children have assembled and are coming." The fourth in vv. 18b-21 is a complex portrayal in five parts of YHWH's oath to return Zion's children. The first is the above-mentioned oath formula and oracle formula in v. 18bα$^{1-4}$ which verifies YHWH's intentions with the oath formula in v. 18bα$^{1-2}$ and the oracle formula in v. 18bα$^{3-4}$. The second is YHWH's two-part statement to Zion in v. 18bα^5-β that "you (Zion) shall wear them (your children) like jewelry" in v. 18bα$^{5-8}$ and that "you (Zion) shall bind them (your children) on like a bride" in v. 18bβ. The third is YHWH's statement in v. 19 that "your ruined land and places will be crowded with inhabitants while your enemies stay far away." The fourth is YHWH's statement in v. 20 that "your children will say that the place is too crowded" as they demand room to live. The fifth in v. 21 presents YHWH's statement that asserts that Zion will say to herself, "where did they come from?" The 2nd-feminine singular speech formula, *wĕʾāmart bilbābēk,* "and you will say in your heart," in v. 21aα$^{1-2}$ introduces Zion's speech. Zion's speech proper in v. 21aα^3-b comprises three parts: "who bore them when I was bereaved and barren, exiled and turned aside?" in v. 21aβ^3-bα$^{1-2}$; "who raised them when I was indeed left alone?" in v. 21bα^3-γ^4; and "where have they been?" in v. 21bγ$^{5-6}$.

The second oracular response in 49:22-23 focuses on YHWH's promise to signal the nations to bring Zion's children home. It begins with the messenger formula in v. 22aα$^{1-4}$, which asserts that the following oracle of deliverance in vv. 22aα^5-23 is from YHWH. YHWH's oracle comprises five components that depict the stages of YHWH's action. The first in v. 22aα^5-β presents YHWH's two-part statement to "raise my hand to the nations" in v. 22aα$^{5-9}$ and to "lift my ensign to the peoples" in v. 22aβ. The second in v. 22b presents YHWH's two-part statement that "they will bring your children home, carrying your sons in their bosoms" in v. 22bα and "carrying your daughters on their shoulders" in v. 22bβ. The third in v. 23aα presents YHWH's twofold statement that "kings and queens will care for your children," including the kings who will be your caretakers in v. 23aα$^{1-3}$ and the queens who will be your wet nurses in v. 23aα$^{4-5}$. The fourth in v. 23aβ-γ presents YHWH's twofold assertion that "they will bow to you" in v. 23aβ and that "they will lick the dust of your feet" in v. 23aγ. The fifth in v. 23b presents a qualified example of the recognition formula, including the recognition formula per se in v. 23bα, "and you (Zion) shall know that I am YHWH," and the qualification in v. 23bβ that "those who wait for me will not be shamed." The recognition formula thus marks the realization of the return of Zion's children, i.e., the people of Israel, as a revelatory act of YHWH's power in the world and it exhorts Jerusalem to continue to wait for the time when YHWH's promise will actually be realized.

The third oracular response in 49:24-26 focuses on YHWH's pledge to ensure Zion's salvation. It begins with the twofold rhetorical questions in v. 24: "can spoil be taken from a warrior?" in v. 24a and "can captives be released from one who is righteous?" in v. 24b. Both rhetorical questions would normally be answered with a "no!" in this context; YHWH pledges to accomplish precisely what cannot normally be done. The presentation of YHWH's oracular answer to these questions in vv. 25-26 begins with the messenger formula in v. 25aα$^{1-4}$ to verify YHWH as the source of the answer. The oracle proper in vv. 25aα^5-26 then follows in four parts that assert YHWH's plans to deliver Israel's captives, i.e., Zion's children, from their captors. The first element in v. 25aα^5-β asserts in two parts that captives and spoil will be taken, including captives taken from a warrior in v. 25aα$^{5-8}$ and spoil retrieved from a tyrant in v. 25aβ. The second element in v. 25b asserts that YHWH will contend with adversaries to deliver the children, including the contention with adversaries in v. 25bα and the deliverance of children in v. 25bβ. The third element in v. 26a presents YHWH's promise to make Zion's oppressors eat their own flesh and drink their own blood, with the flesh appearing in v. 26aα and the blood in v. 26aβ. Finally, the fourth element in v. 26b presents an elaborated recognition formula, with the recognition formula "all will know that I am YHWH your deliverer" in v. 26bα and the elaboration of YHWH's qualities as "your redeemer, the Mighty One of Jacob" in v. 26bβ. As in 49:22-23, YHWH's action appears as a revelatory event.

Isaiah 50:1-11 constitutes a trial scene which presents YHWH's conditions for the salvation or restoration of Israel. The introductory prophetic messenger speech in 50:1-3 constitutes a trial speech which builds on the messenger speech pattern of the disputation speech of 49:14-26 (see 49:22, 24-25). It differs from the earlier promises of salvation in 49:14-26 by focusing on the people's responsibility for their exile. The third Servant Song in 50:4-9 presents the servant's psalm of confidence in YHWH, which functions as a model for the people's outlook and behavior. The unit then concludes with the prophet's presentation of YHWH's conditions for salvation in 50:10-11. Specifically, this unit builds upon the Servant Song by calling upon the people to trust in YHWH.

The trial speech in 50:1-3 argues that the people are responsible for their own exile because they broke their covenant with YHWH. The subunit begins with a prophetic messenger formula in v. 1aα$^{1-3}$, which introduces the trial speech proper in vv. 1aα^4-3 and identifies it as a speech by YHWH. The trial speech comprises two sets of rhetorical questions and their rhetorical answers, which assert the charge of the people's guilt in this matter.

The first set of two rhetorical questions appears in v. 1aα^4-b. The rhetorical questions appear in v. 1aα^4-β, and they assert that YHWH brought punishment on the people because of their sins. The first rhetorical question in v. 1aα$^{4-10}$ asks "where is the divorce document of your mother whom I divorced?" which functions as a means to assert that the grounds for the divorce, the disruption of YHWH's relationship with Israel, would be stated there. The second rhetorical question in v. 1aβ asks "who are my creditors to whom I sold you?" which functions as an assertion that the reason for YHWH's sale of the people, i.e., the mother's children, would be found by consulting the parties to whom the people were sold. The rhetorical answers then follow in v. 1b. The first in v. 1bα charges that the people were sold for their sins, and the second in v. 1bβ charges that your mother was divorced because of the people's (her children's) sins.

The second set of rhetorical questions appears in 50:2-3 and asserts that YHWH is the true power in the universe. Two subsets of rhetorical questions appear in v. 2a. The first subset in v. 2aα asserts that the people did not appear or answer, i.e., v. 2aα$^{1-4}$ asks "why was no one there when I came?" and v. 2aα$^{5-7}$ asks "why did no one answer when I called?" The second subset of rhetorical questions in v. 2aβ-γ asserts that YHWH has the strength to redeem and deliver. The first in v. 2aβ asks, "is my hand too short to redeem?" and the second in v. 2aγ asks, "do I lack the strength to deliver?" Three sets of rhetorical answers follow in vv. 2b-3. The first in v. 2bα presents YHWH's twofold assertion that "I dried up the sea" in v. 2bα$^{1-4}$, and that "I made the rivers a desert" in v. 2bα$^{5-7}$. The second in v. 2bβ-γ portrays the rotting and dead fish that result from YHWH's aforementioned actions concerning the sea and the rivers. Verse 2bβ portrays the fish that rot for lack of water, and v. 2bγ portrays the fish dying of thirst. The third in v. 3 then presents metaphorically the mourning that follows from YHWH's actions against creation by drying up the seas and rivers. YHWH asserts in v. 3a that "I clothe the heavens in darkness," in mourning, and YHWH asserts in v. 3b that "I cover the heavens with sackcloth," the clothing of mourning. Altogether, these rhetorical answers assert YHWH's role as the true power in creation.

Isaiah 50:4-9 then presents a psalm of confidence in YHWH by the servant, which functions as a model for the people's outlook and behavior within the larger context of 50:1-11. The structure of the psalm is based on three syntactically-independent statements concerning YHWH's actions on behalf of the servant and the servant's reactions to YHWH in vv. 4, 5-7 (which contains two such sections in vv. 5-6 and 7 joined by a conjunctive wāw), and 8-9.

The first subunit of the psalm is the servant's assertion in 50:4 that "My L-rd YHWH gives me the tongue of those who are taught," i.e., YHWH instructs me to listen like those who are taught. The first element in this subunit appears in v. 4a, which presents the servant's basic statement of the issue in two parts. The servant states in v. 4aα that "YHWH gave me the tongue (i.e., instruction speech) of those who are taught" (limmûdîm). The servant then defines YHWH's purpose in v. 4aβ, that the servant would know how to give aid to the weary. The second element in v. 4b presents the servant's statements that "YHWH opens my ear to listen like those who are taught." The first element in v. 4bα presents the servant's statement that "YHWH opens my ear every morning," and v. 4bβ presents the purpose, "to listen like those who are taught."

The second subunit of the psalm is the servant's assertion that "My L-rd YHWH opens my ear and helps me" in 50:5-7. This subunit comprises two elements joined by a conjunctive wāw in vv. 5-6 and 7, each of which opens with a reference to "my L-rd YHWH." The servant asserts in the first element in vv. 5-6 that "YHWH opens my ear." The servant presents YHWH's action in v. 5aα, and the servant's reactions then follow in vv. 5aβ-6. The presentation of the servant's reactions comprises four elements, each of which describes a different aspect of the servant's reactions. The servant's assertion that "I did not rebel" constitutes the first reaction in v. 5aβ. The servant's assertion that "I did not flee" constitutes the second reaction in v. 5b. The servant's assertion that "I submitted to insults" constitutes the third reaction in v. 6a, including statements that "I gave my back to beating" in v. 6aα and that "I gave my cheeks to spitting" in v. 6aβ. The servant's assertion that "I did not hide my face from insult and spitting" then concludes the sequence with the fourth reaction in v. 6b. The second element of the subunit appears in v. 7 with the servant's assertion that "my L-rd YHWH helps me." YHWH's action appears in v. 7aα, and the results, that the servant is not ashamed, appear in v. 7aβ-b. The results appear in two parts. The servant states in v. 7aβ that "I am not humiliated." In v. 7b the servant states that "I set my face like flint" and "I am not shamed," with the first part of this statement in v. 7bα and the second part in v. 7bβ.

The third subunit of the psalm in 50:8-9 constitutes the servant's assertions of confidence in YHWH coupled with rhetorical questions that reinforce the servant's assertions. The subunit comprises four basic elements, each of which presents a different but related contention. The first appears in v. 8aα-β^3 in which the servant asserts that "my defender is near so that no one will challenge me." The assertion that "my defender is near" appears in v. 8aα. The rhetorical question "who will contend with me?" in v. 8aβ$^{1-3}$ reinforces the assertion by claiming that "no one will contend with me." The second appears in v. 8aβ^4-b in which the servant asserts that "we stand together so that no one will contest." The assertion per se appears in v. 8aβ$^{4-5}$, and the rhetorical question with a rejoinder appears in v. 8b. The rhetorical question "who brings my case to trial?" in v. 8bα dismisses the ability of anyone to challenge the servant as long as "we," i.e., the servant and YHWH, stand together. The rejoinder "let him approach" in v. 8bβ reinforces the point by indicating that if such a contender approaches, he will lose as long as the servant and YHWH stand together. The third appears in v. 9a in which the servant asserts that "my L-rd YHWH helps me so that no one condemns me." The assertion proper appears in v. 9aα, and the rhetorical question "who will condemn me?" in v. 9aβ reinforces the point by asserting that "no one will condemn me." The fourth element appears in v. 9b in which the servant asserts that "my opponents have no power." The servant presents this assertion metaphorically in two parts. The servant states in v. 9bα that "my opponents wear out like a garment," and the statement "a moth consumes them" then follows to reinforce the point in v. 9bβ.

Isaiah 50:10-11 constitutes the prophet's presentation of YHWH's declaration of conditions for the covenant with Israel. The subunit comprises two basic elements in vv. 10 and 11, each of which is defined by its speaker. Isaiah 50:10 presents the prophet's exhortation to trust in YHWH. This subunit includes two basic elements. The first is the prophet's rhetorical questions in v. 10a-bα that call upon the people to trust in YHWH and listen to the servant. The first rhetorical question in v. 10a, "who among you trusts in YHWH?" functions as an exhortation to trust in YHWH. The second rhetorical question in v. 10bα, "who among you listens to the servant who walks in darkness without light?" functions as an exhortation to listen to the servant. The prophet's twofold exhortation proper then follows in v. 10bβ-γ. The prophet exhorts the people to trust in YHWH in v. 10bβ and to rely on G-d in v. 10bγ. The prophet's statements in v. 10 then introduce YHWH's admonition to "abandon your resistance (to

YHWH)" in v. 11. YHWH's admonition includes three basic elements which employ metaphorical language to warn the people of the danger they are in by resisting YHWH. The first appears in v. 11a, in which YHWH observes that the people are immersed in fire. It includes two components: the statement "you kindle fire" in v. 11aα and the statement that "you gird on sparks" in v. 11aβ. The second is YHWH's challenge to the people in v. 11bα to walk in fire (and see the result). This element includes two basic components: the command to "walk in the light of your fire" in v. 11bα$^{1-3}$ and the command to "walk in the sparks which you have kindled" in v. 11bα$^{4-5}$. The third is YHWH's admonition in v. 11bβ-γ that "you will suffer because this comes from me," including the statement that "this comes to you from my hand" in v. 11bβ and the statement that "you will lie in pain" in v. 11bγ.

Isaiah 51:1–52:12 constitutes a proclamation of salvation for Zion. Its purpose is to provide a culmination for 49:14–52:12 with an announcement of Zion's restoration and YHWH's return to Zion to establish divine worldwide sovereignty. It is demarcated at the outset by the threefold exhortation to listen and see in 51:1-8, which constitutes the first subunit of the passage and addresses the people of Jerusalem/Israel with imperative commands to listen to YHWH and to see YHWH's acts of restoration for Zion. It continues with the second subunit of the passage, the announcement of Zion's restoration, specifically expressed as YHWH's return to Zion, in 51:9–52:12. The unit closes with the culminating subunit of 51:9–52:12, a command to the people to join YHWH and to depart for Jerusalem in 52:11-12. Isaiah 52:13, with its introductory *hinnēh,* "behold!" marks the beginning of the next unit of the text.

The threefold exhortation to listen and see in 51:1-8 comprises three basic subunits, each of which is defined by a masculine plural imperative verb that calls upon its audience to listen in vv. 1, 4, and 7. In the case of the first two instances, a 2nd-masculine plural imperative in vv. 1b and 6 calls upon the addressees to observe YHWH's actions as well. These three subunits in 51:1-3, 4-6, and 7-8 function together to call the exiled people of Jerusalem/Israel to witness YHWH's actions on behalf of Zion. They thereby prepare the audience for the announcement of Zion's restoration in 51:9–52:12.

The first subunit in 51:1-3 begins in v. 1a with the call to attention, which employs the masculine plural imperative verb *šim'û 'ēlî,* "listen to me," to command "those who pursue righteousness, those who seek YHWH," to listen to the prophet. The imperative phrase "listen to me" in v. 1aα constitutes the basic statement of the call to attention, and the addressees appear in v. 1aβ, including "you who pursue justice" in v. 1aβ$^{1-2}$ and "you who seek YHWH" in v. 1aβ$^{3-4}$. The phrase "you who pursue righteousness, you who seek YHWH" functions as a means to address those exiles who would return to Jerusalem by characterizing them in positive terms. It thereby serves as a rhetorical device to persuade the audience that the right thing to do is to seek YHWH and pursue righteousness by returning to Jerusalem. Isaiah 51:1b-2 then follows with a twofold call to see, each of which begins with the imperative verb *habbîṭû 'el,* "look unto," in vv. 1b and 2. The first call to see in v. 1b employs the imperative "look unto" as the basis for two commands. The first in v. 1bα calls upon the audience to "look to the rock from which you were cut," and the second in v. 1bβ supplies a parallel command to "look to the quarry from which you were carved." The second call to see in v. 2 then specifies the first by reference to Abraham and Sarah. The call proper in v. 2a again employs the imperative phrase *habbîṭû 'el,* "look unto," to command the audience to look first to "Abraham your father" in v. 2aα and then to "Sarah who bore you" in v. 2aβ. The basis for the call to see appears in v. 2b, introduced by the particle *kî,* "for, because." The first portion of the basis in v. 2bα explains that "he, Abraham, was only one person when I called him." Apparently, the text presumes that the reference to Abraham covers Sarah as well. The second portion of the basis in v. 2bβ then follows with YHWH's statement that "I blessed and multiplied him." The basis for the entire exhortation in vv. 1-3 then appears in v. 3, again introduced by *kî,* "for, because." The basis falls into three paired components, the first two of which describe YHWH's actions and the third of which describes the outcome for Zion. Verse 3aα presents a paired statement of YHWH's comfort for Zion and its ruins, including the statement of comfort for Zion in v. 3aα$^{1-4}$ and the statement of comfort for Zion's ruins in v. 3aα$^{5-7}$. Verse 3aβ-γ presents a paired statement of YHWH's transformation of the wilderness and the desert, including the wilderness like Eden in v. 3aβ and the desert like the garden of YHWH in v. 3aγ. Verse 3b then presents a paired statement of the results of YHWH's actions including gladness and joy in v. 3bα and thanksgiving and the sound of music in v. 3bβ.

The second exhortation to hear and see addressed to "my nation" appears in 51:4-6. It is demarcated at the outset with the masculine plural imperative verbal expressions *haqšîbû 'ēlay,* "pay attention to me," and *ha'ăzînû,* "give ear," in v. 4a, which introduce the call to attention with basis in 51:4-5. The masculine plural imperative verbal phrases "raise (*śĕ'û*) to the heavens your eyes and look (*wĕhabbîṭû*) to the earth below" in v. 6a introduce the exhortation to see YHWH's victory in 51:6.

The call to attention in 51:4-5 begins with a twofold call to attention in v. 4a based on the above-mentioned imperative phrases, "pay attention to me, my people" in v. 4aα and "my nation, to me give ear" in v. 4aβ. The basis for the call, introduced by the particle *kî,* "for, because," then follows in 51:4b-5. The basic statement of the cause appears in the paired statements in v. 4b, including "because Torah from me goes out" in v. 4bα and "my law for a light to the nations I establish" in v. 4bβ. Isaiah 51:5 then elaborates on the basis for the call by pointing to the nations and coastlands that wait for YHWH's rule. The first part of the elaboration in v. 5a employs the metaphor of YHWH's arm as an expression for YHWH's power to rule. It includes the twofold statement in v. 5aα that "my righteousness is near" in v. 5aα$^{1-2}$ and "my victory goes forth" in v. 5aα$^{3-4}$. Verse 5aβ then concludes with a summary statement, "and my arm will rule nations." Isaiah 51:5b then follows with its portrayal of the coastlands hoping and waiting for YHWH, including the statement that "the coastlands hope for me" in v. 5bα and that "the coastlands wait for my arm," i.e., power, in v. 5bβ.

Isaiah 51:6 then presents the exhortation to see YHWH's victory as the complement to the call to attention in 51:4-5. It begins with the twofold exhortation proper in v. 6a based on the above-mentioned masculine plural imperative phrases, "lift to the heavens your eyes" in v. 6aα and "and look to the earth below" in v. 6aβ. The bases for the exhortation then follow in 51:6b as five statements, introduced by the particle *kî*, "because," and joined by conjunctive *wāw*'s. They include the statements that "the heavens will dissipate like a cloud" in v. 6bα¹⁻⁴; that "the earth will wear out like a garment" in v. 6bα⁵⁻⁷; that "earth's inhabitants will die like gnats" in v. 6bβ¹⁻⁴; that "my victory shall be forever" in v. 6bβ⁵⁻⁷; and that "my righteousness shall not be dismayed" in v. 6bγ.

The third exhortation to hear, but without the exhortation to see, appears in 51:7-8 addressed to "the nation with my Torah in their heart." It begins with the exhortations in 51:7, each of which is expressed with paired masculine plural verbal forms. The first is a twofold call to attention in v. 7a, expressed with imperative verbal expression *šim'û 'ēlay*, "listen to me," addressed to "you who know righteousness" in v. 7aα and to "the nation with my Torah in their heart" in v. 7aβ. A twofold reassurance speech, introduced by an example of the reassurance formula, *'al-tîrē'û*, "do not fear," and the imperative phrase *'al-tēḥāttû*, "do not be dismayed," then follows in v. 7b, including the commands "do not fear the shame of humans" in v. 7bα and "do not be dismayed by their jeers" in v. 7bβ. The bases for these exhortations then appear in v. 8 in two parts. The first in v. 8a asserts that the shaming and jeering of human beings will pass away, including metaphorical statements that "moths will eat them like a garment" in v. 8aα and that "moths will eat them like wool" in v. 8aβ. The second in v. 8b then asserts that YHWH's righteousness and victory are forever, including the statement that "my righteousness is forever" in v. 8bα and that "my victory is for all generations" in v. 8bβ.

Isaiah 51:9–52:12 constitutes an announcement of the restoration of Zion. In contrast to 51:1-8, which employs masculine plural address forms, 51:9–52:12 employs a combination of feminine singular and masculine plural address forms directed to Bat Zion as the metaphorical personification of Jerusalem and to its inhabitants. The unit includes five basic subunits which form the elements of the announcement of Zion's restoration. They include the answered lament in 51:9-16, which asserts that YHWH will act; the salvation speech in 51:17-23, which announces that the suffering of Zion is over; the exhortation of comfort to Zion in 52:1-6; the vision of the herald in 52:7-10, which announces YHWH's return to Zion; and the command to the people to depart Babylon and join YHWH in returning to Zion in 52:11-12.

Isaiah 51:9-16 constitutes an answered lament which sets the sequence of subunits within 51:9–52:12 into motion. Here YHWH responds to the lament of the people to indicate that YHWH will act to restore Zion. The passage comprises two components, including the quotation of the lament in which the people appeal for YHWH to act in 51:9-11 and YHWH's answer in 51:12-16, in which YHWH pledges to deliver the people.

The quotation of the lament in 51:9-11 begins in v. 9a with a metaphorical appeal for YHWH's arm to take action on behalf of Israel as in former times. The metaphor of YHWH's arm signifies YHWH's power to defend Israel as in the past. The passage employs feminine singular imperative verbs, including three examples of *'ûrî*, "awake," and one of *libšî*, "clothe (yourself)," metaphorically addressed to YHWH's arm. The appeal comprises two parts; the first in v. 9aα calls upon YHWH's arm to awaken two times and to clothe itself in strength, and the second in v. 9aβ calls upon YHWH's arm to awaken as it did in days of old and past generations. Rhetorical questions then follow in 51:9b-11 to call to mind YHWH's past actions as a basis to motivate YHWH's actions in the present. In doing so, the rhetorical questions also motivate the audience to have confidence that YHWH will act. The subunit includes two sets of rhetorical questions in vv. 9b and 10-11. The first set in 51:9b metaphorically asks the arm if it has subdued sea monsters. Insofar as the questions are rhetorical, they function as assertions that of course YHWH's arm has subdued sea monsters in the past, including the cleaving of Rahab in v. 9bα and the piercing of the Dragon in v. 9bβ. The second set of rhetorical questions then follows in 51:10-11 with three rhetorical questions that focus on the arm's role in drying the sea, much as in the exodus, so the exiles could return to Zion. The first rhetorical question, "did you not dry the sea?" appears in v. 10aα. The second, "did you not dry the great deep?" appears in v. 10aβ. The third, "did you not make a road for the redeemed to pass?" appears together with elaboration in vv. 10b-11. The question proper appears in v. 10b, and the elaboration on the question appears in v. 11. The elaboration comprises two basic elements. The first is a twofold statement in v. 11a concerning the return of the ransomed people to Zion, including the announcement that the ransomed of YHWH will return in v. 11aα and the following announcement that they will come to Zion with shouting in v. 11aβ. The second is a threefold statement concerning the rejoicing of the ransomed people as they return to Zion in v. 11aγ-b, including the announcement that eternal joy is upon their head in v. 11aγ; that they will attain joy and gladness in v. 11bα; and that worry and groaning will flee in v. 11bβ.

Isaiah 51:12-16 then constitutes YHWH's answer, that "I will deliver you as my people." The unit comprises three basic elements, including YHWH's initial response of comfort in v. 12a; an elaboration concerning YHWH's resolve expressed in the form of rhetorical questions and answers in vv. 12b-14; and the hymnic response that "I am YHWH and you are my people" in vv. 15-16.

YHWH's initial response in 51:12a to the preceding lament in vv. 9-11 is an emphatic statement that "I, I am your comforter." The double use of *'ānōkî*, "I," adds emphasis to indicate that this is YHWH's definitive answer to the lament.

The elaboration in 51:12b-14 employs two rhetorical questions with responses in vv. 12b-13a and 13b-14 to demonstrate YHWH's resolve to deliver the people. The first rhetorical question with answer in 51:12b-13a begins with a twofold rhetorical question concerning "why do you fear mortals?" in v. 12b. The first expression of the question appears in v. 12bα as "why do you fear men who will die?" and the second in v. 12bβ asks "why do you fear humans who are like grass?" The response in 51:13a emphasizes that "you have forgotten YHWH and you therefore fear the oppressor." The first portion of the response in v. 13aα[1-7] indicates that "you have forgotten YHWH your maker who spread out the heavens and founded the earth." The second portion of the response in v. 13aα[8]-β indicates that "you fear all the time the wrath of the oppressor who prepares to destroy you." The second rhetorical question with answer then follows in 51:13b-14. The question per se, "where is the anger of the oppressor?" appears in v. 13b to indicate that the people should not fear the anger of the oppressor. The response, that the oppressed one is freed, appears in v. 14 in three parts, including the statement that "quickly the oppressed is freed" in v. 14a; the statement that "he does not die" in v. 14bα; and the statement that "he does not lack bread" in v. 14bβ.

Isaiah 51:15-16 then constitutes the hymnic response that closes 51:9-16 with YHWH's hymnic assertion that "I am YHWH and you are my people." The hymnic response comprises two basic elements. The first element in v. 15 focuses on YHWH's statement of identity, "I am YHWH your G-d." It includes the basic statement of YHWH's identity in v. 15aα followed by the qualification in v. 15aβ that YHWH is the one who stirs up the sea so that its waves roar and the declaration in v. 15b that YHWH Seba'ot is the divine name. The second element in v. 16 focuses on YHWH's actions, namely, what YHWH will do. It includes four elements: YHWH's statement to the prophet that "I place my words in your mouth" in v. 16aα; YHWH's statement to the prophet in v. 16aβ that "in the shadow of my hand I conceal you"; YHWH's qualification in v. 16bα that YHWH spread out the heavens and founded the earth; and YHWH's qualification in v. 16bβ that YHWH will say to the people, "you are my people."

Isaiah 51:17-23 constitutes the second major element of 51:1–52:12 as a salvation speech that announces that Zion's suffering is over. It includes two basic components. The first is the call to Jerusalem to awaken and rise in 51:17 so that she might hear the salvation speech. The second is the salvation speech proper in 51:18-23 that announces that Zion's suffering is over.

The call to Jerusalem to awaken and rise in 51:17 employs feminine singular address forms to portray Jerusalem metaphorically once again as Bat Zion. The subunit includes two basic components. The first is the commands to Jerusalem to awaken and rise in v. 17aα, each of which is based on a feminine singular imperative verb, including *hit'ôrĕrî*, "awaken," in v. 17aα[1]; *hit'ôrĕrî*, "awaken," once again in v. 17aα[2]; and *qûmî*, "arise, O Jerusalem," in v. 17aα[3-4]. The second is the qualification of Jerusalem as one who has drunk the cup of YHWH's wrath in v. 17aβ-b, including the first component of the qualification that she has drunk the cup of YHWH's wrath in v. 17aβ and the second component of the qualification that she has drained the goblet of reeling in v. 17b.

Isaiah 51:18-23 then constitutes the salvation speech proper, which asserts that Zion's suffering is over. It is structured much like a prophetic judgment speech into two parts, including the basis for salvation in Zion's current state of ruin in vv. 18-20, followed by the announcement of salvation in vv. 21-23. Like a prophetic judgment speech, it therefore points to the current status of the people followed by the anticipated outcome.

The basis for salvation in 51:18-20 focuses on Zion's current state of ruin and includes three basic elements. In all three, the passage employs metaphorical imagery of Zion as woman and mother in relation to her sons. The first in v. 18 focuses on Zion's lack of guidance due to the absence of her sons. In this case, the imagery portrays the city bereft of her inhabitants. It comprises two elements, including the assertion that there is no one to guide her from all the sons that she bore in v. 18a and the assertion that there is no one to hold her hand from all the sons that she raised in v. 18b. The second element in v. 19 portrays the two things that have befallen Zion: destruction and hunger. This is basically stated in v. 19aα and specified in v. 19aβ-b. The specification includes two elements expressed through rhetorical questions. Verse 19aβ focuses on destruction and ruin by asking "who will console you?" and v. 19b focuses on hunger and the sword by asking "who will comfort you?" Finally, the third element in v. 20 asserts that Zion's sons lie punished by YHWH. It includes the portrayal of Zion's sons lying faint like a trapped antelope in v. 20a and the assertion that they are filled with the wrath of YHWH and the rebuke of Zion's G-d in v. 20b. The portrayal of divine punishment likely influenced the decision to structure this oracle in terms much like those of the prophetic announcement of punishment.

Isaiah 51:21-23 then constitutes the announcement of salvation for Zion. It begins with the particle *lākēn,* "therefore," which reinforces the analogy with the prophetic announcement of punishment. The unit comprises two basic components, including the call to attention in 51:21 and the oracle of salvation for Zion in 51:22-23. The call to attention, introduced by *lākēn,* "therefore," in v. 21, employs the feminine singular imperative verb *šim'î-nā',* "hear now," addressed to Zion first as the humbled one in v. 21a and then as the one drunk but not with wine in v. 21b. The oracle of salvation for Zion then follows in 51:22-23. It begins with the prophetic messenger formula in v. 22aα attributed to "your L-rd, YHWH," in v. 22aα$^{1-4}$ and to "your G-d who contends for the people" in v. 22aα$^{5-7}$. The salvation oracle proper then follows in v. 22aβ-23. It includes two basic elements. The first element is YHWH's assertion that "I have taken the cup of reeling from you" in v. 22aβ-b. This includes the twofold basic statement in v. 22aβ-bα that "I have taken the cup of reeling" in v. 22aβ and that "I have taken the goblet of my wrath" in v. 22bα. Verse 22bβ then states the result: "you shall never again drink from the cup." The second element in v. 23 presents YHWH's statement that "I have given the cup of reeling to your oppressors." This is basically stated in v. 23aα and the oppressors are qualified in v. 23aβ-b. The oppressors are qualified as those who told Zion to lie down in v. 23aβ, including the narrative speech formula tag in v. 23aβ$^{1-3}$ and their statement, "lie down that we may cross," in v. 23aβ$^{4-5}$. Verse 23b then states the result of the oppressors' statement to Zion: she lay down so that they could cross.

Isaiah 52:1-6 consttutes the third major subunit of 51:1–52:12 as a proclamation of release for Zion. It is demarcated at the outset by the feminine singular imperative verbs *'ûrî, 'ûrî, libšî,* "awake, awake, put on (your strength)," addressed to Zion personified as Bat Zion. It continues through v. 6, in which YHWH announces to Zion and Israel that "I am the one who speaks, behold, I," which conveys YHWH's readiness to act on Zion's and Israel's behalf. The portrayal of the approaching herald in 52:7 introduces the next subunit of 51:1–52:12.

Isaiah 52:1-6 includes two basic components. The first is a fourfold address to Zion in 52:1-2 which employs feminine singular address forms to call upon Zion to rise from her current state of captivity and humiliation. The second is an explanatory address to Israel in 52:3-6 which employs masculine plural address forms to announce that YHWH will act against Israel's oppressor.

The fourfold address to Zion in 52:1-2 comprises four basic elements, each of which is defined by a distinctive 2nd-feminine singular address form to Zion according to her various designations. The first is an address to Zion in

v. 1a, calling upon her to awaken and clothe herself in strength in anticipation of her deliverance. The second appears in v. 1b, calling upon her as the Holy City Jerusalem to put on her splendid garments. It includes a call to put on her garments proper in v. 1bα, followed by an explanatory statement in v. 1bβ that indicates that the uncircumcised and unclean will not humiliate her again. The third element appears in v. 2a, which calls upon Jerusalem to shake off the dust, rise, and sit. The fourth element in v. 2b calls upon the captive Bat Zion to open the bonds upon her neck.

The explanatory address to Israel in 52:3-6 includes two basic elements, each of which elaborates on the impending release of Zion addressed in 52:1-2. The first explanatory address in Isa 52:3 is an oracular address that announces that Israel was sold for no price and that it will now be redeemed for no price. It begins with the explanatory particle *kî*, "for, because," followed by the prophetic messenger formula in v. 3aα. These elements both establish the relationship with 52:1-2 and identify the following material as an oracle from YHWH. The oracles proper in v. 3aβ-b present the two elements of YHWH's statements that Israel was sold for nothing in v. 3aβ and that Israel would be redeemed for nothing in v. 3b. The purpose of these statements is to establish the analogy between Israel's captivity in Egypt and its subjugation to Assyria. They thereby provide the basis from past experience in the first portion of the book of Isaiah (see, e.g., 10:20-26) for YHWH to release Zion/Israel from Babylonian captivity.

The second explanatory address in 52:4-6 then turns to YHWH's readiness to redeem the captive Israel/Bat Zion. This subunit is also formulated as an oracular speech. It begins in v. 4aα with a conjunctive *wāw* and particle *kî* followed by the prophetic messenger formula which establishes the parallel with v. 3. The oracle proper in vv. 4aβ-6 focuses on YHWH's intent to redeem the captive Israel/Bat Zion. Although the oracle announces restoration for Zion, it is patterned along the lines of a prophetic announcement of judgment. It begins in vv. 4aβ-5 with an announcement of the basis for YHWH's intervention on Zion's behalf. The first portion of this subunit in v. 4aβ-b focuses on Assyria's oppression of Israel like that of Egypt, including statements that Israel originally sojourned in Egypt in v. 4aβ and that Assyria oppressed Israel for nothing in v. 4b. The oracular elaboration of the meaning of this statement in v. 5 then turns to the basis for YHWH's action in three parts. The first is the rhetorical question in v. 5aα that asserts that YHWH gained nothing from these events. The first elaboration in v. 5aβ-bα asserts that the people were carried off for nothing while their oppressors howled, presumably in triumph. The second elaboration in v. 5bβ explains that such an act defiled YHWH's name, thereby establishing motivation for YHWH to act. Verse 6 then follows as the second element of the oracle with a twofold announcement of YHWH's intention to act on behalf of Israel/Bat Zion in v. 6. In the first announcement in v. 6a, YHWH states that "my people shall know my name," i.e., as a result of YHWH's intervention on their behalf. In the second announcement in v. 6b, YHWH announces that "I am the one who speaks, behold, I," in an effort to convince the people that YHWH is their true G-d who delivers them.

The vision of the herald announcing YHWH's return to Zion in 52:7-10 constitutes the fourth subunit of 51:1–52:12. It is demarcated at the outset by the portrayal of the approaching herald in v. 7 and it continues with accounts of the shouting that results from the vision, including the shouting of the watchmen in v. 8 and the call for Jerusalem/Israel to shout for the approach of YHWH in vv. 9-10.

The vision proper of the herald in 52:7 includes five basic elements. The first is the vision statement in v. 7aα that serves as the premise of the whole with its announcement of the approaching herald. The first qualification of this vision then follows in v. 7aβ$^{1-2}$ with a portrayal of the herald's announcement of peace. The second qualification follows in v. 7aβ$^{3-4}$ with the portrayal of the herald's announcement of goodness. The third qualification in v. 7aβ$^{5-6}$ portrays the herald's announcement of deliverance. The presentation of the herald's statement to Zion in v. 7b concludes the vision with the speech formula in v. 7bα and the herald's statement, "your G-d rules," in v. 7bβ.

The presentation of the shout of the watchmen at the approach of the herald in 52:8 includes two basic components. The first is the announcement of the watchmen's shout in v. 8a which includes three elements: the voice of the watchmen in v. 8aα; the statement that they have raised their voices in v. 8aβ; and the statement that together they sing out in v. 8aγ. The reason for their shouting then follows in v. 8b: they see YHWH's return to Zion.

The call for Jerusalem and Israel to shout for YHWH in 52:9-10 then closes the subunit. It begins with the call proper to the ruins of Jerusalem to shout in v. 9a. The bases for this call then follow in vv. 9b-10 with three assertions. The first in v. 9bα asserts that YHWH has comforted the people. The second in v. 9bβ asserts that YHWH has redeemed Jerusalem. The third in v. 10 asserts that YHWH has bared YHWH's arm so that all the nations can see, including statements that YHWH has bared the holy arm in the sight of all the nations in v. 10a and that all the ends of the earth can see the deliverance of our G-d in v. 10b.

Isaiah 52:11-12 constitutes the fifth and final subunit of 51:1–52:12, with a command to the people to depart Babylon and to join YHWH in the return to Jerusalem. The subunit is demarcated by its 2nd-masculine plural address forms which identify the people of Israel/Judah in Babylonian exile as the addressees. The subunit comprises two basic elements. The first is the twofold command proper to the bearers of the vessels of YHWH in v. 11. The identification of the addressees as the bearers of the vessels of YHWH presumes a holy procession led by the priests who would bear the vessels of the temple for restoration in Jerusalem. The first command in v. 11a calls upon the people to turn, go out, and touch nothing impure. The second command in v. 11b then follows with commands to go out and be pure. The bases for the commands then follow in v. 12. The first basis appears in v. 12a with an instruction that the people shall not depart in haste or flee. The statement that they shall not depart in haste appears in v. 12aα, and the statement that they shall not flee follows in v. 12aβ. The second basis for the commands appears in v. 12b with the announcement that "YHWH goes with you." The announcement that "YHWH goes before you" appears in v. 12bα, and the announcement that "the G-d of Israel guards your rear" appears in v. 12bβ.

Genre

Isaiah 49:14-26 is an example of the DISPUTATION speech. Disputations normally challenge a thesis or viewpoint articulated in a text, present a counterthesis or viewpoint, and provide argumentation to support the counterthesis (see Graffy, *A Prophet Confronts His People;* Murray, "The Rhetoric of Disputation"). In the present instance, 49:14-26 disputes Zion's statements in 49:14 that YHWH has abandoned and forgotten her. Such statements presuppose the prophetic marriage metaphor which posits that YHWH and Jerusalem or Israel are bound together in a marriage relationship in which YHWH is identified as the husband and Jerusalem/Zion or Israel functions as the wife (cf. Isaiah 54; Hosea 1–3; Zeph 3:14-20; Ezekiel 16; Baumann, *Love and Violence;* Abma, *Bonds of Love*). Zion's statements to YHWH therefore presuppose her metaphorical portrayal as the wife of YHWH who has been abandoned by her husband. Such a metaphor provides a means to give expression to Jerusalem's destruction by the Babylonian Empire in 587-586 B.C.E. and the exile to Babylonia of much of the city's surviving population.

Isaiah 49:15-26, however, presents YHWH's counterthesis and argumentation to dispute Zion's claims. The fundamental statement of YHWH's counterthesis, "And I will not forget you," appears in 49:15bβ as part of the larger text in vv. 15-26 that is designed to answer and refute Zion's claim. The prophet presents YHWH's answer in three oracular responses in vv. 15-21, 22-23, and 24-26. Each employs oracular language to ensure that the reader understands that YHWH is the source of each respective statement. The first oracular statement in vv. 15-21 employs a combination of the OATH FORMULA, *ḥay-'ānî,* "(as) I live," and the ORACLE FORMULA, *nĕ'um yhwh,* "utterance of YHWH," in v. 18bα to validate YHWH as the speaker. The oath formula confirms YHWH's commitment to restore Zion, and the oracle formula validates YHWH as the source of the commitment. The subunit begins with two RHETORICAL QUESTIONS in v. 15a, "can a woman forget her baby?" and "can a woman forget the child of her womb?" As rhetorical questions, both are considered to be self-evidently answered with "no." But YHWH's initial response in v. 15b is willing to grant that a mother might indeed forget her children in the present circumstance. Such a proposal serves the rhetorical purposes of the argument, however, insofar as the mother's willingness to forget then highlights YHWH's commitment never to forget Zion and to ensure that she will be restored. YHWH's extended response in vv. 16-21 then reiterates the basic counterthesis that YHWH will indeed remember Zion and argues on behalf of this counterthesis by making several key points. First are the metaphorical assertions in v. 16 that Zion is engraved on YHWH's hands and that her walls are before YHWH so that YHWH cannot possibly forget. Verses 17-21 then follow with an extended presentation of the return of Zion's children, which functions as a metaphorical statement that Jerusalem's population will return to reinhabit the city. The above-mentioned OATH FORMULA and ORACLE FORMULA both serve as means to reinforce and validate this assertion. Likewise, the SPEECH FORMULA, "and you (Zion) shall say in your heart," at the outset of v. 21 introduces Zion's speech in which she will express her affirmation at the return of her children by asking questions: "Who bore them? Who raised them? And where have they been?" By placing these questions into Zion's mouth, the passage effectively reinforces the counterargument of the disputation by having Zion herself affirm the argument.

The second oracular response appears in vv. 22-23. The oracle appears in the form of a prophetic MESSENGER SPEECH as indicated by the introductory prophetic MESSENGER FORMULA. The prophetic messenger speech constitutes a speech by YHWH that is delivered to its intended recipients by a prophet who presumably quotes YHWH's speech word for word. Although the genre is characteristically prophetic, it is rooted in diplomatic discourse in which an authority figure, e.g., Abraham in Genesis 24 or the Assyrian King Sennacherib in Isaiah 36–37/2 Kings 18–19, employs a messenger to convey a formal message to its intended party. The prophetic MESSENGER FORMULA, *kōh 'āmar yhwh*, "thus says YHWH," identifies YHWH as the source of the message. The oracle itself is an oracle of deliverance, which is an adaptation of the PROPHETIC ANNOUNCEMENT OF SALVATION. The oracle lacks the customary formula "do not fear," but it nevertheless promises salvation or deliverance for Jerusalem by YHWH. The concluding RECOGNITION FORMULA in v. 23b, "and they shall know that I am YHWH," then identifies the restoration of Zion and the return of the people to the city as a revelatory event by which all witnesses will recognize YHWH as the one who brought about the restoration.

The third oracular response in vv. 24-26 opens once again with a pair of RHETORICAL QUESTIONS in v. 24 that ask if spoil can be taken from a warrior and if captives can be released from one who prevails. The answer once again is presumably "no," but as in vv. 22-23, the oracle presumes that YHWH as the true G-d and creator is capable of such action. Thus, the presentation of YHWH's oracular answer in vv. 25-26 makes precisely that point: YHWH can take spoil and captives from victorious warriors and will demonstrate that capacity by taking the exiles from their Babylonian captors and restoring them to Jerusalem. Again, the oracular answer is formulated as a prophetic MESSENGER SPEECH in which the prophet presents YHWH's words to the intended audience, including both the fictive audience of the Babylonian exiles and the reading audience of the book. The prophetic MESSENGER FORMULA at the outset in v. 25aα$^{1-4}$ identifies YHWH as the source of the message. The elaborated RECOGNITION FORMULA in v. 26b again identifies YHWH's return of the exiles as a revelatory act by which all the world will recognize YHWH.

Isaiah 50:1-11 constitutes a TRIAL SCENE in which YHWH lays out the conditions for the salvation or restoration of Israel that has been at the forefront of (Second) Isaiah's concerns. The trial scene is an element of the TRIAL GENRES in which two parties present their arguments as part of a larger legal or forensic issue that would be settled in a court of law. The TRIAL GENRES are therefore closely related to the DISPUTATION speeches, which themselves present the arguments for or against a given point of contention. The fact that 50:1-11 follows directly upon the DISPUTATION speech in Isa 49:14-26 is no accident. Having announced assurance of salvation for Israel in 49:14-26, the issue now turns to the conditions by which salvation is to be achieved in 50:1-11. As full consideration of 50:1-11 shows, trust in YHWH emerges as the fundamental issue in

YHWH's offer. Such a concern points to the persuasive element of both the TRIAL GENRES and the DISPUTATION speeches. Both are designed to convince their respective audiences of the truth of their claims. In the present instance, that truth is that YHWH is capable of restoring Israel, but that YHWH requires something from Israel, trust in YHWH, in return. Such a strategy points to the aim of the TRIAL SCENE in 50:1-11: to convince its audience, whether that be the people of Israel in the late 6th century B.C.E. or the later readers of the book of Isaiah, to trust in YHWH as the party capable of redeeming or restoring Israel.

Isaiah 50:1-11 employs a number of additional generic elements as part of its overall presentation.

Isaiah 50:1-3 constitutes a TRIAL SPEECH within the overall pattern of the TRIAL GENRES. A TRIAL SPEECH is simply a speech made by one of the parties involved in the forensic dispute at hand. In the present instance, the prophet presents a speech by YHWH as part of the trial scene. The MESSENGER FORMULA in v. 1aα$^{1-3}$ identifies the following speech as a speech by YHWH. YHWH's TRIAL SPEECH proper in vv. 1aα^4-3 argues that the people have suffered on account of their sins and that YHWH is the true power in the universe. Both of these arguments are prefatory to the final argument in 50:10-11 that the people must trust in YHWH to achieve the restoration that YHWH promises. YHWH's TRIAL SPEECH makes extensive use of the RHETORICAL QUESTION to make its points. The RHETORICAL QUESTION is a question whose answer is obvious. The point of such a question is not to achieve an answer; rather, it is designed to win over the audience to the speaker's point of view by having the audience accept the expected answer and thereby accept an element in the line of reasoning that the speaker offers. RHETORICAL QUESTIONS therefore function as a persuasive element within a speech. In the present instance, the rhetorical questions of v. 1aα^4-β — "where is the divorce document of your mother whom I divorced?" and "who are my creditors to whom I sold you?" — are designed to persuade the audience by use of the metaphors of divorce and sale to accept that they were "divorced" and "sold," i.e., that their relationship with YHWH has been disrupted. The purpose of such an argumentative strategy becomes apparent in the RHETORICAL ANSWERS of v. 1b: "for your sins you were sold" and "for your sins your mother was divorced." By prompting the audience to accept the terms of the questions, the RHETORICAL ANSWERS thereby prepare the audience to accept YHWH's power to bring punishment upon them on account of their sins. The second set of RHETORICAL QUESTIONS and RHETORICAL ANSWERS in vv. 2-3 then carries the argument further. The two subsets of rhetorical questions make two different but related points. The first in v. 2aα asks "why was no one there when I came?" and "why did no one answer when I called?" to point to the people's responsibility for their failure to show or respond to YHWH as a cause of their punishment. The second in v. 2aβ-γ, "is my hand too short to redeem?" and "do I lack the strength to deliver?" make the point that YHWH possesses the power to restore the people following the punishment for their failure. The rhetorical answers in vv. 2b-3 underscore the second point by pointing to YHWH's powers over creation, in this instance the sea and the rivers, their fish, and the heavens, to demonstrate YHWH's capacity to redeem and restore Israel.

The second major generic element of 50:1-11 is the servant's SONG OF CONFIDENCE in 50:4-9. The SONG OF CONFIDENCE is generally considered to be an element of the COMPLAINT SONGS, but it can stand as an independent generic unit as well (see Gerstenberger, *Psalms, Part 2,* 535; cf. his treatment of AFFIRMATION OF CONFIDENCE, 508-9). It is essentially a hymnic form that expresses trust or confidence in YHWH. In the present instance, the SONG OF CONFIDENCE expresses the servant's trust in YHWH's support that prompted the servant not to rebel or flee when faced with opposition and oppression, but to trust in YHWH instead to stand behind him and uphold his position. Here, the servant argues that YHWH instructs him to listen like those who are taught, that YHWH opens his ears and helps him, and that, despite the hardships that the servant has suffered, no one will be able to challenge him as a result. The RHETORICAL QUESTION plays an important role in this passage as well to advance the argumentative agenda in the ASSERTIONS OF CONFIDENCE in vv. 8-9. The servant makes three assertions, each of which is followed by a RHETORICAL QUESTION that then builds toward the fourth and final assertion of the subunit. In the first, the servant asserts that "my defender is near" and then asks "who will contend with me?" as a means to assert that no one will do so. In the second, the servant asserts that "we (YHWH and I) stand together," followed by the RHETORICAL QUESTION "who brings my case to trial?" as a means to assert that no one will do so. In the third, the servant asserts that "YHWH helps me" and then asks the RHETORICAL QUESTION "who will condemn me?" as a means to assert that no one will do so. The fourth point, "my opponents have no power," then falls into place as the natural conclusion to the song. Altogether, the servant's SONG OF CONFIDENCE provides a model for the people to emulate as YHWH carries out the restoration.

Isaiah 50:1-11 concludes with its third generic element in 50:10-11, the prophet's concluding PARENESIS which declares YHWH's conditions for redeeming or restoring Israel. PARENESIS is a rhetorical genre that attempts to persuade an audience to adopt a specific set of beliefs or to engage in a specific set of actions with reference to a goal. It typically employs elements of EXHORTATION, an argument to engage in an action or to hold a belief, and ADMONITION, a warning against engaging in undesirable actions or holding undesirable beliefs. The prophet presents the EXHORTATION in v. 10 to trust in YHWH as a means to realize the promised restoration. The EXHORTATION also makes use of RHETORICAL QUESTIONS in v. 10a to make the point. The first, "who among you trusts in YHWH?" is designed to evoke trust among the audience of the passage. The second, "who among you listens to the servant who walks in darkness without light?" is designed to persuade the audience to listen to the servant and thereby to be able to endure the hardships of the exile prior to the realization of the restoration. YHWH's ADMONITION to abandon resistance to YHWH then appears in v. 11. There is no MESSENGER FORMULA to identify the verse as a speech by YHWH, only the 1st-person reference to the fact that this comes from "my hand" to indicate YHWH as speaker. Overall, the ADMONITION to abandon resistance to YHWH is designed to reinforce the charge that the people suffer for their own sins by metaphorically stating that they kindle fire, gird on sparks, and walk through them of their own accord.

The concluding statement that the people's pain comes from "my hand" reinforces the contention that YHWH is the true power and that the people should therefore trust in YHWH.

Isaiah 51:1–52:12 constitutes a PROPHETIC ANNOUNCEMENT OF SALVATION to Zion. The basic pattern for this form in Deutero-Isaiah comprises three elements: the REASSURANCE FORMULA, "fear not!" which appears in 51:7; the basis for reassurance, which appears in 51:1-8, especially in vv. 3, 4b-5, and 8; and the PROPHETIC ANNOUNCEMENT OF SALVATION per se, which appears in 51:9–52:12. This is a highly elaborated example of the genre which employs a metaphorical portrayal of Zion as Bat Zion, "Daughter Zion," as the object or addressee of the passage. Indeed, the passage is designed to convince its audience, exiled Jerusalemites, Judeans, and Israelites, that the time has come to return to Jerusalem and to begin the work of rebuilding the city to display YHWH's power and sovereignty over all creation. Because 51:1–52:12 is a large and complex unit with persuasive intent, a number of other genres also appear within.

A key genre is the EXHORTATION. An EXHORTATION is an address form employed to persuade an audience to adapt a particular viewpoint and course of action. It influences the passage as a whole, insofar as 51:1–52:12 is designed to persuade its audience to accept that YHWH is the true G-d of all creation and that it is now time to return to Jerusalem to rebuild the city and the land of Israel and thereby to demonstrate YHWH's sovereignty to the world. The genre is particularly influential in 51:1-8, which is constituted as a threefold EXHORTATION to listen and to see. As noted in the discussion above, 51:1-8 also functions as the basis for reassurance in the PROCLAMATION OF SALVATION in order to provide the foundations for the ANNOUNCEMENT OF SALVATION to Zion in 51:9–52:13. The exhortational character of the passage speaks to its persuasive function insofar as the purpose of the unit is not simply to announce Jerusalem's restoration but to convince the people to take part in that restoration. As noted in the discussion of structure above, 51:1-8 comprises three basic subunits in vv. 1-3, 4-6, and 7-8, which call upon the audience to hear and to see the bases for the coming restoration of Zion. Consequently, these subunits do double duty by providing both the evidence for reassurance in keeping with the PROPHETIC ANNOUNCEMENT OF SALVATION and the evidence for the EXHORTATION.

A variety of other genres and formulas also appear within 51:1-8. The CALL TO ATTENTION appears in 51:1a, 4a, and 7a. The CALL TO ATTENTION formula typically begins with an imperative verb that calls upon the audience to hear the following announcement. In the present text, several verbs are used, including šim'û, "hear!" in v. 1a; haqšîbû, "pay attention!" and ha'ăzînû, "give ear!" in v. 4a; and šim'û, "hear!" once again in v. 7a. These are coupled with similar imperative verbs for seeing to draw upon the interest in Deutero-Isaiah for calling upon the exile to see and to hear and thereby to open their eyes and ears that were commanded to be shut in ch. 6. Another genre within 51:1-8 is the REASSURANCE SPEECH in 51:7b, which functions as a means to instill confidence in the people that YHWH will indeed act to restore Zion and therefore they must return to Jerusalem to take part in YHWH's action. The REASSURANCE SPEECH typically begins with the REASSURANCE FORMULA, in this case expressed as the negative command form, 'al-tîrĕ'û, "do not fear!" in v. 7b. In this instance, the parallel negative command, *'al-tēḥātû,* "do not be dismayed!" accompanies the REASSURANCE FORMULA.

Isaiah 51:9–52:12 constitutes the ANNOUNCEMENT OF SALVATION for Zion as the second element of the PROPHETIC ANNOUNCEMENT OF SALVATION in 51:1–52:12. This is the key element in the genre insofar as it conveys its basic purpose. Nevertheless as noted above, this passage is designed to persuade its audience as well as inform it. Consequently, a variety of generic elements influence the composition of this text to serve its persuasive purpose to convince the audience that YHWH is indeed restoring Jerusalem and that the exiles must return to Jerusalem to take part in the restoration.

One generic element is the ANSWERED LAMENT in 51:9-16. This is a variation of the classic LAMENTATION or COMPLAINT form that appears so frequently in the Psalms. The ANSWERED LAMENT typically gives voice to a complaint on the part of the psalmist to YHWH in order to ask YHWH for relief from the problem named in the LAMENT. At the most basic level, the purpose of the ANSWERED LAMENT in 51:9-16 is to appeal to YHWH to act to deliver Jerusalem. But it also functions as a means to convince the audience that YHWH will act. Consequently, vv. 9-11 quote the lament per se as an appeal to YHWH to act to restore the city of Jerusalem. Indeed, the ANSWERED LAMENT employs RHETORICAL QUESTIONS in vv. 9b-11 that serve as the basis for the appeal by asserting YHWH's past acts of deliverance and the ordering of creation. YHWH's answer to the lament then follows in 51:12-16, beginning with YHWH's initial response in v. 12a, "I, I am your comforter." Such an answer serves the persuasive function of the passage to convince the audience that YHWH will act and thereby to convince the audience to take part in the restoration. The passage likewise employs two sets of RHETORICAL QUESTIONS, with answers in vv. 12b-13a and 13b-14 that assert that YHWH is the creator who spread out the heavens and established the earth. Why then should the people fear their mortal oppressors (vv. 12a-13a), and why should they fear the anger of their oppressors when YHWH has freed them (vv. 13b-14)? The hymnic response in 51:15-16 further serves the exhortational character of the passage. By employing the HYMN genre in vv. 15-16, the passage draws upon a liturgical form to identify YHWH as "your G-d" and to convince the audience that YHWH will act on Zion's — and their — behalf. Indeed, the HYMN employs an element of the covenant formula by stating that "YHWH is G-d and you are YHWH's people" (Rendtorff, *"Bundesformel"*).

Isaiah 51:17-23 then presents the salvation speech which conveys the generic ANNOUNCEMENT OF SALVATION. It begins with a call to Jerusalem to awaken and arise in v. 17 as a preparation for the salvation speech proper in vv. 18-23. Indeed, these verses employ the PROPHETIC ANNOUNCEMENT OF SALVATION genre, although it is clear that its formulation is heavily influenced by the PROPHETIC ANNOUNCEMENT OF PUNISHMENT. Apparently, the influence of the judgment form is intended to demonstrate YHWH's hand in the entire process from initial punishment to ultimate restoration in keeping with the purposes of the book of Isaiah to depict Jerusalem's experience of punishment and restoration entirely as an act of YHWH. Like the PROPHETIC ANNOUNCEMENT OF PUNISHMENT, vv. 18-20 lay out the basis for salvation by portraying Zion's current state of ruin as a deliberate act of punishment by YHWH. RHETORICAL QUESTIONS play a role in v. 19aβ-b by asserting that YHWH will console and comfort the people in the aftermath of punishment, thereby pointing to YHWH as the sovereign who brings both punishment and restoration. The ANNOUNCE-MENT OF SALVATION proper in vv. 21-23 then serves as the culmination of the subunit by portraying YHWH as the one who brings deliverance to Jerusalem.

Isaiah 52:1-6 constitutes a proclamation of release for Zion. Scholars have struggled to define the generic elements of this text because it does not corre-spond to a recognized form (e.g., Melugin, *Formation,* 159-67). Nevertheless, it appears to be an adaptation of the PROPHETIC ANNOUNCEMENT OF SALVATION. Melugin *(Formation)* characterizes the initial fourfold address in vv. 1-2 as speech to comfort mourners that would be derived from the language of lament (p. 165). But the context here is not mourning. It is instead the end of Zion's oppression, and so the genre must be recognized simply as a COMMAND, in this case to rise from captivity and humiliation as the restoration is about to take place, which takes the place of the reassurance formula that would normally appear in the form. The explanatory oracular address in vv. 3-6 constitutes an adaptation of the ANNOUNCEMENT OF SALVATION in which YHWH announces Zion's/Israel's redemption in v. 3 and the divine intent to act in v. 6. Verse 3 employs the classic oracular form of the PROPHETIC MESSENGER SPEECH, including the MESSENGER FORMULA in v. 3aα and the ORACLE proper in vv. 3aβ-b. A second example of the form appears in vv. 4-6, including the MESSEN-GER FORMULA in v. 4aα and the ORACLE proper in vv. 4aβ-6. A RHETORICAL QUESTION appears in v. 5aα as a means to assert that YHWH had gained nothing from Egypt's and Assyria's oppression of Israel other than the reviling of the divine name.

Isaiah 52:7-10 presents the vision of the herald who announces YHWH's return to Zion. The passage is based on the VISION REPORT genre, which in this case includes both the visual elements of the approach of the herald in v. 7 and the audial elements of the shout of the watchmen in v. 8 and the call for Jerusa-lem/Israel to shout for YHWH in vv. 9-10. The portrayal of YHWH's bared arm that redeems Jerusalem has been identified by some as an element of a HYMN, which appears to be the basis for Zion's/Israel's response to the announcement of YHWH's approach to redeem Zion.

Finally, 52:11-12 constitutes a COMMAND to depart and join YHWH on the return to Zion.

Setting

The overall concern with the restoration of Zion points to the end of the Babylo-nian exile in the late 6th century B.C.E. as the setting for the composition of this text. The portrayal of the Akitu festival procession in ch. 46 reinforces the view that Second Isaiah, the purported composer of this text, was present in Babylon in 539 at the time of Cyrus's enthronement as King of the Babylonian Empire, but the extensive use of disputation speeches in Second Isaiah in general and in Isa 49:14-26 in particular suggests an important need to convince the late-exilic

Jewish community that YHWH is indeed the true G-d of Israel and of creation at large. Such an agenda would be instrumental in attempts to convince exiled Jews to return home to Jerusalem and to convince those who returned or who had remained in the first place to support the building and ongoing function of the Second Temple as the new holy center of Jerusalem and indeed of creation at large. The recognition formulas in vv. 23 and 26 play especially important roles in this regard. Both function as means to convince (Second) Isaiah's audience that YHWH is the true G-d by pointing to the return of Jews from Babylon to Jerusalem as evidence. But readers must recall that only a very few Jews actually returned with Sheshbazzar in 538 and with Zerubbabel and Joshua ben Jehozadak in 522, and so the efforts to convince Jews that YHWH was truly G-d and that they should therefore return to Jerusalem, rebuild the temple, and reconstruct Jewish life in the land of Israel would have been ongoing efforts from the time of Cyrus's ascension to the throne through the building of the Second Temple and beyond.

The return of Nehemiah and Ezra to Jerusalem in the mid-5th through early 4th centuries is testimony to ongoing concern with convincing the people to adhere to YHWH as the true G-d and to support both the building of the temple and its ongoing functioning in the aftermath of its building. And so our present text with its disputational character and its efforts to portray the return of Jews to Jerusalem as a revelatory act of YHWH's power, presence, and sovereignty in the world would have served as an important component of the 5th-century edition of the book of Isaiah as well.

Similar considerations apply to the setting for 50:1-11. The stipulations for YHWH's conditions must be read against the background of the late-6th-century attempts to persuade exiled Jews to return to Jerusalem to carry out the rebuilding of the temple and the overall restoration of Jerusalem and Israel. The contention that the people suffer for their sins provides a basis for the major interest of the passage, namely, to convince the people to show trust in YHWH as the true power of the universe and the only one who can authorize the promised restoration. But YHWH apparently needs the assistance of the people to accomplish the goal of restoration. Such a goal requires that the people trust in YHWH so that they will be able to engage in the efforts at restoration themselves. Such concerns apply to both the 6th-century edition and the 5th-century edition of the book of Isaiah. The 5th-century edition presumes a city in which all of the goals of temple restoration had not yet been met. Although the temple had been rebuilt, it had not regained its status as the center of a fully restored Israel and of creation at large. In the context of the 5th-century edition of the book of Isaiah, 50:1-11 would look forward to the entire people of Israel giving its trust to YHWH and returning to Jerusalem and the land of Israel to carry out Isaiah's full program of restoration.

Isaiah 51:1–52:12 likewise presupposes the end of the Babylonian exile and the beginning of the Second Temple period in the late 6th century B.C.E. as its historical setting. The overarching concern with persuading the exiles that YHWH is acting to restore Zion and that they should likewise return to Jerusalem to take part in the restoration presupposes both the anticipation of return as Babylon falls to Cyrus in 539 and the beginnings of the Second Temple period as the temple is finally rebuilt in 520-515 under Darius. Although many scholars would see the issue as pertaining only to the return, the ongoing function of 51:1–52:12 would continue throughout the entire period of Jerusalem's restoration from the return to Jerusalem and the land of Israel, the rebuilding of the Jerusalem temple, and the continuing rebuilding of the city and restoration of the role of the temple as the holy center of Judah through the periods of Ezra and Nehemiah in the late 5th and early 4th centuries B.C.E. Indeed, the liturgical characteristics of 51:1–52:13 indicate that it may have functioned as part of a liturgy performed in the Jerusalem temple at its dedication in 515 and beyond to celebrate YHWH's ongoing role in sustaining the temple — and the people's ongoing role as well in ensuring that the temple would continue to function as the holy center of creation. Such a liturgy could stand beside psalms such as Exodus 15 or Judges 5 that respectively celebrated YHWH's deliverance at the Red Sea during the time of the exodus or YHWH's deliverance of Israel during the time of the Judges.

Interpretation

Isaiah 49:14-26 presents YHWH's disputation speech to Zion, in which YHWH assures Zion/Jerusalem of her restoration. The passage is designed to build support among the late-exilic Jewish population for YHWH as the true G-d of creation and of Israel and to convince the people to return to Jerusalem from Babylonian exile, to rebuild the temple, and to adhere to YHWH once the temple is built. The disputation form allows for the prophet to challenge the people's views that YHWH had abandoned them as a result of the experiences of the destruction of Jerusalem and the temple as well as the Babylonian exile and to convince them instead to support the efforts at restoration. Overall, the counter arguments here promote the notion that YHWH is indeed in control of creation and human events and that the restoration of Jerusalem will constitute a revelatory event in which all Israel and all the world will recognize YHWH as G-d.

The passage presupposes the metaphorical role of Zion as Bat Zion or Daughter Zion, the bride whom YHWH has abandoned, in chs. 49–54. As an expression of the prophetic marriage tradition, this motif functions as a metaphorical means to express YHWH's judgment against Jerusalem as a husband's abandonment or divorce of his wife (cf. Hosea 1–3; Ezekiel 16; Baumann, *Love and Violence;* Abma, *Bonds of Love*). The metaphor is theologically problematic in that it generally portrays Israel or Jerusalem as a wayward bride who pursues other lovers, which then justifies YHWH's divorce of the bride for infidelity. But such uses of the metaphor simply assume Israel's or Jerusalem's guilt and ignore YHWH's failure to protect Israel or Jerusalem from assault by foreign powers in keeping with the Zion tradition so well represented in the book of Isaiah. In short, such portrayals simply assume the guilt of the injured party in an ironic twist of a basic principle of biblical law, that someone will suffer punishment if they do wrong. When reversed, such a principle presumes that if a party suffers punishment, it must have done something wrong to deserve such suffering, i.e., a woman who is raped must have done something to attract the rapist, but such a contention ignores the criminal intent and action of the rapist who has actually committed the crime. Fortunately, chs. 49–54 do not assign blame to Bat Zion for her suffering, but simply portray YHWH's promises of return and restoration to her after a period of abandonment and suffering.

In the end, 49:14-26 functions as a means to motivate people to take action to restore themselves based upon their belief in the power of YHWH as the true G-d. It functions not only as a means to motivate exiled Jews to return to Jerusalem and the land of Israel to restore Jewish national and religious life in the homeland, but it also functions as a means to motivate the population to continue in their efforts to rebuild Jewish life in the land of Israel in the years after the restoration takes place.

Isaiah 50:1-11 takes the argument of 49:14-26 a step further by stipulating the conditions by which YHWH will restore Jerusalem and Israel. Specifically, YHWH demands trust from the people as a condition for restoration. The passage presents its thesis in three basic subunits: the trial speech in 50:1-3, which asserts that the people were responsible for breaking the covenant; the presentation of the servant's psalm of confidence in YHWH in 50:4-9, which provides a model for the people's relationship with their deity; and the prophet's presentation of YHWH's conditions for restoration, that the people trust in YHWH, in 50:10-11.

The trial scene in 50:1-3 maintains that the people — and not YHWH — are responsible for breaking their covenant with YHWH. This is a very important and controversial assertion within the book of Isaiah, which is so firmly based in the Davidic/Zion covenant tradition that maintains an eternal covenant between YHWH and the house of David/Zion (see, e.g., 2 Samuel 7). In such a relationship, YHWH swears to maintain an eternal relationship in which YHWH will guarantee the security and continuity of the royal house of David and the city of Jerusalem in return for the eternal allegiance of the house of David and Jerusalem. But the Babylonian deportation of King Jehoiachin of Judah in 597 B.C.E. and the destruction of Jerusalem in 587-586 called such a relationship into question by demonstrating that YHWH was somehow unable or unwilling to meet the terms of the eternal covenant. Insofar as the authors of the book of Isaiah hold that YHWH is the true G-d and creator of the universe and protector of Israel, they are unwilling to impugn YHWH's reputation by suggesting that YHWH had failed in meeting the divine obligations of the eternal covenant. Consequently, they argue that the people must be responsible by failing in their obligations to adhere to YHWH. The foundations for such a charge appear largely in the first part of the book in chs. 1–33, in which many of Isaiah ben Amoz's oracles and narratives about him charge infidelity on the part of the house of David or Jerusalem and Israel to YHWH. The narrative concerning King Ahaz's refusal to trust in YHWH during the Syro-Ephraimitic War in 7:1–8:15 is a case in point. When Ahaz refuses to accept Isaiah's demands that he trust in YHWH rather than the city's defenses to protect Jerusalem, Isaiah condemns the king and presents a lengthy set of oracles that envision the Assyrian conquest of Judah (see Sweeney, *Isaiah 1–39*, 143-75).

Interpreters must recognize, however, that the charge of the people's culpability in 50:1-3 is an instance of theodicy: the book of Isaiah presents an attempt to defend YHWH's reputation by asserting that the people — and not YHWH — are the cause of Israel's exile. As noted in the discussion of the rhetorical questions employed in 50:1-3 and throughout 50:1-11, this text is designed to persuade its audience of a set of propositions in order to motivate its audience, either the people of the late 6th century B.C.E. or later readers of the book, to redouble their commitment and efforts to adhere to YHWH. Such an argument would call for 6th-century Jews to reject their alleged abandonment of YHWH so that they might return to Jerusalem from Babylonian exile under the belief that YHWH — and not Marduk — was the true G-d of the universe and redeemer of Israel. They would then be able to begin work on the reconstruction of the temple and the restoration of the city of Jerusalem and Israel at large. Similar concerns would apply for the 5th-century edition of the book of Isaiah as well. Later readers would see this passage as a continuing call for adherence to YHWH so that the full restoration of Jerusalem and Israel could become the ultimate goal of the final form of the book of Isaiah.

The servant's psalm of confidence in YHWH in 50:4-9 builds upon this argument by presenting the servant as the model for trust in YHWH. As noted in the treatment of the earlier Servant Song in 49:1-6, the servant is Israel personified, and so the servant's continued trust in YHWH despite the experience of suffering and humiliation becomes the model for Isaiah's audience to emulate. The initial reference to YHWH's instruction of the servant in v. 4a, by giving the servant "the tongue of teachings," harks back to earlier references in the first part of the book. These earlier references include the prophet's statement of intent to "bind up the testimony and seal the instruction of YHWH among my teachings (lit., 'those [things] that are taught') so that I will wait and trust in YHWH" (8:16-17), the reference to a sealed document that will reveal earlier prophecy (29:11-12), and an instruction to read the book to understand what YHWH has said (34:16-17). All come to realization in 50:4-9. Having been given YHWH's instruction in the form of "the tongue of teachings," the servant in vv. 4b, 5-7 is able to endure the suffering and humiliation of the Babylonian exile because of his trust in YHWH. The servant's ear is opened by YHWH's teachings, so that he might endure the beatings, spitting, and insults that would be the common experience of people taken into captivity and exile in the ancient world. But the servant's confidence in YHWH comes to expression in vv. 7, 8-9, with his statements that "YHWH helps me," that "my defender is near," that "we stand together," that "my opponents have no power," etc. Indeed, the use of rhetorical questions in vv. 8-9 underscores the persuasive dimensions of the song. By asking the obvious, e.g., "who will contend with me? who brings my case to trial? who will condemn me?" the passage prompts the audience, whether the 6th-century audience that hears the passage or later audiences that read it, to identify with the servant as presented in the text. Such an identification then provides a powerful motivation for the audience to see itself as the servant, to show trust in YHWH despite the suffering and humiliation of the Babylonian exile, and to return to Jerusalem from Babylonia to begin the process of restoration.

Isaiah 50:10-11 then provides the key contention of 50:1-11, YHWH's demand that the people trust in YHWH. As noted above, the people's adherence and trust in YHWH are the key elements for the House of David and the people of Jerusalem/Israel in the eternal Davidic/Zion covenant tradition. Again, rhe-torical questions play an important role in the presentation of this contention. By asking "who among you trusts in YHWH?" and "who among you listens to the servant who walks in darkness without light?" the passage again surreptitiously prompts the audience to identify with the text's contentions. Again, reference to the first part of the book is apparent when the servant is described as one who walks in darkness without light. Such a portrayal of the servant Israel draws on 9:1 (NRSV 9:2) that "the people that walk in darkness have seen a great light; a light has shined upon the inhabitants of the land of gloom," which introduces the royal oracle of 9:2-7 (NRSV 9:3-8) concerning the ideal Davidic monarch who will rule over the people on YHWH's behalf. Of course, Second Isaiah envisions no such ideal Davidic monarch. As noted in the discussions Isa 44:28 and 45:1 above, King Cyrus of Persia is YHWH's anointed monarch and temple-builder, and as noted in the discussion of ch. 55 below, the eternal covenant with the house of David will be applied to the people of Israel at large in the absence of a reigning Davidic king. And so the demand for trust in YHWH in 50:10-11 anticipates this new configuration of the Davidic/Zion covenant: the people must trust in YHWH because they are the ones who will enjoy the eternal covenant with YHWH once enjoyed by the house of David. Consequently the passage concludes with YHWH's warnings that the people kindle fire and gird on sparks, i.e., they need to abandon their resistance to YHWH and approach YHWH instead with trust. Otherwise, the people will continue to suffer the pain that comes from YHWH's hand in the first place.

Isaiah 51:1–52:12 then constitutes the culminating and concluding subunit of 49:14–52:12 with the proclamation of salvation for Zion. The passage begins in 51:1-8 with a threefold exhortation to listen and see directed to Bat Zion and her exiled people. It then turns to the announcement of the salvation of Zion in 51:9–52:12, which concludes in 52:11-12 with a command to depart from exile to join YHWH and return to Jerusalem to rebuild the city.

The threefold exhortation to listen and see in 51:1-8 provides the basis for the rhetorical purpose of the larger unit in 51:1–52:12, which is to convince the exiled people of Jerusalem, Judah, and Israel that YHWH is the true G-d of creation and that they should return to Jerusalem to rebuild the city. The persuasive elements of this subunit appear in the modified form of the typical call to attention which expands the formula with a combination of commands to listen to what YHWH has to say and to see what YHWH is going to do. Such language draws on the account of Isaiah's commissioning in ch. 6 in which YHWH calls upon the prophet to render the people blind, deaf, and dumb so that they will be unable to repent and be saved from the impending punishment and thereby thwart YHWH's plans for worldwide recognition as the true G-d of creation and human events. Such a concern permeates Deutero-Isaiah as well which constantly calls upon the exiles to open their eyes, ears, and minds to see what YHWH is doing in the present to restore the people to Jerusalem and thereby establish divine sovereignty throughout the world. The present passage asks its audience to look back to past tradition.

In 51:1-3, YHWH asks the people to remember Abraham and Sarah, how YHWH took Abraham as one man and made him into a great nation as promised in ancestral narratives of Genesis 12–25, particularly in Genesis 12 and 15, which are part of the EJ stratum of the Pentateuch and were likely extant at the time of the Babylonian exile. It likewise asks the audience to understand that although Jerusalem now lies in ruins, YHWH will turn the city into a veritable garden of Eden, thereby recalling the idyllic garden in Genesis 2–3 from which Adam and Eve were expelled. Insofar as the holy of holies of the Jerusalem temple was considered in ancient Judean thought as a representation of the garden of Eden to which the people, led by the high priest identified as Son of Adam, sought to return, such a promise would then constitute the ideal scenario of restoration for YHWH's divine presence at the Jerusalem temple as the holy center of Israel and creation at large (Levenson, *Sinai and Zion;* idem, "The Temple and the World").

In 51:4-6, YHWH asks the people to recognize that once Zion is restored, YHWH's Torah and Law will go out as a light for the nations. Such a claim builds on the imagery of YHWH as monarch of all creation based upon the model of the Achaemenid Persian king Cyrus as the new emperor of the Persian Empire, including Babylonia, Judah, and ultimately even Egypt. The oracle calls for recognition of YHWH's power, here expressed as YHWH's arms and YHWH's victory that will stand forever, much as the Persian Empire would have been viewed as an eternal power at the outset of Cyrus's reign following his accession as the new king of Babylon.

Finally, 51:7-8 asks the people to hold fast just a little while longer until YHWH's plans are realized. The exhortation to hear recognizes the suffering and the humiliation that the people have experienced as exiles in a foreign land, and it employs the typical reassurance formula and oracle to assure the people that their period of subjugation is about to come to an end.

The announcement of the restoration of Zion in 51:9–52:12 then stands as the true culmination of 49:14–52:12. Here, a series of subunits builds the argument that YHWH's actions as sovereign of creation to restore Zion are about to take place; therefore, the people should recognize YHWH's sovereignty and join the restoration by returning to Jerusalem to take part in YHWH's grand plan. Five subunits build the argument, including the answered lament in 51:9-16 that asserts that YHWH will act; the salvation speech in 51:17-23 that asserts that Zion's suffering is over; the exhortation of comfort for Zion in 52:1-6 that calls upon Zion to arise and assume her new role; the herald's vision in 52:7-10 that portrays the announcement of YHWH's return to Zion; and the command to the exiles in 52:11-12 that calls upon them to join YHWH in departing Babylon and returning to Zion.

The answered lament in 51:9-16 leads off the series of the announcement of Zion's restoration in 51:9–52:12 by making the point that YHWH will act to restore Zion. It presupposes a lament made to YHWH by the people to address their current situation of exile and defeat by calling upon YHWH's arm to take action. The image of YHWH's arm is a metaphor for YHWH's strength and capacity to act. The appeal for assistance is a typical element of the lament form. Here, it serves as a platform for recalling YHWH's past actions as a basis for motivating YHWH to act in the present. The references to the slaying of Rahab and the piercing of the Dragon recall the combat myth motif in the Hebrew

Bible in which YHWH defeats the sea monsters of chaos in a bid to bring order into the world of creation (cf. 30:7; Job 9:13; 26:12; 38-41; Psalm 74; 87:4;
89:10). The reference to YHWH's drying up the waters of the sea to make a road
for the redeemed to cross harks back to the crossing of the Red Sea during the
exodus from Egypt in Exodus 14–15 as well as to the various references to this
event in relation to the return of exiles from Assyria and Egypt in 11:16; 27:13;
and 35:10. YHWH answers the lament in 51:12-16 with the assertion that "I am
YHWH who comforts you." Consequently, the people should no longer fear the
mortal Babylonians who will ultimately die nor should they fear the anger of
their oppressors now that YHWH has pledged to act. The hymnic response in vv.
15-16 reinforces YHWH's answer in liturgical form. Here, YHWH responds with
the elements of the covenant formula: "I am YHWH your G-d" and "you are
my people." Such a statement recalls the basic terms of the covenant between
YHWH and Israel (Rendtorff, "Bundesformel").

The salvation speech in 51:17-23 asserts that the suffering of Zion is over
because YHWH is about to act. It calls upon Zion to awaken and arise because
her current state of ruin in which she is bereft of sons to guide and support her
is about to come to an end. YHWH will now take the cup of punishment and
reeling from which she has drunk for so long. Her oppressors, who in the past
demanded that she lie down before them so that they might cross on her back,
will now drink from that cup instead.

The proclamation of release for Zion in 52:1-6 asserts YHWH's commitment to act on Zion's/Israel's behalf. It begins with a fourfold address to Zion to
rise from her captivity and humiliation so that she might prepare for her restoration. The fourfold address in vv. 1-2 employs the metaphorical personification
of a woman who has suffered in captivity, but now looks forward to an end to
her misery. The metaphor of course helps to accentuate Zion's victimization at
the hands of the Babylonians. The four imperative segments move in sequence.
The first in v. 1a addresses her as Zion and calls upon her to awaken and put on
her strength. The second in v. 1b addresses her as the Holy City, Jerusalem, and
asks her to put on her splendid garments, and it clarifies the matter by announcing that she will no longer be subject to rape and humiliation at the hands of
her uncircumcised and unclean oppressors. The third in v. 2a addresses her as
Jerusalem and calls upon her to shake off the dust, rise, and sit, presumably on a
throne or other suitable piece. The fourth in v. 2b addresses her as Bat Zion and
calls upon her to open the bonds of servitude that have been placed upon her
neck. The explanatory address to Israel then points to the purpose for Zion's rise
from humiliation, that YHWH will act against the oppressor. The metaphor shifts
from the feminine singular Bat Zion to the masculine plural Israel to emphasize
that YHWH will act on behalf of the nation Israel at large. The first explanatory
oracular address in v. 3 emphasizes that Israel was sold for no price and it will be
redeemed for no price. This metaphor first emphasizes Israel's victimization by
stating that the nation gained nothing by being sold to Egypt, but only endured
slavery. The shift to YHWH's redemption of Israel/Zion for nothing highlights
that YHWH, too, will gain nothing by acting on Zion's behalf. The second explanatory oracular address to Israel/Bat Zion asserts that YHWH will act on their
behalf as a means to interpret the preceding statements. Following the messenger

formula in v. 4aα, which certifies the oracle as YHWH's, vv. 4aβ-6 lay out both the basis for YHWH's intervention and the announcement of YHWH's intent to act. YHWH's basis for intervention in vv. 4aβ-5 focuses first on Assyria's oppression of Israel as an analogy for Egypt's oppression of Israel in the time of the exodus. The focus on Assyria here has perplexed many scholars, but it draws upon the imagery of the first part of the book, particularly in 10:5–11:16, which portrays Assyria as the oppressing nation that will be brought down by YHWH, and chs. 13–14, which establish the analogy between Babylon and Assyria, especially in 14:24-27; Babylon is viewed as a successor to Assyria who will oppress Israel and in turn merit punishment in 13:1–14:23. The present context in 52:4aβ-b affirms that the vision of Isaiah ben Amoz concerning Assyria and Babylonia is now realized. Verse 5 asserts that YHWH gained nothing from Egypt's or Assyria's oppression of Israel other than a reviled name which YHWH seeks to counteract throughout the book of Isaiah. Finally, 52:6 announces YHWH's intent to act on behalf of Israel/Bat Zion so that the people will know YHWH's name and that YHWH speaks (and acts) on their behalf.

Isaiah 52:7-10 then portrays the vision of the herald who announces YHWH's return to Zion. The vision proper in v. 7 emphasizes that YHWH's return to Zion means that YHWH rules as the sovereign of Israel and all creation. The imagery of the herald of course picks up the imagery of the herald in 40:1-11. The shout of the watchmen in v. 8 points to the herald as the one who announces YHWH's return to Zion. This in turn leads to vv. 9-10, which call upon ruined Jerusalem to sing and shout at YHWH's return. Verses 9b-10 appear to constitute a hymnic element that celebrates YHWH's comforting of the people, YHWH's redemption of Jerusalem, and YHWH's bared arm displayed to the nations of the world as a means to portray YHWH's power.

Finally, 52:11-12 presents the command to the exiled people to depart Babylonian captivity and to join YHWH in returning to Jerusalem. The commands proper in v. 11 are addressed to those who bear the vessels of YHWH as a means to signal the restoration of the temple as the goal of Jerusalem's restoration. The basis for the commands in v. 12 plays on the exodus traditions by emphasizing that the exiles will not depart in haste or flee like escaping slaves. Rather, they will form a holy procession — again like the exodus — in which YHWH will both go before them and act as their rearguard as they journey through the "wilderness" to return to Zion as announced in 40:1-11.

Bibliography

W. Beuken, "Jes. 50, 10-11," *ZAW* 85 (1973) 168-82; H. Bosman, "Myth, Metaphor or Memory? The Allusions to Creation and Exodus in Isaiah 51:9-11 as a Theological Response to Suffering during the Exile," in *Exile and Suffering* (ed. B. Becking and D. Human; OtSt 50; Leiden: Brill, 2009) 71-81; E. Gerstenberger, *Psalms, Part 2, and Lamentations* (FOTL; Grand Rapids: Eerdmans, 2001); F. Holmgren, "Chiastic Structure in Isaiah LI 1-11," *VT* 19 (1969) 196-201; J. G. Janzen, "An Echo of the Shema in Isaiah 51.1-3," *JSOT* 43 (1989) 69-82; idem, "Rivers in the Desert of Abraham and Sarah and Zion," *HAR* 10 (1986) 139-55; K. Koch, "Damnation and Salvation," *ExAud* 6 (1990) 5-13;

J. K. Kuntz, "The Contribution of Rhetorical Criticism to Understanding Isaiah 51:1-16," in *Art and Meaning* (ed. D. J. A. Clines, D. M. Gunn, and A. J. Hauser; JSOTSup 19; Sheffield: Sheffield Academic, 1982) 140-71; J. D. Levenson, *Sinai and Zion: An Entry into the Jewish Bible* (Minneapolis: Winston, 1985); idem, "The Temple and the World," *JR* 64 (1984) 275-98; R. P. Merendino, "Allein und einzig G-ttes prophetisches Wort: Israels Erbe und Auftrag für alle Zukunft (Jesaja 50,4-9a.10," *ZAW* 97 (1985) 344-66; idem, "Jes 50,1-3 (9b.11)," *BZ* 29 (1985) 221-44; R. Rendtorff, *Das "Bundesformel": Eine exegetisch-theologische Untersuchung* (SBS 160; Stuttgart: Katholisches Bibelwerk, 1995); T. Seidl, "J-hwe der Krieger — J-hwe der Tröster: Kritik und Neuinterpretation der Schöpfungsvorstellungen in Jesaja 51,9-16," *BN* 21 (1983) 116-34; O. H. Steck, "Beobachtungen zu den Zion-Texten in Jesaja 51," *BN* 46 (1989) 58-90; idem, "Zions Tröstung," in *Die Hebräische Bibel und ihre zweifache Nachgeschichte (Fest. R. Rendtorff*; ed. E. Blum, C. Macholz, and E. Stegemann; Neukirchen-Vluyn: Neukirchener, 1990) 257-76; idem, "Zur literarischen Schichtung in Jesaja 51," *BN* 44 (1987) 74-86; A. Terian, "The Hunting Imagery in Isaiah li 20a," *VT* 41 (1991) 462-71; N. A. van Uchelen, "Abraham als Felsen (Jes 51 ₁)," *ZAW* 80 (1968) 183-91; H. G. M. Williamson, "Gnats, Glosses and Eternity," in *New Heaven and New Earth (Fest.* A. Gelston; ed. P. J. Harland and C. T. R. Hayward; VTSup 77; Leiden: Brill, 1999) 101-11.

YHWH'S LITURGICAL INSTRUCTION CONCERNING THE EXALTATION OF THE SERVANT 52:13–53:12

Structure

I. YHWH's announcement concerning the exaltation of the servant, Jacob/Israel, despite prior humiliation — 52:13-15
- A. Concerning the servant's exaltation — 52:13
  - 1. He shall succeed — 52:13a
  - 2. He shall be exalted — 52:13b
- B. Concerning the servant's prior humiliation — 52:14-15
  - 1. Protasis: many are aghast over you — 52:14aα
  - 2. First apodosis: because his appearance is marred — 52:14aβ-b
    - a. Because his human appearance is marred — 52:14aβ
    - b. Because his human form is marred — 52:14b
  - 3. Second apodosis: because he purifies many nations — 52:15
    - a. He purifies nations — 52:15aα
    - b. Kings hide their mouths because of him — 52:15aβ-b
      - 1) Basically stated — 52:15aβ
      - 2) Twofold explanation: they see and understand — 52:15b
        - a) They see what was told to them — 52:15bα
        - b) They understand what they did not attend — 52:15bβ
II. Israel's response to YHWH's announcement: concerning the suffering of the servant — 53:1-11aβ¹⁻³
- A. Twofold rhetorical questions asserting YHWH's actions concerning the servant — 53:1
  - 1. First rhetorical assertion: what we have heard is unbelievable — 53:1a

b) He did not open his mouth   53:7aα$^{4-6}$
2) Silent like a lamb/ewe   53:7aα^{7}-b
   a) Like lamb/ewe   53:7aα^{7}-β
    (1) Like lamb led to slaughter   53:7aα$^{7-9}$
    (2) Like ewe silent before shearers   53:7aβ
   b) He did not open his mouth   53:7b
b. He was killed for the transgressions of his people   53:8
1) He was taken   53:8a
   a) He was taken in judgment   53:8aα
   b) His current abode is indescribable   53:8aβ
2) He was killed   53:8b
   a) He was cut off from the land of the living   53:8bα
   b) He was stricken for the transgression of his people   53:8bβ
c. He was buried though he did no wrong   53:9
1) He was buried   53:9a
   a) His grave is with the wicked   53:9aα
   b) His burial mound is with the rich   53:9aβ
2) He did nothing wrong   53:9b
   a) He did no violence   53:9bα
   b) He spoke no deceit   53:9bβ
4. YHWH's punishment leads to the servant's exaltation   53:10-11aβ^{3}
a. YHWH willed the servant's punishment   53:10aα
1) YHWH willed the servant's punishment   53:10aα$^{1-4}$
2) Servant's life would serve as a guilt offering   53:10aα$^{5-8}$
b. Servant will live long and prosper   53:10aβ-b
1) Will live long   53:10aβ
2) Will prosper   53:10b
c. He will redeem the people from his suffering   53:11aα-β^{3}
1) From his suffering he will be satiated   53:11aα
2) He will redeem the people   53:11aβ$^{1-3}$
III. YHWH's announcement concerning the purpose of the servant   53:11aβ^{4}-12
A. Announcement concerning purpose of servant: bears iniquity of many   53:11aβ^{4}-b
1. Servant was for many   53:11aβ$^{4-5}$
2. Bore their iniquity   53:11b
B. Consequence: YHWH will grant him inheritance because he bore sin of many   53:12
1. YHWH will grant him a portion   53:12a
   a. Grant portion because he exposed self to death   53:12aα
   b. Because he is numbered among the transgressors   53:12aβ
2. He will bear the sin of many and interpose for the transgressors   53:12b
   a. Bear the sin of many   53:12bα
   b. Interpose for transgressors   53:12bβ

Isaiah 52:13–53:12 constitutes YHWH's instruction concerning the exaltation of the servant as the third major subunit of 49:1–54:17. The shift in speaker in

52:13 demarcates the beginning of the subunit. Whereas 49:14–52:12 presents the prophet's speech throughout, even when the prophet presents the words of others, 52:13 begins with a 1st-person speech form concerning the servant: "behold, my servant shall prosper," which presupposes YHWH as the speaker. Although the concern with the servant appears throughout 52:13–53:12, the speakers shift. YHWH presents an announcement concerning the exaltation of the servant in 52:13-15; the 1st-person plural pronouns beginning in 53:1 indicate that the people Israel respond to YHWH's announcement in 53:1-11aβ³ with a focus on the suffering of the servant; and the resumption of 1st-person singular pronouns in 53:11aβ⁴⁻⁵ indicates that 53:11aβ⁴-12 constitutes YHWH's announcement concerning the purpose of the servant. The feminine singular address to Bat Zion in 54:1 indicates the beginning of the next subunit in 49:14–54:17. Isaiah 52:13–53:12 focuses on YHWH's exaltation of the servant following his suffering and humiliation.

Isaiah 52:13-15 constitutes YHWH's announcement concerning the exaltation of the servant (Israel/Jacob) despite his prior humiliation. The 1st-person pronouns indicate YHWH is the speaker, and earlier statements throughout the second portion of the book of Isaiah indicate that the servant is Israel/Jacob. The people Israel are the implied audience for YHWH's address. The subunit begins with YHWH's basic twofold statement concerning the exaltation of the servant in 52:13, which includes the statement "behold my servant shall succeed/prosper," in 52:13a and the parallel statement concerning his exaltation, "he shall be exalted, raised up, and very high," in 52:13b.

Isaiah 52:14-15 then focuses on the servant's prior humiliation and suffering as a means to contextualize the initial statement concerning the servant's exaltation — the servant suffered horribly prior to his rise. Isaiah 52:14-15 presents a protasis/apodosis structure in which the phrase introduced by ka'ăšer, "just as," marks the protasis in v. 14aα and the two instances of kēn, "so," mark the two apodoses that follow in vv. 14aβ-b and 15. The protasis in 52:14aα begins with a statement concerning the many who were appalled concerning the servant, here addressed with a 2nd-person masculine pronoun: "just as many were aghast concerning you." Most scholars believe that this pronoun is a textual error introduced by a scribe who remembered the other three constructions of the phrase šāmĕmû 'ālêkā, "they were aghast at you," in Ezek 27:35; 28:19; and 35:12. Most interpreters believe the phrase should be read šāmĕmû 'ālāyw, "they were aghast concerning him," in keeping with the 3rd-person masculine singular address perspective of the immediate context in vv. 14-15. Thus, the protasis in 52:14aα establishes the perspective of those who observed the servant's humiliation and suffering as the basis for the two apodoses that elaborate upon the servant's appearance and purpose in 52:14aβ-b and 52:15, respectively. The first apodosis in 52:14aβ-b then presents a twofold statement concerning the marred appearance of the servant, including statements that his appearance is marred in 52:14aβ and that his human form is marred in 52:14b. The second apodosis in 52:15 then follows with a complex twofold statement concerning the purpose of the servant's humiliation and suffering: he purifies many nations. The first part of this premise is stated in 52:15aα: "so he sprinkles many nations," recalling the sprinkling of blood, water, or oil that is used to purify the temple altar and persons associated with it (e.g., Lev. 5:9; 14:7; 16:14, 19 [blood]; Lev. 8:11 [oil]; Lev. 14:51 [blood and water]). The second part of this premise appears in 52:15aβ-b with the portrayal of kings who cover their mouths in horror at the sight of him. This is basically stated in 52:15aβ, and then 52:15b follows with a twofold explanation indicating that they see the servant and understand, i.e., they see what was told to them in v. 15bα and they understand what they did not attend or hear in v. 15bβ.

Isaiah 53:1-11aβ³ shifts to a 1st-person plural address that responds to YHWH's initial announcement concerning the exaltation of the servant. The present subunit presumes that the people of Israel are the speakers, and they draw out the meaning of YHWH's statements by examining the servant's suffering and positing that it is meant to redeem them from wrongdoing. The subunit comprises two basic elements. The first appears in 53:1, which presents a twofold set of rhetorical questions that assert YHWH as the source of the servant's suffering and posit that YHWH's actions are revealed in relation to the servant. The first rhetorical question in v. 1a asserts that what the people have seen is unbelievable. The second rhetorical question in v. 1b asserts that YHWH's action is revealed in relation to the servant. The second element appears in 53:2-11aβ³, which elaborates on the meaning of YHWH's actions in relation to the servant by asserting that the servant's suffering leads to exaltation.

Isaiah 53:2-11aβ³ is constructed on the basis of a series of poetical doublets that are only sometimes joined by conjunctions but otherwise stand syntactically–independently. The developing concerns of the content allow for a grouping into four subunits in 53:2-3; 53:4-6; 53:7-9; and 53:10-11aβ³.

Isaiah 53:2-3 begins the sequence with a metaphorical portrayal of the servant as an insignificant tree sapling growing from dry ground. The purpose of this portrayal is to point to the unexpected nature of the figure who would restore Israel. Isaiah 11, for example, points to the righteous Davidic king as the shoot that grows from the stump of Jesse and as the figure who will restore Israel in the first part of the book of Isaiah. The present passage, however, employs the tree imagery with very different import: the growing shoot will not become a great, wise, and righteous king, but instead will become a humiliated figure who will suffer and who will nevertheless play the key role in Israel's restoration. Ironically, this figure is Israel itself, who will suffer and ultimately become exalted as a result of YHWH's efforts to be recognized as the sovereign of all creation (cf. ch. 6). The passage proceeds with three subunits, each of which considers a different aspect of the servant portrayed as sapling. The first subunit of this passage appears in 53:2aα, which presents a twofold simile concerning the growth of the servant like a sapling in v. 2aα¹⁻³ and like a root in dry ground in v. 2aα⁴⁻⁶. The second subunit appears in 53:2aβ-b, which portrays the servant/sapling as not yet fully grown. This subunit is more complex than the first, insofar as it comprises two sets of paired statements joined by a conjunctive *wāw,* rather than only one. The first appears in v. 2aβ, which states that the servant/sapling has no form or splendor — it has not grown into its full form — including the statement in v. 2aβ¹⁻³ that it has no form and the statement in v. 2aβ⁴⁻⁵ that it has no splendor. The second appears in v. 2b, which states that "we look, but we are not pleased" to express the people's view that the sapling has not yet fully grown. The first part of the paired statement is that "we look, but there is nothing to see" in v. 2bα, and the second part is that "we are not pleased" in v. 2bβ. The third subunit appears in v. 3, which sums up the sequence by asserting that the servant/sapling is considered as revolting and not worth considering. It appears in two paired couplets. The first in v. 3a focuses on the premise that the people find him/it revolting, including statements that he/it is despised and shunned by the people in v. 3aα and that he/it is injured and sick in v. 3aβ. The second in v. 3b focuses on the premise that the people find the servant/sapling not worth considering, including statements that he is hiding his face in shame and suffering in v. 3bα and that he is despised and not worth considering in v. 3bβ.

The second element in the sequence appears in 53:4-6, which focuses on the premise that the servant is suffering because of the people's sins. Again, it comprises three subunits, each formed by paired statements, that develop this premise. The first subunit appears in 53:4, which employs two sets of paired statements to assert that the servant's suffering is imposed by G-d. The first in v. 4a asserts that "he bore our sickness and pain," including statements that "he bore our sickness" in v. 4aα and that "he endured our pain" in v. 4aβ. The second in v. 4b asserts that "we considered him plagued by G-d," including statements that "we considered him" in v. 4bα and that "he was plagued, stricken by G-d, and humbled" in v. 4bβ. The second subunit appears in 53:5, which again employs two sets of paired statements to assert that "he suffered because of our transgressions." The first appears in v. 5a, which asserts that "he suffered for our transgressions and iniquities," including statements that "he suffered for our transgressions" in v. 5aα and that "he was crushed for our iniquities" in v. 5aβ. The second appears in v. 5b, which asserts that "we were restored by his suffering," including statements that "we were restored because of him" in v. 5bα and that "we were healed because of his wounds" in v. 5bβ. The third subunit appears in 53:6, which asserts that "YHWH imposed punishment on him because of our iniquity." Again, the subunit begins with a paired statement in v. 6a that asserts that "we went astray," including statements that "we went astray like sheep" in v. 6aα and that "we each went our own way (rather than YHWH's)" in v. 6aβ. The second element of the subunit is not a paired statement, however, but a single statement in v. 6b, apparently for climactic stylistic effect, that "YHWH imposed our iniquity on him."

The third subunit appears in 53:7-9, which focuses on the servant's suffering, again with three subunits which develop the theme. The first subunit appears in 53:7, which asserts that the servant was silent. It comprises two sets of paired statements. The first appears in v. 7aα$^{1-6}$, which asserts that the servant did not open his mouth while suffering, including statements that he was oppressed and humbled in v. 7aα$^{1-3}$ and that he did not open his mouth in v. 7aα$^{4-6}$. The second appears in v. 7aα^{7}-b, which employs two sets of statements to assert that he was silent. The first set asserts that he was like a lamb or a ewe, including statements that he was like a lamb led to slaughter in v. 7aα$^{7-9}$ and that he was silent like a ewe before shearers in v. 7aβ. The second set is simply a single statement that he did not open his mouth in v. 7b. The second subunit appears in v. 8, which asserts that he was killed for the transgression of his people. The subunit employs two sets of paired statements to make its point. The first appears in v. 8a, which asserts that he was taken, including statements that he was taken in judgment in v. 8aα and that his current abode or state of being is indescribable in v. 8aβ. The second appears in v. 8b, which states that he was killed, including statements that he was cut off from the land of the living in v. 8bα and that he was stricken for the transgression of his people in v. 8bβ. The third subunit appears in v. 9, which asserts that he was buried although he did nothing wrong. Again, the subunit develops its point with two sets of paired statements. The first in v. 9a asserts that he was buried, including statements that his grave is with the wicked in v. 9aα and that his burial mound is with the rich in v. 9aβ. The second in v. 9b asserts that he did nothing wrong, including statements that he did no violence in v. 9bα and that he spoke no deceit in v. 9bβ.

The fourth and climactic subunit of the series appears in 53:10-11aβ³, which asserts that YHWH's punishment leads to the servant's exaltation. Again, the subunit develops its point in three subunits, each of which is constituted by a set of paired statements. The first appears in v. 10aα, which asserts that YHWH willed the servant's punishment, including statements that YHWH willed the servant's punishment in v. 10aα¹⁻⁴ and that the servant's life would function as an *'āšām* or "guilt offering" (Leviticus 5) in v. 10aα⁵⁻⁸. The second appears in v. 10aβ-b, which asserts that the servant will live long and prosper, including statements that he will live long in v. 10aβ and that he will prosper in v. 10b. The third appears in v. 11aα-β³, which asserts that he will redeem the people from his own suffering, including statements that he will be satiated from his own suffering in v. 11aα and that he will redeem the people in v. 11aβ¹⁻³.

Isaiah 53:11aβ⁴-12 constitutes YHWH's announcement concerning the purpose of the servant: to bear the sin of many as a priest does in the sanctuary (Numbers 17–18). The unit comprises two major subunits. The first is YHWH's announcement in 53:11aβ⁴-b concerning the purpose of the servant, that he bears the iniquity of many. This announcement comprises two statements: that the servant was for many in v. 11aβ⁴⁻⁵ and that he will bear their iniquity in v. 11b. The second element begins with *lākēn,* "therefore," which indicates that it defines the consequences or outcomes of YHWH's announcement, that YHWH will grant him an inheritance because he bore the sin of many. This consequence is defined in two parts. The first in v. 12a asserts that YHWH will grant him a portion, including statements that this is because he exposed himself to death in v. 12aα and that he is numbered among the transgressors in v. 12aβ. The second in v. 12b is that he will bear the sin of many and interpose for the transgressors, including statements that he will bear the sin of many in v. 12bα and that he will interpose for transgressors in v. 12bβ.

Genre

Interpreters have struggled with defining the genre of 52:13–53:12. Jahnow (*Das hebräische Leichenlied,* 256-64) argued that 53:1-12 was an example of a COMMUNAL COMPLAINT SONG, although she was unable to demonstrate a complete correspondence in formal elements and instead relied on the thematic portrayal of the suffering of the servant. Begrich (*Gesammelte Studien,* 62-65) acknowledged the influence of the COMPLAINT SONG, but argued that 53:1-11a constitutes a SONG OF THANKSGIVING, insofar as vv. 2-9 portray the situation of need or threat and vv. 10-11a portray deliverance, but again, the text does not present a full correlation to the THANKSGIVING SONG. Kaiser (*Königliche Knecht,* 88) identifies the text as a SALVATION SPEECH, but his designation is based on thematic rather than formal grounds. Melugin (*Formation,* 73-74) acknowledges all of these influences, but in the end argues that it is a unique composition by the prophet that functions as a speech of salvation even though it differs from the standard form by portraying deliverance in relation to the servant's suffering rather than by YHWH's action. Nevertheless, the passage makes it clear throughout that YHWH imposes the suffering upon the servant and then employs the servant to bring about redemption. In this respect, 52:13–53:12 does function as a SALVATION SPEECH, but its formal elements demand attention.

The structure analysis of the passage points out that 52:13–53:12 constitutes YHWH's announcement concerning the exaltation of the servant in 52:13-15; Israel's response to YHWH's announcement in 53:1-11aβ^3; and YHWH's announcement concerning the servant's purpose in 53:11aβ^4-12, and so the passage has a dialogical or responsive structure involving both YHWH and the people of Israel as speakers. Although some will point to the presence of the word *'ammî,* "my people," in 53:8 as evidence for YHWH's speech, such a term indicates that the prophet employs both 1st-person plural and singular forms to act as spokesperson on behalf of the people. In this instance, the responsive structure of the passage suggests a liturgical purpose or setting in which YHWH and the prophet/people both participate. The passage focuses on the servant's suffering, but it ultimately assigns that suffering a redemptive purpose in which the servant bears the iniquity of the people much like sheep who are led to the slaughter in 53:7. Indeed, 53:10 portrays him as an *'āšām,* "guilt offering" in which animals are offered as part of a process by which human beings atone for some guilty act (Leviticus 5). Isaiah 52:13–53:12 begins as YHWH's speech followed by the people's response and YHWH's statement once again defining the purpose of the suffering of the servant in redemptive terms. It would appear then that 52:13–53:12 is a form of INSTRUCTION speech, which would be typical of the Levites, which defines the suffering servant in sacrificial terms as a part of the means by which the people are purified from their guilt. Although such a form is often considered a wisdom form, all elements in Judean society would employ instruction of some sort or another. Indeed, Lev 10:10-11 defines instruction of the people in what is holy and profane and what is clean and unclean as the basic task of the priests. Isaiah 52:13–53:12 then becomes an example of such instruction, expressed in a liturgical setting, applied to the interpretation of the servant Israel's experience of suffering and presumed redemption as part of the divine plan expressed in the book of Isaiah. Consequently, the genre must be defined as a LITURGICAL INSTRUCTION (cf. Elliger, *Deuterojesaja in seinem Verhältnis,* 19, 291-92; Fohrer, *Das Buch Jesaja,* 160-61, who consider 52:13–53:12 to be a prophetic liturgy).

Isaiah 52:13–53:12 makes use of RHETORICAL QUESTIONS in 53:1 as part of its overall presentation of the purpose of the servant's suffering. RHETORICAL

QUESTIONS function as a means to make an assertion. They do so by actively engaging the audience of the text or speech with a question which has an obvious answer. Such a strategy then aids in drawing the audience in to the speaker's line of reasoning and ultimately to the speaker's position. The rhetorical questions in 53:1 therefore function as a means to assert that YHWH's action is incredible and that YHWH's action is revealed in relation to the servant, both of which surreptitiously convince the audience that YHWH is acting on the servant's (i.e., Israel's) behalf. The initial RHETORICAL QUESTIONS therefore prepare the way for the audience to accept that the servant's suffering was justified and that it would ultimately lead to a redemptive outcome.

Setting

As noted in the discussion of genre above, 52:13–53:12 presents a responsive structure in which Israel, represented by the prophet, responds to YHWH, and YHWH in turn responds to Israel and the prophet. Such a responsive structure suggests a liturgical setting for this text in which the speakers or singers who present the text may perform it in antiphonal fashion. Insofar as 52:13–53:12 identifies the suffering servant, Israel, as an example of an *'āšām,* "guilt offering" (see Leviticus 5), the text presupposes the sacrificial concerns of the Jerusalem priesthood which would oversee the presentation of the *'āšām* offerings as part of their normal service. Both of these factors point to 52:13–53:12 as a liturgical text that is intended together with the rest of the book of Isaiah for performance in the Jerusalem temple. Although this text may well have been composed prior to the completion of the Second Temple in 515 B.C.E., it apparently functioned as part of the temple liturgy, perhaps even as part of the dedication ceremonies for the Second Temple in 515 (Ezra 6).

As part of the book of Isaiah, 52:13–53:12 would function in the temple dedication ceremony as a means to define Israel's experience of suffering from the time of the late-8th-century B.C.E. Assyrian invasions of the land of Israel through the 6th-century Babylonian exile and late-6th-century restoration under Persian rule. Although it does not specifically cite ch. 6, 52:13–53:12 interacts with ch. 6 by virtue of their respective placements and roles in the book of Isaiah as a means to make sense of YHWH's instructions to the prophet to render the people blind, deaf, and dumb so that YHWH's plans for the revelation of divine sovereignty over all creation might ultimately be realized. Isaiah 52:13–53:12 attempts to make sense of YHWH's instructions to Isaiah in ch. 6 by pointing to the redemptive or restorative purposes of the servant's suffering; i.e., 52:13–53:12 presents the suffering servant as a form of *'āšām* offering to demonstrate that the suffering endured by Israel over the course of two centuries would have a positive and purifying effect. Of course in retrospect, such a theological strategy might raise objections concerning YHWH's moral integrity in sacrificing generations of Israelites and Judeans for a teleological goal, but it would represent an early attempt to make sense of suffering to a generation that was only now enjoying the outcome of YHWH's plan. Indeed, the identification of the suffering servant with the *'āšām* offering was a major factor in Elliger's attempt to argue

Isa 52:13–53:12 was written by Trito-Isaiah (Elliger, *Deuterojesaja in seinem Verhältnis,* 6-27), but such a view presupposes that cultic issues would appear in the later postexilic period and not in the work of Deutero-Isaiah. Elliger also pointed to stylistic correspondence between 52:13–53:12 and chs. 56–66. Insofar as Trito-Isaiah is now recognized as the work of multiple writers who ranged from the late 6th century through the completion of the book, such a view is not impossible. Preoccupation with the interpretation of ch. 6 is characteristic of Trito-Isaiah, although Trito-Isaian texts tend to cite ch. 6 explicitly (Sweeney, "Prophetic Exegesis"). It seems more likely that 52:13–53:12 was written as part of the late-6th-century edition of the book of Isaiah for use as part of the liturgy for the dedication of the Second Temple. The ambiguity of the text would then have stimulated reflection on ch. 6 in later texts in Trito-Isaiah.

Interpretation

Isaiah 52:13–53:12 functions as part of the culminating material of the 6th-century B.C.E. edition of the book of Isaiah 2–55; 60–62*, which served as part of the dedication ceremony for the Second Temple. It presupposes that the suffering servant is Jacob/Israel, in keeping with the previous three Servant Songs and the overall context of Deutero-Isaiah. It presents an interpretation of the servant Israel's suffering over the course of centuries from the time of the late-8th-century Assyrian invasions of Israel and Judah during the lifetime of Isaiah ben Amoz through the Babylonian exile in the late-6th-century edition of the book and through the earlier Persian period in the 5th-/4th-century edition of Isaiah. Overall, it maintains that the servant Israel suffered as part of YHWH's plans to reveal divine sovereignty over creation to the nations at large. The servant Israel's suffering is ultimately redemptive insofar as the servant's restoration in the aftermath of such suffering would be the final proof that YHWH had intended such an outcome all along. In this respect, the role of the servant Israel is likened to that of the *'āšām,* "guilt offering," which is presented at the temple as part of an effort to restore good relations with YHWH in the aftermath of some misdeed (Leviticus 5). The passage follows 49:14–52:12, which announced YHWH's restoration of Zion, and it precedes 54:1-17, which proclaims the restoration of the covenant, metaphorically portrayed as a marriage, between YHWH and Bat Zion. Insofar as Bat Zion metaphorically functions as the bride of YHWH, the servant Jacob/Israel functions as the people who will return to Jerusalem/Zion during the course of her restoration. As part of the 6th-century edition of the book of Isaiah, 52:13–53:12 is formulated to justify YHWH's actions in bringing about Israel's suffering and to convince its audience, the people of Israel and Judah, that such action identifies YHWH as the true G-d of creation. On that basis, the people will return to Jerusalem to take part in the restoration.

The liturgical character of the pericope is evident in its antiphonal features. It begins with YHWH's announcement in 52:13-15 of the servant Israel's exaltation in the aftermath of suffering and humiliation. Isaiah 52:13 announces that the servant Israel will succeed and be exalted. Isaiah 52:14-15 then focuses

on the servant's prior suffering and humiliation. It begins in 52:14aα with recognition of the servant's suffering in the form of a protasis that people are
aghast at the sight of him. The first apodosis in 52:14aβ-b explains the people's
reaction by asserting that the servant's appearance is marred beyond normal
human recognition. The second apodosis in 52:15 asserts that the servant's suffering purifies nations. Although kings might cover their mouths in shock at the
servant's appearance, they will come to understand what they had not listened
to, i.e., what they had been taught in the earlier portions of the book of Isaiah.

Israel's response concerning the suffering of the servant then follows in
53:1-11aβ³. The servant's response provides the opportunity to elaborate upon
the servant's suffering and its ultimate redemptive purpose. It begins in 53:1
with rhetorical assertions, first, that what the people have heard is entirely
unbelievable and second, that the entirety of YHWH's action is now revealed
to them. Isaiah 53:2-11aβ³ then elaborates. The elaboration begins in Isa 53:2-3
with a metaphorical portrayal of the servant like an insignificant tree that has
just been planted and is now growing in dry ground. Such an image draws on
the tree imagery of ch. 6, in which Israel is portrayed as an oak or terebinth
that has been chopped down and burned until less than a tenth remains. But
the book of Isaiah correctly presumes that when a tree is cut down, its roots
will enable it to grow once again. Hence, the passage also presupposes ch. 11,
which portrays the emergence of a new monarch who grows out of the stump of
Jesse like a new shoot and who in turn will restore Israel from the power of its
oppressors. Although people do not yet recognize the significance of this new
growth and find it not worth considering, it ultimately portends the restoration
of Israel. The passage continues in 53:4-6, which asserts that the servant was
suffering for the sins of the people. In keeping with the perspective of the book
of Isaiah as a whole, this passage asserts that YHWH brought suffering upon the
servant because of the transgressions of the people. Isaiah 53:7-9 then focuses
on the servant's suffering per se, indicating that he was silent like a lamb going
to slaughter. Such an image enables the passage to draw the analogy between
the servant and the 'āšām, "guilt offering": just as the 'āšām is sacrificed to
play a role in the atonement of the guilty party (Leviticus 5), so the servant was
sacrificed to redeem the people for their alleged transgressions against YHWH.
In the end, 53:10-11aβ³ asserts that YHWH's punishment of the servant Israel
leads to Israel's exaltation. The servant will live long and prosper as a result of
YHWH's action, and he will redeem the people at large.

YHWH's response to the servant in 53:11aβ⁴-12 sums up the passage with
YHWH's announcement concerning the purpose of the servant. The servant
was for many and bore their iniquity. As a consequence, YHWH will grant the
servant Israel an inheritance because he exposed himself to death on behalf of
the transgressors.

Such a theological understanding of the purpose of the servant Israel's
suffering is an attempt to make sense of Israel's experience during the Assyrian
and Babylonian periods. It is a form of theodicy that defends the integrity and
power of YHWH in the face of claims that YHWH had been powerless before
Israel's enemies and that YHWH had abandoned Israel to its fate. Post-Shoah
theological discussion has pointed to the inadequacy of such a theological con-

ceptualization: why should YHWH sacrifice generations of people for greater recognition centuries later? (Sweeney, *Reading the Hebrew Bible after the Shoah*). Nevertheless, we must recognize that the book of Isaiah represents one step in the effort to understand this issue fully. It is up to us to continue the work.

Bibliography

P. Beauchamp, "Lectures et relectures du Quatrième Chant du Serviteur," in Vermeylen, ed., *The Book of Isaiah*, 325-55; C. T. Begg, "Zedekiah and the Servant," *ETL* 62 (1986) 393-98; W. H. Bellinger and W. R. Farmer, eds., *Jesus and the Suffering Servant: Isaiah 53 and Christian Origins* (Harrisburg: Trinity, 1998); A. Bentzen, *King and Messiah* (London: Lutterworth, 1955) 56-59; idem, "On the Ideas of 'the Old' and 'the New' in Deutero-Isaiah," *ST* 1 (1947-48) 183-87; A. R. Ceresko, "The Rhetorical Strategy of the Fourth Servant Song," *CBQ* 56 (1994) 42-55; D. J. A. Clines, *I, He, We, and They: A Literary Approach to Isaiah 53* (JSOTSup 1; Sheffield: JSOT, 1976); J. J. Collins, "The Suffering Servant," *PIBA* 4 (1980) 59-67; C. Conroy, "The Enigmatic Servant Texts in Isaiah in the Light of Recent Study," *PIBA* 32 (2009) 24-48; idem, "The 'Four Servant Poems' in Second Isaiah in the Light of Recent Redaction-Historical Studies," in *Biblical and Near Eastern Essays* (*Fest.* K. J. Cathcart; ed. C. McCarthy and J. F. Healey; JSOTSup 375; London: T. and T. Clark, 2004) 80-94; J. Coppens, "La finale du quatrième chant du serviteur," *ETL* 39 (1963) 114-21; G. Dalman, *Jesaja 53* (Leipzig: Hinrichs, 1914); G. R. Driver, "Isaiah 52:13–53:12," in *In memoriam Paul Kahle* (ed. M. Black and G. Fohrer; BZAW 103; Berlin: Töpelmann, 1968) 90-105; O. Eissfeldt, "Neue Forschungen zum 'Ebed JHWH-Problem," *TLZ* 68 (1943) 273-80; repr. in *Kleine Schriften* (Tübingen: Mohr, 1962-79) 2:443-52; M. Fischer, "Vom leidenden G-ttesknecht nach Jesaja 53," in *Abraham unser Vater* (*Fest.* P. Michel; ed. O. Betz, M. Hengel. and P. Schmidt; AGSU 5; Leiden: Brill, 1963) 116-28; G. Fohrer, "Stellvertretung und Schuldopfer in Jes 52,13–53,12," in *Studien zu alttestamentlichen Texten und Themen* (BZAW 155; Berlin: de Gruyter, 1981) 24-43; G. Gerleman, "Der G-ttesknecht bei Deuterojesaja," in *Studien zur alttestamentlichen Theologie* (Heidelberg: Schneider, 1980) 38-60; M. S. Gignilliat, "Who Is Isaiah's Servant? Narrative Identity and Theological Potentiality," *SJT* 61 (2008) 125-36; H. L. Ginsberg, "The Oldest Interpretation of the Suffering Servant," *VT* 3 (1953) 400-404; B. Gosse, "Isaïe 52,13–53,12 et Isaïe 6," *RB* 98 (1991) 537-43; H. Haag, *Der G-ttesknecht bei Deuterojesaja* (ErF 233; Darmstadt: Wissenschaftliche Buchgesellschaft, 1985); F. Hägglund, *Isaiah 53 in the Light of Homecoming after Exile* (FAT 2/31; Tübingen: Mohr Siebeck, 2008); H. Henning-Hess, "Bemerkungen zum ASCHAM-Begriff in Jes 53,10," *ZAW* 109 (1997) 618-26; H. Jahnow, *Das hebräische Leichenlied im Rahmen der Völkerdichtung* (BZAW 36; Giessen: Töpelmann, 1923); B. Janowski, "Er trug unsere Sünden: Jesaja 53 und die Dramatik der Stellvertretung," *ZTK* 90 (1993) 1-24; idem, *Stellvertretung: alttestamentliche Studien zu einem theologischen Grundbegriff* (SBS 165; Stuttgart: Katholisches Bibelwerk, 1997); B. Janowski and P. Stuhlmacher, eds., *The Suffering Servant: Isaiah 53 in Jewish and Christian Sources;* K. Joachimsen, *Identities in Transition: The Pursuit of Isa. 52:13–53:12;* idem, "Steck's Five Stories of the Servant in Isaiah lii 13-liii 12 and Beyond," *VT* 57 (2007) 208-28; O. Kaiser, *Die königliche Knecht* (FRLANT 70; Göttingen: Vandenhoeck & Ruprecht, 1959); A. S. Kapelrud, "The Identity of the Suffering Servant," in *Near Eastern Studies in Honor of William Foxwell Albright* (ed. H. Goedecke; Baltimore: Johns Hopkins University Press, 1971) 307-14; T. N. D. Mettinger, *A Farewell to the Servant Songs;* A. Neubauer and S. R. Driver, *The Fifty-Third Chapter of Isaiah According to the Jewish Interpreters* (New York: Ktav, 1969); J. W. Olley, "The Many," *Bib* 68 (1987) 330-56; H. M. Orlinsky, *The So-Called 'Suffering Servant' in Isaiah 53* (VTSup 14; Leiden: Brill, 1977) 1-133; S. Sekine, "The Concept of Redemption in Second Isaiah," in *Transcendency and Symbols in the Old Testament* (BZAW 275; Berlin: de Gruyter, 1999) 284-398; C. J. Sharp, "(Re)Inscribing Power through Torah Teaching: Rhetorical Pedagogy in the Servant Songs of Deutero-Isaiah," in *Thus Says the L-rd* (*Fest.* R. R. Wilson; ed. J. J. Ahn and S. L. Cook; London, 2009) 167-78; J. A. Soggins, "Tod und Auferstehung des leidenden G-tteskenechtes," *ZAW* 87 (1975) 546-55; C. Spaller, "Syntaktische und stilistische Relationen im Vierten G-tteskenechtslied und deren exegetische Relevanz," in *Liebe zum Wort* (*Fest.* L. Bernhard; ed. F. V. Reiterer and P. Eder; Salzburg: Müller, 1993) 275-92; H. Spieckermann, "Konzeption und Vorgeschichte des Stellvertretungsgedankens im Alten Testament," in *Congress Volume: Cambridge 1995* (VTSup 66; ed. J. A. Emerton; Leiden: Brill, 1997) 281-95; O. H. Steck, "Aspekte des G-tteskenechts in Jes 52,13–53,12," *ZAW* 97 (1985) 36-58; M. A. Sweeney, *Reading the Hebrew Bible after the Shoah: Engaging Holocaust Theology* (Minneapolis: Fortress, 2008); D. W. Thomas, "A Consideration of Isaiah liii in the Light of Recent Textual and Philological Study," *ETL* 44 (1968) 79-86; M. Treves, "Isaiah liii," *VT* 24 (1974) 98-108; H. Welshman, "The Atonement Effected by the Servant," *Biblical Theology* 23 (1973) 46-49; R. N. Whybray, *Thanksgiving for a Liberated Prophet* (JSOTSup 4; Sheffield: JSOT 1978); W. Zimmerli, "Die Vorgeschichte von Jes liii," in *Congress Volume: Rome 1968* (VTSup 17; Leiden: Brill, 1969) 236-44.

PROCLAMATION OF THE RESTORATION OF THE COVENANT BETWEEN YHWH AND ZION 54:1-17

Structure

I. Prophet's call to Zion: rejoice	54:1
A. Call to rejoice proper	54:1a
1. Shout aloud	54:1aα
2. Break out in song	54:1aβ
B. Basis for call: YHWH's statement concerning Zion's children	54:1b
1. Basis proper	54:1bα
2. YHWH speech formula	54:1bβ
II. Prophet's call to Zion to enlarge tent/dwelling	54:2-3
A. Call proper	54:2
1. Twofold instruction to enlarge tent/dwelling	54:2aα
a. Expand tent	54:2aα$^{1-3}$
b. Extend the curtains of your dwelling	54:2aα$^{4-6}$
2. Prohibition against holding back	54:2aβ
3. Twofold instruction concerning ropes and pegs	54:2b
a. Arrange your ropes	54:2bα
b. Fasten your pegs	54:2bβ

Isaiah 54:1-17 constitutes a proclamation of the restoration of the covenant or marriage between YHWH and Zion. It is formulated throughout as a 2nd-feminine singular address in which the prophet speaks on YHWH's behalf. The macrostructure of 54:1-17 comprises a sequence of five 2nd-person feminine singular address forms, each of which displays a distinctive yet interrelated set of generic characteristics and thematic concerns. The five constituent elements of the unit work together to announce the restoration of the marriage/covenant as the major concern of ch. 54. Although the addressee is never identified by name, the correlation of language pertaining to marriage, divorce, and the restoration of children with that pertaining to covenant indicates that the addressee is intended to be Bat Zion. Following a unit devoted to the restoration of the male servant, Israel, in 52:13–53:12, the identification of the female servant figure in ch. 54 as Bat Zion makes sense because the exiled "children" of Israel would naturally return to her from exile.

The first subunit in ch. 54 is the prophet's call to Zion to rejoice in 54:1. Such a call to rejoice of course anticipates the restoration of the covenant/marriage relationship between YHWH and Zion which will follow. This subunit is hymnic in form insofar as it includes a twofold call to rejoice or sing in v. 1a, including calls to shout aloud in v. 1aα and to break out in song in v. 1aβ. The basis for the call to rejoice then follows in v. 1b with a statement concerning the overwhelming numbers of children who will appear once the bride is restored from her former state of abandonment to her new state of marriage. The basis includes both the basis proper in v. 1bα and the YHWH speech formula in v. 1bβ, which identifies the basis as a quotation by YHWH.

Isaiah 54:2-3 constitutes the prophet's call to the bride Zion to enlarge the size of her tent or dwelling. Such a call builds on the preceding subunit by positing that the return of Zion's children as a result of the restoration of her marriage to YHWH will require the expansion of her dwelling to accommodate the great numbers of returning children. Such a call presumes the common practice in ancient Israel that bedouin women are responsible for setting up the tent in which the family dwells by driving the stakes, extending the cords, and setting up the tent structure that the pegs and cords will support. The structure of vv. 2-3 is analogous to that of v. 1. It begins with the prophet's call proper in v. 2, which comprises three subunits. The first is a twofold feminine singular instruction to enlarge the tent or dwelling per se in v. 2aα, which includes a call to expand the tent in v. 2aα$^{1-3}$ and a call to extend the curtains of the dwelling in v. 2aα$^{4-6}$. The second is a 2nd-feminine singular prohibition against holding back (the size of the tent) in v. 2aβ. The third is a twofold 2nd-feminine instruction in v. 2b concerning the disposition of the ropes and pegs, including instructions to arrange the ropes in v. 2bα and to fasten the pegs in v. 2bβ. The basis for the call, that the children will expand by possessing nations and cities, then follows in v. 3. The basis includes two fundamental elements, each defined by a 2nd-feminine singular address form. The statement that "you shall spread out to the right and to the left" appears in v. 3a, and the twofold statement that "your seed or descendants shall possess nations and inhabit cities" appears in v. 3b, including statements that they will possess nations in v. 3bα and that they will inhabit desolated cities in v. 3bβ.

Isaiah 54:4-6 constitutes the prophet's salvation oracle to Zion to announce to her that YHWH has redeemed her. The structure of this subunit comprises a twofold reassurance formula in v. 4a followed by three basis statements, each introduced by a causative *kî*, "because," in vv. 4b, 5, and 6. The twofold reassurance formula in v. 4a includes two expressions of the formula, each with a basis, in vv. 4aα and 4aβ. The first in v. 4aα presents the classic form of the formula with the "do not fear" formula in v. 4aα$^{1-2}$ and the basis, "for you shall not be ashamed," in v. 4aα$^{3-5}$. The second in v. 4aβ presents an atypical variation, "do not be ashamed," in v. 4aβ, including the formula proper in v. 4aβ$^{1-2}$, followed by the basis, "for you shall not be disgraced," in v. 4aβ$^{3-5}$. The three bases in vv. 4b, 5, and 6 then present extensions of the bases for each reassurance formula. Basis #1 in v. 4b presents a twofold statement concerning the end of the shame of your youth/widowhood, including statements to "forget the shame of your youth" in v. 4bα and to "not remember the shame of your widowhood" in v. 4bβ. Basis #2 in v. 5 asserts that YHWH is redeeming you, including statements that "your husband, YHWH Seba'ot, is your maker" in v. 5a and that "your husband, G-d of all the earth, is your redeemer" in v. 5b. Basis #3 in v. 6 focuses on the portrayal of YHWH calling you back from despair/rejection, including statements that "YHWH has called you back" in v. 6a and the rhetorical question/statement in v. 6b that G-d cannot reject the wife of youth. The rhetorical question/statement in v. 6b in turn comprises two elements, including the rhetorical question/statement proper in v. 6bα and the G-d speech formula in v. 6bβ, which identifies G-d as the speaker of the rhetorical question/statement.

Isaiah 54:7-10 presents the prophet's conveyance of YHWH's promise of a covenant of peace for Zion. The subunit comprises two major elements, including a statement concerning the reversal of YHWH's anger toward Zion concluded by a YHWH speech formula in vv. 7-8 and a statement of the outcome, YHWH's oath of a covenant of peace for Zion, introduced by *kî,* in vv. 9-10. The statement concerning the reversal of YHWH's anger in vv. 7-8 includes two basic components, YHWH's twofold statement proper in vv. 7-8a and the YHWH Redeemer speech formula, which identifies the preceding as a statement by YHWH, in v. 8b. YHWH's statement in vv. 7-8a includes two elements. The first is YHWH's statement in v. 7 that "I abandoned you in haste" (v. 7a) and that "I gather you in love" (v. 7b). The second in v. 8a includes statements that "I hid my face from you momentarily in anger" (v. 8aα) and that "with eternal fidelity I show you love" (v. 8aβ). The second major element is the statement of the outcome in vv. 9-10. Again, this subunit comprises YHWH's twofold oath of fidelity to Zion in vv. 9-10bα and a YHWH speech formula to identify YHWH as the speaker in v. 10bβ. YHWH's twofold oath of fidelity to Zion in vv. 9-10bα begins with the first oath statement in v. 9, which includes the protasis that compares YHWH's oath to Zion to the one sworn by YHWH to Noah (Genesis 9) in v. 9a and the apodosis that "I swear to show you no anger or rebuke" in v. 9b. The second oath statement in v. 10a-bα includes a twofold protasis and a twofold apodosis. The twofold protasis in v. 10a includes statements that mountains may move in v. 10aα and that hills may totter in v. 10aβ as the foundations for the following assertions in the apodosis in v. 10bα that "my fidelity will not move" (v. 10bα$^{1-4}$) and that "my covenant of peace will not totter" (v. 10bα$^{5-8}$).

Isaiah 54:11-17 presents the culminating subunit with the prophet's conveyance of YHWH's promise to adorn and protect Zion. The subunit employs 2nd-feminine singular address language throughout. Following upon the covenant language of 54:7-10, the present subunit employs the metaphorical language of bridal adornment to reinforce the overall message that YHWH's covenant with Zion is secure. The basic structure of the passage includes YHWH's address to Zion in 54:11-17bα and the oracle formula in 54:17bβ to identify the speech as that of YHWH.

YHWH's address to Zion includes seven basic elements that are built from a combination of formal and thematic features to convey the message of adornment and protection. The first is the address formulation in v. 11a, which identifies the feminine singular addressee as the humiliated, storm-tossed, and uncomforted one. Zion is not explicitly mentioned, but the context of Second Isaiah and its use of the marriage metaphor make it clear that Bat Zion is indeed the intended addressee.

The second element in 54:11b-13 is the promise to adorn Jerusalem with jewels and to provide protection. This, of course, is the key element of this section. It includes a sequence of statements, each joined together by a conjunctive *wāw* and addressed to the 2nd-feminine singular addressee, Zion. The sequence of statements includes "I will make carbuncle your building stones" in vv. 11bα; "I will found you with sapphires" in v. 11bβ; "I will make your battlements of rubies" in v. 12aα; "I will make your gates of precious stones" in v. 12aβ; "I will make all your borders of gems" in v. 12b; "all your sons will be taught by YHWH" in v. 13a; and "your children will live in peace" in v. 13b.

The third element in 54:14a actually continues the sequence of the preceding element, but it is not joined by a conjunctive *wāw*. The lack of a conjunction highlights its importance in relation to the other elements insofar as it constitutes YHWH's promise to establish the addressee, Zion, in righteousness.

Isaiah 54:14b constitutes the fourth element as a parenesis that calls upon Zion to keep far from oppression. Parenesis combines positive instruction and negative prohibition in an effort to persuade its audience to follow a particular course of action. The positive statement appears in v. 14bα$^{1-2}$, which calls upon the 2nd-feminine singular addressee to keep far from oppression. The negative element appears in v. 14bα^3-b, which breaks down further into two components. The first is the prohibition per se in v. 14bα$^{3-5}$, which appears in the form of the reassurance formula, "for you shall not fear," and the second in v. 14bβ provides the basis for the reassurance formula with the contention "and from ruin, for it will not come near to you."

Isaiah 54:15 constitutes the fifth element as an announcement that intruders will not come against Zion from YHWH. The announcement comprises two basic elements. The first in v. 15a presents YHWH's assertion that "no harm is done without me," and the second in v. 15b asserts that "whoever would harm you will fall."

Isaiah 54:16-17a constitutes the sixth element in the sequence with an announcement that YHWH annuls all threats to Zion. The announcement again comprises two basic elements. The first in v. 16 presents YHWH's assertion, that "I am the creator," in two parts, i.e., an announcement that "I create the smith to fan the fire and produce implements" in v. 16a and an announcement in v. 16b that "I create a destroyer to inflict pain." The second element in v. 17a presents YHWH's two-part assertion that "what I create will not harm you," i.e., the assertion in v. 17aα that "no weapon formed against you will succeed" and the assertion in v. 17aβ that "you shall defeat any tongue raised against you in judgment."

Isaiah 54:17bα constitutes the seventh and final element in the sequence as a summary appraisal form that summarizes with the statement that this is the inheritance of YHWH's servants.

Again, the oracle formula in 54:17bβ identifies the speech as that of YHWH.

Genre

Isaiah 54:1-17 constitutes a proclamation of restoration of the covenant/marriage between YHWH and Zion. Although this proclamation does not constitute a discrete genre per se, it relies heavily on the HYMN OF PRAISE and the PROPHETIC ANNOUNCEMENT OF SALVATION. In discussing the roles of these genres in constituting this text, it is important to keep in mind the differentiation between the synchronic form of the text, which constitutes its literary formal structure, and its underlying diachronic form, in which the genres play an important role in shaping this text.

The prophet's call to Zion to rejoice in 54:1 draws heavily on the HYMN OF PRAISE. The two basic elements of this subunit, the call to rejoice proper in v. 1a and the basis for the call in v. 1b, correspond to the two basic elements of the HYMN OF PRAISE, the CALL TO PRAISE and the BASIS FOR PRAISE, which normally constitute the genre. The elements are modified here to serve the immediate literary context of introducing a text that proclaims the restoration of the covenant or marriage between YHWH and Zion. The text calls upon Zion to rejoice, but the basis for rejoicing is not YHWH's victory over an enemy. Rather, it is the return of Zion's children, in this case, the exiles of Jerusalem, Judah, and Israel, who will return to the city to rebuild it and restore it to its former position as the holy center of creation. The HYMN OF PRAISE form lends itself to the hymnic character of Deutero-Isaiah and the book of Isaiah as a whole, which functions as a liturgy for the dedication of the Second Temple (see Setting below). The YHWH SPEECH FORMULA, "says YHWH," in v. 1bβ[7-8] aids in verifying that the prophet's announcement comes ultimately from YHWH.

The prophet's call to Zion to enlarge her tent/dwelling in vv. 2-3 has been identified by some as the continuation of the hymnic material in v. 1 (e.g., Melugin, *Formation,* 169-70). There is some basis for such a conclusion, insofar as this text displays a similar structure: call to enlarge in v. 2 followed by the basis for the call in v. 3, that would then continue the motif of v. 1. Nevertheless, the call points only indirectly to YHWH's action that would then serve as the basis for praise. It is clear that INSTRUCTION plays an important role in this segment, insofar as the call constitutes INSTRUCTION to act in v. 2aα and 2b, together with the PROHIBITION against holding back in v. 2aβ. Such a combination suggests a PARENESIS that is designed to convince the reading or hearing audience of the book to act to enlarge Jerusalem and thereby to facilitate the city's restoration.

The prophet's salvation oracle for Zion in 54:4-6 is based upon the prophetic ORACLE OF SALVATION. Such an oracle typically includes an example of the REASSURANCE FORMULA, "do not fear," which appears here in v. 4a, and the basis for the reassurance, which appears both together with the two examples of the REASSURANCE FORMULA in v. 4aα and 4aβ as well as in the sequence of three bases that appear in vv. 4b, 5, and 6. The REASSURANCE FORMULA appears in its typical form, *'al-tîrĕ'î,* "do not fear," in v. 4aα and in an intentional variant of the form, *wĕ'al tikkālĕmî*, "do not be ashamed," in v. 4aβ. The reason for the variant is stylistic, as Deutero-Isaiah tends to present statements in poetic doublets and the REASSURANCE FORMULA only appears typically with one verbal form. The third basis in v. 6 employs a RHETORICAL QUESTION in v. 6bα, "and the wife of youth, is she indeed rejected?" as a means to assert the contrary, "indeed, the wife of youth is not rejected." Such usage tends to draw in an audience to the speaker's position by asking a question with an obvious answer, thereby preparing the audience to accept the speaker's premise, in this case, the assertion that YHWH is renewing the marriage/covenant with Zion. The G-d SPEECH FORMULA in v. 6bβ aids in verifying that the preceding statement was indeed made by YHWH.

The prophet's conveyance of YHWH's promise of a covenant of peace to Zion in 54:7-10 appears to continue the prophetic ORACLE OF SALVATION by specifying the nature of the salvation that YHWH offers. There is no typical form for this element; rather, it employs the metaphor of the restoration of a marriage to make its point concerning the restoration of the covenant between YHWH and Zion. Isaiah 54:7-8 takes up the reversal of YHWH's anger toward Zion with statements of YHWH's eternal fidelity *(ḥesed 'ôlām)* to Zion that presuppose YHWH's covenant with Jerusalem and Israel at large. Isaiah 54:9-10 then presents the outcome: YHWH's OATH of a covenant of peace for Zion. YHWH's twofold OATH of fidelity appears in vv. 9-10bα in terms that recall YHWH's oath to Noah never to destroy the earth by flood again (Genesis 9) and creation itself insofar as YHWH likens divine fidelity to the mountains and hills of creation that will never move. The YHWH SPEECH FORMULA in v. 10bβ functions as a means to verify YHWH as the source of the OATH.

The prophet's conveyance of YHWH's promise to adorn and protect Zion in 54:11-17 likewise continues the PROPHETIC ANNOUNCEMENT OF SALVATION with a metaphorical portrayal of Zion as bride. The bridal motif proceeds with YHWH's promise of protection for Zion expressed by adorning her with jewels and precious stones. Her bridal jewels and precious stones metaphorically portray YHWH's guarantee of the integrity of the various features of the city: the bridal decorations thus represent Zion's building stones, foundations, battlements, gates, and outer borders. Her inhabitants are also portrayed as her sons and children. The promise in v. 14a that Zion will be established with righteousness speaks to the core issue of the restoration of the relationship and YHWH's promise of protection, modeled on a husband's promise of protection for his bride. The PARENESIS employs a positive command to call upon Zion to keep far from oppression, and its negative statement employs the REASSURANCE FORMULA to call upon her not to fear oppression. Verse 15 expresses YHWH's power to guarantee Zion's protection by emphasizing that no harm can come to Zion and anyone who would try to harm her would fail because YHWH as sovereign of creation has complete control over any potentially harmful elements in the created world. YHWH self-identifies as creator in vv. 16-17a. The SUMMARY-APPRAISAL formula in v. 17bα assures the reading or hearing audience that Zion can be assured of YHWH's power to protect. Finally, the ORACLE FORMULA in v. 17bβ assures the reader that YHWH is the source of the preceding guarantee.

Setting

Isaiah 54:1-17 appears as the concluding subunit of 49:1–54:17, which presents the contention that YHWH is renewing the relationship with Zion. As the culminating subunit of both 49:1–54:17 and YHWH's substantiation of the renewal of the covenant with Zion in 40:12–54:17, 54:1-17 presents the claim in vivid metaphorical form concerning the restoration of YHWH's marriage relationship with Bat Zion. Isaiah 54:1-17 follows immediately upon the Servant Song in 52:13–53:12, which anticipated the restoration of Israel, here understood as the exiles of Israel and Judah who would return to Zion. Thus, 54:1-17 completes the imagery by focusing on YHWH's bride, here understood to be Bat Zion, as the metaphorical representation of the city to which the exiles would return.

Isaiah 54 presupposes the social setting of ancient Israelite and Judean wedding ceremonies. Marriage texts, such as Genesis 24 and Genesis 29, presuppose a ceremony in which the bride is brought to the groom with an appropriate celebration and feasting for a week. Although the details of the bride's dress are not given apart from a veil, it seems reasonable to assume that she was dressed in her finest garments and bedecked with whatever jewelry that she and her family possessed for the occasion. Esther 2 envisions a six-month period of preparation with the finest clothing and cosmetics for a royal wedding, whereas Ruth 4 envisions a much simpler affair for a poor widow. Isaiah 3:16-24 gives readers some idea of the clothing and other items available to women in antiquity, but the biblical writers, most likely men, spent little time discussing the preparation and dress of brides.

When read in the context of the 5th-century edition of the book of Isaiah, ch. 54 aids in portraying the restored city of Jerusalem during the appointments of Nehemiah and Ezra. Nehemiah was known for restoring the city walls of Jerusalem to make the city inhabitable again and for a limited set of reforms that would restore the city's population and restore the Jerusalem temple to its role as the holy center of creation and Jewish religious and cultural life under Persian rule. Ezra was known for strengthening Nehemiah's reforms and giving them priestly authorization so as to ensure the integrity of the holy role of the temple. Although we do not know specifically what role the book of Isaiah might have played in the reforms of Nehemiah and Ezra, it seems reasonable to conclude that the book might have played some role in the life of the Jerusalem temple. The hymnic characteristics of the book of Isaiah, and of ch. 54 in particular, point to some liturgical role. Indeed, Ezra 9 in particular indicates that Ezra's return to Jerusalem was conceptualized as fulfillment of the book of Isaiah (Koch). Perhaps the book played a role in the liturgy for the rededication of the temple, and perhaps it was read in conjunction with the regular reading of the Torah instituted by Ezra (Nehemiah 8–10). Readers may note Nehemiah's and Ezra's efforts to engage the Jewish population of Jerusalem and Judah in temple worship. Consequently, the position of ch. 54 immediately prior to chs. 55–66, which call upon the people to play their roles in relation to YHWH's renewed covenant, points to an interest in convincing the people to return to Jerusalem and to reengage the temple and the Jewish tradition in the late 5th and early 4th centuries B.C.E.

When read in relation to the 6th-century edition of the book of Isaiah, ch. 54 appears to function as one of the culminating texts of the book. Although interpreters cannot be certain as to the position and role of chs. 60–62 within Deutero-Isaiah and even the 6th-century edition of the book of Isaiah as a whole, ch. 54 does appear at the conclusion of the prophet's contention that YHWH is restoring the relationship with Israel and Judah and immediately prior to ch. 55, which invites the people to take part in that renewed relationship. As noted before, the hymnic elements of this text, esp. vv. 1, 2-3, suggest a liturgical role for both the chapter and the book as part of the liturgy for the dedication of the newly-built Second Temple. Indeed, the emphasis on the restoration of the relationship between YHWH and Jerusalem would provide a fitting culmination for such a liturgy, insofar as the rebuilding of the temple would signify the restoration of the "marriage" relationship between YHWH and Zion. The adornment of the bride would of course correspond to the adornment of the city for the occasion, and YHWH's promises of fidelity and the return of children would likewise signal such restoration in 515 B.C.E., when the completed temple was dedicated for sacred service (Ezra 6).

Interpretation

Isaiah 54 employs a combination of genre elements, motifs, and intertextual references to present its proclamation of the restoration of the covenant/marriage relationship between YHWH and Zion. Although Zion is never explicitly mentioned as YHWH's bride in this passage, the literary context of Deutero-Isaiah makes it clear that the 2nd-feminine singular addressee of this chapter is indeed Bat Zion. As Tull Willey *(Remember the Former Things)* indicates, Bat Zion functions as a female servant figure in Deutero-Isaiah who interacts with the male servant of the so-called Servant Songs. Whereas the male servant, Israel or Jacob, may be identified with the exiled people of Israel, Judah, and Jerusalem, Bat Zion may be identified as the city of Jerusalem to which the exiled people or children return.

The passage is based on the prophetic announcement of salvation, but it is clear throughout that this genre interacts with other generic, motific, and intertextual elements in presenting its content. Overall, the passage combines the prophetic announcement of salvation with hymnic elements, the marriage metaphor for the relationship between YHWH and Jerusalem, and references to the matriarchal figures, Sarah and Rachel, to portray the restoration of Zion and the return of the exiled people to the city. In this respect, the passage serves as a suitable culminating element for a liturgy that would have celebrated the dedication of the Second Temple in the late-6th-century B.C.E. edition of the book of Isaiah and as a key text in the late-5th- or early-4th-century edition of the book of Isaiah that would have accompanied the restoration programs of Nehemiah and Ezra.

The interaction begins in the prophet's call to Zion to rejoice in 54:1. The liturgical character of the subunit is apparent in its hymnic form, which casts the whole passage as a celebratory song for the return of Zion's lost children. Here, the prophet refers to Zion as the barren one and the one who bore no child in apparent reference to the matriarchs, Sarah and Rachel, who were barren early on their marriages to the patriarchal figures, Abraham and Jacob, respectively. Such a portrayal of barrenness in the matriarchs portended the birth of an important figure in each case, i.e., Isaac for Sarah and Joseph for Rachel, both of whom would play leading roles in the formation of the nation of Israel/Judah. In the present instance, however, they function somewhat differently in that the reference to Zion's barrenness portends the return of her lost children who had been exiled away from their mother city. The barren mother whose children were lost appears in the image of Rachel weeping for her lost children in Jer 31:15 in the context of Jeremiah 30–31, which anticipates the return of the exiles to Jerusalem. The desolate nature of Zion takes up the imagery of the forlorn women of Isa 3:25–4:1, in which seven women would marry one man in the aftermath of the desolation of Jerusalem. It presupposes the rape of the land of Judah by the Assyrian king in 8:1-15. It compares to the forlorn Bat Babylon of ch. 47, although the present context makes it clear that Bat Zion's fortunes will be restored whereas Babylon's will not.

The prophet's call to Zion to enlarge her tent or dwelling in 54:2-3 likewise continues the portrayal of v. 1. Again, the structure of the passage appears to presuppose the hymn of praise, although it focuses on the effects of YHWH's actions on Zion rather than on YHWH's actions per se. Here, Bat Zion is instructed to enlarge the size of her tent or home to accommodate the many children or exiles that will return home in the aftermath of the Babylonian exile as the city of Jerusalem undergoes its restoration as YHWH's wife or covenant partner. The subunit presupposes the role of women as mistresses of the household, which in bedouin culture means that they set up the tent, drive the pegs, and fasten the cords that will hold the tent dwelling upright. A glimpse into this role appears in the portrayal of Jael, who invited the enemy commander Sisera into her tent following his defeat by Israel and killed him by driving a tent peg through his head (Judges 4–5). The use of the marriage metaphor to portray the covenant between YHWH and Zion or Israel draws upon a long tradition in the prophets, including Hosea 1–3; Zeph 3:14-20; Jeremiah 2; Ezekiel 16 and 20; and Isaiah 49–54, either for good or for bad (see Abma, *Bonds of Love;* Baumann, *Love and Violence*). The language of covenant begins to emerge in v. 3, which portrays Zion's children spreading out to the right and to the left and her seed possessing nations and inhabiting desolated (conquered) cities. Such motifs appear explicitly in Isaac's blessing to Jacob in Gen 27:28-29 and YHWH's blessing to Jacob in Gen 35:9-12 and implicitly in YHWH's blessing to Abraham in Gen 12:2-4 and to Jacob in Gen 28:13-15, which mention that "all the families of the land will be blessed through you."

The prophetic announcement of salvation begins to appear in the prophet's salvation oracle to Zion in 54:4-6. Here, the reassurance formula, "do not fear," the characteristic feature of the genre, appears in a modified twofold form in v. 4a with statements that Zion should neither fear nor be ashamed, followed by bases for each. The extended bases of vv. 4b-6 then pick up the marriage metaphor for the covenant once again. Verse 4a calls upon Zion to forget the shame of her youth and the humiliation of her widowhood. Ancient Israelite society presumed that women would be married and therefore protected and supported by their husbands. Insofar as men possessed land in an agricultural economy in which land meant wealth, women who were widowed lived in the households of their sons, returned to the households of their fathers or other male relatives, or fended for themselves. Normally, a widow left childless might engage in a Levirite marriage with a brother or male relative of her husband, who would provide her with offspring who would then inherit the dead man's estate (Deut 25:5-10; Ruth 4). But if a widow had no such options, she was left to her own devices. She might be sold into slavery to marry a man in the master's household (Exod 21:2-11); she might glean the fields for leftover crops to support herself (Exod 23:10-11); she might prostitute herself, which of course would leave her open to abuse (Genesis 38); or she might be subject to rape and murder (cf. Judges 19–21). In the present instance, YHWH informs Zion that those days are over. Isaiah 54:5 indicates that YHWH the creator is redeeming and marrying the forlorn Zion, which is an interesting proposition, given that the marriage metaphor would suggest that they were already married. This motif is developed further in v. 6, which maintains that YHWH is calling the forlorn Zion back because a man cannot reject the wife of his youth. And yet both ancient and modern times indicate that men, including YHWH, do precisely that. Deuteronomy 24:1-4 proposes that a man may not remarry his divorced wife once she has been married to another. Such an instance does not apply in the present case, strictly speaking, but Zion is portrayed as a raped and humiliated woman who was taken by the Assyrians or Babylonians (cf. 8:1-15). Given the fact that other men have had her, what is her status in relation to her (former?) husband YHWH?

The prophet's conveyance of YHWH's promise of a covenant of peace to Zion in 54:7-10 takes up this question. Here, YHWH admits to abandoning Zion in haste and in anger, but now YHWH is ready to take her back. Verse 7a makes the key statement, "for a little while, I abandoned you." One might ask, "what exactly does that mean?" In the present context, it means that YHWH left Jerusalem exposed to enemies while YHWH was doing, what? In human terms, it means the husband abandoned the marriage and left the wife exposed. Judean and Israelite tradition presumes that YHWH had an eternal covenant with Zion, the people of Israel, or the house of David, which calls upon YHWH to defend Zion, Israel, or David and for each of these parties to adhere to YHWH. But this covenant tradition was disrupted when the Assyrians and later the Babylonians destroyed Israel, Judah, and Jerusalem and carried the people into exile. How does YHWH, the sovereign creator, not keep an eternal covenant? Such an event demands an explanation, and here the explanation is that YHWH was angry with Zion, presumably for failing to adhere to her husband. But such an explanation might appear to be a bit contrived during the period when the exiles suffered the humiliation — if they survived — of displacement to a foreign land for some seventy years or three generations, i.e., from the destruction of the temple in 587 B.C.E. to the rededication of the temple in 515. It is only at the end of the exile when the restoration is at hand that such an explanation makes sense; YHWH has returned (from where and doing what?) to take back the bride Zion in love and mercy. Such an explanation plays on the hidden face of YHWH motif in 8:16-17: YHWH hides the divine face when Israel or Judah suffers invasion by enemies but ceases to do so when the time for restoration has come. Such a metaphor becomes a means for explaining disaster while maintaining the continuity of the covenant relationship between YHWH and Israel/Judah/Jerusalem. By claiming that this was YHWH's plan all along, the explanation takes on further credence while leaving open the question, "where were you and what were you doing during the interim?" It qualifies YHWH's promises of fidelity to Zion in vv. 9-10. YHWH's oath of fidelity to Zion is like that sworn to Noah, i.e., "I will not destroy the earth again by flood" (Genesis 9); but what about by fire? Hurricane? Invasion? YHWH's fidelity to Zion and covenant of peace is like that with the mountains and hills of creation, but readers must keep in mind that creation stands only so long as the temple stands. As the holy center of creation, creation is destroyed when the temple is destroyed (Levenson, "The Temple and the World"). The restoration of the temple in Ezekiel 40–48 portends a new creation in which even the waters of the Dead Sea sustain life. Indeed, Isaiah 66 envisions a new creation when the temple is restored. In other words, YHWH's promise of fidelity and a covenant of peace to Zion will last only so long as the temple is able to stand as the holy center of creation. But should it be destroyed again — as it was in 70 C.E. — the same questions of divine fidelity to Israel would emerge once again, and the same expectations of restoration would follow.

The prophet's conveyance of YHWH's promise to adorn and protect Zion in 54:11-17 continues to build on the metaphorical portrayal of YHWH's covenant with Jerusalem as a marriage relationship that had gone awry and is now being restored. Here YHWH portrays the battlements, gates, towers, building stones, etc., of Jerusalem as decked with jewels and precious stones, just as a bride would be so adorned for her wedding. But the motif of a new relationship comes into play when v. 13 portrays her sons as "taught by YHWH" *(limmûdê yhwh)*, which of course plays on Isaiah's earlier statement in 8:16-17, "Bind up the testimony, and seal the instruction *(tôrâ)* among my disciples/teachings *(bĕlimmûdāy)* and I will wait for YHWH who is hiding his face from the house of Jacob, and I will hope in him." Such a statement presents a double entendre for the term *limmûdîm* (lit., "those who are taught"), which might mean "disciples" or "teachings." In the present case in 54:13, it appears to mean "disciples" in reference to the children or people of Jerusalem. Such a citation entails an expectation of the people's fidelity to YHWH as well as YHWH's fidelity to the people, i.e., the disaster happened because the people did not trust in YHWH (like Ahaz in 7:1-9) and therefore suffered the consequences when YHWH hid the divine face from Jerusalem despite the eternal covenant which called for YHWH to defend the city.

In order to underscore YHWH's promises to Zion, the reassurance formula "do not fear" appears once again in v. 14 to signal the presence of the prophetic announcement of salvation working together with the marriage metaphor. YHWH swears that no harm will come to Zion, because YHWH is the creator and therefore controls all that takes place in creation. But of course, readers know that YHWH was the creator before and yet the disaster came nevertheless. But again, readers are asked to believe in the following chapter that YHWH had purposed such a scenario all along to reveal to the world that YHWH is the true creator and sovereign of all creation. Such a contention of course takes up YHWH's purpose as articulated in ch. 6, that the people will be kept blind, deaf, and dumb, so that YHWH's purpose might be worked out before all the world, clearly a teleological interpretation of YHWH's moral stance in which the ends justify the means rather than an ontological stance in which an act is judged as moral or not in and of itself.

In the end, the summary-appraisal form in 54:17b, "this is the inheritance of the servants of YHWH, and their righteousness/indication is from me," presents the Isaian assessment of YHWH's acts. Ultimately, Zion will be redeemed, but she suffers in the interim until YHWH acts to restore her.

Bibliography

K. Koch, "Ezra and the Origins of Judaism," *JSS* 19 (1974) 173-97; M. C. A. Korpel, "The Female Servant of the L-rd in Isaiah 54," in *On Reading Prophetic Texts* (*Fest.* F. van Dijk-Hemmes; ed. B. Becking and M. Dijkstra; BibInt 18; Leiden: Brill, 1996) 153-67; J. D. Levenson, "The Temple and the World," *JR* 64 (1984) 275-98; R. Martin-Achard, "Ésaïe liv et la nouvelle Jérusalem," in *Congress Volume: Vienna 1980* (VTSup 32; ed. J. A. Emerton; Leiden: Brill, 1981) 238-62; S. L. Stassen, "Marriage (and Related) Metaphors in Isaiah 54:1-17," *Journal for Semitics* 6 (1994) 57-73; O. H. Steck, "Beobachtungen zur Anlage von Jes 54,1-8," *ZAW* 101 (1989) 282-85.

EXHORTATION TO JOIN THE RESTORED ISRAEL 55:1–66:24

Structure

2. The people's lament: appeal to YHWH for mercy   63:7–64:11
3. YHWH's answer: restoration for the righteous and death
   for the wicked   65:1–66:24

Most scholars correctly maintain that ch. 55 was composed as the conclusion for the work of Deutero-Isaiah in chs. 40–55. It is fundamentally concerned with exhorting the audience of the text to observe the eternal covenant, which is the subject of both ch. 54 (see esp. vv. 9-10) and 40:1-11 (see esp. v. 8), which attempt to convince the audience that YHWH's word is eternal. But the eternal covenant is also the concern of the work of Trito-Isaiah in chs. 56–66. Indeed, the eternal covenant is explicitly named in 59:21 and 61:8. Trito-Isaiah is concerned throughout with how that covenant will be realized and how the restored exiles will take part in the new nation that the covenant will found. And so at the synchronic level, the exhortation in ch. 55 not only looks retrospectively at the concern for covenant and the divine word in chs. 40–54, but it simultaneously looks forward to the concern with the eternal covenant in chs. 56–66. Indeed, the exhortation of ch. 55 functions as a means to convince the people to take part in the covenant by joining the restored nation outlined in chs. 56–66.

Isaiah 55 differs on formal grounds from what precedes. Isaiah 54 concluded with a summary-appraisal form in v. 17b that looks back on the inheritance of the servants of YHWH. Isaiah 55 begins with a *hôy*-form that attracts the attention of the audience to the following material. Insofar as it is designed to exhort the audience to join YHWH's covenant, and insofar as chs. 56–66 are designed to define YHWH's covenant and the terms by which the people will participate in it, ch. 55 functions synchronically as an introduction to chs. 56–66. Isaiah 55 comprises two major subunits, a metaphorical invitation in v. 1 to buy water and food for free, which functions as a means to invite the people to join in YHWH's covenant, and YHWH's formal exhortation to the people in vv. 2-13, which clarifies the meaning of the metaphor by explicitly inviting the people to join YHWH's covenant.

Isaiah 56–66 is united by its focus on the nature of the reconstituted covenant and the expectations for those who would join the restored nation. Although the segment is constructed diachronically from a variety of textual forms, a combination of formal and thematic features points to three major subunits: the prophetic instruction concerning proper observance of the covenant in chs. 56–59; the prophetic announcement concerning the restoration of the reconstituted nation in chs. 60–62; and the prophetic instruction concerning the process of selection for the reconstituted nation in chs. 63–66.

The prophetic instruction concerning the proper observance of the covenant appears in chs. 56–59, which focus on the behavior expected of the restored nation. It begins with a YHWH speech formula in 56:1, which sets the unit off from the preceding material, and it concludes with a summary-appraisal form in 59:21, which presents a summation of YHWH's covenant. The first subunit is the basic exhortation to observe the covenant in 56:1-8, which begins with a YHWH speech formula and concludes with an oracle formula to define the subunit. The second subunit focuses on YHWH's willingness to forgive those who repent in 56:9–57:21, which is demarcated by its direct address to the wicked and the concluding statement by G-d that there is no peace for the wicked in 57:20-21. The third subunit in 58:1-14 admonishes the people to repent and provides specific criteria for doing so. This subunit is demarcated by its introductory imperatives formulated as a speech by YHWH and by its closing YHWH speech formula in v. 14bβ. The fourth and final subunit appears in the lament in 59:1-21, which focuses on YHWH's ability to forgive those who repent. The subunit is demarcated by its introductory particle, *hēn,* "behold"; its lament form; its concern with YHWH's willingness to forgive those who do repent; and the above-noted summary-appraisal form in 59:21. Some argue that the portrayal of YHWH equipped for battle in 59:17-19 forms a redactional envelope with 63:1-6 around the portrayal of YHWH's restoration of Zion in chs. 60–62. There is little evidence to judge 59:17-19 as a redactional insertion, but it does aid in advancing the plot and argument of the text that YHWH will restore the righteous and punish the wicked.

The prophetic announcement of restoration for the reconstituted nation in chs. 60–62 is a long-recognized formal and thematic unit. It is demarcated formally by its 2nd-person feminine singular address forms directed to Zion/Jerusalem and her people and by its formal character as a proclamation of salvation. It is concerned throughout with YHWH's eternal covenant with Zion and the primary role she will play at the center of a restored Israel as well as the nations of the world.

The prophetic instruction concerning the process of selection for the restored nation in chs. 63–66 focuses on defining how those who are righteous will be included in the restored nation and how those who are wicked will suffer punishment. It functions rhetorically as a means to convince the audience that they want to be included among the righteous and thereby be a part of the restoration rather than lost to punishment. It begins with a portrayal of YHWH as divine warrior in 63:1-6, which portrays YHWH's slaughter of enemies. It continues in 63:7–64:11 with the people's lament in which they appeal to YHWH for mercy and thereby avoid the impending judgment against the wicked. It closes in chs. 65–66, which relate YHWH's answer to the people's lament with divine statements concerning life for the righteous and death for the wicked.

Genre

Insofar as chs. 55–66 comprise a composite unit, it includes a large variety of genres that will be discussed in the treatment of the various subunits of the text. Its overarching concern, however, is EXHORTATION, insofar as the unit is designed to convince its audience to join YHWH's covenant with the restored nation of Israel/Judah at Zion.

Setting

Although ch. 55 was composed in the late 6th century B.C.E. as part of the work of Deutero-Isaiah, the bulk of the unit in chs. 56–66 presupposes the Persian-period restoration of Nehemiah and Ezra in the latter 5th and early 4th centuries. Detailed discussion of this setting appears in the treatment of the individual subunits of this text.

Interpretation

Isaiah 55–66 constitutes the concluding segment of the second half of the book in chs. 34–66, which is concerned with the realization of YHWH's plans for worldwide sovereignty at Zion, as well as of the book of Isaiah as a whole, which is concerned with exhorting the people of Jerusalem/Judah to adhere to YHWH based on divine claims of worldwide sovereignty at Zion. Chs. 55–66 are therefore fundamentally concerned with making the case for adherence to YHWH's covenant.

Isaiah 55–66 proceeds in two segments. The first segment is the exhortation proper in ch. 55, which employs in 55:1 the metaphor of buying water and bread as a rhetorical device to draw the audience into support for the main argument. After all, who wouldn't want to buy water and bread for free? It then continues with YHWH's exhortation to the people in 55:2-13, which transitions from the metaphor to a clear invitation to join YHWH's covenant, based on the sure promises to David.

The second segment is the substantiation of the exhortation in chs. 56–66, which presents prophetic instruction concerning the reconstituted nation in Zion. Isaiah 56–66 comprises three subunits, each of which builds the case for adherence to the covenant by outlining proper adherence to the covenant, the rewards for such adherence, and the consequences for failure to do so.

The first subunit in chs. 56–59 presents prophetic instruction concerning the proper observance of the covenant. It begins in 56:1-8 with a basic instruction or exhortation which calls for observance of Shabbat as a basic criterion for the people, even those who might have been born as foreigners or who have become eunuchs during the period of Babylonian exile. It continues in 56:9–57:21 with a statement of YHWH's willingness to forgive those who repent, which functions rhetorically as a call to repentance directed to the nation that would then open the way for their return to Jerusalem and Judah. The admonition to repent then follows in 58:1-14, which provides specific criteria for covenant observance, such as observance of divine righteousness *(ṣĕdāqâ)* and law *(mišpāṭ)* mentioned in v. 2. Finally, the lament in 59:1-21 focuses on YHWH's intent and ability to deliver those who repent.

The second subunit in chs. 60–62 presents a prophetic announcement of restoration for the reconstituted nation. It addresses the city of Jerusalem to announce to her that the time of oppression has come to an end as the light of YHWH will shine on her and the nations will now flock to her, not as oppressors, but as supplicants. The subunit concludes with YHWH's oath never again to give the city over to enemies. Such a claim of course raises theological questions when one considers the destruction of Jerusalem by the Romans in 70 C.E. as well as the continued occupation of the city by foreign powers, such as Rome, the Muslim conquest, the Ottoman Empire, and the British, until modern times.

The third and final subunit is chs. 63–66, which presents prophetic instruction concerning the process of selection for the reconstituted nation. The text envisions the return and restoration of the righteous, those who repent and return to YHWH, but it also envisions punishment for the wicked who do not. Such a division signals a continuing effort to elicit support for the book's claims and agenda, particularly when read in relation to the restoration of Nehemiah and Ezra in the late 5th through early 4th centuries B.C.E. The text signals the approach of YHWH as divine warrior in 63:1-6, which suggests YHWH's efforts to punish those who stand as obstacles to the divine agenda. It turns to the people's lament and their appeal for mercy in 63:7–64:11, which highlights the importance of choosing to include oneself among the righteous. And finally, YHWH answers that there will be restoration for the righteous and death for the wicked in 65:1–66:24, which provides further rhetorical incentive to make the right choice. Insofar as Ezra 9 presents Ezra's return to Jerusalem as a fulfillment of Isaiah's vision (cf. Koch, "Ezra and the Origins of Judaism"), the final form of the book of Isaiah appears to have been written to support the restoration efforts of Ezra and Nehemiah.

Bibliography

K. Koch, "Ezra and the Origins of Judaism," *JSS* 19 (1974) 173-97; M. A. Sweeney, *Isaiah 1–4*, 87-92.

EXHORTATION SPEECH 55:1-13

Structure

I. Metaphorical invitation to buy water and food for free	55:1
A. First *hôy* address to all who are thirsty: come for water	55:1aα
1. *hôy* address form to thirsty	55:1aα$^{1-3}$
2. Imperative invitation	55:1aα$^{4-5}$
B. Second address to those without money: come, buy, eat	
without money	55:1aβ-b
1. Address form to those without money	55:1aβ
2. Imperative invitation	55:1b
a. Threefold imperatives: come, buy, and eat	55:1bα
b. Imperative elaboration	55:1bβ
II. YHWH's exhortation to people	55:2-13
A. Twofold rhetorical question: why do you spend money for	
nothing?	55:2a
1. First rhetorical question: why spend money for what is not	
bread?	55:2aα
2. Second rhetorical question: why spend money for what	
does not satisfy?	55:2aβ
B. Rhetorical answer: exhortation to follow YHWH	55:2b-13

1. First instruction: listen to me and you shall eat choice
   food: threefold imperative   55:2b
   a. Listen to me   55:2bα$^{1-3}$
   b. Eat well   55:2bα$^{4-5}$
   c. Enjoy rich food   55:2bβ
2. Second instruction: incline your ear and come to eternal
   covenant   55:3-5
   a. Threefold imperatives: incline, come, listen   55:3a
      1) Incline your ear   55:3aα$^{1-2}$
      2) Come to me   55:3aα$^{3-4}$
      3) Hear that you may live   55:3aβ
        a) Imperative: hear   55:3aβ^{1}
        b) Motivation for hearing: so you may live   55:3aβ$^{2-3}$
   b. Expanded motivation for listening: YHWH's announcement of eternal covenant for Israel   55:3b-5
      1) Announcement proper of eternal covenant   55:3b
        a) Announcement of eternal covenant   55:3bα
        b) Qualification of eternal covenant: Davidic promise   55:3bβ
      2) Elaboration of Davidic covenant applied to Israel   55:4-5
        a) I made David the leader of nations   55:4
          (1) I made him a witness to the nations   55:4a
          (2) Leader and commander of nations   55:4b
        b) You will summon nations because of YHWH   55:5
          (1) You will summon a nation that you do not know   55:5aα
          (2) Nation that does not know you will run to you   55:5aβ-b
            (a) Basically stated   55:5aβ
            (b) Reason: because of YHWH   55:5b
              α. Because of YHWH your G-d   55:5bα
              β. Because of Holy One of Israel who
                glorified you   55:5bβ
3. Third instruction with rationale   55:6-13
   a. Third instruction: seek YHWH   55:6-7
      1) First twofold imperative instruction: seek YHWH   55:6
        a) First imperative: seek YHWH while he may be found   55:6a
        b) Second imperative: call YHWH when he is near   55:6b
      2) Second jussive instruction: let wicked abandon his way   55:7
        a) Twofold instruction   55:7a
          (1) Let wicked abandon his way   55:7aα
          (2) Let evil man abandon his plans   55:7aβ
        b) Twofold rationale: return to G-d who forgives   55:7b
          (1) He will return to YHWH who shows him mercy   55:7bα
            (a) Return to YHWH   55:7bα$^{1-3}$
            (b) YHWH shows him mercy   55:7bα^{4}
          (2) He will return to his G-d who will forgive
            abundantly   55:7bβ
            (a) Return to his G-d   55:7bβ$^{1-2}$
            (b) G-d will forgive him abundantly   55:7bβ$^{3-5}$

b. Rationale: YHWH achieves YHWH's plans — you will
   return in peace   55:8-13
   1) Basic premise of rationale: my thoughts/plans are
      higher than yours   55:8
      a) Twofold basic statement   55:8a
        (1) First statement: my plans are higher than yours   55:8aα
        (2) Second statement: my ways are higher than yours 55:8aβ
      b) Oracle formula   55:8b
   2) Elaboration: you will return in peace   55:9-13
      a) Initial premise: my ways/plans are higher than yours 55:9
        (1) Protasis: heavens are higher than earth   55:9a
        (2) Twofold apodosis: my ways/plans higher than
           yours   55:9b
          (a) My ways higher than yours   55:9bα
          (b) My plans higher than yours   55:9bβ
      b) Second premise: I achieve what I set out to do   55:10-11
        (1) Protasis: rain/snow soaks the earth and brings
           vegetation   55:10
          (a) Rain and snow come down from heaven
             and do not return   55:10aα
             α. Rain and snow come down from heaven   55:10aα$^{1\text{-}7}$
             β. They do not return to heaven   55:10aα$^{8\text{-}10}$
          (b) But rain/snow waters the earth, gives birth,
             sprouts, and produces food   55:10aβ-b
             α. It waters the earth   55:10aβ
             β. Earth gives birth and sprouts   55:10aγ
             γ. Gives seed for sowing and bread for eating 55:10b
        (2) Apodosis: my word achieves what I propose   55:11
          (a) Analogy: so is my word that comes from
             my mouth   55:11aα
          (b) But it achieves what I propose   55:11aβ-b
             α. It does not return to me empty   55:11aβ
             β. Twofold statement: achieves what I propose 55:11b
               aa. It achieves what I propose   55:11bα
               bb. It succeeds in what I send it to do   55:11bβ
      c) Third premise: you will return in peace   55:12-13
        (1) Twofold premise   55:12a
          (a) You will go out from exile in joy   55:12aα
          (b) You will return to Jerusalem in peace   55:12aβ
        (2) Elaboration: creation restored   55:12b-13
          (a) Rejoicing of mountains, hills, and trees   55:12b
             α. Mountains and hills will break out in song 55:12bα
             β. Trees of the field will clap hands   55:12bβ
          (b) Creation transformed   55:13a
             α. Cypress will replace briar   55:13aα
             β. Myrtle will replace nettle   55:13aβ
          (c) It will constitute an eternal sign   55:13b

α. It will establish YHWH's name   55:13bα
β. It will become an eternal sign that is not
    cut off   55:13bβ

Most scholars follow Begrich in viewing ch. 55 as a combination of two major units: 55:1-5 and 55:6-13. But Begrich's view is based on a generic distinction between the two subunits. He maintains that 55:1-5 is an invitation of wisdom genre, i.e., an invitation to a meal (Begrich, *Studien,* 59-61; cf. Melugin, *Formation,* 25-26), whereas 55:6-13 begins with a prophetic imitation of priestly Torah followed by other prophetic elements (Begrich, *Studien,* 58; cf. Melugin, *Formation,* 86-87). But the institutional distinction between wisdom and prophecy which justifies the division into two subunits is deceptive insofar as generic elements do not constitute a text, as early form critics such as Begrich would maintain; rather, generic elements function within a text to contribute to its overall form and message. Indeed, the rhetorical or persuasive dimensions of the text must be considered in establishing its literary form. In the present instance, the two generic elements in vv. 1-5 and 6-13 serve within a larger literary and formal framework concerned with exhortation and the persuasion of the audience that YHWH indeed has acted from the beginning to demonstrate divine sovereignty over all creation by restoring Israel in the aftermath of its destruction and exile.

Isaiah 55:1-13 is demarcated at the outset by its initial *hôy* form followed by its masculine plural imperative verbs (see vv. 1, 2, 3, 6) and other 2nd-masculine plural pronoun and verbal forms (see vv. 2, 3, 8, 9, 12) that address the audience throughout the text in an effort to convince the audience to join in YHWH's covenant (v. 3) based on the premise that YHWH will lead the people out from exile and return them to their homeland in peace (v. 12). The reference to the eternal sign in v. 13 concludes the unit, and the prophetic messenger formula which introduces YHWH's oracle in 56:1 opens the next unit.

Isaiah 55:1-13 is an exhortation speech designed to convince its audience to join in YHWH's new covenant. Its formal structure begins in 55:1 with a metaphorical invitation to buy water and food for free, which serves as a means to signal YHWH's covenant which will emerge later in the text. The invitation begins with the first *hôy* address to all who are thirsty in v. 1aα, which invites them to come for water. Normally, *hôy* is an exclamation that means "woe!" but in the present context it simply signals the audience, here portrayed as those who are thirsty, to pay attention to what follows. Isaiah 55:1aα includes two major components: the *hôy* address form to the thirsty in v. 1aα¹⁻³ and the imperative instruction to come for water in v. 1aα⁴⁻⁵. The second address to those without money follows in v. 1aβ-b with an invitation to come, buy, and eat without cost. This subunit comprises two basic elements. The address form to those without money appears in v. 1aβ, and the imperative invitation appears in v. 1b. The invitation in v. 1b in turn comprises two basic elements: the threefold imperatives to come, buy, and eat in v. 1bα and the imperative elaboration in v. 1bβ that indicates that wine and dairy products may be had without cost.

The major element of the passage, YHWH's exhortation to the people, then appears in 55:2-13. The passage is somewhat disputational in character, in that it challenges the proclivities of an audience that would otherwise remain in Babylonian exile because it believes that YHWH is a defeated G-d who could not protect the people of Israel and Judah from Babylonia. Instead, the passage is designed to convince the people to join in YHWH's new covenant so that they might return to their homeland. Such a proposal is based on the premise that YHWH had planned both the exile and the restoration long ago, in part to demonstrate divine sovereignty over all creation.

Isaiah 55:2-13 begins with a twofold rhetorical question in v. 2a that asks the audience "why do you spend your money for nothing?" Such a question of course builds upon the metaphor of v. 1, all the while indicating that the people are wasting their future away by remaining in Babylonian exile as YHWH prepares to bring them home. The first rhetorical question in v. 2aα asks them why they spend money for that which is not bread, and the second rhetorical question in v. 2aβ asks them why they spend money for that which does not satisfy.

The rhetorical answer to these questions then occupies the rest of the passage in 55:2b-13 in the form of an exhortation speech. The exhortation speech includes three basic instructions, each of which is introduced by a masculine plural imperative in vv. 2b, 3-5, and 6-13. Taken together, they constitute the elements of a speech designed to convince the audience to join in YHWH's covenant.

The first instruction appears in 55:2b. It comprises a threefold set of 2nd-masculine plural imperative commands to "listen to me" in v. $2b\alpha^{1-3}$; to "eat well" in v. $2b\alpha^{4-5}$; and to "enjoy rich food" in v. 2bβ. This instruction opens the sequence by calling for the audience's attention and continuing the metaphorical invitation to buy water and food in v. 1.

The second instruction appears in 55:3-5. It constitutes an instruction to "incline your ear" and come to the eternal covenant which YHWH is establishing with the people. The instruction begins in v. 3a with threefold imperatives to "incline your ear" in v. $3a\alpha^{1-2}$; to "come to me" in v. $3a\alpha^{3-4}$; and to "hear that you may live" in v. 3aβ. The last element in v. 3aβ is further subdivided into the imperative command to hear in v. $3a\beta^1$ and the motivation for hearing, i.e., "so that you may live," in v. $3a\beta^{2-3}$. An expanded motivation for listening appears in vv. 3b-5, which convey YHWH's announcement of an eternal covenant for Israel. The announcement proper of the eternal covenant appears in v. 3b, which comprises the announcement of the eternal covenant in v. 3bα followed by the qualification of the covenant as the Davidic promise in v. 3bβ. An elaboration of the Davidic covenant applied to all Israel then follows in vv. 4-5. The first portion of this elaboration appears in v. 4, which constitutes YHWH's statement that "I made David the leader of nations." YHWH's statement comprises two elements: "I made him a witness to the nations" in v. 4a and "I made him a leader and commander of nations" in v. 4b. The reference to David as witness *('ēd)* is considered problematic by some scholars, but interpreters must recall that the house of David ruled on behalf of YHWH and so the Davidic rulers constituted witnesses to YHWH as the true sovereign of Israel. The second portion of the elaboration appears in v. 5, in which the prophet states that "you will summon nations because of YHWH." The first portion of this statement appears in v. 5aα, in which the prophet states that "you will summon a nation that you do not know," and the second portion appears in v. 5aβ-b with a complex statement indicating that "a nation that does not know you will run to you." This statement comprises the basic statement of the issue in v. 5aβ and the reason for the statement, that this happens because of YHWH, in v. 5b. The reason in turn comprises two basic elements: because of "YHWH your G-d" in v. 5bα and because of "the Holy One of Israel who glorified you" in v. 5bβ.

The third instruction, which constitutes the culmination of the unit, appears in 55:6-13. The instruction calls upon the audience to seek YHWH and it provides a rationale for doing so. The instruction to seek YHWH appears in vv. 6-7, and the rationale appears in vv. 8-13.

The instruction to seek YHWH in vv. 6-7 comprises two basic elements. The first is a twofold imperative instruction in v. 6 to seek YHWH. This instruction comprises two sets of imperatives. The first set of imperatives in v. 6a calls upon the audience to seek YHWH while YHWH might yet be found. The second set of imperatives in v. 6b calls upon the audience to call upon YHWH when YHWH is near. The second jussive instruction in v. 7 calls upon the audience to let the wicked abandon his way. It begins with a twofold instruction in v. 7a which asks the audience to let the wicked abandon his way in v. 7aα and then follows by asking the audience to let the evil man abandon his plans in v. 7aβ. The second element of v. 7 is a twofold rationale in v. 7b which calls upon the audience to return to G-d who forgives. Verse 7b comprises two basic elements. The first element in v. 7bα states that "he will return to YHWH who shows him mercy" in two parts: the statement that "he will return to YHWH" in v. 7bα$^{1-3}$ and the statement that "YHWH shows him mercy" in v. 7bα^4. The second element in v. 7bβ states that "he will return to his G-d who will forgive abundantly," including statements that "he will return to his G-d" in v. 7bβ$^{1-2}$ and that "G-d will forgive him abundantly" in v. 7bβ$^{3-5}$.

The rationale for the exhortation to seek YHWH then follows in 55:8-13. The rationale asserts that the audience should seek YHWH because YHWH will achieve YHWH's plans and that the people will consequently return to their homeland in peace. The rationale comprises two basic elements: the basic premise of the rationale that YHWH's plans are higher than the people's plans in v. 8 and the elaboration in vv. 9-13 that the people will return home in peace.

Isaiah 55:8 constitutes the basic premise of the rationale with its assertion that "my (YHWH's) thoughts or plans are higher than your (the people's) thoughts or plans." This becomes a means to state that YHWH's purposes and understanding trump those of the people. The subunit begins with a twofold basic statement of this premise in v. 8a. The first statement, "my plans are higher than your plans," appears in v. 8aα, and the second statement, "my ways are higher than your ways," appears in v. 8aβ. The oracle formula in v. 8b then closes out this subunit by asserting that the previous statement is indeed an oracle from YHWH.

The elaboration of this premise, that "you will return in peace," then follows in vv. 9-13. The initial premise of the elaboration appears in v. 9 in the form of a conditional statement including a protasis and twofold apodosis. The protasis appears in v. 9a with the condition "because the heavens are higher than the earth." The apodosis then follows in v. 9b with a twofold statement of the consequences of the protasis. The first appears in v. 9bα with the statement that "my ways are higher than yours," and the second appears in v. 9bβ with the statement that "my plans are higher than yours."

The second premise of the rationale appears in vv. 10-11, in which YHWH asserts that "I achieve what I set out to do." Again, YHWH's statement is conditional, including both a protasis and an apodosis. The protasis, that rain and snow soak the earth and bring forth vegetation, appears in v. 10 in two parts. The first, in v. 10aα, states the condition that rain and snow come down from heaven in v. 10aα$^{1-7}$ and that rain and snow do not return to heaven in v. 10aα$^{8-10}$. The second portion of the protasis, that rain and snow water the earth, which then gives birth, sprouts, and produces food, appears in v. 10aβ-b. The three elements appear in sequence: rain and snow water the earth in v. 10aβ; the earth gives birth and sprouts in v. 10aγ; and the earth therefore gives seed for sowing and food for eating in v. 10b. The apodosis, that "my word therefore achieves what I propose," then follows in v. 11. The apodosis begins by establishing an analogy with the process of rain and snow described in the protasis: "so is my word that comes from my mouth," in v. 11aα. The second part of the apodosis in v. 11aβ-b then focuses on how YHWH's word achieves what YHWH proposes. It begins with a statement in v. 11aβ that "it (YHWH's word) does not return to me empty," i.e., it is not uttered without purpose or result. A twofold statement describing how YHWH's word achieves what YHWH proposes then follows in v. 11b in two parts. The first part in v. 11bα asserts that "it (YHWH's word) achieves what I propose," and the second part in v. 11bβ asserts that "it succeeds in what I send it to do."

Finally, the third premise of the exhortation, that "you will return in peace," appears in 55:12-13. It begins with a twofold statement of the premise in v. 12a. The first portion of the premise in v. 12aα states that "you will go out (from exile) in joy," and the second portion of the premise in v. 12aβ states that "you shall be led (to Jerusalem) in peace." An elaboration concerning the restoration of creation as a result of the return of the people to the land then follows in vv. 12b-13. This segment comprises three subunits. The first subunit in v. 12b focuses on the rejoicing of the mountains, hills, and trees as a result of Israel's restoration. This subunit comprises two elements: the assertion that the mountains and hills will break out in song in v. 12bα and the assertion that the trees of the field will clap their hands in v. 12bβ. The second subunit in v. 13a focuses in two parts on the transformation of creation. The first part in v. 13aα asserts that cypress will replace briar, and the second part in v. 13aβ asserts that myrtle will replace nettle. The third subunit in v. 13b asserts that the transformation of creation will constitute an eternal sign of what YHWH has done for Israel and creation, again in two parts. The first in v. 13bα asserts that it will establish YHWH's name (as the sovereign of creation), and the second in v. 13bβ asserts that it will become an eternal sign that will not be cut off.

Genre

Interpreters have taken a rather fragmented approach to reading 55:1-13, based in large measure on their inability to correlate the various generic forms that appear within the text. A particularly important issue is the inability to reconcile the wisdom-based INVITATION TO A MEAL that appears in vv. 1-5 with the prophetic genres that appear within vv. 6-13. Verses 6-13 were especially confusing as scholars identified a variety of prophetic forms that seemed not to correlate, such as the prophetic imitation of priestly Torah in vv. 6-7, the DISPUTATIONAL substantiation for the exhortation in vv. 8-9, and a second substantiation in vv. 10-11, followed by an ANNOUNCEMENT OF SALVATION in vv. 12-13 (Melugin, *Formation* 86-87). Because these genres come from different institutional settings, wisdom for the former and prophecy for the latter, they could not possibly work together within a text as conceived in the early stages of form-critical research. As a result, scholars have misread both the literary form of this text and its generic character, offering little insight as to how vv. 1-5 and 6-13 could work together.

But while genres function within the larger formal structure of a given text, they do not always constitute the text. In the present instance, rhetorical criticism, with its attention to argumentative or persuasive intent, aids in discerning the overall form of ch. 55. As the above structure analysis indicates, ch. 55 is formulated to persuade its audience to seek YHWH (v. 6) and to do so because YHWH is acting to bring the people out of Babylonian exile and to return them to their homeland in Jerusalem and the land of Israel (v. 12). The early wisdom-oriented INVITATION TO A MEAL in vv. 1-5 merely functioned as a metaphorical means to express the invitation to seek YHWH as stated in v. 6. Verses 1-5 therefore begin the process of persuasion by employing the metaphor of water and food for nothing, which ultimately gives way to the concern to persuade the people to accept YHWH's sovereignty based on the projected achievement of YHWH's plans for the nation and creation at large.

Given such persuasive intent, 55:1-13 must be recognized as an EXHORTATION. The EXHORTATION is an inherently persuasive genre that is designed to persuade the audience of a given point. In this respect, the interest in persuading the people to seek YHWH based upon YHWH's promise to bring them out of Babylon and home to Jerusalem and Israel is in keeping with the general persuasive intention of chs. 40–55.

Although EXHORTATION constitutes the overarching generic identity of 55:1-13, other generic elements play roles within this text which facilitate the realization of its purposes. We have already noted the INVITATION TO A MEAL in vv. 1-5. Begrich viewed the invitation as an imitation of a wisdom genre (Begrich, *Studien,* 59-61). The form is based on the INVITATION TO A MEAL, which typically appears in wisdom literature as a means to use the metaphor of eating to invite the audience to learn wisdom (Prov 9:5; Sir 24:19). Here, however, the invitation is not to study wisdom, strictly speaking, but to recognize YHWH as the true sovereign of the universe. This is indeed a form of wisdom, particularly since the wisdom tradition maintains that one may recognize YHWH by studying the world of creation. In this respect, the correlation of Israel's redemption from Babylonian exile and repatriation to the land of Israel correlates with the celebration of creation in vv. 12-13. Melugin is correct to observe that vv. 3b-5 do double duty as a form of prophetic SALVATION SPEECH (Melugin, *Formation,* 25), especially since the overall concern of the passage is the restoration of the exiles to the land of Israel.

Other genres also play their roles in vv. 1-5. The RHETORICAL QUESTIONS in v. 2 build the metaphor of eating by asking the audience why they spend their money on bread that does not satisfy, i.e., why do they pursue a wrong course in failing to recognize YHWH's intent to bring them home. Indeed, the pattern of vv. 2-13 is based on the RHETORICAL QUESTIONS in v. 2a and the RHETORICAL ANSWER that explains the intent of the question in vv. 2b-13. The genre INSTRUCTION is also evident in vv. 2b, 3-5, and 6-13, which work together to call upon the audience to "listen to me" so that they might learn YHWH's intent and thereby follow YHWH. In each case, a basic instruction is given: to "listen to me" in v. 2b, to "incline your ear, come to me, and hear so that you may live" in vv. 3-5, and to "seek YHWH" in vv. 6-13. The last instruction also includes the rationale in vv. 8-13, which explains the purpose of the instructional sequence.

The ORACLE FORMULA appears in v. 8b to certify YHWH's speech in v. 8a. This helps to identify the prophetic character of the text at large insofar as the prophet conveys YHWH's words throughout 55:1-13.

Setting

Elliger employs a number of thematic, stylistic, and linguistic observations to maintain that ch. 55 is written by Trito-Isaiah (*Die Einheit;* cf. Muilenburg, "Chapters 40–66," 643; Rofé, "How Is the Word Fulfilled?"). Nevertheless, the arguments for viewing ch. 55 as an epilogue to Deutero-Isaiah point to its origins in the work of the late-exilic-period prophet. The concern with the eternal covenant of the house of David now applied to all Israel in vv. 3-5 corresponds to the concern with the eternal covenant of peace in 54:6-10 as well as the designation of Cyrus as YHWH's temple-builder and messiah in 44:28 and 45:1. The references to an eternal covenant in 59:21 and 61:8 appear in contexts which deliberately take up earlier texts in First Isaiah in keeping with Trito-Isaiah's interpretive character (Sweeney, "Reconceptualization"). Furthermore, ch. 55 displays important parallels with 40:1-11, which demonstrates that the two texts were designed to serve as literary "book ends" for Deutero-Isaiah. Melugin (*Formation,* 87) points to several key parallels: the return to a merciful YHWH in 55:6-7 and 40:1-2; the promise of an exodus from Babylonian exile in 55:12-13 and 40:3-5; the assertions of YHWH's radical differences from human beings in 55:8-9 and 40:6-9; and the reliability of YHWH's word in 55:10-11 and 40:8. We might add the interest in ch. 55 in convincing the reading or listening audience of YHWH's power and role as sovereign of all creation who is fully capable of releasing Israel from Babylonian captivity and restoring them to Jerusalem and the land of Israel.

Thus, it appears that ch. 55 was composed as a concluding text for the work of Second Isaiah in the late 6th century B.C.E. Although it is possible that chs. 60–62 are also a part of Second Isaiah (see below, ad loc), ch. 55 presents a culminating perspective for the arguments offered throughout chs. 40–54, that YHWH brought about the exile of Israel and its restoration as part of a larger effort to demonstrate divine sovereignty over all creation and the nations of the world. In this respect, the emphasis on the reliability of YHWH's word is crucial both at the conclusion of Deutero-Isaiah in 55:13 and at the beginning in 40:8. Likewise, the argument that the Davidic covenant is to be applied to Israel rather than only to the house of David takes up Deutero-Isaiah's announcement that Cyrus is YHWH's temple-builder and messiah in 44:28 and 45:1, roles previously enjoyed by the house of David. In the context of the late-6th-century edition of the book of Isaiah, such arguments would be crucial to convince exiled Jews in Babylonia to return home to Jerusalem and Israel in an effort to begin the reconstruction of the Jerusalem temple and national life, albeit under Persian rule, in the land of Israel. Isaiah 55 maintains that such restoration was part of YHWH's plan from the beginning.

Nevertheless, the diachronic conclusion that ch. 55 was composed as part of the work of Deutero-Isaiah does not preclude the synchronic conclusion that ch. 55 also serves as an introduction to the work of Trito-Isaiah in chs. 56–66. Whereas Deutero-Isaiah makes the case for YHWH's role as the sovereign of all creation and nations, Trito-Isaiah begins to lay out the conditions for those who would be a part of YHWH's eternal covenant promised in ch. 55. Isaiah 56–59 focuses on instructions for the proper observance of the covenant, such as the requirement to observe Shabbat in 56:1-8; the need for repentance and YHWH's willingness to forgive those who repent in 56:9–57:21; specific criteria for repentance and covenant expectations in 58:1-14; and a lament concerned with YHWH's willingness and ability to deliver those who repent in 59:1-21. Isaiah 60–62 presents a proclamation of salvation that points to the glorious expectation of restoration in Jerusalem and the land of Israel and the recognition of the nations. Isaiah 63–66 takes up the process by which the covenant shall be achieved with special attention to differentiating between the righteous, who will be included in the covenant, and the wicked, who will not. Such considerations include YHWH's approach as a divine warrior in 63:1-6 to punish the wicked, such as Edom; the people's appeal for mercy in the lament of 63:7–64:11; and YHWH's answer that deliverance is for the righteous and punishment is for the wicked in 65:1–66:24.

Thus, ch. 55 plays a key role in the 5th-century edition of the book of Isaiah. By introducing chs. 56–66, which are concerned with observance of YHWH's covenant, ch. 55 highlights the conditions of covenant inclusion within the context of the reform efforts of Nehemiah and Ezra. Both were appointed to their respective offices by the Persian Empire, Nehemiah as the governor of the Persian province of Yehud and Ezra as the priest or commissioner for religious affairs who would provide the people with Torah as the basis for their semi-autonomous life under Persian rule (cf. J. Weinberg, *The Citizen-Temple Community* [trans. D. Smith-Christopher; JSOTSup 151; Sheffield: JSOTSup, 1992]). In this respect, ch. 55 functions as a means to convince the 5th-century Judean audience of the book to accept the restoration efforts of Nehemiah and Ezra as expressions of YHWH's will for implementing the eternal covenant of David, now applied to Israel at large. In other words, don't include yourselves among the wicked who will suffer YHWH's punishment; include yourselves among the righteous who will enjoy YHWH's preplanned restoration.

Interpretation

Isaiah 55 is formulated as an exhortation to seek YHWH. It functions simultaneously as the conclusion to chs. 40–54 and as the introduction to chs. 56–66. As the culminating text of chs. 40–54, it draws upon the arguments throughout these chapters that YHWH is the sovereign of Israel, creation, and the nations as part of a larger effort to convince the exiled people of Jerusalem and Judah/ Israel to return to the land of Israel to commence the restoration of Jerusalem. As the introduction to chs. 56–66, it introduces YHWH's eternal covenant with the nation of Israel, like that of the house of David, which then serves as the basis in chs. 56–66 to specify how the nation should go about seeking YHWH.

The chapter begins with a metaphorical invitation to buy water and food for free in 55:1. Such a metaphor is a typical wisdom device that signals an invitation to engagement in study and analysis of the world of creation at large in an effort to discern the divine principles that underlie it. In the present context, the metaphorical invitation serves as a means to engage the people's attention by defining their relationship with YHWH through the eternal covenant that YHWH offers Israel as a basis for their restoration from Babylonian captivity to their new life in the restored city of Jerusalem and the land of Israel. The metaphor presumes that just as water and food are necessary for life, so recognition of YHWH and engagement with YHWH's covenant are the necessary conditions for the life of the nation. Essentially, the metaphor enables the text to use the stomach as a means to engage the mind. The invitation stresses the free nature of the water and food offered to symbolize the fact that YHWH's covenant is open to all Israel.

YHWH's exhortation to the people then follows in 55:2-13. The exhortation continues the metaphor initially by posing rhetorical questions in v. 2a that ask the audience why they spend their money for nothing or for bread that does not satisfy. Such questions serve the disputational character of the passage by challenging the current beliefs of the people who would maintain that they are in Babylonian exile because their G-d, YHWH, was powerless to defend the nation and the city of Jerusalem against the power of the Babylonian Empire and its god, Marduk. To the contrary, ch. 55 aims to convince the audience that YHWH is indeed powerful as the true sovereign of the universe, who planned exile and restoration long ago as part of a larger plan to demonstrate divine sovereignty over all creation and the nations. For the nation Israel, YHWH's sovereignty means an end of the Babylonian exile and a return home to a restored Jerusalem at the center of creation.

The rhetorical answer in 55:2b-13 then offers three sets of instructions to the audience concerning YHWH's true character and the nature of the covenant that YHWH offers the people.

The first set of instructions in v. 2b continues the metaphor of food and provides a basic instruction to listen to YHWH so that the people will eat well and enjoy rich food. Such an instruction serves basically as an introduction to what is to follow.

The second set of instructions in vv. 3-5 then gets to the heart of the matter by delineating the eternal covenant that YHWH offers the people. Again, the second instruction begins with a set of imperatives in v. 3a that instructs the people to incline their ears, come to YHWH, and hear that they might live. The motivation for such attention then follows in vv. 3b-5 with YHWH's announcement of the eternal covenant offered to Israel, including both the announcement proper in v. 3b and an elaboration of the covenant in vv. 4-5. This passage addresses one of the key theological problems of the book of Isaiah: what does one make of the eternal Davidic covenant (2 Samuel 7) when it is clear that there will be no Davidic king on the throne and that the nation will be ruled by the Persian monarchy? Isaiah 44:28 and 45:1 had already prepared for this outcome by announcing that King Cyrus of Persia would be recognized as YHWH's temple-builder and anointed monarch, roles that the royal house of David had filled throughout the monarchic period in Judah. Essentially, the passage redefines the covenant by focusing on the role that the people would have played during the period of the Davidic monarchy: if the house of David was secured by an eternal covenant, then the people of Israel were likewise secured by YHWH's promise that a Davidic king would rule perpetually in Jerusalem. In the aftermath of the Babylonian exile, Jerusalem, the temple, and Israel would be restored, the people would be returned to Jerusalem, Judah, and Israel, and YHWH's sovereignty would be recognized throughout creation and the nations. The only difference would be that there would no longer be a Davidic monarch on the throne; rather, the Achaemenid monarchs of Persia, Cyrus and his successors, would be recognized as YHWH's royal agents in place of the house of David. In this respect, chs. 40–55 — and indeed, the book of Isaiah as a whole — identify YHWH with the Achaemenid dynasty and counsels submission to the Persian Empire as an expression of YHWH's will. Of course, other biblical books dispute such a claim, such as the Book of the Twelve Prophets, which consistently calls for warfare against the nations that threaten Jerusalem and the nation of Israel at large until those nations recognize YHWH and cease their oppression of Israel (cf. E. Bosshard-Nepustil, *Die Rezeptionen von Jesaja 1–39 im Zwölfpropheten-buch* [OBO 154; Göttingen: Vandenhoeck & Ruprecht, 1997]). Such a position is, however, in keeping with that of the book of Ezra-Nehemiah, which posits Ezra and Nehemiah as legitimate authorities in the restored Jerusalem and Judah, appointed by the Persian Empire and working on YHWH's behalf.

The third instruction then follows in 55:6-13 with the culminating instruction to seek YHWH. The imperatives in v. 6 present the basic instruction to seek YHWH, and the jussive statements in v. 7 then elaborate by specifying that those who seek YHWH will constitute the righteous in Israel who will enjoy YHWH's eternal covenant. Verse 7a is exhortational in character, insofar as it counsels those who are evil to abandon their ways and plans in order that they might embrace YHWH and therefore be recognized as righteous, and v. 7b emphasizes that YHWH will forgive those who return. Such a scenario presumes that wickedness entails the rejection of YHWH as G-d, whereas righteousness entails the recognition of YHWH's divine sovereignty.

The rationale for the instruction to seek YHWH then follows in 55:8-13. YHWH's basic premise appears in v. 8: "my plans and ways are higher than yours." This is more than just an adolescent power play; it is a fundamental statement of YHWH's role as sovereign of creation: YHWH's plans and ways supersede those of human beings. On the surface, this is a valid argument, but when one considers the generations of Jews who suffered Assyrian and Babylonian invasion, death, deportation, and subjugation, the argument rings hollow. Does one die and suffer for the greater glory of G-d to be revealed to later generations? That is the argument of the book of Isaiah. It is a teleological argument, one that is realized and justified when its goals are reached, but it is not an ontological moral argument, in that such a process does not represent an inherently moral act to those who had to suffer until the process reached its end. In this respect, it is an argument designed to interpret history and to appeal to those who live at the time when YHWH's sovereignty is to be realized, i.e., to the generations that do not have to pay the bill in suffering that their ancestors paid.

The elaboration, which promises the people that they will return to Jerusalem in peace, then follows in 55:9-13 with three major premises. The first in v. 9 reiterates YHWH's point from v. 8 that YHWH's plans and ways are higher than those of the people. The second in vv. 10-11 makes the point that YHWH achieves what YHWH sets out to do. Here, the reliance on imagery from creation, such as rain and snow that bring about vegetation and life, underscores YHWH's role as the sovereign over all creation who brings life to those who inhabit it. Such analogy with creation then underscores YHWH's major point in v. 11: "my word achieves what I propose and it succeeds in what I send it to do," i.e., YHWH is reliable. Just as the first part of Isaiah promised a restoration following the period of punishment, so that restoration is realized now. The third premise then follows in vv. 12-13: "you will return (to Jerusalem) in peace." The basic statements of this premise appear in v. 12a: "you will go out (from exile) in joy and you will return (to Jerusalem) in peace." The elaboration in vv. 12b-13 again underscores the point by pointing to the role of creation, i.e., the mountains and hills and the cypress and myrtle, that will appear to celebrate the achievement of YHWH's plans and word to establish YHWH's name as an eternal sign that will not be cut off. In other words, YHWH will be recognized as the true sovereign of creation, Israel, and the nations of the world.

Bibliography

W. A. M. Beuken, "Is 55,3-5: The Reinterpretation of David," *Bijdr* 35 (1974) 49-64; W. Brueggemann, "Isaiah 55 and Deuteronomic Theology," *ZAW* 80 (1968) 191-203; idem, "A Poem of Summons," in *A Social Reading of the Old Testament* (Minneapolis: Fortress 1994) 134-46; A. Caquot, "Les 'graces de David,'" *Sem* 15 (1965) 45-59; R. J. Clifford, "Isaiah 55: Invitation to a Feast," in *The Word of the L-rd Shall Go Forth* (*Fest.* D. N. Freedman; ed. C. L. Meyers and M. O'Connor; Winona Lake: Eisenbrauns, 1983) 27-35; J. Coppens, "Le messianisme royale iv," *NRTh* 90 (1968) 622-50; O. Eissfeldt, "The Promises of Grace to David in Isaiah 55:1-5," in Anderson and Harrelson, eds., *Israel's Prophetic Heritage,* 196-207; W. C. Kaiser, "The Unfailing Kindnesses Promised to David," *JSOT* 45 (1989) 91-98; M. C. A. Korpel, "Metaphors in Isaiah LV," *VT* 46 (1996) 43-55; idem, "Second Isaiah's Coping with the Religious Crisis: Reading Isaiah 40 and 55," in *The Crisis of Israelite Religion* (OtSt 42; ed. B. Becking and Korpel; Leiden: Brill, 1999) 90-113; S. Paganini, "Who Speaks in Isaiah 55.1? Notes on Communication

Structure in Isaiah 55," *JSOT* 30 (2005) 83-92; A. Rofé, "How Is the Word Fulfilled? Isaiah 55:6-11 Within the Theological Debate of Its Time," in *Canon, Theology, and Old Testament Interpretation (Fest.* B. S. Childs; ed. G. M. Tucker, D. L. Petersen, and R. R. Wilson; Philadelphia: Fortress, 1988) 246-61; W. Schniedewind, "The Way of the Word: Textualization in Isaiah 55:6-11," in *Bringing the Hidden to Light (Fest.* S. A. Geller; ed. K. F. Kravitz and D. M. Sharon; Winona Lake: Eisenbrauns, 2007) 237-48; H. C. Spykerboer, "Isaiah 55:1-5: The Climax of Deutero-Isaiah," in Vermeylen, ed., *The Book of Isaiah/Le livre d'Isaïe,* 357-59; H. G. M. Williamson, "The Sure Mercies of David," *JSS* 23 (1978) 31-49.

PROPHETIC INSTRUCTION CONCERNING THE INCLUSION OF OBSERVANT FOREIGNERS AND EUNUCHS IN YHWH'S TEMPLE 56:1-8

Structure

A. Prophet's presentation of YHWH's oracle   56:4-5
   1. Prophetic messenger formula   56:4aα$^{1-4}$
   2. YHWH's instruction speech concerning assured place of
     observant foreigners and eunuchs in temple   56:4aα^5-5
     a. To the eunuchs   56:4aα^5-b
      1) Who observe my Shabbats   56:4aα$^{5-9}$
      2) And choose what I want   56:4aβ
      3) And hold fast to my covenant   56:4b
     b. YHWH's promise: monument and name   56:5
      1) Monument and name in my Temple and walls better
       than sons and daughters   56:5a
      2) An eternal name   56:5b
B. Concerning place of observant foreigners in temple   56:6-8
   1. To the foreigners who join YHWH   56:6
     a. Qualification of foreigners who join YHWH   56:6a
      1) To serve YHWH   56:6aα
      2) To love the name of YHWH   56:6aβ
      3) To be a servant to YHWH qualified   56:6aγ
     b. Appositional specification   56:6b
      1) All who observe Shabbat   56:6bα
      2) All who hold fast to my covenant   56:6bβ
   2. Presentation of YHWH's oracular promise: they are wel-
     come in my temple   56:7-8
     a. YHWH's oracular statement   56:7
      1) Promise: I will include them in my temple   56:7a
       a) I will bring them to my holy mountain   56:7aα$^{1-4}$
       b) I will have them rejoice in my house of prayer   56:7aα$^{5-7}$
       c) Their whole burnt offerings and peace offerings
        are welcome on my altar   56:7aβ
      2) Basis for promise: my house of prayer is for all
       the peoples   56:7b
     b. Expanded oracle formula   56:8
      1) Oracle formula proper   56:8aα
      2) Qualification: YHWH gathers exiles of Israel   56:8aβ-b
       a) Prophet's qualification: YHWH gathers exiles of
        Israel   56:8aβ
       b) YHWH's statement: I will gather more to those
        already gathered   56:8b

Isaiah 56:1-8 constitutes prophetic instruction concerning the inclusion of observant foreigners and eunuchs in YHWH's temple. It is demarcated at the outset
by the introductory messenger formula in v. 1aα, which identifies the prophet
as the speaker who conveys YHWH's speech. YHWH's speech then follows in
vv. 1aβ-2 with YHWH's instructions concerning proper observance. Some argue
that only vv. 1-2 constitute a unit separate from the following material in vv. 3-8
(e.g., Westermann, *Isaiah 40–66,* 309-16). But such a view fails to account for
the fact that YHWH's speech in vv. 1-2 expresses the basic principles of justice

and righteousness, here defined as Shabbat observance and refraining from evil, that serve as the foundation for the following elaboration on YHWH's instruction by the prophet in vv. 3-8. The prophet quotes YHWH throughout vv. 3-8 in elaborating on the inclusion of foreigners and eunuchs who observe Shabbat and YHWH's covenant at large. Consequently, the expanded oracle formula in v. 8 closes the unit. The metaphorical references to wild beasts and blind watchmen in 56:9 pen a new unit concerned with YHWH's forgiveness of those who repent.

The prophetic report concerning YHWH's instructions for proper observance in 56:1-2 begins with the prophetic messenger formula in v. 1aα, which identifies the following material as a speech by YHWH. The 1st-person references in v. 1aβ-b confirm YHWH's identity as a speaker, but such references are lacking in vv. 2-3. Indeed, the 3rd-person references to YHWH in v. 3 appear as part of the purported speech by the foreigner. Lacking any indication of a shift in speaker, vv. 2-3 must be considered as part of YHWH's speech. The second instance of the prophetic messenger formula in v. 4 indicates the voice of the prophet once again. YHWH's instruction speech in vv. 1aβ-3 consequently comprises two major subunits. The first in v. 1aβ-b constitutes YHWH's instruction proper concerning justice and righteousness. This segment begins with a twofold instruction in v. 1aβ to do justice and righteousness, which includes individual statements for each in v. 1aβ$^{1-2}$ and v. 1aβ$^{3-4}$, respectively. The twofold rationale, introduced by the particle *kî*, "because, for," follows in v. 1b with YHWH's statements that "my deliverance is near" in v. 1bα and that "my righteousness is to be revealed" in v. 1bβ.

The second subunit in vv. 2-3, which begins with no conjunctive element, then specifies what is meant by justice and righteousness. After all, these are very general terms that do not lend themselves to inherent definition. Consequently, vv. 2-3 specifies these general principles by stating that observant foreigners and eunuchs will not be excluded or cut off from the nation by YHWH. The first element in this subunit is the beatitude in v. 2, which specifies that justice and righteousness in this instance constitute observance of Shabbat and refraining from doing evil. The first element or protasis of the beatitude in v. 2a states that "happy is the man who does this" in v. 2aα and "happy is the person who holds fast to this or grasps this" in v. 2aβ. Because the reader does not yet know what "this" is, v. 2b steps in as the beatitude apodosis to state that "this" refers to Shabbat observance and refraining from doing evil. Verse 3, linked to v. 2 by a *wāw*-consecutive verbal formation, then follows with prophetic instruction concerning the inclusion of foreigners and eunuchs, in two statements. The first in v. 3a instructs that foreigners should not have to say that YHWH excludes them, and the second in v. 3b instructs that eunuchs should not have to say that they are withered trees, i.e., that they have no progeny or legacy among Israel. Nevertheless, readers must recognize that observance and the foreigners and eunuchs have not yet been put together.

The basis for the prophet's instruction then follows in 56:4-8 with a report of YHWH's instructions concerning the place of the observant foreigners and eunuchs in the temple community. This section begins with an introductory *kî*, which signals its explanatory role in relation to 56:1-3. The introductory prophetic messenger formula in v. 4aα¹⁻⁴ and the closing expanded oracle formula in v. 8 indicate that the prophet is the speaker. The passage comprises two major subunits. The first is the prophet's presentation of YHWH's oracle concerning the observant eunuchs in vv. 4-5, and the second is the prophet's discussion concerning the place of observant foreigners in vv. 6-8.

The prophet's presentation of YHWH's oracle concerning observant eunuchs in vv. 4-5 begins with the prophetic messenger formula in v. 4aα¹⁻⁴, which introduces YHWH's instruction speech in vv. 4aα⁵-5. The instruction speech comprises two subunits. The first is the reference to the eunuchs in v. 4aα⁵-b, which identifies them as the subject of discussion. The subunit presents YHWH's three qualifications for the eunuchs: "they observe my Shabbats" in 4aα⁵⁻⁹; "they choose what I want" in v. 4aβ; and "they hold fast to my covenant" in v. 4b. YHWH's promise to the eunuchs then follows in v. 5. Verse 5a states that they will have a monument and a name in YHWH's temple and walls which is better than sons or daughters, and v. 5b states that they will have an eternal name.

The prophet's discussion concerning the place of observant foreigners in the temple then follows in vv. 6-8. Verse 6 presents the prophet's statements concerning observant foreigners. The 3rd-person reference to YHWH confirms that the prophet is the speaker. The prophet begins in v. 6a with a statement of the qualification of the foreigners who would join YHWH: they will serve YHWH in v. 6aα, they will love the name of YHWH in v. 6aβ, and they will be servants to YHWH in v. 6aγ. Verse 6b then presents two appositional specifications for the foreigners: they are those who observe Shabbat in v. 6bα and they are all who hold fast to "my" covenant in v. 6bβ. The reference to "my" suggests that the prophet quotes a fragment of a YHWH speech, although it is possible that an original reading of "his covenant" became "my covenant" under the influence of YHWH's oracular statement in v. 7 and the reference to "my covenant" in v. 4b. The prophet then presents YHWH's oracular promise in vv. 7-8. YHWH's oracular statement appears first in v. 7. It includes YHWH's basic promise in v. 7a that "I will include them in my temple," specified in three successive statements: "I will bring them to my holy mountain" in v. 7aα¹⁻⁴; "I will have them rejoice in my house of prayer" in v. 7aα⁵⁻⁷; and "their whole burnt offerings and peace offerings are welcome on my altar" in v. 7aβ. The basis for YHWH's promise, that "my house of prayer is for all peoples," then follows in v. 7b. Finally, the expanded oracle formula in v. 8 identifies vv. 6-8 as an oracle by YHWH. The oracle formula proper appears in v. 8aα, and the qualification of YHWH as the one who gathers exiles appears in v. 8aβ-b. The prophet's qualification proper appears in v. 8aβ, and then the prophet includes a quotation from YHWH, "I will gather more to those already gathered," in v. 8b to reinforce YHWH's identity as a powerful and trustworthy G-d.

Genre

Past interpreters have identified a number of generic elements in 56:1-8, but the basic genre of the passage is prophetic INSTRUCTION concerning the inclusion of observant foreigners and eunuchs in YHWH's temple community. To arrive at this generic character, the passage combines several generic elements, such as the prophet's REPORT of YHWH's speeches, the ORACLES which constitute YHWH's speeches, and the basic generic character of the passage as an INSTRUCTION, which provides proper guidance concerning the inclusion of observant foreigners and eunuchs in the temple.

First is the REPORT. The passage combines 3rd-person statements about YHWH and the issue of foreigners and eunuchs with 1st-person statements attributed to YHWH to provide the relevant instruction. Although the prophet is not named, the use of oracular forms in the passage, e.g., the MESSENGER FORMULA, "Thus says YHWH," and its variants in vv. 1aα and 4aα$^{1-4}$ together with the closing expanded ORACLE FORMULA, "utterance of my L-rd, YHWH" (read as "utterance of my L-rd, G-d") in v. 8a points to the prophetic identity of the basic speaker in the passage. In all cases, these formulae refer to YHWH in the 3rd-person as do the statements in vv. 3, 6a-bα (although v. 6bβ is formulated in 1st-person, it may originally have been a 3rd-person statement), and 8a.

The second is an ORACLE by YHWH. The oracles reported by the prophet in the passage include vv. 1aβ-2, 4aα^{5}-5, 7, and 8b. All are identified as oracular material by the combination of MESSENGER FORMULAE in vv. 1aα and 4aα$^{1-4}$, the expanded ORACLE FORMULA in v. 8a, and by the 1st-person language presupposing YHWH as the speaker found in each of the oracular speeches noted above.

The third is INSTRUCTION by YHWH as conveyed by the prophet. INSTRUCTION is "a writing or discourse . . . that offers guidance to an individual or group by setting forth particular values or prescribing rules of conduct" (Sweeney, *Isaiah 1–39*, 522). In the present instance, that INSTRUCTION calls for the inclusion of observant foreigners and eunuchs in YHWH's temple. Interpreters must be clear as to the full parameters of this instruction. It does not simply call for the inclusion of foreigners and eunuchs; it specifies that such foreigners and eunuchs must be observant, and it specifies that such observance constitutes doing what is just and right, observing the Shabbat, refraining from doing evil, doing what YHWH wills, holding fast to YHWH's covenant, serving YHWH, loving the name of YHWH, and being servants to YHWH (see vv. 1, 2, 4 and 6). Although Deut 23:2-9 specifies that certain foreign groups and anyone with crushed testicles or a cut-off member shall be excluded from the congregation, the present passage specifies that such persons shall be admitted to the congregation if they are observant of YHWH's covenant. In the case of foreigners, the passage does not go into the details of whether they are Ammonite, Moabite, Edomite, or Egyptian, which hold different status in Deuteronomy. Instead, it appears to presuppose Deuteronomy's commands to allow "resident aliens" *(gērîm)* certain rights of observance in Israel. In later periods, such "resident aliens" are considered as converts to Judaism. In the case of eunuchs, the passage apparently considers that such status may not be a matter of personal choice and that the decision to observe YHWH's covenant in fact constitutes observance of YHWH's covenant — and possibly repentance — as envisioned by Deuteronomy. Thus, the passage appears to presuppose Deuteronomy, but it also appears to have expanded or interpreted the meaning of Deuteronomy in keeping with the views expressed throughout the larger context of the book.

Finally, the BEATITUDE also plays a role in this passage in v. 2. A BEAT-

ITUDE is "a short formulaic speech that extols the fortunate or blessed state of an individual or whole people" (Sweeney, *Isaiah 1–39*, 515). It typically begins with *'ašrê*, "happy are," which is the case in v. 2. In the present instance, the BEATITUDE follows the basic INSTRUCTION to do justice and righteousness. The BEATITUDE in v. 2 reinforces the INSTRUCTION in v. 1 by specifying in part what doing justice and righteousness means: it constitutes Shabbat observance and refraining from doing evil. This constitutes INSTRUCTION or guidance in proper conduct, and the rest of the passage continues to offer further INSTRUCTION concerning the meaning of the initial statement in v. 1.

Setting

Although past interpreters have attempted to argue that 56:1-8 is a composite text (Westermann, *Isaiah 40–66*, 309-16; Sekine, *Die tritojesajanische Samm-lung*, 31-41; Koenen, *Ethik und Eschatologie*, 11-15), more recent discussion, including the present analysis, points to the literary unity of this passage (e.g., Stromberg, *Isaiah after Exile*, 40-42; Blenkinsopp, *Isaiah 56–66*, 131; Smith, *Rhetoric and Redaction*, 51-54). In most cases, the grounds for dividing the passage into discrete components were generic, but form-critical scholarship has come to recognize that genre is not the fundamental defining criterion for a distinct text, but functions as an element within textual form, often in combination with other generic elements, to constitute the text and to serve its purposes. In the present text, 56:1-8 is an example of prophetic INSTRUCTION, but it employs a variety of other generic elements to facilitate its basic form and task of instruction.

The passage is clearly interested in the status of foreigners and eunuchs within the Jewish temple community. The laws in Deut 7:1-6; 23:2-9(NRSV 1-8) indicate that questions were raised about the status of both groups within the Jewish community. Deuteronomy was likely composed in the late 7th century B.C.E. and presupposes a settled kingdom of Judah that could presume a largely Judean or Israelite population and control admission to the Jerusalem temple, but the demise of the kingdom of Judah and the experience of the Babylonian exile would have reopened questions concerning the status of foreigners and eu-nuchs within the Jewish community and its temple environs. The experience of foreign invasion on the one hand and Babylonian exile on the other would have opened the way for far greater numbers of intermarriages and foreign births among the people of Israel and Judah as they were exposed in both contexts to foreign cultures. In the case of eunuchs, service, whether forced or not, in various Babylonian contexts would have required eunuch status. With the possi-bility of the return of both eunuchs and Jews born of one or two foreign parents, the issue of the status of such persons in Judaism would have risen once again in the early Persian period when both returning exiles and Jews who remained in the land would have turned to the newly-built Second Temple in Jerusalem.

The issue of the status of foreigners in the Jewish community — and particularly in relation to the temple — comes to a head in the times of Nehe-miah and Ezra during the late 5th and early 4th centuries B.C.E. In both cases,

Nehemiah and Ezra forbid intermarriage with foreigners as recorded in Ezra 9–10 and Neh 13:23-31. Most interpreters presuppose that Isa 56:1-8 is opposed to the practice of forbidding foreign marriage, but closer examination of the issue indicates that this is not necessarily the case. The prohibition of intermarriage by Ezra and Nehemiah is based on the above-mentioned laws in Deut 7:1-6, which forbid marriage with the Canaanites because they will cause the people to follow their foreign gods. But Deut 21:10-14 specifies the procedure for an Israelite man to marry a foreign woman in the aftermath of war. Likewise, Deuteronomy continuously calls for the inclusion of *gērîm* or "resident aliens" in the celebration of Israelite holidays (see Deut 16:11-12) and guarantees them equal legal rights and care (Deut 1:16; 10:17-19). In rabbinic times, *gērîm* were understood to refer to converts to Judaism.

Given Ezra's (and Nehemiah's) observance of Torah, consideration of the law of the Passover offering in Exod 12:43-49 is especially instructive. The law specifies that no "foreigner" *(ben-nēkār)* may eat of the Passover offering. But it goes on to specify that slaves who have been circumcised and resident aliens *(gērîm)* who have been circumcised may eat of the Passover offering. Those who remained uncircumcised are excluded from eating the Passover offering. Here, circumcision appears to be the defining characteristic of who might eat of the Passover offering. A foreigner is uncircumcised. A resident alien has the option to become circumcised. And a foreigner can presumably become a resident alien. It appears that we see in Exod 12:43-49 a process by which foreigners might become part of the people of Israel or Judah. Such a process appears to constitute an early form of conversion to Judaism as later recognized by rabbinic Judaism.

Similar considerations may be brought to bear on Ezra and Nehemiah. Marriages to foreign women are forbidden, but foreign women in Ezra-Nehemiah appear to be women who continue to speak the languages of their former cultures and who continue to worship foreign gods (Neh 13:23-31). But what about those women who assimilate into Jewish culture, learning to speak the Hebrew language and worshipping YHWH exclusively, as stipulated by Deuteronomy? Do they remain foreigners? Or do they become part of Israel?

This question returns us to 56:1-8. The passage specifies that foreigners who uphold YHWH's covenant with Israel, specifically including the observance of Shabbat, will be admitted to the temple. At this point, we must consider such persons to be converts in some form or another to Judaism. Such persons would have been considered part of the Jewish community in the time of Ezra and Nehemiah as well. Our passage appears to complement Ezra-Nehemiah, not oppose it.

Consequently, 56:1-8 appears to be set in the period of Ezra and Nehemiah, the late 5th or early 4th century B.C.E., about a century following the building of the Second Temple, when Nehemiah made observance of the covenant, particularly Shabbat, the defining characteristic of the Jewish people in Jerusalem, and when Ezra made observance of Torah the criterion by which proper Jewish observance would be measured.

As many have observed, 56:1-8 functions as an introduction to the Trito-Isaian materials in chs. 56–66, and it relates intertextually to chs. 65–66, which envision the restoration of the righteous nation of Israel at the end of the book. The question of inclusion in the Jewish community is of paramount interest in these chapters. Isaiah 56:1-8 defines the parameters for inclusion in the Jewish community: adherence to the covenant, observance of the Shabbat, doing what is considered to be just *(mišpāṭ)* and right *(ṣĕdāqâ)*, and refraining from doing what is wrong. These characteristics define the people of Israel who will be returned to Jerusalem and the land of Israel throughout Trito-Isaiah. As Rendtorff observes, reference to those who display such characteristics, particularly those who do what is considered to be just *(mišpāṭ)* and right *(ṣĕdāqâ)*, permeate the entire book of Isaiah and suggest that the materials in Trito-Isaiah, chs, 56–66, constitute a major portion of the final redaction of the book. Indeed, he notes that *mišpāṭ* and *ṣĕdāqâ* appear frequently together in chs. 1–39, but never in chs. 40–55, which prefer the combination *ṣĕdāqâ,* "righteousness," and *yĕšû'â,* "deliverance," instead. The different conceptualizations of *ṣĕdāqâ,* one which emphasizes justice and the other which emphasizes divine deliverance, point to a Trito-Isaian redaction of the book of Isaiah which presupposed a core in chs. 40–55 for which chs. 1–39 and 56–66 would provide a broader literary context (Rendtorff, "Isaiah 56:1"; idem, "Zur Komposition des Buches Jesajas").

Interpretation

Isaiah 56:1-8 sets the theme for chs. 56–66 by specifying who is eligible for inclusion in the restored Jewish community of the Jerusalem temple. It stipulates that foreigners and eunuchs, two groups whose status among the Jewish people might come into question, are included insofar as they do what is just and right, choose what YHWH desires, hold fast to YHWH's covenant, observe the Shabbat, and avoid doing what is wrong. In the case of the foreigners, such persons would constitute converts to Judaism insofar as these foreigners affirm the covenant between YHWH and the Jewish people. In the case of the eunuchs, who likely served in some capacity as part of the Babylonian administration, such persons would be granted status in the Jewish community by adhering to the covenant. Isaiah 56:1-8 is therefore in dialogue with pentateuchal texts, such as Deut 7:1-6; 23:2-9(NRSV 1-8); and Exod 12:43-49, which provide guidance on the admission of foreigners and eunuchs into the people of Israel. Isaiah 56:1-8 presupposes the debate concerning the admission of foreigners into the community in the time of Nehemiah and Ezra. Although many view 56:1-8 as opposed to Ezra's policy against intermarriage with foreign women, 56:1-8 stipulates that foreigners undertake action that amounts to conversion to Judaism. Nehemiah and Ezra are opposed to intermarriage with women who maintain foreign identity and religious practice, and so there is little basis for concluding that 56:1-8 and the texts concerning intermarriage in Ezra 9–10 and Neh 13:23-31 are in conflict with each other. Isaiah 56:1-8 appears to support the policies of Nehemiah and Ezra by stipulating how foreigners become a part of Israel and are therefore no longer viewed as foreign. The book of Ruth likewise supports the practice of conversion to Judaism, in this case by a woman.

Isaiah 56:1-8 constitutes the prophet's report concerning the inclusion of observant foreigners and eunuchs in the temple community. Within the literary context of the book of Isaiah, the prophet must be Isaiah ben Amoz. Diachronically speaking, the prophet is one of the anonymous prophets from the Persian period whose works appear in chs. 56–66, commonly identified with Trito-Isaiah. Following ch. 55, which functions as an introduction to chs. 56–66 by inviting the people to take part in YHWH's covenant conceived as a continuation of the Davidic covenant (cf. Stromberg, *Isaiah after Exile,* 77-79), 56:1-8 states the conditions for the inclusion of foreigners and eunuchs in the temple community. Overall, chs. 56–66 expect that the people will be righteous servants of YHWH (Blenkinsopp, "The Servant and the Servants"; cf. Stromberg, *Isaiah after Exile,* 79-82), insofar as they observe YHWH's covenant. These chapters also charge that the wicked in the community, those who do not observe the covenant, impede the full realization of the ideals of the book of Isaiah.

Isaiah 56:1-8 begins in vv. 1-3 with the prophet's report concerning YHWH's instructions for proper observance. The prophetic messenger formula in v. 1aα identifies the following material in vv. 1aβ-3 as YHWH's oracular instruction speech concerning proper observance. The speech presents a very general overview statement of YHWH's expectations in v. 1aβ-b, that the people should observe justice and do righteousness because YHWH's deliverance is near and YHWH's righteousness is about to be revealed. Such a statement anticipates the fulfillment of the ideals of the book of Isaiah, but it does little to specify what exactly YHWH requires. Verses 2-3 then specify the general statement. Verse 2 employs a beatitude to specify that "the happy man," i.e., the ideal Jew from the standpoint of our oracle, is one who observes the Shabbat and refrains from doing evil. Observance of the Shabbat is a fundamental command in Judaism; Genesis 1:1–2:3 presents the Shabbat as an inherent component of the divine creation of the world, and Exod 31:12-17 identifies observance of the Shabbat as an "eternal covenant" or "covenant of creation" (*bĕrît 'ôlām*) between Israel and YHWH. Verse 3 then presents prophetic instruction concerning the inclusion of foreigners and eunuchs who observe these conditions in the form of rhetorical statements respectively made by the foreigner and eunuch that they will not be excluded from the community nor considered a withered tree. The withered tree of course serves as a metaphor for a person who cannot produce seed and therefore cannot produce offspring.

Isaiah 56:4-8 then presents the basis for the instruction in the form of the prophet's report of YHWH's instruction concerning the place of observant foreigners and eunuchs in the temple community. The passage begins in vv. 4-5 with the prophet's presentation of YHWH's oracle, introduced in v. 4aα[1-4] with the prophetic messenger formula. YHWH's oracular instruction speech in vv. 4aα[5]-5 stipulates that eunuchs who observe Shabbat, choose what YHWH wants, and hold fast to YHWH's covenant will have a place in YHWH's house and walls, i.e., within YHWH's temple. That place comes in the form of a monument *(yād,* lit., "hand"), which is better than sons and daughters, and an eternal name. The term *yād* can be used to describe a monument, such as the sacred pillar that sometimes appears in Israelite temples or a monument for a grave site (1 Sam 15:12; 2 Sam 18:18). It can also be used as a metaphor for the phallus, which is the organ of reproduction that is missing in the eunuchs (Isa 57:8). The combination of terms in this passage, *Yad veShem,* "Hand/Monument and Name," is employed as the name for the modern Holocaust Museum in Jerusalem to signify that those lost in the Shoah (Holocaust) would forever have a place among the people of Israel despite the fact that their murders deprived them of the chance to produce descendants for the future of Judaism.

Isaiah 56:6-8 then presents the prophet's statements concerning the place of foreigners in the temple. Verse 6 speaks of the qualifications of such observant foreigners, initially in v. 6a that they are to serve YHWH, love the name of YHWH, and be servants to YHWH. Verse 6b specifies that they are to observe the Shabbat and hold fast to YHWH's covenant. Verses 7-8 then constitute the prophet's presentation of YHWH's oracular promise. YHWH's oracular statement in v. 7 indicates that YHWH will include them in the temple by bringing them to the holy Temple Mount, having them rejoice or worship in the house of prayer, and having them present their offerings. The basis for this promise is that YHWH's temple is the temple for all the peoples; it stands as the holy center of creation, and Israel's worship there aids in securing all creation (J. D. Levenson, "The Temple and the World" *JR* 64 [1984] 275-98). The expanded oracle formula in v. 8 identifies YHWH as the source of the oracle and the one who gathers the exiles of Israel. The quotation of YHWH's statement in v. 8b indicates that YHWH's efforts to gather in the diaspora are ongoing, i.e., there are more to come. Apparently, 56:8 draws on images of YHWH's holy mountain in 11:9, and it anticipates 66:20. Isaiah 56:6-8 likewise points to the gathering of the exiles in 11:12 and 66:20 (Sweeney, "Reconceptualization"; idem, "Prophetic Exegesis"; Stromberg, *Isaiah after Exile,* 82-86).

Bibliography

K. Koenen, *Ethik und Eschatologie,* 11-32; H. Odeberg, *Trito-Isaiah,* 32-62; K. Pauritsch, *Die neue Gemeinde,* 31-51; G. Polan, *In the Ways of Justice,* 43-90; R. Rendtorff, "Isaiah 56:1 as a Key"; J. Schaper, "Rereading the Law: Inner-Biblical Exegesis of Divine Oracles in Ezekiel 44 and Isaiah 56," in *Recht und Ethik im Alten Testament* (ed. B. M. Levinson and E. Otto; Münster: LIT, 2004) 124-44; B. Schramm, *The Opponents of Third Isaiah,* 17-20, 115-25; S. Sekine, *Die tritojesajanische Sammlung,* 31-42; P. A. Smith, *Rhetoric and Redaction,* 50-66; O. H. Steck, *Studien zu Tritojesaja,* 34-44, 169-86, 229-65; J. Stromberg, *Isaiah after Exile,* 40-42, 74-86; S. S. Tuell, "The Priesthood of the 'Foreigner': Evidence of Competing Polities in Ezekiel 44:1-14 and Isaiah 56:1-8," in *Constituting the Community* (*Fest.* S. D. McBride Jr.; ed. J. Strong and Tuell; Winona Lake: Eisenbrauns, 2005) 185-206; R. D. Wells, "'Isaiah' as an Exponent of Torah: Isaiah 56:1-8," in Melugin and Sweeney, eds., *New Visions of Isaiah,* 140-55; D. W. Van Winkle, "An Inclusive Authoritative Text in Exclusive Communities," in Broyles and Evans, eds., *Writing and Reading the Scroll of Isaiah,* 423-40; idem, "Isaiah LVI 1-8," in *SBL 1997 Seminar Papers* (SBLSP 36; Atlanta: Scholars 1997) 234-52; idem, "The Meaning of *yād wašem* in Isaiah LVI 5," *VT* 47 (1997) 378-85; J. L. Wright and M. J. Chan, "Isaiah 56:1-8 in Light of Honorific Royal Burial Practices," *JBL* 131 (2012) 99-119.

PROPHETIC INSTRUCTION CONCERNING
YHWH'S WILLINGNESS TO FORGIVE
THOSE WHO REPENT 56:9–57:21

Structure

I. Concerning the failure of the watchmen/prophets	56:9-12
A. Address to animals: come and eat	56:9
1. Wild animals	56:9a
2. Animals of the forest	56:9b
B. Portrayal of the watchmen/prophets	56:10-12
1. They are blind	56:10aα
a. The watchmen are all blind	56:10aα$^{1-3}$
b. They do not know	56:10aα$^{4-5}$
2. They are incompetent	56:10aβ-12
a. They are dogs	56:10aβ-11aα
1) They are all dumb lazy dogs	56:10aβ-b
a) They are dumb dogs	56:10aβ
b) They cannot bark/warn	56:10aγ
c) They watch while lying down	56:10bα
d) They love to snooze	56:10bβ
2) They are greedy dogs	56:11aα
a) They are greedy	56:11aα$^{1-3}$
b) They are never satisfied	56:11aα$^{4-6}$
b. They are drunken shepherds	56:11aβ-12
1) They are shepherds	56:11aβ
2) They do not know understanding	56:11aγ
3) They turn to their own paths/they are selfish	56:11bα
4) They each turn to their own gain	56:11bβ-12
a) Basically stated	56:11bβ
b) Quote of their statement: let's get drunk	56:12
(1) Proposal to drink	56:12a
(a) Come, let me drink wine	56:12aα
(b) Let us get drunk on brandy	56:12aβ
(2) Basis for proposal: it won't hurt	56:12b
(a) Tomorrow will be like today	56:12bα
(b) Tomorrow will be even better	56:12bβ
II. YHWH's promise to deliver the righteous	57:1-21
A. Initial premise: the righteous suffers, but they will have peace	57:1-2
1. Twofold statement of righteous suffering	57:1
a. The righteous suffers and no one pays attention	57:1a
1) The righteous suffers	57:1aα
2) No one pays attention	57:1aβ
b. Men of fidelity perish because of evil	57:1b
1) Men of fidelity perish	57:1bα$^{1-3}$
2) Reason: for lack of understanding that they perish because of evil	57:1bα^{4}-b

(a) With oil	57:9aα
(b) You multiplied perfume	57:9aβ
(2) You sent envoys as far as Sheol	57:9b
(a) You sent envoys afar	57:9bα
(b) As far as Sheol	57:9bβ
2) You didn't care	57:10-11
a) Twofold accusation	57:10
(1) Though you were weary, you never said "enough!"	57:10a
(2) You satisfied your lust so you didn't care	57:10b
b) Rhetorical questions	57:11
(1) Whom do you fear that you lie and do not remember me?	57:11a
(2) Was I too patient that you do not fear me?	57:11b
b. Announcement of judgment	57:12-13a
1) I declare your judgment	57:12a
2) Your idols will not do you any good	57:12b
3) When you cry for help, the wind will blow them away	57:13aα
4) A breeze will take them	57:13aβ
C. Prophetic announcement of salvation for the righteous	57:13b-21
1. Announcement of salvation proper	57:13b
a. Those who trust in me shall inherit the earth	57:13bα
b. Those who trust in me shall possess my holy mountain	57:13bβ
2. Prophet's report of YHWH's command to build highway for return of people	57:14
a. Speech formula	57:14aα^1
b. Speech: commands to build the road	57:14aα^2-b
1) Build the highway	57:14aα$^{2-3}$
2) Prepare the road	57:14aβ
3) Remove obstacles from the road of my people	57:14b
3. Prophetic messenger speech concerning salvation of righteous	57:15-21
a. Modified expanded messenger formula	57:15aα
1) Messenger formula proper: high and uplifted	57:15aα$^{1-5}$
2) Dwelling forever and holy of name	57:15aα$^{6-8}$
b. YHWH's speech proper	57:15aβ-21
1) I dwell on high to give life to the downtrodden	57:15aβ-b
a) I dwell high and lofty	57:15aβ
b) Purposes	57:15b
(1) To give life to those low of spirit	57:15bα
(2) To give life to those of crushed heart	57:15bβ
2) Concerning divine anger and mercy	57:16-21
a) I am not always angry, but also give life	57:16
(1) I will not always be angry	57:16a
(a) I will not always contend	57:16aα
(b) I will not be angry forever	57:16aβ
(2) I give soul to one who becomes faint before me	57:16b

b) I was angry because of their iniquity   57:17
  (1) I was angry and struck them because of their
     iniquity   57:17a
    (a) I was angry because of their iniquity for gain   57:17aα
    (b) I struck them and hid in my anger   57:17aβ
  (2) And they went about in the way of their hearts   57:17b
c) I will heal them   57:18-19
  (1) I see their way and I heal them   57:18a
  (2) I guide them and restore comfort to their
     mourners   57:18b
  (3) I create the fruit of their lips   57:19a
  (4) YHWH's statement: peace to them and I will
     heal them   57:19b
    (a) Peace, peace to those far and near   57:19bα
    (b) Speech formula   57:19bβ$^{1-2}$
    (c) I will heal them   57:19bβ^3
d) But the wicked will have no peace   57:20-21
  (1) Wicked are like the raging sea   57:20
    (a) Basically stated   57:20a
    (b) Reason: can't be still and kick up mud   57:20b
     α. Can't be still   57:20bα
     β. Always kick up mud and silt   57:20bβ
  (2) Conclusion: there is no peace for the wicked   57:21
    (a) There is no peace   57:21aα
    (b) Speech formula   57:21aβ
    (c) For the wicked   57:21b

Isaiah 56:9–57:21 constitutes prophetic instruction concerning YHWH's willingness to forgive those who repent. The unit is demarcated at the outset by its direct address to wild animals in the forest to come and eat, immediately following the oracle formula that closed the previous unit. The reference to the animals forms the basis in 56:9-12 for charging that the watchmen of the people are not doing their jobs, which leaves the people open to danger. The following material in 57:1-13a focuses primarily on judgment of the wicked whereas the material in 57:13b-21 focuses on restoration of the righteous, but the conjunctive *wāw* in 57:13b binds these two texts together to constitute a unit that is concerned with the interrelationship between judgment against the wicked and restoration for the righteous. Altogether, 57:1-21 presents YHWH's commitment to deliver the righteous despite the failure of the watchmen, but it emphasizes that the wicked will suffer judgment even as the righteous are restored. The unit concludes with the statement by G-d that there is no peace for the wicked.

Isaiah 56:9-12 is prophetic instruction concerning the failure of the watchmen or prophets to guard their people. It begins with a twofold address to the animals in v. 9 to come and eat, including the wild animals in v. 9a and the animals of the forest in v. 9b. The following portrayal of the watchmen in vv. 10-12, apparently the leaders of the people, explains the reason for the address to the animals: the watchmen are not doing their job in protecting the people, and so the animals are free to come in and eat whatever they like. The subunit begins in v. 10aα with a charge that the watchmen are blind, including the basic charge in v. 10aα$^{1-3}$ and the following charge in v. 10aα$^{4-5}$ that they do not know. The balance of the subunit in vv. 10aβ-12 lacks an introductory conjunction and focuses on the incompetence of the watchmen. The first portion of this subunit in vv. 10aβ-11aα portrays the watchmen as dogs, who are dumb and lazy as well as greedy. Verse 10aβ-b emphasizes the dumbness and laziness of the dogs in four consecutive statements, none of which is linked by a conjunction. Verse 10aβ states that they are dumb dogs: they cannot speak; v. 10aγ indicates that they cannot bark or warn the people; v. 10bα indicates that they lie down while they watch; and v. 10bβ indicates that they love to snooze. Verse 11aα, which begins with an introductory *wāw*, focuses on the greed of the dogs, including statements that they are greedy in v. 11aα$^{1-3}$ and that they are never satisfied in v. 11aα$^{4-6}$. Isaiah 56:11aβ-12 then turns to the portrayal of the watchmen as drunken shepherds, in a sequence of four statements. The first in v. 11aβ simply states that they are shepherds. Verse 11aγ states that they do not know understanding. Verse 11bα states that they turn to their own paths, i.e., that they are selfish. The last statement in vv. 11bβ-12 indicates that each turns to his own gain, but this statement is more complex. It begins in v. 11bβ with the basic statement that each turns to his own unjust gain. Verse 12 then quotes the drunken watchmen. Verse 12a quotes in two parts their proposal to drink: "come, let me drink wine" in v. 12aα and "let us get drunk on brandy" in v. 12aβ. Verse 12b then quotes the basis for their proposal, including the proposition that tomorrow will be just like today — nothing will change or be harmed — in v. 12bα and that tomorrow will be even better in v. 12bβ.

Isaiah 57:1-21 then presents prophetic instruction concerning YHWH's promise to deliver the righteous. This unit builds upon 56:9-12 by presenting YHWH's promise despite the incompetence of the wicked watchmen of the people.

The first element of 57:1-21 appears in vv. 1-2, which state the initial premise of the passage: the righteous suffer, but they will have peace. The subunit begins in v. 1 with a twofold statement concerning the suffering of the righteous. The first portion in v. 1a states that the righteous suffers in v. 1aα and that no one pays attention in v. 1aβ. The second portion in v. 1b then states the consequence, that men of fidelity perish in v. 1bα$^{1-3}$ and that the reason for this situation is that they lack understanding that the righteous perish because of evil in v. 1bα^4-b. Verse 2 then follows with the assertion that the one who walks forward will have peace and rest on his bed, including statements that he will have peace in v. 2a and that the one who walks forward will have peace on his bed in v. 2b.

The second element of 57:1-21 appears in vv. 57:3-13a, which focus on the condemnation of the wicked. The entire subunit takes the form of an extended prophetic judgment speech. It begins in v. 3 with a summons to approach directed to the evil, who are portrayed as sons of a sorceress in v. 3a and as sons of an adulteress and whore in v. 3b. Verses 4-6 follow with a disputational section constructed from rhetorical questions that are designed to assert that YHWH, portrayed as the 1st-person speaker, will not back down before the taunts of the wicked. The first set of questions appears in v. 4a, which asks "whom do you mock and insult?" The question "whom do you mock?" appears in v. 4aα. The question "whom do you insult?" appears in v. 4aβ in two parts. Verse 4aβ¹⁻⁴ asks "to whom do you open your mouth wide?" and v. 4aβ⁵⁻⁶ asks "to whom do you extend your tongue?" The second set of questions, which focuses on the charge that the people are rebellious and lying children, then follows in vv. 4b-6 in a sequence of five rhetorical questions. The first appears in v. 4bα, which simply states the basic theme of the subunit: "are you not rebellious children?" The second in v. 4bβ complements the first with the question "are you not lying seed?" The third in v. 5a asks "are you not inflamed with lust under the trees?" including two locations: "under the terebinths" in v. 5aα and "under every green tree" in v. 5aβ. The fourth, "do you not slaughter children by the streams under rocks?" in vv. 5b-6bα has a more complex structure. It begins in v. 5b with a set of two questions: "do you not slaughter children by the streams?" in v. 5bα and "under clefts of rocks?" in v. 5bβ. A set of accusations then follows in v. 6a-bα. The first in v. 6a charges that "your share or lot is with that of the stream," including the reference to "your share" in v. 6aα and "your lot" in v. 6aβ. The second accusation, that "you offer libations and grain offerings to them," appears in v. 6bα, including the reference to libations in v. 6bα¹⁻⁴ and grain offerings in v. 6bα⁵⁻⁶. Finally, the fifth rhetorical question, "shall I relent at these things?" concludes the subunit in v. 6bβ.

The third element of 57:3-13a appears in vv. 57:7-13a, which is a prophetic judgment speech against the wicked. This subunit begins with an extended statement concerning the basis for judgment in vv. 7-11. The basis for judgment includes two basic charges: "you committed apostasy/adultery with other gods" in vv. 7-9 and "you didn't care" in vv. 10-11. The charge that "you committed apostasy/adultery" in vv. 7-9 includes three basic elements. The first is the charge that "you set your bed for sacrifice on a high hill" in v. 7, which includes the basic charge that "you set your bed on a high hill" in v. 7a and that "you offered sacrifice" in v. 7b. The second is the charge that "behind the door you made a covenant with them" in v. 8, which includes the charges that "you set your remembrance, i.e., you forgot about me (G-d)" in v. 8a, that "when you left me you widened your bed and made a covenant" in v. 8bα, and that "you loved their bed and saw their *yād* (penis)" in v. 8bβ. The third is that "you approached the king and sent envoys" in v. 9. The first portion of this charge focuses on the approach to the king with oil and perfume in v. 9a, including the reference to oil in v. 9aα and the reference to multiplying perfume in v. 9aβ. The second portion of this charge claims that "you sent envoys as far as Sheol" in v. 9b, including the charge that "you sent envoys afar" in v. 9bα and that "they went as far as Sheol" in v. 9bβ. The charge that "you didn't care" in vv. 10-11 includes two basic charges. The first in v. 10 is a twofold accusation that "though you were weary (with making illicit love), you never said enough" in v. 10a and that "you satisfied your lust so you didn't care" in v. 10b. The second in v. 11 appears in the form of rhetorical questions, including "whom do you fear that you lie and do not remember me?" in v. 11a and "was I too patient that you do not fear me?" in v. 11b. Finally, the announcement of judgment appears in vv. 12-13a in four statements: "I declare your judgment" in v. 12a; "your idols will not do you any good" in v. 12b; "when you cry for help, the wind will blow them (your idols) away" in v. 13aα; and "a breeze will take them (your idols)" in v. 13aβ.

The third element of 57:1-21 appears in vv. 57:13b-21, which constitute the prophetic announcement of salvation for the righteous. It begins with YHWH's basic announcement of salvation proper in v. 13b, which includes statements that "those who trust in me shall inherit the earth" in v. 13bα and that "those who trust in me shall possess my holy mountain" in v. 13bβ. The prophet's report of YHWH's command to build the highway for the return of the people then follows in v. 14. It begins with the speech formula in v. 14aα¹ and the speech proper in v. 14aα²-b, which presents YHWH's three-part command to build a highway for the people to return. The first part in v. 14aα²-³ is the command to "build the highway"; the second part in v. 14aβ is the command to "prepare the road"; and the third part in v. 14b is the command to "remove the obstacles from the road of my people." Finally, the complex prophetic messenger speech concerning the salvation of the righteous concludes the subunit in vv. 15-21. It begins with the modified and expanded messenger formula in v. 15aα, which includes the messenger formula proper in v. 15aα¹-⁵, which refers to YHWH as high and uplifted as well as the reference to YHWH in v. 15aα⁶-⁸ as dwelling forever and holy of name. YHWH's speech proper concerning the salvation of the righteous then follows in vv. 15aβ-21. The first element of YHWH's speech is the assertion in v. 15aβ-b that "I dwell on high to give life to the downtrodden." It includes the statement that "I dwell high and holy" in v. 15aβ and a statement of the purposes in v. 15b that includes "to give life to those low of spirit" in v. 15bα and "to give life to those crushed of heart" in v. 15bβ. The balance of the subunit then turns to the interrelationship between divine anger and mercy in vv. 16-21, in four parts. The first part in v. 16 focuses on YHWH's assertion that "I am not always angry, but also give life." The focus on YHWH's anger appears in v. 16a in two parts: a statement that "I will not always contend" in v. 16aα and a statement that "I will not be angry forever" in v. 16aβ. The focus on YHWH's life-giving role appears in v. 16b with the statement that "I give soul (life) to one who becomes faint before me." The second part appears in v. 17 which focuses on YHWH's claim to be angry because of the people's iniquity. The first element of this assertion in v. 17a states in two parts that YHWH was angry and struck the people because of their iniquity: "I was angry because of their iniquity for gain" in v. 17aα and "I struck them and hid in my anger" in v. 17aβ. The second element in v. 17b states that "they went about in the way of their hearts," i.e., they did as they pleased. The third part in vv. 18-19 presents YHWH's claim that "I will heal them," in four parts. The first in v. 18a asserts that "I see their way and I heal them"; the second in v. 18b asserts that "I guide them and restore comfort to their mourners"; the third asserts that "I create the fruit of their lips" in v. 19a; and the fourth presents YHWH's statement that "there will be peace upon them" and that "I will heal them" in v. 19b. This last element includes three parts: a statement that there will be peace to those far and near in v. 19bα; a speech formula identifying YHWH as the speaker in v. 19bβ¹-²; and YHWH's statement that "I will heal them" in v. 19bβ³. Finally, the fourth part in vv. 20-21 presents the statement of exception that the wicked will have no peace. It begins with the assertion in v. 20 that wicked are like the raging sea. This is basically stated in v. 20a. The reason for the statement follows in v. 20b: "they can't be still and kick up mud," i.e., one sees mud (guilt) and so there must be a cause. Verse 20bα presents the statement that they can't be still, and v. 20bβ presents the statement that they always kick up mud and silt if they are not still. Verse 21 concludes with the prophet's presentation that there is no peace for the wicked. This verse includes the assertion that there is no peace in v. 21aα; the speech formula identifying "my G-d" as the speaker in v. 21aβ; and the concluding element, for the wicked, in v. 21b.

Genre

Isaiah 56:9–57:21 is configured as a prophetic INSTRUCTION concerning YHWH's willingness to forgive those who repent. Prophetic INSTRUCTION is based upon the INSTRUCTION genre which offers guidance to an individual or group by setting forth particular values or prescribing rules of conduct. Prophetic INSTRUCTION tends to be employed for persuasive purposes by focusing on adherence to YHWH. INSTRUCTION has no specified formal structure or vocabulary. In the present instance, it focuses on adherence to YHWH as the definition of righteous behavior that will result in the restoration of Jerusalem and Judah as well as peace for the righteous. Wicked behavior is here defined as abandonment of YHWH for other gods and participation in foreign religious practice. Although not explicitly addressed, the passage appears to accept the political agenda of the book of Isaiah as a whole to submit to the Persian Empire as an act of adherence to YHWH. Efforts to foment revolt against Persia in cooperation with other nations would constitute wicked behavior in this passage and in the book of Isaiah as a whole.

Isaiah 56:9–57:21 also employs a variety of other genres within the overall framework of Prophetic INSTRUCTION.

Isaiah 56:9 employs an ADDRESS form to address the wild animals of the forest in order to invite them to come and eat. An ADDRESS is nothing more than a speech addressed to a particular audience. Here the ADDRESS is employed both metaphorically and sarcastically as a means to critique the watchmen of Jerusalem who are not doing their jobs by protecting the city from outside threat. Hence, wild animals can come in at any time to eat what they like. The use of METAPHOR, the portrayal of one thing in terms like that of another, in 56:9-12 applies not only to the wild animals addressed in this passage, but also to the watchmen themselves. The wild animals here appear to indicate foreign nations, such as Egypt, which might like to foment revolt against the Persian Empire. The portrayal of the watchmen as dogs likewise employs METAPHOR as a means to depict the incompetence, dumbness, greed, and laziness of the watchmen or leaders of the city. The use of drunken shepherds also constitutes a form of METAPHOR, again to emphasize the selfishness and absence of good judgment among the leaders of the people who are responsible for watching over their charges much as a shepherd watches sheep. Of course if the shepherd is drunk, the sheep are not adequately protected.

YHWH's promise to deliver the righteous in 57:1-21 employs a variety of genres in an effort to convince its audience to include themselves among the righteous by adhering to YHWH and submitting to the Persian Empire as an expression of YHWH's rule. The DISPUTATION genre is especially influential in this passage. This genre is employed to examine contrasting points of view and to argue in favor of a particular viewpoint. Elements of the DISPUTATION include the premise to be contested or supported, the counter thesis for which the text argues, and the argumentation proper. The initial premise of the passage appears in 57:1-2, which portrays the suffering of the righteous. Such a premise articulates the thesis against which the passage argues, that the righteous should suffer and that no one should care. Instead, 57:1-21 argues that the righteous who adhere to YHWH will ultimately receive peace as their reward whereas the wicked will know no peace.

The condemnation of the wicked in 57:3-13a functions as the argumentation against the premise that the righteous should suffer. Instead, the passage argues that the wicked will suffer. The subunit begins with a SUMMONS TO APPROACH in 57:3, which appears to presuppose a forensic setting in a court of law in which a defendant is summoned to come forward to submit to examination. METAPHOR appears within the SUMMONS. By portraying the wicked as sons of a sorceress and sons of an adulteress and whore, the passage signals its view that the wicked who refuse to adhere to YHWH are the ones who are guilty and therefore actually deserve to suffer. Isaiah 52:4-6 employs RHETORICAL QUESTIONS to advance the DISPUTATION by stating first that "I" (YHWH) will not back down against the taunts of the wicked. Here, the RHETORICAL QUESTIONS are employed to assert first in v. 4a that the wicked would mock and insult YHWH, the Holy G-d of Israel. A second set of RHETORICAL QUESTIONS in vv. 4b-5 asserts that the wicked are nothing more than rebellious and lying children who are inflamed with lust and who sacrifice children by the streams under a cleft of rock. Such persons of course have no real standing to challenge YHWH. The charges then lead to further accusations that the wicked share their lot with that of the stream; they sacrifice children by the stream and dump their remains there, and then they offer libation and grain offerings to accompany their child sacrifices. After portraying such evil, YHWH concludes this segment by asking the RHETORICAL QUESTION, "Should I relent at these things?" The answer of course is "No!"

Isaiah 57:7-13a then presents a PROPHETIC JUDGMENT SPEECH as part of the larger DISPUTATION pattern. The PROPHETIC JUDGMENT SPEECH is a genre in which a prophet announces YHWH's judgment against an individual or collective group, such as a nation. It typically consists of two basic elements, the BASIS FOR JUDGMENT and the ANNOUNCEMENT OF JUDGMENT proper. The BASIS FOR JUDGMENT appears in vv. 7-11, which charge the wicked with having committed apostasy with other gods in vv. 7-9 and with failing to care that they did so in vv. 10-11. Again, METAPHOR plays an important role in this passage insofar as the wicked are portrayed as adulterous women who abandon their husband, YHWH, to engage in relations with another lover. They are portrayed as setting their beds upon a high hill to engage in sacrifice to other gods. They are charged with using their beds to make a covenant with other gods and apparently other nations. And they are charged with using oil and perfume to approach a foreign king and to send envoys to foreign countries. In these instances, apostasy runs hand in hand with establishing relations with another nation and its gods, apparently to challenge YHWH's favored Persian Empire. The METAPHOR of adultery continues in vv. 10-11 with the charge that the wicked didn't care about their betrayal of YHWH. The RHETORICAL QUESTIONS in v. 11 indicate that the wicked show no fear nor respect for YHWH and suggest that YHWH was too patient with them. The ANNOUNCEMENT OF JUDGMENT appears in vv. 12-13a in four cryptic statements indicating that YHWH declares the judgment of the wicked, that their idols will do them no good, that the wind will blow their cries for help away, and that a breeze will take them.

Finally, 57:13b-21 closes the unit with a PROPHETIC ANNOUNCEMENT OF SALVATION for the righteous. The PROPHETIC ANNOUNCEMENT OF SALVATION typically presents an ANNOUNCEMENT OF SALVATION proper to an individual or group, followed by a BLESSING. The ANNOUNCEMENT OF SALVATION proper appears in v. 13b with statements that those who trust in YHWH will inherit the earth and G-d's holy mountain. Succeeding subunits then build upon the ANNOUNCEMENT OF SALVATION proper. Isaiah 57:14 presents the prophet's report of YHWH's command to build a highway for the return of the people. The SPEECH FORMULA in v. 14aα¹ introduces YHWH's speech, formulated as a COMMAND, in v. 14aα²-b. Isaiah 57:15-21 then presents a PROPHETIC MESSENGER SPEECH concerning the salvation of the righteous. The modified and expanded PROPHETIC MESSENGER FORMULA in v. 15aα certifies the following speech as a speech by YHWH. The speech proper in vv. 15aβ-21 then presents the details of YHWH's promises to bring restoration to the righteous, culminating in peace. The promise of peace in v. 19b might be construed as a BLESSING. The reference to the fate of the wicked in vv. 20-21 serves the instructional and disputational character of the passage by reiterating that there will be no peace for the wicked.

Setting

Isaiah 56:9–57:21 provides prophetic instruction concerning YHWH's willingness to forgive those who repent. Such an agenda suggests that the passage is primarily concerned with religious adherence to YHWH's will, particularly since the passage follows 56:1-8, which identified Shabbat observance as the key criterion by which to observe Judah's covenant with YHWH. Observance of Shabbat emerges as a form of righteousness that permits both foreigners and eunuchs to be included in YHWH's covenant, although as we noted above, such observance on the part of foreigners constitutes conversion to Judaism. Consequently, when readers encounter the distinction between the righteous and the wicked in 56:9–57:21, they will naturally assume that Shabbat observance and the other religious requirements of Judaism constitute the basis by which one might be considered righteous or wicked in this passage. Such criteria might apply at any point in the Second Temple period, which would complicate attempts to establish a setting for this passage.

But a closer reading of 56:9–57:21 suggests that there is more to the conceptualization of righteousness and wickedness than only adherence to YHWH's religious expectations. The passage of course begins with a condemnation of the watchmen in 56:9-12, identifying them as dumb, lazy, and greedy dogs who sleep on their watch and thereby expose the people to danger. Such an analogy is consistent with Ezekiel's role as watchman as defined in Ezekiel 3 and 33, in which the prophet and priest is tasked with the responsibility for ensuring that the people understand their obligations to YHWH. Isaiah 56:9-12 tells readers little about what issues the watchmen have failed to see. Isaiah 57:1-2 points to the righteous *(haṣṣadîq)* who perishes and the man of fidelity *('anšê-ḥesed)* who is gathered, i.e., who perishes like the righteous, but again, the text does little to identify what it means by righteous or to what a man of fidelity adheres. Readers will correctly assume it is YHWH, but what exactly does this text mean by adherence to YHWH?

The condemnation of the wicked in 57:3-13a begins to provide some criteria. As noted above, the passage begins by addressing the wicked metaphorically as sons of a sorceress and sons of an adulteress and whore. Such metaphors suggest the practice of divination, which is forbidden in the Bible (see, e.g., Deuteronomy 13), and sexual infidelity, which is a common means to depict Israel's or Judah's apostasy against YHWH among prophets who employ the marriage metaphor for the relationship between the husband YHWH and the bride Israel, Judah, or Jerusalem (e.g., Hosea 1–3; Ezekiel 16; Isaiah 54; Zeph 3:14-20). The passage develops the motif by portraying Israel as rebellious children, inflamed with lust under the trees and slaughtering children by the streams under the clefts of rock in 57:4-5. Such accusations are formally made in 57:6 and constitute a common means to portray the people turning to other gods through some sort of sexual rites and child sacrifice common in antiquity (see S. Ackerman, *Under Every Green Tree: Popular Religion in Sixth-Century Judah* [HSM 46; Atlanta: Scholars, 1992]). Indeed, the references to libations and grain offerings in 57:6 reinforce the charge that the people have turned to the worship of other gods.

The prophetic judgment speech against the wicked in 57:7-13a appears to continue in this line of accusation. It employs the metaphor of adultery to express religious apostasy in the basis for judgment in vv. 7-9. It charges that the people have set their bed on a high hill, a reference to the "high places," where illicit worship of foreign gods might take place. It charges that the people have offered sacrifice, that they have widened their bed to make a covenant with them, and that they have even seen the *yād* of the foreign gods. The Hebrew term *yād,* literally, "hand," is a double entendre that refers simultaneously to the sexual image of a penis during sex and to the religious image of a monument to a deity, which of course continues the correlation of adultery with apostasy in this passage. But 57:9 includes some very telling language when it refers to the people approaching the king covered with perfume and oil and sending envoys to Sheol. The approach to the king with perfume and oil continues the sexual metaphor, and interpreters have noted that "king"*(melek)* may well be a cryptic reference to the Moabite god Molech, to whom children are purportedly sacrificed. The following reference to "sending your envoys *(ṣîrayik)* afar to Sheol" would seem to refer to sending children to their deaths as sacrifices to this cannibalistic deity. But is the image of approaching a king and sending envoys also a double entendre that would suggest a political dimension to the people's abandonment of YHWH, particularly in a prophetic book like Isaiah that makes submission to Cyrus and the Achaemenid Persian dynasty an expression of observance of YHWH's will (44:28; 45:1)? Such a scenario emerges when interpreters consider the significance of the building of the Jerusalem temple in the late 6th century B.C.E., the rumblings of revolt against the Persian Empire, and the intertextual debate that takes place between the Book of the Twelve Prophets, especially in Haggai and Zechariah, and Isaiah over the question of YHWH's will for Israel's response to the Persian Empire.

It is well known that the temple was rebuilt during the reign of the Persian monarch Darius in 520-515 B.C.E. It is also well known that Darius supported the rebuilding of the temple by sending a party of exiled Jews led by Zerubbabel ben Shealtiel and Joshua ben Jehozadak back to Jerusalem in 522 to carry out the work. Zerubbabel ben Shealtiel was the grandson of King Jehoiachin ben Jehoiakim of Judah, the last legitimate monarch of the Davidic line, and Joshua ben Jehoazadak was destined to become the high priest in the Jerusalem temple (see his ordination ceremony as portrayed in Zechariah 3). Darius authorized this work at the outset of his reign, when revolt had broken out against him throughout the Persian Empire. Authorizing the rebuilding of the temple was a means to gain support from Judah in western Asia at a time when he would have needed to have stable lines of communication and supply for his invasion of Egypt to put down the revolt there.

The instability of the Persian Empire at the outset of the reign of Darius is a key factor influencing the understanding of the significance of the rebuilding of the Jerusalem temple and the return to Jerusalem of a member of the house of David together with the next high priest of the temple. The prophet Haggai maintains that such an event portends the restoration of the Davidic monarchy and Judah's independence as brought about YHWH. In his brief book, Haggai maintains that YHWH is shaking the nations, who will bring gifts to acknowledge YHWH as the true deity at the Jerusalem temple. In his concluding oracle in Hag 2:20-23, Haggai asserts that YHWH will overthrow the throne of the nations, i.e., the Persian Empire, and designate Zerubbabel as YHWH's signet ring, which of course means that Zerubbabel will rule in Jerusalem as YHWH's designated monarch. Zechariah, too, appears to hold such views concerning the significance of the return of the Davidic Zerubbabel and the high priest Joshua. He portrays both as YHWH's anointed in Zechariah 4, but when it comes to the vision of the coronation of a figure who will be crowned and enthroned on a throne with a priest beside him, the figure is not Zerubbabel but Joshua ben Jehozadak the priest.

Many presuppose that Darius recognized the threat posed by Zerubbabel and somehow removed him from the scene, leaving only the priest Joshua ben Jehozadak to be crowned and enthroned with a priest beside him. Indeed, Ezra 3 includes Zerubbabel at the dedication ceremony for the altar at the outset of construction on the Jerusalem temple, whereas Ezra 6 does not include Zerubbabel at the dedication ceremony of the completed temple. Even the so-called protoapocalyptic material in Zechariah 9-14 envisions YHWH's war against the nations, apparently led by the house of David, in which the nations will ultimately recognize YHWH in Jerusalem at the festival of Sukkot. Although early scholars understood Zechariah 9–14 to refer to a war against the Greeks, more recent scholarship has recognized that Zechariah 9–14 dates to the Persian period (C. L. Meyers and E. M. Meyers, *Zechariah 9–14* [AB 25C; New York: Doubleday, 1993]; D. L. Petersen, *Zechariah 9–14 and Malachi* [OTL; Louisville: Westminster John Knox, 1995]; M. A. Sweeney, *The Twelve Prophets* [Berit Olam; Collegeville: Liturgical, 2000]). The passage does not portray conflict between Judah and Alexander the Great. Alexander had good relations with Judah during his campaign against the Near East to the extent that he sponsored offerings for the Jerusalem temple.

But the portrayal of conflict between Jews and Persians in Haggai and Zechariah is particularly pertinent for the interpretation of Isa 56:9–57:21. The book of Isaiah in general and this passage in particular envision the righteous as those who adhere to YHWH's expectations. Those expectations include the observance of Shabbat as a religious requirement, but they also appear to include submission to the Persian Empire, beginning with Cyrus, as an expression of YHWH's will. Consequently, the portrayal of an approach to a king, the making of a covenant, and the sending of envoys raises a question: does 56:9–57:21 envision the wicked as including those who would support a revolt against the Persian Empire at the time of the rebuilding of the Jerusalem temple? Haggai and apparently Zechariah call for revolt against Persia in a scenario that highlights the role of the house of David. If such a revolt was planned, interpreters might expect some overture to a country like Egypt, which had just been pacified by Cambyses immediately prior to his death. Darius had to return to Egypt in 518-517 to put down revolt there once again at the outset of his reign. His march to Egypt would take him through Israel, and that would constitute the perfect opportunity to deal with Zerubbabel and put an end to any possibilities for revolt in Judah.

Isaiah 56:9–57:21 appears to be opposed to any such overtures to foreign gods and their human counterparts. Insofar as the book of Isaiah views Cyrus as YHWH's anointed monarch and temple-builder, it would seem that 56:9–57:21 views apostasy against YHWH as including any moves to establish a political relationship with another nation, such as Egypt, in an attempt to overthrow Persian rule. By submitting to Persian rule in accordance with the will of YHWH, 56:9–57:21 can conclude that peace will come to the righteous, but the wicked will know no peace. Such a perspective holds true from the late-6th-century period of the rebuilding of the Jerusalem temple during the reign of Cyrus through the late-5th- and early-4th-century periods of Nehemiah and Ezra, both of whom are appointed to their positions of leadership in the Judean community by the Persian king.

Interpretation

Isaiah 57:6–57:21 presents prophetic instruction concerning YHWH's willingness to forgive those who repent. Its purpose, therefore, is to encourage repentance among the Jewish community of the early Persian period so that they will return to YHWH. Although the passage expresses the matter largely in religious terms, i.e., adherence to YHWH rather than to the various foreign deities who might be available at the time, there appears to be a political dimension to the text as well. Adherence to YHWH in the book of Isaiah also entails adherence to the Persian Empire as an expression of YHWH's will.

The passage begins in 56:9-12 with the prophet's instruction concerning the failure of the watchmen of the people. "Watchmen" in this case appears to refer to the leadership of the people, which would include the Persian-appointed governor, Zerubbabel ben Shealtiel, the high priest, Joshua ben Jehozadak, and the prophets, Haggai and Zechariah. As noted in the discussion of setting, a potential revolt was brewing in Judah during the period of the reconstruction of the Second Temple that would overthrow Persian rule and reestablish the house of David. A Judean revolt at this time would have coincided with the revolt in Egypt. It seems likely that Egypt and Judah would have been in contact about such plans, although we have no such clear evidence. Haggai was clearly a supporter of such revolt, and Zechariah appears to support it as well, although his book appears to have been rewritten in the aftermath of the failure of any such attempt.

Isaiah 57:9-12 opposes such revolt and chides the watchmen of the people for not doing their jobs. It portrays them as blind, lazy, and incompetent dogs and shepherds who let wild animals come and eat whatever they like. The passage begins in v. 9 with a summons to the wild animals of the forest to come and eat. The cause for such a summons then follows in vv. 10-12 as the watchmen are portrayed first as blind figures who do not know anything in v. 10aα and then as incompetent dogs and shepherds in vv. 10aβ-12. Verses 10aβ-11aα focus on the metaphor of dogs, who are dumb and do not bark, who lie down and snooze while they are on guard, and who are greedy and never satisfied in pursuing their own interests rather than doing their job by keeping watch. Verses 11aβ-12 then employ the metaphor of drunken shepherds as a means to describe the watchmen. The shepherd metaphor develops the portrayal of greed by pointing to the shepherds as those who do not know what they are doing, who turn to their own selfish paths or interests, who would therefore rather spend their time drinking than doing their jobs. The concluding statement of the passage, that tomorrow will be like today and even better than today, indicates that they are not concerned with any threat to their charges — they are not doing their jobs because they don't take seriously the possibility of a threat.

The major subunit of the text then follows in 57:1-21 with the prophet's announcement of YHWH's promise to deliver the righteous. The passage is disputational in character because it challenges the initial premise that the righteous should suffer and instead argues that the righteous will know peace. It is also exhortational in character because it attempts to convince its audience to identify with the righteous and thereby share in the peace that it promises to the righteous.

The initial premise of the passage appears in 57:1-2. Verse 1 presents the premise that the righteous suffers because no one pays attention and the men of fidelity perish because of evil and lack of understanding. Verse 2 presents the counterthesis that those who go forward, i.e., the righteous, will have peace and rest on their own beds.

The condemnation of the wicked in 57:3-13a constitutes a form of counterargument to the initial premises of the passage. The wicked here must once again be the leadership of the community. They are summoned to approach and are caricatured as sons of a sorceress and sons of an adulteress and whore in v. 3 to highlight the charge that they have abandoned YHWH. As they approach, they are met with a series of disputational rhetorical questions from YHWH in vv. 4-6 that emphasize that YHWH will not back down in the face of their taunts. YHWH first demands to know "whom do you mock and insult?" which is based on the premise that YHWH is the G-d of creation and of Israel who cannot be challenged by the wicked. The second question is "are you not rebellious children?" which intertextually recalls the very first oracle of the book of Isaiah in 1:2-3, which portrays the people as rebellious children. The third question, "do you not slaughter children by streams under the clefts of rock?" takes up a common charge of Moabite wrongdoing in an attempt to portray the people as apostate. YHWH's fourth question, "shall I relent at these things?" is rhetorically answered with a resounding "No!"

The prophetic judgment speech against the wicked then follows in 57:7-13a to conclude the condemnation of the wicked. Its function is to seal the argument that the wicked will face punishment and thereby to convince the audience that they should identify themselves with the righteous. The basis for judgment in vv. 7-11 emphasizes the metaphorical portrayal of the wicked as adulterous women who have sought out other lovers, here characterized as other gods, although the characterization of their lovers as other nations lies below the surface of the text. Verses 7-9 present a double entendre that emphasizes sexual betrayal and religious apostasy. The charge that "you set your bed on a high hill" in v. 7 of course presents sexual betrayal by use of the image of the bed, but the location on the top of a high hill calls to mind the "high places" where gods are commonly worshipped. The reference to a sacrifice makes this aspect clear. The charge in v. 8 that "behind the door you made a covenant" indicates sexual betrayal by use of the closed-door imagery, whereas the covenant would be understood as a covenant with another god. But given the political dimensions of covenants and treaties in the ancient world, the term also suggests a political alliance that runs contrary to YHWH's interests and expectations. Such an alliance might be made with Egypt in preparation for a revolt against the Persian Empire. The charge in v. 9 that "you approached the king and sent envoys" again combines metaphors. The portrayal of the wicked as a woman covered with perfume and oil again suggests sexual betrayal, and dispatch of envoys to Sheol suggests the death cult of the Moabite god Molech, to whom children were allegedly sacrificed in antiquity (see G. C. Heider, "Molech," *ABD* 4:895-98). The reference to envoys, however, also surreptitiously suggests a political dimension that is doomed to failure. The charges that "you didn't care" in vv. 10-11 continue the sexual metaphor by portraying the wicked as a woman who cannot satisfy her lust. These verses also employ YHWH's rhetorical questions to charge that the wicked do not fear or respect YHWH. Finally, the prophetic announcement of judgment in 57:12-13a closes the issue with YHWH's declaration of judgment followed by the claims that the people's idols will not be able to save them.

The final segment of the passage is the prophetic announcement of salvation for the righteous in 57:13b-21. It begins with the prophetic announcement of salvation proper in 57:13b, which states that those who trust in YHWH will inherit the earth and possess YHWH's holy sanctuary, the Jerusalem temple. The following report of YHWH's command to build a highway for the return of the people reinforces the announcement of salvation. It also builds upon previous references to the return of the people, often by highway, throughout the book of Isaiah, i.e., 11:16; 27:12-13; 35:1-10; 40:1-11; 48:20-22. The prophetic messenger speech concerning the salvation of the righteous in 57:15-21 then constitutes the culmination of the subunit and the passage at large with YHWH's declarations. First, YHWH declares that "I dwell high and lofty," which recalls the imagery of Isaiah 6, where YHWH is described in similar terms, and that "I give life to those low of spirit and crushed of heart." Such a claim of course reinforces the initial promises to grant peace to the righteous. Verses 16-21 then reflect on the interplay between YHWH's anger and mercy. YHWH claims in v. 16 that the granting of soul or life will follow divine anger. YHWH attempts to explain that anger in v. 17 by pointing out the iniquity of the people. And YHWH claims in vv. 18-19 to heal the people once the punishment is over. But vv. 20-21 reiterate that the wicked continue to rage like the sea. Therefore, there will be no peace for the wicked.

Bibliography

W. A. M. Beuken, "Isa. 56,9–57,13: An Example of the Isaianic Legacy of Trito-Isaiah," in *Tradition and Re-interpretation in Jewish and Early Christian Literature* (*Fest.* J. C. H. Lebram; ed. J. W. van Henten et al.; StPB 36; Leiden: Brill, 1986) 48-64; J. Blenkinsopp, "Who Is the *Saddiq* of Isaiah 57:1-2?" in *Studies in the Hebrew Bible, Qumran, and the Septuagint Presented to Eugene Ulrich* (ed. P. W. Flint, E. Tov, and James C. Vanderkam; VTSup 101; Leiden: Brill, 2006) 109-20; S. W. Flynn, "Where Is YHWH in Isaiah 57,14-15?" *Bib* 87 (2006) 358-70; K. Koenen, *Ethik und Eschatologie*, 32-58; H. Odeburg, *Trito-Isaiah*, 14-20, 100-118; K. Pauritsch, *Die neue Gemeinde*, 66-73; G. J. Polan, *In the Ways of Justice*, 91-172; B. Schramm, *The Opponents of Third Isaiah*, 17-20, 125-33; P. A. Smith, *Rhetoric and Redaction*, 67-96; O. H. Steck, *Studien zu Tritojesaja*, 69-86, 192-214.

PROPHETIC INSTRUCTION CONCERNING REPENTANCE: SPECIFIC CRITERIA FOR COVENANT EXPECTATIONS 58:1-14

Structure

I. YHWH's instruction to the prophet: instruct the people concerning the proper observance of a fast to YHWH   58:1-7
    A. YHWH's threefold command to the prophet: declare to the people their transgression   58:1

1. Cry out without restraint — 58:1aα
2. Raise your voice like a shofar — 58:1aβ
3. Declare to my people transgression and sin — 58:1b
   a. Declare to my people their transgression — 58:1bα
   b. Declare to the house of Jacob their sin — 58:1bβ
B. YHWH's elaboration to the prophet concerning the misunderstanding of the people — 58:2-7
  1. Introductory statement: the people attempt to be observant — 58:2
   a. Twofold basic statement — 58:2a
    1) They seek me daily — 58:2aα
    2) They desire knowledge of my ways — 58:2aβ
   b. Twofold simile for nation attempting to do what is right — 58:2bα
    1) Like a nation that does what is right — 58:2bα$^{1-4}$
    2) Like a nation that does not abandon the law of its G-d — 58:2bα$^{5-8}$
   c. They desire to do right by G-d — 58:2bβ
    1) They ask me for righteous law — 58:2bβ$^{1-3}$
    2) They desire the nearness of G-d — 58:2bβ$^{4-6}$
  2. First set of rhetorical questions: assertion — you misunderstand your fasts — 58:3-4
   a. Twofold rhetorical question by people — 58:3a
    1) Why did you not see our fast? — 58:3aα
    2) Why did you not know that we afflicted ourselves? — 58:3aβ
   b. YHWH's rhetorical answer — 58:3b-4
    1) Because you do normal business and oppress your
employees — 58:3b
     a) On your fast day, you do what you want — 58:3bα
     b) On your fast day, you oppress your employees — 58:3bβ
    2) Because your fast is not adequate to make yourselves
heard — 58:4
     a) You fast for conflict and contention — 58:4a
      (1) You fast for conflict and contention — 58:4aα
      (2) You fast to strike the wicked with your fist — 58:4aβ
     b) Your fast today is not adequate to be heard — 58:4b
  3. Second set of rhetorical questions: I do not desire your fast — 58:5
   a. First rhetorical question: I do not want you to afflict
yourselves — 58:5a
   b. Second rhetorical question: I don't want bowing and
sackcloth — 58:5bα
    1) I do not want bowing — 58:5bα$^{1-3}$
    2) I do not want sackcloth and ashes — 58:5bα$^{4-6}$
   c. Third set of rhetorical questions: what you call a fast is
not what I want — 58:5bβ
    1) This is not a fast — 58:5bβ$^{1-3}$
    2) This is not a day that YHWH wants — 58:5bβ$^{4-6}$
  4. Third set of rhetorical questions: I desire just actions — 58:6
   a. Basic rhetorical question: is this not the fast that I desire? — 58:6aα$^{1-4}$
   b. Fourfold specifications — 58:6aα^{5}-b

I) To release the bonds of wickedness — 58:6aα$^{5\text{-}7}$
2) To loosen the cords of the yoke — 58:6aβ
3) To set the oppressed free — 58:6bα
4) To break every yoke — 58:6bβ
5. Fourth set of rhetorical questions: it is to do what is just — 58:7
    a. Is it not to share bread with the hungry? — 58:7aα
    b. To bring the poor into your house? — 58:7aβ
    c. To clothe the naked? — 58:7bα
    d. To not hide yourself from your own people? — 58:7bβ
II. The prophet's announcement of the results of correct action:
light will shine and YHWH will answer — 58:8-14
A. The prophet's exposition — 58:8-12
    I. First statement: light will shine — 58:8
        a. Light will shine and healing will quickly sprout — 58:8a
            I) Light will shine — 58:8aα
            2) Healing will quickly sprout — 58:8aβ
        b. Righteousness will lead you and glory of YHWH will
        protect your rear — 58:8b
            I) Righteousness will lead you — 58:8bα
            2) Glory of YHWH will protect your rear — 58:8bβ
    2. Prophet's second statement: YHWH will answer you — 58:9-12
        a. Basic premise: YHWH will answer when you call — 58:9a
            I) When you call, YHWH will answer — 58:9aα
            2) When you cry out, G-d will say, "Here I am!" — 58:9aβ
        b. Prophet's elaboration — 58:9b-12
            I) Protasis: if you do these things — 58:9b-10a
                a) If you remove the yoke from your midst — 58:9bα
                b) If you cease pointing fingers and speaking evil — 58:9bβ
                c) If you provide for the hungry — 58:10aα
                d) If you feed a famished person — 58:10aβ
            2) Apodosis: then your light will shine — 58:10b-12
                a) Your light will shine and your gloom will be like
                noon — 58:10b
                    (1) Your light will shine — 58:10bα
                    (2) Your gloom will be like noon — 58:10bβ
                b) YHWH will guide you always — 58:11
                    (1) YHWH will guide you — 58:11a
                        (a) YHWH will guide you — 58:11aα$^{1\text{-}3}$
                        (b) YHWH will satisfy your thirst in dry places — 58:11aα$^{4\text{-}6}$
                        (c) YHWH will strengthen your bones — 58:11aβ
                    (2) You will be like a watered garden — 58:11b
                        (a) You will be like a watered garden — 58:11bα
                        (b) You will be like a spring whose waters do
                        not fail — 58:11bβ
                c) You will rebuild — 58:12
                    (1) Men from among you will rebuild ancient ruins — 58:12aα
                    (2) You will restore old foundations — 58:12aβ

(3) They will call you repairer and restorer	58:12b
α. They will call you repairer of breached walls	58:12bα
β. They will call you restorer of paths for habitation	58:12bβ
B. YHWH's exposition	58:13-14
1. Protasis: if you do these things	58:13
a. If you refrain from doing your will on Shabbat	58:13a
1) If you don't go about on Shabbat	58:13aα
2) If you don't do your will on my holy day	58:13aβ
b. If you call Shabbat delightful and honored	58:13bα
1) Delightful	58:13bα$^{1-3}$
2) Honored	58:13bα$^{4-6}$
c. If you honor it and don't go about business	58:13bβ-γ
1) Honor it and not go on your own ways	58:13bβ
a) Honor it	58:13bβ^{1}
b) Refrain from going on your own ways	58:13bβ$^{2-3}$
2) Doing your will and speaking about business	58:13bγ
a) Doing your will	58:13bγ$^{1-2}$
b) Speaking about business	58:13bγ$^{3-4}$
2. Apodosis: you can delight in YHWH	58:14
a. Apodosis proper	58:14a-bα
1) You can delight in YHWH	58:14aα
2) I will let you ride the high places and let you eat the inheritance of Jacob	58:14aβ-bα
a) I will let you ride the high places of the land	58:14aβ
b) I will let you eat the inheritance of Jacob your father	58:14bα
b. YHWH authorization formula	58:14bβ

Isaiah 58:1-14 constitutes prophetic instruction concerning the repentance of the people insofar as it presents specific criteria for YHWH's covenant expectations. The unit is demarcated at the outset by its introductory 2nd-person masculine imperatives in v. 1 with which YHWH addresses the prophet to announce to the people their transgressions and sins. Although the prophet's voice appears in vv. 8-12, YHWH's voice returns in vv. 13-14bα followed by an example of the Prophetic authorization formula in v. 14bβ, which closes the unit. The appearance of the prophet's voice in vv. 8-12, 14bβ indicates that the unit is constituted as the prophet's presentation of YHWH's instructions and elaboration upon them. Although some scholars maintain that the unit should include 59:1-21 because of its stylistic features and continued focus on the sins of the people (e.g., Polan, *In the Ways,* 243-319; Seitz, "Isaiah 40–66," 498-503; Steck, *Studien zu Tritojesaja,* 177-82), the introductory exclamation forms in 59:1, its generic character as a lament, and its concluding summary-appraisal form in 59:21 set 59:1-21 off as the fourth subunit of chs. 56–59, which present the prophet's instruction concerning observance of YHWH's covenant with specific focus on the observance of Shabbat and other holy requirements. The concern with Shabbat observance in 58:13-14bα picks up the concern with Shabbat in 56:1-8.

The first subunit of the passage appears in 58:1-7. It is formulated as YHWH's speech directed to the prophet. The speech is formulated as YHWH's instruction to the prophet to address the people in an effort to announce to them their transgressions and sins and to instruct them instead in proper conduct as expected by YHWH. The appearance of the prophet's voice in v. 8 points to the beginning of the next subunit in the passage.

Isaiah 58:1 constitutes the first element of YHWH's speech. It is a three-fold command, formulated in 2nd-masculine singular imperatives addressed by YHWH to the prophet. YHWH's identity is apparent in the 1st-person singular formulation of the passage. YHWH issues three commands to the prophet. The first in v. 1aα is to "cry out without restraint." The second in v. 1aβ is to "raise your voice like a shofar," the ram's horn used in the Jerusalem temple to signal important holy occasions. The third in v. 1b is to "declare to my people their transgression and sin" in two parts: their transgression in v. 1bα and their sin in v. 1bβ.

Isaiah 58:2-7 constitutes YHWH's elaboration to the prophet concerning the people's misunderstanding of their obligations to YHWH. It builds upon v. 1 by specifying what the sins of the people are and what remedies they should pursue. It presumes throughout that the people are anxious to meet YHWH's demands, but that they are doing it wrong. Five elements in vv. 2, 3-4, 5, 6, and 7, an introduction and four elements each introduced by a rhetorical question, develop the theme of the subunit.

The passage begins in v. 2 with an introductory statement concerning the people's attempts to observe YHWH's expectations. The first portion of the subunit is the twofold basic statement of the issue in v. 2a, that the people "seek me (YHWH) daily" in v. 2aα and that "they desire knowledge of my (YHWH's) ways" in v. 2aβ. A twofold form designed to express the nation's attempts to do what is right then follows in v. 2bα, including statements that "they are like a nation that does what is right" in v. 2bα$^{1-4}$ and that "they are like a nation that does not abandon the law of its G-d" in v. 2bα$^{5-8}$. Finally, v. 2bβ presents the third element in the sequence with a statement that they desire to do right by G-d, including statements that "they ask me for righteous law" in v. 2bβ$^{1-3}$ and that "they desire the nearness of G-d" in v. 2bβ$^{4-6}$.

The first set of rhetorical questions, which asserts that the people misunderstand their fasts, appears in vv. 3-4. The twofold rhetorical questions by the people appear in v. 3a, including "why did you (YHWH) not see our fast?" in v. 3aα and "why did you not know that we afflicted ourselves?" in v. 3aβ. YHWH's rhetorical answer to the questions then follows in vv. 3b-4 in two parts. The first part in v. 3b answers that the reason YHWH neither sees nor knows about the people's efforts is that the people go about their normal business and oppress their employees on fast days. The statement that they do what they want on fast days appears in v. 3bα, and the statement that they oppress their employees on fast days appears in v. 3bβ. YHWH's second rhetorical answer, because the people's fast is not adequate to make them heard, appears in v. 4. The first part of the answer, that "you fast for the sake of conflict and conten-tion," appears in v. 4a, including the statements that "you fast for conflict and contention" in v. 4aα and that "you fast to strike the wicked with your fist" in v. 4aβ. The second part of the answer in v. 4b asserts that "your fast is not adequate to be heard."

The second set of rhetorical questions, which asserts that YHWH does not desire the fast of the people, appears in v. 5. The first rhetorical question in v. 5a asserts that YHWH does not want the people to afflict themselves. The second rhetorical question in v. 5b asserts that YHWH does not want bowing and sackcloth, including statements that "I do not want bowing" in v. 5bα$^{1-3}$ and that "I do not want sackcloth and ashes" in v. 5bα$^{4-6}$. The third set of rhetorical questions in v. 5bβ asserts that what the people call a fast is not what YHWH wants. It includes two statements: "this is not a fast" in v. 5bβ$^{1-3}$ and "this is not a day that YHWH wants" in v. 5bβ$^{4-6}$.

The third set of rhetorical questions, in which YHWH asserts that "I desire just actions," appears in v. 6. The subunit begins with the basic rhetorical question, "is this not the fast that I desire?" in v. 6aα$^{1-4}$. Fourfold specifications then follow in v. 6aα^5-b which state that the people's obligation is to do what is just. The first asserts that it is to release the bonds of wickedness in v. 6aα$^{5-7}$; the second asserts that it is to loosen the cords of the yoke in v. 6aβ; the third asserts that it is to set the oppressed free in v. 6bα; and the fourth asserts that it is to break every yoke in v. 6bβ.

The fourth and final set of rhetorical questions, which asserts that the people's obligation is to do what is just, appears in v. 7 in four parts. The first is the obligation to share bread with the hungry in v. 7aα; the second is the obligation to bring the poor into your house in v. 7aβ; the third is the obligation to clothe the naked in v. 7bα; and the fourth is the obligation not to hide yourself from your own people in v. 7bβ.

The prophet's announcement of the anticipated results of the people's correct actions then follows in 58:8-14. As noted above, this subunit is formulated as the prophet's address, including the presentation of YHWH's words in vv. 13-14bα. The message of this section is optimistic: light will shine and YHWH will answer the people. The basic structure of the unit includes the prophet's exposition in vv. 8-12 and the prophet's presentation of YHWH's exposition in vv. 13-14.

The prophet's exposition in vv. 8-12 begins in v. 8 with the first statement, that light will shine. This statement appears in two basic parts. The first in v. 8a asserts that light will shine and that healing will quickly sprout, including the statements that light will shine in v. 8aα and that healing will quickly sprout in v. 8aβ. The second part of the statement then follows in v. 8b: "righteousness will lead you and the glory of YHWH will protect your rear," including the statements that "righteousness will lead you" in v. 8bα and that "the glory of YHWH will protect your rear" in v. 8bβ.

The prophet's second statement, that "YHWH will answer you," appears in vv. 9-12. The basic premise appears in v. 9a: "YHWH will answer when you call," including statements that "when you call, YHWH will answer" in v. 9aα and that "when you cry out, G-d will say, 'Here I am!'" in v. 9aβ. The prophet's elaboration then follows in vv. 9b-12 in the form of a conditional statement that states the results of the people's correct actions. The conditions of the statement or the protasis appear in vv. 9b-10a with a statement of the conditions that the people must meet: if you do these things, then the results will follow. Four conditions then appear in sequence, including "remove the yoke from your midst" in v. 9bα; "cease pointing fingers and speaking evil" in v. 9bβ; "provide for the hungry" in v. 10aα; and "feed a famished person" in v. 10aβ. The anticipated results of these actions then appear as the apodosis in vv. 10b-12 in three elaborated statements. The first elaborated statement appears in v. 10b which asserts that "your light will shine and your gloom will be like noon," including statements that "your light will shine" in v. 10bα and that "your gloom will be like noon" in v. 10bβ. The second elaborated statement appears in v. 11 with the statement that "YHWH will guide you always." The premise appears in two parts. The first in v. 11a asserts in three parts that "YHWH will guide you": "YHWH will guide you" in v. 11aα$^{1-3}$; "YHWH will satisfy your thirst in dry places" in v. 11aα$^{4-6}$; and "YHWH will strengthen your bones" in v. 11aβ. The second appears in v. 11b with the assertion that "you will be like a watered garden" in two parts, including "you will be like a watered garden" in v. 11bα and "you will be like a spring whose waters do not fail" in v. 11bβ. The third elaborated statement appears in v. 12, which asserts that the people will rebuild. The statement appears in three parts: "men from among you will rebuild ancient ruins" in v. 12aα; "you will restore old foundations" in v. 12aβ; and "they will call you repairer and restorer" in v. 12b. Verse 12b is further divided into two parts: "they will call you repairer of breached walls" in v. 12bα and "they will call you restorer of paths for habitation" in v. 12bβ.

The prophet's presentation of YHWH's exposition then concludes the unit in 58:13-14. The passage likewise appears in a conditional form with anticipated results. The protasis in v. 13 specifies the conditions that the people must meet, in three parts. The first appears in v. 13a which asserts that the people must refrain from doing their will on the Shabbat: "if you don't go about on Shabbat" in v. 13aα and "if you don't do your will on my holy day" in v. 13aβ. The second appears in v. 13bα, which asserts that the people must call the Shabbat delightful and honored, including the assertion that Shabbat be delightful in v. 13bα$^{1-3}$ and that it be honored in v. 13bα$^{4-6}$. The third condition in v. 13bβ-γ is that the people should honor the Shabbat and not go about their normal business. The first part of this statement in v. 13bβ asserts that the people must honor the Shabbat and not go on their normal way, including statements that they should honor it in v. 13bβ^{1} and that they refrain from going on their normal ways in v. 13bβ$^{2-3}$. The second statement in v. 13bγ asserts that the people must not do their will or speak about business, including statements that they not do their will in v. 13bγ$^{1-2}$ and that they not speak about business in v. 13bγ$^{3-4}$. The apodosis in v. 14 asserts that if the people meet the above-named conditions in v. 13, that they can delight in YHWH. The apodosis proper, formulated in 1st-person form as a speech by YHWH, appears in v. 14a-bα in two parts. The first is the assertion that "you can delight in YHWH" in v. 14aα. The second is that YHWH will let the people ride the high places and eat the inheritance of Jacob in v. 14aβ-bα, including statements that "I will let you ride the high places of the land" in v. 14aβ and that "I will let you eat the inheritance of Jacob your father" in v. 14bα. The YHWH authorization formula, which appears in 3rd-person form as a statement by the prophet about YHWH, closes the subunit in v. 14bβ.

Genre

Isaiah 58:1-14 is formulated as a prophetic INSTRUCTION concerning repentance. Its generic character as a prophetic INSTRUCTION is based on two fundamental premises. The first is the goal to offer proper instruction concerning the repentance of the people. INSTRUCTION typically appears as an imperative text that offers guidance to individuals or groups concerning rules of conduct or values. In the present instance, the text notes the desire of the people to seek and serve YHWH properly and to do what is right, but it offers a critique of the people's efforts by pointing out that their observance of fast days is improper. The text argues that the people do observe fast days, but notes in vv. 3-4 that the people continue to go about their normal business on those days, thereby undermining the purpose of the fast to repent and reflect upon holy obligations to G-d. Specific charges are that the people act in accordance with their own will and not with YHWH's will on those days, that they continue to oppress their employees on those days, that they promote conflict and contention on their fast days, and that their purpose is to punish those considered wicked. But YHWH argues instead that afflicting oneself, bowing, and sackcloth and ashes are not what YHWH wants unless such acts are accompanied by efforts to engage in issues of social justice. Examples of proper behavior then follow in vv. 6 and 7. Verse 6 specifies desired actions as releasing the bonds of wickedness, loosening the cords of the yoke, setting the oppressed free, and breaking every yoke. Verse 7 in turn specifies sharing bread with the hungry, bringing the poor into one's home, clothing the naked, and not hiding oneself from one's own people when they are in need.

The second premise for the definition of the genre of this text as prophetic INSTRUCTION is the prophetic context in which it functions. Although vv. 1-7 present YHWH's instruction speech concerning proper observance, the prophet presents an exposition of the anticipated results of the people's proper observance of YHWH's expectations in vv. 8-12. In general, the prophet makes two points: that light will shine if the people follow YHWH's will and that YHWH will answer them. But in doing so, the prophet provides further specification concerning proper repentance before YHWH in vv. 9b-10a: the people must remove the yoke from their midst, they must cease their efforts to blame others for problems, they must provide for the hungry, and they must feed a famished person. The prophet's presentation of YHWH's exposition in vv. 13-14 provides further specification as well. Here YHWH points specifically to the observance of Shabbat in terms much like those of the above-noted fast days: the people must honor or observe the Shabbat and refrain from going their own way and they must not go about doing their own will and speaking about normal business on Shabbat.

Overall, the text provides instruction concerning the proper observance of YHWH's will. Ritual action alone is inadequate unless it is accompanied by the people's efforts to do YHWH's will with respect to the moral issues of social justice that prompt the fast days and Shabbat in the first place.

The extensive use of RHETORICAL QUESTIONS well serves the instructional agenda of this passage. A RHETORICAL QUESTION is a question that has an obvious response. It therefore functions as a form of assertion for the issue at hand. In the context of instruction, the party to whom the question is addressed already knows and affirms the answer so that no statement of the answer is necessary. Insofar as the addressee already knows the answer, the rhetorical effect of the question is to aid in persuading the addressee of the correctness of the argument at hand. Since the answer to the question is obvious, the addressee joins in the assertion and thereby joins the speaker in the argument that the speaker is attempting to make. RHETORICAL QUESTIONS appear throughout the present context in vv. 3-4, where they function as a platform for justifying YHWH's refusal to acknowledge the people's fasts; in v. 5, where they aid in articulating YHWH's rejection of the people's fast; v. 6, where they give expression to YHWH's desire for just action; and v. 7, where they again give expression to YHWH's desire for just action. In this respect, the RHETORICAL QUESTIONS in vv. 3-7 serve the instructional agenda of the passage by expressing both what YHWH does not want and what YHWH wants.

Other generic elements also appear in this passage. YHWH addresses the prophet in v. 1 with a COMMAND to declare to the people their transgression. YHWH's COMMAND thereby initiates the plot sequence and therefore the instructional agenda of this text. The use of the SIMILE in v. 2bα likens the people to a nation that does what is right and that does not abandon the law of its G-d. Here, it helps to characterize the people's desire to do what YHWH wants, but this is preparatory to YHWH's critique of the people that will follow. By declaring that the people are like a nation that does what is right, the simile expresses that they are not actually a nation that does what is right — only that they are like one — and thereby rhetorically opens the way for YHWH's critique. Finally, the PROPHETIC AUTHORIZATION FORMULA in v. 14bβ identifies YHWH as the speaker of the foregoing statement in vv. 13-14bα. But it also points to YHWH's statement as the basis for the realization of what YHWH has said: because YHWH has said it, it will happen. Insofar as the preceding statement guarantees the people control of the land if they observe YHWH's expectations, the PROPHETIC AUTHORIZATION FORMULA guarantees that the promise will be realized.

Setting

Some interpreters, e.g., Seitz, "Isaiah 40–66," 498; Steck, *Studien zu Tritojesaja,* 182-86; Polan, *In the Ways,* 315, and others, have recognized that ch. 58 is related to the following text in ch. 59, based especially on the inclusio in 58:1 and 59:20 with its focus on the people's rebellion *(pešaʻ).* Although the interrelationship between chs. 58 and 59 is justified, interpreters must also recognize that ch. 58 is part of a sequence of texts in 56:1-8; 56:9–57:21; 58:1-14; and 59:1-21 that is concerned with articulating the means by which the people will be included in the Persian-period Jewish community. Although rebellion and sin are part of the equation, observance of the covenant, particularly the Shabbat, comes to the forefront as well as instruction to observe the moral requirements of the covenant together with the ritual. Although modern interpreters, particularly Protestant interpreters, carefully distinguish between the two, the ancients viewed morality and ritual action as intimately linked (see, e.g., Leviticus 19, which includes a combination of moral and ritual instruction), and such conceptualization is central to the message of ch. 58 as well as the other texts in the sequence.

Isaiah 58 presupposes the observance of fast days, which would be an important feature of temple worship, particularly at Yom Kippur and other fast days in the Jewish tradition. The observance of such fasts and Shabbat therefore points to the period following the rebuilding of the temple when the people were becoming more and more accustomed to participating in the temple's liturgy and observances. The passage also presupposes that religious instruction is taking place, insofar as it goes to special efforts to instruct the people in proper moral action and the value of social justice. Although some might see this as a replacement for the ritual action of the temple, particularly if they are formed by NT images of temple ritual as the exclusive concern of the temple, observance of temple ritual presupposes the observance of moral teachings as well. The so-called "entrance liturgies" in Psalms 15 and 24 call for the people to do what is right (Ps 15:2), to stand by their oath (15:4), to refuse bribes against the innocent (15:5), and to have clean hands and a pure heart (Ps 24:4), all of which are examples of YHWH's moral teachings, before appearing in the temple. Isaiah 58 promotes such concerns as doing what is right, observing the laws of G-d, treating employees properly, feeding the hungry, giving shelter to the poor and clothing to the naked, etc. Such principles are necessary for admittance to the temple and are therefore necessary to observe together with the fasts and other ritual or liturgical action that takes place there. The instructions presuppose a religious authority, such as a priest, who would then expound upon divine Torah as a means to teach the people their proper obligations to YHWH in the covenant. Although our spokesperson here appears to be the prophet, it appears that the prophet is taking on the role of the priest by conveying such instruction. Perhaps it is because the prophet is a priest, although we have no way to know that, or is emulating a priest, which seems much more likely.

Given the emphasis on moral teachings of social justice that accompany the ritual observance of fasts and Shabbat, it appears that ch. 58 is set in the period of Nehemiah and Ezra during the late 5th century and early 4th century B.C.E. Both figures instituted temple worship, observance of Shabbat and fast days, and observance of divine torah as the basis for their understanding of Jewish practice. The teachings found in ch. 58 are perfectly compatible with the agendas of both figures as represented in Ezra-Nehemiah. Nehemiah, for example, made sure to close the city of Jerusalem on Shabbat (Neh 13:15-22), and Ezra read the Torah to the people and reinstituted the observance of the festival of Sukkot (Nehemiah 8–10). The instruction offered in ch. 58 would likely support the observance of temple fasts and Shabbat and thereby support the interests of both of these figures in establishing the Jerusalem temple as the central institution for Jewish life and identity in the early Persian period.

Interpretation

Isaiah 58:1-14 presents prophetic instruction to the people concerning repentance with specific criteria for observing covenant expectations. The passage puts the prophet in the place of the priest, who would normally give such instruction to the people concerning their observance of the holy requirements of temple worship and practice. The fact that the prophet plays such a role indicates some ambiguity in the roles of prophets and priests. Prophetic figures such as Isaiah ben Amoz, Second Isaiah, Hosea, Amos, Elijah, Elisha, and others frequently offer divine instruction to the people from the context of a temple setting or temple practice without ever having any priestly identity. Insofar as prophets served as temple singers in the Jerusalem temple, the later shift to identify them as Levites may indicate that prophetic figures eventually came to be absorbed into the Levitical priesthood at some point during the Second Temple period (D. L. Petersen, *Late Israelite Prophecy: Studies in Deutero-Prophetic Literature and in Chronicles* [SBLMS 23; Missoula: Scholars, 1977], 55-96). Although some might argue that the prophet introduces a moral perspective into an otherwise ritually- or cultically-oriented temple practice, study of priestly literature, such as Leviticus 19, demonstrates that the temple and priesthood always combined moral with ritual concerns.

The basic purpose of the passage is to instruct the people to combine moral practice with ritual practice. The passage comprises two basic segments: YHWH's instruction to the prophet to instruct the people in the proper observance of a fast to YHWH in vv. 1-7 and the prophet's announcement that correct action will lead to beneficial results, i.e., light will shine and YHWH will answer the people, in vv. 8-14.

The passage throughout presupposes that the people are willing to observe YHWH's expectations appropriately but they are doing so incorrectly. Hence, YHWH's instruction in vv. 1-7 is designed to prompt the prophet to point out the wrongdoing of the people so that their actions might be corrected. Isaiah 58:1 presents YHWH's initial commands to the prophet to raise his/her voice and to declare to the people their transgression. YHWH's elaboration to the prophet concerning the misunderstanding of the people makes it clear that they do not sin deliberately, but do so out of ignorance of YHWH's expectations. The prophet's task is therefore to correct the problem. YHWH notes in v. 2 the people's attempts at proper observance, i.e., "they seek me daily, they desire knowledge of my ways," etc. But YHWH's first set of rhetorical questions to the prophet identifies the problem. YHWH does not answer the people's supplications when they conduct public fasts. Such a situation fits the early Persian period, when the reconstruction of the temple in 520-515 B.C.E. did not result in worldwide recognition of YHWH by the nations nor in the good times projected by the prophet Haggai if the people would build the temple. In conjunction with the reforms of Nehemiah and Ezra in the late 5th and early 4th centuries, YHWH points out that the people do as they please, charging that they oppress their employees, promote conflict, and use their fasting as a basis for accusing others of wrongdoing. Consequently, the people's supplications to YHWH when they fast are not heard.

YHWH offers counterinstruction in 58:5. YHWH makes it clear that the people's fasts and self-affliction are not what YHWH wants. The counterinstruction continues in v. 6 with the next set of rhetorical questions indicating that YHWH desires just actions. This does not mean that fasting and other forms of ritual action are to be rejected; it means that moral action must accompany ritual action as indicated in the temple entrance liturgies, such as Psalms 15 and 24. YHWH calls for moral action in v. 6, e.g., release the bonds of wickedness, loosen the cords of the yoke, set the oppressed free, and break every yoke. The last set of rhetorical questions in v. 7 makes YHWH's expectations even more explicit: share bread with the hungry, bring the poor into your house, clothe the naked, and do not hide from your own people when they need your aid. Such actions serve the moral agenda of YHWH's instruction and aid in building a holy and a just society which looks to the needs of its people.

The prophet's exposition of the results of correct action in 58:8-14 indicates that light will shine and that YHWH will answer the people if they conduct themselves in accordance with YHWH's instructions. The prophet's exposition proper appears in vv. 8-12. The prophet begins in v. 8 with the contention that light will shine and that healing will "sprout" for the people. These references indicate some intertextual links with the first part of the book of Isaiah. The light metaphor draws upon 9:1(NRSV 9:2), which describes the great light to be seen by the people after walking for so long in darkness. The sprouting of healing draws upon the imagery of the shoot that sprouts from the stump of Jesse in ch. 11 to indicate the emergence of a righteous Davidic monarch. Insofar as YHWH proves to be the true monarch in 66:1, these images indicate that YHWH will fulfill the roles of the righteous monarch as announced in 9:1-6 and 11:1-16 to bring security and peace to the people. The prophet then turns to the second element of the exposition in vv. 9-12, that YHWH will answer the people when they call. The basic premise appears in v. 9a, in which the prophet depicts YHWH as responding, "Here I am," when the people call for help. Ironically, this was Isaiah's response to YHWH in 6:8 when YHWH asked for someone to speak on YHWH's behalf to the people. The irony is compounded by the fact that YHWH's message in ch. 6 was one of judgment; the prophet's task was to ensure that the people remained blind, deaf, and ignorant so that they would not repent and thereby avoid the punishment that YHWH decreed as part of the scenario by which YHWH would be recognized as the sovereign master of creation and human events. Here toward the end of the book, YHWH is ready to respond to the people, who have suffered invasion and exile before returning to a desolate land, but only if they conduct themselves properly. One might legitimately ask if YHWH's conduct has been exemplary from the time of the late 8th century on! The prophet's elaboration in vv. 9b-12 lays out the conditions by which the people will see YHWH's light: they must remove the yoke from their midst, cease denouncing others, provide for the hungry, and feed the famished. Then they will receive YHWH's divine light, here defined as YHWH's guidance, satisfaction of thirst, strengthening of bones, etc., so the people will be like a watered garden ready to rebuild Jerusalem. The reference to rebuilding ruins and breached walls of course points to Nehemiah's efforts to restore the breached walls of Jerusalem when he returned to the city in 445.

YHWH's own exposition in 58:13-14 adds further clarification. Should the people observe Shabbat properly by not going about their normal business and by honoring it instead, they will be able to delight in YHWH, who will in turn grant them the inheritance of Jacob, i.e., the land of Israel. The YHWH authorization formula in v. 14bβ certifies YHWH's offer.

Bibliography

M. L. Barré, "Fasting in Isaiah 58:1-12: A Reexamination," *BTB* 15 (1985) 94-97; L. J. Hoppe, "Isaiah 58:1-12: Fasting and Idolatry," *BTB* 13 (1983) 44-47; K. Koenen, *Ethik und Eschatologie*, 88-103; H. Kosmala, "Form and Structure of Isaiah 58," *ASTI* 5 (1967) 69-81; W. Lau, *Schriftgelehrte Prophetie*, 240-61; G. J. Polan, *In the Ways of Justice*, 173-242; W. Schottroff, "'Unrechtmässige Fesseln auftun, Jochstricke lösen': Jesaja 58,1-12, Ein Textbeispiel zum Thema 'Bibel und Ökonomie,'" *BibInt* 5 (1997) 263-78; P. A. Smith, *Rhetoric and Redaction*, 97-114; O. H. Steck, *Studien zu Tritojesaja*, 177-82.

THE PROPHET'S PRESENTATION OF YHWH'S RESPONSE TO THE PEOPLE'S CONFESSION: YHWH WILL DELIVER THOSE WHO REPENT 59:1-21

Structure

I. The prophet's presentation of the people's confession	59:1-15a
A. Prophetic instruction concerning the people's iniquities as barrier between them and G-d	59:1-8
1. Announcement concerning YHWH's capacity to deliver	59:1
a. YHWH's arm not too short to deliver	59:1a
b. YHWH's ear not too heavy to hear	59:1b
2. Announcement concerning the people's iniquity	59:2-8
a. Announcement of YHWH's refusal to see or hear the people	59:2
1) Your iniquities are a barrier between you and G-d	59:2a
2) Your sins prompt G-d to hide the divine face from you and refuse to hear you	59:2b
b. Basis for YHWH's refusal: people's iniquities	59:3-8
1) Your hands and fingers are defiled	59:3a
a) Your hands are defiled with blood	59:3aα
b) Your fingers are defiled with iniquity	59:3aβ
2) Your lips and tongue speak dishonestly	59:3b
a) Your lips speak lies	59:3bα
b) Your tongue mutters treachery	59:3bβ
3) There is no justice	59:4a
a) No one calls out in justice	59:4aα
b) No one is judged with honesty	59:4aβ
4) They rely on falsehood and give birth to trouble	59:4b
a) Rely on chaos and falsehood	59:4bα
b) Give birth to violence and trouble	59:4bβ
5) Metaphor of adder's eggs and spider's webs	59:5a
a) Adder's eggs	59:5aα
b) Spider's webs	59:5aβ
6) Elaboration concerning adder's eggs	59:5b
a) Whoever eats them will die	59:5bα

b) If an egg is crushed, it hatches a viper	59:5bβ
7) Elaboration concerning spider's web	59:6a
a) Webs cannot serve as garment	59:6aα
b) Their product cannot clothe anyone	59:6aβ
8) Uselessness of their creations and deeds	59:6b
a) Their creations are troublesome	59:6bα
b) Their deeds create violence	59:6bβ
9) Perversity of their feet	59:7a
a) Their feet run after evil	59:7aα
b) They run to shed innocent blood	59:7aβ
10) Their plans are destructive and injurious	59:7b
a) Their plans are problematic	59:7bα
b) Destruction and injury are on their roads	59:7bβ
11) They do not know peace or justice	59:8
a) They do not know the path of peace	59:8aα
b) There is no justice in their wagon tracks	59:8aβ
c) Their paths are crooked	59:8bα
d) Those who walk their paths know no peace	59:8bβ
B. Prophet's presentation of the people's confession	59:9-15a
1. Confession: justice and righteousness are far from us	59:9-11
a. Basically stated	59:9a
1) Justice is far from us	59:9aα
2) Righteousness does not reach us	59:9aβ
b. Elaborated metaphorically by people walking in darkness	59:9b-11
1) We hope for light, but get darkness	59:9b
a) Hope for light, but get darkness	59:9bα
b) Hope for brilliance, but walk in gloom	59:9bβ
2) We are like the blind	59:10a
a) We grope like the blind along a wall	59:10aα
b) We grope like those without eyes	59:10aβ
3) We are like the twilight	59:10b
a) We stumble at noon as if in darkness	59:10bα
b) We are like the twilight	59:10bβ
4) We growl and moan like bears and doves	59:11a
a) We growl like bears	59:11aα
b) We moan like doves	59:11aβ
5) We hope for justice and righteousness, but there is neither	59:11b
a) We hope for justice, but there is none	59:11bα
b) Righteousness is far from us	59:11bβ
2. Explanation: our sins and iniquities are the cause	59:12-15a
a. Basic explanation: our sins are many and testify against us	59:12a
1) Many are our transgressions against you	59:12aα
2) Our sins testify against us	59:12aβ
b. Elaborated explanation: we know our sins and iniquities as cause for lack of justice and righteousness among us	59:12b-15a
1) We know our iniquities	59:12b-13

286

a) We know our transgressions and iniquities 59:12b
  (1) Our transgressions are with us 59:12bα
  (2) We know our iniquities 59:12bβ
b) Catalog of transgressions and iniquities 59:13
  (1) Rebellion against G-d 59:13a
    (a) Rebellion and lying to YHWH 59:13aα
    (b) Turning away from G-d 59:13aβ
  (2) Speaking fraud and treachery 59:13bα
  (3) Teaching and uttering false words 59:13bβ
2) Consequences resulting from the people's
transgressions 59:14-15a
a) Justice and righteousness are turned aside 59:14a
  (1) Justice is turned aside 59:14aα
  (2) Righteousness stands far away 59:14aβ
b) Causes: truth and integrity are lacking 59:14b-15a
  (1) Basically stated: truth and integrity are lacking 59:14b
    (a) Truth stumbles in the street 59:14bα
    (b) Integrity is not able to enter 59:14bβ
  (2) Results: truth is lacking and those refraining
    from evil are plundered 59:15a
    (a) Truth is lacking 59:15aα
    (b) Anyone refraining from evil is plundered 59:15aβ

II. The prophet's account of YHWH's response: YHWH will
deliver those who repent 59:15b-21
  A. YHWH saw that there was no justice 59:15b-16
    1. YHWH sees and is displeased 59:15b
      a. YHWH sees and is displeased 59:15bα
      b. Basis: there is no justice 59:15bβ
    2. YHWH sees that no one approaches to deliver in
    righteousness 59:16
      a. YHWH sees that no one approaches 59:16a
        1) YHWH sees that there is no man 59:16aα
        2) YHWH observes that no one arrives 59:16aβ
      b. There is no one to deliver in righteousness 59:16b
        1) There is no one whose arm will deliver 59:16bα
        2) There is no one whose righteousness supports him 59:16bβ
  B. YHWH dresses for battle 59:17
    1. YHWH dresses in righteousness 59:17a
      a. YHWH dresses in righteous armor 59:17aα
      b. A helmet of salvation on YHWH's head 59:17aβ
    2. YHWH dresses for vengeance 59:17b
      a. YHWH dresses in garments of vengeance 59:17bα
      b. YHWH dons a robe of zeal 59:17bβ
  C. YHWH's declaration: repay foes and redeem Zion/Jacob 59:18-20
    1. Presentation of YHWH's oracular declaration 59:18-20a
      a. Declaration of requital to enemies 59:18
        1) According to their deeds, YHWH will repay foes 59:18a

2) YHWH will repay the deeds of enemies in the
    coastlands   59:18b
  b. YHWH comes as redeemer for Zion and Jacob   59:19-20a
    1) From west and east, they will revere YHWH   59:19a
      a) From west they will revere YHWH's name   59:19aα
      b) From east they will revere YHWH's glory   59:19aβ
    2) Basis: YHWH comes as redeemer   59:19b-20a
      a) YHWH comes like wind-driven flood   59:19b
        (1) YHWH comes like rushing river   59:19bα
        (2) The wind of YHWH drives it on   59:19bβ
      b) YHWH comes as redeemer to Zion and to those
        who repent in Jacob   59:20a
        (1) Redeemer to Zion   59:20aα
        (2) To those who repent from transgression in Jacob   59:20aβ
  2. Oracle formula   59:20b
  D. YHWH's summary-appraisal: eternal covenant with Zion/Jacob   59:21
    1. Introduction to YHWH's promise   59:21aα
    2. Substance of YHWH's promise: my spirit and words will
      never depart from you and your descendants   59:21aβ-b

Isaiah 59:1-21 constitutes the prophet's presentation of YHWH's response to the people's confession in which YHWH states the intention to deliver those who repent. The passage is demarcated at the outset by the introductory exclamation by the prophet, "Indeed *(hēn),* the arm of YHWH is not too short to deliver, and his ear is not too dull *(kābĕdâ,* lit., 'heavy') to hear!" The passage then comprises two primary subunits. The first is the prophet's presentation of the people's confession in 59:1-15a. Although many interpreters render this text as two subunits in vv. 1-8 and 9-15a, the introductory "therefore" *('al-kēn)* in v. 9 holds the two subunits together, insofar as vv. 1-8 constitute prophetic instruction concerning the people's iniquities as a barrier between them and G-d, whereas vv. 9-15a, introduced by the particle *'al-kēn,* "therefore," then introduces the prophet's presentation of the people's confession as a means to address the iniquities identified in vv. 1-8. The second primary subunit appears in 59:15b-21, which is joined to 59:1-15a by an introductory *wāw*-consecutive formation. Isaiah 59:15b-21 constitutes the prophet's account of YHWH's response, including YHWH's pledge to redeem the righteous. The concluding summary-appraisal form in v. 21 closes the unit with a summation of YHWH's covenant with those who repent, which will be established for all succeeding generations.

    The prophetic instruction concerning the people's iniquities as a barrier between them and G-d in 59:1-8 includes two primary segments. The first is the above-mentioned exclamation in v. 1, which begins with the introductory particle *hēn,* "behold! indeed!" The exclamation announces YHWH's capacity to deliver in the form of two rhetorical questions: "is YHWH's arm too short to deliver?" in v. 1a and "is YHWH's ear not too heavy (dull) to hear?" in v. 1b. The passage establishes YHWH's efficacy, which the people apparently deny or disregard in the following segment.

    The second segment of 59:1-8 appears in vv. 2-8, which constitute an announcement of the people's iniquity. This segment begins with a twofold announcement of YHWH's refusal to see or hear the people in v. 2, including charges directed by the prophet to the people that "your iniquities are a barrier between you and G-d" in v. 2a and that "your sins prompt G-d to hide the divine face from you and refuse to hear you" in v. 2b. The basis for YHWH's refusal then follows in vv. 3-8 in a series of paired statements, each of which articulates a charge against the people. The first in v. 3a charges that "your hands and fingers are defiled," including charges that "your hands are defiled with blood" in v. 3aα and that "your fingers are defiled with iniquity" in v. 3aβ. The second in v. 3b charges that "your lips and tongue speak dishonestly," including charges that "your lips speak lies" in v. 3bα and that "your tongue mutters treachery" in v. 3bβ. The third in v. 4a charges that there is no justice, including charges that no one calls out for justice in v. 4aα and that no one is judged with honesty in v. 4aβ. The fourth in v. 4b charges that they rely on falsehood and give birth to trouble, including charges that they rely on chaos and falsehood in v. 4bα and that they give birth to violence and trouble in v. 4bβ. The fifth in v. 5a employs the metaphors of adder's eggs and spider's webs to charge that the people hatch adder's eggs in v. 5aα and weave spider's webs in v. 5aβ. The metaphor continues in v. 5b with the sixth paired statement that elaborates on the preceding metaphor of adder's eggs by charging that whoever eats them will die in v. 5bα and that if an egg is crushed, it hatches a viper (that will then strike) in v. 5bβ. The metaphor again continues in v. 6a with the seventh paired statement that elaborates on the metaphor of the spider's webs. It charges that webs cannot serve as a garment in v. 6aα and that their product cannot clothe anyone in v. 6aβ. The eighth paired statements in v. 6b focus on the uselessness of their creations and deeds with the charges that their creations are troublesome in v. 6bα and that their deeds create violence in v. 6bβ. The ninth in v. 7a focuses on the perversity of their feet, including charges that their feet run after evil in v. 7aα and that they run to shed innocent blood in v. 7aβ. The tenth in v. 7b states that their plans are destructive and injurious, including charges that their plans are problematic in v. 7bα and that destruction and injury are on their roads in v. 7bβ. The eleventh and final set in v. 8 culminates with four charges: they do not know the path of peace in v. 8aα, there is no justice in their wagon tracks in v. 8aβ, their paths are crooked in v. 8bα, and those who walk in their paths know no peace in v. 8bβ.

The prophet's presentation of the people's confession in 59:9-15a comprises two major subunits. The first in 59:9-11 comprises the people's confession that justice and righteousness are far from them. The second in 59:12-15a begins with the causative particle *kî* and offers the explanation that the people's sins and iniquities are the cause of their problems.

The presentation of the people's confession in 59:9-11 begins with a twofold basic statement of the confession in v. 9a, that "justice is far from us" in v. 9aα and that "righteousness does not reach us" in v. 9aβ. Verses 9b-11 then elaborate metaphorically by portraying the people walking in darkness with five successive assertions based on paired statements. The first in v. 9b indicates that the people hope for light but get darkness, including statements that they hope for light but get darkness in v. 9bα and that they hope for brilliance but walk in gloom in v. 9bβ. The second in v. 10a asserts that the people are blind, including statements that they grope like the blind along the wall in v. 10aα and that they grope like those without eyes in v. 10aβ. The third in v. 10b asserts that the people are like the dead, including statements that they stumble at noon as if in darkness in v. 10bα and that they are like the dead in v. 10bβ. The fourth in v. 11a asserts that the people growl and moan like bears and doves, including statements that "we growl like bears" in v. 11aα and that "we moan like doves" in v. 11aβ. The fifth in v. 11b asserts that the people hope for justice and righteousness but there is none, including statements that "we hope for justice, but there is none" in v. 11bα and that "righteousness is far from us" in v. 11bβ.

The second subunit in 59:12-15a explains the people's situation by stating that "our sins" and "our iniquities" are the cause. The basic explanation appears in v. 12a with a twofold statement that "many are our transgressions against you" in v. 12aα and that "our sins testify against us" in v. 12aβ. The elaborated explanation then follows in vv. 12b-15a, which asserts that "we know our sins and iniquities are the cause of the lack of justice and righteousness among us." Verses 12b-13 assert that the people know their iniquities. The basic assertion that "we know our transgressions and iniquities" appears in v. 12b, including statements that "our transgressions are with us" in v. 12bα and that "we know our iniquities" in v. 12bβ. A catalog of transgressions and iniquities then follows in v. 13, which includes rebellion against G-d in v. 13a, which in turn comprises rebellion and lying to YHWH in v. 13aα and turning away from G-d in v. 13aβ. The second segment of the catalog focuses on speaking fraud and treachery in v. 13bα, and the third focuses on teaching and uttering false words in v. 13bβ. Verses 14-15a then turn to the consequences that follow from the people's transgressions. The first segment in v. 14a asserts that justice and righteousness are turned aside, including the statement that justice is turned aside in v. 14aα and the statement that righteousness stands far away in v. 14aβ. The second segment in vv. 14b-15a focuses on the causes of the people's problems, that truth and integrity are lacking. Verse 14b basically states this assertion in two parts, including the statement that truth stumbles in the street in v. 14bα and that integrity is not able to enter in v. 14bβ. Verse 15a then states the results of this situation, that truth is lacking and those refraining from evil are plundered. This statement appears in two parts: that truth is lacking in v. 15aα and that anyone refraining from evil is plundered in v. 15aβ.

The second major segment of 59:1-21 appears in 59:15b-21, which constitutes the prophet's account of YHWH's response to the people's confession, that YHWH will deliver those who repent. The passage comprises four major sections which portray a progression of images that lead ultimately to YHWH's declaration of an everlasting covenant with those who repent.

The first appears in vv. 15b-16a, which indicate that YHWH saw that there was no justice. The segment includes two parts. The first in v. 15b indicates that YHWH sees and is displeased, including statements that YHWH sees and is displeased in v. 15bα and the basis for YHWH's displeasure, that there is no justice, in v. 15bβ. The second in v. 16 indicates that YHWH sees that no one approaches to deliver in righteousness. This segment includes the assertion that YHWH sees that no one approaches in v. 16a, including statements that YHWH sees that there is no man in v. 16aα and that YHWH observes that no one arrives in v. 16aβ. The second assertion in v. 16b indicates that there is no one to deliver righteousness, including statements that there is no one whose arm will deliver in v. 16bα and that there is no one whose righteousness supports him in v. 16bβ.

The second appears in v. 17, which indicates that YHWH dresses for battle to deal with the problems outlined above. This segment includes two subunits. The first in v. 17a asserts that YHWH dresses in righteousness, including a statement that YHWH dresses in righteous armor in v. 17aα and that a helmet of salvation is on YHWH's head in v. 17aβ. The second in v. 17b asserts that YHWH dresses for vengeance, including statements that YHWH dresses in garments of vengeance in v. 17bα and that YHWH dresses in a robe of zeal in v. 17bβ.

The third appears in vv. 18-20, which present YHWH's declaration that YHWH will repay foes and redeem Zion and Jacob. The passage appears as an oracle, including the presentation of YHWH's oracular declaration in vv. 18-20a and the concluding oracle formula in v. 20b. The oracular declaration in vv. 18-20a includes two basic components. The first is the declaration of requital to YHWH's enemies in v. 18, including statements that YHWH will repay foes according to their deeds in v. 18a and that YHWH will repay the deeds of enemies in the coastlands in v. 18b. The second in vv. 19-20a asserts that YHWH comes as a redeemer for Zion and Jacob. The first segment of this text in v. 19a asserts that the people will revere YHWH from west and east, including statements that they will revere YHWH's name from the west in v. 19aα and that they will revere YHWH's glory from the east in v. 19aβ. The second in vv. 19b-20a presents the basis for these assertions, that YHWH comes as a redeemer. Verse 19b asserts that YHWH comes like a wind-driven flood, including assertions that YHWH comes like a rushing river in v. 19bα and that the wind of YHWH drives it on in v. 19bβ. Verse 20a then asserts that YHWH comes as a redeemer to Zion and to those who repent in Jacob, including YHWH's role as redeemer to Zion in v. 20aα and to those who repent from transgressions in Jacob in v. 20aβ. As noted above, the oracle formula closes the subunit in v. 20b.

The fourth appears in v. 21 as a summary-appraisal form that asserts YHWH's eternal covenant with Zion and Jacob. The first segment of this section in v. 21aα constitutes the introduction to YHWH's promise, and the second segment in v. 21aβ-b presents the substance of YHWH's promise, YHWH's statement that "my spirit and words will never depart from you and your descendants."

Genre

Isaiah 59:1-21 constitutes the prophet's presentation of YHWH's response to the people's confession. Consequently, the passage is built around the people's CONFESSION OF SIN in 59:9-15a, although the CONFESSION does not constitute the entire unit. Rather, the prophet's presentation of the issue influences the overall generic character of the passage.

Isaiah 59:1-21 begins with prophetic INSTRUCTION concerning the people's iniquities as a barrier between them and YHWH. As an example of the INSTRUCTION genre, the passage offers guidance to the people concerning the impediments to their realization of a full relationship with YHWH. The behaviors identified in this passage tend to be general characterizations: the people pursue evil, they walk in darkness, they eat adder's eggs, they don't know the paths to peace, etc. The reader does not see specific sets of accusation; rather, the passage focuses on the general characterization of the people as the problematic figures in the relationship. The reader is left to search the broader context of the passage for hints of specific issues, such as the observance of Shabbat and YHWH's covenant in 56:1-8. Nevertheless, the interest in identifying the people as the culpable party in the relationship points to an underlying generic pattern in the prophet's INSTRUCTION: the PROPHETIC JUDGMENT SPEECH. Following the prophet's ANNOUNCEMENT concerning YHWH's capacity to deliver in v. 1, vv. 2-8 turn to an ANNOUNCEMENT of the people's iniquity which is patterned on the PROPHETIC JUDGMENT SPEECH. Verse 2 constitutes an ANNOUNCEMENT of the people's iniquity, i.e., their iniquities are a barrier between them and G-d and their sins prompt G-d to hide the divine face and refuse to hear them, which corresponds to the ANNOUNCEMENT OF JUDGMENT in the PROPHETIC JUDGMENT SPEECH. The basis for YHWH's refusal then follows in vv. 3-8 with an eleven-part delineation of the people's iniquities that prompt YHWH to refuse relationship with them. Such a passage corresponds closely with the PROPHETIC ANNOUNCEMENT of the BASIS FOR JUDGMENT in the PROPHETIC JUDGMENT SPEECH. In the present instance, the prophet's INSTRUCTION conveys the basis for YHWH's refusal to enter into relationship with the people, and it therefore provides the background for the following presentation of the people's CONFESSION OF SIN.

Isaiah 59:9-15a constitutes the prophet's presentation of the people's CONFESSION OF SIN. The basic Confession appears in v. 9a in the form of 1st-person plural statements by the people: "justice is far from us," and "righteousness does not reach us." In other words, the people admit that they lack justice and righteousness. Verses 9b-11 then elaborate on this Confession with a series of five METAPHORS that play on the motifs of the people walking in darkness (cf. 9:1) and the people's blindness (cf. ch. 6), and culminate in the absence of justice and righteousness among them. The explanation that the people's sins and iniquities are the cause of YHWH's refusal to enter into relationship with them constitutes a further example of the CONFESSION OF SIN in vv. 12-15a. Again, the Confession is basically stated in v. 12a with 1st-person plural statements in which the people assert that "many are our transgressions against you," and "our sins testify against us." The elaborated explanation in vv. 12b-15a likewise expands upon the Confession genre with a combination of statements in vv. 12b-13 that the people know their iniquities, including both the statement per se in v. 12b and a short catalog in v. 13 of the transgressions and iniquities of the people. Verses 14-15a again show the influence of the prophetic ANNOUNCEMENT OF JUDGMENT by pointing to the consequences of the people's behavior: justice and righteousness are turned aside in v. 14a and truth and integrity are lacking in vv. 14b-15a.

The prophet's account of YHWH's response, that YHWH will deliver those who repent, in 59:15b-21 is built around a PROPHETIC ANNOUNCEMENT OF SALVATION in vv. 18-20. The first portions of the passage appear as notices of YHWH's observation that there was no justice among the people in vv. 15b-16 and that YHWH dresses for battle in v. 17 prior to acting to redeem the righteous. The key generic element then appears in vv. 18-20 with an ORACLE that constitutes a PROPHETIC ANNOUNCEMENT OF SALVATION for the righteous. The oracular character of this text is evident in the appearance of the concluding ORACLE FORMULA in v. 20b, *nĕ'um yhwh*, "oracle of YHWH," which concludes and characterizes the passage. The ORACLE per se appears in vv. 18-20a, which declare YHWH's requital or punishment of enemies in v. 18 and YHWH's role as redeemer for Zion and those who repent in Jacob in vv. 19-20a. The passage concludes with the SUMMARY-APPRAISAL form in v. 21, which summarizes the process outlined in the passage as the establishment of YHWH's eternal covenant with Zion and Jacob. Here YHWH promises that "my spirit and words will never depart from you," i.e., the righteous among Zion and Jacob, nor will they depart from their descendants.

Setting

Isaiah 59:1-21 is closely tied into the prophet's instruction concerning the proper observance of YHWH's covenant in chs. 56–59. Some interpreters have argued that 59:1-21 and 58:1-14 are two segments of the same passage (see Polan, *In the Ways*, 243-319; Steck, *Studien zu Tritojesaja*, 177-82; Seitz, "Isaiah 40–66," 498-503), but the full literary context includes the entire block of chs. 56–59. These passages are concerned throughout with proper observance of YHWH's covenant, particularly Shabbat, although the general language of justice and righteousness supports observance of all of YHWH's Torah or instruction to the people. Such an interest then provides the foundation for the passage's rhetorical agenda to persuade the people to observe YHWH's covenant and thereby earn YHWH's protection by being counted among the righteous.

Isaiah 59:1-21 presupposes the social setting of the Jerusalem temple. The prophet's presentation of the people's confession and the explanation of that confession in vv. 9-15a point to this conclusion. The temple is the holy center of creation and of Israel, and it thereby serves as the locus at which human beings are expected to take action when their failure to observe the divine will compromises the sanctity of the temple, creation, and the nation itself. Such action comes in the form of confession of sins, the presentation of offerings at the temple altar, and the resulting efforts of the people to ensure that they live in conformance with divine instruction. The organization of the passage makes this agenda clear. Within the prophet's presentation of the people's confession in vv. 1-15a, the first part of the passage in vv. 1-8 identifies the iniquities that the people need to address together with YHWH's capacity to deliver, whereas vv. 9-15a present both the confession proper in vv. 9-11 and an explanation in vv. 12-15a that the people's iniquities are the cause of the lack of justice and righteousness in the land. The presentation of YHWH's response in vv. 15b-21 reiterates the problems identified in the first portions of the passage and then asserts YHWH's capacity to deliver those in Zion and Jacob (Israel) who are righteous. Such assertions serve as a means to motivate a positive response from the people to YHWH's expectations of observance. The concluding summary-appraisal in v. 21 emphasizes YHWH's intent to conclude an eternal covenant with those in Zion and Jacob who are righteous, therefore reinforcing the rhetorical agenda of the passage to secure the observance of the people. The liturgical character of other elements in chs. 56–59 suggests that 59:1-21 constitutes part of a prophetic liturgy designed for performance in the Jerusalem temple. Although some claim that 59:17-19 is an editorial insertion meant to form a redactional envelope with 63:1-6 around chs. 60–62, the structure analysis indicates that it is an integral part of 59:1-21. It does aid in advancing the argument of chs. 56–66 that YHWH will deliver the righteous and punish the wicked.

The central role of the people's confession in this passage could point to any historical setting in which the temple would be featured, but interpreters must recognize that the emphasis on confession corresponds well to the period of Nehemiah and Ezra in the late 5th and early 4th centuries B.C.E. The building of the temple in 520-515 could provide the context for the prophet's interest in the people's confession, but the sources concerning the building of the temple in Haggai, Zechariah, and Ezra-Nehemiah appear to celebrate the building of the temple rather than focus on the people's sins. The presentation of Nehemiah and Ezra, however, presupposes an effort to purge the people of wrongdoing by reading the Torah publically before them in Nehemiah 8–10 and then enforcing the observance of the Torah's provisions. The goal of Nehemiah's and especially Ezra's reforms was to create a cohesive and holy Jewish community in Jerusalem and Judah whose identity and practice would be based upon YHWH's torah. The efforts to enforce observance of the Shabbat and the holidays, to move one-tenth of the population into the city, and to prohibit intermarriage without conversion, were ways to build the identity of the community based upon YHWH's torah. The emphasis on the people's confession in ch. 59 would play an appropriate role in any efforts to secure the people's observance of YHWH's torah as the basis for Nehemiah's and Ezra's reforms. Such efforts would then help to secure the role of the Jerusalem temple as the holy center of creation and the people of Israel and Judah in the early Persian period.

Interpretation

The prophet's presentation of YHWH's response to the people's confession in 59:1-21 is designed to persuade the people that they should repent and turn to YHWH and thereby be counted among the righteous who will be granted YHWH's eternal covenant. The means by which they will achieve their repentance is to confess their sins in the context of the now-rebuilt Jerusalem temple and thereby to rededicate themselves to YHWH and support of YHWH's temple.

The prophet's presentation of the people's confession in 59:1-15a serves this agenda well. The prophet's instruction concerning the people's iniquities in vv. 1-8 serves as a means to identify the people as sinful and therefore requiring repentance and return to YHWH. The passage begins with an enticement in v. 1 which focuses on YHWH's capacity to deliver. Such a statement stands as an incentive to the people to accept the claims made in this passage, that YHWH has the capacity to deliver and will do so if the people follow the recommendations laid out in this passage. The announcement concerning the people's iniquity in

vv. 2-8 establishes the basis for the claim that the people need to repent. Again, this subunit begins with a twofold statement in v. 2 that functions as incentive to the people: "your iniquities are a barrier between you and YHWH" (v. 2a) and "your sins prompt YHWH to hide the divine face from you and refuse to listen to you" (v. 2b). Such statements actually complement those in v. 1. Whereas v. 1 presents positive incentive, v. 2 presents negative incentive. Verses 3-8 then specify the people's sins, but they do so in a very general manner that suggests flaws in their worldview and practice in daily life rather than specific sets of charges. Thus, the people are charged with having been defiled, speaking dishonestly, lacking justice, relying on falsehood, giving birth to trouble, acting uselessly, etc. There is no real, corroborating evidence to sustain these charges; rather, they appear to be statements of principle. Indeed, interpreters must bear in mind the perspective of the text that charges the people with these shortcomings as a means to justify its call for repentance. Many interpreters take such charges at face value, but there is little basis to do so insofar as the charges function primarily to sustain a persuasive agenda in this text.

The prophet's presentation of the people's confession in vv. 9-15a further serves the persuasive agenda of this text by placing words in the mouths of the people that are intended to illustrate the contention that they need to confess and repent. Verses 9-11 present a confession in which the people assert in v. 9a that they lack justice and righteousness. Verses 9b-11 elaborate on this assertion by portraying the people metaphorically as walking in darkness as if they are blind. The assertions made in vv. 9b-11 must be viewed in intertextual perspective. The assertion that the people walk in darkness in v. 9b relates intertextually to 9:1(NRSV 9:2), in which the people walking in darkness now see a bright light in the form of a new Davidic king (see also 42:7, 16). Insofar as Deutero- and Trito-Isaiah lack such a king, the present context entails that the restoration of the temple and the people's return to YHWH as the true king (see 66:1) constitute the true fulfillment of Isaiah's oracle. Likewise, the claim that the people are blind and groping along a wall in v. 10a recalls Isaiah's commission from YHWH in 6:9-10 to render the people blind, deaf, and dumb so that the people would not repent and thereby thwart YHWH's efforts to be recognized as G-d of all creation. It also recalls Deutero-Isaiah's repeated calls for the people to open their eyes, ears, and minds and to perceive that YHWH has accomplished the purposes originally outlined in the first part of the book (see, e.g., 42:7, 16, 18-20; 43:8). The reference to "the people of the dead in a time of darkness" in 59:10b recalls Isaiah's critiques of the people for consulting the dead on behalf of the living and thereby denying them the possibility to see the light of dawn (8:17-23[NRSV 8:16–9:1]). The reference to the growling of bears and the murmuring of doves recalls the growling of a lion that does not deter YHWH in 31:4 and the murmuring of the heart in anticipation of the king in 33:17-18. The hope for justice and righteousness in 59:11b is a theme that underlies the entire book of Isaiah (e.g., 1:17, 27; 9:6[NRSV 7]; 28:17; 42:1, 3, 4; 49:4; 56:1; 58:2; 61:8; Rendtorff, "Isaiah 56:1"). The explanation that the people's sins are the cause of their lack of justice in vv. 12-15a reinforces the view that they require repentance. The passage portrays the people as stating that their many sins testify against them in v. 12a, and the elaboration in vv. 12b-15a develops this point by painting a picture of the people as recognizing that their own iniquities explain their lack of justice and righteousness. The catalog of iniquities in v. 13 — rebellion against G-d, speaking fraud and treachery, and teaching and uttering false words — is expressed in general terms. Likewise, vv. 14-15a portray the lack of justice and righteousness in equally general terms, building the case that the people need to repent on principle; specific sins do not appear.

Finally, the prophet's account of YHWH's response in 59:15b-21 brings the argument home by asserting that YHWH will act to deliver those who repent. Such a claim constitutes the epitome of motivation for those addressed in this passage. The passage begins in vv. 15b-16 with assertions that YHWH sees that there is no justice and is displeased by its absence and sees that no one approaches to do anything about this situation. And so the groundwork is laid for the claim that YHWH must act on behalf of the righteous, i.e., those who repent, because no one else is prepared to do so. Verse 17 portrays YHWH dressing for battle as a means to certify that YHWH will act — and so the people had best repent. Verses 18-20 present YHWH's oracular declaration that YHWH will repay foes and enemies according to their deeds. The assertion that YHWH comes as redeemer for Zion and Jacob reinforces the argument of the passage that the people must repent, and it envisions the people as greater than only Jerusalem by including Jacob, the ancestor of all the tribes of Israel, in the scenario of repentance and deliverance. The portrayal of YHWH's approach like a rushing river pushed on by the winds highlights YHWH's role as creator to give greater credence to the claims of deliverance. The concluding statement in v. 20a reiterates that YHWH will redeem Zion and all who repent in Jacob as a means of encouraging the people to accept the claims of the passage and turn to YHWH and the temple for repentance and validation. The oracle formula in v. 20b aids in certifying that these claims come from YHWH. Verse 21, the final element in the passage, summarizes YHWH's promise of an eternal covenant for Zion and Jacob, thereby underscoring the promises of ch. 55 which asserted that the eternal Davidic covenant would be applied to all Israel. The promise appears here as well, underscoring the appeal to repent and to support the temple, thereby to be counted among the righteous.

Bibliography

B. Gosse, "Les introductions des Psaumes 93–94 et Isaïe 59,15b-20," *ZAW* 106 (1994) 303-6; P. D. Hanson, *The Dawn of Apocalyptic,* 119-34; D. Kendall, "The Use of *Mišpat* in Isaiah 59," *ZAW* 96 (1984) 391-405; K. Koenen, *Ethik und Eschatologie,* 59-76; K. Pauritzsch, *Die neue Gemeinde,* 87-103; G. J. Polan, *In the Ways of Justice,* 243-75; A. Rofé, "Isaiah 59:19 and Trito-Isaiah's Vision of Redemption," in Vermeylen, ed., *The Book of Isaiah/Le livre d'Isaïe,* 407-10; idem, "The Piety of the Torah-Disciples and the Winding-up of the Hebrew Bible: Josh 1:8; Ps 1:2; Isa 59:21," in *Bibel in jüdischer und christlicher Tradition (Fest.* J. Maier; ed. H. Merklein, K. Müller, and G. Sternberger; Frankfurt am Main: Hain, 1993) 78-85; S. Sekine, *Die tritojesajanische Sammlung,* 136-39; P. A. Smith, *Rhetoric and Redaction,* 97-128; O. H. Steck, *Studien zu Tritojesaja,* 169-86, 187-91, 203-9.

PROPHETIC ANNOUNCEMENT OF
RESTORATION FOR JERUSALEM 60:1–62:12

Structure

I. Prophet's presentation of YHWH's words to Zion: return of Zion's exiles and restoration of Zion	60:1-22
II. Prophet's presentation of the words of the speech of the anointed priest concerning the restoration of Zion	61:1–62:12

Isaiah 60–62 has long been recognized as a discrete unit within Trito-Isaiah (Stromberg, *Isaiah after Exile,* 11-13). The passage is clearly demarcated by the initial announcement in 60:1, "Arise, shine, for your light has come," the focus throughout on Zion's restoration, and the concluding announcements in 62:10-12 concerning the arrival of the deliverer and the restoration of Zion. Isaiah 63:1 begins a new unit that focuses on YHWH's return from victory over Edom. The basic structure of the passage is easily established by the prophet's presentations of the words of two different speakers: YHWH's words to Zion in 60:1-22 and the speech of the anointed priest in 61:1–62:12. The two subunits are interrelated by the role played by the priest in the temple as spokesperson to the people on behalf of YHWH: YHWH makes the initial announcement of Zion's restoration and the priest reiterates and elaborates upon YHWH's words.

Genre

The overarching genre of chs. 60–62 is the PROPHETIC ANNOUNCEMENT OF SALVATION. Insofar as the genre is derived from an earlier priestly form (Westermann, *Prophetic Oracles of Salvation,* 39-66), perhaps from oracular inquiry, the passage employs the anointed priest as speaker in chs. 61–62.

Setting

The unit presupposes the dedication of the rebuilt Jerusalem temple and the ordination of Joshua ben Jehozadak as high priest of the temple in 515 B.C.E. (see Ezra 1–6; Haggai; Zechariah 1–6, esp. Zechariah 3). For detailed discussion, see below.

Interpretation

The passage announces restoration for Zion as a result of the restoration of the Jerusalem temple. The passage was composed to celebrate the rebuilding and dedication of the temple in the 6th century B.C.E. It thereby serves as the literary culmination of the 6th-century edition of the book of Isaiah. It functions redactionally as a means to hold First and Second Isaiah together, especially with reference to its portrayals of YHWH and the exiles returning to Jerusalem in 62:10-12 (cf. 11:15-16; 27:12-13; 35:1-10; 49:22-23; see Kiesow, *Exodustexte im Jesajabuch;* Steck, "Tritojesaja im Jesajabuch," in *Studien zu Tritojesaja*, 1-45; idem, "Die Heimkehr Redaktion des Jesajabuches in Tritojesaja," in *Studien zu Tritojesaja*, 143-66). For detailed discussion, see below.

Bibliography

C. J. Dempsey, "From Desolation to Delight: The Transformative Vision of Isaiah 60–62," in Everson and Kim, eds., *The Desert Will Bloom*, 217-32; K. Kiesow, *Exodustexte im Jesajabuch;* O. H. Steck, "Die Heimkehr Redaktion des Jesajabuches in Tritojesaja," in *Studien zu Tritojesaja*, 143-66; idem, "Tritojesaja im Jesajabuch," in *Studien zu Tritojesaja*, 1-45; J. Stromberg, *Isaiah after Exile*, 11-13; C. Westermann, *Prophetic Oracles of Salvation in the Old Testament* (tr. K. R. Crim; Louisville: Westminster John Knox, 1991).

THE PROPHET'S PRESENTATION OF YHWH'S WORDS TO ZION: RETURN OF ZION'S EXILES AND RESTORATION OF ZION 60:1-22

Structure

I. Prophet's address to Zion: rise and see shining presence of YHWH 60:1-3
  A. Call to attention: rise to see shining presence of YHWH   60:1
    1. Command to Zion to rise and shine   60:1aα
    2. Twofold basis for command: shining presence of YHWH   60:1aβ-b
      a. Your light has come   60:1aβ
      b. Presence/glory of YHWH shines upon you   60:1b
  B. Elaboration concerning the nations: darkness turns to light   60:2-3
    1. Darkness in the world   60:2a
      a. Darkness covers the earth   60:2aα
      b. Deep darkness covers the nations   60:2aβ
    2. YHWH shines upon you   60:2b
      a. YHWH shines upon you   60:2bα
      b. YHWH's glory/presence appears over you   60:2bβ
    3. Result: nations and kings shall walk to your light   60:3
      a. Nations shall walk to your light   60:3a
      b. Kings shall walk to your shining brilliance   60:3b
II. Presentation of YHWH's address to Zion: announcement of
    Zion's restoration   60:4-22
  A. Command to Zion to see the approach of children and
    wealth from the nations   60:4-7
    1. Command to see approach of children   60:4
      a. Command proper   60:4aα
      b. Approach of children from afar   60:4aβ-b

1) Approach   60:4aβ
   a) All of them are gathered   60:4aβ$^{1\text{-}2}$
   b) They come to you   60:4aβ$^{3\text{-}4}$
2) Specification of approach: sons and daughters   60:4b
   a) Your sons come from afar   60:4bα
   b) Your daughters are secure on the hip   60:4bβ
2. You will see the wealth of the nations come to you   60:5-7
  a. You will see and shine with amazement   60:5
    1) Basically stated   60:5a
      a) You will see and shine   60:5aα
      b) You will stand in awe and swell   60:5aβ
    2) Basis for reaction: wealth of sea and nations will
       come to you   60:5b
      a) Riches of the sea will be turned over to you   60:5bα
      b) Wealth of the nations will come to you   60:5bβ
  b. Elaboration concerning wealth of nations   60:6-7
    1) Approach of caravans from afar   60:6
      a) Dust clouds from dromedaries of Midian and
        Ephah will cover you   60:6aα
      b) All of them come from Sheba   60:6aβ
      c) They bear gold and frankincense   60:6bα
      d) They proclaim the praises of YHWH   60:6bβ
    2) Flocks from afar will become offerings for the temple   60:7
      a) Flocks of Kedar will be gathered for you   60:7aα
      b) Rams of Nebaioth will serve you   60:7aβ
      c) They will go up with favor upon my altar   60:7bα
      d) I will glorify my beautiful temple   60:7bβ
B. Announcement of the restoration of Zion   60:8-18
  1. Concerning the approach of the coastlands   60:8-12
    a. Rhetorical question: assertion of coastlands' approach
      to YHWH   60:8
      1) Simile: who are these who fly by cloud?   60:8a
      2) Simile: who are these who fly to their shelter?   60:8b
    b. Approach proper and results   60:9-12
      1) Coastlands approach   60:9
       a) Coastlands look to YHWH   60:9aα
        (1) Coastlands anticipate YHWH   60:9aα$^{1\text{-}4}$
        (2) Ships of Tarshish are in the lead   60:9aα$^{5\text{-}7}$
       b) Purposes   60:9aβ-b
        (1) To bring your sons and wealth from afar   60:9aβ
         (a) To bring your sons from afar   60:9aβ$^{1\text{-}3}$
         (b) To bring gold and silver with them   60:9aβ$^{4\text{-}6}$
        (2) For YHWH   60:9b
         (a) For the Name of YHWH your G-d   60:9bα
         (b) For the Holy One of Israel who glorifies you   60:9bβ
      2) Results: nations will rebuild walls and your gates
       will remain open   60:10-12

a) Nations will rebuild your walls and kings will
   serve you   60:10

   (1) Basically stated   60:10a

     (a) Nations will rebuild your walls   60:10aα

     (b) Kings will serve you   60:10aβ

   (2) Reasons: YHWH's atonement   60:10b

     (a) In anger I struck you   60:10bα

     (b) In favor I show you mercy   60:10bβ

b) Your gates shall always remain open to admit
   wealth and kings   60:11-12

   (1) Basically stated   60:11

     (a) Gates remain open   60:11a

       α. Your gates will always remain open   60:11aα

       β. Day and night they will not be shut   60:11aβ

     (b) Purposes: admit wealth of nations and kings 60:11b

       α. To admit the wealth of the nations   60:11bα

       β. To admit kings in procession   60:11bβ

   (2) Qualification: those nations and kings who
     refuse will be destroyed   60:12

     (a) The nation or kingdom that does not serve
       you will perish   60:12a

     (b) (These) nations will surely be destroyed 60:12b

2. Portrayal of Zion's restoration   60:13-18

  a. Glory of Lebanon shall come to restore YHWH's temple 60:13

   1) Glory/trees of Lebanon shall come to you   60:13a

   2) Purpose: to beautify and glorify temple   60:13b

    a) To beautify the place of my sanctuary   60:13bα

    b) So that I might glorify the place of my feet 60:13bβ

  b. Results: Zion's restoration   60:14-18

   1) You will be called the City of YHWH   60:14

    a) Enemies will approach you prostrate   60:14a

     (1) The sons of your oppressors will come bowing
       to you   60:14aα

     (2) All your tormentors will bow at the soles of
       your feet   60:14aβ

    b) Result: they will call you City of David and Zion
     of the Holy One of Israel   60:14b

     (1) City of David   60:14bα

     (2) Zion of the Holy One of Israel   60:14bβ

   2) You will know that I am YHWH your deliverer and
    redeemer   60:15-16

    a) Statement of reversal   60:15

     (1) Protasis: whereas you were abandoned and hated 60:15a

     (2) Apodosis: I will make you a pride and joy 60:15b

      (a) Eternal pride   60:15bα

      (b) Eternal joy   60:15bβ

    b) Elaboration of good fortune   60:16

Isaiah 60:1-22 constitutes the prophet's presentation of YHWH's words to Zion concerning the return of Zion's exiles and the restoration of Zion. Although it includes a major speech by YHWH in vv. 4-22, the prophet's words in 60:1-3 and 60:19-20 indicate that the unit is formulated as the prophet's presentation of YHWH's speech. The unit is demarcated at the outset by the prophet's feminine singular address to Zion in vv. 1-3, which also refers to YHWH in the 3rd-person masculine singular form. The 1st-person statements and 2nd-feminine singular address forms throughout vv. 4-22 identify the speech by YHWH conveyed by the prophet. Insofar as YHWH's speech focuses on the return of Zion's children and her restoration, the speech must be recognized as YHWH's address to Zion concerning her restoration. YHWH's statement in v. 22, "I, YHWH, will hasten it in its time," provides an appropriate culmination for YHWH's speech. The 1st-person speech beginning in 61:1 employs 2nd-masculine plural address forms and again refers to YHWH in 3rd-person form. Isaiah 61:1 therefore also signals the concluding demarcation of 60:1-22 by introducing a new subunit.

Isaiah 60:1-3 constitutes the first major subunit of 60:1-22. It appears as the prophet's address to Zion to rise and see the shining presence of YHWH. The introductory feminine singular imperatives, *qûmî 'ôrî*, "arise, shine," together with the overall 2nd-feminine singular address forms and the 3rd-person references to YHWH identify this subunit as the prophet's address to Zion. Although vv. 1-3 do not explicitly identify Zion as the addressee, the references to Zion in v. 14, "my altar" in v. 7, and "my sanctuary" in v. 13 indicate that Zion is the addressee. The identification of the prophet as the speaker is achieved by recognizing Zion as the addressee and YHWH as a 3rd-person referent within the address.

Isaiah 60:1-3 comprises two major subunits. The first is the call to attention form in v. 1, which begins with the above-noted feminine singular imperatives and address forms. The command to Zion to rise and shine appears in v. 1aα, and the twofold basis for the command, introduced by the particle *kî,* "for, because," then follows in v. 1aβ-b. The basis for the command focuses on the imagery of the shining presence of YHWH in two statements, that "your light has come" in v. 1aβ and that "the presence or glory of YHWH shines upon you" in v. 1b. Verses 2-3 then constitute the second element of the passage by elaborating on the metaphorical identification of YHWH's presence as light. The passage again begins with a causative *kî,* which establishes the syntactical relationship with v. 1, and then proceeds with three elements, all of which are joined by *wāw*'s, that define the sequence of the metaphorical imagery. The first in v. 2a focuses on the metaphor of darkness in the world as a means to prepare the reader for the emergence of YHWH's presence. Verse 2a includes two elements, the portrayal of darkness covering the earth in v. 2aα and the portrayal of deep darkness covering the nations in v. 2aβ. The second element in v. 2b focuses on the metaphor of "YHWH shining upon you," including statements that "YHWH shines upon you" in v. 2bα and that "YHWH's glory or presence appears over you" in v. 2bβ. The third element in v. 3 focuses on the result of the sequence presented thus far, an assertion that "nations and kings shall walk to your light," including statements that "the nations shall walk to your light" in v. 3a and that "kings shall walk to your shining brilliance" in v. 3b.

Altogether, the prophet's address to Zion in vv. 1-3 prepares the reader for the presentation of YHWH's address in vv. 4-22.

The prophet's presentation of YHWH's address to Zion concerning her restoration then follows in 60:4-22. Although the bulk of the passage is formulated with 1st-person subject pronouns and 2nd-feminine singular object pronouns to indicate the addressee, vv. 19-20 break the sequence with 3rd-person references to YHWH, indicating that the prophet speaks in these verses as the voice that conveys YHWH's speech to the reader. The formal structure of the subunit comprises three major elements, each of which is syntactically discrete within the larger structure of the passage and internally coherent on both syntactic and thematic grounds. The first is the command to Zion to see the approach of her children and wealth from the nations in vv. 4-7. The second is the announcement of the restoration of Zion in vv. 8-18. And the third is the prophet's presentation of YHWH's promise of eternal possession of the land of Israel in vv. 19-22. Altogether, these three elements constitute the prophet's presentation of YHWH's address to Zion announcing her restoration.

Isaiah 60:4-7 constitutes the first element in the sequence as the command to Zion to see the approach of her children and wealth from the nations. The subunit builds a sense of suspense as it prepares for the following announcement of restoration by portraying the approaching children and the nations bearing wealth. The passage begins with the feminine singular imperative command to see the approach of the children in v. 4. The command proper, formulated with feminine singular imperative verbs, "raise *(śĕ'î)* round about your eyes and see *(rĕ'î),*" appears in v. 4aα. Verse 4aβ-b then follows by defining the object of the command: to see the approach of children from afar. Verse 4aβ defines the approach proper with two elements: the statement that "all of them are gathered" in v. 4aβ$^{1-2}$ and the statement that "they come to you" in v. 4aβ$^{3-4}$. Verse 4b then specifies the approach by pointing specifically to the sons and daughters, including statements that "your sons come from afar" in v. 4bα and that "your daughters are secure on the hip," indicating a means of carrying children on the hips, in v. 4bβ.

The second element focuses on Zion's viewing of the wealth of the nations coming to her in vv. 5-7. This segment is joined syntactically to v. 4 by the introductory particle *'az,* "then," which indicates that vv. 4 and 5-7 together form the elements of the larger subunit in 60:4-7. The subunit then comprises two components. The first is the focus on the assertion that "you will see and shine with amazement at the sight of the approaching children and wealth" in v. 5. This assertion is basically stated in v. 5a in two parts: "you will see and shine" in v. 5aα and "you will stand in awe and swell" in v. 5aβ. The basis for this reaction, that "the wealth of the sea and the nations will come to you," then

303

follows in v. 5b in two parts: the statement that "the riches of the sea will be turned over to you" in v. 5bα and the statement that "the wealth of the nations will come to you" in v. 5bβ. The second element is the elaboration on the wealth of the nations in vv. 6-7. This subunit comprises two elements. The first in v. 6 focuses on the approach of the caravans from afar in four statements: "the dust clouds from the dromedaries of Midian and Ephah will cover you" in v. 6aα; "all of them come from Sheba" in v. 6aβ; "they bear gold and frankincense" in v. 6bα; and "they proclaim the praises of YHWH" in v. 6bβ. The second in v. 7 focuses on the flocks from afar that will become offerings to YHWH for the temple. Again, this element includes four statements: "the flocks of Kedar will be gathered to you" in v. 7aα; "the rams of Nebaioth will serve you" in v. 7aβ; "they will go up with favor upon my altar" in v. 7bα; and "I will glorify my beautiful temple" in v. 7bβ.

Isaiah 60:8-18 then presents the centerpiece of the unit with YHWH's announcement concerning the restoration of Zion. The subunit includes two major components, each of which is defined by a combination of theme and syntactical features. The first focuses on the approach of the coastlands in vv. 8-12, and the second focuses on the portrayal of Zion's restoration in vv. 13-18.

Isaiah 60:8-12 focuses on the approach of the coastlands as part of the larger concern with the restoration of Zion in vv. 8-18. The subunit comprises two basic elements. The first is the rhetorical question in v. 8 which asserts that the coastlands are approaching YHWH. The question includes two parts: the metaphorical question "who are those that fly by cloud?" in v. 8a and the metaphorical question, "who are these who fly to their shelter?" in v. 8b.

The second is the focus on the approach proper and its results in vv. 9-12. This subunit begins with the approach of the coastlands in v. 9, in two parts. The first is the assertion that the coastlands look to YHWH in v. 9aα, including assertions that the coastlands anticipate YHWH in v. 9aα$^{1-4}$ and that the ships of Tarshish are in the lead in v. 9aα$^{5-7}$. Verse 9aβ-b then focuses on the purposes of the coastlands' approach, in two parts. The first purpose is "to bring your sons and wealth from afar" in v. 9aβ, including statements that the purpose is "to bring your sons from afar" in v. 9aβ$^{1-3}$ and "to bring gold and silver with them" in v. 9aβ$^{4-6}$. The second purpose is that the approach is done for YHWH in v. 9b, including statements that "it is done for the Name of YHWH your G-d" in v. 9bα and that "it is done for the Holy One of Israel who glorifies you" in v. 9bβ. The second basic element of the subunit appears in vv. 10-12, which discuss the results of the coastlands' approach: "the nations will rebuild your walls and the gates of the city will remain open." This subunit includes two elements. The first element is v. 10, which asserts that "the nations will rebuild your walls and kings will serve you." This is basically stated in v. 10a with statements that "the nations will rebuild your walls" in v. 10aα and that "kings will serve you" in v. 10aβ. Verse 10b presents the reasons for these assertions in relation to YHWH's atonement for past punishment of Jerusalem, including YHWH's statements that "in anger I struck you" in v. 10bα and "in favor I show you mercy" in v. 10bβ. The second element is vv. 11-12, which asserts that "your gates shall always remain open to admit wealth and kings." This is basically stated in v. 11 in two parts. The first part in v. 11a asserts that the gates will remain open, including two parts, that "your gates will always remain open" in v. 11aα and that "day and night they will not be shut" in v. 11aβ. The second part in v. 11b defines the purposes of the open gate: to admit the wealth of nations and kings, including statements that "they will admit the wealth of the nations" in v. 11bα and that "they will admit the kings in procession" in v. 11bβ. The second part in v. 12 qualifies v. 11 by specifying that those nations and kings who refuse will be destroyed, including statements that "the nation or kingdom that does not serve you will perish" in v. 12a and that "(these) nations will surely be destroyed" in v. 12b.

Isaiah 60:13-18 focuses on the portrayal of Zion's restoration. The basic thesis of this subunit appears in v. 13, which asserts that the glory of Lebanon shall come to restore YHWH's temple. Verse 13a asserts that "the glory or trees of Lebanon shall come to you," and v. 13b asserts in two parts that their purpose is to beautify and glorify the temple, "to beautify the place of my sanctuary" in v. 13bα and "so that I might glorify the place of my feet" in v. 13bβ.

Isaiah 60:14-18 then defines the results of this move with a portrayal of Zion's restoration, in three parts. The first in v. 14 asserts that "you will be called the City of YHWH." This part includes an announcement that "enemies will approach you prostrate" in v. 14a, including statements that "the sons of your oppressors will come bowing to you" in v. 14aα and that "all of your tormentors will bow at the soles of your feet" in v. 14aβ. Verse 14b then describes the result, that "they will call you the City of David and Zion of the Holy One of Israel," including statements that "they will call you the City of David" in v. 14bα and that "they will call you Zion of the Holy One of Israel" in v. 14bβ.

The second part of vv. 14-18 is vv. 15-16, which employs the recognition formula "you will know that I am YHWH your deliverer and redeemer." The first element of this subunit is v. 15 which presents a statement of reversal to portray Jerusalem's reversal of fortune. The protasis in v. 15a begins with a "whereas" clause, "whereas you were abandoned and hated," and the apodosis in v. 15b asserts that "I will make you a pride and joy," including eternal pride in v. 15bα and eternal joy in v. 15bβ. Verse 16 then elaborates in two parts on Zion's good fortune. The first in v. 16a asserts that "you will suck the breasts of nations and kings," including sucking the milk of nations in v. 16aα and sucking the breasts of kings in v. 16aβ. The second in v. 16b presents the recognition formula to portray the outcome: "you will know that I am YHWH," including "YHWH your deliverer" in v. 16bα and "the Mighty One of Jacob your redeemer" in v. 16bβ.

The third part of vv. 14-18 appears in 60:17-18, which portrays peace for Jerusalem as the culmination of the subunit. It includes two parts. The first is the portrayal of peace and righteousness for Jerusalem in v. 17. Verse 17 begins with a statement of reversal to portray the reversal of Jerusalem's fortunes with four statements, including "instead of copper, I bring gold" in v. 17aα; "instead of iron, I bring silver" in v. 17aβ; "instead of wood, I bring bronze" in v. 17aγ; and "instead of stones, I bring iron" in v. 17aδ. Verse 17b describes the results of the reversal, i.e., peace and righteousness for Jerusalem, in two parts: "I will appoint peace as your punishment" in v. 17bα and "I will appoint righteousness as your oppressors" in v. 17bβ. Verse 18 then elaborates on the results by portraying the deliverance and praise due to Jerusalem. It begins with an assertion in v. 18a that there will be no more violence, plunder, and injury in the city, including statements that "there will be no more violence in our land" in v. 18aα and that "there will be no more plunder or injury in our borders" in v. 18aβ. Verse 18b then closes with a portrayal of deliverance and praise: "you shall call your walls deliverance" in v. 18bα and "you shall call your gates praise" in v. 18bβ.

The third and final element of 60:4-22 is vv. 19-22, in which the prophet presents YHWH's promise for eternal possession of the land. The subunit includes two basic elements identified by speaker. The first is the prophet's portrayal of YHWH as the eternal light for Jerusalem in vv. 19-20. This passage begins in v. 19 with the prophet's assertion that there is no need for sun or moon as YHWH is Jerusalem's eternal light. The assertion that there is no need for sun or moon appears in v. 19a in two parts: that there is no need for sun by day in v. 19aα and that there is no need for moon by night in v. 19aβ. The assertion in v. 19b that YHWH will serve as light and beauty for Jerusalem likewise appears in two parts: that "YHWH will be eternal light" in v. 19bα and that "YHWH will be your beauty" in v. 19bβ. Verse 20 then describes the results, that because YHWH is eternal light for Jerusalem, mourning in the city is ended. Verse 20a asserts that sun and moon will not set, including assertions that the sun will set no more in v. 20aα and that the moon will not set in v. 20aβ. Verse 20b defines the reason for such phenomena: that YHWH is eternal light, including statements in v. 20bα that YHWH is eternal light and in v. 20bβ that mourning is ended. YHWH's speech then emerges in vv. 21-22 with YHWH's promise of eternal possession of the land, in four parts. The first in v. 21a asserts that the people will possess the land forever, including statements in v. 21aα that "all your people will be righteous or innocent" and in v. 21aβ that "they will possess the land forever." The second in v. 21b asserts that "they are my planting and work," including statements by YHWH that "they are my planting" in v. 21bα and that "they are the beautiful work of my hand" in v. 21bβ. The third in v. 22a takes up the reversal of Jerusalem's status, including statements in v. 22aα that the smallest will become a thousand and in v. 22aβ that the youngest will become a strong nation. The fourth and final statement that concludes the entire unit appears in v. 22b with YHWH's promise that "I will make it happen quickly."

Genre

Most interpreters correctly follow Westermann (*Isaiah 40–66*, 356) in understanding 60:1-22 as a PROPHETIC ANNOUNCEMENT OF SALVATION. Such an observation is based on the recognition that the passage anticipates the return of Babylonian exiles to Jerusalem and the consequent restoration of Zion and the Jerusalem temple. The PROPHETIC ANNOUNCEMENT OF SALVATION typically includes a proclamation of deliverance or restoration followed by a blessing. The ANNOUNCEMENT OF SALVATION appears in vv. 8-18, and the BLESSING, which in this instance constitutes the prophet's presentation of YHWH's promise of the land, appears in vv. 19-22. In the present instance, the BLESSING lacks the frequent term *bārûk*, "blessed," but this term is not always necessary to the form.

Rather, the content of the genre is determinative. In this case, YHWH's promise of support and the land for the people constitutes the basis for the BLESSING.

A number of other genres also appear within 60:1-22. The first is the CALL TO ATTENTION in v. 1 together with the elaboration in vv. 2-3. The CALL TO ATTENTION typically begins with imperative verbs that call upon the audience to listen, but in the present instance, the imperatives call upon Zion to "arise" *(qûmî)* and "shine" *('ôrî)*. Like commands to listen, these verbs also call for a response from the audience, but the present literary context emphasizes the intertextual fulfillment of an earlier passage in 9:1-2, which announces that the people walking in darkness have seen a great light. In the present passage, Zion is now asked to recognize that great light in the form of YHWH's restoration of the exiles to Jerusalem and to respond to that light accordingly. The elaboration in vv. 2-3 aids in making the interpretation of the initial imagery of the CALL TO ATTENTION clear. The contrast with darkness highlighted in the passage in v. 2 recalls the darkness of the holy of holies of the Jerusalem temple, where YHWH and the now absent ark of the covenant would reside in Solomon's temple. Now that YHWH has acted from the depths of the darkness in the (presumably restored) holy of holies, the light of the presence of YHWH shines forth as Zion resumes her role as the holy center of creation.

The PROPHETIC ANNOUNCEMENT OF SALVATION in 60:4-22 begins with the prophet's COMMAND to Zion in vv. 4-7 to see the approach of the children of Zion and the wealth of the nations to the restored city. Such a COMMAND is not a necessary element of the PROPHETIC ANNOUNCEMENT OF SALVATION, but it functions here as a means to provide the context for Zion's restoration. Insofar as Zion was conceived in ancient Judean theology as the holy center of creation, the recognition of this role by the nations at large plays an important role in signaling Jerusalem's restoration to this status at the beginning of the Persian period, when the Jerusalem temple is rebuilt. Insofar as the nations return Jerusalem's exiles to her and approach her from the ends of the earth or the coastlands of the sea with their gifts of gold, frankincense, and animals to be offered at the Jerusalem temple, Zion's role as the holy center of creation — or the temple of all creation — then becomes clear and aids in supporting YHWH's claims throughout the book of Isaiah to be the true G-d of creation and the nations at large as well as the true G-d of Israel, Judah, and Jerusalem. Verse 7 makes the temple context clear, insofar as the approach of the exiled Jews, the nations, and the goods that they bear are intended to support temple worship in Jerusalem; the gold, frankincense, and animals are to be offered at the temple as recognition of YHWH's role as creator of the universe and master of human events.

The PROPHETIC ANNOUNCEMENT OF SALVATION proper appears in 60:8-18. It begins with a portrayal of the approach of the coastlands, which would function as part of the evidence that typically appears in the genre that the restoration is at hand. This segment of the passage begins with a RHETORICAL QUESTION in v. 8 that is designed to assert that the coastlands — the farthest reaches of the inhabited world in ancient thought — are approaching Jerusalem to demonstrate that all of the world, including those at its furthermost points, have recognized the significance of the restoration and have come to participate and to make their offerings to YHWH. Insofar as RHETORICAL QUESTIONS elicit their response from the audience at hand, they play a role in persuading the audience that the claims made in the text are true. In this case, the RHETORICAL QUESTION would play a role in convincing the Jerusalemite audience of the time that the restoration of Jerusalem was indeed at hand and that YHWH was the party responsible for bringing it about.

The ANNOUNCEMENT or DESCRIPTION OF (Jerusalem's) SALVATION proper in 60:13-18 would then constitute the core of the PROPHETIC ANNOUNCEMENT OF SALVATION in this passage. Elements of the restoration include the reference to the "glory of Lebanon" in v. 13, which signals the wooden interior paneling of the restored temple; the naming of Zion as "the city of YHWH" in v. 14 to signal that YHWH is responsible for the restoration and that Zion serves as YHWH's domicile; the instance of the RECOGNITION FORMULA, "and you will know that I am YHWH," in vv. 15-16, which identifies YHWH as Zion's deliverer and redeemer; and the portrayal of peace for Jerusalem in vv. 17-18, which signals the idyllic future for Jerusalem now that YHWH is acting and recalls the basis for Jerusalem's name as "a possession of *(yĕrûš)* peace *(šālôm/šālēm)*."

As noted above, the prophet's presentation of YHWH's promise for eternal possession of the land by the people constitutes the BLESSING that frequently plays a role in the PROPHETIC ANNOUNCEMENT OF SALVATION.

Setting

Although chs. 60–62 are a part of Trito-Isaiah, interpreters have repeatedly noted their correspondence with Deutero-Isaiah (Smith, *Rhetoric and Redaction,* 22-49; Sekine, *Die tritojesajanische Sammlung*). Like Deutero-Isaiah, these chapters emphasize the restoration of Zion with a particular emphasis on the return of the exiles to Jerusalem. In many cases, interpreters argue that chs. 60–62 are either written by Deutero-Isaiah or that they are closely associated with the late-6th-century prophet, perhaps as the product of the prophet's disciples (Westermann, *Isaiah 40–66,* 352-53; Koenen, *Ethik und Eschatologie,* 216-17; cf. W. Zimmerli, "Zur Sprache Tritojesajas," 217-33).

As a component of chs. 60–62, ch. 60 shows clear indications of its interest in Jerusalem's restoration in the aftermath of the Babylonian exile and its special interest in the restoration of the Jerusalem temple. But whereas Deutero-Isaiah appears to be situated in the Babylonian exile when calling upon the exiles to return to Jerusalem (see chs. 48; 49), ch. 60 appears to be situated in Jerusalem, watching as the exiles return from afar and the nations approach with gold, frankincense, and animals to be offered to YHWH at the temple. Although many note that Trito-Isaiah throughout is concerned with the restoration of Jerusalem, ch. 60 does not indicate an interest like that seen in chs. 56–59 and 63–66 in distinguishing between the righteous and the wicked as part of its understanding of the process of restoration. Rather, ch. 60 is interested in the return of all Zion's children, and it makes no effort to charge any of them with any particular wrongdoing that would bar them from entry into the temple.

Such a perspective is consistent with the portrayal of the restoration of the temple as seen in the book of Haggai. Haggai and Zechariah are the two prophets identified in Ezra-Nehemiah as the prophets who supported the restoration of the Jerusalem temple during the early reign of Darius (Ezra 5:1; 6:14); indeed, both prophets are dated to the outset of the second year of Darius, 520 B.C.E., the year in which construction on the temple commenced (Hag 1:1; Zech 1:1). Haggai portrays the nations bringing their precious things as gifts to be offered in the soon-to-be-rebuilt Jerusalem temple in Hag 2:6-9, and he states in the same context that such offerings will restore the glory of Jerusalem and grant peace to the place. Isaiah 60 shares such aspirations. Isaiah 60:4-7 portrays the approaching nations who bear gifts for offering at the temple; vv. 8-18 portray not only the incoming wealth of the nations but their submission to YHWH at Zion as well; and 60:17 in particular proclaims peace for Jerusalem. Such a correspondence indicates that like Haggai, ch. 60 is written in the late 6th century at the time of the reconstruction of the temple.

Isaiah 60 is written in relation to the reconstruction of the temple, and it appears to take up the themes of restoration in the earlier portions of the book. The focus on the nations walking in light appears to relate intertextually to the portrayal of the people of Israel walking in darkness prior to coming upon a great light in 9:1-2. Interpreters might also note the role that the restoration of the exiles to Zion plays in 11:11-16; 27:12-13; 35:1-10; and throughout chs. 40–55. As Steck has observed, these passages appear to form the basis for a late-6th-century redaction that binds together the "Great Isaiah Book" at the end of the Babylonian exile (Steck, *Bereitete Heimkehr;* idem, *Studien zu Tritojesaja,* 3-166; Koenen, *Ethik und Eschatologie,* 137-57; cf. Sweeney, *Isaiah 1–39,* 55-57), although his thesis that chs. 60–62 include redactional layers that made this association possible has been refuted (Smith, *Rhetoric and Redaction,* 22-49). In this late-6th-century edition of the book, ch. 60 would form part of the concluding segment in chs. 60–62 that would celebrate the restoration of Jerusalem with the building of the Jerusalem temple and return of its exiled people. Given the key role played by liturgical texts throughout the book of Isaiah (e.g., 2:2-4; 12; 24-27; 40-55), it would appear that this edition of the book played a role in a liturgy for the restoration of the temple. Indeed, chs. 60–62 would have formed the climax and culmination of such a liturgical presentation of the book of Isaiah.

But ch. 60 also plays a role in the final edition of the book of Isaiah during the reforms of Nehemiah and Ezra in the late 5th and early 4th century B.C.E. The reforms of Ezra and Nehemiah emphasized proper observance of the covenant with YHWH, including proper temple worship and support, observance of the Shabbat, and other practices, which were designed to distinguish those who were righteous from those who were not. Nevertheless, the portrayal of the restoration of Zion and the temple played key roles in the reforms of Nehemiah and Ezra as well, insofar as both took action to ensure the central role of the restored Jerusalem temple as the sacred center of Jerusalem and Jewish life in the world of the Persian Empire. Consequently, the restoration of Zion and the temple as portrayed in ch. 60 would have contributed to the restoration program of Nehemiah and Ezra as well and would therefore have ensured their place in the final edition of the book.

Interpretation

When read as part of the late-6th-century edition of the book of Isaiah, ch. 60 forms part of the larger text in chs. 60–62 that constitutes the conclusion of the book with a portrayal of a restored Zion with the exiles returning to the city of Jerusalem, the nations bringing their offerings to the temple, and YHWH promising peace and eternal possession of the land of Israel. In the final late-5th- to early-4th-century edition of the book, chs. 60–62 form part of the segment in chs. 55–66 that is concerned with convincing the people to adhere to YHWH's covenant in the context of the restoration of Nehemiah and Ezra. Isaiah 60–62 demonstrates the benefits of the restoration and adherence to YHWH's expectations, whereas other texts point to the consequences for failing to observe YHWH's covenant. In both cases, the portrayal of Jerusalem's restoration in ch. 60 serves a rhetorical purpose to convince Jewish readers of the book to return to Jerusalem and to adhere to YHWH's covenant.

The formal structure of ch. 60 and its intertextual relationships within the book of Isaiah point to its interest in persuading Isaiah's readers to return to Jerusalem and to observe YHWH's covenant. Its formal character as the prophet's presentation of YHWH's words to Zion concerning the return of Zion's exiles and the restoration of Zion serves these purposes by certifying that the restoration is authorized by YHWH, who is recognized in the book at large as the true G-d of all creation and human events.

The prophet's initial address to Zion in 60:1-3 to rise and see the shining presence of YHWH provides the means to call the reader's attention to the central message of the text, to recognize that YHWH is acting to restore Zion and that the people should respond by returning to Jerusalem and observing the covenant. It draws upon earlier images in the book of Isaiah, such as the procession of the nations to Zion in 2:2-4 to learn YHWH's torah; the portrayal of the people walking in darkness who now see a great light in 9:1-2; and the portrayals of exiled Israelites and Judeans returning to Jerusalem in 11:11-16; 27:12-13; 35:1-10; and throughout chs. 40–55 (cf. Lau, *Schriftgelehrte Prophetie,* 22-66). Although these texts portray either nations streaming to Zion (2:2-4) or the return of Jewish exiles (11:11-16; 27:12-13; 35:1-10; 40–55), ch. 60 combines these images to portray the nations approaching Jerusalem to facilitate the return of the exiles and the presentation of their offerings at the Jerusalem temple. Such a portrayal aids in building the overall claims of the book that YHWH is the true G-d of all creation and human events, as demonstrated by YHWH's role in bringing about both punishment and restoration for Zion and the people of Israel and Judah.

The portrayal of YHWH as a manifestation of brilliant light draws upon a long tradition in both Mesopotamia and Israel of associating divine theophanies with light (Langer, *G-tt als "Licht"*). The imagery of YHWH's brilliant presence emerging out of darkness of course draws upon the imagery of the darkened holy of holies of the Jerusalem temple, where the ark of the covenant resided during the time of Solomon's temple, and where YHWH is invisibly manifested during the time of the Second Temple. The holy of holies is portrayed as an abode of deep darkness that signals YHWH's presence in the heavenly realm beyond earthly experience, but YHWH emerges from this darkness at times of liturgical worship to receive the offerings and prayers of the people. Insofar as the interior of the temple is lit with ten *menorot* or candelabra, each with seven lamps, the brilliance of the interior of the temple serves as the backdrop for the claims in this text that YHWH represents a shining presence to be seen by Zion and her people.

The presentation of YHWH's address to Zion in 60:4-22 announces the restoration of Zion. The introductory command to Zion in 60:4-7 to observe the approach of her children and the wealth of the nations serves as a means to signal both the restoration of Zion and the recognition of YHWH as the true G-d of creation and human events by the nations. In the context of the early Persian period, such a claim of course identifies YHWH with the Persians, but it also signals the Persians' subservience to YHWH. It presupposes Cyrus's decree to allow Jews to return to Jerusalem to rebuild the temple and Darius's efforts to facilitate the restoration by financing and authorizing the expedition by Zerubbabel ben Shealtiel and Joshua ben Jehozadak to carry out the task. The portrayal of exiles and wealth coming in from all the world — from the sea, Midian, Ephah, Sheba, Kedar, Nebaioth, etc. — points to YHWH's worldwide power, and the designation of these offerings for YHWH's altar points to the rebuilt Jerusalem temple as YHWH's Holy Center of Creation to which all of the nations respond as a manifestation of YHWH's glory or presence in the world.

The announcement of the restoration of Zion in 60:8-18 reiterates the theme of the nations' approach to Zion, but it takes the theme even further than the previous verses. Here, the coastlands are identified as the source of the nations who bring exiles and wealth to Jerusalem from over the seas in ships of Tarshish. The coastlands function as a means of designating the farthest reaches of the earth in Mesopotamian maps of the world (see W. Horowitz, *Mesopotamian Cosmic Geography* [MC 8; Winona Lake: Eisenbrauns, 1998] 20-43), and they function similarly here as well. "Ships of Tarshish" is an expression that designates ocean-going ships, although we must recognize that they were actually small vessels that hugged the coast but nevertheless carried on sea trade and transportation in antiquity. The text defines the purposes of the nations' journey in v. 9, "to bring your sons, gold, and silver from afar" and to do so in the name of YHWH. Here, the nations serve YHWH by rebuilding the walls of the temple and by the service rendered to YHWH and the people of Jerusalem by their kings. Verse 10b indicates some theological atonement and explanation on YHWH's part, insofar as YHWH admits to striking the people in anger, but attempts to atone by stating the intent to show the people mercy now that the judgment is over. Much like the Babylonian Akitu or New Year's festival in which the nations and their gods process through Babylon to honor Marduk and the Babylonian king, vv. 11-12 portray the nations processing through Jerusalem with their offerings of wealth to honor YHWH. Should they fail to do so, judgment awaits, just as it did for those who did not show up for the Akitu festival.

The portrayal of Zion's restoration in 60:13-18 begins with the imagery of the glory of Lebanon as a means to portray YHWH's glory. This would refer to the use of cedar and acacia wood from Lebanon as the means to construct the interior walls and floors of the temple on the model of Solomon's older structure. Such wood was expensive and tended to be used in royal residences, which also served as the patterns for building temples in Western Asia in antiquity. With the restoration of the temple, Zion is now called the City of YHWH as her enemies bow down to her and call her the City of David and Zion of the Holy One of Israel. Such names recall the power and independence of the early Davidic monarchy and YHWH as the G-d who installed the House of David as Israel's monarchy. Such references might hint at an interest in the restoration of Judean independence and Davidic restoration along the lines of Hag 2:20-22, but no explicit claims are made here in Isaiah. Instead, the text turns to lauding YHWH as Zion's redeemer and deliverer so that all of Zion's people will recognize YHWH as the one who redeems and delivers Jerusalem and brings her peace.

The prophet's presentation of YHWH's promise for eternal possession of the land of Israel in 60:19-22 serves as a means to assert that YHWH will fully restore Zion and the land of Israel together with its people. The prophet argues that there is no need for the sun and the moon of the old creation, as YHWH will now serve as Zion's light, which is another way of signaling YHWH's eternal presence in the city and the end of Zion's mourning. YHWH's promise of eternal possession of the land draws upon the vineyard parables of 5:1-7 and 27:2-6 to signal the "replanting" of Israel in the land forever.

Bibliography

K. Koenen, *Ethik und Eschatologie,* 137-57; B. Langer, *G-tt als "Licht" in Israel und Mesopotamien;* W. Lau, *Schriftgelehrte Prophetie,* 22-66; G. J. Polan, "Zion, the Glory of the Holy One of Israel: A Literary Analysis of Isaiah 60," in *Imagery and Imagination in Biblical Literature* (CBQMS 32; ed. L. Boadt and M. S. Smith; Washington: Catholic Biblical Association of America, 2001) 50-71; S. Sekine, *Die tritojesajanische Sammlung,* 68-74; P. A. Smith, *Rhetoric and Redaction,* 22-49; O. H. Steck, *Studien zu Tritojesaja,* 3-166; J. Stromberg, *Isaiah after Exile,* 11-13, 27-30; J. Vermeylen, *Du prophète Isaïe,* 471-78; W. Zimmerli, "Zur Sprache Tritojesajas," 217-33.

THE PROPHET'S PRESENTATION OF THE
SPEECH OF THE ANOINTED PRIEST 61:1–62:12

Structure

I. The anointed one's statement of his commission to release the
captives so that they might serve in Jerusalem as priests to the
nations   61:1-9
  A. The anointed one's statement of his commission to release
    the captives   61:1-4
    1. Initial statement of divine spirit upon the anointed one   61:1a
    2. Elaborated statement of anointing   61:1b-3a
      a. Statement of YHWH's anointing   61:1bα$^{1-4}$

a. For the sake of Zion I will not be silent   62:1aα
b. For the sake of Jerusalem I will not be quiet   62:1aβ
   2. Twofold statement of goal of pledge: righteousness and
      deliverance   62:1b
      a. Until her righteousness goes forth   62:1bα
      b. Until her deliverance burns like a torch   62:1bβ
B. Address to Jerusalem: announcement of salvation/restoration   62:2-7
   1. You shall be a crown and diadem in the hand of YHWH   62:2-3
      a. Nations and kings shall see your righteousness and glory   62:2a
         1) Nations shall see your righteousness   62:2aα
         2) Kings shall see your glory   62:2aβ
      b. You will be called by a new name   62:2b
         1) Basically stated   62:2bα
         2) Qualified: which the mouth of YHWH will designate   62:2bβ
      c. You shall be a crown/diadem in YHWH's hand   62:3
         1) You shall be a beautiful crown in the hand of YHWH   62:3a
         2) You shall be a royal diadem in the palm of your G-d   62:3b
   2. You shall be renamed from "Forsaken" to "Married"   62:4-5
      a. You will not again be called abandoned and desolate   62:4aα
         1) You will not again be called abandoned   62:4aα$^{1-5}$
         2) Your land will not again be called desolate   62:4aα$^{6-10}$
      b. First qualification: you will be called Hephzibah and
         Married   62:4aβ
         1) You will be called Hephzibah/My Desire is in Her   62:4aβ$^{1-4}$
         2) Your land will be called Married   62:4aβ$^{5-6}$
      c. Second qualification: for YHWH desires you   62:4b
         1) For YHWH desires you   62:4bα
         2) And your land will be married/owned   62:4bβ
      d. Two metaphors for rejoicing over Jerusalem   62:5
         1) Young man rejoicing over a virgin   62:5a
            a) As a young man rejoices over a bride   62:5aα
            b) So your sons will rejoice over you   62:5aβ
         2) A bridegroom rejoices over a bride   62:5b
            a) As a bridegroom rejoices over a bride   62:5bα
            b) So your G-d will rejoice over you   62:5bβ
   3. I have posted watchmen to ensure your security until
      YHWH acts   62:6-7
      a. Concerning appointment of watchmen of Jerusalem's
         walls   62:6a
         1) Basically stated   62:6aα
         2) Qualification: they shall not be silent all day   62:6aβ
      b. Instructions to watchmen: no rest until Jerusalem estab-
         lished   62:6b-7
         1) First instruction to watchmen: do not remain silent   62:6b
         2) Second instruction: do not allow YHWH to be silent   62:7
            a) Basically stated   62:7a
            b) Qualification: until YHWH establishes Jerusalem   62:7b

Isaiah 61:1–62:12 constitutes the prophet's presentation of the speech of an anointed figure. The unit begins in 61:1, in which the anointed figure begins with a 1st-person speech in vv. 1-4 that announces his anointing by YHWH and his commission to proclaim good tidings to the people of Jerusalem and Judah. Although the 1st-person form of the speech indicates that the anointed one is the speaker, the larger context in chs. 60–62 indicates that the prophet is the one who transmits the anointed one's speech. The 1st-person speech form continues all the way through 62:12. Isaiah 63:1 opens a new unit with a rhetorical question concerning the approach of YHWH from Bozrah. Although a 1st-person address form appears in 64:7, it is no longer clear that the anointed figure of 61:1–62:12 is the speaker.

The formal structure of the anointed one's speech comprises five syntactically-discrete elements that proceed from an announcement of the anointed priest's commission in 61:1-9 through the anointed one's psalm of rejoicing in 61:10-11, his pledge to Jerusalem to enable her restoration in 62:1-7, the presentation of YHWH's oath in 62:8-9, and finally the announcement of Zion's restoration in 62:10-12. Insofar as the anointed one appears to be the high priest of the Jerusalem temple, chs. 61–62 constitute the high priest's speech that announces his commission by YHWH and his task to carry out the restoration of Jerusalem so that it might once again serve as the holy center of creation and all the world.

The passage begins in 61:1-9 with the anointed one's announcement of his commission to release the captives so that they might serve in Jerusalem as priests for the nations. Such a role is consistent with the conceptualization of the Jerusalem temple as the holy center of all creation and the ideology of the final form of the Pentateuch that identifies Israel as a kingdom of priests in the midst of the nations of the world (Exod 19:5-6). The subunit is defined throughout by the 1st-person speech forms employed by the speaker and the focus on the anointing of the priests and his concern to fulfill his tasks in keeping with divine expectation. Although the passage begins by portraying the people of Jerusalem and Judah in 3rd-person form as if they were a third party, the anointed one's use of the 1st-common plural, "for our G-d," in v. 2, indicates that he does indeed address the people of Jerusalem and Judah. The speech continues in vv. 5-9, which are joined to vv. 1-4 by the *wāw*-consecutive form, *wĕ'āmĕdû,* "and they (strangers) will stand," to describe the nations that will tend to Zion's flocks and fields. Verses 5-9 display a subtle shift in their use of address forms. Whereas vv. 1-4 employ 3rd-person language to portray the people who will benefit from the anointed one's commission, vv. 5-9 shift to a 2nd-person plural address form for the people that continues through v. 7aα before it reverts back to the 3rd-person descriptive form through the balance of the subunit. The purpose of such a shift appears to be rhetorical: the anointed one employs a combination of 2nd-person plural address forms in vv. 5 and 7aα; a 1st-person common plural address form, "our G-d," once again in v. 6aβ; and 3rd-person address forms in vv. 7aβ-9 to address both his immediate audience and a larger audience beyond. Insofar as v. 3aα deliberately mentions "the mourners of Zion" as the objects of his concern, it seems that the people of Jerusalem/Zion are his primary audience but that the people of Judah or even Israel at large constitute the broader audience for the anointed one's remarks.

The anointed one's speech comprises two major elements. The first is the anointed one's statement of his anointing and commission to release the captives in 61:1-4. The second element is his presentation of YHWH's words to the people in 61:5-9. As noted above, these verses are joined to vv. 1-4 by the introductory *wāw*-consecutive form, *wĕ'āmĕdû,* "and they (strangers) will stand."

Isaiah 61:1-4 constitutes the anointed one's statement of his anointing and commission to release the captives. The subunit begins with the initial 1st-person statement in v. 1a that "the spirit of my L-rd, YHWH, is upon me."

Such a statement sets the tone for the following sequence that announces the anointing and the purposes for which the anointing is done. Verses 1b-3a present an elaborated statement of the anointing that begins with a basic statement of the figure's anointing in v. 1bα$^{1-4}$ followed by a sequence of statements, each introduced by a form of the particle *lě,* "to," in vv. 1bα^{5}-3a that define the purposes of the figure's anointing. The sequence includes seven elements, some of which include multiple statements that elaborate on the point at hand. The first appears in v. 1bα$^{5-7}$ which states that YHWH has sent the anointed one to proclaim good tidings to the humble. The second in v. 1bα$^{8-10}$ asserts that the anointed one is to bind those broken of heart. The third in v. 1bβ is a twofold statement joined by a conjunctive *wāw* that focuses on captives and prisoners, to proclaim the release of the captives in v. 1bβ$^{1-3}$ and to proclaim freedom to the prisoners in v. 1bβ$^{4-6}$. The fourth is another twofold statement in v. 2a that focuses on stating divine purpose, favor, and vindication, "to proclaim a year of favor for YHWH" in v. 2aα and "to proclaim a day of vindication for our G-d" in v. 2aβ. The fifth in v. 2b asserts that the purpose is to comfort all who mourn. The sixth in v. 3aα$^{1-3}$ asserts that the purpose is to install the mourners of Zion. And the seventh and concluding element in v. 3aα^{4}-β asserts that it is to clothe them as priests, including specifications that they will have a turban instead of ashes in v. 3aα$^{4-8}$, that they will have oil of rejoicing instead of mourning in v. 3aα$^{9-11}$, and that they will have a garment of praise instead of a faint spirit in v. 3aβ. Verses 3b-4, which are joined to the preceding elements by an introductory *wāw,* then describe the results of the anointing for the people of Jerusalem in three paired statements defined by the use of finite verbs. The first in v. 3b states that they will be called righteous terebinths in v. 3bα and glorified plantings in v. 3bβ. The second in v. 4a states that they will rebuild ancient ruins in v. 4aα and reestablish former places in v. 4aβ. And the third in v. 4b states that they will renew ruined cities in v. 4bα and long desolated places in v. 4bβ.

The second major element is the anointed one's presentation of YHWH's words to the people in 61:5-9 in which he states that the people will serve as priests of YHWH. The subunit comprises two basic elements.

The first appears in 61:5-6, which continues the interest in the results of the anointing that concluded vv. 1-4, but these verses are distinguished by their 2nd-person masculine address form. The passage includes three paired statements concerning the results of the anointing. The first in v. 5 presents a twofold statement that foreigners will tend the flocks and fields, including statements that "strangers will stand to shepherd your sheep" in v. 5a and that "foreigners will tend your fields and vineyards" in v. 5b. The second in v. 6a asserts that "you will be called priests of YHWH and ministers of our G-d," including statements that "you will be called priests of YHWH" in v. 6aα and "you will be designated as ministers of our G-d" in v. 6aβ. And the third in v. 6b asserts that "you will be celebrated," including statements that "you will eat the wealth of the nations" in v. 6bα and that "you will enjoy their glory" in v. 6bβ.

The second appears in 61:7-9, which constitutes an oracle of salvation for the people of Jerusalem. The passage employs a classic structure including the basis for salvation in v. 7a and resulting announcement of salvation in vv. 7b-9.

The basis for salvation in v. 7a begins with a twofold statement of the causes of YHWH's decision to grant salvation to the people, "because *(taḥat)* of your double shame" in v. 7aα and "(because) in humiliation they celebrated their portion" in v. 7aβ. Verses 7b-9 then describe the results in the form of an announcement of salvation. The basic announcement appears in v. 7b with a twofold statement that they will inherit double in their land in v. 7bα and they will have eternal joy in v. 7bβ. Verses 8-9 then elaborate on this announcement by proclaiming YHWH's eternal covenant with the people. The elaboration comprises two basic components. The first in v. 8 presents YHWH's announcement of an eternal covenant. It begins in v. 8a with a twofold 1st-person statement that YHWH loves justice in v. 8aα and that YHWH hates a corrupted whole burnt offering *('ôlâ)* in v. 8aβ. Verse 8b then follows with YHWH's statement that "I will make an eternal covenant with them," including the statement that "I act with integrity" in v. 8bα and that "I will make an eternal covenant with them" in v. 8bβ. The second in v. 9 presents the results, that their descendants will be known throughout the world. The first portion appears in v. 9a in the form of a twofold statement that their descendants will be known throughout the world, including the statement that their seed will be known among nations in v. 9aα and that their offspring will be known in the midst of people in v. 9aβ. The second is a twofold statement in v. 9b that everyone will recognize them, including that all who see them will recognize them in v. 9bα and that the reason is that they are seed blessed by YHWH in v. 9bβ.

The second major subunit of chs. 61–62 is the anointed one's psalm of rejoicing over the restoration of YHWH's righteousness before the nations in 61:10-11. The short psalm takes the basic form of the hymn of praise. The announcement for praise appears in v. 10aα in the form of the anointed one's twofold declaration of rejoicing, including his statement that "I will surely rejoice in YHWH" in v. 10aα[1-3] and that "I will celebrate in my G-d" in v. 10aα[4-7]. The first statement of the basis for praise appears in v. 10aβ-b, in which the anointed one asserts that "YHWH clothes me in garments of righteousness." This segment begins in v. 10aβ-γ with a twofold statement that "YHWH clothes me in garments of deliverance" in v. 10aβ and that "YHWH wraps me with a cloak of righteousness" in v. 10aγ. The elaboration in v. 10b relates this imagery to a groom and bride, including statements that "he will look like a groom with a priestly turban" in v. 10bα and that "she will resemble a bride decked in her ornaments" in v. 10bβ. The second basis for praise then follows in v. 11 with an allegorical portrayal of YHWH making the earth bloom with righteousness and praise. The basis for the allegory appears in v. 11a with a portrayal that "he is like the earth blooming," including the assertion that "he is like the earth which sprouts its growth" in v. 11aα and that "he is like a garden that sprouts its sowings" in v. 11aβ. The application of the allegory then concludes the subunit in v. 11b with the assertion that YHWH will cause righteousness and praise to sprout before all the nations.

The anointed priest's pledge to Jerusalem to enable her restoration, in the form of her righteousness and deliverance, to be realized appears in 62:1-7. This unit is demarcated at the outset by the priest's statement of a pledge not to remain silent in 62:1 and his address in 62:2-7 that culminates in his statement that he will make sure that neither the watchmen posted on the walls nor YHWH will remain silent until Jerusalem is established. The unit is syntactically independent both at its beginning and its conclusion.

The first segment of this unit is the anointed priest's statement of his pledge in 62:1. The subunit comprises two major twofold elements that define the purpose of the pledge in v. 1a and the goal of the pledge in v. 1b. The twofold statement of the purpose of the pledge in v. 1a includes statements that "for the sake of Zion I will not be silent" in v. 1aα and "for the sake of Jerusalem I will not be quiet" in v. 1aβ. The twofold statement of the goal of the pledge in v. 1b includes the goal that the lack of silence will continue until Jerusalem's righteousness goes forth in v. 1bα and that her deliverance will burn like a torch in v. 1bβ.

The anointed priest's address to Jerusalem in 62:2-7 announces her salvation or restoration. It is joined to v. 1 by a *wāw*-consecutive verbal form, *wĕrā'û,* "and they (the nations) shall see (her righteousness)," at the beginning of v. 2, and it includes three major syntactically-unconnected elements in vv. 2-3, 4-5, and 6-7 that successively describe the priest's efforts to ensure her restoration.

Isaiah 62:2-3 states that Jerusalem will become a crown and diadem in the hand of YHWH. The elements of this subunit are linked together by the *wāw*'s in vv. 2b and 3 that bind the subunit together. Verse 2a asserts that nations and kings shall see Jerusalem's righteousness and glory, including the elements that "the nations shall see your righteousness" in v. 2aα and that "kings shall see your glory" in v. 2aβ. Verse 2b asserts that Jerusalem will be called by a new name, including a basic statement of this principle in v. 2bα and a qualification in v. 2bβ that the mouth of YHWH will designate this name. Verse 3 asserts that Jerusalem will become a diadem in YHWH's hand, including statements that "you shall be a beautiful crown in the hand of YHWH" in v. 3a and that "you shall be a royal diadem in the palm of your G-d" in v. 3b.

Isaiah 62:4-5 then constitutes the second subunit that asserts that Jerusalem shall be renamed from "Forsaken" to "Married." This subunit comprises four elements, including the initial statement concerning the name change in v. 4aα, followed by three qualifications, each introduced by the particle *kî,* "for, because," in vv. 4aβ, 4b, and 5. Verse 4aα begins the sequence with the assertion that Jerusalem will not again be called "Abandoned" and "Desolate," including the assertions that she will not be called "Abandoned" in v. 4aα$^{1-5}$ and that her land will not be called "Desolate" in v. 4aα$^{6-10}$. The first qualification in v. 4aβ asserts that Jerusalem will be called "Hephzibah/My Desire is in Her" and "Married," including "Hephzibah/My Desire is in Her" in v. 4aβ$^{1-4}$ and "Married" in v. 4aβ$^{5-6}$. The second qualification in v. 4b asserts that YHWH desires Jerusalem, including the statements that "YHWH desires you" in v. 4bα and that "your land will consequently be married or owned" in v. 4bβ. The final qualification in v. 5 presents two metaphors for rejoicing over Jerusalem. The first focuses on a young man rejoicing over a virgin in v. 5a, including the statement of the simile in v. 5aα that "this is like a young man rejoicing over a virgin" and the result that "so Jerusalem's sons will rejoice over their mother" in v. 5aβ. The second metaphor in v. 5b focuses on a bridegroom rejoicing over his bride, including the simile statement in v. 5bα that "this is like a bridegroom who rejoices over his bride" and the result that "your G-d will rejoice over Jerusalem" in v. 5bβ.

Isaiah 62:6-7 presents the anointed priest's statements that he has posted watchmen to ensure Zion's security until YHWH acts. The first element of this subunit in v. 6a focuses on his stationing of watchmen on Jerusalem's walls, including a basic statement of this act in v. 6aα and the qualification in v. 6aβ that they will not be silent all day, i.e., they will call out when the time for restoration comes. The second element in vv. 6b-7 presents the instructions to the watchmen that there will be no rest until Jerusalem is reestablished. The first instruction in v. 6b is to the watchmen that they are not to remain silent. The second instruction is that they are not to allow YHWH to remain silent either, including a basic statement of this instruction in v. 7a and the qualification that this absence of silence will continue until YHWH establishes Jerusalem in v. 7b.

The fourth major element of the anointed priest's speech appears in 62:8-9, which constitutes an announcement of YHWH's oath of protection for Jerusalem. This unit is syntactically-unconnected and simply structured. It begins in v. 8a with a twofold introduction to the oath, including the statement in v. 8aα that YHWH has sworn by the right hand and the statement in v. 8aβ that YHWH has sworn by the strong arm. The oath proper then follows in vv. 8b-9 in two portions. The negative expression of the oath appears in v. 8b with YHWH's twofold statement that "I will not give your grain to enemies" in v. 8bα and that "I will not give your *tirosh* or grape juice to foreigners" in v. 8bβ. The positive element of the oath then follows in v. 9. The first portion in v. 9a asserts that those who harvest the grain shall eat it, including a basic statement of this premise in v. 9aα and a statement of the result in v. 9aβ, that they shall praise YHWH. The second portion in v. 9b asserts that those who gather the grapes shall drink in YHWH's holy courts.

The fifth and final portion of the anointed priest's address is the announcement and signal in 62:10-12 that Jerusalem's deliverance has arrived. The unit begins in v. 10 with a fivefold command, each introduced by a masculine plural imperative verb, concerning preparations for the return of the people. The sequence includes a command to pass through the gates in v. 10aα, to clear the road for the people in v. 10aβ, to build the highway in v. 10bα$^{1-3}$, to clear the stones (from the road) in v. 10bα$^{4-5}$, and to raise a flag over the peoples to signal their deliverance in v. 10bβ. The second portion of the unit is the announcement of YHWH's restoration of Zion in vv. 11-12. This portion begins with the anointed priest's presentation of YHWH's announcement in v. 11. The introduction in v. 11aα indicates YHWH's announcement to the ends of the earth. The announcement proper then follows in v. 11aβ-b. It begins with the masculine imperative command to "say to Bat Zion" in v. 11aβ, followed by the content of the command or announcement in v. 11b. The announcement includes two components. The first is the announcement in v. 11bα, introduced by *hinnēh*, "behold!" that "your deliverer comes." The second is the announcement in v. 11bβ, again introduced by *hinnēh*, that "his reward is with him and his deed before him," including statements that "his reward is with him" in v. 11bβ$^{1-3}$ and that "his deed is before him" in v. 11bβ$^{4-5}$. Verse 12 then presents the priest's announcement of the results of YHWH's announcement: Zion is restored. He states in v. 12a that the people will be called holy and redeemed of YHWH, including the statement that they will be called "holy people" in v. 12aα and "redeemed of YHWH" in v. 12aβ. His second statement in v. 12b asserts that Jerusalem will be called "Sought Out" and "City Not Abandoned," including the statement that the city will be called "Sought Out" in v. 12bα and "City Not Abandoned" in v. 12bβ.

Genre

Isaiah 61:1–62:12 constitutes the prophet's presentation of the speech of an anointed figure to the people of Jerusalem and Judah. Insofar as the imagery and language associated with that figure are priestly in character, the figure appears to be a priest. As indicated in the discussion of setting below, the priest would be Joshua ben Jehozadak, the first high priest commissioned to serve in the newly-rebuilt Jerusalem temple in 515 B.C.E. (see Ezra 6; Zechariah 3). The present text appears to represent a presentation of Joshua on the occasion of his ordination and commission to serve as high priest in the temple.

The first portion of the text in 61:1-9 constitutes the anointed one's statement of his commission to release the captives. A COMMISSION speech presupposes an authoritative charge given by a superior to a subordinate. In the case of the commission of the high priest, the authoritative figure would be YHWH and any ordained priests who would be available to play the appropriate role in the ordination of a high priest when no such figure had officiated in the temple since its destruction in 587/586 B.C.E. Zechariah 3 and perhaps Zechariah 6 portray the ordination of Joshua ben Jehozadak, including a statement of his commission to oversee the new temple on YHWH's behalf (see Zech 3:6-10; M. A. Sweeney, *The Twelve Prophets* [Berit Olam; Collegeville: Liturgical, 2000] 2:592-604). The present text appears to presuppose the charge given to Joshua ben Jehozadak in Zechariah 3, but it differs insofar as he is commissioned to oversee the temple in Zechariah 3 while in Isa 61:1-9 he is commissioned to proclaim the release of the captives and to oversee their return to Zion and the temple. The commission to release the captives in 61:1-4 makes it clear that he is anointed to proclaim good tidings to the people, to bind those broken of heart, to proclaim the release of the captives, to proclaim a year of favor for YHWH, to comfort the mourners, to install the mourners of Zion, and to clothe them as priests in vv. 1b-3a. Such a task points to the role that the people of Jerusalem will play as priests to the people at large; just as the priesthood functions as the sacred center of Jerusalem, so the people of Jerusalem will serve as the sacred center for Judah and Israel. The high priest of the temple is to sanctify the restored people of Jerusalem, and their task is to sanctify the people of Judah and Israel. As a result of this commission, the people are then to serve symbolically as righteous terebinths and plantings to restore the ruined cities and places of the land at large in vv. 3b-4.

The anointed one's presentation of YHWH's words to the people in 61:5-9 provides the divine basis for such a COMMISSION, which the priest is tasked to convey to the people. This segment expands the people's task to sanctify the nations of the world as well, which are expected to tend the flocks and fields of Jerusalem for a people who will then serve as priests and ministers of G-d. The oracular ANNOUNCEMENT OF SALVATION to the people of Jerusalem in vv. 7-9 underscores this commission with YHWH's own words. The ANNOUNCE-MENT OF SALVATION is structured much like a PROPHETIC ANNOUNCEMENT OF PUNISHMENT, insofar as v. 7a provides the BASIS FOR SALVATION in the twofold punishment of the people (see 40:2; much like a thief caught with stolen goods in his possession, Exod 22:3). The ANNOUNCEMENT OF SALVATION proper then follows in vv. 7b-9, insofar as the people will inherit double from their land and have eternal joy. YHWH's statement in vv. 8-9 elaborates on the announcement by presenting the divine pledge of an eternal covenant for the people based on the premise of YHWH's integrity and the promise that the descendants of the people will be known throughout the world.

Isaiah 61:10-11 appears as the anointed one's psalm of rejoicing over the restoration of YHWH's righteousness before the nations. This psalm is based on the HYMN OF PRAISE, which typically includes two basic elements, the CALL TO PRAISE and the BASIS FOR PRAISE. Both elements appear in the present context insofar as declaration of rejoicing by the anointed one in v. 10aα corresponds to the CALL TO PRAISE, and vv. 10aβ-11 then follow with two BASES FOR PRAISE. The first BASIS FOR PRAISE in v. 10aβ-b identifies YHWH's act in clothing the newly-anointed priest in garments of deliverance. Such an act corresponds to the priest's anointing, in which his profane garments are exchanged for holy vestments (see Exodus 28; Zechariah 3). The second BASIS FOR PRAISE in v. 11 focuses on YHWH's role in causing the earth to bloom. Such an act is a consequence of the anointing of the priest, which in turn enables the temple to function as the holy center of creation, one result of which is the fertility and growth of all creation.

The lack of any indication of a change of speaker indicates that 62:1-7 continues the speech of the anointed priest. These verses constitute the priest's PLEDGE to enable Jerusalem's righteousness and deliverance to be realized. A PLEDGE is a formalized promise in which one party promises or pledges to do something for another. Other examples of the PLEDGE would include the promises to Israel's ancestors of a covenant that promises their relationship with YHWH, that they will become a great nation, that they will possess the land of Israel, etc. (see Gen 12:2-3, 7; 15:18-21; 17:4-8; 28:13-15; 35:11-12); YHWH's pledge never again to destroy the earth by flood (Gen 9:9-11); or YHWH's promise that David will have a dynasty (2 Sam 7:12-16). In the present instance, YHWH's pledge to Jerusalem entails that YHWH will serve as Zion's advocate to ensure her righteousness and deliverance in 62:1, and it includes the AN-NOUNCEMENT OF SALVATION in 62:2-7 which functions as a major portion of YHWH's pledge. The ANNOUNCEMENT OF SALVATION here includes three major elements. The first is YHWH's promise in 62:2-3 that Jerusalem will become a crown or diadem in YHWH's hand, i.e., a tangible symbol of Zion's restored status that will be seen by the nations and that will result in a new name for the city. The second is in 62:4-5, which specifies the new names for Zion; Zion's name shall be changed from "Forsaken" to "Married" and from "Desolate" to "Hephzibah" ("My Delight is in Her"), as she is now restored as YHWH's bride. The third element appears in 62:6-7, in which YHWH promises to post watchmen to ensure the security of Jerusalem until YHWH acts. In the context of the anointed priest's speech, the watchmen would refer to the posting of the priestly watches which would oversee the sanctity of the Jerusalem temple (cf. 1 Chr 23:32–24:31).

Isaiah 62:8-9 constitutes the announcement of YHWH's oath of protection for Jerusalem. The OATH is a formal pronouncement which binds the oath-taker to a particular course of action. In the present text, the OATH is signaled by the introductory statements in v. 8a, "YHWH has sworn *(nišbaʿ)* by his right hand and by his strong arm." The OATH proper then follows in vv. 8b-9. The negative portion of the oath, which states what YHWH will not do, appears as a twofold statement in v. 8b in which each element is introduced by the particle *ʾim,* "if." In each case, *ʾim* signals the negation, "if I give (i.e., I will not give) your grain again as food for your enemies and if foreigners will drink (i.e., foreigners will not drink) your *tirosh*/grape juice on which you have labored." The positive elements then appear in v. 9, introduced by the particle *kî,* "for, indeed": "for those who harvest it shall eat and those who gather it shall drink it," etc.

Finally, the announcement and signal that the deliverer has arrived appears in 62:10-12. This passage appears to function as a form of the ANNOUNCEMENT OF SALVATION. It includes a set of five COMMANDS in v. 10 that prepare for the return of the people. The formal ANNOUNCEMENT OF SALVATION appears in vv. 11-12, in which YHWH announces the restoration of Zion, including the anointed priest's presentation of YHWH's announcement in v. 11 followed by the results of YHWH's announcement, the restoration of Zion, in v. 12.

Setting

The question of the setting of 61:1–62:12 is dependent upon the relationship of these chapters to the work of Deutero-Isaiah in chs. 40–55, particularly 61:1-9, which has some affinities to the Servant Songs. Because these chapters appear to share a common base of ideas and language with Deutero-Isaiah, most interpreters view them as the work of Deutero-Isaiah or as the work of a disciple closely associated with the prophet. In some cases, the affinities between these chapters and Deutero-Isaiah prompt scholars to argue that there is no Trito-Isaiah and that chs. 56–66 therefore continue the work of the great late-6th-century prophet (e.g., Paul, *Isaiah 40–66;* Sommer, *A Prophet Reads Scripture;* Tiemeyer, *For the Comfort of Zion*). Others maintain that these chapters play an important role in redactionally binding Proto-Isaiah and the work of Deutero-Isaiah together (e.g., Steck, *Studien zu Tritojesaja,* 1-166; Sweeney, *Isaiah 1–39,* 51-57). Still others assign these chapters entirely to Trito-Isaiah (Duhm, *Das Buch Jesaia;* Elliger, *Die Einheit des Tritojesaia*).

Most interpreters assume the prophetic identity of the speaker in these chapters, and that assumption in turn influences conclusions concerning authorship and setting. To a large extent, such a conclusion is based upon the often-observed affinities between 61:1-4 or 61:1-9 and the Servant Songs of Deutero-Isaiah. But a closer examination of this material raises questions about such an identification. In principle, the narrator of the book, identified with the superscriptions of 1:1; 2:1; 13:1, etc., continues to function throughout the entire work as does the narrator's identification of the prophet, Isaiah ben Amoz, as the prophet whose vision the book presents. When historical-critical work is taken into consideration, the prophet who speaks in chs. 40–55 must be identified as the anonymous prophet Deutero-Isaiah, and the speaker of chs. 60–62 must be identified as the prophet Trito-Isaiah, even if Trito-Isaiah proves to be a cover term for a variety of prophets whose works appear in chs. 56–66.

But questions arise at the very outset of the passage in 61:1 when the speaker self-identifies as one anointed by YHWH. Prophets are not anointed. They may experience the spirit of YHWH upon them and they may be commissioned to serve as heralds of good tidings for the people, as our speaker notes in v. 1, but prophets are normally commissioned to serve YHWH in a visionary experience that may involve visionary or audial elements or even both (see Exodus 3; 1 Kings 22; Isaiah 6; Jeremiah 1; Ezekiel 1; Amos 7–9; etc.). Kings and priests are anointed, but prophets are not anointed. Indeed, the language employed in the passage points to the priestly identity of the speaker. This anointed one is tasked with proclaiming release *(dĕrôr)* for the captives and a year of YHWH's favor *(šĕnat-rāṣôn lyhwh)*. Such terminology is consistent with that employed for the Jubilee or Sabbatical Year of the temple, the fiftieth year which stands as the culmination of the seven times seven years of release announced in Leviticus 25. Time in the temple is measured in periods of seven years in which the people will farm their land for six years and allow the land to lie fallow in the seventh year so that the land will renew itself and serve as a source of food for those who are poor and destitute (see Exod 23:10-11; cf. Ruth 2). After seven such periods of seven years pass, the fiftieth year is then designated the year of Jubilee, in which land lies fallow once again (Leviticus 25) and other measures are enacted to release debtors or slaves from their debts (Deut 15:1-18) and to return land to its ancestral owners (Lev. 27:14-21). Leviticus 25:10 specifically identifies the year of Jubilee as the year of release *(dĕrôr;* cf. Jer 34:8, in which King Zedekiah proclaims a release *(dĕrôr)* of slaves so that they might aid in the defense of Jerusalem). The term *rāṣôn,* "favor," is also employed in priestly literature to indicate divine acceptance of offerings in the temple (see Exod 28:38; Lev. 1:3; 19:5; 22:19-21; 23:11).

Other language in the passage also points to the priestly role of the speaker. Isaiah 61:3 continues the anointed one's commission with tasks to give to the mourners of Zion a turban *(pĕ'ēr)* instead of ashes, oil *(šemen)* instead of mourning, and a garment of praise *(ma'ăṭēh tĕhillâ)* instead of a weak spirit. Turbans are worn by priests (see Ezek 24:17; 44:18), priests and temple fixtures are anointed with oil (Exod 25:6; 30:24, 25; Lev. 8:2, 10, 12; 10:7; 14:10; 21:12; etc.), and although the term *ma'ăṭēh,* "garment," is a hapax, priests serve in the temple choirs and lead the people in singing the praises of YHWH. Likewise, the anointed figure designates the returning people as "the priests of YHWH" and "ministers of our G-d" in Isa 61:6. Priests are not ordained by prophets, but only by other priests acting on YHWH's behalf. The psalm of praise in 61:10-11 depicts the singer, here identified with the anointed speaker of 61:1, as a figure dressed in priestly fashion *(yĕkahēn)* with a turban like a bridegroom. The verb employed here, *yĕkahēn,* literally means "to act like a priest." Finally, YHWH's promise in 62:6-7 to post watchmen to ensure the security of Jerusalem points to the appointment of the twenty-four priestly courses who watch over the Jerusalem temple to ensure its sanctity and security (1 Chr 23:32–24:31).

Altogether, the language employed here identifies the speaker in the passage as a priest, not as a prophet. This observation has implications for establishing the setting of the passage. Overall, the imagery of the passage indicates that the anointed figure is a priest who is being commissioned for a task that will result in the return of the exiled people to the Jerusalem temple and the recognition of their holy status as priests by the rest of the people of the world. Such a task suggests that the passage presupposes an ordination ceremony for a priest in the temple, much like the ordination of Joshua ben Jehozadak as high priest in the newly-rebuilt Jerusalem temple in Zechariah 3. Joshua is stripped of his profane garments, presumably anointed with oil, dressed in the holy garments of the high priesthood, and commissioned to have charge over the holy temple of YHWH. Haggai posits that the restoration of the Jerusalem temple will result in recognition of YHWH by the nations of the world, who will then bring their offerings to Jerusalem, and even the quasi-apocalyptic scenario laid out in Zechariah 9–14 results in the recognition of YHWH at the temple by the nations of the world on Sukkot. Such parallels suggest that our passage likewise presupposes the ordination of Joshua ben Jehozadak as high priest in the newly-restored Jerusalem temple who proceeds to describe the tasks to which he is commissioned. Indeed, the ordination of Joshua ben Jehozadak as high priest of the newly-rebuilt Jerusalem temple would ensure the temple's sanctity, integrity, and protection as well as that of Jerusalem. The portrayal of Jerusalem in 62:1-7 as the restored or "married" bride of YHWH in whom YHWH delights (Hephzibah) metaphorically expresses the restoration of the temple. Likewise, YHWH's oath of protection in 62:8-9 and the concluding announcement and signal of the arrival of Jerusalem's deliverer would point to the liturgical procession that would signal YHWH's return to Zion and the rebuilt temple. Such processions take place when David brings the ark to Jerusalem (2 Samuel 6; 1 Chronicles 16), when Ezra returns to Jerusalem and the temple (Ezra 9), when the people ascend to Jerusalem to celebrate the festivals at the Jerusalem temple (see the Songs of Ascent in the book of Psalms), and when the people bring their offerings to the temple in Ezekiel's vision of the restored Jerusalem (Ezekiel 40–48).

Such a scenario indicates that chs. 61–62 were composed in the late 6th century B.C.E. to portray the ordination of Joshua ben Jehozadak as high priest in the newly-restored temple. The passage does not presuppose authorship by Deutero-Isaiah, but its affinities with the work of Deutero-Isaiah, particularly its portrayal of returning exiles to an eternal covenant in Jerusalem, suggest that it was composed as the culminating text of the late-6th-century edition of the book of Isaiah (Steck, *Studien zu Tritojesaja,* 1-166; Sweeney, *Isaiah 1–39,* 51-57). As part of the late-6th-century edition of Isaiah, it would build upon portrayals of returning exiles in 11:11-16; 27:12-13; and 35:1-10 to bind Proto-Isaiah and Deutero-Isaiah together into a single book to celebrate the restoration of the Jerusalem temple and the ordination of Joshua ben Jehozadak as high priest.

Indeed, the liturgical elements of the passage and the book suggest that the book may have played a role in the inaugural liturgy of the newly-rebuilt temple.

A late-6th-century temple setting for this passage — and the book of Isaiah as a whole — indicates that the passage would have played a role in the late-5th-/early-4th-century edition of the final form of the book of Isaiah as well. The portrayal of a newly-anointed priest announcing his commission to uphold the people and to commission them to serve as priests to the world at large also corresponds to the agenda of Nehemiah and Ezra. Although the temple had already been standing for about a century in their time, the ideals articulated in the late 6th century stand as the basis of the reform programs of first Nehemiah and then Ezra. By establishing the Jewish identity of the early Persian period in relation to observance of divine Torah, both figures would have laid the groundwork for the priestly role of the people of Jerusalem articulated in chs. 61–62.

Interpretation

The prophet's presentation of the words of the anointed priest in 61:1–62:12 is designed to motivate its Judean audience to return to Jerusalem and to support the newly-built Second Temple. The words of the priest build upon the earlier words of the servant in Second Isaiah so that the anointed priest in the Jerusalem temple emerges as YHWH's servant, both at the conclusion of the 6th-century edition of the book of Isaiah and the late-5th- and early-4th-century final edition of the book. Such a presentation is designed to demonstrate that the rebuilding of the temple is done as a result of YHWH's promise of an eternal covenant to the people of Jerusalem and Judah in which all the nations of the earth will recognize YHWH, the temple, and the people at the holy center of creation. It also attempts to demonstrate YHWH's credibility as the G-d of creation and human events, much like Deutero-Isaiah, now that the temple is rebuilt and the exiles are to return to Jerusalem.

The passage begins with the anointed priest's statement of his anointing and commission to release the captives. As noted above, the priest may well have originally been Joshua ben Jehozadak, the figure who was anointed as high priest in the temple following its building in 520-515 B.C.E. (see Ezra 3; 6; Zechariah 3; 6). In both the 6th-century and the final edition of the book, the identity of the anointed priest is unimportant to the interpretation of the passage. He simply functions as the priest whose role is to convince the people of the legitimacy of the building of the temple and thus to prompt the people to return to Jerusalem to support the new institution. He begins his speech with a notice in v. 1a that the divine spirit has descended upon him as a result of his anointing by YHWH. Such a notice signals his identity as the ordained priest who then speaks on YHWH's behalf. The purposes of the anointing in vv. 1b-3a make clear his role to serve as herald of good tidings, initially identified in 40:9-11. Although the prophet Deutero-Isaiah would likely have self-identified as the herald, the present passage makes it clear that the priest will serve this function. Interpreters must remember that the role of the priest in some respects is like that of the prophet; he stands as mediator in the temple between YHWH and the people and thereby serves as interpreter and spokesman of each to the other. In the present instance, he speaks on YHWH's behalf, through the agency of the prophet, to the people. The message is one of comfort, restoration, and return from exile in keeping with Deutero-Isaiah. Indeed, now that the temple is built, it is appropriate for the priest to serve in this capacity. As noted above, the anointed priest's announcement of release and a year of favor for YHWH is in keeping with the celebration of the temple Jubilee Year, in which debtors and slaves are released from their debts and obligations and land is returned to its original owners so that they might start anew. The Jubilee Year therefore serves as a suitable analogy for the release and return of the captives who have now repaid their obligation to YHWH (40:2) and can now return to Jerusalem to reclaim their city, homeland, and lives in vv. 3b-4. One aspect of the return and restoration is the expectation that the people will be clothed as priests. Such a role accentuates the role of Jerusalem with its newly-rebuilt temple as the holy center of all creation, including all the nations of the world.

The anointed priest's presentation of YHWH's words to the people in 61:5-9 serves an important role in legitimizing the restoration of the temple and the return of the people as an act of YHWH. The above-mentioned role as the holy center of creation and thus of the nations as well as of Israel/Judah comes to the forefront in vv. 5-6 insofar as foreigners will tend the flocks and fields of the people of Jerusalem/Judah, who in turn serve as priests and ministers for YHWH. Such a role is in keeping with the expectation of Exod 19:6, which identifies Israel as a kingdom of priests for YHWH. The precise role of the people is not entirely clear in the passage, but the reestablishment of the temple would entail that the people of Jerusalem would constitute the holy congregation of the temple and would therefore be expected to observe YHWH's expectations for holy conduct. Given that the priest is the speaker, such a role makes sense, particularly since Lev. 10:10-11 identifies the role of the priest as to teach the difference between sacred and profane and between clean and unclean. Just as the priests serve as a model for the people and teach them proper observance of YHWH's will, so the people will serve a similar function at the center of the nations at large. It is not entirely clear that such efforts were made when the temple was rebuilt in the late 6th century, but the late-5th- and early-4th-century reforms of Nehemiah and Ezra are designed specifically for such a task. The oracle of salvation to the people of Jerusalem in vv. 7-9 then makes clear that this is YHWH's expectation. Because the people have suffered double for their alleged wrongdoing (cf. 40:2), they will inherit double in the land and live in eternal joy. YHWH's announcement of an eternal covenant with the people then builds upon the expectation of an eternal covenant for David and Zion, but in the absence of a Davidic king, the people then become the recipients of that covenant in keeping with ch. 55. YHWH's announcement is designed to reinforce the view that YHWH is just and acts with integrity. The reference to a corrupted whole burnt offering does not reject the practice per se; it serves as a reminder to the people to respond to YHWH themselves with justice and integrity by presenting a suitable offering and by remembering that their obligations go beyond the simple offering of sacrifices, i.e., they must observe all of YHWH's expectations, moral and ritual alike.

As a result, they and their descendants will be recognized among the nations throughout the world of creation. And of course YHWH will be recognized as the true G-d of creation as well.

The anointed priest's psalm of rejoicing over the restoration of YHWH's righteousness in 61:10-11 again functions as a means to convince the Jerusalemite/Judean audience that YHWH is the true G-d and that the rebuilding of the temple and the return to Jerusalem are acts of YHWH. The psalm follows the basic structure of the psalm of praise with a proclamation of praise and statements of the basis for praise. The first basis for praise focuses on what YHWH does for the people: by restoring them to the holy temple, YHWH treats them like a bride and bridegroom who celebrate their marriage in garments like those of priests. Insofar as the garments are characterized with deliverance and righteousness, they celebrate and reinforce qualities identified with YHWH. The second basis recognizes YHWH's role as G-d of creation. With the temple restored and functioning properly, creation itself responds with new growth and the sprouting of plants, trees, and general fertility for all.

There is no indication of a change of speaker in 62:1, and so 62:1-7 continues with the anointed priest's pledge to Jerusalem that her righteousness and deliverance will be realized. With a twofold statement of the pledge in v. 1, the priest maintains that he will neither be quiet nor silent until Jerusalem's righteousness goes forth and her deliverance burns like a torch. Both of these statements speak to Jerusalem's restoration with the temple at its center. Her righteousness speaks to her integrity as the holy site of YHWH's temple, and her deliverance points to YHWH's capacity to deliver her from threat. The priest's address to Jerusalem then continues in vv. 2-7 with an announcement of salvation that promises Jerusalem's restoration as the holy center of creation. It begins in vv. 2-3 with the statement that Jerusalem will be the crown or diadem in YHWH's hand. Such language points to the new status of Jerusalem as the site for YHWH's temple, to be observed by her new names as designated by YHWH. The new names then appear in vv. 4-5. Here, Jerusalem's names are changed in a series of statements that mark her changed status as YHWH's bride. The first states in v. 4aα that she will no longer be named "Forsaken," i.e., signifying her status as the abandoned wife of YHWH, nor will she be named "Desolate," signifying her status as a mother bereft of her children. The second in v. 4aβ qualifies the first by stating that she will be called "Hephzibah," a Hebrew term that means "My Desire is in Her," to signify YHWH's desire for the city as a bride. The name Hephzibah is a known proper name for a woman, as indicated by its use as the name for King Manasseh's mother in 2 Kgs 21:1. Her land will also now be called "Married," to signify her status as the restored wife of YHWH. The term "married" *(bĕ'ûlâ)* also means, "owned," to signify the status of the land of Jerusalem as owned or belonging to YHWH. The third statement in v. 4b qualifies the preceding statements by asserting that YHWH desires Jerusalem and that her land will be married or owned. The fourth statement in v. 5 then completes the sequence with metaphors that signify rejoicing over the restored Jerusalem. The first maintains that, as a young man rejoices over a virgin, so Jerusalem's sons will rejoice over her. The metaphor here is not sexual, but celebratory. The second maintains that as a bridegroom rejoices over his bride, so G-d will rejoice over Jerusalem. Finally, the priest states in vv. 6-7 that he has posted watchmen to ensure the security of the city until YHWH acts. Such an act entails the posting of twenty-four priestly courses that stand watch over the temple compound to ensure its sanctity (see 1 Chr 23:27–24:31; cf. Zech 3:6-10). This segment begins in v. 6a with the basic statement of the priest's action and the qualification that they will not remain silent; they will do their duty and ensure the city's sanctity and protection. Here, we may note the charge of Joshua ben Jehozadak that he would oversee the sanctity of the newly-restored Jerusalem temple when he was ordained as high priest in Zechariah 3. Verses 6b-7 then elaborate with instructions to the watchmen that they will not rest; they will remain vigilant in ensuring the sanctity of the city until such time as YHWH acts to establish Jerusalem as the site of the restored temple.

Isaiah 62:8-9 continues with the priest's announcement of YHWH's oath of protection for the city of Jerusalem. The twofold oath formula in v. 8a introduces the oath, and the oath proper follows in vv. 8b-9 in two parts. The negative portion of the oath in v. 8b presents YHWH's guarantee that enemies will not eat Jerusalem's grain and that foreigners will not drink her *tirosh,* grape juice that has not yet been fermented into wine. The positive portion of the oath in v. 9 presents YHWH's guarantees that the people of Jerusalem will consume her produce; those who harvest the grain will eat it and praise YHWH, and those who gather the grapes shall drink the *tirosh* in the holy temple courts.

The anointed priest's speech concludes in 62:10-12 with the announcement and signal that the deliverer, i.e., the holy presence of YHWH, has arrived. Verse 10 opens this announcement with a fivefold command to prepare for the return of the people from exile as they pass through the gates over the newly-prepared roads with flags that signal their entry into the city. The waving of such flags recalls the flags under which the tribes of Israel marched in the wilderness. It also recalls the ensign in 11:10 that signals the restoration of the Davidic king, but in chs. 40–66 there is no Davidic king; only YHWH is recognized as king at the end of the book in ch. 66. The announcement of the restoration of Zion then follows in vv. 11-12. The announcement proper appears in v. 11, in which the priest announces to Bat Zion, Daughter Zion, that her husband and deliverer, YHWH, comes with an appropriate announcement to all creation. He then announces the results of YHWH's return in v. 12, that Jerusalem is restored, that her people will be called "Holy" and "Redeemed by YHWH," and that the city will be called "Sought Out," to signify her role as the destination of sacred pilgrimage once again at the holy times of the year, and as "City Not Abandoned," to signify her restoration as the city espoused to her husband and G-d with her children, the people, all about her.

Bibliography

T. D. Anderson, "Renaming and Wedding Imagery in Isaiah 62," *Bib* 67 (1986) 75-80; W. A. M. Beuken, "Servant and Herald of Good Tidings: Isaiah 61 as an Interpretation of Isaiah 40–55," in Vermeylen, ed., *The Book of Isaiah/Le livre d'Isaïe,* 411-42; W. W.

Cannon, "Isaiah 61,1-3: An Ebed-Jahweh Poem," *ZAW* 47 (1929) 284-88; K. Elliger, *Die Einheit des Tritojesajas*, 24-26; A. J. Everson, "Isaiah 61:1-6 (To Give Them a Garland Instead of Ashes)," *Int* 32 (1978) 69-73; P. Grelot, "Sur Isaïe LXI: La première consécration d'un grand-prêtre," *RB* 97 (1990) 414-31; H.-W. Jüngling, "'Die Eichen der Gerechtigkeit': 'Protojesajanisches' in Jes 61," in *Biblische Theologie und gesellschaftlicher Wandel* (*Fest.* N. Lohfink; ed. G. Braulik, W. Gross, and S. McEvenue; Freiburg im Breigau: Herder, 1993) 199-219; U. Kellermann, "Tritojesaja und das Geheimnis des G-ttesknechts. Erwägungen zu Jes 59,21; 61,1-3; 66,18-24," *BN* 58 (1991) 46-82; K. Koenen, *Ethik und Eschatologie*, 103-12, 115-28, 131-37; W. Lau, *Schriftgelehrte Prophetie*, 66-80, 90-102, 108-15; J. C. de Moor, "Structure and Redaction: Isaiah 60,1–63,6," in van Ruiten and Vervenne, eds., *Studies in the Book of Isaiah*, 325-46; J. A. Sanders, "From Isaiah 61 to Luke 4," in *Christianity, Judaism, and Other Greco-Roman Cults* (*Fest.* M. Smith; ed. J. Neusner; SJLA 12; Leiden: Brill, 1975) 75-106; J. J. Schmitt, "The Motherhood of G-d and Zion as Mother," *RB* 92 (1985) 557-69; P. A. Smith, *Rhetoric and Redaction*, 33-38; O. H. Steck, "Der Rachetag in Jesaja lxi 2: Ein Kapitel redaktionsgeschichtlicher Kleinarbeit," *VT* 36 (1986) 323-38; idem, *Studien zu Tritojesaja*, 106-66; P. de Vries, "Structural Analysis of Isaiah 61 with a Special Focus on verses 1-3," *OTE* 26 (2013) 298-314; W. Zimmerli, "Zur Sprache Tritojesajas," 226-28.

PROPHETIC ANNOUNCEMENT CONCERNING THE DELIVERANCE OF THE RIGHTEOUS 63:1–66:24

Structure

I. Concerning YHWH's punishment of Edom and the nations	63:1-6
II. The prophet's lament: appeal for mercy	63:7–64:11
III. Report of YHWH's response: YHWH will act to requite the evil and to deliver the righteous in a new creation at Zion	65:1–66:24

Isaiah 63–66 is the concluding unit of the book of Isaiah. It is formulated as a prophetic announcement concerning the deliverance of the righteous as a means to point to the promises of restoration found throughout the book of Isaiah as a whole and the second part of the book in chs. 34–66 in particular. It also builds upon the distinction between the righteous and the wicked articulated throughout the so-called Trito-Isaiah materials in chs. 56–66 which are designed to establish criteria for who will be included in the restored covenant with Israel as announced in ch. 55.

Isaiah 63–66 is demarcated thematically from the preceding announcement of restoration in chs. 60–62 by its focus on the process of differentiating the righteous who will be included in the restored nation from the wicked who will perish. It is also distinguished formally by the syntactically-independent dual rhetorical questions, beginning with "Who is this coming from Edom?" that appear at the outset of the unit in 63:1a. The questions are posed by a sentry at the gate to one who approaches dressed for battle and covered with blood. The answer to the question, of course, is YHWH, and the unit proceeds by making it clear that YHWH is returning from the defeat of Edom, which represents the wicked of the world. Insofar as YHWH is described as speaking in righteousness and ready to save, YHWH appears to the righteous as a deliverer. Insofar as YHWH also appears as a warrior slaughtering the nations in vengeance, YHWH is also a threat to the wicked. Isaiah 63:1-6 at the head of the unit recalls the initial oracles of ch. 34, which introduce the second half of the book of Isaiah within the structure of the whole.

The second subunit in 63:7–64:11 appears in the form of a lament in which the prophet appeals for mercy, apparently to the approaching warrior, YHWH, on behalf of the nation Israel. This subunit is distinguished by its 1st-person speech perspective and its addresses to both 3rd- and 2nd-person audiences that extend throughout the subunit. Although it appeals to YHWH, it is actually addressed to the audience of the book in an effort to convince them to adopt the behavior desired by YHWH in order to be included among the righteous and thereby delivered from the impending judgment.

The third subunit in chs. 65–66 presents YHWH's response to the preceding appeal by the prophet, indicating that YHWH will act to requite evil and deliver the righteous in the new creation that will emerge at Zion. The subunit is presented as an announcement by the prophet, who in turn is conveying YHWH's words. Although the subunit focuses on the deliverance of the righteous within Israel, it has a worldwide perspective insofar as the righteous among the nations are the ones who will return the exiled Israelites to Jerusalem and the land of Israel at large.

Genre

Isaiah 63–66 includes a wide variety of generic elements that will be discussed in the detailed exegesis of each subunit. The overarching genre of the unit, however, is the PROPHETIC ANNOUNCEMENT, insofar as the prophet is the speaker throughout who conveys the words of YHWH in 63:1-6 and 65–66 and who appeals to YHWH on behalf of the people in 63:7–64:11.

Setting

Isaiah 63–66 comprises the conclusion to Trito-Isaiah, chs. 34–66, and indeed the book of Isaiah as a whole. In the first instance, its announcement of YHWH's return to deliver the righteous and to bring judgment against the wicked is consistent with the overall perspective of chs. 56–66, which call upon the people to observe YHWH's covenant in order that they might be included in the covenant with YHWH that will see to the restoration of Jerusalem and the nation Israel. Isaiah 63–66 also comprises the conclusion to the second half of the book of Isaiah in chs. 34–66, which begin in ch. 34 with an announcement of judgment against Edom, as representative of wickedness among the nations of the world, as a prelude to the announcement in ch. 35 of the return of the exiled people of Israel to Jerusalem. And again, chs. 65–66 comprise the conclusion to the entire book of Isaiah, which presents an overview of YHWH's plans for the establishment of divine sovereignty over all creation from Zion, beginning with the judgment or purging of Jerusalem and culminating in its restoration as anticipated throughout the book.

Such a scenario of restoration of the righteous and judgment against the wicked in Jerusalem is consistent with the reform efforts of Nehemiah and Ezra, who sought to restore the rebuilt Jerusalem temple as the holy center of creation at large and Israel in particular. Nehemiah saw to the defenses, repopulation, and early efforts at religious reform for the city, and Ezra returned with the Torah of YHWH to provide priestly instruction concerning the observance of YHWH's covenant. When considered in relation to Nehemiah's and Ezra's efforts to persuade the people to observe YHWH's covenant, the distinction between the righteous and the wicked in chs. 63–66 was designed to motivate the audience of the book to observe YHWH's covenant and thereby be considered among the righteous, rather than to neglect the covenant and suffer the fate of the wicked. Insofar as so much of the book of Isaiah demonstrates liturgical formulation, it would appear that the final form of the book of Isaiah was written for liturgical performance to support the reform efforts of Ezra (see Koch, "Ezra and the Origins of Judaism").

Interpretation

Isaiah 63–66 is designed to serve as the conclusion of the book of Isaiah by pointing to the restoration of Israel to Jerusalem as the culmination of the book. It thereby serves as a means to interpret the suffering experienced by Jerusalem during the ca. three- to four-hundred-year period covered by the book, beginning with the Assyrian invasions of Israel and Judah in the late 8th century B.C.E., the Assyrian subjugation of Judah during the early 7th century, the failed efforts at national restoration mounted by King Josiah of Judah in the late 7th century, the subjugation of Judah to Babylonia and the Babylonian exile in the 6th century, the Persian period restoration with the rebuilding of the temple in the late 6th century, and finally the reform and restoration efforts of Nehemiah and Ezra in the 5th and early 4th centuries. Isaiah 63–66 is therefore designed to defend YHWH by portraying the restoration of Zion and the recognition of YHWH's sovereignty over Israel, all the nations, and all creation as the ultimate goal of YHWH's efforts.

The unit begins in 63:1-6 by portraying YHWH's destruction of Edom as a means to signal YHWH's role as deliverer of the righteous and judge of the wicked to set the theme for the unit. It then turns to the prophet's lament on behalf of the people with its appeal to deliver the people from oppression. It then culminates with the prophet's announcement of YHWH's restoration of Zion, including YHWH's plans to requite the wicked and to restore the righteous in the newly-restored Jerusalem, which in turns serves as the new holy center of Israel, the nations, and all creation. The goal of such a distinction, of course, is to convince the people that they will want to be included among the righteous by observing YHWH's covenant and thereby avoid the fate of the wicked portrayed at the end of the book.

Bibliography

K. Koch, "Ezra and the Origins of Judaism," *JSS* 19 (1974) 173-97; M. A. Sweeney, *Isaiah 1–4,* 91-92; A. J. Tomasino, "Isaiah 1.1–2.4 and 63–66, and the Composition of the Isaianic Corpus," *JSOT* 57 (1993) 81-98.

PROPHETIC ANNOUNCEMENT CONCERNING YHWH'S PUNISHMENT OF EDOM AND THE NATIONS 63:1-6

Structure

I. First question and response: Watchman questions approaching figure	63:1
A. Watchman's threefold first question: who is this coming in red-stained garments from Edom/Bozrah?	63:1a
1. Who is this coming from Edom?	63:1aα^{1-3}
2. Who is this coming in red-stained garments from Bozrah?	63:1aα^{4-6}
3. Who is this marching in great might?	63:1aβ
B. (YHWH's) answer: I speak in righteousness, great to deliver	63:1b
II. Second question and response: watchman questions color of garments	63:2-6
A. Watchman's twofold second question: why are your garments red?	63:2
1. Why is your garment red?	63:2a
2. Why is your clothing like one who treads in a grape press?	63:2b
B. (YHWH's) answer: I alone am taking vengeance against peoples	63:3-6
1. Announcement of punishment against peoples: I punished the peoples due to my planned day of vengeance	63:3-4
a. Concerning punishment of peoples	63:3
1) I trod the vintage alone	63:3aα
a) Basically stated	63:3aα^{1-3}
b) Elaborated: no one was with me from the peoples	63:3aα^{4-7}
2) I trod in anger staining my clothing	63:3aβ-b
a) Concerning treading in anger	63:3aβ
(1) I trod them in my anger	63:3aβ^{1-2}
(2) I trampled them in my wrath	63:3aβ^{3-4}
b) I stained my garments	63:3b
(1) Their blood stained my garments	63:3bα
(2) I stained all my clothing	63:3bβ
b. Basis for punishment: day of vengeance and year of redemption	63:4
1) Day of vengeance was in my heart	63:4a
2) Year of redemption had come	63:4b
2. Continued announcement of punishment: I punish nations alone	63:5-6

a. There was no one to help   63:5a
    1) I looked but there was no one helping   63:5aα
    2) I searched but there was no one supporting   63:5aβ
b. My arm and anger were my help and support   63:5b
    1) My arm gave me deliverance   63:5bα
    2) My anger was my support   63:5bβ
c. I trampled them in punishment   63:6
    1) I trampled peoples in my anger   63:6aα
    2) I made them drunk in my wrath   63:6aβ
    3) I brought their blood down to earth   63:6b

The prophetic announcement concerning YHWH's punishment of the nations is demarcated by the question-answer format that defines the structure of the entire passage. The scenario presupposes a watchman at the gate, who might be either a military guard for the city or a priestly gatekeeper for the temple, who questions an approaching figure whose garments are stained red with blood or the juice of trampled grapes. Although the passage never identifies YHWH as the approaching figure, the claim of punishment against the peoples ensures that YHWH is the intended figure in this scenario.

The passage comprises two basic subunits, each of which is based on a question and answer schema. Together, they implicitly identify the approaching figure as YHWH and portray YHWH's punishment of the nations as an act of judgment. Although the cause of the punishment is never made clear apart from YHWH's need to take vengeance and to bring about redemption, the passage hints that the nations have not abided by YHWH's will insofar as YHWH is left alone. Consequently, punishment is mandated. It is portrayed metaphorically as a time for the treading of grapes, presumably after they are gathered for the fall festival of Sukkot, "Booths" or "Tabernacles," when the fruit harvest is brought in prior to the onset of the fall rains. In order to provide adequate long-term storage of the grape harvest, they are trampled into grape juice or *tirosh* and allowed to ferment so that they will become wine, which can then be consumed throughout the year.

The first question and answer sequence in the text appears in 63:1, where the basic identity of the one approaching is established. The watchman asks a threefold question of one seen approaching in v. 1a, "who is this coming from Edom?" in v. 1aα[1-3]; "who is this coming in red-stained garments from Bozrah?" in v. 1aα[4-6]; and "who is this marching in great might?" in v. 1aβ. The passage of course portrays the approach of a figure apparently returning from battle in Edom with garments stained red with blood. The answer then follows in v. 1b in which the speaker does not self-identify but simply states, "I speak in righteousness, great to deliver." Such an answer suggests that the figure is YHWH, returning from having carried out judgment against Edom (cf. chs. 21; 34).

The second question and answer sequence appears in 63:2-6, in which the watchman questions the red color of the approaching figure's garments. The watchman's twofold question appears in v. 2, including the question, "why is your garment red?" in v. 2a and "why is your clothing like one who treads in a grape press?" in v. 2b. The second question shifts the significance of the color from battle to the grape harvest and thereby signals the time of Sukkot, which is viewed as a time of great rejoicing and deliverance in ancient Judah as the year's fruit harvest comes in. The answer, however, ensures that the speaker is YHWH and that the issue at hand remains YHWH's punishment against the nations who do not abide by YHWH's will.

YHWH's answer begins with an announcement of punishment in 63:3-4, in which YHWH lays out a brief rationale for judgment against the nations. The announcement of punishment against the peoples appears in v. 3 in two major subunits. The first in v. 3aα focuses on YHWH's claim to have trod the vintage alone, an act that would be unthinkable in Judean society, where everyone would cooperate to ensure that the fruit harvest was in before the rains came. YHWH's statement in turn falls into two parts: a basic statement that "I trod the vintage alone" in v. 3aα$^{1-3}$, followed by an elaboration on the issue in v. 3aα$^{4-7}$ that no one from the peoples was with YHWH. The second subunit in v. 3aβ-b focuses on YHWH's anger at having been left alone, thereby staining the clothing. The first part of this subunit focuses on YHWH's anger in v. 3aβ, including statements by YHWH that "I trod them in my anger" in v. 3aβ$^{1-2}$ and that "I trampled them in my wrath" in v. 3aβ$^{3-4}$. The second part of the subunit in v. 3b focuses on the stained garments, including YHWH's statements that "their blood (or juice) stained my garments" in v. 3bα and that "I stained all my clothing" in v. 3bβ. A statement of the basis for the punishment of the peoples then follows in v. 4, including YHWH's claims that "a day of vengeance was in my heart" in v. 4a and that "a year of redemption has come" in v. 4b. Together, these statements suggest wrongdoing on the part of the nations against Jerusalem or Judah that had to be righted.

A continued announcement of punishment against the nations then follows in 63:5-6, in which YHWH announces that "I punish nations alone." This subunit comprises three basic elements. The first in v. 5a announces that there was no one to help YHWH, i.e., no one had sided with YHWH. The announcement includes two elements: YHWH's statement that "I looked but there was no one helping" in v. 5aα and that "I searched but there was no one supporting" in v. 5aβ. The second element appears in v. 5b with YHWH's assertion that "my arm and my anger were my help and my support," including YHWH's assertion that "my arm gave me deliverance" in v. 5bα and that "my anger was my support" in v. 5bβ. The third element is YHWH's assertion in v. 6 that "I trampled them in punishment," including statements that "I trampled peoples in my anger" in v. 6aα, that "I made them drunk in my wrath" in v. 6aβ, and that "I brought their blood (juice) down to earth" in v. 6b. These last statements combine the metaphors of spilt blood and grape juice.

Genre

The prophetic announcement concerning YHWH's judgment against Edom and the nations in Isa 63:1-6 is based especially in the QUESTION AND ANSWER SCHEMA in the Hebrew Bible and ancient Near Eastern literature. The genre functions as a literary device that projects a question and its response as a means of describing a future situation. Normally, the genre assumes a disaster, and by means of its questions and answers attempts to explain the disaster and assign responsibility for it. In this case, the text presupposes the setting of a watchman at the gate of the city or the temple who makes inquiry of an approaching figure who would enter. The questions are basic: "who is this coming from Edom and Bozrah?" and "why are your garments stained red?" The genre thereby establishes several premises. The first is that Edom and Bozrah, one of the major cities of Edom, are under threat. The second is that the approaching figure is responsible for the threat, particularly since his garments are stained red with what is presumably blood. The third is that there is indeed a temple setting associated with this oracle, insofar as the metaphor of trampled grapes is employed to express the motif of blood-stained garments; i.e., the trampling of grapes is associated with the fruit harvest celebrated in ancient Judah at the festival of Sukkot, "Booths" or "Tabernacles," in the fall. Such an association entails an element of deliverance for the people of Jerusalem and Judah so that the threat leveled against Edom and Bozrah must result in deliverance for Judah and its temple. The fourth is that YHWH is the figure in question who will bring punishment against Edom and Bozrah and thereby bring deliverance to Jerusalem and Judah.

The second major generic pattern in 63:1-6 is the PROPHETIC ANNOUNCE-MENT OF JUDGMENT. A modified form of the pattern is apparent in vv. 3-6, in which YHWH announces judgment against the nations as the answer to the watchman's second set of questions, "why are your garments stained red?" The formal ANNOUNCEMENT OF JUDGMENT appears in v. 3, and the BASIS FOR PUNISHMENT appears in v. 4. Verses 5-6 then continue the PROPHETIC AN-NOUNCEMENT OF PUNISHMENT. There are two modifications. The first is that the basis for punishment does not specify wrongdoing on the part of the nations to be punished. Instead, the reference to a day of vengeance in v. 4a presumes some act that merits punishment. The following reference in v. 4b to the year of redemption indicates that the act of punishment against the nations will play a role in redeeming Jerusalem and Judah. The second is the continuation of the announcement of punishment against the nations in vv. 5-6. The reason for these modifications is that the text is designed to make the points that Edom is currently suffering punishment, that YHWH is responsible for the punishment, and that Edom's punishment is emblematic for all of the nations that oppressed Jerusalem and Judah. The motif that YHWH acts alone because there is no one to help underscores the claim that all of the nations will suffer punishment because no one came to the aid of Jerusalem and Judah. All are therefore culpable and subject to divine punishment.

Setting

The social setting for 63:1-6 appears to lie in a watchman's query to an approaching figure who would seek entry into the city or temple guarded by the watchman. The initial setting presupposes a city gate in which the watchman questions a figure approaching from Edom and Bozrah with clothing stained in blood. The stains suggest that the figure has returned from warfare in Edom and Bozrah. But as the passage continues, it introduces the motif of garments stained with the juice of grapes resulting from the ingathering of the grape harvest and the subsequent treading of grapes into *tirosh* or grape juice that will be drunk or stored in jars and fermented to produce wine. Such imagery suggests a temple setting for the watchman who would then function as one of the Levitical gatekeepers for the temple (see 1 Chronicles 26) and the entrance (Psalms 15; 24). The festival of Sukkot, held at the end of the dry summer season prior to the fall rains, would celebrate the bounty of the fruit harvest which would supply the people's needs for the coming year. Such celebration would entail deliverance from drought and want as well as deliverance from an enemy, such as Edom or the nations at large.

This points to the historical setting as well, insofar as the passage presupposes a threat against Edom and Bozrah, one of Edom's major cities, as well as against the nations at large which did nothing to protect Jerusalem and Judah during their own times of threat. Other biblical texts presuppose that Edom actively cooperated with the Babylonian Empire in the destruction of Jerusalem and the temple (see ch. 34; Ezek 25:12; Joel 4:19[NRSV 3:19]; Obadiah; Ps 137:7; Lam 4:21-22). Although interpreters frequently dismiss these references as speculation that lacks proof, the pervasiveness of this tradition points to long-lasting resentment against Edom for actions against Jerusalem and the temple at the time of the Babylonian assault. The Nabonidus Chronicle indicates that the Babylonian monarch, Nabonidus, besieged a place known as "the city of Edom," which many interpreters judge to be Bozrah, in the mid-6th century B.C.E. Biblical sources likewise refer to Edom's suffering during this period (Jer 49:7-22; Ezek 25:12-14; Obad 1, 8; Mal 1:2-5). Although Edom recovered from its mid-6th century reverses, by the 4th and 3rd centuries, the Nabateans, possibly linked to Nebaioth, were displacing the Edomites (see J. R. Bartlett, "Edom," *ABD* 2:287-95; idem, *Edom and the Edomites;* K. Mellish, "Edom," *EBR* 7:403-11). The social setting of the Jerusalem temple and the celebration of Sukkot, the motif of deliverance for Jerusalem and Judah, and the decline of the Edomites therefore point to the mid-5th to early 4th century, when Nehemiah and Ezra were restoring the temple to its place as the holy center of Jewish life in Jerusalem and Judah under Persian rule.

The literary setting appears to be the late-5th- through early-4th-century final edition of the book of Isaiah produced during the time of Ezra and Nehemiah. Isaiah 63:1-6 introduces the last major unit of the book in chs. 63–66 where, following the announcement of Zion's restoration in chs. 60–62, the text turns to the question of the judgment against the wicked and the restoration of the righteous. Isaiah 63:1-6 looks to judgment against Edom and the nations for their role in the oppression of Jerusalem and Judah, and this concern leads in turn to the projected punishment of the wicked within Jerusalem and Judah itself, who would be viewed as impeding the restoration of the city and the nation. The reforms of Ezra and Nehemiah were designed to correct the behavior of the people so that they might be considered worthy of YHWH's restoration. Isaiah 63:1-6 establishes the principle that Edom and the nations had sinned and therefore merited punishment. The balance of the unit in chs. 63–66 would apply a similar measure to Jerusalem and Judah as a means to persuade the people to observe divine expectations and thereby not find themselves among those who merit punishment.

Some interpreters contend that 63:1-6 forms, with 59:17-19, a redactional envelope around chs. 60–62. Given the relationship of both 63:1-6 and 59:17-19 with their immediate literary contexts, there is little basis to conclude that they represent a redactional thread that has been added secondarily for such a purpose. Nevertheless, 59:17-19 does anticipate some of the imagery of 63:1-6 so that the two passages function within the larger blocks in chs. 56–59 and 63–66 to form the redactional envelope for chs. 60–62. Isaiah 56–59 and chs. 63–66 aid in building the basic plot and argument of chs. 56–66, that YHWH comes to restore and deliver Zion together with the righteous therein, but those who fail to meet YHWH's expectations will suffer death.

Interpretation

Isaiah 63:1-6 employs the motif of a watchman's questions to one approaching the gates for entry to convey YHWH's announcement of judgment against the nations of the world. This text relates to the initial portrayal of an ideal scenario in ch. 2, in which Jacob is invited to join the nations in streaming to Zion to learn divine torah and thereby to produce a world in which nations would turn their swords into plowshares and their spears into pruning hooks to learn war no more. But ch. 2 also maintains that the means to attain such an ideal scenario is through YHWH's punishment of the world at large. Isaiah 63:1-6 takes up the question of the punishment of the nations, beginning with Edom, which is highlighted in ch. 34 at the introduction to the second half of the book.

Isaiah 63:1-6 presents no concrete reason for Edom's punishment; its motivation is simply YHWH's perception of a day of vengeance. Other biblical references indicate that Edom played a role in carrying out the destruction of Jerusalem and the temple by the Babylonians in 587-586 B.C.E. (see Isaiah 34; Ezek 25:12; Joel 4:19[NRSV 3:19]; Obadiah; Ps 137:7; Lam 4:21-22), and Isa 63:1-6 indicates that the time of punishment has come. Insofar as Edom and Bozrah in particular suffered attack by the Babylonians led by Nabonidus in the mid-6th century and declined into the 4th and 3rd centuries as the Nabateans supplanted the Edomites, the passage appears to presuppose that YHWH was in fact behind the reverses in Edom's fortunes during this period. As in ch. 34, the nations are also included in the judgment, but the only hints of wrongdoing are YHWH's statements that none of the nations joined to aid the divine purpose and so the nations would suffer punishment as well.

As the lead text in the last major subunit of the book of Isaiah in chs. 63–66, 63:1-6 introduces a concern with the welfare of Jerusalem and Judah as well. The passage indicates that restoration is part of the overall scenario insofar as YHWH's motivation in bringing about the punishment is that the year of redemption had come. As noted above, the passage presupposes the in-gathering of the grape harvest as part of its scenario of judgment and restoration — Edom and the nations would be cut down and trampled like grapes at the time of the fruit harvest (for analogous imagery applied to those who threaten Jerusalem, see Joel 1–2). But the fruit harvest in the fall signals the celebration of the festival of Sukkot, which marks the end of the dry summer season and the beginning of the rainy fall season in the land of Israel. The ingathering of the fruit at Sukkot therefore marks a time of celebration and redemption, as the fruit harvest signals the ingathering of food, the production of *tirosh,* wine, olive oil, dates, etc. that would support the people for the coming year. As the lead subunit of chs. 63–66, our passage signals judgment against the wicked, which will include those considered wicked within Jerusalem and Judah as well, that would ultimately signal the realization of the initial vision of 2:2-4, in which Jerusalem would stand as the center of holiness, learning of divine torah, and peace, among Israel and all the nations of the world, thereby signaling YHWH's role as creator and sovereign of all creation and the nations that reside therein.

Bibliography

J. R. Bartlett, *Edom and the Edomites* (JSOTSup 77; Sheffield: JSOT, 1989); C. Carvalho, "The Beauty of the Bloody G-d: The Divine Warrior in Prophetic Literature," in *Aesthetics of Violence in the Prophets* (ed. C. Franke and J. M. O'Brien; LHBOTS 517; New York: T. & T. Clark, 2010) 131-52; B. Gosse, "Détournement de la vengeance du Seigneur contre Edom et les nations en Isa 63,1-6," *ZAW* 102 (1990) 105-10; F. C. Harding, "The Oracle against Edom (Isa 63:1-6 and 59:16-17)," *JBL* 33 (1914) 213-17; F. Holmgren, "YHWH the Avenger: Isaiah 63:1-6," in *Rhetorical Criticism (Fest.* J. Muilenburg; ed. J. J. Jackson and M. Kessler; PTMS 1; Pittsburgh: Pickwick, 1974) 133-48; K. Koenen, *Ethik und Eschatologie,* 76-87; W. Lau, *Schriftgelehrte Prophetie,* 279-86; M. J. Lynch, "Zion's Warrior and the Nations: Isaiah 59:15b-63:6 in Isaiah's Zion Traditions," *CBQ* 70 (2008) 244-63; J. C. de Moor, "Structure and Redaction: Isaiah 60,1–63,6," in van Ruiten and Vervenne, eds., *Studies in the Book of Isaiah,* 325-46; J. M. Myers, "Edom and Judah in the Sixth-Fifth Centuries B.C.," in *Near Eastern Studies (Fest.* W. F. Albright; ed. H. Goedicke; Baltimore: Johns Hopkins University Press, 1971) 377-92; K. Pauritsch, *Die neue Gemeinde,* 138-44; H. G. L. Peels, *The Vengeance of G-d: The Meaning of the Root NQM and the Function of the NQM Texts in the Context of Divine Revelation in the OT* (OtSt 31; Leiden: Brill, 1995); S. Sekine, *Die tritojesanische Sammlung,* 140-47; P. A. Smith, *Rhetoric and Redaction,* 38-49; O. H. Steck, *Studien zu Tritojesaja,* 106-18; E. C. Webster, "The Rhetoric of Isaiah 63–65," *JSOT* 47 (1990) 89-102; W. Zimmerli, "Das Gnadenjahr des H-rrn," in *Archäologie und Altes Testament (Fest.* K. Galling; ed. A. Kuschke and E. Kutsch; Tübingen: Mohr Siebeck, 1970) 321-32.

THE PROPHET'S LAMENT APPEAL TO YHWH FOR MERCY 63:7–64:11(NRSV 12)

Structure

I. First address to YHWH: prophet's historical review concerning YHWH's acts in support of Israel to make an eternal name   63:7-14

A. Prophet's historical review proper   63:7-14a
    1. Introduction: prophet recalls YHWH's fidelity to house of
       Israel   63:7
       a. Twofold announcement of intention to recall YHWH's
          fidelity   63:7aα
          1) I will recall fidelities of YHWH   63:7aα$^{1-3}$
          2) (I will recall) praises of YHWH   63:7aα$^{4-5}$
       b. Threefold specification   63:7aβ-b
          1) According to all the goodness that YHWH bestowed
             upon house of Israel   63:7aβ-bβ^2
          2) According to YHWH's mercies   63:7bβ$^{3-4}$
          3) According to YHWH's many fidelities   63:7bβ$^{5-6}$
    2. Review of YHWH's role as deliverer of people   63:8-9
       a. Concerning YHWH's decision to become Israel's
          deliverer   63:8
          1) YHWH says to Self: they are my people who do
             not betray   63:8a
             a) Narrative tag: and he said (to himself)   63:8aα^1
             b) Content of thought: they are my people who do
                not betray   63:8aα^2-β
                (1) Indeed, they are my people   63:8aα$^{2-4}$
                (2) They are my children who will not betray   63:8aβ
          2) So YHWH became their deliverer   63:8b
       b. Concerning YHWH's actions on behalf of Israel as
          deliverer   63:9
          1) YHWH's deliverance of Israel   63:9aα
             a) In all their trouble, YHWH was troubled   63:9aα$^{1-4}$
             b) And so the angel of YHWH's presence delivered
                them   63:9aα$^{5-7}$
          2) YHWH's redemption of Israel   63:9aβ-b
             a) In all his love and pity, YHWH redeemed them   63:9aβ
             b) YHWH carried and bore them all the days of old   63:9b
    3. YHWH becomes enemy to people because of their rebellion   63:10
       a. Concerning people's rebellion against YHWH   63:10a
          1) People rebelled   63:10aα
          2) People grieved YHWH's holy spirit   63:10aβ
       b. YHWH changes to enemy of people   63:10b
          1) YHWH becomes enemy of people   63:10bα
          2) YHWH fights against them   63:10bβ
    4. YHWH remembers the days of old to make Self a name
       by delivering people   63:11-14a
       a. YHWH remembers days of old, drawing out the people   63:11a
          1) YHWH remembers days of old   63:11aα
          2) Specification: drawing out the people   63:11aβ
       b. Rhetorical questions concerning YHWH's actions on
          behalf of Israel to deliver them from Egypt: assertions
          of YHWH's acts on behalf of Israel   63:11b-14aα

1) Twofold explicit questions   63:11b
   a) Where is the one who brought them up from the
      sea with the shepherds of his flock?   63:11bα
   b) Where is the one who placed in Israel's midst his
      holy spirit?   63:11bβ
2) Threefold implicit rhetorical questions   63:12-14aα
   a) (Who) led his glorious arm at the right hand of
      Moses?   63:12a
   b) (Who) divided the sea before them to make him-
      self an eternal name?   63:12b
   c) (Who) led them in the depths like a horse that
      does not stumble and a beast that goes down to the
      valley?   63:13-14aα
     (1) Like a horse that does not stumble?   63:13
     (2) Like a beast that goes down to the valley?   63:14aα
  c. Rhetorical answer: the spirit of YHWH gives us rest   63:14aβ
 B. Prophet's address to YHWH: so you guided your people to
   make for yourself a glorious name   63:14b
II. Second address to YHWH: prophet's appeal to YHWH to
deliver and redeem the people   63:15–64:11
 A. Prophet's appeal to YHWH to observe destitute state of
  temple and people   63:15-19a
   1. Appeal proper to look down from heaven and see from
     your holy and glorious height   63:15a
    a. Look down from heaven   63:15aα
    b. See from your holy and glorious height   63:15aβ
   2. First rhetorical question with answer: you are our Father   63:15b-16
    a. Question proper: where is your zeal and power?   63:15bα
    b. Answer: your empathy and mercy are withheld though
     you are our Father   63:15bβ-16
     1) Basically stated: your empathy and mercy are with-
      held from me   63:15bβ
     2) Motivation to change: twofold assertion that you are
      our Father   63:16
      a) First assertion: you are our Father   63:16a
       (1) Basically stated: you are our Father   63:16aα
       (2) Counterpoints: though Abraham and Israel
         wouldn't know us   63:16aβ-γ
         (a) Though Abraham would not know us   63:16aβ
         (b) Though Israel (Jacob) wouldn't recognize us   63:16aγ
      b) Second assertion: you, YHWH, are our Father   63:16b
       (1) Basically stated: you, YHWH, are our Father   63:16bα
       (2) Your name from old is "Our Redeemer"   63:16bβ
   3. Second rhetorical question with answer: return to us   63:17-19a
    a. Twofold rhetorical questions: why do you make us stray
     and harden our hearts?   63:17a
     1) Why do you make us stray from your ways?   63:17aα

2) Why do you harden our hearts from revering you?   63:17aβ
b. Rhetorical answer: return to us   63:17b-19a
    1) Rhetorical answer proper: return for the sake of your
      servants, the tribes of your heritage   63:17b
    2) Substantiation/motivation   63:18-19a
      a) Your temple is trampled   63:18
        (1) Your holy people possessed (the temple) only
          briefly   63:18a
        (2) Our enemies have trampled your sanctuary   63:18b
      b) We are devoid of your identity   63:19a
        (1) We are like a people that you never ruled   63:19aα
        (2) We are like a people that lack your name   63:19aβ
B. Prophet's appeal to YHWH to come down and make name
  known to enemies   63:19b–64:3
   1. Appeal proper: come down and make name known to
     enemies   63:19b–64:1
     a. Conditional appeal to tear heavens and come down   63:19bα
      1) Tear heavens   63:19bα$^{1-3}$
      2) Come down   63:19bα^{4}
     b. Basis for appeal: mountains and nations would fear you   63:19bβ–64:1
      1) Mountains would quake before you   63:19bβ–64:1aα
       a) Basically stated   63:19b
       b) Twofold metaphorical comparison   64:1aα
        (1) As when fire kindles brush   64:1aα$^{1-3}$
        (2) As when fire boils water   64:1aα$^{4-6}$
      2) Nations will tremble before you   64:1aβ-b
       a) Purpose: to make your name known to enemies   64:1aβ
       b) Basically stated   64:1b
   2. Past substantiation for appeal: you have done it before   64:2-3
     a. When you act, mountains quake   64:2
      1) When you did wonders, we did not expect you to
       come down   64:2a-bα^{1}
      2) Mountains quaked before you   64:2bα^{2}-β
     b. No one but you acts for those who wait for you   64:3
      1) No one has ever heard such a thing   64:3a
       a) No one has ever heard   64:3aα
       b) We have not noticed   64:3aβ
      2) The eye has not seen a G-d apart from you who acts
       for those who wait   64:3b
C. Appeal for action   64:4-11
   1. YHWH punished one who would act righteously   64:4aα
   2. Appeal for action because the people will remember you
     for your ways   64:4aβ-11
     a. Premise: people will remember you for your ways   64:4aβ-b
      1) Basically stated: the people will remember you for
       your ways   64:4aβ
      2) Twofold illustration of principle   64:4b

a) You are angry when we sin — 64:4bα
b) We walk in your ways and we are delivered — 64:4bβ
b. Past punishment contrasted with present appeal for
deliverance — 64:5-11
1) Past punishment — 64:5-6
   a) We are unclean and carried off — 64:5
      (1) We are all unclean — 64:5a
         (a) Basically stated — 64:5aα
         (b) Our righteousness is unclean like a men-
            strual cloth — 64:5aβ
      (2) We all wither like leaves — 64:5b
         (a) Basically stated — 64:5bα
         (b) Our iniquities are lifted up like wind — 64:5bβ
   b) No one calls on your name because you hide your
     face — 64:6
      (1) No one calls on you — 64:6a
         (a) No one calls upon your name — 64:6aα
         (b) No one awakens to grasp you — 64:6aβ
      (2) Reason: you hide your face and punish us — 64:6b
         (a) You hide your face from us — 64:6bα
         (b) You dissolve us for our iniquities — 64:6bβ
2) Appeal for present deliverance — 64:7-11
   a) Assertion of father/children relationship between
     YHWH and people: foundation for appeal — 64:7
      (1) YHWH, you are our father — 64:7a
      (2) We are clay and you are potter — 64:7bα
         (a) We are clay — 64:7bα$^{1-2}$
         (b) You are the potter — 64:7bα$^{3-4}$
      (3) We are all the work of your hands — 64:7bβ
   b) Appeal for attention: do not be angry; look — 64:8
      (1) Do not be angry or remember iniquity forever — 64:8a
         (a) Do not be angry — 64:8aα
         (b) Do not remember iniquity forever — 64:8aβ
      (2) Look at all of your people — 64:8b
   c) What you will see: ruin — 64:9-10
      (1) Ruined holy cities — 64:9
         (a) Your holy cities are wilderness — 64:9a
         (b) Zion has become wilderness — 64:9bα
         (c) Jerusalem has become desolate — 64:9bβ
      (2) Ruined temple — 64:10
         (a) Our holy and glorious temple is burned
            with fire — 64:10a
         (b) Our delightful temple has become a ruin — 64:10b
   d) Appeal for action by twofold rhetorical questions — 64:11
      (1) Will you restrain yourself over this, YHWH? — 64:11a
      (2) Will you remain silent and allow us to suffer
         so much? — 64:11b

Isaiah 63:7–64:11 constitutes the prophet's lament: appeal to YHWH for mercy, to act on behalf of the people of Israel and to restore their ruined cities, particularly Jerusalem and the Jerusalem temple. The passage is demarcated by the 1st-person speaker who first appears in 63:7. Whereas the 1st-person speaker of 63:1-6 is YHWH, the 1st-person speaker in 63:7–64:11 addresses YHWH throughout the passage. Likewise, the 1st-person speaker of 65:1 is YHWH once again. Although the speaker in 63:7 appears to address the people initially in vv. 7-14a, the statement to YHWH in 63:14b, "Thus you have guided *(nihagtā)* your people to make for yourself a glorious name," indicates that the 3rd-person references to YHWH's past actions on behalf of the people are actually addressed to YHWH in an effort to motivate YHWH to act on the people's behalf once again. Following the portrayal of YHWH's slaughter of the nations and Edom in 63:1-6, the appeal to YHWH to act on Israel's behalf follows naturally from the defeat of Israel's oppressors. The portrayal of the nations bringing exiled Israelites back to Jerusalem in chs. 65–66 then completes the scenario of anticipated restoration.

Isaiah 63:7–64:11 constitutes the prophet's address to YHWH. The formal structure of the passage comprises two basic addresses to YHWH, each of which serves a distinctive purpose. The first address to YHWH in 63:7-14 presents the prophet's historical review concerning YHWH's past acts to support Israel which resulted in making an eternal and glorious name for YHWH. The second address to YHWH in 63:15–64:11, signaled by the imperative clause *habbēṭ . . . ûrĕ'ēh,* "look . . . and see," constitutes the prophet's appeal to YHWH to deliver and redeem the people.

The presentation of the prophet's first address to YHWH in 63:7-14 is demarcated at the outset by the 1st-person singular address form, which points to the prophet as the speaker. Although the 3rd-person historical review of YHWH's acts on behalf of the people in vv. 7-14a would seem to indicate that the people are the addressees, the above-noted address to YHWH in 63:14b indicates that the whole of vv. 7-14 indeed functions as an address to YHWH. The introductory particle *kēn,* "thus," is inherently conjunctive and thereby indicates continuity with the preceding verses. It also indicates the conclusion that they presume the prophet's historical review as an address to YHWH. In the present context, the historical review functions as a means to motivate YHWH to act on behalf of the people. Consequently, the formal structure of the unit breaks down into two primary subunits. The first is the prophet's 3rd-person historical review of YHWH's past acts on behalf of Israel in 63:7-14a. The second is the address to YHWH in 63:14b indicating the purpose of the summary: to indicate how YHWH obtained a glorious name by acting on behalf of Israel. Although unstated, the context suggests that YHWH's eternal and glorious name is now in question.

The prophet's historical review of YHWH's past acts on behalf of Israel in 63:7-14a comprises four basic subunits, each of which is defined by a combination of thematic and syntactical features. The four subunits are each joined by a *wāw*-formation to indicate continuity.

The first subunit is 63:7, which functions as the prophet's introduction to the review, which recalls YHWH's past acts on behalf of Israel. The prophet makes a twofold statement of the intent to recall YHWH's acts in v. 7aα, including the statement "The fidelities of YHWH I will recall *('azkîr)*" in v. 7aα$^{1-3}$ and "the praises of YHWH (I will recall)" in v. 7aα$^{4-5}$. A threefold specification of the prophet's purposes in recalling YHWH's acts then follows in v. 7aβ-b, each of which begins with the preposition *kĕ-*, "like, as, according to," to indicate the positive portrayal of YHWH's actions. Thus, v. 7aβ-bβ^2 indicates "according to all the goodness that YHWH bestowed on the house of Israel"; v. 7bβ$^{3-4}$ indicates "according to YHWH's mercies"; and v. 7bβ$^{5-6}$ indicates "and according to YHWH's many fidelities."

The second subunit is 63:8-9, in which the prophet reviews YHWH's role as deliverer of the people. This subunit focuses specifically on YHWH's acts, in two components. The first is a portrayal of YHWH's concerns for the people in v. 8. This segment begins with a presentation of YHWH's thoughts in v. 8a, signaled by the narrative tag in v. 8aα^1, "and he said (to himself)," and the content of YHWH's thoughts in v. 8aα^2-β. The quotation of YHWH's thoughts appears in two parallel syntactic statements: "indeed, they are my people," in v. 8aα$^{2-4}$ and "they are my children who will not betray" in v. 8aβ. The syntactically-joined *wāw*-consecutive statement in v. 8b, "and He (YHWH) became their deliverer," points to the conclusion drawn by YHWH as a result of these thoughts. The second component in v. 9 then turns to YHWH's actions on behalf of Israel that follow from YHWH's decision to become Israel's deliverer in v. 8. The relationship between vv. 9 and 8 is signaled at the outset of v. 9 by the phrase "in all their trouble, He (YHWH) was troubled," which indicates that YHWH was motivated to act by witnessing Israel's past affliction. Verse 9 portrays two roles for YHWH: "deliverer of Israel" in v. 9aα and "redeemer of Israel" in v. 9aβ-b. The portrayal of YHWH as deliverer in v. 9aα comprises two basic elements, an assertion that in all their trouble YHWH was troubled in v. 9aα$^{1-4}$ and the following statement that the angel of YHWH's presence delivered them in v. 9aα$^{5-7}$, apparently as a consequence of YHWH's distress over the troubles of the people. The portrayal of YHWH as redeemer of Israel in v. 9aβ-b likewise comprises two components, including the assertion in v. 9aβ that in all his love and pity for Israel, YHWH redeemed them and the following statement, joined by a *wāw*-consecutive, in v. 9b that YHWH carried and bore them as in days of old.

The third subunit in 63:10 shifts to a focus on how YHWH became an enemy to the people as a consequence of their rebellion. The subunit comprises two elements joined together by a *wāw*-consecutive formation, each of which is distinguished by a distinctive concern. The first in v. 10a focuses on the people's rebellion against YHWH, including two elements, the statement that the people rebelled in v. 10aα and the statement that the people grieved YHWH's holy spirit in v. 10aβ. The second in v. 10b focuses on how YHWH becomes an enemy of the people as a result of their rebellion, including two elements, the statement that YHWH becomes the enemy of the people in v. 10bα and the statement that YHWH fights against them in v. 10bβ.

The fourth subunit in 63:11-14a focuses on YHWH's memory of the days of old in which YHWH made a name by delivering the people. This subunit functions as a means to prompt YHWH to recall the older days of deliverance and redemption in an effort to prompt YHWH to resume such roles. The subunit comprises three elements based on formal and thematic features. The first element in v. 11a states how YHWH should remember the days of old when YHWH drew out the people. It includes two components, the statement that YHWH should remember the days of old in v. 11aα and the statement that YHWH drew out *(ma'ălēm)* the people in v. 11aβ. The second element in vv. 11b-14aα comprises two sets of rhetorical questions that assert YHWH's actions on behalf of Israel to deliver them from Egypt. The first set of two, explicitly formulated as rhetorical questions, appears in v. 11b, including the first question, "where is the one who brought them up from the sea with the shepherds of his flock?" in v. 11bα and the second question, "where is the one who placed in Israel's midst his holy spirit?" in v. 11bβ. The answer to each question is "YHWH," which is meant to establish the premise that YHWH acted on behalf of the people in the past. The second set of three rhetorical questions, which are only implicitly identified as questions by the lack of an interrogative at the outset of each, appears in vv. 12-14aα. The first question in v. 12a asks, "(who) led his glorious arm at the right hand of Moses?" The second question in v. 12b asks, "(who) divided the sea before them to make himself an eternal name?" And the third question in vv. 13-14aα asks, "(who) led them in the depths like a horse that does not stumble and a beast that goes down to the valley?" The first component to this question, concerning the simile of a horse that does not stumble, appears in v. 13, and the second component, concerning the simile of a beast that goes down to the valley, appears in v. 14aα. Of course, the answer to each question is "YHWH." Isaiah 63:14aβ, which functions as the third element of 63:11-14a, provides this answer with the statement "The spirit of YHWH gives us rest."

As noted above, 63:14b shifts the prophet's speech to a direct address to YHWH with the statement "Thus you guided your people to make for yourself a glorious name." The particle *kēn,* "thus," establishes formal continuity with the historical review of vv. 7-14a by pointing to YHWH's efforts to establish a glorious name as the result of the above-stated actions. Such a statement implies that YHWH's good name and reputation depend on YHWH's efforts to deliver and redeem the people. Consequently, the review establishes motivation for YHWH to act in the present as well.

The prophet's second address to YHWH in 63:15–64:11 constitutes an appeal to YHWH to deliver and redeem the people. The passage comprises three distinct subunits, each beginning with a syntactically-independent 2nd-person masculine singular address to YHWH, in 63:15-19a; 63:19b–64:3; and 64:4-11. The first in 63:15-19a calls upon YHWH to observe the destitute state of the temple and the people. The second in 63:19b–64:3 appeals to YHWH to come down and make the divine name known to YHWH's and Israel's enemies. The third in 64:4-11 appeals to YHWH for action so that the people remember YHWH's ways. Altogether, the sequence builds upon the prior unit, which rehearsed YHWH's past actions on behalf of Israel, in an effort to compel YHWH to act on their behalf in the present.

The first subunit in 63:15-19a appeals to YHWH to observe the destitute state of the temple and the people. It comprises three components: an initial appeal in v. 15a to observe the situation below, followed by two sets of rhetorical questions with answers that assert that "YHWH is our father" in vv. 15b-16 and that "YHWH should return to us" in vv. 17-19a. The first component in v. 15a comprises a twofold masculine singular imperative statement directed to YHWH to "look down *(habbēṭ)* from heaven" in v. 15aα and to "see *(ûrĕ'ēh)* from your glorious and holy place" what the situation is down below in v. 15aβ. The second component in vv. 15b-16 constitutes a first rhetorical question with rhetorical answer addressed to YHWH which asserts that "YHWH is our father." The question proper, "where is your zeal and power?" appears in v. 15bα, and the rhetorical answer, which charges that "YHWH withholds empathy and mercy despite the fact that YHWH is our father," appears in vv. 15bβ-16. The 2nd-person masculine singular charge that YHWH withholds empathy and mercy appears as a basic statement in v. 15bβ. Verse 16, introduced by an explanatory *kî,* "for, because," then follows with a twofold assertion that "YHWH is our father," which functions as a means to persuade YHWH to change and intervene on behalf of the people. The first assertion that "YHWH is our father" appears in v. 16a, which makes the basic statement that "you are our father" in v. 16aα. Two counterpoints, introduced by a limiting *kî,* "although," and joined by a conjunctive *waw,* then follow in 16aβ-γ: "although Abraham wouldn't know us" in v. 16aβ and "(although) Israel (Jacob) wouldn't recognize us" in v. 16aγ. Both statements play on the ancestral promise that YHWH would make Israel a great nation, although the present circumstances of the people would undermine such a claim. The second assertion that "YHWH is our father" appears in v. 16b in the form of a direct 2nd-person masculine singular address including the basic statement "you, YHWH, are our father," in v. 16bα followed by the syntactically-independent assertion that "your name from old is 'Our Redeemer'" in v. 16bβ. The second set of rhetorical questions and answers then follows in vv. 17-19a in an effort to appeal to YHWH to "return to us." The twofold presentation of the rhetorical questions concerning "why YHWH makes us stray and harden our hearts" appears in v. 17a, including the question "why do you make us stray from your ways?" in v. 17aα and "why do you harden our hearts from revering you?" in v. 17aβ. Both function as charges that "YHWH makes us stray and hardens our hearts." The rhetorical answer asking YHWH to "return to us" then follows in vv. 17b-19a. The rhetorical answer proper, which appeals to YHWH to return "for the sake of your servants, the tribes of your heritage," appears in v. 17b. The substantiation and motivation for this answer then follows in vv. 18-19a in two parts. The first in v. 18 asserts that "your temple is trampled," including the statement in v. 18a that "your holy people possessed (the temple) only briefly" in v. 18a and that "our enemies have trampled your sanctuary" in v. 18b. The second in v. 19a asserts that "we are devoid of your identity," including statements that "we are like a people that you never ruled" in v. 19aα and that "we are like a people that lack your name" in v. 19aβ.

The second subunit in 63:19b–64:3 appeals to YHWH to come down and make the divine name known to YHWH's and Israel's enemies. The subunit comprises two elements, including the appeal proper in 63:19b–64:1 and a statement of the past substantiation for the appeal in 64:2-3. The appeal proper in Isa 63:19b–64:1 begins with the conditional particle *lû'-,* "if," which expresses the prophet's desire for YHWH's action. In this case, the appeal in 63:19bα to "tear open the heavens and come down" appears in two parts: "tear open the heavens" in v. 19bα¹⁻³ and "come down" in v. 19bα⁴. The basis for the appeal then follows in 63:19bβ–64:1 with assertions that "the mountains and nations would fear you." The first basis, that "mountains would quake before you," appears in 63:19bβ–64:1aα. It is basically stated in v. 19bβ, and a twofold metaphorical expansion follows in 64:1aα: "as when fire kindles brush" in v. 1aα¹⁻³, a phenomenon all too well known in Southern California, and "as when fire boils water" in v. 1aα⁴⁻⁶. The second basis in v. 1aβ-b, that "nations will tremble before you," appears in two parts: that the purpose of the action is "to make your name known to enemies" in v. 1aβ followed by a basic statement of this principle in v. 1b. The past substantiation for the ideal, the claim that YHWH has undertaken such action on behalf of Israel in the past, follows in 64:2-3 in two parts. The first in v. 2 asserts that "when you act, mountains quake," including statements in v. 2a-bα¹ that "when you did wonders, we did not expect you to come down" and in v. 2bα²-β that mountains quaked before you. The second in v. 3 asserts that "no one but you acts for those who wait for you," in two parts. The first part in v. 3a asserts that "no one has ever heard of such a thing" in v. 3aα and that "we have not noticed" in v. 3aβ. The second part in v. 3b asserts that "the eye (i.e., no one) has not seen a G-d apart from you who acts for those who wait," i.e., only YHWH acts for those who wait.

The third subunit in 64:4-11 constitutes an appeal for YHWH to act. It begins with a 2nd-masculine singular charge that YHWH punished one who would act righteously in v. 4aα. The moral disjunction in this charge then constitutes the reason why YHWH must act, to redeem the divine name and reputation. The remainder of the passage in 64:4aβ-11 constitutes a 2nd-masculine singular appeal to YHWH for action because "the people will remember you for your ways." This segment comprises two elements, a statement of the premise that "the people will remember you for your ways" in v. 4aβ-b and contrast of past punishment of Israel compared with the present appeal for deliverance in vv. 5-11. The premise that "people will remember you for your ways" in v. 4aβ-b comprises two basic elements. The first is a basic statement of the premise in v. 4aβ, and the second in v. 4b is a twofold illustration of the principle, including statements that "you are angry when we sin" in v. 4bα and that "we walk in your ways and we are delivered" in v. 4bβ. Isaiah 64:5-11 then turns to a portrayal of past punishment for Israel contrasted with the present appeal for deliverance. The portrayal of past punishment in vv. 5-6 includes two segments. The first in v. 5 presents the prophet's statement on behalf of the people that "we are unclean and carried off" — we have committed some wrongdoing and are punished for having done so. The statement that "we are unclean" appears in v. 5a in two parts, a basic statement in v. 5aα and an elaboration that "our righteousness is unclean like a menstrual cloth" in v. 5aβ, i.e., we are not righteous. The statement that "we all wither like leaves" in v. 5b comprises a basic statement in v. 5bα followed by an elaboration that "our iniquities are lifted up like the wind" in v. 5bβ, i.e., our iniquities have left us like dead leaves. The second in v. 6 presents the prophet's statement that "no one calls on your name because you hide your face," which constitutes a charge that "YHWH punishes us." The charge appears in two parts. The first in v. 6a asserts that "no one calls on you," including the assertion that "no one calls your name" in v. 6aα and that "no one awakens to grasp you" in v. 6aβ. The reason for the refusal to call upon YHWH appears in v. 6b in two parts: "you hide your face from us" in v. 6bα and "you dissolve us for our iniquities" in v. 6bβ.

The appeal by the prophet to YHWH for present deliverance follows in 64:7-11, beginning with the conjunctive phrase "and now" *(wĕ'attâ),* which links the subunit to the preceding 64:5-6. The passage proceeds in four syntactically-independent parts that function together in an attempt to motivate YHWH to act. The first appears in v. 7, which is an assertion of a father-child relationship between YHWH and the people that constitutes a foundation for YHWH's action. The subunit comprises three elements: the initial direct appeal to "YHWH, our father" in v. 7a, an assertion in v. 7bα that "we are clay" (v. 7bα¹⁻²) and "you are the potter" (v. 7bα³⁻⁴), and the concluding assertion that "we are all the work of your hands" in v. 7bβ. The second appears in v. 8, which constitutes an appeal for attention that asks YHWH to look. It includes an appeal not to be angry or remember iniquity forever in v. 8a, including appeals not to be angry in v. 8aα and not to remember iniquity forever in v. 8aβ. The appeal to "look at all of your people" follows in v. 8b. The third in vv. 9-10 asserts that YHWH will see ruin when looking at the people. The first part in v. 9 focuses on ruined holy cities, including statements that YHWH's holy cities are wilderness in v. 9a, that Zion has become wilderness in v. 9bα, and that Jerusalem has become desolate in v. 9bβ. The second part in v. 10 focuses on the ruined temple, including statements that "our holy and glorious temple is burned with fire" in v. 10a and that "our delightful temple has become a ruin" in v. 10b. The fourth and final part of the passage appears in v. 11, which constitutes an appeal for action by YHWH expressed in two rhetorical questions. The first asks, "will you restrain yourself over this, O YHWH?" in v. 11a, and the second asks, "will you remain inactive and allow us to suffer so much?" in v. 11b. Both questions are obviously answered in the negative with the expectation that YHWH will answer the appeal and act to deliver and to redeem the people.

Genre

Interpreters generally agree that 63:7–64:11 constitutes a form of a Lament, i.e., a COMPLAINT, although they also maintain that it represents a unique form of the genre. Gunkel and Mowinckel maintain that laments, also known as complaints, are liturgical compositions that typically include historical reminiscence, praise of YHWH, a description of the present unsatisfactory conditions of the people, attempts to motivate YHWH to act, a petition, assurance of a hearing, and a commitment to offer a vow or thanksgiving offering (H. Gunkel, *Einleitung in die Psalmen* [Göttingen: Vandenhoeck & Ruprecht, 1933] 125; S. Mowinckel, *The Psalms in Israel's Worship* [Nashville: Abingdon, 1962], 1:195-219). Most of the typical elements appear in 63:7–64:11. It appears to presuppose a liturgical setting, such as the laments that would have been performed at the site of the ruined temple (see Lamentations; Zechariah 7) or liturgies that would have appealed to YHWH to aid in a time of distress (Psalm 106; Nehemiah 9; cf. Ezra 9; see Williamson, "Isaiah 63,7–64,11").

Isaiah 63:7–64:11 includes a HISTORICAL REVIEW; praise of YHWH; description of the present unsatisfactory conditions of the people, the temple, and the cities of the land; attempts to motivate YHWH to act; and a petition. The HISTORICAL REVIEW in 63:7-14a rehearses YHWH's acts on behalf of Israel in providing bounty for Israel and in delivering Israel at the time of the exodus from Egypt, as well as YHWH's punishment of Israel for their rebellions in the wilderness (cf. Deuteronomy 26; 28–30). The HISTORICAL REVIEW is designed to remind YHWH of the means by which YHWH attained a great name (63:14b) as well as to praise YHWH for fidelity to Israel. In order to drive the point home, both to YHWH and to the Israelite audience, it employs RHETORICAL QUESTIONS in 63:11b-14a which assert and reinforce the claim of YHWH's past acts of fidelity on behalf of the nation.

But the HISTORICAL REVIEW is also designed to motivate YHWH to act to address the present suffering of the people as indicated by the APPEAL to YHWH in 63:15–64:11 to look down from heaven and to do something on behalf of the people. The first APPEAL in 63:15-19a begins with the APPEAL proper, which appears in 63:15a, followed again by RHETORICAL QUESTIONS in 63:15b-16 that assert that "YHWH is our Father" and in 63:17-19a that call upon YHWH to "return to us." The prophet's APPEAL to YHWH resumes in 63:19b–64:3 with a call for YHWH to come down and make the divine name known to Israel's enemies. Such an appeal constitutes a petition to act, and it is again reinforced by a review of YHWH's past acts of wonders in creation. Finally, the last element of the APPEAL follows in 64:4-11 in which the prophet appeals to YHWH to take action on behalf of the people so that the people will remember YHWH's ways. As noted above, the passage acknowledges Israel's past guilt, but it also holds YHWH culpable and demands that YHWH act in the present. This segment functions somewhat like Lamentations 1, which calls upon YHWH to look at the plight of Bat Zion, insofar as the present passage calls upon YHWH to look at the desolate cities, including Zion, the ruined temple, and the desolate Jerusalem. Again, RHETORICAL QUESTIONS in 64:11 demand to know whether YHWH will remain passive and inactive or whether YHWH will act on behalf of the people and for the sake of the divine name.

But 63:7–64:11 lacks the assurance of a hearing and the commitment to offer a vow or thanksgiving offering. The missing elements should cause little concern, as genres function within texts to serve the needs of the text at hand. In the present case, 63:7–64:11 displays a unique interest in putting YHWH on the spot for the people's suffering. Although the passage acknowledges the people's guilt as a basis for the punishment they have suffered, it points to YHWH as the culpable party who "causes the people to stray from your ways" and who "hardens our hearts from revering you" in 63:17; indeed, the verse calls upon YHWH to "return (i.e., relent, šûb) for the sake of your servants, the tribes of your heritage." Likewise, 64:4 charges that "you have struck one who rejoices and does justice, who remembers you in your ways," which suggests that YHWH has punished the righteous. Such statements are in keeping with other texts in Isaiah which charge that YHWH is hiding the divine face from the house of Jacob in 8:17 and that YHWH has commissioned Isaiah to make sure that the people remain blind, deaf, and dumb so that they cannot repent and be saved from the punishment that YHWH has in store for them in ch. 6. Indeed, the passage presupposes YHWH's culpability in the plight of the people and the ruined temple. The fact that neither Abraham nor Jacob would recognize them in 63:16 calls to mind the so-called promises to the ancestors that envisioned Israel as a great nation like the stars of the heavens and sands of the sea. But the present circumstances belie such a claim and raise questions about YHWH's own fidelity to the covenant.

Setting

The prophet's lament and appeal for mercy to YHWH in 63:7–64:11 appears immediately following the portrayal of YHWH's punishment of Edom and the nations in 63:1-6 and prior to the presentation of YHWH's response concerning the intention to bring death to the wicked and deliverance to the righteous in chs. 65–66. In the present literary context, 63:7–64:11 provides a transition within the larger context of chs. 63–66. It explains the past suffering and punishment of Israel as the result of rebellion, analogous to the punishment portrayed of Edom and the nations in 63:1-6, and it portends YHWH's deliverance of the righteous in chs. 65–66 as a response to the appeal for YHWH's action on behalf of the people in 63:7–64:11. Isaiah 63:7–64:11 therefore functions as a means to negotiate the interplay between punishment and deliverance for Israel, in that it anticipates the death of the wicked in chs. 65–66 as well as the deliverance of the righteous. Such a function conforms to the overall concern with the distinction between the wicked and the righteous among Israel in chs. 55–66.

When read in the present literary context of chs. 55–66, 63:7–64:11 functions as part of the final late-5th- or early-4th-century edition of the book of Isaiah. Insofar as the final edition of the book is set in the context of the restoration and reforms of Nehemiah and Ezra, it therefore provides a rationale for the past suffering and misfortunes of the Jewish people throughout the monarchic period, the Babylonian exile, and even the period following the building of the Second Temple, when the temple had not yet succeeded in emerging as the holy center of Judaism. The restoration and reforms of Ezra and Nehemiah were intended to address this issue, and the final form of the book of Isaiah functions as a means to provide rationale and support for the restoration efforts. The liturgical form of the passage as a lament suggests that the final form of the book of Isaiah functioned as part of a temple liturgy that would provide such rationale and support for the efforts of both Nehemiah and especially the priest and scribe Ezra, who succeeded in establishing the temple as the holy center of Judaism.

Nevertheless, 63:7–64:11 does not appear to have been composed as part of the final form of the book of Isaiah. Williamson ("Isaiah 63,7–64,11") demonstrates that it is an earlier composition that must have functioned as part of a liturgical lamentation ceremony based on parallels with Psalm 106 and Nehemiah 9. Isaiah 63:7–64:11 was later edited into its place in the present form of the book of Isaiah. Isaiah 63:18 and 64:9-10 indicate that the temple has been destroyed and that Jerusalem/Zion and the cities of Judah have also been laid waste. Such a scenario indicates that 63:7–64:11 was composed at some point following the Babylonian destruction of Jerusalem and the temple in 587 B.C.E. and prior to the rebuilding of the temple in 520-515. There is little indication of any literary relationship to the rest of the book of Isaiah. The parallels with Isaiah identified by Aejmelaeus ("Der Prophet als Klageliedsänger") — YHWH's role as Israel's creator, references to the exodus and wilderness, and YHWH's incomparability — do not hold up when one considers that YHWH is culpable for leading the people astray in this text, whereas in chs. 40–55; 60–62 YHWH is only portrayed as Israel's and Jerusalem's redeemer, not as the figure who led them astray. The charges that "you (YHWH) caused us to stray from your ways" and that "you (YHWH) hardened our hearts from revering you" in 63:17 might suggest a reaction to YHWH's commission of Isaiah to make the people blind, deaf, and dumb in ch. 6, but the absence of lexical parallel indicates that there is no explicit intertextual relationship with ch. 6.

Altogether, 63:7–64:11 appears to constitute a lamentation text akin to the book of Lamentations. Zechariah 7 makes it clear that weeping and fasting took place at the site of the ruined temple during the years of the Babylonian exile until its reconstruction in 520-515. The lack of explicit intertextual relationship with the rest of the book of Isaiah and the interest in charging YHWH with wrongdoing in causing the people to stray from divine ways suggest that 63:7–64:11 is a non-Isaian text that was perhaps employed in relation to lamentation rituals for the lost temple during the period of the Babylonian exile (Williamson, "Isaiah 63,7–64,11"). Such a text might have played a role in relation to the reconstruction of the Jerusalem temple and perhaps even in relationship to the 6th-century edition of the book, including the work of Second Isaiah in chs. 40–55 and the later-6th-century materials in chs. 60–62. It is possible that 63:7–64:11 might have had a place in the 6th-century edition of the book; perhaps chs. 40–55 or 60–62 functioned as responses to the appeals posed to YHWH in the text, but no firm proof for such a role is evident. When 63:7–64:11 is considered as an independent text, the speaker would not have been the prophet; the identification of the speaker with the prophet is only possible when the passage is read as an integral part of the book of Isaiah.

Interpretation

Within the final form of the book of Isaiah, and especially within chs. 63–66, the prophet's lament and appeal for mercy in 63:7–64:11 pose questions concerning YHWH's capacity to deliver and redeem Israel that are answered by the portrayal of the return of Israel's exiles to Jerusalem in chs. 65–66. Following 63:1-6, which portrays YHWH's return from punishing Edom and the nations, 63:7–64:11 turns to the question of YHWH's role in punishing Israel and appeals to YHWH to begin the process of deliverance and redemption as in times past when YHWH delivered Israel from Egyptian bondage. YHWH's answer to the appeal then follows in chs. 65–66, in which YHWH claims to have responded to those who did not ask with announcement that YHWH intends to bring punishment on those who sin but that YHWH will also restore the righteous to Jerusalem when the process of punishment is complete.

Isaiah 63:7–64:11 is ideally formed, as the prophet's lament and appeal to YHWH for mercy, to serve such a role. Although the prophet is never explicitly identified as the speaker, the literary context of the book of Isaiah demands that the prophet be recognized as such, even though the text appears to have been originally written for a very different context. The prophet's first address to YHWH in 63:7-14 begins with a historical review of YHWH's past acts of support for Israel during the exodus and wilderness periods, when YHWH formed the relationship with Israel and thereby forged a great name and reputation as the deliverer and redeemer of Israel. Although the review is couched initially in v. 7 in the general language of YHWH's acts of fidelity toward Israel as the deliverer of Israel, the focus on bringing the people out of Egypt, dividing the sea, and providing guidance through the wilderness speaks to the origins of Israel as a nation. The passage is clearly aware of Abraham and Israel (Jacob) as the ancestral figures of Israel, but the exodus from Egypt was a national experience celebrated at Passover that functions as a form of Israel's Independence Day. Verses 8-9 thereby focus on YHWH's role as deliverer of the people, invoking words of the covenant relationship, "indeed, they are my people" in v. 8aα$^{2-4}$ that form part of the covenant formula: "they shall be my people and I will be their G-d" (e.g., Gen 17:7-8; Exod 6:7; Jer 7:23; 11:4; see R. Rendtorff, *"Die Bundesformel": Eine exegetisch-theologische Untersuchung* [SBS 160; Stuttgart: Katholisches Bibelwerk, 1995]). But the relationship presumes fidelity from Israel as well in v. 8aβ, and this will emerge as an issue in the next verse. Verse 10 recalls Israel's rebellions against YHWH, presumably in the wilderness, and states that YHWH became an enemy to them, presumably to bring about punishment for their rebellion. Verses 11-14a then present the culmination and purpose of the historical review, i.e., that YHWH should remember the days of old as a basis for acting to deliver the people in the present. The rhetorical questions of vv. 11b-14a make that memory explicit: "where is the one who brought them up from the sea with the shepherds of his flock? Where is the one who placed his holy spirit in Israel's midst?" The answer of course is "YHWH," and the following three inexplicit rhetorical questions underscore the point: "who led his glorious arm at the right hand of Moses? Who divided the sea before them to make an eternal name? Who led them in the depths (of the sea)?" Throughout the sequence of questions, the answer of course is "YHWH." Although the voice of the speaker and the identity of the audience were ambiguous throughout vv. 7-14a — was it the people? a priest? a prophet? — v. 14b makes it clear that the speaker addresses YHWH directly, even though only the literary context of the book of Isaiah makes it clear that the speaker is the prophet.

The prophet's second address to YHWH in 63:15–64:11 presents the prophet's appeal to deliver and redeem the people. The address begins in 63:15-19a with the prophet's demand in v. 15a that YHWH look down from heaven and see the destitute state of the temple and the people. In this respect, the passage is analogous to Lamentations 1, in which Bat Zion demands that YHWH look and see what has happened to her as a result of YHWH's punishment. The address plays on YHWH's relationship with the people as their father by asking more rhetorical questions in vv. 15b-16: "where is your zeal and power?" indicating that YHWH has withheld mercy even though YHWH is the father of the people. Such a claim functions as a charge against YHWH, i.e., YHWH, too, has violated the relationship by failing to protect the people who look to YHWH as father. The prophet presses the issue further by asserting that Abraham and Israel (Jacob) wouldn't recognize the people whom YHWH promised to make into a great nation like the stars in the heavens or the sands of the sea in the ancestral promise tradition of the Pentateuch (e.g., Genesis 12; 15; 17; 28; 35). By v. 16b the prophet shifts from images of YHWH as father to the question of YHWH's great name: the prophet appeals to YHWH's reputation as well as the relationship with Israel. A second set of rhetorical questions in vv. 17-19a are designed to prompt YHWH to "return to us": "why do you make us stray and harden our hearts?" The questions level a charge against YHWH: YHWH causes us to sin and then punishes us for doing so. The rhetorical answers underscore the appeal for YHWH to return "for the sake of your servants. Your temple is trampled by enemies, your people have lost their identity established through YHWH." In the end, they are a people who lack YHWH's holy name, again, an appeal to the integrity of YHWH's reputation.

The prophet's second address to YHWH continues in 63:19b–64:3, to come down and make the divine name known to Israel's (and YHWH's) enemies. Given the concerns expressed in the previous section, it is clear that YHWH's reputation remains at stake. The appeal proper in 63:19b–64:1 provides its own basis: the mountains, i.e., creation at large, and the nations would quake and tremble before YHWH. All creation, including the mountains and humanity, will recognize their creator and respond accordingly, but the first thing that must happen is that the creator must act. Motivation comes in 64:2-3, which points to past actions by YHWH that have had the desired results: you've done it before and you can do it again. Just as the mountains quaked when you acted in the past, they will do so again. The passage underscores a fundamental point, no one but you can do this; there is no other G-d who can do such a thing. And so it is time to act.

The prophet's second address to YHWH concludes with the appeal for action in 64:4-11. Again, the question of YHWH's integrity is paramount, as the passage begins in v. 4aα with the prophet's claim that YHWH punished one who has acted righteously, i.e., the prophet points to the claim that YHWH is one who caused Israel to stray. The appeal then proceeds in vv. 4aβ-11 based on the premise that "the people will remember you for your ways" — YHWH's name is still at stake. Verse 4aβ-b states the ideal premise: "you are angry when we sin, and we walk in your ways and we are delivered." Essentially, the prophet asks that this ideal paradigm be put into play; the punishment is over, the time for restoration has come. Verses 5-11 contrast past punishment with present circumstances. Past punishment as described in vv. 5-6 entails that the people are unclean and carried off because they wither like dried leaves. Consequently, "no one calls upon your name" because "you are hiding your face." The hiding of the divine face is a constant issue in the psalms of lament (S. Balentine, *The Hidden G-d: the Hiding of the Face of G-d in the Old Testament* [Oxford: Oxford University Press, 1983]), insofar as the suffering of the people is explained as instances in which G-d hides the divine face from them. It is a key issue in Isaiah as well, as indicated in 8:17, in which the prophet makes the statement "I will wait for YHWH who hides his face from the house of Jacob, and I will trust in him." The appeal for deliverance in the present follows in vv. 7-11. Verse 7 returns to the father/child relationship between YHWH and Israel as the basis for the prophet's appeal to YHWH to act, reiterating that "you are our father, we are clay and you are the potter, we are the work of your hands" — we depend upon you and only you can do it. Verse 8 appeals for attention, asking YHWH not to hold to anger and to look, as in Lamentations. Verses 9-10 point out what YHWH will see, i.e., the ruin of your cities, including Zion/Jerusalem and the ruined temple. Finally, v. 11 returns to the core issue of YHWH's reputation with two rhetorical questions: "will you restrain yourself over this, YHWH? Will you remain silent and allow us to suffer so much?" By pointedly addressing YHWH by name in the first question, the passage thereby closes by implicitly raising the question of YHWH's good name once again.

Bibliography

A. Aejmelaeus, "Der Prophet als Klageliedsänger — Zur Funktion des Psalms Jes 63,7–64,11 in Tritojesaja," *ZAW* 107 (1995) 31-50; M. A. Beek, "Das Mit-leiden G-ttes: Eine masoretische Interpretation von Jes 63.9," in *Symbolae Biblicae et Mesopotamicae.* (*Fest.* F. M. T. de Ligare Böhl; ed. M. A. Beek et al.; Leiden: Brill, 1973), 23-30; R. J. Clifford, "Narrative and Lament in Isaiah 63:7–64:11," in *To Teach the Text: Biblical and Related Studies (Fest.* J. A. Fitzmyer, S.J. (ed. M. P. Horgan and P. J. Kobelski; New York: Crossroad, 1989), 93-102; E. W. Conrad, "Isaiah and the Abraham Connection," *Australian Journal of Theology* 2 (1988) 382-93; P. W. Ferris, Jr., *The Genre of Communal Lament in the Hebrew Bible and the Ancient Near East* (SBLDS 127; Atlanta: Scholars, 1992); I. Fischer, *Wo ist JHWH? Das Volksklagelied Jes 63,7–64,11 als Ausdruck des Ringens um eine gebrochene Beziehung* (SBB 19; Stuttgart: Katholischer Biblewerk, 1989); J. Goldenstein, *Das Gebet der G-ttesknechte: Jes 63,7–64,11 im Jesajabuch* (WMANT 92; Neukirchen-Vluyn: Neukirchener, 2001); P. D. Hanson, *The Dawn of Apocalyptic,* 81-100; G. Hoaas, "Passion and Compassion of G-d in the Old Testament: A Theological Survey of Hos 11:8-9; Jer 31:20; and Isa 63:9-15," *SJOT* 11 (1997) 138-59; K. Koenen, *Ethik und Eschatologie,* 159-61; R. Kuntzmann, "Une relecture du "salut" en Is 63,7-14: Étude du vocabulaire," *RSR* 51 (1977) 22-39; W. Lau, *Schriftgelehrte Prophetie,* 286-315; E. Lipinski, *La Liturgie Pénitentielle dans la Bible* (Paris: Cerf, 1969); J. Morgenstern, "Isaiah 63:7-14," *HUCA* 23 (1950/51) 187-203; S. Mowinckel, *The Psalms in Israel's Worship* (2 vols.; Nashville: Abingdon, 1962); J. H. Newman, *Praying by the Book: The Scripturalization of Prayer in Second Temple Judaism* (EJL 14; Atlanta: Scholars, 1999); P. Niskanen, "YHWH as Father, Redeemer, and Potter in Isaiah 63:7–64:11," *CBQ* 68 (2006) 397-407; K. Pauritsch, *Die neue Gemeinde,* 144-71; S. Sekine, *Die tritojesa-janische Sammlung,* 148-64; O. H. Steck, *Studien zu Tritojesaja,* 229-65; T. Veijola, "Das Klagegebet in Literatur und Leben der Exilsgeneration am Beispiel einiger Prosatexte," in *Congress Volume: Salamanca, 1983* (ed. J. A. Emerton; VTSup 36; Leiden: Brill, 1985), 286-307; E. C. Webster, "The Rhetoric of Isaiah 63–65," *JSOT* 47 (1990) 89-102; R. A. Werline, *Penititential Prayer in Second Temple Judaism: The Development of a Religious Institution* (EJL 13; Atlanta: Scholars, 1998); C. Westermann, *Praise and Lament in the Psalms* (Atlanta: John Knox, 1981); H. G. M. Williamson, "Isaiah 63,7–64,11: Exilic Lament or Post-Exilic Protest?" *ZAW* 102 (1990) 48-58.

REPORT OF YHWH'S RESPONSE: YHWH WILL ACT TO REQUITE THE EVIL AND TO DELIVER THE RIGHTEOUS IN A NEW CREATION AT ZION 65:1–66:24

Structure

I. Report of YHWH's announcement that YHWH will requite evil
(prophetic judgment speech pattern)   65:1-7
  A. YHWH was ready, but people did not call: rejected overtures
(grounds for punishment)   65:1-5
    1. I was ready for inquiry by those who did not ask   65:1aα
    2. I was available to those who did not seek me   65:1aβ
    3. I said "Here I am" to a nation that does not call my name   65:1b
    4. I spread out my hands all day to a rebellious people   65:2-5
     a. Basically stated   65:2a
     b. Specification of rebellious people   65:2b-5a
      1) Who walk in a wrong path after their own thoughts   65:2b
      2) Who always provoke me to my face   65:3a
      3) Who sacrifice in gardens and offer incense on
pavements   65:3b
       a) Who sacrifice in gardens   65:3bα
       b) Who offer incense on pavements   65:3bβ
      4) Who sit in graves and reside in enclosures   65:4a
       a) Who sit in graves   65:4aα
       b) Who reside in enclosures   65:4aβ
      5) Who eat pig's flesh and the broth of filth in their bowls   65:4b
       a) Who eat pig's flesh   65:4bα
       b) (Who eat) the broth of filth in their bowls   65:4bβ
      6) Who say I come near to you, but don't touch me,
because I would set you apart   65:5a
       a) Who say I come near to you, but don't touch me   65:5aα
       b) Basis: I would set you apart   65:5aβ
     c. Summation: these things offend me   65:5b
      1) These things are smoke in my nose   65:5bα
      2) (These things) are a burning fire all day long   65:5bβ
  B. YHWH will requite evil (announcement of punishment)   65:6-7
    1. Statement of recording: behold it is written before me   65:6a
    2. Statement of principle: I will requite   65:6b-7aα
     a. I will not be idle, but I will requite   65:6bα

1) I will not be idle   65:6bα$^{1-2}$
2) I will requite   65:6bα$^{3-5}$
b. How: I will requite upon their bosom your iniquities and the iniquities of your ancestors together   65:6bβ-7aα
  1) Statement of requital   65:6bβ-7aα^{4}
    a) Statement of requital proper: I will requite upon their bosom   65:6bβ
    b) Object of requital: your iniquities and the iniquities of your ancestors together   65:7aα$^{1-4}$
  2) YHWH speech formula   65:7aα$^{5-6}$
3. Specification: prophetic judgment speech   65:7aβ-b
a. Grounds for punishment: burned incense on mountains and shamed me on hills   65:7aβ
  1) They burned incense on the mountains   65:7aβ$^{1-4}$
  2) They shamed me on the hills   65:7aβ$^{5-8}$
b. Announcement of punishment: I shall measure their former deed upon their bosom   65:7b
II. Report of YHWH's address to the wicked: the seed of Jacob will be restored in new creation on Zion, but the wicked will be punished   65:8-25
A. Statement of principle that not all will be destroyed, only the wicked   65:8-12
1. Prophetic messenger formula   65:8aα$^{1-3}$
2. YHWH's address proper: analogical instruction concerning preservation of righteous and slaughter of the wicked   65:8aα^{4}-12
a. Concerning preservation of seed from Jacob   65:8aα^{4}-10
  1) Basis for analogy: juice in grape cluster   65:8aα^{4}-β
    a) Basis for analogy: juice found in grape cluster   65:8aα$^{4-7}$
    b) Expected statement/action: don't destroy it   65:8aβ
  2) Application to righteous servants of YHWH   65:8b-10
    a) Statement of principle: not destroy everything   65:8b
      (1) Statement of application: so I will do for my servants   65:8bα
      (2) Specification: not destroy everything   65:8bβ
    b) Bring out seed from Jacob and heirs to my mountain from Judah   65:9
      (1) Basically stated   65:9a
        (a) Bring out seed from Jacob   65:9aα
        (b) Heirs to my mountain from Judah   65:9aβ
      (2) My chosen ones shall possess and dwell there   65:9b
        (a) My chosen ones shall possess it   65:9bα
        (b) My servants shall dwell there   65:9bβ
    c) Sharon and Valley of Achor for my people who seek me   65:10
      (1) Sharon will become a sheep pasture   65:10aα
      (2) Valley of Achor for grazing cattle for my people who seek me   65:10aβ-b

b. Concerning slaughter of the wicked/those who abandon
   YHWH   65:11-12
  1) Address to those who abandon YHWH   65:11
    a) Basically stated   65:11aα
    b) Specification: those who forget my holy mountain   65:11aβ
    c) Specification: who arrange a table for Gad   65:11bα
    d) Specification: who mix a drink for Meni   65:11bβ
  2) Announcement of punishment   65:12
    a) Announcement of punishment proper   65:12aα
      (1) I will number you for the sword   65:12aα^{1-3}
      (2) All of you will kneel for slaughter   65:12aα^{4-6}
    b) Bases for punishment   65:12aβ-b
      (1) You did not answer or listen   65:12aβ-γ
        (a) You did not answer when I called   65:12aβ
        (b) You did not listen when I spoke   65:12aγ
      (2) You did evil and chose what I do not desire 65:12b
        (a) You did evil in my eyes   65:12bα
        (b) You chose what I do not desire   65:12bβ
B. Announcement of punishment for the wicked and restoration
 of the righteous   65:13-25
 1. Prophetic messenger speech formula joined by "therefore" 65:13aα^{1-5}
 2. YHWH's speech: punishment for the wicked and restoration for the righteous   65:13aα^{6}-25bα
  a. Concerning punishment of the wicked   65:13aα^{6}-15a
   1) My servants shall eat, but you shall starve 65:13aα^{6-10}
   2) My servants shall drink, but you will thirst   65:13aβ
   3) My servants shall rejoice, but you will be shamed 65:13b
   4) My servants shall shout for goodness of heart, but you
    shall cry for a pained heart and wail for a broken spirit 65:14-15a
    a) Basically stated   65:14
      (1) My servants shall shout for goodness of heart 65:14a
      (2) You shall cry for a pained heart and wail for a
        broken spirit   65:14b
        (a) You shall cry for a pained heart   65:14bα
        (b) You shall wail for a broken spirit   65:14bβ
    b) You have ruined your name   65:15a
      (1) You have left your name for an oath by my chosen 65:15aα
      (2) Oath: my L-rd G-d will kill you   65:15aβ
  b. Prophet's comment concerning contrasting name of
   YHWH's servants   65:15b-16
   1) Basically stated: YHWH's servants will have another
    name   65:15b
   2) Elaboration: a blessed name in the land   65:16a
    a) Blessing in land by G-d   65:16aα
      (1) Protasis: whoever blesses oneself in the land 65:16aα^{1-3}
      (2) Apodosis: shall bless oneself by the true G-d 65:16aα^{4-6}
    b) Swearing in the land by G-d   65:16aβ

(1) Protasis: whoever swears in the land   65:16aβ$^{1-2}$
(2) Apodosis: swears by true G-d   65:16aβ$^{3-5}$
3) YHWH's statement of bases: former troubles forgotten and hidden   65:16b
a) Former troubles forgotten   65:16bα
b) (Former troubles) hidden from my eyes   65:16bβ
c. Basis: YHWH's announcement of new creation/restoration of Jerusalem; announcement of restoration   65:17-25bα
1) Address to people: announcement of new creation and command to rejoice   65:17-18
a) Announcement of new creation   65:17
(1) I am creating a new heaven and earth   65:17a
(2) Former things will not be remembered nor come to mind   65:17b
(a) Former things will not be remembered   65:17bα
(b) (Former things) will not come to mind   65:17bβ
b) Command to rejoice   65:18
(1) Command proper   65:18a
(a) Rejoice   65:18aα
(b) Celebrate forever what I create   65:18aβ
(2) Basis for celebration: create Jerusalem   65:18b
(a) I am creating Jerusalem   65:18bα
(b) Celebration ensues   65:18bβ
2) YHWH's announcement of celebration   65:19-25bα
a) Announcement proper: I will celebrate and rejoice   65:19a
(1) I will celebrate over Jerusalem   65:19aα
(2) I will rejoice over my people   65:19aβ
b) Elaboration: basis for celebration   65:19b-25bα
(1) No more weeping and wailing   65:19b
(2) Full lives for everyone   65:20
(a) Infants and old people will fulfill their days   65:20a
(b) Explanation   65:20b
α. Youth will live to one hundred   65:20bα
β. One-hundred-year-old sinner will be cursed   65:20bβ
(3) They shall build and plant for their offspring   65:21-23
(a) They shall build houses and plant vineyards   65:21
α. Build houses   65:21a
β. Plant vineyards   65:21b
(b) They will not build for others   65:22
α. They will not build or plant for others   65:22a
aa. They do not build for others to dwell   65:22aα
bb. They do not plant for others to eat   65:22aβ
β. They will live long   65:22b
aa. My people will live long like a tree   65:22bα
bb. My people will outlive the work of their hands   65:22bβ

β) I will send fugitives from them to
the nations that have not seen my
glory   66:19aβ-bα

  cc. Fugitives' actions: they shall declare
my glory among the nations   66:19bβ

  dd. Nations' actions: they shall return the
fugitives to my holy mountain as an
offering   66:20aα

  (b) YHWH speech formula   66:20aβ

(2) YHWH's second speech: selection of priests
and Levites from returned fugitives   66:20b-21

  (a) Speech proper   66:20b-21a

    α. Just as Israel brings offering to the temple   66:20b

    β. I will choose from them/fugitives priests
and Levites   66:21a

  (b) YHWH speech formula   66:21b

b) Promise of Israel's continued seed and name as
nations come to worship YHWH   66:22-23

  (1) Statement of analogy: just as the new heavens
and earth stand before me   66:22a

    (a) Statement proper   66:22aα

    (b) Oracle formula   66:22aβ

  (2) Statement of application: Israel's seed and
name will stand   66:22b-23

    (a) Statement proper   66:22b-23bα

     α. Basically stated   66:22b

     β. Elaboration: all flesh will worship regu-
larly before me   66:23a-bα

    (b) YHWH speech formula   66:23bβ

c) Portrayal of nations viewing corpses of the wicked   66:24

  (1) They will go out to see corpses of those who
rebelled against YHWH   66:24a

  (2) What they will see: continued sign of rebellion
against YHWH   66:24b

    (a) Their worm will not die   66:24bα[1-4]

    (b) Their fire will not go out   66:24bα[5-7]

    (c) They shall be horror to all flesh   66:24bβ

Isaiah 65–66 is demarcated by its consistent formulation as the prophet's report of YHWH's speeches concerning the fate of the righteous and the wicked. This demarcation is evident from the prophetic messenger speech formulas and other YHWH speech formulas that appear throughout these chapters and the 1st-person singular formulation of the speeches which clearly refer to YHWH. This stands in contrast to the preceding lament in 63:7–64:11(NRSV 64:12), in which the prophet appeals for YHWH to act against Israel's oppressors. Isaiah 65–66 appears at the conclusion of the book of Isaiah as part of the larger block of material in chs. 55–66 that exhorts the book's addressees to join the restored nation at Zion. It forms part of the textual subunit in chs. 63–66 which presents YHWH's approach against Edom as the Divine Warrior who destroys the wicked (63:1-6) and the prophet's lament in which he appeals for mercy (63:7–64:11[NRSV 64:12]). Isaiah 65–66 constitutes the report of YHWH's response to the lament, in which YHWH reiterates the decision to provide deliverance for the righteous and death for the wicked who refuse YHWH's offer. By outlining the future for those who accept or reject the invitation to become a part of the restored nation in Zion, chs. 65–66 play a major role in defining the goals and agenda of the book of Isaiah and thereby constitute a fitting conclusion for the book.

The structure of chs. 65–66 is determined by a combination of thematic and formal features, including the identifications of the addressees of each textual subunit and the various YHWH speech formulas that define each subunit. Overall, three major subunits constitute chs. 65–66, including 65:1-7, 65:8-25, and 66:1-24. The units work together to state the basic problem of the refusal by some to seek YHWH (65:1-7) and to address both the wicked (65:8-25) and the righteous (66:1-24) concerning their contrasting fates for refusing or accepting YHWH's invitation to join the restored nation at Zion.

The first major subunit of the passage is 65:1-7. These verses are demarcated by their formulation as the prophet's report of a speech by YHWH. This is evident from the YHWH speech formula, *'āmar yhwh,* "says YHWH," which appears in v. 7 and the 1st-person singular formulation of the verb forms and pronouns that indicate the speaker. The speech is not addressed to any specific party, but employs 3rd-person objective address forms to describe the refusal by the wicked to call upon YHWH. Two 2nd-person masculine plural suffix pronouns appear in v. 7aα, *'ăwōnōtêkem wa'ăwōnōt 'ăbôtêkem yaḥdāyw,* "(and I will requite) your iniquities and the iniquities of your ancestors together," but the rest of v. 7 employs 3rd-person masculine plural forms to designate the "sinners," which is consistent with vv. 1-7 as a whole. The shift to 2nd-person plural address forms in v. 7 constitutes a rhetorical device in which a direct address to the wicked is incorporated into a larger address to the audience at large.

Isaiah 65:1-7 breaks down into two basic components based upon the prophetic judgment speech pattern. Verses 1-5 comprise the report of YHWH's statement concerning readiness to be sought by those who were not asking, including statements concerning YHWH's attempts to offer aid to the people and the people's refusal to acknowledge YHWH. Consequently, vv. 1-5 function as the grounds for punishment of the people for wrongdoing. Verses 6-7 constitute a second component, initially identified by the exclamatory statement "Behold! It is written before me," which conveys YHWH's intentions not to remain silent in the face of rejection by the people, but to requite their evil deeds. Verses 6-7 thereby constitute the announcement of punishment in the overall prophetic judgment speech pattern. Nevertheless, the introductory statement in vv. 1-2, in which YHWH states, "I was ready to be sought by those who did not ask," etc., indicates that the passage is designed not only to announce judgment against the wicked, but to appeal to the audience to accept YHWH's offer and not to be included among the wicked.

The presentation of the grounds for punishment in 65:1-5 comprises four basic subunits based on YHWH's 1st-person singular, syntactically-independent statements in vv. 1aα, 1aβ, 1b, and 2. The first subunit therefore is YHWH's statement in v. 1aα that "I was ready for inquiry by those who did not ask." The second subunit is YHWH's statement in v. 1aβ that "I was available to those who did not seek me." The third subunit is YHWH's statement in v. 1b that "I said 'Here I am' to a nation that does not call my name." The fourth subunit is vv. 2-5, which begins with YHWH's statement that "I spread out my hands all day to a rebellious people." The four subunits thereby constitute a progressive set of statements concerning YHWH's willingness to engage the people, together with the people's refusal to do so. The fourth subunit in vv. 2-5 constitutes the culmination of the unit, and it therefore includes a basic statement of YHWH's stance in v. 2a, followed by an appositional specification of the rebellious people in vv. 2b-5a and a summation statement in v. 5b. The specification includes six elements, each of which begins with a participle formation that defines an aspect of the rebellious people *('am sôrēr)* mentioned in v. 2a. The first element in v. 2b defines them as "those who walk in a wrong path after their own thoughts." The second element in v. 3a defines them as "those who always provoke me to my face." The third element in v. 3b defines them with two statements joined by a conjunctive *wāw* as "those who sacrifice in gardens" in v. 3bα and as "those who offer incense on pavements" in v. 3bβ. The fourth element in v. 4a again defines them with two statements joined by a conjunctive *wāw,* including "those who sit in graves" in v. 4aα and "those who reside in enclosures" in v. 4aβ. The fifth element in v. 4b defines them as "those who eat pig's flesh" in v. 4bα and as "those who eat the broth of filth in their bowls" in v. 4bβ. Finally, the sixth element in v. 5a defines them as "those who say 'I come near to you, but don't touch me'" in v. 5aα, adding the basis "because I would set you apart" in v. 5aβ. The summation statement in v. 5b employs the metaphor of an irritating fire in YHWH's statements "these things are smoke in my nose" in v. 5bα and "these things are a burning fire all day long" in v. 5bβ.

The announcement of punishment in vv. 6-7 presents YHWH's statements concerning the punishment of the wicked in an elaborated form comprising three elements in vv. 6a, 6b-7aα, and 7aβ-b. The first element in v. 6a constitutes YHWH's statement that "the punishment is recorded before me." The second element in vv. 6b-7aα constitutes the presentation of YHWH's statement of principle concerning the requiting of the wicked. The first part of this statement appears in v. 6bα, which includes two basic elements: YHWH's statements that "I will not be idle" in v. 6bα[1-2] and that "I will requite" in v. 6bα[3-5]. The second part of this statement in vv. 6bβ-7aα focuses on how YHWH will requite the wicked. It includes two basic elements. The first element in vv. 6bβ-7aα[4] is YHWH's statement of requital, including the statement of requital proper, "I will requite upon their bosom," in v. 6bβ and a statement of the object of YHWH's requital, "your iniquities and the iniquities of your ancestors together," in v. 7aα[1-4]. The YHWH speech formula in v. 7aα[5-6] closes the second part by identifying it as a speech by YHWH. The third element in v. 7aβ-b specifies the prior elements in the form of a generically complete prophetic judgment speech. The grounds for punishment appear in v. 7aβ, including charges that "they burned incense on the mountains" in v. 7aβ$^{1-4}$ and "they shamed me on the hills" in v. 7aβ$^{5-8}$. The announcement of punishment, "I shall measure their former deed upon their bosom," appears in v. 7b.

The second major subunit is 65:8-25. This section is demarcated by two different features. The first is the various YHWH speech formulas, including the messenger speech formulas in vv. 8, *kōh 'āmar yhwh,* "thus says YHWH," and 13, *lākēn kōh 'āmar 'ǎdōnāy yhwh,* "therefore, thus says my L-rd, YHWH," and the concluding YHWH speech formula, *'āmar yhwh,* "says YHWH," in v. 25. The second is the formulation of the passage as a 1st-person singular speech by YHWH which addresses the wicked, i.e., "those who abandon YHWH" (v. 11), with 2nd-person masculine plural verbal and pronoun forms. The speeches by YHWH also discuss the righteous, but they employ 3rd-person objective language, indicating that the righteous are described to the wicked, who are directly addressed.

Isaiah 65:8-25 falls into two basic components, each of which is introduced by a version of the prophetic messenger speech formula. Verses 8-12 articulate the principle that not all of the people will be destroyed, and this modifies the perspective of vv. 1-7, which make no distinction within the people. Rather, vv. 8-12 maintain that YHWH will preserve a portion of the people to act as the "seed" from Jacob, who will "possess my mountain" from Judah (v. 9). This principle is articulated on the basis of an analogy with the harvest of grapes: just as the cluster of new grapes *(hattîrôš bā'eškôl)* is not destroyed as there might be some value that will come from it, so YHWH will not destroy the people entirely so that the "seed" for a new beginning might emerge. Isaiah 65:8-12 comprises two basic subunits: the prophetic messenger formula in v. 8aα$^{1-3}$ and the following address by YHWH proper in vv. 8aα^4-12. YHWH's address is formulated as analogical instruction concerning the preservation of the righteous and the slaughter of the wicked. Verses 8aα^4-10 are formulated in objective address language to describe the principle, whereas vv. 11-12 are formulated in 2nd-person masculine plural address language directed to "those who abandon YHWH" (v. 11) in order to inform them that they have been designated for the sword because of their evil deeds.

Isaiah 65:8aα^4-10 presents YHWH's analogical instruction concerning the preservation of the righteous, which is defined as seed from Jacob. The basis for the analogy, the observation of juice in a grape cluster, appears in v. 8aα^4-β, including a statement of the basis for the analogy proper in v. 8aα$^{4-7}$ and the expected statement of action that will proceed from the observation, "don't destroy it," in v. 8aβ. The application of the analogy then follows in vv. 8b-10, which includes three basic subunits in vv. 8b, 9, and 10. The first in v. 8b is a statement of the principle at hand, i.e., do not destroy everything, including a statement of the application by YHWH, "so I will do for my servants," in v. 8bα and a basic statement which specifies the implications of the principle, "do not destroy everything," in v. 8bβ. The second in v. 9 then calls for bringing out the seed from both Jacob and "the heirs to my mountain from Judah." The first element in this subunit is the basic statement in v. 9a, "bring out the seed from Jacob" in v. 9aα and "bring out the seed from the heirs to my mountain from Judah" in v. 9aβ. Verse 9b then follows with the explication that "my chosen ones will possess it" in v. 9bα and "my servants shall dwell there" in v. 9bβ. The third in v. 10 focuses on two plains or valleys in Israel, the Sharon plain in northern Israel, south and east of the Carmel mountain range, and the Valley of Achor, which some identify with the Wadi Qelt, running from Jerusalem down to the Jordan Valley and the Dead Sea. Both areas will be designated for those who seek YHWH, including the Sharon plain in v. 10aα, which will be used as a pasture for sheep, and the Valley of Achor in v. 10aβ-b, which will be used for grazing cattle.

Isaiah 65:11-12, joined to vv. 8-10 by a conjunctive *wāw* and a masculine plural address form, then addresses those who abandon YHWH, in order to announce their punishment to them. The address form appears in v. 11 with four elements. The first in v. 11aα is a basic statement of the address, "and you who abandon YHWH." The second in v. 11aβ specifies "those who forget (me on) my holy mountain." The third in v. 11bα specifies "those who arrange a table for Gad," an ancient deity associated with luck. The fourth in v. 11bβ specifies "those who mix a drink for Meni," a deity associated with destiny. The announcement of punishment then follows in v. 12 in the form of an inverted prophetic judgment speech. The announcement of punishment proper appears in v. 12aα with a twofold statement that "I will number you for the sword" in v. 12aα[1-3] and that "all of you will kneel for slaughter" in v. 12aα[4-6]. The basis for the punishment follows in v. 12aβ-b in two parts. The first appears in v. 12aβ-γ, which charges that "you did not answer when I called" in v. 12aβ and that "you did not listen when I spoke" in v. 12aγ. The second appears in v. 12b, which charges that "you did evil in my eyes" in v. 12bα and that "you chose what I do not desire" in v. 12bβ.

The second component of 65:8-25, vv. 13-25, likewise begins with a version of the prophetic messenger speech form, *lākēn kōh 'āmar 'ădōnāy yhwh,* "therefore, thus says my L-rd, YHWH," in v. 13aα[1-5], and it closes with a YHWH speech formula in v. 25bβ. The YHWH speech proper therefore appears in vv. 13aα[6]-25bα. The introductory *lākēn,* "therefore," indicates that this unit follows upon vv. 8-12 by defining the practical consequences of the principle articulated in these verses, i.e., vv. 13-25 describe the punishment for the wicked and the restoration of the righteous. The first subunit of the presentation of the YHWH speech reported in vv. 13aα[6]-15a employs 2nd-person masculine plural verbal and pronoun forms to address the wicked directly and to describe their upcoming suffering in contrast to the experience of the righteous. The second element of the presentation of the YHWH speech in vv. 15b-16 constitutes the prophet's comment concerning the contrasting name of YHWH's servants. The third element of the presentation of the YHWH speech in vv. 17-25bα employs 3rd-person objective forms to describe the restoration and benefits of the righteous in great detail. Especially noteworthy are references at the end of the passage which tie it into the larger framework of chs. 65–66. Verse 23b identifies the righteous as "the seed blessed by YHWH," thereby tying this unit into vv. 8-12, in which YHWH states that a seed from Jacob will be preserved as a possible blessing. Verse 24a states that "when they (the righteous) call, I will answer," which contrasts with the situation described in vv. 1-7, where YHWH stood ready but the people did not call.

The presentation of YHWH's speech concerning the punishment of the wicked and the restoration of the righteous in vv. 13aα⁶-25bα begins in vv. 13aα⁶-15a with YHWH's statement concerning the punishment of the wicked. YHWH's statement comprises four basic elements, each of which begins with the introductory interjection *hinnēh,* "behold," and contrasts the positive experience of YHWH's servants with the negative experience of the wicked. The first in v. 13aα⁶⁻¹⁰ states that "my servants shall eat, but you shall starve." The second in v. 13aβ states that "my servants shall drink, but you will thirst." The third in v. 13b states that "my servants shall rejoice, but you will be shamed." The fourth in vv. 14-15a presents an expanded statement that "my servants shall shout for goodness of heart, but you shall cry for a pained heart and you shall wail for a broken spirit." This is basically stated at length in v. 14. The basic statement includes the statement in v. 14a that "my servants shall shout for goodness of heart" and the twofold statement in v. 14b that "you shall cry for a pained heart" in v. 14bα and that "you shall wail for a broken spirit" in v. 14bβ. Verse 15a then expands the basic statement with the charge that "you have ruined your name," in two parts: "you have left your name for an oath by my chosen" in v. 15aα and the oath in v. 15aβ that "my L-rd G-d will kill you."

The prophet's comment concerning the contrasting name of YHWH's servants appears in 65:15b-16, which is distinguished by its 3rd-person portrayal of YHWH. The basic statement "YHWH's servants will have another name" appears in v. 15b. An elaboration concerning their blessed name in the land follows in v. 16a in two parts. The first in v. 16aα presents a blessing in the land by G-d, including the protasis in v. 16aα¹⁻³, "whoever blesses oneself in the land," and the apodosis in v. 16aα⁴⁻⁶, "shall bless oneself by the true G-d." The second in v. 16aβ focuses on swearing in the land by G-d, including the protasis in v. 16aβ¹⁻², "whoever swears in the land," and the apodosis in v. 16aβ³⁻⁵, "swears by the true G-d." Finally, the presentation of YHWH's statement of the bases, that former troubles will be forgotten and hidden, appears in v. 16b in two parts. The first in v. 16bα states that "the former troubles are forgotten," and the second in v. 16bβ states that "the former troubles are hidden from my eyes."

Isaiah 65:17-25bα presents the basis for YHWH's speech: YHWH's announcement of a new creation and restoration of Jerusalem. The passage proceeds in two parts. The first part is YHWH's address to the people in vv. 17-18 announcing a new creation and commanding them to rejoice. The announcement of the new creation appears in v. 17, including YHWH's twofold statement that "I am creating a new heaven and earth" in v. 17a and the following statement in v. 17b that "the former things will not be remembered" in v. 17bα, "nor will they come to mind" in v. 17bβ. The command to rejoice follows in v. 18. It begins with the command proper in v. 18a, including the command to "rejoice" in v. 18aα and the command to "celebrate forever what I create" in v. 18aβ. The basis for the celebration, the creation of Jerusalem, follows in v. 18b with statements that "I am creating Jerusalem" in v. 18bα and that the celebration ensues in v. 18bβ.

The second part concerning YHWH's announcement of celebration follows in 65:19-25bα. The passage begins with YHWH's announcement proper, "I will celebrate and rejoice," in v. 19a, including statements that "I will celebrate over Jerusalem" in v. 19aα and "I will rejoice over my people" in v. 19aβ.

Verses 19b-25bα then present an elaboration on the basis for the celebration, in four parts. The first is an announcement that there will be no more weeping and wailing in v. 19b. The second is that there will be full lives for everyone in v. 20. The segment includes assertions that infants and old people will fulfill their days in v. 20a. The following explanation in v. 20b states that youths will live to be one hundred in v. 20bα and that a one-hundred-year-old sinner will be cursed in v. 20bβ. The third part in vv. 21-23 focuses on the building and the planting of the righteous for their offspring, in three segments. The first segment in v. 21 focuses on building houses in v. 21a and planting vineyards in v. 21b. The second segment in v. 22 asserts that they will not build for others. This segment includes the basic concern in v. 22a that they will not build for others, including assertions that they will not build for others to dwell in v. 22aα and that they do not plant for others to eat in v. 22aβ. Verse 22b follows with assertions that they will live long, including assertions that "my people will live long like a tree" in v. 22bα and that "my people will outlive the work of their hands" in v. 22bβ. The third segment in v. 23 focuses on the assertion that they will be blessed with offspring. The first segment in v. 23a asserts that they do not work for nothing in v. 23aα and that they do not bear for naught in v. 23aβ. The second segment in v. 23b asserts that they are blessed seed of YHWH in v. 23bα and that their offspring are blessed seed of YHWH in v. 23bβ. The fourth part in vv. 24-25bα presents the results of the process in which YHWH states that "I will answer and there will be peace." YHWH asserts in the first segment in v. 24 that "when they call, I will answer" in v. 24a and that "when they speak, I will hear" in v. 24b. YHWH asserts that "my holy mountain will be peaceful like Eden" in v. 25a-bα, including four assertions that "the wolf and lamb will graze together" in v. 25aα¹⁻⁴, that "the lion and the bovine will eat straw" in v. 25aα⁵⁻⁸, that "the food of the snake will be dirt" in v. 25aβ, and that "there will be no evil nor destruction in all my holy mountain" in v. 25bα.

As noted above, the YHWH speech formula in v. 25bβ closes 65:8-25.

The third major subunit is 66:1-24. Again, this subunit is demarcated both by its thematic and formal features. The first is the prophetic messenger formula in 66:1, kōh 'āmar yhwh, "Thus says YHWH," which introduces the subunit and identifies the following material as a speech by YHWH. The second is the call to attention formula in 66:5, šimě'û děbar-yhwh haḥărēdîm 'el děbārô, "Hear the word of YHWH, you who tremble at his word," which again introduces the following material and identifies it as a speech by YHWH. Other formulas that identify this material as a report of YHWH's speeches include the oracle formulas of vv. 2, 17, and 22, ně'um yhwh, "oracle of YHWH"; the subordinate messenger formula of v. 12, kî kōh 'āmar yhwh, "for thus says YHWH"; the YHWH speech formulas of vv. 20, 21, and 23, 'āmar yhwh, "says YHWH"; and modified forms of the YHWH speech formula in v. 9, yō'mar yhwh, "says YHWH," and 'āmar 'lhyk, "says your G-d." The speeches by YHWH are all formulated in characteristic 1st-person singular form, but they differ from the preceding material in ch. 65 in that the 2nd-person masculine plural address forms are no longer directed to the wicked but to the righteous. When the speeches shift to 3rd-person objective language, they now describe the wicked and not the righteous as in ch. 65.

Isaiah 66:1-24 comprises two major subunits. The first is the prophet's presentation in Isa 1–4 of YHWH's statement that the humble who tremble at YHWH's word will be restored and the wicked will be punished. Isaiah 66:1-4 is introduced by its own prophetic messenger speech formula in v. 1aα, and the presentation of YHWH's speech follows in 66:1aβ-4. The addressee of the speech is unclear: the 2nd-person masculine address form in 66:1b, "what is this house that you would build *(tibnû)* for me?" is somewhat ambiguous in that the context provides no clue as to whether the question is addressed to the righteous or the wicked. It simply addresses those who would build the temple for YHWH. Nevertheless, the reference to "the one who trembles *(wĕḥārēd)* at my word," in v. 2b indicates that this pericope is to be read in relation to 66:5-24, which is addressed to "those who tremble *(haḥărēdîm)* at His word." Overall, the passage reports YHWH's statement that the humble or those who tremble at YHWH's word will be restored and the wicked will be punished.

Isaiah 66:1aβ-4 comprises two basic components. The first in vv. 1aβ-2 describes YHWH's intentions to look to the humble. It comprises two elements, distinguished by the closing oracle formula in v. 2aβ$^{4-5}$, in vv. 1aβ-2a and 2b. Isaiah 66:1aβ-2a focuses on YHWH's claims to be the creator. The YHWH speech proper appears in vv. 1aβ-2aβ^3, and it includes three basic elements. The first in v. 1aβ asserts YHWH's right to rule over heaven and earth, including YHWH's statements that "heaven is my throne" in v. 1aβ$^{1-2}$ and that "earth is my footstool" in v. 1aβ$^{3-5}$. The second is YHWH's assertion that the temple is limited when one considers that YHWH is the creator. YHWH's assertion appears in the form of two rhetorical questions: "where is this temple that you would build me?" in v. 1bα and "where is this place for my residence?" in v. 1bβ. The third is YHWH's assertion that YHWH is the creator, in v. 2aα-β^3, including assertions that "my hand made all these things" in v. 2aα and that "my hand caused all these things to exist" in v. 2aβ$^{1-3}$. The oracle formula in v. 2aβ$^{4-5}$ closes 66:1aβ-2a. The second element in 66:2b focuses on the presentation of YHWH's declaration to look to those deemed righteous. It comprises two basic elements. The first is YHWH's assertion in v. 2bα that "I will look into this." The second is YHWH's definition of the objects of concern in v. 2bβ, including the humble in v. 2bβ$^{1-2}$, the stricken of spirit in v. 2bβ$^{3-4}$, and the one who respects or trembles at YHWH's word in v. 2bβ$^{5-6}$.

The second element of 66:1aβ-4 appears in vv. 3-4, which employ 3rd-person objective language to describe YHWH's intention to punish the evil. The concluding statements in v. 4, "because I called and no one answered, I spoke and they did not hear," recall YHWH's waiting to be called by the people in 65:1-7. Likewise, the reference in v. 4b, "and they did evil in my eyes and that in which I did not delight they chose," recalls the similar statement in 65:12 addressed to the wicked. The passage focuses on YHWH's punishment of the wicked. This subunit is an example of a modified prophetic judgment speech in which the basis for punishment appears at the beginning in v. 3a, the announcement of punishment appears in vv. 3b-4aα, and a second set of bases for punishment appears in v. 4aβ-b. The first announcement of the basis for punishment in v. 3a comprises four charges, including slaughtering a bull and killing a man in v. 3aα, sacrificing a sheep and breaking the neck of a dog in

v. 3aβ, presenting the blood of a pig as an offering in v. 3aγ, and offering incense and blessing an abomination in v. 3aδ. The announcement of punishment in vv. 3b-4aα comprises two elements based on the analogy between the actions of the wicked and the corresponding punishment chosen by YHWH. The first in v. 3b charges that the wicked chose to commit wrong, including charges that they chose their way in v. 3bα and that they desired their abominations in v. 3bβ. Verse 4aα then presents YHWH's announcement that "I choose to punish them," including statements that "I choose to humiliate them" in v. 4aα$^{1-4}$ and that "I bring terror to them" in v. 4aα$^{5-7}$. The second set of bases for punishment in v. 4aβ-b comprises two elements. The first in v. 4aβ-γ charges that "they didn't answer when I called" in v. 4aβ and that "they didn't listen when I spoke" in v. 4aγ. The second in v. 4b charges that "they did what was wrong" in v. 4bα and that "they chose what I didn't want" in v. 4bβ.

The second major component of 66:1-24 appears in vv. 5-24. The passage constitutes the prophet's presentation of YHWH's announcement of restoration in the new creation at Zion. The prophet is the speaker throughout, as indicated by the call to attention formula in v. 5a and the prophetic messenger formula in v. 12, as well as the various speech and oracle formulas as well as 3rd-person references to YHWH that appear throughout the passage and function as indications of the prophet's presentation of YHWH's speeches. YHWH's speeches are evident by their formulation in 1st-person singular speaker's form and their use of 2nd-person masculine forms to address the righteous. The text includes two basic components, each of which begins with a statement by the prophet that introduces the speeches by YHWH. Isaiah 66:5-14 reports YHWH's announcements concerning the birth of a new world at Zion, and 66:15-24 announces YHWH's approach to purge the wicked and to create the new world at Zion.

The announcement of restoration in the new creation at Zion in 66:5-14 comprises two basic elements. The first in vv. 5-6 announces the upcoming shame of the wicked. The passage is addressed to the righteous as indicated by the call to attention formula in v. 5a, which is directed to those who respect or tremble at YHWH's word. Verse 5b then focuses on the shame of the wicked as a basis for motivating the righteous. It begins with a quote of the wicked who mock YHWH in v. 5bα, including the speech formula identifying "those who hate you and reject YHWH's name" as the speakers in v. 5bα$^{1-6}$ and the quotation of their speech in v. 5bα^{7}-β^{2}. The speech includes two basic elements: the statement by the wicked to let YHWH manifest glory in v. 5bα$^{7-8}$ and a statement of the purpose of such manifestation, "that we may see your joy" in v. 5bβ$^{1-2}$. Verse 5bβ$^{3-4}$ then closes v. 5b with a statement of the result, that the wicked will be shamed. The third element then appears in v. 6 as an exclamation concerning the sound of YHWH's requital of enemies, including exclamations of the sound of tumult in the city in v. 6aα, the sound from the temple in v. 6aβ, and the sound of requital for YHWH's enemies in v. 6b.

The second element of 66:5-14 appears in vv. 7-14, which employ the imagery of childbirth to announce the creation of the new world order and call for the rejoicing of the righteous. The passage comprises two major subunits. The first is the portrayal of Jerusalem giving birth in vv. 7-9. The subunit begins with an announcement of Jerusalem giving birth in v. 7, including statements that she gave birth before she labored in v. 7a and that she delivered a son before the labor pains came in v. 7b. The second subunit comprises a set of rhetorical questions in vv. 8-9 that affirms the occurrence of the birth to Jerusalem. The first set of rhetorical assertions in v. 8aα announces that the birth to Jerusalem is new, including questions, "who ever heard of this?" in v. 8aα$^{1-3}$ and "who has seen anything like this?" in v. 8aα$^{4-6}$. A second set of rhetorical assertions in v. 8aβ-b maintains that Jerusalem did indeed give birth. This subunit begins with rhetorical questions in v. 8aβ-γ that ask and assert "can a land labor in one day?" in v. 8aβ and "can a nation be born at one time?" in v. 8aγ. The rhetorical answers appear in v. 8b, which asserts that Zion labored in v. 8bα and that Zion bore her children in v. 8bβ. A third set of rhetorical assertions in v. 9 then closes the subunit by maintaining that YHWH brought this about. It comprises two rhetorical questions, each identified by a YHWH speech formula to affirm YHWH's role. The first in v. 9a asks "shall I bring labor and not birth?" including the question proper in v. 9aα and the YHWH speech formula in v. 9aβ. The second in v. 9b asks "shall I cause birth and then stop it?" including the question proper in v. 9bα and the divine speech formula in v. 9bβ.

The second element of 66:7-14 appears in vv. 10-14, which constitute a call to rejoice for Jerusalem, together with the basis for doing so. The passage begins with the prophet's calls to rejoice over Jerusalem in vv. 10-11. The calls proper appear in v. 10. The first set of calls to rejoice appears in v. 10a in two parts, including the call to rejoice with Jerusalem in v. 10aα and the call to celebrate with her in v. 10aβ. The second call to rejoice appears in v. 10b, directed to those who mourned for her. The purpose for the calls then follows in v. 11, including statements that the people may suck from the breast of consolation in v. 11a and that they may suck from the teat of glory in v. 11b. The basis for the calls to rejoice for Jerusalem then follows in vv. 12-14 in the form of the prophet's presentation of YHWH's speech. The passage begins in v. 12aα with a prophetic messenger formula that is joined to the preceding material by a conjunctive kî, "for, because." It functions as the means to identify the following material in vv. 12aβ-14a as a speech by YHWH. YHWH's speech is an announcement of restoration for Jerusalem that comprises four basic elements. The first is a statement that "I extend the glory of the nations that you may drink" in v. 12aβ. The second is YHWH's statement in v. 12b that "you shall be carried on the side" in v. 12bα and that "you shall be played with on the knees" in v. 12bβ. The third is YHWH's statement in v. 13 that "I will comfort you like a mother" in v. 13a and that "you shall be comforted" in v. 13b. The fourth is YHWH's statement in v. 14a that "you will see" in v. 14aα^1, that "your heart will rejoice" in v. 14a$^{2-3}$, and that "your bones will flourish like grass" in v. 14aβ. The prophet then closes the subunit with a twofold statement in v. 14b indicating that the hand and anger of YHWH will be known respectively to YHWH's servants in v. 14bα and to YHWH's enemies in v. 14bβ.

The second basic component of 66:5-24 appears in vv. 15-24, which present the prophet's announcement concerning YHWH's coming to purge the wicked and create the new world at Zion. The passage begins with the introductory connective kî, "for," which ties this text to vv. 5-14. It comprises two basic subunits. The first appears in vv. 15-16 with the prophet's statements concerning the approach of YHWH. Isaiah 66:15-16 begins in v. 15a with an announcement of YHWH's approach proper, which includes YHWH's approach with fire in v. 15aα and a statement that YHWH's chariots are like a whirlwind in v. 15aβ. An elaboration then follows in vv. 15b-16, which indicates that the ultimate purposes of YHWH's appearances are to vent anger and to judge. Verse 15b announces that the purpose is to vent YHWH's anger, including statements in v. 15bα that the purpose is to vent anger and in v. 15bβ that it is to rebuke with fire. Verse 16 then follows with a statement that the ultimate purpose is to judge, including statements in v. 16a that YHWH comes to judge with fire and sword against all flesh and in v. 16b that those slain by YHWH will be many.

The second component of 66:15-24 appears in vv. 17-24, which announce YHWH's purge and restoration. This passage comprises two basic elements. The first in v. 17 presents an announcement that all the wicked will come to an end, including YHWH's announcement proper in v. 17a-bα and the oracle formula identifying the preceding as a statement by YHWH in v. 17bβ.

The second element of 66:17-24 appears in vv. 18-24, which present a portrayal of the restoration and the purge. The passage includes three basic elements: a portrayal of YHWH's restoration of Israel/Judah from among the nations in vv. 18-21, a promise joined by *kî* of Israel's continuing seed as the nations come to worship YHWH in vv. 22-23, and a portrayal of the nations viewing the corpses of the wicked in v. 24.

The portrayal of YHWH's restoration of Israel/Judah in 66:18-21 begins in vv. 18-20a with a presentation of YHWH's first speech, an announcement of restoration. The speech proper appears in vv. 18-20aα, which includes two basic components. The first is the statement of the premise in v. 18aα that "I know their deeds and thoughts." The second is the announcement of restoration proper in vv. 18aβ-20aα, which proceeds in four parts. The first in v. 18aβ-b asserts that "the time has come to gather all the nations to see my glory," including a statement in v. 18aβ that "the time has come to gather all the nations" and a twofold statement in v. 18b that "the nations will come" in v. 18bα and that "they will see my glory" in v. 18bβ. The second in v. 19a-bα states YHWH's actions, including YHWH's announcement that "I will place a sign upon them" in v. 19aα and that "I will send fugitives from them to the nations that have not seen my glory" in v. 19aβ-bα. The third in v. 19bβ turns to the fugitives' actions with an announcement that "they shall declare my glory among the nations." The fourth in v. 20aα then turns to the nations' actions with an announcement that "they shall return the fugitives to my holy mountain as an offering." The YHWH speech formula in v. 20aβ closes the account of YHWH's first speech. YHWH's second speech then follows in vv. 20b-21 with an announcement concerning the selection of priests and Levites from among the returned fugitives. The speech proper appears in v. 20b-21a with an analogical statement. The protasis in v. 20b states that "just as Israel brings offerings to the temple," and the apodosis in v. 21a states that "so I will choose from them (i.e., the fugitives returned by the nations) for priests and Levites." Although many interpreters read "and I will also take from them" in v. 21a as a reference to the nations, the antecedent to this phrase is "and the sons of Israel shall bring an offering in vessels of pure gold to the house of

YHWH" — i.e., it refers to the fugitives returned by the nations. The YHWH speech formula in v. 21b closes the presentation of YHWH's second speech.

Isaiah 66:22-23 constitutes an announcement of Israel's continued seed and name as the nations come to worship YHWH. As noted above, this subunit is joined to vv. 18-21 by a conjunctive *kî,* "for." The passage comprises two elements. The first in v. 22a presents a statement of analogy, "just as the new heavens and earth stand before me," including the statement proper in v. 22aα and the oracle formula in v. 22aβ. The statement of application, "Israel's seed and name will stand," follows in vv. 22b-23. The segment includes YHWH's twofold statement proper in v. 22b-23bα, including the basic statement in v. 22b and an elaboration that "all flesh will worship regularly before me" in v. 23a-bα. The YHWH speech formula in v. 23bβ closes the account of the speech.

Finally, 66:24, joined to vv. 22-23 by a *wāw*-consecutive formation, presents the concluding portrayal of the nations viewing the corpses of the wicked, in two parts. The first in v. 24a indicates that they will go out to see the corpses of those who rebelled against YHWH, and the second in v. 24b indicates what they will see, a continued sign of their rebellion against YHWH.

Genre

Isaiah 65–66 employs a number of generic and formulaic elements in its construction of YHWH's response concerning YHWH's anticipated actions to requite the evil and to deliver the righteous. No one genre or formula dominates the whole. Rather, they function within the text to enable it to achieve its rhetorical purposes.

Perhaps the best represented genres in this text are the various instances of the PROPHETIC JUDGMENT SPEECH pattern and the PROPHETIC ANNOUNCEMENT OF SALVATION. Both genres are to be expected in a text that deliberately contrasts the impending punishment of the wicked and the restoration of the righteous. Indeed, they serve a larger purpose to persuade the audience of the text to count themselves among the righteous rather than among the wicked. By holding out the threat of punishment to those who would forsake YHWH and the promise of restoration for those who would adhere to YHWH's expectations as envisioned in this text, the text is designed to persuade its audience to adopt the desired course of action — to support the restoration of the Jewish people at the restored Jerusalem temple.

The PROPHETIC JUDGMENT SPEECH pattern plays an especially important role in chs. 65–66 in portraying the impending judgment of the wicked. The pattern normally contains two basic elements, the BASIS FOR PUNISHMENT, which lays out the reasons that punishment or judgment has been decreed by YHWH, and the PROPHETIC ANNOUNCEMENT OF PUNISHMENT, which provides a detailed announcement of the consequences that the wicked will suffer as a result of their actions. When considering the rhetorical goals of this genre within chs. 65–66, the prophetic judgment speech serves as a means to identify undesirable behavior among the people and thereby to dissuade them from engaging in it. Examples of the prophetic judgment speech occur at a number of key points within this text. Isaiah 65:1-7 presents an example to introduce the text, particularly the charge that the people did not answer when YHWH called, even though YHWH was allegedly prepared to act on the people's behalf. Isaiah 65:1-5 presents the grounds for punishment in detail. In addition to their not answering when YHWH was ready, the text identifies various forms of pagan or illicit worship practice, such as worship in gardens for various nature deities, rituals associated with the dead and their tombs, the consumption of swine's flesh, and others. The announcement of punishment in 65:6-7 then makes a general statement that YHWH will act to requite the wicked. A YHWH SPEECH FORMULA closes the text in 65:7aα[5-6].

A second example of the PROPHETIC JUDGMENT SPEECH appears in 65:8-12, albeit in modified form. A prophetic MESSENGER FORMULA introduces the subunit to identify it as a word from YHWH, and an example of analogical INSTRUCTION employs experience with grape vines to make the point that those who are righteous must be preserved, whereas those who are wicked must be cast off. Grounds for punishment appear in v. 11, an announcement of punishment in v. 12aα, and another set of bases for punishment in v. 12aβ-b, which returns to the theme that the people did not listen. A similarly formulated example of the PROPHETIC JUDGMENT SPEECH appears in 66:3-4, in which v. 3a offers a series of bases for punishment, vv. 3b-4aα present the announcement for punishment, and v. 4aβ-b returns to the grounds for punishment, which again emphasizes the people's refusal to listen. The concern with listening to YHWH is pervasive in all three examples of the PROPHETIC JUDGMENT SPEECH and indicates a rhetorical interest in motivating the people to listen and thereby to persuade them to adopt the desired behavior, in this case, observance of YHWH at the Jerusalem temple.

The PROPHETIC ANNOUNCEMENT OF SALVATION also plays a key role insofar as it identifies the anticipated benefits that will accrue to the righteous who observe YHWH's will. Although full expressions of the form may present a blessing or a reassurance formula, the examples in chs. 65–66 include only the announcement of restoration. YHWH's announcement of celebration in 65:19-25bα appears to be based on the prophetic announcement of restoration, insofar as it calls upon the people to celebrate the restoration of the city of Jerusalem and its people. Like the examples of the prophetic judgment speeches, the passage displays a concern with listening to YHWH, insofar as it ends with the righteous doing exactly that. A YHWH SPEECH FORMULA closes the unit in 65:25bβ.

The primary example of the PROPHETIC ANNOUNCEMENT OF SALVATION appears in 66:1-24, which closes the book of Isaiah. The passage actually includes elements of both the prophetic announcement of restoration and the PROPHETIC JUDGMENT SPEECH. Isaiah 66:1-4 begins with a prophetic MESSENGER FORMULA in v. 1aα, which identifies YHWH as the source of the following oracle. The oracle itself announces that the humble, i.e., those who tremble at the word of YHWH, will enjoy the restoration, whereas the wicked will suffer. The passage presents an argument for why one should observe YHWH's word: YHWH is the creator, whose presence is manifested throughout the world, not only in the Jerusalem temple. This point is made by a set of RHETORICAL

QUESTIONS in v. 1b which question the typical understanding of the temple as the sole home of YHWH when in fact YHWH is manifested throughout all creation. The closing ORACLE FORMULA in v. 2aβ[4-5] reinforces the notion that this statement does indeed come from YHWH.

Isaiah 66:5-24 returns to the PROPHETIC ANNOUNCEMENT OF SALVATION with a lengthy set of oracles that encourage the righteous. The passage begins with the CALL TO ATTENTION formula in v. 5a directed to those who tremble at the word of YHWH, and vv. 5b-6 employ a SPEECH FORMULA to quote the wicked who will suffer YHWH's wrath. Isaiah 66:7-14 employs the imagery of a woman in childbirth to announce the restoration of Zion, and the RHETORICAL QUESTIONS in vv. 8-9 function as assertions that the rebirth or restoration of Jerusalem is indeed taking place. The YHWH SPEECH FORMULA in v. 9aβ and the divine SPEECH FORMULA in v. 9bβ assert that these speeches indeed come from YHWH.

Isaiah 66:15-24 combines the PROPHETIC JUDGMENT SPEECH and the PROPHETIC ANNOUNCEMENT OF SALVATION in an effort to summarize the contrasting fates of the righteous and the wicked and thereby to reinforce the rhetorical interest in motivating the audience to observe YHWH's will. Following the theophanic announcement of YHWH's approach in vv. 15-16, 66:17 announces the end of all the wicked with an ORACLE FORMULA in v. 17bβ to underscore the point, whereas 66:18-24 portrays the restoration of Israel's seed, in which Jewish exiles will be returned to Jerusalem by the nations. Indeed, the passage emphasizes that some of the returned exiles will serve as Levites and priests. Again, YHWH SPEECH FORMULAS appear in vv. 20aβ, 21b, and 23bβ together with an ORACLE FORMULA in v. 22aβ to underscore the point that these developments will come directly from YHWH.

Setting

The report of YHWH's response in 65:1–66:24 dates to the late-5th- or early-4th-century edition of the final form of the book of Isaiah. It is marked by a clear concern to differentiate between the evil and the righteous in Jerusalem and Judah during the period of Nehemiah's and Ezra's reforms, which were designed to garner support for reestablishing the Jerusalem temple as the holy center of Jerusalem and Judah, as well as creation at large. Although Hanson had argued that the differentiation between the wicked and the righteous in this text indicated polemic by visionary prophetic circles who challenged the Zadokite priesthood of the temple (Hanson, *The Dawn of Apocalyptic*, 161-85), his model is based upon an outmoded Wellhausenian model of conflict between the prophets and the priesthood that in turn presupposes Protestant polemics against the Roman Catholic Church. More recent scholarship points to the constructive role that prophets play in relation to temples; D. L. Petersen notes how prophets were ultimately incorporated into the Levitical priesthood in Chronicles (*Late-exilic Prophecy: Studies in Deutero-Prophetic Literature and in Chronicles* [SBLMS 23; Missoula: Scholars 1977] 55-96), and my own work stresses that many prophetic figures, especially from later periods, such as Jeremiah, Ezekiel, and Zechariah, are priests (e.g., M. A. Sweeney, *The Prophetic Literature* [IBT; Nashville: Abingdon, 2005]). Indeed, F. Flannery-Dailey's work (*Dreamers, Scribes, and Priests: Jewish Dreams in the Hellenistic and Roman Eras* [JSJSup 90; Leiden: Brill, 2004]) demonstrates that oracular activity is most commonly associated with temples. Insofar as prophets were ultimately identified as the Levitical singers of the temple, chs. 65–66 — and indeed, the final form of the book of Isaiah as a whole — would easily function as part of a liturgy designed to celebrate the restoration of the Jerusalem temple as the holy center of creation and Israel in the aftermath of the Babylonian exile and the reconstruction of the temple itself.

The differentiation between the righteous and the wicked in ch. 65–66 plays a key role in garnering support for the late-5th- and early-4th-century temple reforms of Nehemiah and Ezra. The 6th-century edition of Isaiah did not differentiate between the righteous and the wicked among Israel and Judah in exile because it sought the full support of the people in returning to Jerusalem and restoring the temple in the aftermath of the Babylonian exile. But the reforms of Nehemiah and Ezra were based on convincing an already resident Jerusalemite and Judean population actively to engage the sanctity of the temple by moving one-tenth of the population into the city, closing the city on Shabbat and holidays, and supporting the temple with their presence and offerings at the holy times of the week and year. It is noteworthy, therefore, that 66:2, 5 employ the Hebrew term *ḥārēdîm*, "those who tremble" at YHWH's word (i.e., those who stand in awe of YHWH and will do what YHWH expects), insofar as it is the same term employed for the self-designation of the community under Ezra (Ezra 9:3; 10:4; J. Blenkinsopp, *Ezra-Nehemiah* [OTL; Philadelphia: Westminster, 1988] 178-79). Convincing the people to support such an enterprise, particularly in the aftermath of the Babylonian exile and the rebuilding of the temple, was a key challenge for a people that continued to live in economic hardship and under threat by the various brigands and marauders of western Asia during the Persian period. Consequently, the differentiation between the wicked and the righteous served a rhetorical end to convince the people that they would not want to be accounted among the wicked who ignored YHWH and the temple, but instead among those who supported YHWH, the creator of the universe and the redeemer of Israel, in YHWH's efforts to restore the temple to its proper role as the holy center of the Jewish people in Jerusalem and as the holy center of creation at large.

In short, chs. 65–66 were written as part of the final late-5th-/early-4th-century edition of the book of Isaiah in an effort to support the temple reforms of Nehemiah and Ezra.

Interpretation

Isaiah 65–66 functions as the conclusion to the book of Isaiah as a whole by pointing to the anticipated restoration of Jerusalem that will follow from the punishment and exile suffered by the city since the Assyrian period. In addition to providing a response to the lament in 63:7–64:11, chs. 65–66 take up issues raised in various texts throughout the book of Isaiah beginning with ch. 1. The pattern of intertexual citation and allusions focuses on several major issues, including the distinction between the righteous and the wicked in Israel; the pilgrimage of the nations to Zion in order to return the exiled people; the imagery of the tree in relation to the new growth of the "seed"; and YHWH's readiness to accept the people in contrast to the people's unwillingness to accept YHWH and YHWH's sovereignty. Overall, the citations indicate a major interest in reading the book of Isaiah in order to point to the rebirth of the "seed" of Israel in a new creation centered around Zion.

The interrelationship between chs. 65–66 and ch. 1 is well-known. In general, ch. 1 points to the rebellious nature of the people who reject YHWH (vv. 2-9); the abuse of cultic sacrifice (vv. 10-17); the need to purify the people (vv. 18-20); the need to purify Jerusalem (vv. 21-26); the distinction between the righteous who will be redeemed and the wicked who will be destroyed (vv. 27-28); and the use of imagery pertaining to withered trees and gardens to portray the destruction and shame of the wicked (vv. 29-31). Isaiah 65–66 likewise points to the distinction between the righteous and the wicked (65:8-12; 66:1-4); the presence of cultic abuse (65:1-7; 66:3-4, 17); the need to preserve the righteous seed of the people and the need to destroy the wicked among them (65:8-25; 66:18-24); and the use of tree and garden imagery to illustrate the pruning process (65:8-25).

These thematic connections are reinforced by a number of lexical associations. The reference to the people's abandonment of YHWH in 65:11, *'ōzĕbê yhwh*, "those who abandon YHWH," echoes the language of 1:4, *'āzĕbû 'et yhwh*, "they have abandoned YHWH," and 1:28, *wĕ'ōzĕbê yhwh yiklû*, "and those who abandon YHWH will perish." The reference to the rebellious nature of the people in 65:2, *'am sōrēr*, "rebellious people," takes up language from 1:4, *'am kebed 'āwōn*, "a people heavy with sin," and 1:5, *tôsîpû sārâ*, "they continue rebellion." The statements in 65:12 and 66:4 that the people have chosen to act in a manner that YHWH does not want, *ûba'ăšer lō'-ḥāpaṣtî bĕḥartem/bāḥārû*, "and in what I did not delight you have chosen/they have chosen," take up language from 1:11, "and (in) lambs and goats, I do not delight *(lō'-ḥāpaṣtî)*." The references in 65:3 to the people sacrificing in the gardens, *zōbĕḥîm baggannôt*, "sacrificing in the gardens," and in 66:17 to their sanctifying themselves in the gardens, *hammitqaddĕšîm wĕhammiṭahărîm 'el-haggannôt*, "those who sanctify themselves and purify themselves unto the gardens," combine the language of sacrifice in 1:11, *lāmmâ-lî rōb-zibḥêhem*, "why multiply to me your sacrifices?" with the reference in 1:29 to cultic apostasy in the gardens, *wĕtaḥpĕrû mēhaggannôt*, "and you were embarrassed by the gardens." The reference to the shame of the apostates appears again in 1:29, *kî yēbōšû mē'êlîm*, "for they will be ashamed from the oaks," and in 66:5, *wĕhēm yēbōšû*, "and they will be ashamed," and in 65:13, *wĕ'attem tēbōšû*, "and you will be ashamed." The reference in 66:17 to the destruction of the apostates together, *yaḥdāyw yāsupû*, "together they will be brought to an end," corresponds to the statements that the wicked will be destroyed together in 1:28, *wĕšeber pōšĕ'îm wĕḥaṭṭā'îm yaḥdāyw*, "and the breaking of the rebellious and sinners together," and 1:31, *ûbā'ărû šĕnêhem yaḥdāyw*, "and the two of them shall burn together." Likewise, the statement in 66:24 that the fire that consumes the rebels will not be quenched, *wĕ'iššām lō' tikbeh,* "and their fire will not be quenched," takes up the language of 1:31, *wĕ'ên mĕkabbeh,* "and there is no quenching." The passage also contains elements of reversal. In contrast to the reference in 1:15 to people who spread their hands to YHWH in unwanted sacrifice, *ûbĕpāriśkem kappêkem,* "and when you spread your hands," 65:2 indicates that YHWH's hands were spread to the people all along, *pēraśtî yāday kol hayyôm,* "I spread my hands all day." In contrast to the reference in 1:15 that YHWH would be unwilling to hear unwanted prayer, *gam kî-tarbû tĕpillâ 'ênennî šōmē'a,* "indeed, when you multiply prayer, there is no one listening," 65:24 indicates that YHWH will listen when the people call, *wa'ănî 'ešmā',* "and I will listen."

These correspondences demonstrate the interrelationship between ch. 1 and chs. 65–66, but they do not explain all of the intertextual allusions between First Isaiah and chs. 65–66. For example, 1:4 refers to the rebellious people as *zer'a mĕrē'îm,* "rebellious seed," whereas 65:9 refers to the "seed" that YHWH will bring out from Jacob, *wĕhôṣē'tî miyya'ăqōb zera',* "and I will bring out from Jacob a seed." The association between these verses must be considered in relation to 6:13, which draws upon the imagery of a burnt tree to speak of the emergence of the "holy seed" *(zera' qōdeš)* that will emerge from its stump to constitute the remnant of Israel. This likewise informs the reference in 65:22 that the days of YHWH's people will be like the days of a tree, *kîmê hā'ēṣ yĕmê 'ammî,* "for the days of the tree are like the days of my people," which expresses the longevity of the restored people. It also aids in establishing the analogy between YHWH's statement of readiness in 65:1 to accept the people, *'āmartî hinnēnî hinnēnî,* "I said, 'here I am, here I am,'" and the statement by the prophet in 6:8 that he was prepared to accept YHWH's call, *wā'ōmar hinĕnî šĕlāḥēnî,* "and I said, 'here I am, send me.'"

The interrelationship between ch. 6 and chs. 65–66 likewise points to other textual associations. YHWH's reference to the desolation of the land in 6:11, *'ārîm mē'ên yôšēb ûbāttîm mē'ên 'ādām,* "cities without inhabitant and houses without a person," stands behind the statement in 65:21-22, *ûbānû bāttîm wĕyāšābû wĕnāṭĕ'û kĕrāmîm wĕ'ākĕlû piryām lō' yibnû wĕ'aḥēr yēšēb lō' yiṭṭĕ'û wĕ'aḥēr yō'kēl,* "and they shall build houses and dwell in them and they shall plant vineyards and eat their fruit, they shall not build and another inhabit, they shall not plant and another eat." The fact that this statement appears immediately prior to the above-mentioned analogy between the days of the tree and the days of the restored people aids in establishing the association. But the language and imagery of 65:21-22 also presupposes that of 5:1-7, which contains the vineyard allegory, and that of vv. 8-10, which contain the first of the woe oracles. Isaiah 5:1-7 points to YHWH's destruction of the "vineyard" *(kerem)* which produced poor fruit, and 5:8-10 condemns those who appropriate the houses of the poor so that "surely many houses will be left desolate, great and good without inhatbi-tant" *('im-lō' bātîm rabbîm lĕšammâ yihyû gĕdōlîm wĕṭôbîm mē'ên yôšēb).* The reference to "the work of their hands" *(ûma'ăśēh yĕdêhem)* in 65:22 likewise takes up a phrase that appears in 5:12 *(ûma'ăśēh yādāyw,* "and the work of his hands") and elsewhere throughout the book (cf. 2:8; 17:8; 19:25; 29:23; 37:19; 60:21; 64:7).

The relationship between the "tree" and "seed" imagery of chs. 6 and 65–66 likewise points to other texts that play a role in chs. 65–66. Scholars have long noted that 65:25 contains a condensed version of the paradisial imagery of 11:6-9, in which the "wolf" *(zĕ'ēb)* and "lamb" *(ṭāleh)* will graze together, the "lion" *('aryēh)* and "cattle" *(bāqār)* will eat chaff, and the serpent *(nāḥāš)* will be included with all of the others on YHWH's holy mountain. In fact, two statements from both passages are identical, *wĕ'aryēh kabbāqār yō'kal-teben,* "and the lion shall eat chaff like cattle," and *lō'-yārē'û wĕlō'-yašḥîtû bĕkol-har qodšî,* "and no one will harm them and no one will destroy them in all of my holy mountain." The term *har qodšî,* "my holy mountain," is sufficiently important in chs. 65–66 that it appears in 65:11 and 66:20 in reference respectively to "those who have abandoned YHWH, forgetting my holy mountain," and to the return of the exiles "upon my holy mountain Jerusalem." Like ch. 6, ch. 11 employs tree imagery to express the potential regrowth of the people after they have been cut down. Isaiah 11:1 states that "a new shoot shall go forth from the stump of Jesse and a shoot shall sprout from his roots." This new growth leads to the idyllic picture of the animals grazing together in 11:6-9, and it leads to the scenario in 11:10-16, in which the nations will return the exiles of Israel to the land. This is a major motif of 66:18-24, which portrays the nations bringing the exiled people of Israel back to Zion. The passage must be read in relation to other texts that express the same motif, such as 2:2-4 and 60–62, but scholars often overlook the association with 37:30-32, which conveys Isaiah's sign that Jerusalem will be saved from Sennacherib. Isaiah 37:30-32 calls for the remnant of the people to "take root below and make fruit above," in comparison to the new root of Jesse mentioned in 11:1. But the sign also calls for the people to plant new vineyards in the third year after the siege: *wĕnāṭĕ'û kĕrāmîm wĕ'ākĕlû piryām,* "and they shall plant vineyards and eat their fruit," which corresponds precisely to 65:21. The preceding command in 37:30 to "sow seed and harvest" *(zir'û wĕqiṣrû)* likewise aids in establishing the relationship of this text with the reference to "seed" in 6:13 and 65:9.

Isaiah 66:5-24 also makes extensive reference to earlier Isaianic texts. This is evident first of all in 66:7-9. The passage describes the birth of a new land and nation, and Zion's giving birth to new sons. The characteristic language of this passage includes the verbs *ḥwl,* "to be in labor" (vv. 7, 8), and *yld,* "to give birth" (vv. 7, 8 [2x], 9 [2x]), and the noun *ḥbl,* "labor pain" (v. 7). Pfisterer Darr (*Isaiah's Vision,* 205-25) treats the motif of birthing in the book of Isaiah, particularly as it relates to the present passage. She points to birthing imagery as a motif that appears throughout the book of Isaiah, noting especially the role of Hezekiah's proverb in 37:3, "babes are positioned for birth, but there is no strength to deliver." In the context of the narrative concerning Sennacherib's siege of Jerusalem, the proverb signifies the imperilment of Jerusalem, which is ultimately delivered by YHWH after Hezekiah turns to YHWH in the temple. Pfisterer Darr also notes the appearance of this motif in 26:17-18, in which the distressed people appeal to YHWH to deliver them by describing themselves in analogy to a woman in childbirth who brings forth nothing. Because they are unable to deliver themselves, they appeal to YHWH. The passage continues with a reference to the resurrection of the dead in 26:19 and to YHWH's approach to punish the wicked, who have brought about the distress of the people. She likewise notes the use of the imagery in 66:7-9, but concludes that it is impossible to know whether the author of 66:7-9 wrote with 37:3 specifically in mind. Nevertheless, it is clear that 66:7-9 takes up a major motif that is developed throughout the book of Isaiah. Isaiah 3:25–4:1, for example, portrays the defeated Jerusalem as a mother whose sons have all been killed around her. Isaiah 7:1–9:6(NRSV 7) portrays the birth of Isaiah's sons as important signs concerning YHWH's deliverance of the city of Jerusalem. Isaiah 13 portrays the downfall of Babylon to YHWH's holy warriors as a symbol for the birth of a new world. Especially noteworthy is 13:8, which describes the agony of the city's defenders with imagery of childbirth: "and they are dismayed, pangs and labor pains seize them, like a birthing woman they give birth." Likewise, 13:5 employs a wordplay on the verb *ḥbl* to portray YHWH's destruction of the land: "YHWH and the weapons of his wrath (come) to destroy/give labor pain to *(lĕḥabbēl)* all the earth." Finally, ch. 54 portrays Zion as a barren mother whose children will now be gathered around her as a means to announce the restoration of Jerusalem that YHWH is bringing about. It would seem that 66:7-9 draws upon these themes in its own portrayal of the restoration of Zion. In this regard, it seems to have a precursor in 65:23, "They will not labor in vain, and they will not give birth for disaster, because they are seed blessed of YHWH, and their offspring are with them." Here it is noteworthy that 65:23 combines the imagery of childbirth as a metaphor for the restoration of Zion with that of the seed from 6:13; 37:30-32; and 65:9.

The second example is 66:10-14. This section extends the metaphor of childbirth from 66:7-9 by portraying the redeemed people as the babies of mother Jerusalem who suck at her breast. This imagery appears in v. 11, "in order that you may suck and be sated from her consoling breast, in order that you may suck and be delighted from the fullness of her glory," and vv. 12aβ-13bα, "and you will suck, upon the hip you will be carried, and upon the knees you will be played with, like a man whose mother comforts him, I will comfort you." But 66:10-14 also shifts its intertextual references from the childbirth imagery that appears in ch. 13 and other texts to the imagery of rejoicing and flowing water that appears in 8:6-8. Although the commands to rejoice in 66:10 draw upon the language and imagery of 35:1-2, the phrase *śîśû 'ittâ māśôś*, "rejoice with her in exultation," draws explicitly on 8:6, in that it is the only other instance in the Hebrew Bible in which the verb *śwś* and the noun *māśôś* are employed together with the particle *'et*, "with." Isaiah 8:6 reads, *ûmĕśôś 'et-rĕṣîn ûben-rĕmalyāhû*, "and exultation with the son of Rezin and the son of Remaliah." Furthermore, 66:10-14 draws on other vocabulary from 8:6-8 in order to present the image of YHWH's glory restored to Jerusalem. Thus, 66:12aβ reads *hinĕnî nōṭeh-'ēlêhā kĕnāhār šālôm ûkĕnaḥal šôṭēp kĕbôd gôyim*, "behold, I am extending unto her peace like a river and the glory of the nations like an overflowing stream." This draws especially on the language and imagery of Assyrian conquest as a flood that "overflows and passes by" *(šāṭap wĕ'ābar)*, and it presents the Assyrian king as one who "extends his wings/skirts" to fill the land. The portrayal of overflowing waters and the "spreading of his wings/skirts" in 8:7b-8 conveys the imagery of sexual intercourse — or, more precisely, rape. Although it employs the vocabulary and imagery of 8:6-8, 66:10-14 reverses the imagery of rape by the Assyrian monarch to the imagery of YHWH as the father who brings about the new birth in Jerusalem and thereby provides the cause for rejoicing. Furthermore, it appears to build upon the statement in 65:18-19a, "Indeed, rejoice and be glad *(śîśû wĕgîlû)* forever (over) what I am creating, for behold, I am creating for Jerusalem gladness *(gîlâ)* and for her people exultation *(māśôś)*, and I will be glad *(wĕgaltî)* with Jerusalem and I shall rejoice *(wĕśaśtî)* with her people."

The final example is 66:15-24. Scholars have noted that this passage draws upon the pilgrimage imagery of chs. 60–62 and other texts from Deutero- and Trito-Isaiah, but texts from First Isaiah appear to play the constitutive role. As noted above, the portrayal in v. 17 of illicit worship in the gardens draws upon 1:29-31. The imagery in vv. 15-16 of YHWH's coming in fire to judge the apostates draws upon the imagery of the burning gardens/tree of 1:29-31 as well. The passage also depends upon 5:28, insofar as its imagery of the approach of YHWH's chariots "like a whirlwind" *(kassûpâ)* corresponds to the imagery and language of 5:28, "his horses' hooves are like flint, and his wheels like the whirlwind *(kassûpâ).*" But the "flowing river" imagery of 66:10-14 is operative here as well, in that it establishes a connection between the portrayal of the pilgrimage of the nations to Zion in 66:18-24 and a similar portrayal in 2:2-4. In portraying the imagery of the nations' pilgrimage to Zion, 2:2b employs the language of flowing waters, "and all the nations shall flow *(wĕnāhărû)* unto it." The verb "flow" *(wĕnāhărû)* is based on the same root as river *(nāhār)* in 66:12, "peace like a river *(kĕnāhār šālôm).*" Many scholars see 66:18-24 as a prophecy that the nations will come to Zion and that YHWH will choose priests and Levites from them (see esp. vv. 20-21), but as Schramm's recent analysis of this passage demonstrates, the passage refers to YHWH's choosing priests and Levites from the exiled Israelites who are returned by the nations to Zion. This is completely consistent with the perspective of 2:2-4 in the context of chs. 2–4 as a whole; 2:5 invites Jacob to become a part of the procession, and 2:6-22 portrays YHWH's destruction of evil in the land. The ultimate result is a cleansed Jerusalem in which the remnant of Israel will be established in Jerusalem (4:2-6). The reference to the establishment of "your seed and your name" in v. 22 indicates that the passage draws upon 65:8-9, which portrays YHWH's intentions to preserve a "seed" from Jacob (and Judah) to possess the holy mountain, and 65:15b-16, which indicates that YHWH's servants will have another name.

Bibliography

B. W. Anderson, "The Apocalyptic Rendering of the Isaiah Tradition," in *The Social World of Formative Christianity and Judaism (Fest.* H. C. Kee; ed. J. Neusner et al.; Philadelphia: Westminster, 1988) 17-38; W. A. M. Beuken, "Does Trito-Isaiah Reject the Temple? An Intertextual Inquiry into Isaiah 66:1-6," in *Intertextuality in Biblical Writings (Fest.* B. van Iersel; ed. S. Draisma; Kampen: Kok, 1989) 53-66; idem, "Isaiah Chapters LXV–LXVI: Trito-Isaiah and the Closure of the Book of Isaiah," in *Congress Volume:*

Leuven 1989 (ed. J. A. Emerton; VTSup 43; Leiden: Brill, 1991) 204-21; idem, "The Main Theme of Trito-Isaiah"; idem, "Yhwh's Sovereign Rule and His Adoration on Mt. Zion: A Comparison of Poetic Visions in Isaiah 24–27, 52, and 66," in Everson and Kim, eds., *The Desert Will Bloom,* 91-107; J. Blenkinsopp, "A Jewish Sect of the Persian Period," *CBQ* 52 (1990) 5-20; idem, "The Servant and the Servants in Isaiah and the Formation of the Book"; idem, "The 'Servants of the L-rd' in Third Isaiah," in *"The Place Is Too Small for Us": The Israelite Prophets in Recent Scholarship* (ed. R. P. Gordon; Winona Lake: Eisenbrauns, 1995), 392-412; W. H. Brownlee, *The Meaning of the Qumran Scrolls for the Bible,* 234-35; D. M. Carr, "Reading Isaiah from Beginning (Isaiah 1) to End (Isaiah 65–66): Multiple Modern Possibilities," in Melugin and Sweeney, eds., *New Visions of Isaiah,* 188-218; M. J. Chan, "Isaiah 65–66 and the Genesis of Reorienting Speech," *CBQ* 72 (2010) 445-63; E. U. Dim, *The Eschatological Implications of Isa 65 and 66 as the Conclusion of the Book Of Isaiah* (Berne: Lang, 2005); C. A. Franke, "'Like a Mother I Have Comforted You': The Function of Figurative Language in Isaiah 1:7-26 and 66:7-14," in Everson and Kim, eds., *The Desert Will Bloom,* 35-55; A. E. Gardner, "Isaiah 66:1-4: Condemnation of Temple and Sacrifice or Contrast Between the Arrogant and the Humble," *RB* 113 (2006) 506-28; P. Hanson, *The Dawn of Apocalyptic,* 134-50; S.-H. Jang, "Hearing the Word of G-d in Isaiah 1 and 65–66," in *The One Who Reads May Run (Fest.* E. W. Conrad; ed. R. Boer, M. Carden, and J. Kelso; LHBOTS 553; London: T. & T. Clark, 2012) 41-58; H. G. Jefferson, "Notes on the Authorship of Isaiah 65 and 66," *JBL* 68 (1949) 225-30; U. Kellermann, "Tritojesaja und das Geheimnis des G-ttesknechts: Erwägungen zu Jes 59,21; 61,1-3; 66,18-24," *BN* 58 (1991) 46-82; K. Koenen, *Ethik und Eschatologie,* 168-205; W. Lau, *Schriftgelehrte Prophetie,* 126-42, 168-202; L. J. Lieb-rich, "The Compilation of the Book of Isaiah," *JQR* 46 (1955-56) 259-77; idem, "The Compilation of the Book of Isaiah," *JQR* 47 (1956-57) 114-38; C. M. Maier, "Zion's Body as a Site of G-d's Motherhood in Isaiah 66:7-14," in *Daughter Zion: Her Portrait, Her Response* (ed. M. J. Boda, C. J. Dempsey, and L. S. Flesher; AIL 13; Atlanta: Society of Biblical Literature, 2012), 225-42; K. Nielsen, *There Is Hope for a Tree* (JSOTSup 65; Sheffield: JSOT, 1989) 201-22; K. Pauritsch, *Die neue Gemeinde,* 171-218; K. Pfisterer Darr, *Isaiah's Vision and the Family of G-d;* A. Rofé, "Isaiah 66:1-4: Judean Sects in the Persian Period as Viewed by Trito-Isaiah," in *Biblical and Related Studies Presented to Samuel Iwry* (ed. A. Kort and S. Morschauser; Winona Lake: Eisenbrauns, 1985), 205-17; B. Schramm, *The Opponents of Third Isaiah,* 161-70; E. Sehmsdorf, "Studien zur Redaktionsgeschichte"; S. Sekine, *Die tritojesajanische Sammlung,* 43-45, 54-65; P. A. Smith, *Rhetoric and Redaction,* 128-32, 144-67; O. H. Steck, ". . . ein kleiner Knabe kann sie leiten: Beobachtungen zum Tierfrieden in Jesaja 11,6-8 und 65,25," in *Alttes-tamentlicher Glaube und biblische Theologie (Fest.* H. D. Preuss; ed. J. Hausmann and H.-J. Zobel; Stuttgart: Kohlhammer, 1992) 104-13; idem, "Der Neue Himmel und die neue Erde: Beobachtungen zur Rezeption von Gen 1–3 in Jes 65:16b-25," in van Ruiten and Vervenne, eds., *Studies in the Book of Isaiah,* 349-65; idem, *Studien zu Tritojesaja,* 217-28; U. Stegemann, "Der Restgedank bei Isaias," *BZ* 13 (1969) 161-86; J. Stromberg, *Isaiah after Exile,* 40-73, 87-141; M. A. Sweeney, "On *ûměśôś* in Isaiah 8:6," in *Form and Intertextuality,* 36-45; idem, "Prophetic Exegesis in Isaiah 65–66," in *Form and Intertextuality,* 46-62; A. J. Tomasino, "Isaiah 1.1–2.4 and 63–66 and the Composition of the Isaianic Corpus," *JSOT* 57 (1993) 81-98; E. C. Webster, "The Rhetoric of Isaiah 63–65," *JSOT* 47 (1990) 89-102; idem, "A Rhetorical Study of Isaiah 66," *JSOT* 34 (1986) 93-108; H. G. M. Williamson, *The Book Called Isaiah,* 1-29.

Glossary

GENRES

ACCOUNT (Erzählung, Bericht). A term nearly synonymous with (→) Report. Generally long and more complex than a simple Report, an Account may consist of several briefer reports, statements, descriptions, or even fragments of (→) Story, organized according to a common theme. Accounts may aim at some degree of explanation rather than simple narration of events. However, like Reports, Accounts show matter-of-fact 3rd person narrative style and few literary, imaginative, or artistic features. Examples of Account are: Judg 1:16-17; 1 Kgs 6:1–7:51.

ACCUSATION (Anklage). One of the (→) Trial Genres. The Accusation functions as a part of the Trial Speech in which the accuser acts as prosecutor and the accused acts as defendant. The Accusation normally specifies the offense for which the accused is being brought to trial. The Accusation often serves as an element of the (→) Prophetic Judgment Speech, the (→) Prophetic Announcement of Punishment Against an Individual, or the (→) Prophetic Announcement of Punishment Against the People. In this capacity, the Accusation functions as a means for the prophet to convey the reasons for YHWH's punishment of the accused.

Related genres: (→) Trial Genres

ADDRESS (Anrede). A speech directed to a particular audience. The audience is specified either in the speech itself, normally as a vocative, or in the literary context in which the speech is placed.

ADMONITION (Ermahnung gegen . . .). A speech designed to dissuade an individual or a group from a certain kind of behavior. It is closely related to (→) Instruction, and, together with (→) Exhortation, it constitutes (→) Parenesis. It is not easily distinguished from statements that prohibit certain actions. Admonition appears in both prophetic discourse (e.g., Isa 1:16-17; Jer 25:3-7; Amos 5:4-5, 6-7) and didactic literature (e.g., Prov 6:20-21; 7:1-15). The genre is probably not the creation of either the prophets or the wisdom teachers, but more likely reflects modes of discourse that stem from a family or tribal setting.

Related genres: (→) Exhortation; (→) Instruction; (→) Parenesis; (→) Prohibition

AFFIRMATION OF CONFIDENCE (Vertrauensäusserung). A particular passage of

386

individual and communal (→) Complaint that voices trust in G-d (cf. Pss 22:4-6, 10-11; 31:7-9; 56:4-5; 71:5-7). "You are my G-d" (Pss 22:11[NRSV 10]; 25:5; 31:15[14]; 43:2; 44:5[4]; 63:2[1]; 68:25[24]; 89:27[26]; 118:28; 140:7[6]; cf. Pss 7:2[1]; 13:4[3]; 25:2; 30:3[2]; 59:6[5]) thus may be considered a formulaic expression of confidence. Some psalms concentrate on the trust motif to the exclusion of others (cf. Pss 11; 23; 62; (→) Song of Confidence). The trust element dwells on past salvific experiences which grow out of a group's relationship with G-d (Smith; Alt); analogies can be found in many cultures (see Vorländer, contra Begrich). In fact, all (→) Prayer is based on the supplicant's and the group's basic trust in the accessibility and benevolence of the deity invoked. This confidence has to be articulated liturgically, although it is implicit in the fact of praying itself and in each element of the prayer.

A. Alt, "The G-d of the Fathers," (1929) in *Essays on Old Testament History and Religion* (trans. R. A. Wilson; Oxford: Blackwell, 1966) 1-100; J. Begrich, "Die Vertrauenäusserungen im israelitischen Klagelied des Einzelnen und in seinem babylonsichen Gegenstück," *ZAW* 46 (1928) 221-60 (repr. *Gesammelte Studien* [TB 21; Munich: Kaiser, 1964] 168-216); E. S. Gerstenberger, *THAT* 1:300-305; *Psalms Part 1* (FOTL; Grand Rapids: Eerdmans, 1988) 244; *Psalms Part 2* (FOTL; Grand Rapids: Eerdmans, 2002) 508-9; H. Gunkel and J. Begrich, *Einleitung in die Psalmen* (2nd ed.; Göttingen: Vandenhoeck & Ruprecht, 1966) 232-36, § 6, no. 19, 27; see Eng. ed. (Macon: Mercer University Press, 1998) §C for additional bibliog.; W. R. Smith, *Lectures on the Religion of the Semites* (London: Black, 1889); H. Vorländer, *Mein G-tt* (AOAT 23; Kevelaer: Butzon & Bercker, 1975).

ALLEGORY (Allegorie). Not strictly a genre, but rather a speech form closely related to figurative or metaphorical language. The details of an allegory are chosen and shaped against the background of the interpretation or application so that each detail of the allegory recurs in the interpretation. The shortest form of the allegory is the metaphor, with just one motif calling for interpretation (Isa 3:14; Ezek 18:2); a longer form is the allegorical story, where each detail has its bearing on the interpretation (Isa 5:1-7; Ezekiel 16; 34). An allegorical form of speech calls for allegorical interpretation. Allegory occurs in a variety of contexts, such as a Dream Report (cf. Gen 37:7; 41:17-24; Dan 7:2-14), a (→) Vision Report (cf. Dan 8:1-14 and the visions of Zechariah), a Psalm (cf. Ps 80:9-20[NRSV 8-19]), a prophetic discourse (Isa 5:1-7; Ezekiel 16; 34), and a self-contained narrative (Judg 9:8-15).

ANNOUNCEMENT (Ankündigung). A public proclamation, either oral or written, of particular issues, circumstances, actions, decisions, etc. The announcement is generally specified for example as a (→) Prophetic Announcement of Punishment, (→) an Announcement of Salvation, (→) an Announcement of a Royal Savior, etc.

ANNOUNCEMENT OF JUDGMENT (Gerichtsankündigung, Gerichtsansage). Ordinarily, the element in the (→) Prophetic Judgment Speech in which punishment is announced. Also occurs as an independent genre. Its essence is the statement that a disaster (death, war, captivity, etc.) is imminent as YHWH's punishment for crimes or sins. Most frequently, the Announcement of Judgment is framed and styled as a speech of YHWH through a prophet; thus it is usually introduced by means of the (→) Messenger Formula and concluded with the (→) Oracle Formula. The most common style is a 1st-person speech of YHWH which states what YHWH is about to do. Passive or impersonal formulations are known as well (cf. Amos 4:2-3). In older terminology, the genre was known as the "threat."

Related genre: (→) Prophetic Judgment Speech

E. Balla, *Die Droh und Scheltwörte des Amos* (Leipzig: Edelmann, 1926); C. Westermann, *Basic Forms of Prophetic Speech.*

ANNOUNCEMENT OF SALVATION. A major element of (→) the Prophetic Announcement of Salvation that typically appears in the oracle together with (→) the Reassurance Formula and (→) the Basis for Salvation.

ANSWERED LAMENT (Antwortete Klagen) The ANSWERED LAMENT is a variation of the classic LAMENTATION OR COMPLAINT form that appears so frequently in the Psalms. The ANSWERED LAMENT typically gives voice to a complaint on the part of the psalmist to YHWH in order to ask YHWH for relief from the problem named in the LAMENT. At the most basic level, the purpose of the ANSWERED LAMENT is to appeal to YHWH to act on behalf of the psalmist's lament, but it also functions as a means to convince the audience that YHWH will act. Indeed, the ANSWERED LAMENT may employ RHETORICAL QUESTIONS that serve as the basis for the psalmist's appeal by asserting YHWH's past acts of deliverance and the ordering of creation. YHWH's answer to the lament then follows. See Isa 51:9-16.

APPEAL (Anrufung, Berufung). An urgent request for action, assistance, intervention, or the like. Unlike (→) Command, (→) Prohibition, (→) Petition, and (→) Parenesis, an Appeal may assume no special relationship of obligation between the person making the Appeal and the party to whom it is made.

ASSERTION OF CONFIDENCE. See (→) Affirmation of Confidence.

AUDITION REPORT (Auditionsbericht). In terms of structure, setting, and intention, simply one kind of (→) Vision Report. The Audition Report is distinguished only by the use of auditory means, rather than visual, to convey the vision.

Related genre: (→) Vision Report

AUTOBIOGRAPHICAL CHRONICLE (Selbtsbiographische Chronik). A chronologically-arranged autobiographical account of a person's life. Such 1st-person chronicles should be considered in terms of Memoirs.

AUTOBIOGRAPHY (Selbstbiographie). The narration of a person's life or major life events, written by him- or herself in 1st-person form. No full Autobiography occurs in the Hebrew Bible, but accounts of specific events do occur in autobiographical form (e.g., Isaiah 6; 8:1–9:6[7]; Neh 1:1–7:5; 11–13). Such 1st-person accounts should be considered in terms of Memoirs.

BASIS FOR JUDGMENT (Gerichtsgrund). A major element of (→) the Prophetic Judgment Speech, which announces the reasons for judgment.

BASIS FOR PRAISE. A basic element of the (→) Hymn of Praise which provides the reasons for the Call or (→) Summons to Praise, oftentimes introduced by the particle *kî,* "for, because" (e.g., Exod 15:1, "I will sing to YHWH, for he has triumphed magnificently!"

BASIS FOR PUNISHMENT. See (→) Accusation.

BASIS FOR REASSURANCE. See (→) Prophetic Announcement of Salvation.

BASIS FOR SALVATION. See Basis for Reassurance in (→) the Prophetic Announcement of Salvation.

CALL FOR A COMMUNAL COMPLAINT SONG (Aufruf zur Volksklage). A call to
the community to assemble for a complaint service. It may be triggered by any
crisis of wide and devastating impact upon the community (e.g., drought, Jer
14:1ff; locust plague, Joel 1:5ff; military threat, 2 Chronicles 20). The fundamental
intention is to convene the community for an appropriate cultic response to the
crisis at hand. This response normally leads to a petition for YHWH to intervene
in order to remove the source of danger. The genre is highly stylized and usually has three constituent elements: 1) the Call itself in the form of a sequence
of imperatives; 2) the direct address to the specific groups involved; and 3) the
reason or motivation for the complaint service (cf. Joel 1:5-14). The genre is often
found in the prophetic literature (cf. Isa 14:31; 23:1-14; 32:11-14; Jer 6:26; 25:34;
49:3; Zeph 1:10-11; Zech 11:2).

Related genres: (→) Call to Mourn; (→) Communal Complaint

H. W. Wolff, "Der Aufruf zur Volksklage," *ZAW* 76 (1964) 48-56.

CALL NARRATIVE. See (→) Vocation Account

CALL TO PRAISE. See (→) Summons to Praise, a major element of (→) the Hymn
of Praise.

COMMAND (Gebot). A direct commission, based on authority such as custom, law,
or decree. It is usually expressed by an imperative or by forms with an imperative
function, and it may be accompanied by a motive clause (cf. Isa 1:16-17; Prov
4:1-2). Command is the opposite of (→) Prohibition and a subgenre of (→) Order,
which combines Command and Prohibition.

COMMISSION (Beauftragung, Sendung). An authoritative charge given by a superior
to a subordinate. Commission may include a variety of elements such as direct
command or specific instructions, depending upon the particular role envisioned
by the one who gives order, e.g., military envoy (2 Sam 11:18-21, 25), messenger
(Gen 32:3-5; 1 Kgs 14:7-11), a royal official (2 Kgs 19:2-7). Commission often
appears in narratives about prophets (e.g., Exod 3:7-10; 1 Kgs 12:22-24; 19:15-
16; 21:17-19; Amos 7:15-17) and in the prophetic (→) Vocation Accounts (e.g.,
Isa 6:9-10; Jer 1:4-10; Ezek 3:1-11). Thus, commission became an important way
to represent the prophet as YHWH's messenger and to organize collections of
prophetic words. In this context, reports of a prophet's mission display several
typical elements: 1) the (→) Prophetic Word Formula, "the word of the L-rd came
to . . ."; 2) the (→) Commissioning Formula, "go, speak,"; 3) the (→) Messenger
Formula, "Thus says the L-ord,"; and 4) the message itself, usually some kind of
(→) Oracle addressed to individuals or the nation (see Isa 7:3-9; Jer 2:1-3; 7:1-7;
26:1-6; 1 Kgs 12:22-24; 19:15-18; 21:17-19; cf. 2 Kgs 9:1-3).

COMMUNAL COMPLAINT SONG (Volksklagelied, Klagelied des Volkes). A Psalm
sung by the Israelite/Judean community in which YHWH is petitioned to avert
the forthcoming disaster. Both the genre elements and the formulaic language of
the Communal Complaint Song are similar to those in the (→) Complaint of the
Individual. In both genres, the plea or petition for help is the decisive element
which all other features support. The cultic ceremonies in which the genre was
used were not regularly scheduled, but occurred when the community as a whole
was threatened by death, drought, famine, plague, or the like. The ceremonies
included the seeking of (→) Oracles (to determine the reason for the danger and
the means to avert it), processions, sacrifices, and ablutions (cf. Jer 14:2-22; Joel;

Psalms 44; 60; 79; 80; 83). The (→) Lamentation (cf. Lamentations; Psalms 44; 60; 79; 89) is a closely related genre, but different primarily in that it was sung after a calamity had occurred.

H. Gunkel and J. Begrich, *Einleitung in die Psalmen* (Göttingen: Vandenhoeck & Ruprecht, 1933) 117-39; S. Mowinckel, *The Psalms in Israel's Worship* (trans. D. R. Ap-Thomas; 1962; repr. Grand Rapids: Eerdmans and Livonia: Dove, 2004) 1:193-246.

COMMUNAL THANKSGIVING SONG (Danklied des Volkes). A Psalm sung at a special service following a recent intervention by YHWH on behalf of the people. The song celebrates the event and praises YHWH for saving activity. The main elements are: 1) a call to sing (or to give thanks or to praise); 2) an account of the past trouble and salvation; 3) praise for YHWH (or YHWH's works); 4) announcement of sacrifice; 5) blessings; and 6) a vow or pledge. Often the song is antiphonal. Examples include Psalms 66 and 118. Special types of the Communal Thanksgiving Song are the Victory Song (cf. Psalm 68; Exod 15:1-21; Judges 5), and the Harvest Hymn (cf. Psalms 65; 67). The ceremonies that called for Communal Thanksgiving Songs were not part of the regular ritual calendar, but were held to celebrate a victory, a deliverance from calamity, a bountiful harvest, or the like. The Psalm was sung by a priest, a leader, a choir, and/or the people as a whole. The genre is closely related to the (→) Hymn of Praise, differing primarily in terms of its special setting and its frequent inclusion of an account of past trouble and salvation. It is related to the (→) Communal Complaint Song in that the community, when threatened with disaster, often vowed to give thanks if YHWH heard their complaint and delivered them.

F. Crüsemann, *Studien zur Formgeschichte von Hymnus und Danklied in Israel* (WMANT 32; Neukirchen-Vluyn: Neukirchener, 1969); C. Westermann, *Praise and Lament in the Psalms* (trans. K. R. Crim and R. N. Soulen; Atlanta: John Knox, 1981).

COMPENDIUM (Kompendium). A collection of items ordered according to a specific conceptualization, such as the Book of the Twelve Prophets in either its Masoretic or Septuagint form.

M. A. Sweeney, *The Twelve Prophets* (Berit Olam; Collegeville: Liturgical, 2000) 1:xv-xliii.

COMPLAINT (Klage). A statement that describes personal or communal distress, often addressed to G-d with a plea for deliverance (Job 3; Hab 1:2-4; etc.). The description of the distress is characterized by vivid language (cf. the so-called "confessions" of Jeremiah, e.g., Jer 12:1ff), and by the use of the question "why?"

CONFESSION OF GUILT (Schuldgeständnis). A statement in which a defendant formally acknowledges guilt, and often discloses the culpable action and/or the circumstances. While a Confession of Guilt can consist mostly of a plea of guilt (expressed predominantly by *ḥāṭā'tî*, "I have sinned, Exod 10:16; 1 Sam 15:30; 26:21; 2 Sam 12:13; 24:10; 2 Kgs 18:14), it can also contain both the plea and the statement of the offense (cf. Josh 7:20; 1 Sam 14:24; 2 Sam 19:20; Ezra 10:2). A Confession of Guilt can be said when an offense was committed unintentionally (cf. Num 22:34). The Confession of Guilt may occur in the course of (royal, local, sacral, prophetic) legal or judicial proceedings, following either an actual or implicit indictment (cf. 2 Kgs 18:14; Ezra 9:1; 10:2) or a conviction (cf. Josh 7:20; 1 Sam 15:24, 30; 2 Sam 12:13; 19:21[NRSV 20]). However, it may also occur in situations conceived judicially, though indicating no specific court setting (cf. Exod 9:27; 10:16; 1 Sam 24:12; 26:21; 2 Sam 24:10, 17). Its proximity to the judicial setting and language (trials against individuals) account for the fact that the Confession of Guilt occurs — with few exceptions (e.g. Ezra 10:2) — in the 1st-person singular. The function of the Confession when made after the conviction or sentence is to conclude the trial (cf. Josh 7:20; 1 Sam 15:24), whereas its intention is not infrequently to effect mercy or a turn for the better (cf. Exod 9:27; 10:16; 1 Sam 15:24, 30; 26:21; 2 Sam 12:13; 19:21[NRSV 20]; 24:10, 17; 2 Kgs 18:14). Although similar or identical in formulation, the Confession of Sin is different in terms of context and setting, and in view of its frequently communal character. The opposite of the confession of guilt is the Plea of Innocence.

Related genres: (→) Trial Genres

H. J. Boecker, *Redeformen des Rechtslebens im alten Testament* (WMANT 14; Neukirchen-Vluyn: Neukirchener, 1964) 111-17; R. Knierim, *Die Hauptbegriffe für Sünde im alten Testament* (Gütersloh: Mohn, 1965) 20-38.

CONFESSION OF SIN. See (→) Confession of Guilt.

DESCRIPTION OF PUNISHMENT (Strafbeschreibung). A subgenre of (→) Prophetic Announcement, which in turn is an element of the (→) Prophetic Announcement of Punishment. The punishment is normally announced as YHWH's intervention, which is then followed by results. Occasionally, the description of the results occurs as an independent genre. It essentially portrays the disaster that will come as the result of YHWH's punishment for crimes or sins (see 1 Kgs 21:23-24; 2 Kgs 9:36; Ezek 9:1-11).

DESCRIPTION OF SALVATION (Heilsbeschreibung). A subgenre of the (→) Prophetic Announcement of Salvation. The salvation is not announced in a sentence with YHWH speaking in the 1st-person; rather, it constitutes only the second part of the announcement of salvation or, when included together with the results, the third part (cf. Jer 31:23-25).

DIALOGUE (Dialog, Zweigespräch). An exchange of speech between two parties, each in response to the other. Dialogue may be verbal or written, and it may occur in various social settings and literary contexts, such as wisdom disputation (e.g., Job), prophetic speech (e.g., Hab 1:2–2:20), and narrative literature (e.g., Genesis 24; cf. Isaiah 36–37). There is no specific literary genre of dialogue in the Hebrew Bible; rather, dialogue serves as a literary device that aids in defining the structure of a text or the social reality reflected in a text.

DIRGE (Leichenlied, Leichenklage, Leichenklagelied). A funeral song that bewails the loss of the deceased, describes his/her merits, and calls for further mourning. The Dirge typically appears in the 3/2 *qinah* meter. Its characteristic formulation includes the exclamation, *'êk* (or *'êkâ*), "how," "alas," a contrast between former glory and present tragedy, and imperatives which call for mourning. The Dirge was ordinarily performed by hired women or gifted individuals after a death, and it was usually sung in the presence of the corpse as part of the funeral preparations. Examples appear in 2 Sam 1:19-27; 3:33-34. Prophets frequently adapted the Dirge, often mockingly, to announce the fate of a king or personified nation (e.g., Isa 14:4-23; Ezek 19:1-14; 27:1-36; Amos 5:1-3).

E. Gerstenberger, *Psalms, Part 1; with an Introduction to Cultic Poetry* (FOTL; Grand Rapids: Eerdmans, 1988) 10-11; H. Jahnow, *Das hebräische Leichenlied* (BZAW 36; Giessen: Töpelmann, 1923).

DISPUTATION (Disputationswort, Streitgespräch). A general term used to designate a dispute between two or more parties. The genre is rooted in the wisdom tradition, where it is employed as a device to examine contrasting points of view (e.g., Job), and it functions in a legal setting as a means to resolve conflicting legal claims (cf. Gen 31:36-43). Most examples appear in prophetic literature and present only the prophet's speech, which attempts to persuade the audience to abandon its position or belief and adopt that of the prophet (Isa 8:16–9:6[NRSV 7]; 40:12-17, 18-20, [+25-26], 21-24, 27-31; 44:24-28; 45:9-13, 18-25; 46:5-11; 48:1-11, 12-15; 49:14-25; 50:1-3; Jer 2:23-28; 3:1-5; 31:29-30; 33:23-26; Ezek 11:2-12; 11:14-17; 12:21-28; 18:1-20; 20:32-44; 33:10-20; 33:23-29; 37:11b-13; Mic 2:6-11; Hag 1:2-11; Mal 1:2-5; 1:6–2:9; 2:10-16; 2:17–3:5; 3:6-12; 3:13-21[NRSV 3:13–4:3]; cf. Nahum). The genre is based in a two-part structure that includes a statement of the opponent's viewpoint and argumentation in which the speaker attempts to refute that viewpoint and argue for another. Constitutive elements of prophetic examples of the genre include: 1) the thesis to be disputed; 2) the counterthesis for which the speaker argues; and 3) the dispute or argumentation proper.

Related genres: (→) Trial Genres; (→) Dialogue

J. Begrich, *Studien zu Deuterojesaja,* 48-53; A. Graffy, *A Prophet Confronts His People;* D. F. Murray, "The Rhetoric of Disputation"; E. Pfeiffer, "Die Disputationsworte im Buche Maleachi," *EvT* 19 (1959) 546-68; M. A. Sweeney, "Concerning the Structure and Generic Character of the Book of Nahum," *ZAW* 104 (1992) 364-77.

DOXOLOGY (Doxologie). A pithy, highly lyrical acclamation of divine glory and righteousness (e.g., 2 Sam 7:29; 1 Chr 17:27) that often functions in relation to (→) Hymns of Praise (e.g., Psalm 135) and (→) Communal Thanksgiving Songs (e.g., Psalms 118; 136). The Doxology appears to be rooted in cultic poetry, but it can serve as a device that aids in defining the structure and liturgical character of prophetic books (e.g., Amos 1:2; 4:13; 5:8-9; 8:8; 9:5-6; cf. Isa 42:10-13; 44:23; 45:8; 48:20-21; 49:13; 51:3; 52:9-10; 54:1-3).

Related genres: (→) Hymn; (→) Communal Thanksgiving Song

J. L. Crenshaw, *Hymnic Affirmation of Divine Justice: The Doxologies of Amos and Related Texts in the Old Testament* (SBLDS 24; Missoula: Scholars, 1975); K. Koch, "Die Rolle der hymnischen Abschnitte in der Komposition des Amos-Buches," *ZAW* 86 (1974) 504-37; F. Matheus, *Singt dem H-rrn ein neues Lied;* C. Westermann, *Sprache und Structur der Prophetie Deuterojesajas* (2nd ed.; CTM 11; Stuttgart: Calwer, 1981).

EXHORTATION (Ermahnung zu . . . , Mahnrede). An (→) Address form employed to persuade an audience to adopt a particular course of action. It is the opposite of (→) Admonition, which attempts to persuade an audience against a particular course of action. Together, Exhortation and Admonition constitute (→) Parenesis. The form appears to derive from wisdom or cultic instruction (see Prov 1:8-19; Psalms 1; 50; 95), although it may appear in any situation of public or private address in which the speaker attempts to persuade the audience to follow a course of action (e.g., Deuteronomy 6–11; Josh 1:2-9; 1 Kgs 2:2-9; 1 Chr

28:8, 20-21; 2 Chr 15:7). Exhortation appears in prophetic literature (e.g., Isaiah 1; 31; 55; Zeph 2:1-3), although its status as an independent prophetic genre is contested. The debate is bound up with the issue of whether the prophets called for repentance from their audiences, in which case Exhortation serves as a viable prophetic form, or whether they simply announced judgment against them.

Related genres: (→) Admonition; (→) Parenesis

A. Vanlier Hunter, *Seek the L-rd!* (Baltimore: St. Mary's Seminary and University, 1982); K. A. Tångberg, *Die prophetische Mahnrede* (FRLANT 143; Göttingen: Vandenhoeck & Ruprecht, 1987); T. M. Raitt, "The Prophetic Summons to Repentance," *ZAW* 83 (1971) 30-49; G. Warmuth, *Das Mahnwort* (BBET 1; Frankfurt: Lang, 1976); H. W. Wolff, "Das Thema 'Umkehr' in der alttestamentlichen Prophetie," *ZTK* 48 (1951) 129-48.

HISTORICAL REVIEW (Geschichtliche Revue). The rehearsing of salient facts in the past experience of Israel or of the individual being addressed. The genre normally appears in narrative form. DtrH employs it as a testimonial farewell speech for Joshua (Josh 24:2-13) and Samuel (1 Sam 12:7-12) and as a rationale for the dynastic promise to David (2 Sam 7:6-9; cf. 1 Chr 17:5-8). It also appears in the Chronicler's History (2 Chr 15:2-7; 2 Chr 20:7-9) and in Nehemiah's prayer (Neh 9:7-31). It frequently aids in persuading people to follow a specific course of action or to adopt a specific viewpoint. It can therefore appear in prophetic literature as a means to justify an (→) Announcement of Judgment (e.g., Isa 9:7-20[NRSV 8-21]) or as a means to persuade YHWH to deliver the people from threat (Isa.63:7-14a).

HYMN OF PRAISE (Hymn, Loblied). A joyful song of choir or community extolling the greatness, kindness, and righteousness of YHWH and YHWH's dwelling place. Hymns function in various capacities: they praise creation and creator (Psalms 8; 19; 104); they praise YHWH's glorious deeds in history (Psalms 68; 105); they admire YHWH's abode in Mt. Zion (Psalms 46; 48; 76); and they jubilate at YHWH's just reign (Psalms 24; 47; 93; 96). They sometimes appear in the prophetic literature, where they aid in defining the liturgical character and literary structure of the prophetical books (e.g., Isa 12; 42:10-13; 44:23; 45:8; 48:20-21; 49:13; 51:3; 52:9-10; 54:1-3; Amos 1:2; 4:13; 5:8-9; 8:8; 9:5-6).

Related genres: (→) Doxology

F. Crüsemann, *Studien zur Formgeschichte von Hymnus und Danklied in Israel* (WMANT 32; Neukirchen-Vluyn: Neukirchener, 1969); E. Gerstenberger, *Psalms, Part 1; with an Introduction to Cultic Poetry* (FOTL; Grand Rapids: Eerdmans, 1988) 16-19; C. Westermann, *Praise and Lament in the Psalms* (trans. K. R. Crim and R. N. Soulen; Atlanta: John Knox, 1981).

INCLUSION. Often known as Inclusio. A rhetorical device in which a compositional unit begins and ends with the same or similar theme, refrain, vocabulary, or other mode of expression.

INDICTMENT SPEECH (Anklageerhebung). One of the (→) Trial Genres. The Indictment Speech is a component of the Trial Speech. It is a statement formally handed down by a judicial authority charging a person with committing an act that is punishable under the provisions of the law. It is presented either upon approval of an accusation or in its own right. Due to the particular structure of Israel's and Judah's judicial system, the judicial authorities who issue an indictment may function as both accuser and judge, such as a king or a tribal judge (cf. 1 Sam 15:17-19; 22:13; 1 Kgs 2:42-43; 18:17; 22:18). Other officials may also bring an indictment against someone before a judicial authority (cf. Jer 36:20; 2 Sam 19:22[NRSV 21]). A modified form of the Indictment Speech can also be employed in prophetic literature, where it functions as the accusation or the reason for punishment in the (→) Prophetic Judgment Speech (Isa 8:6; Jer 11:9-10; Mic 3:9-11), the (→) Prophetic Announcement of Punishment Against an Individual (Amos 7:16; Jer 23:1), and the (→) Prophetic Announcement of Punishment against the People (Isa 30:12; Hos 2:7-8[NRSV 5-6]).

Related genres: (→) Prophetic Announcement of Punishment against an Individual; (→) Prophetic Announcement of Punishment against the People; (→) Prophetic Judgment Speech; (→) Trial Genres; (→) Trial Speech.

H. J. Boecker, *Redeformen des Rechtslebens im Alten Testament* (2nd ed.; WMANT 14; Neukirchen-Vluyn: Neukirchener, 1970); J. Harvey, *Le plaidoyer prophétique contre Israël après la rupture de l'alliance* (Montreal: Bellarmin, 1967); C. Westermann, *Basic Forms of Prophetic Speech*.

INSTRUCTION (Instruktion, Unterweisung). A writing or discourse, chiefly in imperative mode, which offers guidance to an individual or group by setting forth certain values or prescribing rules of conduct. Instruction typically tends to deal with universals: broad values, traditional rules for conduct, or aphoristic knowledge drawn from wide experience. The settings and occasions of use for Instruction must have been quite diverse. In Israel and Judah, Instructions were probably created by persons of some official or aristocratic standing, such as lawgiver, priest, prophet, scribe, wisdom teacher, or even king. In Egypt, the best examples derive from scribes who formulated didactic works to summarize accepted knowledge or, in some cases, produced instruction in the guise of an after-the-fact testament from a king to his successor, with propagandistic overtones (*ANET,* 414-19; more generally, see M. Lichtheim, *Ancient Egyptian Literature* I [3 vols.; Berkeley: University of California Press, 1973-81] 58-80). Similarly, the clearest examples from the Hebrew Bible are in the didactic literature (e.g., Prov 1-9; 22:17–24:22). Prophetic examples tend to be employed for persuasive purposes, and they become somewhat more specific by focusing on the wisdom of continued adherence to YHWH, who promises to defend Zion and the Davidic house, and on the opportunities for national restoration presented to Judah by YHWH's bringing about catastrophe (e.g., Isa 8:16–9:6[NRSV 7]; 28–33).

Related genres: (→) Admonition; (→) Exhortation; (→) Parenesis

INVITATION TO A MEAL (Einladung zu einer Mahlzeit). A metaphorical device frequently employed in wisdom literature to partake in the study of wisdom. The form frequently appears as a public invitation to the hungry and thirsty to come to Wisdom's table to partake of her food and drink (Prov 9:5; Sir 24:19). Such an invitation may culminate in a promise of life (Prov 9:11). The form appears in Isa 55:1 as a means to invite the exiles of Israel and Judah to join YHWH's eternal promise of restoration. Although this promise was once directed to the house of David, it now applies to all Israel.

C. Westermann, *Isaiah 40–66* (trans. D. M. G. Stalker; OTL; Philadelphia: Westminster, 1969) 281-83.

LAMENTATION (Volksklage, Untergangsklage, Klagelied, Klage). A song in which the community bewails its fate following a national catastrophe. Typical elements include a description of the former bliss and happiness and an account of the present desolation. (→) Exhortations to mourn and (→) Petitions to save the remnant are also frequently employed. The formulaic expressions *'êk* and *'êkâ* ("how," "alas"), as used in the (→) Dirge, are common. The setting of the genre was a public service following a disaster such as a plague or the destruction of a city or tribe. The people were called to mourn, repent, and possibly to move G-d to save the remnant. The ritual usually included fasting (cf. 1 Sam 7:6; Joel 1:14; Judg 20:26). The Lamentation itself could be sung by the people as a whole, a choir, or a soloist. Examples include Lamentations 1; 2; 4; and 5. Psalms 44; 60; and 79 reflect similar situations. The Lamentations should be distinguished on the one hand from the (→) Dirge, which mourns the death of an individual, and on the other hand from the (→) Communal Complaint Song, which is used before the calamity. Consequently, in the Complaint Song the plea predominates; in the Lamentation it is subdued (if it occurs at all).

E. Gerstenberger, *Psalms, Part 1; with an Introduction to Cultic Poetry* (FOTL; Grand Rapids: Eerdmans, 1988) 10-11.

LITURGICAL INSTRUCTION. Instruction expressed in a liturgical setting.

LITURGY (Liturgie). A comprehensive category that denotes widely varying complexes of cultic acts and words set in a stylized sequence and normally intended for use in worship. The constitutive elements may themselves be originally independent genres (e.g., → Hymn, → Prayer, → Complaint, → Oracle, → Thanksgiving Song, → Blessing, → Doxology) which are now interwoven into different patterns depending on setting and intention. Examples include: Liturgies of Complaint (see Psalms 12; 60; Joel 1–2; Jeremiah 14); Liturgies of Praise (see Psalms 66; 95); Liturgies of Thanksgiving (see Psalm 118); Processional Liturgies (see Psalms 24; 132) and Entrance Liturgies (see Psalms 15; 24); and Prophetic Liturgies (see Isaiah 33; Habakkuk; Nahum).

E. Gerstenberger, *Psalms, Part 1; with an Introduction to Cultic Poetry* (FOTL XIV; Grand Rapids: Eerdmans, 1988) 2-22; H. Gunkel and J. Begrich, *Einleitung in die Psalmen* (Göttingen: Vandenhoeck & Ruprecht, 1933, 1966); J. Jeremias, *Kultprophetie und Gerichtsverkündigung* (WMANT 35; Neukirchen-Vluyn: Neukirchener, 1970); A. R. Johnson, *The Cultic Prophet and Israel's Psalmody* (Cardiff: University of Wales Press, 1979); S. Mowinckel, *Psalmenstudien III* (repr.; Amsterdam: Schippers, 1966); R. Murray, "Prophet and the Cult," in *Israel's Prophetic Tradition* (*Fest.* P. R. Ackroyd; ed. R. Coggins, A. Philips, and M. Knibb; Cambridge: University Press, 1982) 200-16.

MESSENGER SPEECH (Botenspruch, Botenrede). The message delivered by a messenger. It is styled as a literal repetition of the words that were given to the messenger at the time that the messenger was commissioned by the sender (cf. Gen 32:1-5). The Messenger Speech begins with the (→) Messenger Formula, and the message itself takes the form of a direct speech by the sender. Use of the form presupposes that the person who delivers the message speaks on behalf of the sender.

S. A. Meier, *The Messenger in the Ancient Semitic World* (HSM 45; Atlanta: Scholars, 1988); idem, *Speaking of Speaking,* 273-98; R. Rendtorff, "Botenformel und Botenspruch," *ZAW* 74 (1962) 165-77; C. Westermann, *Basic Forms of Prophetic Speech,* 98-115.

METAPHOR (Metapher). Not strictly speaking a genre, Metaphor is a literary device in which a term is transferred from the object it normally designates to one that it designates only by implicit comparison or analogy. The (→) Invitation to a Meal is a case in point in which the invitation to eat and drink is employed in wisdom literature as a means to engage in the study of wisdom (Prov 9:5; Sir 24:19) and prophetic literature as a means to take part in YHWH's eternal covenant with all Israel (Isa 55:1).

MOTIVE CLAUSE (Begründungssatz). A statement often employed with another genre, such as a Law, (→) Prohibition, (→) Instruction, or (→) Exhortation that is designed to reinforce the persuasive thrust of the statement. It is generally introduced by *kî,* "for, because," or *pēn,* "lest, unless," and it provides the authoritative basis for the statement, the reason for adopting its viewpoint, or the reason for acting in accordance with its recommendation or instructions.

B. Gemser, "The Importance of the Motive Clause in Old Testament Law," *Congress Volume, Copenhagen 1953,* VTSup 1; ed. G. W. Anderson et al.; Leiden: Brill, 1953) 50-66; R. Soncino, *Motive Clauses in Hebrew Law* (SBLDS 45; Chico: Scholars, 1980).

OATH (Eid, Schwur). A formal pronouncement, cast as either cohortative or indicative, which binds the oath-taker to a particular course of action, attitude, or stance by invoking sanctions by the deity. Typically, an Oath is introduced by the (→) Oath Formula, "As YHWH lives" (*ḥāy yhwh;* e.g., Judg 8:19; cf. Ezek 18:3). Then follows what the person who takes the Oath will or will not do. Most frequently, an Oath is a form of self-curse.

ORACLE (Orakel). A broad generic category that designates communication from a deity, often through an intermediary such as a priest, seer, or prophet. It has no specific form, although it may include the (→) Oracle Formula, *nĕ'um yhwh,* "utterance of YHWH." An Oracle may be delivered in response to an oracular inquiry (Num 22:7-12; Josh 7:6-15; 2 Sam 5:23-24; Ezek 14:1-3), but it may also come unsolicited. Prophetic speeches presented as YHWH's own words may be classified as unsolicited Oracles. The Oracle appears to have originated in a setting of formal inquiry of the deity through a priest or prophet, which may include the divinatory use of lots *(Urim)* or incubation rituals. 1 Sam 28:6 mentions dreams, *Urim,* and prophets as possible sources for seeking an Oracle.

J. Begrich, "Das priesterliche Heilsorakel," in *Gesammelte Studien zum alten Testament* (TB 21; Munich: Kaiser, 1964) 217-31 (repr. from *ZAW* 52 [1934] 81-92); K. Koch, *The Growth of the Biblical Tradition,* 171-82.

ORACLE OF SALVATION (Priesterliches Heilsorakel). An oracle form, postulated by Begrich, from which the (→) Prophetic Announcement of Salvation is believed to have developed. Prophetic forms of the genre occur in Isa 41:8-13, 14-16; 43:1-7; and 44:1-5 (cf. Isa 7:4-9; 37:5-7). The form is typically introduced by the formula "Do not fear," followed by a formal statement by a priest or other cultic official that assures divine favor. Because no independent examples of the priestly form occur in the Hebrew Bible, Kilian has challenged the existence of the form in a setting of individual complaint. But the regularized use of the (→) Reassurance Formula in prophetic contexts and frequent references to divine response in the Psalms (cf. Psalms 12; 35; 91; 121) suggest the likelihood of such an oracle. In this regard, it is noteworthy that the oracle in Isa 37:5-7 apparently comes in response to an inquiry made to the prophet Isaiah, who elsewhere responds to Hezekiah's prayer in the temple (Isa 37:14-35).

Related genre: (→) Prophetic Announcement of Salvation

J. Begrich, "Das priesterliche Heilsorakel," in *Gesammelte Studien zum alten Testament* (TB 21; Munich: Kaiser, 1964) 217-31 (repr. from *ZAW* 52 [1934] 81-92); E. Gerstenberger, *Psalms, Part 1; with an Introduction to Cultic Poetry* (FOTL; Grand Rapids: Eerdmans, 1988) 253; R. Kilian, "Ps 22 und das priesterliche Heilsorakel," *BZ* 12 (1968) 172-85.

PARENESIS (Paräneses). An address to an individual or a group which seeks to persuade with reference to a goal. It may be composed of several genre elements and characteristic stylistic features, in a flexible arrangement (cf. Deuteronomy 6–11; Prov 1:8-19; Isaiah 1; 31). It generally combines (→) Admonition, which aims to dissuade an audience from a particular course of action or belief, with (→) Exhortation, which attempts to persuade an audience to adopt a particular course of action or set of beliefs. (→) Commands, (→) Prohibitions, (→) Instructions, etc., may also be mixed into a parenetic address. Parenesis may exhort, admonish, command, or prohibit in its intent to persuade, and (→) Motive Clauses are frequently included.

PETITION (Petition, Bittrede, Bittschrift). A request or plea from one person to another asking for some definite response. The Petition may occur in contexts that express ordinary day-to-day situations. In such cases, the structure of the petition includes both the basis for the Petition and the Petition proper, expressed directly or indirectly (e.g., Gen 18:3-4; 23:4; 1 Kgs 2:15-17; 5:17-20). The Petition also occurs as the central element of all (→) Complaints, in which the supplicant asks for divine help. It is usually formulated in the imperative, but the jussive, imperfect, and cohortative are also employed to express the supplicant's "wish."

E. Gerstenberger, *Psalms, Part 1; with an Introduction to Cultic Poetry* (FOTL; Grand Rapids: Eerdmans, 1988) 254; B. O. Long, *2 Kings* (FOTL; Grand Rapids: Eerdmans, 1991) 307.

PLEDGE (Pfand). A Pledge is a formalized promise in which one party promises or pledges to do something for another. Examples of the Pledge would include the promises to Israel's ancestors of a covenant that promises their relationship with YHWH, that they will become a great nation, that they will possess the land of Israel, etc. (see Gen 12:2-3, 7; 15:18-21; 17:4-8; 28:13-15; 35:11-12); YHWH's pledge never again to destroy the earth by flood (Gen 9:9-11); YHWH's promise that David will have a dynasty (2 Sam 7:12-16); or YHWH's pledge to Jerusalem that YHWH will serve as Zion's advocate to ensure her righteousness and deliverance in Isa 62:1-7. The (→) Announcement of Salvation in Isa 62:2-7 functions as a major portion of YHWH's pledge.

PRAYER (Gebet). Any communication by a human being toward a deity. Ordinarily, it is a direct address to G-d in the 2nd-person singular. In the Hebrew Bible, Prayer encompasses a great variety of modes of expression, motivations, and intentions, and reflects many distinct settings. Consequently, it includes many different specific genres. While all Prayer tends to be more or less ritualistic, one may distinguish broadly between free, personal Prayer and cultic Prayer. The latter is predominant in the Hebrew Bible; furthermore, the free, personal Prayers usually employ modes of expression and motifs known in the cult. Hezekiah's Prayer to YHWH in Isa

37:14-20, e.g., is a standard (→) Complaint form set in the temple, which presents a (→) Petition to YHWH for deliverance from the Assyrian invasion.

PRESENCE VISION REPORT. See (→) Vision Report

PRIESTLY TORAH (Priesterliche Tora). An authoritative instructional form, postulated by Begrich, from which prophetic (→) Instruction (Prophetic Torah) is believed to have developed. The priestly form seems to have focused on instruction concerning cultic purity, i.e., proper separations between clean and unclean and between holy and profane. Priestly Torah was given by priests in response to a question about such matters. Haggai 2:11-13 demonstrates both this teaching aspect of the priestly office and prophetic utilization of the form. The instruction could take various shapes, and these were often employed by prophets: a command or prohibition (Isa 1:11; Ezek 45:8b-9; Amos 5:5a); a statement of YHWH's desire (Amos 5:21-22); the determination of a judgment (Isa 1:13); or a description of consequences (Amos 4:5).

Related genre: prophetic (→) Instruction

J. Begrich, "Die priesterliche Tora," in *Werden und Wesen des Alten Testaments* (BZAW 66; ed. P. Volz et al.; Berlin: Töpelmann, 1936) 63-88; C. Westermann, *Basic Forms of Prophetic Speech,* 203-4.

PROHIBITION (Verbot). A direct forbidding of an action or a thing, based upon an authority such as custom, law, or decree. It is usually expressed by the phrase "you shall not," which employs *lō'* or *'al* with the jussive (vetitive or prohibitive form). It carries its force within itself, but is frequently accompanied by a (→) Motive Clause (e.g., Prov 22:22–23:18). A Prohibition can appear alone (e.g., Exod 22:17; Isa 1:13) or in a series (e.g., Exod 20:2-17). The opposite of Prohibition is (→) Command. Both Prohibition and Command are subgenres of Order (cf. 2 Sam 13:28). The Prohibition occurs frequently in the wisdom teaching (→ Instruction, → Admonition), as well as in legal narratives. It may also be employed by prophets, generally in conjunction with instructional or persuasive forms. The authoritative character of the prohibition, the absence of specific legal penalties for its violation, and its frequent association with instructional forms indicate that the basic function of the Prohibition is to instruct or to persuade. The setting presupposes an authoritative source, such as the family, clan, or tribe, the priesthood, the monarchy, the wisdom teachers, or the prophets.

Related genres: (→) Command; (→) Admonition; (→) Instruction

J. Bright, "The Apodictic Prohibition: Some Observations," *JBL* 92 (1973) 185-204; E. Gerstenberger, *Wesen und Herkunft des "apodiktischen Rechts"* (WMANT 20; Neukirchen-Vluyn: Neukirchener, 1965); W. Richter, *Recht und Ethos* (SANT 15; Munich: Kösel, 1966).

PROPHECY (Prophetische Ankündigung). See (→) Prophetic Announcement

PROPHECY CONCERNING A FOREIGN NATION (Fremdvolkerorakel, Fremdvölkerspruch). A prophetic speech form that announces punishment or disaster against a foreign nation. It presents the destruction as an act of YHWH that is presently taking place or that will take place in the immediate future. Although the form is generally styled as an address to the foreign nation or its king, the actual addressee is Israel or Judah. Prophecies concerning Foreign Nations usually appear in series (Isaiah 13–23; Jeremiah 46–51; Ezekiel 25–32; Amos 1–2; Zeph 2:4-15), but they may also appear individually (Isa 10:5-34; 34; Obadiah; Nahum). There is no specific structure, and they may employ a variety of forms, including the (→) Taunt (Isa 14:4-23); the (→) Prophetic Pronouncement (Isaiah 13–23); the (→) Dirge (Ezek 27:1-36; 32:1-16); and the (→) Lamentation (Isa 15:1-9); the (→) Summons to War (Isa 13:2-5); and other forms. The setting lies initially in execration rituals to curse enemies (1 Kings 22; Numbers 22–24) and later in liturgical announcements of YHWH's sovereignty (Psalms 2; 46; 48; 76). The form flourished in the Assyrian, Babylonian, and Persian periods, when Israel and Judah experienced invasion by outside armies composed of units from nations throughout the ancient Near East. The various series of Prophecies Concerning Foreign Nations presuppose YHWH's world sovereignty on the pattern of imperial rulers of the time and YHWH's capacity to visit destruction on Israel's and Judah's enemies.

Related genres: (→) Prophetic Announcement, (→) Prophetic Pronouncement

D. L. Christensen, *Transformations of the War Oracle in Old Testament Prophecy* (HDR 3; Missoula: Scholars, 1975); J. H. Hayes, "The Oracles against the Nations in the Old Testament," (Diss. Princeton Theological Seminary, 1964); D. L. Petersen, "The Oracles against the Nations: A Form-Critical Analysis," in *SBL 1975 Seminar Papers* (ed. G. McRae; Missoula: Scholars, 1975) 1:39-61; C. Westermann, *Basic Forms of Prophetic Speech.* 204-5.

PROPHECY OF PUNISHMENT AGAINST AN INDIVIDUAL (Gerichtsankündigung über den Einzelnen). See (→) Prophetic Announcement of Punishment against an Individual

PROPHECY OF PUNISHMENT AGAINST THE PEOPLE (Gerichtsankündigung über das Volk). See (→) Prophetic Announcement of Punishment against the People

PROPHECY OF SALVATION (Prophetische Heilsankündigung). See (→) Prophetic Announcement of Salvation

PROPHETIC ANNOUNCEMENT (Prophetische Ankündigung). A broad collective generic term for an unsolicited (in contrast to a solicited Prophetic Oracle) announcement of a prophet concerning future events or future actions of YHWH. Prophetic Announcement includes a variety of subgenres: (→) Prophetic Announcement of Punishment; (→) Prophetic Announcement of Punishment against an Individual; (→) Prophetic Announcement of Punishment against the People; (→) Prophetic Announcement of Salvation; (→) Prophetic Announcement of a Sign; (→) Pronouncement of a Blessing; (→) Pronouncement of a Curse; (→) Announcement of a Royal Savior; (→) Prophecy Concerning a Foreign Nation; (→) Prophetic Proof Saying.

PROPHETIC ANNOUNCEMENT OF JUDGMENT. See (→) Prophetic Announcement of Punishment.

PROPHETIC ANNOUNCEMENT OF PUNISHMENT (Prophetische Gerichtsankündigung). The essential element of the (→) Prophetic Judgment Speech, the (→) Prophetic Announcement of Punishment Against an Individual, and the (→) Prophetic Announcement of Punishment Against the People. When employed as a part of these genres, the Prophetic Announcement of Punishment follows an (→) Accusation or other indication of the grounds for the punishment (Isa 22:17-24; Ezek 16:3-34, 36-43). It may also appear by itself as an independent genre (Isa 37:29; Ezek 5:14-15, 16-17). It is typically introduced by the (→) Messenger Formula, and it typically is comprised of intervention and results. The former heralds

YHWH's coming acts in the 1st-person, often introduced by *hinnēh,* "behold," and the latter presents the consequences of those acts in the 2nd- or 3rd-person.

Related genres: (→) Prophetic Announcement of Punishment Against an Individual; (→) Prophetic Announcement of Punishment Against the People; (→) Prophetic Judgment Speech

C. Westermann, *Basic Forms of Prophetic Speech,* 149-61.

PROPHETIC ANNOUNCEMENT OF PUNISHMENT AGAINST AN INDIVIDUAL (Gerichtsankündigung an den Einzelnen). A subgenre of the (→) Prophetic Announcement that announces disaster against an individual (cf. 1 Sam 2:27-36; Isa 22:16-24; Amos 7:14-17; Jer 20:1-6) or a group of individuals (cf. 1 Kgs 14:7-11; Jer 23:2, 9-12, 13-15) as punishment for a specified offense. It is distinguished from the (→) Prophetic Judgment Speech in that it employs a more direct form of the (→) Accusation against the individual. The basic two-part structure appears to be based on the sequence of an Israelite or Judean judicial proceeding: 1) the Accusation in which the individual is confronted with the offense; and 2) the (→) Prophetic Announcement of Punishment proper, which specifies YHWH's punishing actions as the consequence of the offense. The latter is typically introduced by *lākēn,* "therefore," and the (→) Messenger Formula. The genre serves as the basis for the (→) Prophetic Announcement of Punishment Against the People.

Related genres: (→) Prophetic Announcement; (→) Prophetic Announcement of Punishment Against the People

K. Koch, *The Growth of the Biblical Tradition,* 210-13; C. Westermann, *Basic Forms of Prophetic Speech,* 129-68.

PROPHETIC ANNOUNCEMENT OF PUNISHMENT AGAINST THE PEOPLE (Gerichtsankündigung über das Volk). A subgenre of the (→) Prophetic Announcement that announces punishment against the entire nation (Amos 2:1-3, 4-5; 4:1-3; Hos 2:7-9; Isa 30:12-14; Mic 3:1-4) for a specified offense. It appears to be a later development from the (→) Prophetic Announcement of Punishment Against an Individual. The structure is much more varied, but the basic components are the same and continue to reflect the sequence of Israelite and Judean court procedure: 1) a statement of the reasons for the punishment, generally in the form of an (→) Accusation which accuses the nation of some offense deserving punishment; and 2) a (→) Prophetic Announcement of Punishment proper which specifies the consequences of the offense. Again, the latter is typically introduced by *lākēn,* "therefore," and the (→) Messenger Formula. The two components may be inverted to produce the (→) Prophetic Explanation of Punishment (e.g., Isa 3:1-11; Jer 2:26-28; Amos 9:8-10).

Related genres: (→) Prophetic Announcement, (→) Prophetic Announcement of Punishment Against an Individual; (→) Prophetic Explanation of Punishment

K. Koch, *The Growth of the Biblical Tradition,* 210-13; C. Westermann, *Basic Forms of Prophetic Speech,* 169-89; H. W. Wolff, "Die Begründungen der prophetischen Heils- und Unheilssprüche."

PROPHETIC ANNOUNCEMENT OF SALVATION (Prophetische Heilsankündigung). A subgenre of the (→) Prophetic Announcement that announces salvation or blessing to individuals, groups, or the nation (Isa 7:7-9; 29:22-24; Jer 28:2-4; 31:2-6; 34:4; Amos 9:11-12, 13-15; Mic 5:9-14[NRSV 10-15]). Westermann maintains that the genre is properly termed the "proclamation of salvation," and argues that the basic pattern includes a proclamation of deliverance followed by a blessing. The form has a long history, and it is employed to express the promise of the land (Exod 3:6-8), the promise of a king (Gen 49:10-12), the promise of a son (1 Sam 1:17-20, 21-28), and the promise of rescue from enemies (1 Sam 7:3-15). A crucial development in the genre takes place in the exilic period, when Deutero-Isaiah derives the (→) Oracle of Salvation (Isa 41:8-13, 14-16; 43:1-7; 44:1-5) from an earlier priestly form. The new form includes three elements: 1) the (→) Reassurance Formula, "fear not"; 2) the "basis of reassurance in the perfect tense or nominal form"; and 3) the "future-oriented basis" which is identical with the "proclamation of salvation" (Westermann, *Prophetic Oracles of Salvation*, 42-43). This sets the pattern for the independent examples of the form that announce deliverance from exile throughout the exilic and postexilic periods. The original setting is uncertain, although the association with the Oracle of Salvation suggests cultic oracular inquiry.

Related genres: (→) Prophetic Announcement; (→) Oracle of Salvation

K. Koch, *The Growth of the Biblical Tradition*, 206-15; C. Westermann, *Prophetic Oracles of Salvation in the Old Testament* (trans. K. R. Crim; Louisville: Westminster John Knox, 1991); H. W. Wolff, "Die Begründungen der prophetischen Heils- und Unheilssprüche."

PROPHETIC BOOK (Prophetisches Buch). The literary presentation of the sayings of a particular prophet. There is some question concerning the number of prophetic books in the Hebrew Bible because of uncertainty as to whether the "Book of the Twelve Prophets" constitutes a single Prophetic Book or twelve individual books. Each book begins either with a (→) Superscription that identifies the following material as the "words," "vision," "pronouncement," of the prophet or with some variation that associates the following material with the prophet. The (→) Superscription may also identify the historical circumstances of the prophet. Narratives may also be provided that aid in establishing the context of the prophet's activity and in expressing the prophet's message (e.g., Isa 6:1–9:6[NRSV 7]; 36–39; Jeremiah 26–29; 32–44; Ezekiel 1–11; Hosea 1–3; Amos 7:10-17; Jonah; Haggai; Zechariah 1–8). The examples of Isaiah and Zechariah clearly demonstrate that it is not necessary that all of the material in the book is written by or about the prophet, even though the Prophetic Books present their contents as such. The form of the Prophetic Book varies considerably because of the large number of generic elements that may be included. Prophetic books are collections only in the broadest sense of the term, insofar as they constitute a collection of the prophet's sayings. Research into the specific forms of entire prophetic books is just beginning, but it suggests that they are deliberately organized in accordance with the intentions of the editors who composed them. Thus, Isaiah focuses on the fate or destiny of Zion; Jeremiah is portrayed as a prophet like Moses; and Ezekiel focuses on the purification of Jerusalem as the necessary prelude for restoration of the Temple. Many scholars presuppose that prophetic books are organized according to a typical three-part pattern including: 1) judgment against Israel; 2) judgment against the nations; and 3) eschatological blessings for Israel and the world (cf. Ezekiel; Jeremiah [LXX]). Other organizing principles may be implemented, such as the chronological arrangement (Ezekiel; Haggai; cf. Zechariah 1–8), a narrative sequence (Jonah), or generic patterns such as the (→)

GLOSSARY

Exhortation (Isaiah; Zephaniah), the (→) Disputation (Nahum), or the (→) Prophetic Pronouncement (Habakkuk). The liturgical character or contents of many of the Prophetic Books (e.g., Isaiah 12; 33; Joel; Habakkuk 3; Nahum) suggests that the setting for their composition and use was in the Temple. During the Second Temple period, prophets appear to have served as functionaries in the Temple rituals, and Prophetic Books appear to have been read as part of the liturgy.

R. E. Clements, "Patterns in the Prophetic Canon," in *Canon and Authority* (*Fest.* W. Zimmerli; ed. G. W. Coats and B. O. Long; Philadelphia: Fortress, 1977) 42-55; idem, "The Prophet and His Editors," in *The Bible in Three Dimensions* (JSOTSup 87; ed. D. J. A. Clines et al.; Sheffield: JSOT, 1990) 203-20; R. M. Hals, *Ezekiel* (FOTL; Grand Rapids: Eerdmans, 1989) 352-53.

PROPHETIC EXPLANATION OF PUNISHMENT (Prophetische Erklärung für Bestrafung). A modification of the (→) Prophetic Announcement of Punishment in which the prophet explains that a current situation of disaster is a punishment imposed by YHWH and provides the reason for that punishment. Essentially, the form reverses the two constituent elements of the Prophetic Announcement of Punishment by presenting the announcement of punishment first, followed by the reasons for the punishment. Examples appear in Isa 3:1-11; Jer 2:26-28; Ezek 22:23-31; 23:5-10; and Amos 9:8-10. The genre is both analytical and instructional, in that it presupposes a current or past situation of disaster, identifies it as an act of YHWH, and then determines the causes that prompted YHWH to bring about the punishment in the first place. The setting is unclear, although it appears to relate to oracular or prophetic inquiry.

Related genres: (→) Prophetic Announcement; (→) Prophetic Announcement of Punishment Against an Individual; (→) Prophetic Announcement of Punishment Against the People

PROPHETIC JUDGMENT SPEECH (Prophetische Urteilsrede, Prophetische Urteilswort). A subgenre of the (→) Prophetic Announcement in which the prophet speaks on behalf of YHWH to announce judgment against an individual, group, or nation. Examples appear in Isa 8:5-8; Jer 11:9-12; and Mic 3:9-12. The main elements of the genre are: 1) a statement of the reasons for judgment; 2) a logical transition, such as *lākēn,* "therefore," with the (→) Messenger Formula; and 3) the (→) Prophetic Announcement of Punishment. Other elements, such as the (→) Call to Attention or the (→) Oracle Formula, may also appear. The Prophetic Judgment Speech is often styled as a speech by the prophet, in which the prophet presents the reasons for judgment in his/her own words, followed by the prophet's report of the Announcement of Punishment by YHWH. This indirect means of stating the punishment and its grounds is the chief distinction between this genre and the (→) Prophetic Announcement of Punishment, which generally employs direct address language to accuse and announce punishment.

Related genres: (→) Prophetic Announcement; (→) Prophetic Announcement of Punishment Against an Individual; (→) Prophetic Announcement of Punishment Against the People

G. M. Tucker, *Form Criticism of the Old Testament* (Philadelphia: Fortress, 1971); C. Westermann, *Basic Forms of Prophetic Speech,* 129-209.

PROPHETIC LITURGY (Prophetische Liturgie). See (→) Liturgy.

PROPHETIC MESSENGER SPEECH. A prophetic speech form in which the prophet

402

employs the (→) Messenger Formula to identify the following message as a speech by YHWH. The prophetic messenger speech presupposes a (→) Commission of the prophet by YHWH to convey the message to a particular audience. The form is known from other ancient Near Eastern cultures, such as Assyrian prophecy and the Mari letters. It is based in the practice of commissioning a messenger to deliver a message formally to another party, both in the personal or family realm (e.g., Abraham's sending Eliezer to secure a bride for Isaac in Genesis 24) or the international realm (e.g., Sennacherib's sending the Rab Shakeh to demand the unconditional surrender of Hezekiah in Isaiah 36–37/2 Kings 18–19). The prophetic use of the form presupposes that the prophet functions as the emissary of YHWH.

M. Nissinen et al., *Prophets and Prophecy in the Ancient Near* East (WAW 12; Atlanta: SBL, 2003); J. F. Ross, "The Prophet as YHWH's Messenger," in *Israel's Prophetic Heritage* (*Fest.* J. Muilenburg; ed. B. W. Anderson and W. Harrelson; New York: Harper, 1962) 98-107; C. Westermann, *Basic Forms of Prophetic Speech,* 98-128.

PROPHETIC PROOF SAYING (Prophetisches Erweiswort). A subgenre of the (→) Prophetic Announcement in which the prophet, speaking on behalf of YHWH, announces punishment against an individual, group, or nation, and argues that this punishment will convince the recipient to recognize YHWH's sovereign identity. This genre appears in 1 Kgs 20:13, 28; very frequently in Ezekiel (e.g., Ezek 25:2-3, 6-7, 8-11, 15-17; 26:2-6); and in Isa 41:17-20; 49:22-26. The main elements are: 1) the (→) Prophetic Announcement of Punishment and 2) the (→) Self-Identification Formula. These two combine to constitute a two-part Prophetic Proof Saying (e.g., Ezek 12:19-20). When, as is often the case, a statement of the reason for punishment and a logical transition are prefixed to the Prophetic Announcement of Punishment, the result is a three-part Prophetic Proof Saying (e.g., Ezek 25:6-7, 8b-11).

Related genre: (→) Prophetic Announcement

R. M. Hals, *Ezekiel* (FOTL; Grand Rapids: Eerdmans, 1989) 353-54; W. Zimmerli, "The Word of Divine Self-Manifestation (Proof-Saying): A Prophetic Genre," in *I Am YHWH* (trans. D. W. Stott; Atlanta: John Knox, 1982) 99-110; idem, *Ezekiel* 1 (trans. R. E. Clements; Hermeneia; Philadelphia: Fortress, 1979) 38-39.

PROPHETIC SPEECH (Prophetische Rede). Any speech given by a prophet. The term is thus a broad functional one, defined sociologically. Because it has no other specific defining characteristics, it is too comprehensive to serve as a specific genre designation. Prophetic speech may be formulated as any specific speech form, such as (→) Messenger Speech, (→) Oracle, (→) Prophetic Announcement, etc.

K. Koch, *The Growth of the Biblical Tradition,* 183-220; S. A. Meier, *Speaking of Speaking;* G. M. Tucker, "Prophetic Speech," *Int* 32 (1978) 31-45; C. Westermann, *Basic Forms of Prophetic Speech;* idem, *Prophetic Oracles of Salvation in the Old Testament* (trans. K. Crim; Louisville: Westminster John Knox, 1991).

PROPHETIC TORAH (Prophetische Tora). See (→) Priestly Torah.

QUESTION AND ANSWER SCHEMA (Frage und Antwort Schema). A literary device that projects a question and its answer as a means of describing a future situation. One type assumes a disaster and assigns reasons and responsibility for it, thus elaborating on implicit admonitions to avoid the behavior which will lead to such an end. Typical are Jer 22:8-9; 1 Kgs 9:8-9; and Deut 29:21-24. All of these are from the Deuteronomistic writers, who placed national destruction in the context of broken covenant realized as covenantal curses. Parallels are in the commemorative royal inscriptions of Ashurbanipal (e.g., *ANET*³, 300). A second type appears as a divine speech addressed to a prophet, envisions a situation in which someone will ask a question, and suggests the answer that will be given. Examples are Jer 23:33; 5:19; 13:12-14; Ezek 21:12; 37:19. Literary function, of course, varies according to biblical context. Models for this device apparently derive from situations in which a person sought oracles through a prophet.

   B. O. Long, "Two Question and Answer Schemata in the Prophets," *JBL* 90 (1971) 129-39.

REASSURANCE SPEECH (Beruhigungsrede, Bestätigungsrede). A speech that employs the (→) Reassurance Formula, *'al tîrā'*, "do not fear!" The Reassurance Speech generally appears in the context of a (→) Prophetic Announcement of Salvation.

REPORT (Bericht). A brief self-contained prose narrative, usually in 3rd-person style, about a single event or situation in the past. In contrast to Story or (→) Legend, there is no developed plot or imaginative characterization. Insofar as there is action, Report differs from statement or description. Varying in length from a very short notice to a longer, even composite account, reports can carry diverse content. Certain types of Report, defined by structure and content, take on special importance in the Hebrew Bible, such as (→) Theophany Report, (→) Vision Report, or (→) Report of a Symbolic Action. Naturally, the setting for Report would vary according to content and purpose.

RHETORICAL ANSWER (Rhetorische Antwort). A stated answer to a (→) RHETORICAL QUESTION.

RHETORICAL QUESTION (Rhetorische Frage). A question asked for its rhetorical or telling effect, which does not require a reply. It is found frequently in argument and persuasion and occurs as a subgenre in numerous genres of the Hebrew Bible. It appears frequently in Isaiah's speeches (e.g., Isa 1:5a, 12b; 3:15a; 5:4; 8:19b; 10:8-9; etc.). The supposition is that the answer is clear, usually the only one possible, and a deeper impression is made upon the hearer by the question form than by the statement.

   D. Sweeney, "What's a Rhetorical Question?" *Lingua Aegyptia* 1 (1991) 315-31.

ROYAL COMMISSION. A (→) Commission directed to a royal figure.

SALVATION SPEECH. See (→) Announcement of Salvation.

SATIRE. Not a genre strictly speaking, but a polemical literary device that employs irony, derision, and mockery to undermine and expose folly or wickedness. The idolatry speeches in Deutero-Isaiah (e.g., Isa 44:9-20) are a primary example.

SELF-DISCLOSURE ORACLE (Prophetisches Erweiswort). See (→) Prophetic Proof Saying.

SIMILE (Gleichnis). A figure of speech in which two essentially different things are explicitly compared with the use of expressions such as "like," "as," and others.

SONG (Lied). A poetic composition intended for public performance by an individual singer or a group. The performance of Songs could be accompanied by musical instruments. The Hebrew Bible includes various noncultic songs, such as working songs (Num 21:17-18; Judg 9:27); love songs or wedding songs (Canticles; Psalm 45); drinking songs (Amos 6:4-6; cf. Isa 5:11-13); battle songs (Exod 15:20-21; Num 10:35-36; 1 Sam 18:6-7); funeral songs (→ Dirge); and mocking songs (Isa 14:4b-23; 23:15-16; Num 21:27-30).

SONG OF CONFIDENCE (Vertrauenlied). A subgenre of the (→) Individual Complaint Song applied by Gunkel to Psalms 4; 11; 16; 23; 27:1-6; 62; 131 (Gunkel and Begrich, 254n10). In fact, (→) Affirmation of Confidence constitutes an integral part of complaint. If the text divisions of the HB psalter are correct, at least some of the indicated songs of confidence formed independent liturgical units to be used in various types of worship services (see Psalms 16; 23; 62; 131). The form may also appear in prophetic texts, e.g., Isa 50:4-9.

H. Gunkel and J. Begrich, *Einleitung in die Psalmen* (2nd ed.; Göttingen: Vandenhoeck & Ruprecht, 1966) 254-256.

SONG OF PRAISE (Loblied). See (→) Hymn of Praise.

SPEECH (Rede). A general term employed for any oral communication. Speeches may appear in a wide variety of forms depending on the circumstances of the speaker, the addressee, the situation addressed, and the setting of the speech.

SUMMONS TO APPROACH. Related to the (→) Trial Genres, a Summons to Approach functions as a means to initiate a legal proceeding by inviting the parties involved in a legal case to approach the judge in order to offer legal arguments. The form appears in Isa 57:3 as part of YHWH's initiation of a legal proceeding against those engaged in idolatry. It is characterized by the use of the verb *qirbû-hēnnâ,* "come here, approach."

SUMMONS TO HEAR. See (→) Call to Attention.

SUMMONS TO PRAISE (Aufruf zu Lob). Also known as Call to Worship. The summons to praise is a basic element of the (→) Hymn of Praise, which begins with a summons to join in singing, playing, giving thanks, shouting, or clapping hands in honor of YHWH. The Summons to Praise is typically followed by the (→) Basis for Praise. A typical form is:

> Sing to YHWH
> For He is great!

Examples appear in Exod 15:21; Deut 32:43; Jer 20:13; Pss 9:11-12(NRSV 12-13); 106:1; 107:1; 117:1-2; 118:1-4; 136:1.

E. Gerstenberger, *Psalms, Part 2, and Lamentations* (FOTL; Grand Rapids: Eerdmans, 2001) 511-12.

SUPERSCRIPTION (Überschrift). A statement prefixed to a literary work, such as a book, collection, song, oracle, etc. The term refers to the place of this statement in the structure of a work, namely, preceding its body (as opposed to a subscription, which follows the conclusion of the body). The Superscription may consist of a variety of elements, such as author, addressee, title, date, location, or genre. While the composition of most of these elements can vary, Superscriptions in the Hebrew Bible ordinarily identify the character of the work, either in the concise definition form of a title ("This is the book of the generations of Adam," Gen 5:1; 2:4a; "A Psalm of David," Ps 101:1; "The Proverbs of Solomon, son of David, King of Israel," Prov 1:1), or in a more elaborate form (e.g., Jer 1:1-3). Superscriptions normally appear at the beginning of the prophetic books in various forms, which generally include a brief indication of author, date, and subject (e.g., Isa 1:1; Amos 1:1; Mic 1:1; Zech 1:1). They also may appear before textual blocks within the book (e.g., Isa 2:1 [Isaiah 2–4]; 13:1 [Isaiah 13–23]; Jer 46:1 [Jeremiah 46–51]) or before individual compositions within the book (e.g., Isa 14:28; 15:1; 38:9; Jer 7:1; 11:1; Hab 3:1; Hag 2:1; Zech 1:7; 9:1; 12:1). Although Superscriptions may function as a title (cf. 2 Chr 32:32; Isa 1:1), they differ from titles generically in that a title refers to the distinguishing name of a work, whether it is a Superscription or not. Superscriptions apparently find their setting in the scribal activity of the tradents of biblical literature, who studied, interpreted, composed, and transmitted the works to which Superscriptions were added.

G. M. Tucker, "Prophetic Superscriptions and the Growth of the Canon," in *Canon and Authority* (*Fest.* W. Zimmerli; ed. G. W. Coats and B. O. Long; Philadelphia: Fortress, 1977) 56-70.

TAUNT (Verspottung, Verhöhnung). An utterance or composition designed to denigrate its object. The Taunt may appear in a war setting, in which opponents battle with words prior to the actual combat (e.g., 1 Sam 17:43, 44; 1 Kgs 20:11), in the context of negotiations in which one party wishes to intimidate the other (e.g., 1 Kgs 12:10b), or in prophetic speech in which the prophet attempts to belittle the addressee (Isa 23:15-16; Jer 22:14-15). The Taunt may also take the form of a mocking or taunting song (e.g., Isa 14:4-23).

THANKSGIVING SONG OF THE INDIVIDUAL (Danklied des Einzelnen). A psalm sung by or on behalf of an individual recently delivered from personal distress, which expresses gratitude to YHWH for intervention and deliverance. The elements are the same as those of the (→) Communal Thanksgiving Song: 1) a call to sing (or to give thanks or praise); 2) an account of the past trouble and salvation; 3) praise for YHWH (or YHWH's works); 4) announcement of sacrifice; 5) blessings; and 6) a vow or pledge. The (→) Thanksgiving Formula, "I thank you . . . ," commonly appears as part of the Song. The setting appears to have been in the context of the temple, in which the individual presented thanks and sacrifices to YHWH for deliverance. Examples appear in Psalms 30; 32; 92; and Jonah 2. The (→) Royal Psalm is a special type reserved for the king (e.g., Isa 9:1-6[2-7]; 38:9-20).

Related genres: (→) Communal Thanksgiving Song; (→) Hymn of Praise

W. Beyerlin, "Die tôdâ der Heilsvergegenwärtigung in den Klageliedern des Einzelnen," *ZAW* 79 (1967) 208-44; F. Crüsemann, *Studien zur Formgeschichte von Hymnus und Danklied in Israel* (WMANT 32; Neukirchen: Neukirchener, 1969); E. Gerstenberger, *Psalms, Part 1; with an Introduction to Cultic Poetry* (FOTL; Grand Rapids: Eerdmans, 1988) 14-16; C. Westermann, *Praise and Lament in the Psalms* (trans. K. R. Crim and R. N. Soulen; Atlanta: John Knox, 1981).

TRIAL GENRES (Gerichtsreden). A collective term for generic elements related to legal procedure and the context of the law court. The setting may be the jurisdiction of the civil courts held at the gates of a city (cf. Ruth 4:1-12), the sacral jurisdiction of the sanctuaries (Joshua 7; Jeremiah 26), or the royal court (2 Sam 12:1-6; 1 Kgs 3:16-28). Legal genres and formulas appear in many situations of daily life; they are especially prevalent in the prophets, where they appear to have had some influence on the (→) Prophetic Announcements of Punishment, the (→) Prophetic Judgment Speech, and prophetic forms of (→) Instruction. One characteristic prophetic form of the Trial Genres is the so-called Trial Speech, often identified as the "*rîb*-pattern" or the "(covenant) lawsuit" form. Examples appear in Isaiah 1; Jeremiah 2; Hosea 4; Micah 6; and various other texts, especially in Deutero-Isaiah. The term *rîb* means "controversy" and can refer to a legal case brought by one party against another; in the case of the prophets, it typically refers to YHWH's case against Israel for violation of the terms of the covenant between YHWH and Israel (cf. Isa 3:13; Jer 2:9; Hos 4:1; Mic 6:1-2). Characteristic elements might include a (→) Call to Attention (Isa 1:2; Hos 4:1; Jer 2:4; Mic 6:1-2); an (→) Appeal for a legal proceeding (Isa 1:18-20); an (→) Accusation speech (Isa 1:2-20; 3:12-15; Hos 4:4-8; Jer 2:5-34); (→) Rhetorical Questions (Isa 1:5, 12; 3:15; Jer 2:5, 14, 31-32); and, finally, an (→) Announcement of Judgment (Jer 2:35-37; Hos 4:4-10) or some form of (→) Instruction in proper behavior (Isa 1:10-17; Mic 6:6-8).

H. J. Boecker, *Redeformen des Rechtslebens im Alten Testament* (2nd ed.; WMANT 14; Neukirchen-Vluyn: Neukirchener, 1970); J. Harvey, *Le plaidoyer prophétique contre Israël après la rupture de l'alliance* (Montreal: Bellarmin, 1967); K. Nielsen, *YHWH as Prosecutor and Judge* (JSOTSup 9; Sheffield: JSOT, 1978).

TRIAL SCENE. A scene of a court setting derived from the (→) TRIAL GENRES.

TRIAL SPEECH. A forensic speech that employs the (→) Trial Genres.

VISION REPORT (Visionsbericht, Visionsschilderung). The description by a prophet of what he/she sees (vision) or hears (audition) in an inner prophetic perception. Visual elements are frequently introduced by *hinnēh*, "behold," and auditory elements are frequently introduced by *qôl*, "listen," or an indication of a speech by YHWH. Horst identifies three basic types: 1) the "presence vision," which recounts the prophet's experience of the presence of YHWH (Isaiah 6; Jer 1:4-10; Ezek 1:4-28); 2) the "word assonance vision," in which the vision is based on a wordplay or an object that symbolizes a word of YHWH (Jer 1:11-12, 13-15; Amos 8:1-3); and 3) the "event vision," in which the vision is conveyed through the depiction of a future event (Isa 13:4-5; 21:1-9; Nah 3:1-3). Long's analysis likewise results in three types: 1) the "oracle vision," which employs a question-and-answer dialogue to present the meaning of a simple image (Amos 7:7-8; Jer 1:11-14); 2) the "dramatic word vision," which depicts a heavenly scene to convey a word of YHWH (Amos 7:1-6; Isaiah 6; Ezek 9:1-10); and 3) the "revelatory-mysteries-vision," in which a divine guide conveys the secrets of YHWH's activity and future events (Zech 2:3-4; 4:1-6a; cf. Daniel 8; 10–12). The original setting of prophetic Vision Reports may have been in the context of divination, oracular inquiry, or participation in a liturgy at a temple or other sacred site. In their literary contexts, they authenticate and convey the prophetic message.

F. Horst, "Die Visionsschilderungen der alttestamentlichen Propheten," *EvT* 20 (1960) 193-205; B. O. Long, "Reports of Visions Among the Prophets," *JBL* 95 (1976) 353-65; M. Sister, "Die Typen der prophetischen Visionen in der Bibel," *MGWJ* 78 (1934) 399-430.

VOCATION ACCOUNT (Prophetischer Berufungsbericht). A genre in which a prophet or the prophetic tradition refers to the initiatory commission of the prophet. The Vocation Account may be presented in an autobiographical (e.g., Isaiah 6; Jeremiah 1; Ezekiel 1) or an objective narrative form (e.g., Exodus 3; Judges 6; 1 Kings 22). There are two basic types: the first focuses on the visionary element in which the prophet sees the heavenly court of YHWH (1 Kings 22; Isaiah 6; Ezekiel 1); the second subordinates all elements to the word of YHWH (Exodus 3; Jeremiah 1; Ezek 2:1–3:15). Habel identifies a number of relatively consistent elements, including: 1) a divine confrontation; 2) an introductory word; 3) a (→) Commission; 4) an objection by the prophet; 5) a reassurance; and 6) a sign. In general, the Vocation Account authenticates the prophet as a spokesperson for YHWH and aids in expressing the prophet's overall message.

N. Habel, "The Form and Significance of the Call Narratives," *ZAW* 77 (1965) 297-323; W. Richter, *Die sogenannten vorprophetischen Berufungsberichte* (FRLANT 101; Göttingen: Vandenhoeck & Ruprecht, 1970); H. Wildberger, *Jesaja 1–12* (BKAT X/1; Neukirchen-Vluyn: Neukirchener, 1972) 234-39; W. Zimmerli, *Ezekiel 1* (trans. R. E. Clements; Hermeneia; Philadelphia: Fortress, 1979) 97-100.

WARNING. See Admonition.

WOE SPEECH (Wehe Spruch). A derivation from the (→) Woe Oracle. A Woe speech employs the typical particle *hôy,* "woe!" but deviates from the standard Woe Oracle form. An example appears in Isa 45:9-10.

ZION HYMN (Zionshymnus). A derivative form of the (→) Hymn of Praise that focuses upon Zion as the abode of YHWH and the principal locale of Israelite and Judean worship (e.g., Psalms 46; 48; 76; 84; 87; 122; 132; 137; cf. Isa 2:2-4). Because of the interrelationship between monarchy and temple, Zion Hymns are generally considered as part of the Royal Psalms.

E. Gerstenberger, *Psalms, Part 1; with an Introduction to Cultic Poetry* (FOTL; Grand Rapids: Eerdmans, 1988) 19, 258.

FORMULAS

ASSISTANCE FORMULA (Beistandsformel). The formula affirming YHWH's presence with the people or an individual. The basic form is YHWH's statement "I am with you," with appropriate variations depending upon the speaker and the context. Three main usages appear: 1) In an (→) Oracle as part of a divine promise. In such cases the Assistance Formula ordinarily is introduced by the (→) Reassurance Formula, "Fear not!" See Isa 43:5; Jer 30:11; 46:28; Judg 6:12, 16.2) Spoken by humans as a promise, wish, or question (in slightly different form). See Gen 28:20; 48:21; Exod 10:10; 18:19; Num 14:43; Deut 20:1. 3) As an assertion or confession. See Gen 39:23; Num 23:21; Deut 2:7; Josh 6:27; 1 Sam 16:18; 2 Chr 13:12; Ps 46:8, 12(NRSV 7, 11). This formula originated perhaps in the situation of migrating nomads, where it was related to the idea that the deity was traveling with the people and providing guidance, protection, or victory in battle.

H. D. Preuss, ". . . ich will mit dir sein," *ZAW* 80 (1968) 139-73; D. Vetter, *JHWHs Mit-Sein; ein Ausdruck des Segens* (*AzT* 1/45; Stuttgart: Calwer, 1971).

BEATITUDE, FELICITATION (Seligspreisung, Gratulation). Beatitude is a short, formulaic speech that extols the fortunate or blessed state of an individual or whole people, such as Israel. Typically, the utterance begins with *'ašrê*, "happy" or "fortunate," followed by the subject and any special qualifiers, often in the form of relative clauses (e.g., 1 Kgs 10:8, "Happy [*'ašrê*] are these your servants who continually stand before you . . ."; cf. Ps 2:12; Prov. 8:34; 16:20). These basic elements can be expanded with the addition of elaborate clauses (e.g., Ps 1:1-2; Prov. 3:13-14) or worked up into more lengthy collections of sayings, as in the NT (e.g., Matt 5:3-11). Beatitude is related to (→) Blessing and Hymn of Praise, but it remains distinct. It does not invoke YHWH's blessing or utter YHWH's praises, but describes a person who is fortunate by reason of upright behavior or blessings already received from G-d. Egyptian parallels are known. Beatitude perhaps was originally a type of spontaneous exclamation. Most examples in the HB, however, suggest that it became a form of wisdom teaching, a description turned into didactic example or precept by those "wise men" whose instructions and learning live on in the books of Proverbs, Qohelet, and certain Psalms (e.g., Psalms 1; 119:1-2; 128).

   G. Dupont, "Beatitudes égyptiennes," *Bib* 47 (1966) 185-222; W. Janzen, "'*Ašrê* in the Old Testament," *HTR* 58 (1965) 215-26; E. Lipiński, "Macanisme et psaumes de congratulation," *RB* 75 (1968) 321-67.

BLESSING (Segen, Segnung). A pronouncement cast in either the imperative (Gen 24:60) or indicative mode (Num 24:5-9), designed to call down divine power through the spoken word. Blessing can be introduced or concluded with a formula employing the participle *bārûk*, "blessed," followed by the person who is to be blessed. Blessing derives from a tribal ethos (see Gen 24:60; 27:27-29), but it is especially associated with liturgical functions (e.g., 1 Kgs 8:14). Blessing may also function within the (→) Prophetic Announcement of Salvation, such as Isa 60:8-22, where the Blessing in Isa 60:19-22 follows the announcement of salvation in Isa 60:8-18. Here, the participle *bārûk* is lacking, but YHWH's promise of support and land constitutes the blessing. Blessing differs from (→) Beatitude (e.g., Ps 2:12; 1 Kgs 10:8), which acclaims blessings already deemed to be received and functions as a type of didactic saying (e.g., Jer 17:7). Blessing also differs from Praise (e.g., Ps 72:18; Exod 18:10), which begins with *bārûk* but offers praise to G-d insofar as G-d is its object (Westermann, *Prophetic Oracles of Salvation,* 62).

   C. Westermann, *Prophetic Oracles of Salvation in the Old Testament* (trans. K. R. Crim; Louisville: Westminster John Knox, 1991).

CALL TO ATTENTION (Aufmerksamkeitsruf, Aufforderung zum Hören, Lehreröffnungsformel). A formula that opens a public presentation or address and intends to attract the attention of the hearers to the speech that follows. The constituent elements are: 1) an invitation to listen; 2) mention of the addressee(s); and 3) an indication of what is to be heard.

   This call would commonly be employed by a singer (cf. Judg 5:3), a wisdom teacher (cf. Prov. 7:24), or an official envoy (cf. 2 Kgs 18:28-29). It appears frequently in the prophetic literature in various forms, often expanded by relative clauses (see Amos 3:1; Hos 4:1; Mic 6:1; Isa 1:10; Ezek 6:3).

   K. Koch, *The Growth of the Biblical Tradition* (trans. S. Cupitt; New York: Scribner's, 1969) 205; B. O. Long, *2 Kings* (FOTL; Grand Rapids: Eerdmans, 1991) 319; I. Lande, *Formelhafte Wendungen der Umgangssprache im Alten Testament* (Leiden: Brill, 1949) 13-14; H. W. Wolff, *Hosea* (trans. G. Stansell;

Hermeneia; Philadelphia: Fortress, 1974) 65-66; S. J. de Vries, *1 and 2 Chronicles* (FOTL; Grand Rapids: Eerdmans, 1989) 437.

CALL TO MOURN (Aufforderung zum Trauern). See (→) Call for a Communal Complaint.

CALL TO A PUBLIC COMPLAINT SERVICE (Aufruf zur Volksklage). A public announcement that calls the population to a public complaint ceremony in cases of a national emergency (drought, Jer 14:1ff; enemy from the outside, 2 Chronicles 20). In this ceremony, YHWH is invoked to intervene in order to "proclaim" or to "sanctify a fast" (*qārā'* or *qiddaš ṣôm;* cf. 1 Kgs 21:9, 12; Joel 1:14; 2:15).

The call has three constituent parts: 1) a sequence of imperatives; 2) mention of the people being called; and 3) mention of the reason for the complaint service. This genre is frequently employed by the prophets (cf. Isa 14:31; 23:1-14; 32:11-14; Jer 6:26; 25:34; 49:3; Ezek 21:17; Joel 1:5-14; Zeph 1:11; Zech 11:2).

A cognate genre is the Call to Mourn, to lament, or to conduct funeral rites, consisting of two components: the imperatives and the reason (cf. Jer 4:8; 6:26; 7:29; 9:16-21[NRSV 17-22]; 22:10, 20-23; 25:34-36).

H. W. Wolff, "Der Aufruf zur Volksklage," *ZAW* 76 (1964) 48-56.

COMMISSIONING FORMULA (Aussendungsformel). The essential part of an authoritative charge to a messenger or emissary to deliver a message on behalf of the sender. The standard wording is "Go and say to PN" plus the identification of the addressee. The (→) Messenger Formula and message then normally follow. Examples appear in Gen 32:5(NRSV 4); 1 Kgs 14:7a; 2 Kgs 18:19; 19:6; Isa 7:3-4; 36:4; 37:6; 38:4; Ezek 3:1b, 4b, and 11a.

MESSENGER FORMULA (Botenformel). The formula *kōh 'āmar* PN, "Thus says PN," which normally introduces a (→) Messenger Speech. It seems to have originated in the ancient and widespread practice of the oral transmission of a message by means of a third party. The formula normally occurs twice in the following sequence: 1) it is spoken by the sender who commissions and instructs the messenger (cf. Gen 32:5[NRSV 4]; 45:9); 2) it is reiterated by the messenger at the delivery of the message (cf. 2 Kgs 18:29/Isa 36:14; Num 22:15-16).

In some prophetic books, the specific Messenger Formula "Thus says YHWH" *(kōh 'āmar yhwh)* frequently occurs (especially in Jeremiah and Ezekiel, but not in Hosea, Joel, Habakkuk, or Zechariah). This usage implies that a prophet delivering a message is understood as analogous to the practice of commissioning, instructing, and sending a messenger. The shorter formula, *'āmar yhwh,* "says YHWH," which is derived from the Messenger Formula, is used like the (→) Oracle Formula in the beginning, at the end, or in the middle of a word of G-d.

Related genre: (→) Messenger Speech

S. A. Meier, *The Messenger in the Ancient Semitic World* (HSM 45; Atlanta: Scholars, 1988); idem, *Speaking of Speaking,* 273-98; C. Westermann, *Basic Forms of Prophetic Speech,* 98-115.

OATH FORMULA (Schwurformel). The formula "As YHWH lives" *(ḥay yhwh),* with which an (→) Oath is usually introduced.

ORACLE FORMULA (G-ttesspruchformel). The formula *nĕ'um yhwh,* "utterance of YHWH," which labels a prophetic speech (or a part of it) as a word of G-d. Its place may be at the beginning, the middle, or the end of a prophetic speech. The setting of the formula appears to be the (→) Vision Report of the seer (cf. 2 Sam 23:1; Num 24:3).

Related genre: (→) Oracle

F. Baumgartel, "Die Formel *ne'um JHWH*," *ZAW* 73 (1961) 277-90; S. A. Meier, *Speaking of Speaking*, 298-314; R. Rendtorff, "Zum Gebrauch der Formel *ne'um jhwh* im Jeremiabuch," *ZAW* 66 (1954) 27-37.

PROPHETIC AUTHORIZATION FORMULA (Prophetische Genehmigung Formel). The formula *kî pî yhwh dibbēr,* "for the mouth of YHWH has spoken" (Isa 1:20; 40:5; 58:14b; Mic 4:4), which functions as a means to indicate that YHWH has authorized the action or scenario with which the formula is associated. The formula appears to be a modification of the standard YHWH speech formula, *kî yhwh dibbēr,* "for YHWH has spoken," and its variants. The addition of *pî,* "mouth," gives greater emphasis to YHWH's own mouth as the source of the action or scenario in question.

S. A. Meier, *Speaking of Speaking,* 156-58.

PROPHETIC UTTERANCE FORMULA (Prophetische Offbarungsformel). See (→) Oracle Formula.

PROPHETIC WORD FORMULA (Wortereignisformel, Offenbarungsformel). A combination of the phrase *dĕbar yhwh,* "the word of YHWH," with the verb *hāyâ,* "to be, happen," plus the preposition *'el,* "to," followed by the name of the prophet or a pronoun suffix that refers to the prophet. It may be employed in narratives which relate the reception of a prophetic word (e.g., 1 Sam 15:10; 1 Kgs 6:11) or as the introduction to a prophetic word in prophetic literature (e.g., Jer 7:1; 11:1). It may serve as a redactional device (e.g., Jer 33:19, 23; 35:12; 42:7), or it may be formulated as a 1st-person report of a prophet (e.g., Jer 1:4, 11; 2:1; Ezek 6:1; 7:1). It may also appear in the (→) Superscription to a (→) Prophetic Book (Hos 1:1; Joel 1:1; Mic 1:1; Zeph 1:1).

S. A. Meier, *Speaking of Speaking,* 314-19.

REASSURANCE FORMULA (Beruhigungsformel, Bestätigungsformel). The formula *'al tîrā',* "fear not," sometimes with name and object, followed by *kî,* "because," which introduces the reason. Often, the reason is expressed with the (→) Assistance Formula, "I am with you." The intention is to encourage a person (or persons) in fear to regain composure.

No original setting can be defined; the formula appears in very different situations. The examples in Isaiah (7:4-9; 10:24-27; 37:6-7) are delivered as part of (→) Prophetic Announcements of Salvation which promise relief from a foreign oppressor. The speaker can be a prophet, speaking for him/herself or for YHWH (cf. 2 Kgs 6:16; Isa 7:4-9; 10:24-27; 35:4; 40:9; 41:10); YHWH (cf. Gen 15:1; 26:24; Deut 3:2; Josh 8:1); or people from all ways of life (cf. Gen 35:17; 43:23; Num 14:9; 1 Sam 22:23; 23:17; Job 5:21-22).

Related genres: (→) Oracle of Salvation; (→) Prophecy of Salvation

E. W. Conrad, *Fear Not Warrior: A Study of 'al tîra' Pericopes in the Hebrew Scriptures* (BJS 75; Chico: Scholars, 1985); P. E. Dion, "The 'Fear Not' Formula and Holy War," *CBQ* 32 (1970) 565-70.

RECOGNITION FORMULA. See (→) SELF-IDENTIFICATION FORMULA

SELF-IDENTIFICATION FORMULA (Selbsterkenntnis Formel). An element of the Recognition Formula in which YHWH self-identifies as the agent for divine action in the world: "I am YHWH."

See also (→) Prophetic Proof Saying.

R. M. Hals, *Ezekiel* (FOTL; Grand Rapids: Eerdmans, 1989) 353-54, 362; W. Zimmerli, "I am YHWH," in *I Am YHWH* (ed. W. Brueggemann; Atlanta: John Knox, 1982) 1-28.

SPEECH FORMULA (Redeformel). A broad general term to indicate a formal marker of a (→) Speech. Speech Formulas may employ any verb or noun that indicates speech, especially the verbs *'mr,* "to say," *dbr,* "to speak," and *'nh,* "to answer," or nouns such as *dābār,* "word," and *n'm,* "utterance." Specific generic types are included, such as the (→) Messenger Formula, the (→) Oracle Formula, and the (→) Prophetic Word Formula. S. A. Meier, *Speaking of Speaking.*

SUMMARY-APPRAISAL FORMULA (Zusammentassende Abschlussformel). A statement attached to the end of a literary unit which offers both a summary and an appraisal of the preceding material. The formula consists of a demonstrative pronounce (e.g., *zeh, zō't,* "this") and usually has a bicolon structure. It is reflective and didactic in character, and it often contains technical wisdom terminology. Its setting appears to be in wisdom instruction (see Prov. 1:19; Job 8:13; 18:21; 20:29; Eccl 4:8; Ps 49:14[NRSV 13]), but it is also employed by prophets (cf. Isa 14:26; 17:14; 28:29; Jer 13:25).

B. S. Childs, *Isaiah and the Assyrian Crisis* (SBT 3; London: SCM, 1967) 128-36; J. W. Whedbee, *Isaiah and Wisdom* (Nashville: Abingdon, 1971) 75-79.